1995

HISTORIC
DOCUMENTS
OF
1995

1995

HISTORIC DOCUMENTS

OF

1995

Cumulative Index, 1991–1995

Congressional Quarterly Inc.

Historic Documents of 1995

Editors: Marty Gottron, John Felton, Bruce Maxwell
Production and Associate Editor: Kerry V. Kern
Indexer: Victoria Agee

Copyright © 1996 Congressional Quarterly Inc.
1414 22nd Street, N.W.
Washington, D.C. 20037

Printed in the United States of America

The Library of Congress cataloged the first issue of this title as follows:

Historic documents. 1972–
    Washington. Congressional Quarterly Inc.

    1. United States — Politics and government — 1945– — Yearbooks.
2. World politics — 1945– — Yearbooks. I. Congressional Quarterly Inc.

E839.5H57   917.3'03'9205   72-97888

ISBN 0-87187-895-X
ISSN 0892-080X

PREFACE

The year 1995 saw major initiatives toward settling long-standing, often bloody conflicts in the Middle East, Northern Ireland, and Bosnia. It witnessed celebrations of the fiftieth anniversaries of the end of World War II and the founding of the United Nations, the establishment of diplomatic relations between the United States and Vietnam, and tentative moves by the Clinton administration toward reestablishing ties with Cuba. But these steps, large and small, toward peace were overpowered by violence and the images it left in its wake.

In January prosecutors began their opening arguments in the trial of football celebrity O. J. Simpson by showing photographs of the brutalized bodies of Simpson's former wife and a friend, found murdered outside her Los Angeles townhouse in June 1994. In October the nation witnessed Simpson's elation as he heard a jury acquit him of the murders.

In November an Israeli extremist assassinated Prime Minister Itzhak Rabin, who only weeks before had signed a peace agreement with Palestine Liberation Organization leader Yasir Arafat. In an unprecedented show of unity, President Hosni Mubarak of Egypt and King Hussein of Jordan joined President Bill Clinton and others to honor Rabin at his funeral. The image the world would remember was that of Rabin's eighteen-year-old granddaughter, who moved even stoic security guards to tears as she spoke eloquently of her family's personal grief.

For most Americans, the most searing image of 1995 was that of the limp and bloodied body of a baby girl thrust into the arms of a clearly anguished firefighter. The baby was one of 168 casualties of the bombing of a federal building in Oklahoma City in April.

The bombing was the most violent terrorist incident in recent U.S. history, the apparent work of two men who harbored deep-seated animosity toward the federal government, particularly the Federal Bureau of Investigation (FBI) and the Bureau of Alcohol, Tobacco, and Firearms (ATF). It took place on the second anniversary of the Waco, Texas, disaster in which several dozen members of a cult under siege by the FBI and ATF died in a fire.

The bombing focused new attention on the right-wing, antigovernment militias that had sprung up in recent years and on the National Rifle Association (NRA). The powerful gun lobby, like the militias, was extremely critical

How to Use This Book

The documents are arranged in chronological order. If you know the approximate date of the report, speech, statement, court decision, or other document you are looking for, glance through the titles for that month in the table of contents.

If the table of contents does not lead you directly to the document you want, turn to the index at the end of the book. There you may find references not only to the particular document you seek but also to other entries on the same or a related subject. The index in this volume is a five-year cumulative index of *Historic Documents* covering the years 1991-1995. There is a separate volume, *Historic Documents Index, 1972–1995* which may also be useful.

The introduction to each document is printed in italic type. The document itself, printed in roman type, follows the spelling, capitalization, and punctuation of the original or official copy. Where the full text is not given, omissions of material are indicated by the customary ellipsis points.

---

of the FBI and the ATF, charging that the two federal law enforcement agencies were overstepping their authority and harassing law-abiding citizens. Former president George Bush was so incensed by an NRA fundraising letter in which federal agents were referred to as "jack-booted thugs" that he resigned his lifetime membership in the organization.

Congress failed to act in 1995 on a new round of antiterrorism legislation urged by President Clinton or on the NRA's push to repeal two recently passed gun control laws. Even so, the year was an exceptionally busy one on Capitol Hill, where Republicans controlled both chambers of Congress for the first time in more than forty years after sweeping the 1994 elections. Proclaiming themselves antiliberal "revolutionaries," conservatives in the House of Representatives set out to pass a long list of legislation aimed at ending or curtailing government programs enacted since the New Deal.

The Republicans called their agenda the Contract with America, and they promised the House would pass all its elements within the first one hundred days of the 104th Congress. They came close to achieving that goal, but most of the legislation died in the Senate, was vetoed by President Clinton, or at year's end was awaiting negotiations between Congress and the president.

The Republicans did force Clinton to bow to their demand for a plan to balance the federal budget within seven years, but the two sides could not agree on specific steps to achieve that goal. The resulting bitter partisan feuding forced two partial government shutdowns in November and December that severely damaged the Republicans politically.

House Speaker Newt Gingrich (R-Ga.) also suffered political damage in 1995, the result of charges by the House ethics committee that he abused his congressional privileges for personal gain. The architect of the Republican revolution saw his poll ratings plummet; at year's end, one major poll put Gingrich's disapproval rating at 65 percent. Another prominent Republican, Sen. Bob Packwood of Oregon, was forced to resign from Congress in October when it became clear that he would be expelled for repeated incidents of sexual harassment. A record number of legislators decided that the Washington political scene had lost its allure; thirteen senators and twenty-six House members announced they would not stand for reelection in 1996.

Race and racial divisions were a major public issue in 1995. The nationally televised trial of Simpson, an African-American charged with murdering his white wife and a friend of hers, polarized blacks and whites as had few other incidents in recent memory. Whites tended to believe that Simpson was guilty as accused, apparently convinced by genetic evidence linking him to the crime scene. Many African-Americans thought Simpson was the innocent victim of a legal system that was habitually unfair to blacks. Those perceptions were heightened during the trial when one of the chief police investigators was shown to be a racist who had bragged about planting evidence in previous cases.

On October 16, an estimated 400,000 African-American men rallied on the Mall in Washington, D.C., in a day of solidarity; it was the largest civil rights demonstration in the nation's history. The Million Man March had been organized by Louis Farrakhan, the controversial Nation of Islam leader, who exhorted the men to atone for their past sins and to take personal responsibility for themselves, their families, and their communities. The march was shunned by many black leaders, who condemned Farrakhan for his antiwhite and anti-Semitic views.

Speaking in Austin, Texas, the same day, President Clinton urged Americans to try to understand the fears and anxieties that prompted each race to react to the other with suspicion and distrust. The Austin speech was one of several thoughtful talks the president delivered throughout the year on social issues dividing the nation. In August he spoke of civility both in everyday life and among politicians. In July he had reaffirmed his commitment to affirmative action, setting out his reasons for believing that programs giving preferences to minorities and women were still necessary.

The Supreme Court also spoke on affirmative action in 1995, ruling that such laws were constitutional only if they were narrowly tailored to meet a compelling government interest. This test was the strictest one the Court had yet applied to any civil rights law, and it seemed likely that some affirmative action programs would be found to have been too broadly drawn to survive such scrutiny.

The Court also applied this strict scrutiny test to congressional redistricting in which boundaries were deliberately drawn to give blacks or other minorities a majority of voters within the district. Such race-based districts were constitutionally suspect, the Court said, and could be justified only if they were shown to meet a compelling state interest. Many proponents of race-based districting worried that the ruling would jeopardize the historic gains that African-Americans and Hispanics had made in Congress in recent years.

In another case with potentially far-reaching implications, the Supreme Court held that Congress had exceeded its power to regulate commerce when it passed a law prohibiting anyone from carrying a gun within 1,000 feet of a school building. It was the first time the Court had curbed Congress's expansive interpretation of the commerce clause since the New Deal and was certain to add to the debate about the limits of congressional power, particularly in areas such as law enforcement, a matter traditionally left to the states.

Citing its authority to regulate drugs and medical devices, the Food and Drug Administration in 1995, with President Clinton's blessing, proposed regulations that would heighten restrictions on the marketing and sale of tobacco products, especially to children. The proposed regulations were issued after internal memos from cigarette manufacturers were made public showing that the cigarette makers knew nicotine was addictive and deliberately controlled levels of nicotine in their products.

Internationally, the world focused much of its attention during 1995 on efforts to bring peace to Bosnia and the Middle East.

The ethnic conflict in Bosnia produced the most savage fighting and the biggest dislocation of people in Europe since World War II. Until the Clinton administration stepped up diplomatic pressure on all sides, there seemed little hope to break the cycle of violence.

With the fighting turning against the Bosnian Serbs by mid-1995, all three sides—Serbs, Muslims, and Croats—appeared willing to grasp at a chance for peace. That chance came during a round of U.S.-brokered peace talks in November at Wright-Patterson Air Force Base near Dayton, Ohio. The three sides eventually agreed to a complex peace agreement dividing Bosnia into two sectors (one controlled by Muslims and Croats, the other by Serbs) under one multiethnic national government. The warring parties were to be separated by NATO-led peacekeeping forces. The Dayton accord was signed in Paris later in November, and at Christmastime troops from the United States, Britain, Germany, France, and other countries began pouring into Bosnia for one of the most complex and dangerous peacekeeping missions in history.

In the Middle East, nearly twenty years of peacemaking efforts by the United States paid off with a substantial new agreement between Israel and the Palestinians. Signed in September, the agreement provided for Israel to turn over administration of much of the West Bank of the Jordan River to an elected Palestinian authority. Negotiations on long-term issues, including the status of Jerusalem (claimed by both Israel and the Arabs), were to begin in 1996.

Barely six weeks after Rabin and Arafat signed that agreement, violence returned. This time it was Israeli versus Israeli, as a right-wing former Israeli soldier assassinated Rabin at the close of a peace celebration in Tel Aviv. The killing plunged Israel into a gloomy self-assessment but failed to achieve its goal of throwing the peace process off track. Rabin's interim successor, Shimon Peres, himself a former prime minister, promised to carry out the commitments to peace.

The Clinton administration helped nudge efforts toward peace in Northern Ireland by bolstering the position of the political wing of the Irish Republican Army, which declared a cease-fire in its terrorist campaign against British forces. To encourage the peace process, Clinton visited Northern Ireland; he was the first sitting U.S. president to do so. Negotiations proceeded fitfully, and it was unclear whether the militant Catholic and Protestant opponents would be willing to make the concessions necessary to end more than twenty-five years of conflict.

The United States in 1995 finally came to grips with one of the most painful episodes in its recent history: the Vietnam War. Twenty years after communists overran the remnants of the U.S.-backed government of South Vietnam, President Clinton officially recognized the Vietnamese government based in Hanoi. Clinton's action brought bitter protests from some veterans groups and conservative Republicans, but the lack of public response seemed to lend support to the president's assertion that it finally was time to close the wounds of America's most unpopular war.

Worldwide commemorations took place in 1995 to mark the fiftieth anniversary of the end of World War II. Several world leaders took the opportunity to make public apologies for the actions taken during and after the war by their predecessor generations. The Japanese prime minister apologized for the brutal Japanese occupation of Asian countries during the 1930s and into the war years. The new French president apologized to Jewish leaders for his country's complicity with Nazi Germany in the deportation of French Jews to concentration camps. President Clinton apologized for the U.S. government's postwar radiation experiments on thousands of American citizens, many of whom were not told they were being subjected to dangerous testing.

The year also marked the fiftieth anniversary of the founding of the United Nations. That institution had many successes to celebrate, but by 1995 it was facing worldwide criticism for its failures, especially its inability to prevent or bring an end to conflicts in Bosnia, Central Africa, and other regions.

Throughout the year, the world watched as Russia continued to stumble through its messy transition from a communist dictatorship to something resembling democracy. Russian president Boris Yeltsin, in failing health, grew weaker politically by the day. In December former communists swept parliamentary elections, further dimming chances that Yeltsin would be able to sustain reforms that were intended to salvage the economy but had the immediate effect of forcing millions of Russians into poverty.

These are but some of the topics of national and international interest chosen by the editors for *Historic Documents of 1995*. This edition marks the twenty-fourth volume of a Congressional Quarterly project that began with *Historic Documents of 1972*. The purpose of this series is to give students, librarians, journalists, scholars, and others convenient access to documents on a wide range of topics that lay out some of the most important issues of the year. In our judgment, the official statements, news conferences, speeches, special studies, and court decisions presented here will be of lasting interest.

Each document is preceded by an introduction that provides background information and, when relevant, an account of continuing developments during the year. We believe these introductions will become increasingly useful as memories of current times fade.

John Felton and Marty Gottron

CONTENTS

January

February

March

April

May

June

CONTENTS

July

CONTENTS

August

September

October

November

December

January

OPENING OF THE
104TH CONGRESS
January 4, 1995

In the opening speeches of the 104th Congress on January 4, as the two political parties were about to embark on a historic reversal of roles, Speaker of the House Newt Gingrich (R-Ga.) and his Democrat counterpart, Minority Leader Richard A. Gephardt of Missouri, pledged mutual cooperation and partnership. The two leaders were taking part in the most dramatic political upheaval on Capitol Hill in more than a generation, as the Republicans took control of both houses of Congress for the first time since 1955. (1994 election results, Historic Documents of 1994, p. 513)

Despite the tension inherent in the turnover of political power, the two House leaders promised that their parties would work together as much as possible. Those pledges would prove difficult to carry out, however, as during 1995 the two parties clashed daily over major economic and social issues.

Republicans Take Control of the House

After defeating Gephardt in the election for Speaker on a party-line vote of 228–202, Gingrich won broad praise from his Republican colleagues, the vast majority of whom appeared to share his conservative political philosophy and admire his combative approach to politics.

Gephardt, who had served as majority leader when the Democrats were in power, had little trouble mustering support from his colleagues, although a few advocated a new, more conservative course for the party. Two of them, Gene Taylor and Mike Parker of Mississippi, abstained on the vote for Speaker, saying they opposed Gephardt but could not vote for Gingrich. Parker was quoted as saying that voting for Gephardt was like asking the captain of the Titanic *for a boat ride. (On November 10, Parker would switch his affiliation and become a member of the Republican party.)*

Upon accepting the Speaker's gavel from Gephardt, Gingrich launched into a rambling, mostly extemporaneous, thirty-five-minute lecture on history and politics, replete with anecdotes, personal reminiscences, and even a few book recommendations. Perhaps the speech was most remarkable for

*what it was not: one of the fiery partisan attacks on Democrats for which
Gingrich was famous. For once, Gingrich repeatedly offered complimenta-
ry remarks about Democrats, not scathing condemnation. He praised
Franklin Delano Roosevelt, for three generations the scourge of conservative Republicans, as "the greatest president of the twentieth century."
Gingrich also paid tribute to Rep. Ronald Dellums (D-Calif.), another frequent target of conservative scorn, for the "great work" he had done "to
extend freedom across the planet."*

*Gingrich took time to assure his colleagues that, although they would
have to work hard, their family lives would not suffer. His principle prescription would be to allow only seventeen minutes for each roll call vote.
As with many other promises, this one turned out to be almost impossible
to enforce in practice, and many workdays in the House during 1995
extended well into the evening.*

Balanced Budget, Welfare Reform

*A former college history teacher, Gingrich used his nationally televised
speech to expound broad philosophical concepts and lay out a formidable
agenda based on the Republicans' Contract with America. The contract
included several relatively noncontroversial reforms of congressional procedure (such as banning proxy votes in committees) as well as such major
policy items as welfare reform and a constitutional amendment requiring
a balanced budget.* (House Republican Contract with America, Historic
Documents of 1994, p. 374)

*The new Speaker devoted much of his speech to the latter two subjects,
calling them the "giant challenges" for Congress and the country. Gingrich
skirted the details of both issues but talked in general terms about the need
for bipartisan cooperation to get legislation passed.*

*The Speaker sought to assure his audience that Social Security would be
"off limits" to budget-cutters, "at least for the first four to six years."
Everything else was up for grabs, he said, citing in particular Medicare,
agricultural subsidies, and defense spending.*

*Obviously seeking to reach out for Democratic support, Gingrich
recalled, in the context of his remarks on the budget, President Franklin
Delano Roosevelt's famous first inaugural statement that "we have nothing
to fear but fear itself." In the same context, Gingrich told his Republican
colleagues that they have "much to learn from studying what the Democrats
did right" on such issues as civil rights.*

*The Speaker offered little in the way of specifics on welfare reform. He
instead related stories of children killing each other and infants left abandoned in dumpsters.*

*In a general word of advice, Gingrich admonished both Republicans and
Democrats to examine carefully their own assumptions. "I would say to
those Republicans who believe in total privatization [of welfare], you can't
believe in the Good Samaritan and explain that as long as business is making money, we can walk by a fellow American who's hurt and not do some-*

thing. And I would say to my friends on the left who believe that there's never been a government program that wasn't worth keeping, you can't look at some of the results we now have and not want to reach out to the humans and forget the bureaucrats."

Gingrich repeatedly used the phrase "reach out" in his speech, closing with a plea for his colleagues to "reach out prayerfully and try to genuinely understand the other. . . ."

In his brief address immediately before passing the Speaker's gavel to Gingrich, Gephardt took the role of a gracious loser, using the occasion to celebrate the vitality of the American political system. "We may not all agree with today's changing of the guard. We not all like it, but we enact the peoples' will with dignity, and honor, and pride," Gephardt said.

Gephardt made no mention of specific policy or political issues, except to say that Democrats had an obligation to fight on behalf of "America's hard-working middle-income families."

Following are excerpts of speeches made January 4, 1995, by Minority Leader Richard A. Gephardt (D-Mo.) and Speaker of the House Newt Gingrich (R-Ga.) at the opening session of the 104th Congress:

GEPHARDT'S REMARKS

Ladies and gentlemen of the House, I first want to thank my Democratic colleagues for their support and their confidence. I noted we were a little short, but I appreciate your friendship and your support.

As you might imagine, this is not a moment that I had been waiting for. (Laughter.)

When you carry the mantle of progress there is precious little glory in defeat. But sometimes we spend so much time lionizing the winners and labeling the losers, that we lose sight of the victory we all share in this crown jewel of democracy. You see, Mr. Speaker, this is a day to celebrate a power that belongs not to any political party, but to the people, no matter the margin, no matter the majority.

All across the world, from Bosnia, to Chechnya, to South Africa, people lay down their lives for the kind of voice we take for granted. Too often the transfer of power is an act of pain and carnage, not one as we see today, of peace and decency. But here in the House of Representatives, for 219 years, longer than any democracy in the world, we heed the peoples' voice with peace and civility, and respect. Each and every day on this very floor we echo the hopes and dreams of our people, their fear and their failures, their abiding belief in a better America.

We may not all agree with today's changing of the guard. We may not all like it, but we enact the peoples' will with dignity, and honor, and pride. And in that endeavor, Mr. Speaker, there can be no losers and there can be no defeat.

5

Of course, in the 104th Congress there will be conflict and compromise. Agreements will not always be easy. Agreement sometimes is not even possible. But while we may not agree on matters of party and principle, we all abide with the will of the people. That is reason enough to place our good faith and our best hopes in your able hands.

I speak from the bottom of my heart when I say that I wish you the best in these coming two years. For when this gavel passes into your hands, so do the futures and fortunes of millions of Americans. To make real progress, to improve real peoples' lives we both have to rise above partisanship. We have to work together where we can and where we must. It is a profound responsibility, one which knows no bounds of party or politics. It is a responsibility not merely for those who voted for you, not merely for those who cast their fate on your side of the aisle, but also for those who did not.

These are the responsibilities I pass, along with the gavel I hold, or will hold in my hand. But there are some burdens that the Democratic Party will never cease to bear. As Democrats we came to Congress to fight for America's hard-working middle-income families, the families who are working often for longer hours, for less pay, for fewer benefits in jobs they are not sure they can keep.

We, together, must redeem their faith that if they work hard and they play by the rules, they can build a better life for their children.

Mr. Speaker, I want this entire House to speak for those families. The Democratic Party will. That mantle we will never lay to rest.

So, with partnership, but with purpose, I pass this great gavel of our government. With resignation but with resolve I hereby end 40 years of Democratic rule of this House.

With faith and with friendship, and the deepest respect, you are now my Speaker, and let the great debate begin.

I now have the high honor and distinct privilege to present to the House of Representatives our new Speaker, the Gentleman from Georgia, Newt Gingrich.

GINGRICH'S REMARKS

We're starting the 104th Congress. I don't know if you ever thought about just the concept. For 208 years we gathered together the most diverse country in the history of the world. We sent all sorts of people. Each of us could find at least one member we thought was weird, and I'll tell you, if you went around the room, the person we chose to be weird would be different for virtually every one of us because we do allow and insist upon the right of a free people to send an extraordinary diversity of people here.

Brian Lamb of C-SPAN read to me Friday a phrase from [Alexis] de Toqueville that was so central to the House. I've been reading [Robert V.] Remini's biography of Henry Clay, and Henry Clay always preferred the House. He was the first strong Speaker. And he preferred the House to the Senate, although he served them both. And he said the House was more vital, more active, more dynamic, more common. And this is what de Toqueville wrote: "Often there is not a distinguished man in the whole number. Its members are almost all obscure individuals whose names bring no associations to mind. They are mostly village lawyers, men in trade, or even persons belonging to the lower classes of society." Now, if you put women in with men, I don't know that we've changed much.

But the word "vulgar" in de Toqueville's time had a very particular meaning, and it's a meaning the world would do well to study in this room. You see, de Toqueville was an aristocrat. He lived in a world of kings and princes. And the folks who come here come here by the one single act that their citizens freely chose them. And I don't care what your ethnic background, what your ideology, I don't care whether you're younger or older, I don't care whether you were born in America or you're a naturalized citizen; every one of the 435 people have equal standing because their citizens freely sent them, and their voice should be heard, and they should have a right to participate.

And it is the most marvelous act of a complex, giant country trying to argue and talk, and as Dick [House Minority Leader Richard A. Gephardt, D-Mo.] said, to have a great debate, to reach great decisions not through a civil war, not by bombing one of our regional capitals, not by killing a half million people, not by having snipers. And let me say unequivocally, I condemn all acts of violence against the law by all people for all reasons. This is a society of law and a society of civil behavior.

['Commoners' in Congress]

And so here we are as commoners together, to some extent Democrats and Republicans, to some extent liberals and conservatives—but Americans all. Steve Gunderson [R-Wis.] today gave me a copy of *The Portable Abraham Lincoln* and suggested there's much for me to learn about our party. But I would also say, as I have since the election, it doesn't hurt to have a copy of *The Portable FDR*. This is a great country of great people.

If there's any one factor or act of my life that strikes as I stand up here as the first Republican in 40 years to do so, when I first became whip in 1989, Russia was beginning to change, the Soviet Union as it was then, and into my whip's office one day came eight Russians and a Lithuanian, members of the Communist Party, newspaper editors. And they asked me, "What does a whip do?" They said, "You know, in Russia we've never [had] a free parliament since 1917 and that was only for a few months. So what do you do?"

And I tried to explain, as Dave Bonior [D-Mich., the House minority whip] or Tom DeLay [R-Texas, the House majority whip] might now, and it's a little strange if you're from a dictatorship, to explain you're called the whip but you don't really have a whip; you're elected by the people you're supposed to pressure; if you pressure them too much they won't reelect you; if you don't pressure them enough they won't reelect you. You've got to somehow find this—it's a—democracy's hard; it's frustrating.

And so we came in the chamber, and the Lithuanian was a man in his late 60s, and I allowed him to come up here and sit and be Speaker. That's something many of us have done with constituents. Remember, this is the very beginning of *perestroika* and *glasnost*. He came out of the chair; he was physically trembling; he was almost in tears. And he said, "You know, ever since World War II, I've remembered what the Americans did and I've never believed the propaganda," but he said, "I have to tell you, I did not think in my life that I would be able to sit at the center of freedom."

Now, it was one of the most overwhelming, compelling moments of my life. And what struck me, and it's something I couldn't help but think of when we were here with [South African] President [Nelson] Mandela and I went over and saw Ron Dellums [D-Calif.] and thought of the great work Ron had done to extend freedom across the planet, and that sense of emotion when you see something so totally different than you'd expected.

And here was a man, he reminded me first of all that while presidents are important, they are in effect an elected kingship; that this and the other body across the way are where freedom has to be fought out. And that's the tradition I hope that we'll take with us as we go to work.

Today we had a bipartisan prayer service. Frank Wolf [R-Va.] made some very important points. He said we have to recognize that many of our most painful problems as a country are moral problems, problems of dealing with ourselves and with life. He said character is the key to leadership, and we have to deal with that. He preached a little bit—I don't think he thought it was preaching, but it was—about a spirit of reconciliation. And he talked about caring about our spouses and our children and our families, because if we're not prepared to model that, beyond just having them here for one day—if we're not prepared to care about our children and we're not prepared to care about our families, then by what arrogance do we think we will transcend our behavior to care about others?

And that's why, with Congressman Gephardt's help, we've established a bipartisan task force on the family. We've established the principle that we're going to set schedules we stick to so families can count on times to be together, built around the school schedules, so that families can get to know each other—and not just on C-SPAN.

I will also say that means one of the strongest recommendations of the bipartisan family committee—I don't want this to be seen as Gingrich acting as a Speaker on his own here—is that we have 17 minutes to vote. They pointed out that if you take the time we spent in the last Congress where we had one more and then one more, at one point we had a 45-minute vote, that you literally can shorten the business and get people home if we will be strict and firm. I say that with all of my colleagues, I hope, paying attention, because we're in fact going to work very hard to have 17 minutes and it's over. So leave at the first bell, not the second bell.

[Carrying Out the Contract]

This may seem particularly appropriate to say on the first day, because this will be the busiest day on opening day in congressional history. I want to read just a part of the "Contract with America," not as a partisan act, but to remind all of us of what we're about to go through and why, because those of us who ended up in a majority stood on these steps and signed a contract, and here's part of what it says, quote:

"On the first day of the 104th Congress, the new Republican majority will immediately pass the following major reforms aimed at restoring the faith and trust of the American people in their government:

"First, require all laws that apply to the rest of the country also apply equally to the Congress.

"Second, select a major independent auditing firm to conduct a comprehensive audit of Congress for waste, fraud or abuse.

"Third, cut the number of House committees and cut committee staffs by a third.

"Fourth, limit the terms of all committee chairs.

"Fifth, ban the casting of proxy votes in committees.

"Sixth, require committee meetings to be open to the public.

"Seventh, require a three-fifths majority vote to pass a tax increase.

"Eighth, guarantee an honest accounting of our federal budget by implementing zero baseline budgeting."

Now, I told Dick last night that, if I had to do it over again, we would have pledged within three days we'll do these things, but that's not what we said. So we've got ourselves in a little bit of a box. But then we go a step further, and I carry the *TV Guide* version of the contract with me at all times. We then said, thereafter, "within the first 100 days of the 104th Congress, we shall bring to the House floor the following bills, each to be given full and open debate, each to be given a clear and fair vote, each to be immediately available for inspection."

We made it available that day. And we listed 10 items: a balanced-budget amendment and line-item veto; to stop violent criminals, emphasizing among other things an effective, enforceable death penalty; third was welfare reform; fourth was protecting our kids; fifth was tax cuts for families; sixth was a stronger national defense; seventh was raising the senior citizens' earning limit; eighth was rolling back government regulations; ninth was commonsense legal reform; and 10th was congressional term limits.

Now, our commitment on our side, and I think we have this absolute obligation, is first of all to work today until we're done. And that, I know, is going to inconvenience people who have families and supporters, but we were hired to do a job, and we have to start today to prove we'll do it.

Second, I would say to our friends in the Democratic Party that we're going to work with you, and we're really laying out a schedule working with the minority leader to make sure that we can set [a] date certain to go home. That does mean two or three weeks out. If we are running short, we'll frankly have longer sessions on Tuesday, Wednesday and Thursday. We'll try to work this out in a bipartisan basis to a workmanlike way to get it done. It's going to mean the busiest early months since 1933.

Beyond the contract, I think there are two giant challenges, and I really— I know I'm a very partisan figure, but I really hope today that I can speak for a minute to my friends in the Democratic Party as well as my own colleagues, speak to the country, about these two challenges, and I hope we can have a real dialogue.

One is to achieve a balanced budget by 2002. I think both Democratic and Republican governors will tell you it's doable, but it's hard. I don't think it's doable in a year or two. I don't think we ought to lie to the American people. This is a huge, complicated job.

Second, I think we have to find a way to truly replace the current welfare state with an opportunity society. Let me talk very briefly about both.

[Balanced-Budget Amendment]

First, on the balanced budget, I think we can get it done. I think the baby boomers are now old enough that we can have an honest dialogue about priorities, about resources, about what works, about what doesn't. Let me say I have already told Vice President Gore we are going to invite him—we would have invited him in December, but he had to go to Moscow—we are going to invite him up to address the Republican Conference on Reinventing Government.

I believe there are grounds for us to talk together and work together, to have hearings together, to have task forces together. And I think if we set priorities, if we apply the principles of [William Edwards] Deming and of Peter Drucker, if we build on the vice president's "reinventing government" effort, if we focus on transforming—not just cutting, not just do you want more or do you want less, but are there ways to do it better, can we learn from the private sector, can we learn from Ford and from IBM, from Microsoft, from what General Motors has had to go through—I think on a bipartisan basis, we owe it to our children and grandchildren to get this government in order and to be able to actually pay our way. I think 2002 is a reasonable time frame, and I would hope that together we could open a dialogue with the American people.

And I've said I think Social Security ought to be off limits, at least for the first four to six years of this process, because I think it will just destroy us if we try to bring it into the game. But let me say about everything else, whether it's Medicare or it's agricultural subsidies or it's defense or anything, that I think the greatest Democratic president of the 20th century, and in my judgment the greatest president of the 20th century, said it right on March 4th, 1933, when he stood in the braces, as a man who had polio at a time when nobody who had that kind of disability could be anything in public life, and he was president of the United States, and he stood in front of this Capitol on a rainy March day, and he said we have nothing to fear but fear itself.

I believe if every one of us will reach out in that spirit and will pledge—and I think frankly on a bipartisan basis—I would say to the member of the Black and Hispanic caucus, I hope we could arrange by late spring to genuinely share districts where you'll have a Republican who frankly may not know a thing about your district agree to come for a long weekend with you, and you'll agree to go for a long weekend with them, and we begin a dialogue and an openness that is totally different than people are used to seeing in politics in America. And I believe if we do that, we can then create a dialogue that can lead to a balanced budget.

But I think we have a greater challenge. And I do want to pick up directly on what Dick Gephardt said, because he said it right, and no Republican here should kid themselves about it. The greatest leaders in fighting for an integrated America in the 20th century were in the Democratic Party. The fact is it was the liberal wing of the Democratic Party that ended segregation. The fact is that it was [President] Franklin Delano Roosevelt who gave hope to a nation that was in despair and could have slid into dictatorship. And the fact is every Republican has much to learn from studying what the Democrats did right.

But I would say to my friends in the Democratic Party that there is much to what [President] Ronald Reagan was trying to get done; there is much to what is being done today by Republicans like [governors] Bill Weld [Mass.] and John Engler [Mich.] and Tommy Thompson [Wis.] and George Allen [Va.] and Christie Whitman [N.J.] and Pete Wilson [Calif.]. And there's much we can share with each other. We must replace the welfare state with an opportunity society.

[Welfare Reform]

The balanced budget is the right thing to do. But it doesn't, in my mind, have the moral urgency of coming to grips with what's happening to the poorest Americans. I commend to all of you Marvin Olasky's *The Tragedy of American Compassion*. Olasky goes back for 300 years and looks at what has worked in America, how we have helped people rise beyond poverty, how we have reached out to save people. And he may not have the answers, but he has the right sense as to where we have to go as Americans.

I don't believe that there is a single American who can see a news report of a 4-year-old thrown off of a public housing project in Chicago by other children and killed and not feel that a part of your heart went. I think of my nephew in the back, Kevin. I mean, how would any of us feel about our children? How can any American read about an 11-year-old buried with his teddy bear because he killed a 14-year-old and then another 14-year-old killed him and not have some sense of, "My God, where [has] this country gone?" How can we not decide that this is a moral crisis equal to segregation, equal to slavery, and how can we not insist that every day we take steps to do something?

I have seldom been more shaken than I was shortly after the election when I had breakfast with two members of the Black Caucus, and one of them said to me, "Can you imagine what it's like to visit a first-grade class and realize that every fourth or fifth young boy in that class may be dead or in jail within 15 years, and they're your constituents, and you're helpless to change it?"

And that just, for some reason, I don't know why, but—maybe because I visit a lot of schools—that got through. I mean, that personalized it. That made it real, not just statistics, but real people.

11

And then I tried to explain part of my thoughts by talking about the need for alternatives to the bureaucracy, and we got into what I think has frankly been a distorted and cheap debate over orphanages.

Let me say, first of all, my father, who's here today, was a foster child who was adopted as a teenager. I am adopted. We have relatives who are adopted. We are not talking out of some vague, impersonal, Dickens, Bleak House, middle-class, intellectual model. We have lived the alternatives. I believe when we are told that children are so lost in the city bureaucracies that there are children in dumpsters, when we are told that there are children doomed to go to school where 70 or 80 percent of them will not graduate, when we're told of public housing projects that are so dangerous that if any private sector ran them they would be put in jail, and we're giving them "Well, we'll study it. We'll get around to it," my only point is we can find ways immediately to do things better and to reach out and to break through the bureaucracy and to give every young American child a better chance.

And let me suggest to you Morris Shechtman's new book—and I don't agree with all of it, but it's fascinating—it's entitled *Working Without a Net*. It's really an effort to argue that in the 21st century, we have to create our own safety nets, but he draws a distinction worth every American reading: between caring and caretaking. He says caretaking's when you bother me a little bit, so I do enough that I feel better because I think I took care of you and may not have done any good to you at all. You may in fact be an alcoholic, and I just gave you the money to buy the bottle that kills you. But I feel better, and I go home. He said caring is actually stopping and dealing with the human being and trying to understand enough about them to genuinely make sure you improve their life, even if you have to start with a conversation like, "If you'll quit drinking, I'll help you get a job," which is a lot harder conversation than, "Oh, I feel better, I gave him a buck, or I gave him five bucks."

And I want to commend every member on both sides to look carefully. I would say to those Republicans who believe in total privatization, you can't believe in the Good Samaritan and explain that as long as business is making money, we can walk by a fellow American who's hurt and not do something. And I would say to my friends on the left who believe that there's never been a government program that wasn't worth keeping, you can't look at some of the results we now have and not want to reach out to the humans and forget the bureaucracies. And if we could build that attitude on both sides of this aisle, we would be an amazingly different place, and the country would begin to be a different place.

You know, we have to create a partnership. We have to reach out to the American people. We're going to do a lot of important things. As of today, we are going to thanks to the House Information System and Congressman Vern Ehlers [R-Mich.], we are going to be online for the whole country—every amendment, every conference report. We're working with C-SPAN and others, and Congressman Gephardt has agreed to help on a bipartisan basis to make the building more open to television, more accessible to the American people. We have talk radio hosts here today for the first time, and I hope to have a bipartisan effort to make the place accessible for all talk radio hosts of all backgrounds, no matter what their ideology. The House historian's office is going to be much more aggressively run on a bipartisan basis to reach out to others, to teach what the legislative struggle's about.

[The Measures of Success]

I think over time we can—and will this spring—rethink campaign reform and lobbying reform and review all ethics, including the gift rule, and rethink what our role should be; but that ain't enough. Our challenge shouldn't be to balance the budget, to pass the contract; our challenge shouldn't be anything that's just legislative. We're supposed to, each one of us, be leaders. I think our challenge has to be to set as our goal—and we're not going to get here in two years, but this ought to be the goal that we go home and we tell people we believe in—that there will be a Monday morning when for the entire weekend not a single child was killed anywhere in America, that there will be a Monday morning when every child in the country went to a school that they and their parents thought prepared them as citizens and prepared them to compete in the world market, that there will be a Monday morning when it was easy to find a job or create a job, and your own government didn't punish you if you tried.

We shouldn't be happy just with the language of politicians and the language of legislation. We should insist that our success for America is felt in the neighborhoods, in the communities, is felt by real people living real lives who can say, "Yeah, we're safer, we're healthier, we're better educated, America succeeds."

This morning's closing hymn at the prayer service was "The Battle Hymn of the Republic." It's hard to be in this building and look down past Grant to the Lincoln Memorial and not realize how painful and how difficult that battle hymn is. A key phrase is, "As he died to make men holy, let us live to make men free."

It's not just political freedom, although I agree with everything Congressman Gephardt said earlier. If you can't afford to leave the public housing project, you're not free. If you don't know how to find a job and you don't know how to create a job, you're not free. If you can't find a place that'll educate you, you're not free. If you're afraid to walk to the store because you could get killed, you're not free.

And so, as all of us over the coming months sing that song, "As he died to make men holy, let us live to make men free," I want us to dedicate ourselves to reach out in a genuinely nonpartisan way, to be honest with each other. I promise each of you that, without regard to party, my door is going to be open. I will listen to each of you; I will try to work with each of you; I will put in long hours, and I'll guarantee that I'll listen to you first and I'll let you get it all out before I give you my version, because you've been patient with me today and you've given me a chance to set the stage.

But I want to close by reminding all of us of how much bigger this is than us. Beyond talking with the American people, beyond working together, I

13

think we can only be successful if we start with our limits. I was very struck this morning with something Bill Emerson [R-Mo.] used. It's a fairly famous quote of Benjamin Franklin at the point where the Constitutional Convention was deadlocked, and people were tired, and there was a real possibility that the convention was going to break up. And Franklin, who was quite old and had been relatively quiet for the entire convention, suddenly stood up and was angry. And he said, "I have lived, sir, a long time, and the longer I live the more convincing proofs I see of this truth, that God governs in the affairs of men. And if a sparrow cannot fall to the ground without his notice, is it probable that an empire can rise without his aid?"

And at that point, the Constitutional Convention stopped. They took a day off for fasting and prayer and then, having stopped and come together, they went back and they solved the great question of large and small states, and they wrote the Constitution, and the United States was created.

If each of us—and all I can do is pledge you from me—if each of us will reach out prayerfully and try to genuinely understand the other, if we'll recognize that in this building we symbolize America writ small, that we have an obligation to talk with each other, then I think a year from now we can look on the 104th as a truly amazing institution, and without regard to party, regard to ideology, we can say here America comes to work and here we are preparing for those children a better future.

Thank you. Good luck and God bless you. . . .

REPORT ON THE FUTURE OF LABOR-MANAGEMENT RELATIONS
January 9, 1995

A presidential commission studying labor-management relations released its final report January 9, 1995, recommending several reforms that would make it easier for workers to organize unions and for employers to set up teams of workers and managers to deal with productivity, quality, and other workplace issues.

The report by the Commission on the Future of Worker-Management Relations, known as the Dunlop Commission, seemed to please nobody. Elements that appealed to business were castigated by organized labor; the parts that labor supported were rejected by business. The Clinton administration did not commit itself to proposing any legislation based on the report. Labor Secretary Robert B. Reich and Commerce Secretary Ronald H. Brown, receiving the final report from commission chairman and former labor secretary John T. Dunlop at a formal press conference, said only that they would study the commission's findings. The only recommendations the Republican-controlled Congress seemed likely to take up dealt with how to make it easier for employers to form work teams.

The report was the result of twenty months of study, in which the commission held twenty-one public hearings, heard from more than four hundred witnesses, and received numerous studies, reports, and statements from business groups, professional associations, labor unions, academics, women's organizations, and other interested parties. The panel published a fact-finding report in June 1994. Among the commission members were two other former labor secretaries, William J. Usery Jr. and F. Ray Marshall, and a former commerce secretary, Juanita M. Kreps.

In its introduction, the report called the workplace "a centerpiece of the nation's economic performance" and noted that changes in the nature and location of work had blurred the traditional distinctions between worker and supervisor. Furthermore, neither federal and state laws and regulations nor attitudes among management and labor have changed to keep in step with a more flexible workplace. As a result, workplaces "are far too

*adversarial in tone and substance for the good of the American economy,"
the report said. "Changes must be made in the way firms, employees, and
unions interact, and in workplace laws, and regulations, to enable them to
carry out successfully the vital tasks society places on them."*

Goals and Recommendations

*The commission listed ten goals for modernizing labor-management rela-
tions and fifteen recommendations for achieving those goals. Several of the
reforms were aimed at reducing workplace disputes and litigation by
expanding the use of negotiated rulemaking, mediation, and alternative dispute resolution procedures. It proposed giving individual workplaces more
responsibility to tailor regulatory guidelines to their own circumstances.*

*The two main sets of recommendations concerned work teams and
union representation rights. Work teams—committees of workers and
supervisors set up to deal with productivity and quality issues—have
become increasingly popular in recent years. According to a survey conducted for the commission, 53 percent of the employees surveyed reported
that some form of employee participation program operated in their workplace and 31 percent said they were involved in such programs. Seventy-
nine percent of those surveyed said the programs gave them a greater say
in their jobs. Two of every three employees at workplaces without participation programs said they would like such a program.*

*Work teams that incidentally discuss conditions of work, such as work
schedules, might, however, be in violation of the 1935 National Labor
Relations Act (NLRA), which forbids "company unions" (committees set
up by management to deal with wages and other work conditions). The
commission urged that the NLRA be clarified to ensure that work teams not
be found unlawful simply because they involved "terms and conditions" of
work. At the same time, the commission said that such work teams should
not be used as a substitute for independent unions and that company
unions continue to be banned.*

*To ensure workers their right to choose union representation, the com-
mission recommended that elections be held within two weeks after workers petition the National Labor Relations Board (NLRB) for the election.
Under current law, management can delay elections by raising legal issues
about such matters as the scope of the bargaining unit. The commission
suggested that all such issues be resolved after the elections have taken
place. The commission also recommended that the NLRB be given authority to issue injunctions against employers who fire or otherwise penalize
workers engaged in organizing activities. According to the survey conducted for the panel, improper dismissals related to organizing activities
occurred in one of every four certification elections.*

*The commission proposed methods for resolving some of the problems
associated with "contingent workers"—independent contractors and part-
time, temporary, seasonal, and leased workers. This category is among the
fastest-growing class of workers; some estimates put the number of con-*

tingent workers at 25 percent of the labor force. While this type of work arrangement offers both the workers and their employers flexibility, it can lead to abuses. Unscrupulous employers may attempt to save money by not contributing anything to a contingent worker's social security or health insurance while still receiving the same quality and quantity of work. The commission suggested that the definition of employee be changed to clarify the distinction between independent contractors and employees. Workers would be considered employees if they were economically dependent on the company they performed services for. Low wages, low skill levels, and working for only one or a few employers would indicate economic dependence, the commission said.

Republican Work Team Legislation

Over objections of pro-labor groups, Republicans in the House of Representatives pushed through legislation on September 27 that would modify the NLRA to encourage the creation of employer-employee work teams. The teams would be prohibited in companies where workers were represented by unions. Republicans said workplace cooperation was needed for companies to be competitive. "What we have here," Rep. Harris W. Fawell (R-Ill.) said of the NLRA, "is a fossilized sixty-year-old definition of labor organization, colliding head-on with dynamic new concepts of doing business in today's fast evolving, information-centered economy and society."

Opponents said that the measure was aimed at undermining organized labor. In a statement, the Clinton administration threatened to veto the bill. The Senate had not acted on the legislation by the end of the year.

Following is the text of the executive summary of the final report of the Commission on the Future of Worker-Management Relations, released January 9, 1995:

The Commission on the Future of Worker-Management Relations was appointed by Secretary of Commerce Ronald H. Brown and Secretary of Labor Robert B. Reich to address three questions:

"1. What (if any) new methods or institutions should be encouraged, or required, to enhance work-place productivity through labor-management cooperation and employee participation?

2. What (if any) changes should be made in the present legal framework and practices of collective bargaining to enhance cooperative behavior, improve productivity, and reduce conflict and delay?

3. What (if anything) should be done to increase the extent to which work-place problems are directly resolved by the parties themselves, rather than through recourse to state and federal courts and governmental bodies?"

Over its twenty months of work, the Commission heard testimony and evaluated the experiences of many employers and employees, and received advice for answering its charge from many groups and individuals. This testimony, and various survey and other evidence, guides the recommendations and suggestions that we offer to the Secretaries, and to the nation.

As reported in the Commission's May 1994 Fact-Finding Report, there is a solid base of experience on which to build more cooperative and productive workplace relations in the United States—the innovative partnerships in collective bargaining and the array of employee involvement programs operating in many workplaces across the country. There are also disconcerting patterns—increased earning inequality, difficulties for contingent workers, increased litigation, rigid and complex regulations, and conflict in union organizing campaigns.

Our recommendations build on the positive experiences with productive and cooperative worker-management relations, support their adoption in additional employment settings, and encourage further experimentation and learning. At the same time we face squarely and propose remedies for the problems of too much conflict, litigation, inequality, and regulatory complexity.

We take an integrated approach to modernizing American labor and employment law and administration for the future. Taken together, these recommendations give workers and managers the tools and flexibility to do what they say they want to do and are capable of doing to improve workplace performance. We recommend flexibility in employee participation while insuring respect for workers' rights to choose unions, if desired. We encourage the development and use of fair systems for resolving disputes quickly closest to their source without going to court or to a government agency. We propose to modernize labor law to deliver through a prompt and simplified process what the law promises: a free choice for workers on whether or not to join a union of their choosing. Our proposals define employees and employers in ways consistent with economic reality. We encourage continued learning and dialogue among private and public sector leaders to improve the quality of policy making on employment issues.

The Commission could not address all the problems or proposed solutions presented to us. This does not imply that those left out are unimportant or not valid. Instead, some need to be left to other groups and to further discussion. Moreover, the recommendations we offer here are presented as starting points for improving the workplace experiences and results for all Americans.

The full set of recommendations are contained in the separate sections of this report. Here we present fifteen key conclusions and recommendations as they relate to each of our three charges.

1. New Methods or Institutions to Enhance Workplace Productivity

The evidence presented to the Commission is overwhelming that employee participation and labor-management partnerships are good for workers, firms, and the national economy. All parties want to encourage expansion and growth of these developments. To do so requires removing the legal uncertainties affecting some forms of employee participation while safeguarding and strengthening employees' rights to choose whether or not they wish to be represented at the workplace by a union or professional organization. Accordingly we recommend:

(1) Clarifying the National Labor Relations Act (NLRA) and its interpretation by the National Labor Relations Board (NLRB) to insure nonunion employee participation programs are not found to be unlawful simply because they involve discussion of "terms and conditions" of work or compensation as long as such discussion is incidental to the broad purposes of these programs. At the same time, the Commission reaffirms the basic principle that these programs are not a substitute for independent unions. The law should continue to make it illegal to set up or operate company-dominated forms of employee representation.

(2) Updating the definitions of supervisor and manager to insure that only those with full supervisory or managerial authority and responsibility are excluded from coverage of the law. We further recommend that no individual or group of individuals should be excluded from coverage under the statute because of participation in joint problem-solving teams, self-managing work groups, or internal self-governance or dispute resolution processes.

(3) Reaffirming and extending protections of individuals against discrimination for participating in employee involvement processes and for joining or drawing on the services of an outside labor or professional organization.

These recommendations are linked to those that follow in important ways. In addition to eliminating the legal uncertainties associated with many of the forms of employee participation underway today, these changes allow and encourage use of worker-management participation in applying government regulations to the workplace and resolving disputes through private resolution procedures. Moreover, these changes remove the threat that workers might lose the protections of collective bargaining by taking on supervisory or managerial responsibilities. These changes, therefore, should open up workplaces to a variety of new experiments with employee participation and labor-management partnerships and bring the benefits of these innovations to more workers and workplaces.

2. Changes in Collective Bargaining to Enhance Cooperation and Reduce Conflict and Delay

The evidence reviewed by the Commission demonstrated conclusively that current labor law is not achieving its stated intent of encouraging collective bargaining and protecting workers' rights to choose whether or not to be represented at their workplace. Rectifying this situation is important to insure that these rights are realized for the workers who wish to exercise them, to de-escalate workplace conflicts, and to create an overall climate of trust and cooperation at the workplace and in the broader labor and management community. Accordingly, the Commission recommends:

(4) Providing for prompt elections after the NLRB determines that sufficient employees have expressed a desire to be represented by a union. Such elections should generally be held within two weeks. To accomplish this objective we propose that challenges to bargaining units and other legal disputes be resolved after the elections are held.

Beyond the reversal of the Supreme Court's decision in Lechmere so that employees may have access to union organizers in privately-owned but publicly-used spaces such as shopping malls, access questions are best left to the NLRB. The Commission urges the Board to strive to afford employees the most equal and democratic dialogue possible.

(5) Requiring by statute that the NLRB obtain prompt injunctions to remedy discriminatory actions against employees that occur during an organizing campaign or negotiations for a first contract.

(6) Assisting employers and newly certified unions in achieving first contracts through an upgraded dispute resolution system which provides for mediation and empowers a tripartite advisory board to use a variety of options to resolve disputes ranging from self-help (strike or lockout) to binding arbitration for relatively few disputes.

(7) Encouraging railroad and airline labor and management representatives to implement their stated willingness to seek their own solutions for improving the performance of collective bargaining in their industries.

These changes are essential to de-escalating the level of conflict, fear, and delays that now too often surround the process by which workers decide whether or not to be represented on their jobs. We distilled our recommendations down to these basic and simplified changes in the law and procedures from an extensive array of proposals offered to the Commission in this area. Therefore, it is vitally important to monitor the effects of these recommendations over time to see if they are adequate to achieve the goals stated in our national labor law and shared by the American public.

3. Increase the Extent to which Workplace Problems Are Resolved by the Parties

The Commission's findings and recommendations regarding workplace regulations, litigation, and dispute resolution fall into three categories: (1) encouraging development of high quality private dispute resolution procedures, (2) encouraging experimentation with workplace self-regulation procedures in general and with specific reference to workplace safety and health, and (3) protecting the employment rights and standards of contingent workers.

The Commission endorses and encourages the development of high quality alternative dispute resolution (ADR) systems to promote fair, speedy, and efficient resolution of workplace disputes. These systems must be based on the voluntary acceptance of the parties involved. The courts and regulatory agencies should hold these systems accountable for meeting high quality standards for fairness, due process, and accountability to the goals and remedies established in the relevant law. The Commission also encourages experimentation with internal responsibility systems for adapting workplace regulations to fit different work settings. Accordingly, we recommend:

(8) Encouraging regulatory agencies to expand the use of negotiated rule making, mediation, and alternative dispute resolution (ADR) procedures for resolving cases that would otherwise require formal adjudication by the agency and/or the courts.

(9) Encouraging experimentation and use of private dispute resolution systems that meet high quality standards for fairness, provided these are not imposed unilaterally by employers as a condition of employment.

(10) Encouraging individual regulatory agencies (e.g., OSHA, Wage and Hour Division, EEOC, etc.) to develop guidelines for internal responsibility systems in which parties at the workplace are allowed to apply regulations to their circumstances.

America's workplaces must be made safer and more healthful and workers' compensation costs need to be reduced. Workplace safety and health is an ideal starting point for experimenting with internal responsibility systems for meeting public policy objectives, given the long-standing and widespread experience with employee participation and labor-management committees in safety and health matters and the shared interests all parties have in improving safety and health outcomes. Evidence presented to the Commission shows that properly structured joint committees and participation plans can significantly improve safety and health protection. Accordingly, we recommend:

(11) Developing safety and health programs in each workplace that provide for employee participation. Those workplaces that demonstrate such a program is in place with a record of high safety and health performance would receive preferential status in OSHA's inspection and enforcement activities.

The growth of various forms of contingent work poses opportunities for good job matches between workers with differing labor force attachments and employers needing flexibility in response to changing market conditions. At the same time, some contingent work arrangements relegate workers to a second class status of low wages, inadequate fringe benefits, lack of training and, most importantly, loss of protection of labor and employment laws and standards. This is a very complex set of developments for which adequate data are not yet available to do more than address the most obvious problems. Our recommendations are therefore cautious in this area, recognizing the need to continue to monitor and evaluate the labor market experiences of all forms of contingent work and to derive policy recommendations as these data and analyses become available. Accordingly, we recommend:

(12) Adopting a single definition of employer for all workplace laws based on the economic realities of the employment relationship. Furthermore, we encourage the NLRB to use its rule-making authority to develop an appropriate doctrine governing joint employers in settings where the use of contract arrangements might otherwise serve as a subterfuge for avoiding collective bargaining or evading other responsibilities under labor law.

(13) Adopting a single definition of employee for all workplace laws based on the economic realities of the employment relationship. The law should confer independent contractor status only on those for whom it is appropriate—entrepreneurs who bear the risk of loss, serve multiple clients, hold themselves out to the public as an independent business, and so forth. The law should not provide incentives for misclassification of employees as independent contractors, which costs federal and state treasuries large sums in uncollected social security, unemployment, personal income, and other taxes.

Implementing the recommendations in this report would open up employment policy and practice to a period of experimentation and opportunities for further learning. To channel this learning into constructive policy making we recommend:

(14) Creating a National Forum on the Workplace involving leaders of business, labor, women's, and civil rights groups to continue discussing workplace issues and public policies. In addition, we recommend establishment of a national Labor-Management Committee to discuss issues of special concern to the future of collective bargaining and worker-management relations. We encourage development of similar forums in communities, states, and industries to further promote grass roots experimentation and learning.

(15) Improving the data base for policy analysis of workplace developments, evaluation of labor-management experiments in the private sector, and for assessment of the economic condition of contingent workers. This requires amalgamation of existing data sets within the NLRB and Department of Labor, and among these and other agencies as well as coordination of research on workplace topics for the National Forum and other interested parties.

The Challenges Ahead

From the views presented to us emerged a vision of the Workplace of the 21st Century that is shared widely across all sectors of society and the workforce. These goals appear at the end of this Executive Summary. Achieving some of them requires updating and modernizing labor and employment law; others can be addressed through changes in administrative processes to give more power and flexibility to the parties at the workplace to govern their relationships and solve problems closest to the source. All will require leadership and sustained commitment to learning and experimentation on the part of individual workers and the labor and management leaders who shape employment practices. We urge that progress toward achievement of these goals be assessed systematically on a continuous basis and the results shared widely with the American public.

We can summarize the challenges facing America to improve the quality and performance of workplace relations quite simply. They are to sustain the momentum underway in the most innovative workplaces, to bring these innovations to and share their benefits among more workers and managers, and to overcome the countervailing forces that stand in the way of achieving the goals of the 21st Century workplace. We see three such countervailing forces, two of which are reflected directly in the charges to this Commission and in our recommendations.

The first of these countervailing forces is the high level of conflict and tension surrounding the process by which workers decide whether or not to be represented by a union for the purpose of collective bargaining. Our recommendations should result in a significant de-escalation of these conflicts and a restoration of workers' promised rights in this area, and thereby improve the overall climate for cooperative labor-management relations.

The second countervailing force is the frustration that managers experience in trying to respond to complex workplace regulations and mounting litigation, and that workers experience in trying to enforce their legal rights on the job. Our recommendations provide workers and managers with the tools and flexibility to replace the command and control system of regulation and the litigious system for enforcing rights with opportunities for greater self-governance and private, high quality, dispute resolution.

The third force limiting the momentum toward higher quality workplaces was highlighted in our Fact Finding Report but its solution lies well beyond the mandate of this Commission. We refer here to the widening earnings inequality and stagnant real earnings that have characterized the American labor market over the past ten to fifteen years. While the Commission makes no direct recommendations focused on this serious problem, a number of our recommendations should contribute to reducing this growing disparity. Among these recommendations are our support for increased training at the workplace; increased opportunities for employee participation to enhance productivity, quality, and worker development; protections against the use of contractors or contingent workers to evade responsibilities under labor and employment law; and changes to provide workers the opportunity for representation and collective bargaining if they want it.

The recommendations of this Report are designed to contribute to the achievement of the goals and relationships required for the 21st Century workplace.

STATE OF THE UNION ADDRESS AND REPUBLICAN RESPONSE
January 24, 1995

Acknowledging that "I have made my mistakes," a chastened President Bill Clinton appealed for bipartisanship in his State of the Union address January 24; challenged the Republican-controlled Congress to work with him toward a "leaner, not meaner" government; and asked the American people to "forge a new social compact" committed to both opportunity and civic responsibility.

In an eighty-two-minute speech, the longest State of the Union address in history, Clinton outlined his position on more than a score of issues. In trying to appeal both to conservative Republicans and liberal members of his own party, several commentators said, the president's speech failed to set a direction for the last two years of his term. "It was a speech about everything, and therefore about nothing," Washington Post *columnist David S. Broder wrote.*

The first Democratic president since Harry S. Truman to address a Republican-controlled Congress, Clinton acknowledged that he had gotten the message from the voters' rebuke of his party in the 1994 elections. "[W]e didn't hear America singing," the president said, "we heard America shouting." He indicated agreement, at least in principle, with some of the more visible Republican proposals, including giving the president the line-item veto, paring back unnecessary regulation, and cutting the federal bureaucracy. His endorsement of these traditional Republican themes brought repeated applause from the new majority in Congress.

On several elements of the Republican Contract with America, Clinton took a conciliatory tone even as he tried to set limits on what he would find acceptable. He told those favoring the proposed constitutional amendment requiring a balanced budget that they had "to be straight with the American people. They have a right to know what you're going to cut—and how it's going to affect them." He also asked Congress to remember that, in cutting the budget, "government still has important responsibilities. Our young people . . . still hold our future in their hands. We still owe a debt to

*our veterans. And our senior citizens have made us what we are." In urg-
ing Congress not to go too far in cutting programs, he singled out funding
for education, veterans affairs, Social Security, Medicare, immunization
programs, school lunches, Head Start, and nutrition programs for infants
and pregnant women.*

*The president said he wanted to work with Congress to pass welfare
reform. "We should require work and mutual responsibility," he said. "But
we shouldn't cut people off [the welfare rolls] just because they're poor,
they're young, or even because they're unmarried." Clinton was indirectly
referring to the proposed House GOP reform bill that, among other things,
would deny cash benefits to unwed mothers under age eighteen.*

*On a few issues, Clinton drew a figurative line in the sand. He declared
that he would not let the ban on nineteen assault weapons, enacted in 1994,
be repealed and that he would not accept a tax cut "that explodes the deficit
or puts our [economic] recovery at risk. We ought to pay for our tax cuts
fully and honestly."*

*Clinton conceded defeat on comprehensive health care reform. Where he
had once attacked those who had pushed for incremental changes in health
care, he now acknowledged that might be the only way to achieve any
reform. "I know that last year . . . we bit off more than we could chew," he
said of his comprehensive health care reform plan. "So I'm asking you that
we work together. Let's do it step by step. Let's do whatever we have to do to
get something done."*

*The president proposed a few new legislative initiatives but offered few
specifics on them. He asked for an increase in the minimum wage, for
example, but did not stipulate what that increase should be. White House
officials later said that the president would like the minimum wage to
move from its current level of $4.25 an hour to $5.00.*

The Republican Response

*In the traditional televised response from the opposing party, Gov.
Christine Todd Whitman of New Jersey repeated many of the campaign
themes that propelled Republicans into the congressional majority in
November 1994. "The election in November was a beginning, not an end,"
she said. "And we are committed to fulfilling the verdict of the voters and
enacting our agenda of hope for the families of America."*

*Whitman also suggested that the president's actions did not always
match his words. "[W]hile at times tonight some of the president's ideas
sounded pretty Republican . . . ," she said, "the fact remains that he has
been opposed to the balanced budget requirement, he proposed even more
government spending, and he imposed the biggest tax increase in American history."*

*Speaking informally, the normally combative House Speaker, Republi-
can Newt Gingrich of Georgia, was not so dismissive of the president.
"Every single policy proposal will be looked at; a number we support," the
Speaker said.*

Other Reaction to the Speech

Moderate Democrats hailed the generally centrist themes that Clinton sounded, saying that a move to the center was crucial if the president intended to reclaim the support of the voters who elected him. "I thought he tried to get back to the things that got him elected—expanding opportunity and not bureaucracy. I liked the fact that it wasn't a whole new laundry list of new programs," said Sen. John B. Breaux (D-La.). To some Democrats, Clinton's emphasis on less government, personal responsibility, and private charity grated. "I don't want my president sounding like a Republican. I want him sounding like a Democrat," said Rep. Charles B. Rangel (D-N.Y.).

Several political pundits agreed that, in trying to coopt popular Republican themes, the president missed his opportunity to lay down a clear agenda for his presidency and his party. "Defenders argue that the speech did serve the important purpose of putting the president back into the argument. By accepting some of the opposition's themes while seeking to modulate and bend them, he suggested the Republicans might be right about some things and made himself a player in a way he otherwise could not hope to be," said an editorial in the Washington Post. *"The question is, a player to what end? How hard is he going to fight, and for what? Eighty-two minutes of speech, and you still don't know."*

Following are the White House text of President Bill Clinton's State of the Union address, as delivered to a joint session of Congress on January 24, 1995, and excerpts from the text of the televised Republican response by Gov. Christine Todd Whitman of New Jersey:

STATE OF THE UNION ADDRESS

Mr. President, Mr. Speaker, members of the 104th Congress, my fellow Americans:

Again we are here in the sanctuary of democracy, and once again, our democracy has spoken. So let me begin by congratulating all of you here in the 104th Congress, and congratulating you, Mr. Speaker.

If we agree on nothing else tonight, we must agree that the American people certainly voted for change in 1992 and 1994. And as I look out at you, I know how some of you must have felt in 1992.

I must say that in both years we didn't hear America singing, we heard America shouting. And now all of us, Republicans and Democrats alike, must say: We hear you. We will work together to earn the jobs you have given us. For we are the keepers of the sacred trust, and we must be faithful to it in this new and very demanding era.

Over 200 years ago, our founders changed the entire course of human history by joining together to create a new country based on a single powerful idea: "We hold these Truths to be self-evident, that all Men are created equal, endowed by their Creator with certain inalienable Rights, and among these are Life, Liberty, and the Pursuit of Happiness."

It has fallen to every generation since then to preserve that idea—the American idea—and to deepen and expand its meaning to new and different times: To Lincoln and his Congress, to preserve the Union and to end slavery. To Theodore Roosevelt and Woodrow Wilson, to restrain the abuses and excesses of the Industrial Revolution, and to assert our leadership in the world. To Franklin Roosevelt, to fight the failure and pain of the Great Depression, and to win our country's great struggle against fascism. And to all our presidents since, to fight the Cold War.

Especially, I recall two who struggled to fight that Cold War in partnership with Congresses where the majority was of a different party. To Harry Truman, who summoned us to unparalleled prosperity at home, and who built the architecture of the Cold War. And to Ronald Reagan, whom we wish well tonight, and who exhorted us to carry on until the twilight struggle against communism was won.

In another time of change and challenge, I had the honor to be the first president to be elected in the post-Cold War era, an era marked by the global economy, the information revolution, unparalleled change and opportunity and insecurity for the American people.

I came to this hallowed chamber two years ago on a mission—to restore the American Dream for all our people and to make sure that we move into the 21st century still the strongest force for freedom and democracy in the entire world. I was determined then to tackle the tough problems too long ignored. In this effort I am frank to say that I have made my mistakes, and I have learned again the importance of humility in all human endeavor. But I am also proud to say tonight that our country is stronger than it was two years ago.

Record numbers of Americans are succeeding in the new global economy. We are at peace and we are a force for peace and freedom throughout the world. We have almost 6 million new jobs since I became president, and we have the lowest combined rate of unemployment and inflation in 25 years. Our businesses are more productive, and here we have worked to bring the deficit down, to expand trade, to put more police on our streets, to give our citizens more of the tools they need to get an education and to rebuild their own communities.

But the rising tide is not lifting all boats. While our nation is enjoying peace and prosperity, too many of our people are still working harder and harder, for less and less. While our businesses are restructuring and growing more productive and competitive, too many of our people still can't be sure of having a job next year or even next month. And far more than our material riches are threatened; things far more precious to us—our children, our families, our values.

Our civil life is suffering in America today. Citizens are working together less and shouting at each other more. The common bonds of community which have been the great strength of our country from its very beginning are badly frayed. What are we to do about it?

More than 60 years ago, at the dawn of another new era, President [Franklin D.] Roosevelt told our nation, "New conditions impose new requirements on government and those who conduct government." And from that simple proposition, he shaped the New Deal, which helped to restore our nation to prosperity and define the relationship between our people and their government for half a century.

That approach worked in its time. But we today, we face a very different time and very different conditions. We are moving from an Industrial Age built on gears and sweat to an Information Age demanding skills and learning and flexibility. Our government, once a champion of national purpose, is now seen by many as simply a captive of narrow interests, putting more burdens on our citizens rather than equipping them to get ahead. The values that used to hold us all together seem to be coming apart.

So tonight, we must forge a new social compact to meet the challenges of this time. As we enter a new era, we need a new set of understandings, not just with government, but even more important, with one another as Americans.

[Forging the 'New Covenant']

That's what I want to talk with you about tonight. I call it "the New Covenant." But it's grounded in a very, very old idea—that all Americans have not just a right, but a solid responsibility to rise as far as their God-given talents and determination can take them; and to give something back to their communities and their country in return. Opportunity and responsibility: They go hand in hand. We can't have one without the other. And our national community can't hold together without both.

Our New Covenant is a new set of understandings for how we can equip our people to meet the challenges of a new economy, how we can change the way our government works to fit a different time, and, above all, how we can repair the damaged bonds in our society and come together behind our common purpose. We must have dramatic change in our economy, our government and ourselves.

My fellow Americans, without regard to party, let us rise to the occasion. Let us put aside partisanship and pettiness and pride. As we embark on this new course, let us put our country first, remembering that regardless of party label, we are all Americans. And let the final test of everything we do be a simple one: Is it good for the American people?

Let me begin by saying that we cannot ask Americans to be better citizens if we are not better servants. You made a good start by passing that law which applies to Congress all the laws you put on the private sector, and I was proud to sign it yesterday.

But we have a lot more to do before people really trust the way things work around here. Three times as many lobbyists are in the streets and corridors of Washington as were here 20 years ago. The American people look at their capital and they see a city where the well-connected and the well-protected can work the system, but the interests of ordinary citizens are often left out.

As the new Congress opened its doors, lobbyists were still doing business as usual—the gifts, the trips, all the things that people are concerned about haven't stopped. Twice this month you missed opportunities to stop these practices. I know there were other considerations in those votes, but I want to use something that I've heard my Republican friends say from time to time—there doesn't have to be a law for everything. So tonight, I ask you to just stop taking the lobbyists' perks. Just stop.

We don't have to wait for legislation to pass to send a strong signal to the American people that things are really changing. But I also hope you will send me the strongest possible lobby reform bill, and I'll sign that, too.

We should require lobbyists to tell the people for whom they work what they're spending, what they want. We should also curb the role of big money in elections by capping the cost of campaigns and limiting the influence of PACs [political action committees].

And as I have said for three years, we should work to open the airwaves so that they can be an instrument of democracy, not a weapon of destruction by giving free TV time to candidates for public office.

When the last Congress killed political reform last year, it was reported in the press that the lobbyists actually stood in the halls of this sacred building and cheered. This year, let's give the folks at home something to cheer about.

More important, I think we all agree that we have to change the way the government works. Let's make it smaller, less costly and smarter—leaner, not meaner.

I just told the Speaker the equal time doctrine is alive and well.

The New Covenant approach to governing is as different from the old bureaucratic way as the computer is from the manual typewriter. The old way of governing around here protected organized interests. We should look out for the interests of ordinary people. The old way divided us by interest, constituency or class. The New Covenant way should unite us behind a common vision of what's best for our country. The old way dispensed services through large, top-down, inflexible bureaucracies. The New Covenant way should shift these resources and decision-making from bureaucrats to citizens, injecting choice and competition and individual responsibility into national policy.

The old way of governing around here actually seemed to reward failure. The New Covenant way should have built-in incentives to reward success. The old way was centralized here in Washington. The New Covenant way must take hold in the communities all across America. And we should help them to do that.

Our job here is to expand opportunity, not bureaucracy; to empower people to make the most of their own lives; and to enhance our security here at home and abroad. We must not ask government to do what we should do for ourselves. We should rely on government as a partner to help us to do more for ourselves and for each other.

[Beyond Yesterday's Government]

I hope very much that as we debate these specific and exciting matters, we can go beyond the sterile discussion between the illusion that there is somehow a program for every problem on the one hand, and the other illusion that the government is a source of every problem we have. Our job is to get rid of yesterday's government so that our own people can meet today's and tomorrow's needs. And we ought to do it together.

You know, for years before I became president, I heard others say they would cut government and how bad it was. But not much happened. We actually did it. We cut over a quarter of a trillion dollars in spending, more than 300 domestic programs, more than 100,000 positions from the federal bureaucracy in the last two years alone. Based on decisions already made, we will have cut a total of more than a quarter of a million positions from the federal government, making it the smallest it has been since John Kennedy was president, by the time I come here again next year.

Under the leadership of Vice President [Al] Gore, our initiatives have already saved taxpayers $63 billion. The age of the $500 hammer and the ashtray you can break on David Letterman is gone. Deadwood programs, like mohair subsidies, are gone. We've streamlined the Agriculture Department by reducing it by more than 1,200 offices. We've slashed the small-business loan form from an inch thick to a single page. We've thrown away the government's 10,000-page personnel manual. And the government is working better in important ways: FEMA, the Federal Emergency Management Agency, has gone from being a disaster to helping people in disasters.

You can ask the farmers in the Middle West who fought the flood there or the people in California who have dealt with floods and earthquakes and fires, and they'll tell you that. Government workers, working hand in hand with private business, rebuilt Southern California's fractured freeways in record time and under budget. And because the federal government moved fast, all but one of the 5,600 schools damaged in the earthquake are back in business.

Now, there are a lot of other things that I could talk about. I want to just mention one because it will be discussed here in the next few weeks. University administrators all over the country have told me that they are saving weeks and weeks of bureaucratic time now because of our direct college loan program, which makes college loans cheaper and more affordable, with better repayment terms for students, costs the government less, and cuts out paperwork and bureaucracy for the government and for the universities. We shouldn't cap that program. We should give every college in America the opportunity to be a part of it.

Previous government programs gather dust. The reinventing government report is getting results. And we're not through. There's going to be a second round of reinventing government. We propose to cut $130 billion in spending by shrinking departments, extending our freeze on domestic spending, cutting 60 public housing programs down to three, getting rid of over 100 programs we do not need, like the Interstate Commerce Commission and the Helium Reserve Program. And we're working on getting rid of unnecessary regulations and making them more sensible. The programs and regulations that have outlived their usefulness should go. We have to cut yesterday's government to help solve tomorrow's problems.

And we need to get government closer to the people it's meant to serve. We need to help move programs down to the point where states and communities and private citizens in the private sector can do a better job. If they can do it, we ought to let them do it. We should get out of the way and let them do what they can do better.

Taking power away from federal bureaucracies and giving it back to communities and individuals is something everyone should be able to be for. It's time for Congress to stop passing on to the states the cost of decisions we make here in Washington.

I know there are still serious differences over the details of the unfunded mandates legislation, but I want to work with you to make sure we pass a reasonable bill which will protect the national interests and give justified relief where we need to give it.

For years, Congress concealed in the budget scores of pet spending projects. Last year was no different. There was $1 million to study stress in plants, and $12 million for a tick removal program that didn't work. It's hard to remove ticks; those of us who have had them know. But, I'll tell you something; if you'll give me the line-item veto, I'll remove some of that unnecessary spending.

But I think we should all remember, and almost all of us would agree, that government still has important responsibilities. Our young people—we should think of this when we cut—our young people hold our future in their hands. We still owe a debt to our veterans. And our senior citizens have made us what we are.

Now, my budget cuts a lot. But it protects education, veterans, Social Security and Medicare—and I hope you will do the same thing. You should, and I hope you will.

And when we give more flexibility to the states, let us remember that there are certain fundamental national needs that should be addressed in every state, north and south, east and west: immunization against childhood disease; school lunches in all our schools; Head Start, medical care and nutrition for pregnant women and infants; All these things are in the national interest.

I applaud your desire to get rid of costly and unnecessary regulations. But when we deregulate, let's remember what national action in the national interest has given us: safer foods for our families, safer toys for our children, safer nursing homes for our parents, safer cars and highways, and safer workplaces, clean air and cleaner water. Do we need common sense and fairness in our regulations? You bet we do. But we can have common sense and still provide for safe drinking water. We can have fairness and still clean up toxic dumps, and we ought to do it.

Should we cut the deficit more? Well, of course, we should. Of course, we should. But we can bring it down in a way that still protects our economic recovery and does not unduly punish people who should not be punished, but instead should be helped.

I know many of you in this chamber support the balanced-budget amendment. I certainly want to balance the budget. Our administration has done more to bring the budget down and to save money than any in a very, very long time. If you believe passing this amendment is the right thing to do, then you have to be straight with the American people. They have a right to know what you're going to cut—and how it's going to affect them.

We should be doing things in the open around here. For example, everybody ought to know if this proposal is going to endanger Social Security. I would oppose that, and I think most Americans would.

Nothing has done more to undermine our sense of common responsibility than our failed welfare system. This is one of the problems we have to face here in Washington in our New Covenant. It rewards welfare over work. It undermines family values. It lets millions of parents get away without paying their child support. It keeps a minority, but a significant minority of the people on welfare, trapped on it for a very long time.

I've worked on this problem for a long time, nearly 15 years now. As a governor I had the honor of working with the Reagan administration to write the last welfare reform bill back in 1988. In the last two years we made a good start in continuing the work of welfare reform. Our administration gave two dozen states the right to slash through federal rules and regulations to reform their own welfare systems, and to try to promote work and responsibility over welfare and dependency.

Last year I introduced the most sweeping welfare reform plan ever presented by an administration. We have to make welfare what it was meant to be—a second chance, not a way of life. We have to help those on welfare move to work as quickly as possible, to provide child care and teach them skills if that's what they need for up to two years. And after that, there ought to be a simple hard rule: anyone who can work must go to work. If a parent isn't paying child support, they should be forced to pay. We should suspend driver's licenses, track them across state lines, make them work off what they owe. That is what we should do. Governments do not raise children, people do. And the parents must take responsibility for the children they bring into this world.

I want to work with you, with all of you, to pass welfare reform. But our goal must be to liberate people and lift them up, from dependence to independence, from welfare to work, from mere childbearing to responsible parenting. Our goal should not be to punish them because they happen to be poor.

We should require work and mutual responsibility. But we shouldn't cut people off just because they're poor, they're young, or even because they're unmarried. We should promote responsibility by requiring young mothers to live at home with their parents or in other supervised settings, by requiring them to finish school. But we shouldn't put them and their children out on the street.

And I know all the arguments, pro and con, and I have read and thought about this for a long time. I still don't think we can in good conscience punish poor children for the mistakes of their parents. My fellow Americans, every single survey shows that all the American people care about this without regard to party or race or region. So let this be the year we end welfare as we know it. But also let this be the year that we are all able to stop using this issue to divide America.

No one is more eager to end welfare. I may be the only president who has actually had the opportunity to sit in a welfare office, who's actually spent hours and hours talking to people on welfare. And I am telling you, people who are trapped on it know it doesn't work. They also want to get off. So we can promote together education and work and good parenting. I have no problem with punishing bad behavior or the refusal to be a worker or a student, or a responsible parent. I just don't want to punish poverty and past mistakes. All of us have made our mistakes, and none of us can change our yesterdays. But every one of us can change our tomorrows.

And America's best example of that may be Lynn Woolsey, who worked her way off welfare to become a [Democratic] congresswoman from the state of California.

[Crime and Gun Control]

I know the members of this Congress are concerned about crime, as are all the citizens of our country. And I remind you that last year, we passed a very tough crime bill—longer sentences, "three strikes and you're out," almost 60 new capital punishment offenses, more prisons, more prevention, 100,000 more police. And we paid for it all by reducing the size of the federal bureaucracy and giving the money back to local communities to lower the crime rate.

There may be other things we can do to be tougher on crime, to be smarter with crime, to help to lower that rate first. Well, if there are, let's talk about them and let's do them. But let's not go back on the things that we did last year that we know work; that we know work because the local law enforcement officers tell us that we did the right things, because local community leaders who have worked for years and years to lower the crime rate tell us that they work.

Let's look at the experience of our cities and our rural areas where the crime rate has gone down and ask the people who did it how they did it. And if what we did last year supports the decline in the crime rate and I am convinced that it does let us not go back on it. Let's stick with it, implement it. We've got four more hard years of work to do, to do that.

I don't want to destroy the good atmosphere in the room or in the country tonight, but I have to mention one issue that divided this body greatly last year. The last Congress also passed the Brady bill and, in the crime bill, the ban on 19 assault weapons. I don't think it's a secret to anybody in this room that several members of the last Congress who voted for that aren't here tonight because they voted for it. And I know, therefore, that some of you who are here because they voted for it are under enormous pressure to repeal it. I just have to tell you how I feel about it.

The members of Congress who voted for that bill—and I would never do anything to infringe on the right to keep and bear arms to hunt and to engage in other appropriate sporting activities. I've done it since I was a boy, and I'm going to keep right on doing it until I can't do it anymore. But a lot of people laid down their seats in Congress so that police officers and kids wouldn't have to lay down their lives under a hail of assault weapon attack—and I will not let that be repealed. I will not let it be repealed.

I'd like to talk about a couple of other issues we have to deal with. I want us to cut more spending, but I hope we won't cut government programs that help to prepare us for the new economy, promote responsibility and are organized from the grass roots up, not by federal bureaucracy. The very best example of this is the National Service Corps—Americorps.

It passed with strong bipartisan support. And now there are 20,000 Americans, more than ever served in one year in the Peace Corps, working all over this country, helping people person to person in local, grass-roots volunteer groups, solving problems and, in the process, earning some money for their education. This is citizenship at its best. It's good for the Americorps members, but it's good for the rest of us, too. It's the essence of the New Covenant, and we shouldn't stop it.

All Americans, not only in the states most heavily affected, but in every place in this country, are rightly disturbed by the large numbers of illegal aliens entering our country. The jobs they hold might otherwise be held by citizens or legal immigrants. The public service they use impose burdens on our taxpayers. That's why our administration has moved aggressively to secure our borders more by hiring a record number of new border guards, by deporting twice as many criminal aliens as ever before, by cracking down on illegal hiring, by barring welfare benefits to illegal aliens.

In the budget I will present to you, we will try to do more to speed the deportation of illegal aliens who are arrested for crimes, to better identify illegal aliens in the workplace as recommended by the commission headed by former Congresswoman Barbara Jordan.

We are a nation of immigrants. But we are also a nation of laws. It is wrong and ultimately self-defeating for a nation of immigrants to permit the kind of abuse of our immigration laws we have seen in recent years, and we must do more to stop it.

[Expanding the Middle Class]

The most important job of our government in this new era is to empower the American people to succeed in the global economy. America has always been a land of opportunity, a land where, if you work hard, you can get ahead. We've become a great middle-class country. Middle-class values sustain us. We must expand that middle class, and shrink the underclass, even as we do everything we can to support the millions of Americans who are already successful in the new economy.

America is once again the world's strongest economic power, almost 6 million new jobs in the last two years, exports booming, inflation down, high-wage jobs are coming back. A record number of American entrepreneurs are living the American Dream. If we want it to stay that way, those who work and lift our nation must have more of its benefits.

Today, too many of those people are being left out. They're working harder for less. They have less security, less income, less certainty that they can even afford a vacation, much less college for their kids or retirement for themselves. We cannot let this continue.

If we don't act, our economy will probably keep doing what it's been doing since about 1978, when the income growth began to go to those at the very top of our economic scale and the people in the vast middle got very little growth, and people who worked like crazy but were on the bottom then fell even further and further behind in the years afterward—no matter how hard they worked.

We've got to have a government that can be a real partner in making this new economy work for all of our people; a government that helps each and every one of us to get an education, and to have the opportunity to renew our skills. That's why we worked so hard to increase educational opportunities in the last two years, from Head Start to public schools, to apprenticeships for young people who don't go to college, to making college loans more available and more affordable. That's the first thing we have to do. We've got to do something to empower people to improve their skills.

The second thing we ought to do is to help people raise their incomes immediately by lowering their taxes. We took the first step in 1993 with a working family tax cut for 15 million families with incomes under $27,000; a tax cut that this year will average about $1,000 a family. And we also gave tax reductions to most small and new businesses.

Before we could do more than that, we first had to bring down the deficit we inherited, and we had to get economic growth up. Now we've done both. And now we can cut taxes in a more comprehensive way. But tax cuts should reinforce and promote our first obligation—to empower our citizens through education and training to make the most of their own lives.

The spotlight should shine on those who make the right choices for themselves, their families and their communities. I have proposed the Middle Class Bill of Rights, which should properly be called the Bill of Rights and Responsibilities because its provisions only benefit those who are working to educate and raise their children and to educate themselves. It will, therefore, give needed tax relief and raise incomes in both the short run and the long run in a way that benefits all of us.

There are four provisions. First, a tax deduction for all education and training after high school. If you think about it, we permit businesses to deduct their investment, we permit individuals to deduct interest on their home mortgages, but today an education is even more important to the economic well-being of our whole country than even those things are. We should do everything we can to encourage it. And I hope you will support it.

Second, we ought to cut taxes, $500 for families with children under 13.

Third, we ought to foster more savings and personal responsibility by permitting people to establish an Individual Retirement Account and withdraw from it tax-free for the cost of education, health care, first-time home-buying or the care of a parent.

And fourth, we should pass a G.I. Bill for America's workers. We propose to collapse nearly 70 federal programs and not give the money to the states, but give the money directly to the American people; offer vouchers to them so that they, if they're laid off or if they're working for a very low wage, can get a voucher worth $2,600 a year for up to two years to go to their local community colleges or wherever else they want to get the skills they need to improve their lives. Let's empower people in this way. Move it from the government directly to the workers of America.

Now, any one of us can call for a tax cut, but I won't accept one that explodes the deficit or puts our recovery at risk. We ought to pay for our tax cuts fully and honestly.

Just two years ago, it was an open question whether we would find the strength to cut the deficit. Thanks to the courage of the people who were here then, many of whom didn't return, we did cut the deficit. We began to do what others said would not be done. We cut the deficit by over $600 billion, about $10,000 for every family in this country. It's coming down three years in a row for the first time since Mr. Truman was president, and I don't think anybody in America wants us to let it explode again.

In the budget I will send you, the Middle Class Bill of Rights is fully paid for by budget cuts in bureaucracy, cuts in programs, cuts in special-interest subsidies. And the spending cuts will more than double the tax cuts. My budget pays for the Middle Class Bill of Rights without any cuts in Medicare. And I will oppose any attempts to pay for tax cuts with Medicare cuts. That's not the right thing to do.

I know that a lot of you have your own ideas about tax relief, and some of them I find quite interesting. I really want to work with all of you. My test for our proposals will be: Will it create jobs and raise incomes? Will it strengthen our families and support our children? Is it paid for? Will it build the middle class and shrink the underclass? If it does, I'll support it. But if it doesn't, I won't.

The goal of building the middle class and shrinking the underclass is also why I believe that you should raise the minimum wage. It rewards work. Two and a half million Americans—2.5 million Americans, often women with children, are working out there today for $4.25 an hour. In terms of real buying power, by next year that minimum wage will be at a 40-year low. That's not my idea of how the new economy ought to work.

Now, I've studied the arguments and the evidence for and against a minimum wage increase. I believe the weight of the evidence is that a modest increase does not cost jobs, and may even lure people back into the job market. But the most important thing is, you can't make a living on $4.25 an hour. Especially if you have children, even with the working families tax cut we passed last year. In the past, the minimum wage has been a bipartisan issue, and I think it should be again. So I want to challenge you to have honest hearings on this; to get together; to find a way to make the minimum wage a living wage.

Members of Congress have been here less than a month, but by the end of the week, 28 days into the new year, every member of Congress will have earned as much in congressional salary as a minimum wage worker makes all year long.

Everybody else here, including the president, has something else that too many Americans do without, and that's health care. Now, last year, we almost came to blows over health care. But we didn't do anything. And the cold, hard fact is that, since last year, since I was here, another 1.1 million Americans in working families have lost their health care. And the cold, hard fact is that many millions more, most of them farmers and small-business people and self-employed people, have seen their premiums skyrocket, their co-pays and deductibles go up. There's a whole bunch of people in this country that, in the statistics have health insurance, but really what they've got is a piece of paper that says they won't lose their home if they get sick.

Now, I still believe our country has got to move toward providing health security for every American family. But I know that last year, as the evidence indicates, we bit off more than we could chew. So I'm asking you that we work together. Let's do it step by step. Let's do whatever we have to do to get something done. Let's at least pass meaningful insurance reform so that no American risks losing coverage for facing skyrocketing prices. That nobody loses their coverage because they face high prices or unavailable insurance, when they change jobs or lose a job, or a family member gets sick.

I want to work together with all of you who have an interest in this, with the Democrats who worked on it last time, with the Republican leaders like Sen. [Bob] Dole [of Kansas, majority leader] who has a longtime commitment to health care reform and made some constructive proposals in this area last year. We ought to make sure that self-employed people in small businesses can buy insurance at more affordable rates through voluntary purchasing pools. We ought to help families provide long-term care for a sick parent or a disabled child. We can work to help workers who lose their jobs at least keep their health insurance coverage for a year while they look for work. And we can find a way—it may take some time, but we can find a way—to make sure that our children have health care.

You know, I think everybody in this room, without regard to party, can be proud of the fact that our country was rated as having the world's most productive economy for the first time in nearly a decade. But we can't be proud of the fact that we're the only wealthy country in the world that has a smaller percentage of the work force and their children with health insurance today than we did 10 years ago, the last time we were the most productive economy in the world. So let's work together on this. It is too important for politics as usual.

[Security Abroad]

Much of what the American people are thinking about tonight is what we've already talked about. A lot of people think that the security concerns of America today are entirely internal to our borders. They relate to the security of our jobs and our homes, and our incomes and our children, our streets, our health and protecting those borders. Now that the Cold War has passed, it's tempting to believe that all the security issues, with the possible exception of trade, reside here at home. But it's not so. Our security still depends upon our continued world leadership for peace and freedom and democracy. We still can't be strong at home unless we're strong abroad.

The financial crisis in Mexico is a case in point. I know it's not popular to say it tonight, but we have to act. Not for the Mexican people, but for the sake of the millions of Americans whose livelihoods are tied to Mexico's well-being. If we want to secure American jobs, preserve American exports, safeguard America's borders, then we must pass the stabilization program and help to put Mexico back on track.

Now let me repeat: It's not a loan; it's not foreign aid; it's not a bailout. We will be given a guarantee like co-signing a note with good collateral that will cover our risks. This legislation is the right thing for America. That's why the bipartisan leadership has supported it. And I hope you in Congress will pass it quickly. It is in our interest, and we can explain it to the American people, because we're going to do it in the right way.

You know, tonight, this is the first State of the Union address ever delivered since the beginning of the Cold War when not a single Russian missile is pointed at the children of America. And along with the Russians, we're on the way to destroying the missiles and the bombers that carry 9,000 nuclear warheads. We've come so far so fast in this post-Cold War world that it's easy to take the decline of the nuclear threat for granted. But it's still there, and we aren't finished yet.

This year I'll ask the Senate to approve START II, to eliminate weapons that carry 5,000 more warheads. The United States will lead the charge to extend indefinitely the Nuclear Non-proliferation Treaty; to enact a comprehensive nuclear test ban; and to eliminate chemical weapons. To stop and roll back North Korea's potentially deadly nuclear program, we'll continue to implement the agreement we have reached with that nation. It's smart; it's tough; it's a deal based on continuing inspection with safeguards for our allies and ourselves.

This year I'll submit to Congress comprehensive legislation to strengthen our hand in combating terrorists—whether they strike at home or abroad. As the cowards who bombed the World Trade Center found out, this country will hunt down terrorists and bring them to justice.

Just this week, another horrendous terrorist act in Israel killed 19 and injured scores more. On behalf of the American people and all of you, I send our deepest sympathy to the families of the victims. I know that in the face of such evil, it is hard for the people in the Middle East to go forward. But the terrorists represent the past, not the future. We must and we will pursue a comprehensive peace between Israel and all her neighbors in the Middle East.

Accordingly, last night I signed an executive order that will block the assets in the United States of terrorist organizations that threaten to disrupt the peace process. It prohibits financial transactions with these groups. And tonight I call on our allies and peace-loving nations throughout the world to join us with renewed fervor in a global effort to combat terrorism. We cannot permit the future to be marred by terror and fear and paralysis.

From the day I took the oath of office, I pledged that our nation would maintain the best-equipped, best-trained and best-prepared military on Earth. We have, and they are. They have managed the dramatic downsizing of our forces after the Cold War with remarkable skill and spirit. But to make sure our military is ready for action, and to provide the pay and the quality of life the military and their families deserve, I'm asking the Congress to add $25 billion in defense spending over the next six years.

I have visited many bases at home and around the world, since I became president. Tonight, I repeat that request with renewed conviction. We ask a very great deal of our armed forces. Now that they are smaller in number, we ask more of them. They go out more often to more different places and stay longer. They are called to service in many, many ways. And we must give them and their families what the times demand and what they have earned.

Just think about what our troops have done in the last year, showing America at its best, helping to save hundreds of thousands of people in Rwanda, moving with lightning speed to head off another threat to Kuwait, giving freedom and democracy back to the people of Haiti.

We have proudly supported peace and prosperity and freedom from South Africa to Northern Ireland, from Central and Eastern Europe to Asia, from Latin America to the Middle East. All these endeavors are good in those places, but they make our future more confident and more secure.

Well, my fellow Americans, that's my agenda for America's future: Expanding opportunity, not bureaucracy; enhancing security at home and abroad; empowering our people to make the most of their own lives. It's ambitious and achievable, but it's not enough. We even need more than new ideas for changing the world or equipping Americans to compete in the new economy; more than a government that's smaller, smarter and wiser; more than all the changes we can make in government and in the private sector from the outside in.

Our fortunes and our posterity also depend upon our ability to answer some questions from within, from the values and voices that speak to our hearts as well as our heads; voices that tell us we have to do more to accept responsibility for ourselves and our families, for our communities, and, yes, for our fellow citizens. We see our families and our communities all over this country coming apart. And we feel the common ground shifting from under us.

The PTA, the town hall meeting, the ballpark, it's hard for a lot of over-worked parents to find the time and space for those things that strengthen the bonds of trust and cooperation. Too many of our children don't even have parents and grandparents who can give them those experiences that they need to build their own character and their sense of identity.

[Making a Difference]

We all know that while we here in this chamber can make a difference on those things, that the real differences will be made by our fellow citizens where they work and where they live. And it will be made almost without regard to party. When I used to go to the softball park in Little Rock to watch my daughter's league, and people would come up to me, fathers and mothers, and talk to me, I can honestly say I had no idea whether 90 percent of them were Republicans or Democrats. When I visited the relief centers after the floods in California—Northern California—last week, a woman came up to me and did something that very few of you would do. She hugged me and said, "Mr. President, I'm a Republican, but I'm glad you're here."

Now, why? We can't wait for disasters to act the way we used to act every day. Because as we move into this next century, everybody matters; we don't have a person to waste. And a lot of people are losing a lot of chances to do better. That means that we need a New Covenant for everybody.

For our corporate and business leaders, we're going to work here to keep bringing the deficit down, to expand markets, to support their success in every possible way. But they have an obligation when they're doing well to keep jobs in our communities and give their workers a fair share of the prosperity they generate.

For people in the entertainment industry in this country, we applaud your creativity and your worldwide success, and we support your freedom of expression. But you do have a responsibility to assess the impact of your work and to understand the damage that comes from the incessant, repetitive, mindless violence and irresponsible conduct that permeates our media all the time.

We've got to ask our community leaders and all kinds of organizations to help us stop our most serious social problem: the epidemic of teen pregnancies and births where there is no marriage. I have sent to Congress a plan to target schools all over this country with anti-pregnancy programs that work. But government can only do so much. Tonight, I call on parents and leaders all across this country to join together in a national campaign against teen pregnancy to make a difference. We can do this, and we must.

And I would like to say a special word to our religious leaders. You know, I'm proud of the fact the United States has more houses of worship per capita than any country in the world. These people who lead our houses of worship can ignite their congregations to carry their faith into action; can reach out to all of our children, to all of the people in distress, to those who have been savaged by the breakdown of all we hold dear. Because so much of what we've done must come from the inside out, and our religious leaders and their congregations can make all the difference. They have a role in the New Covenant as well.

There must be more responsibility for all of our citizens. You know, it takes a lot of people to help all the kids in trouble stay off the streets and in school. It takes a lot of people to build the Habitat for Humanity houses that the Speaker celebrates on his lapel pin. It takes a lot of people to provide the people power for all of the civic organizations in this country that made our communities mean so much to most of us when we were kids. It takes every parent to teach the children the difference between right and wrong and to encourage them to learn and grow; and to say no to the wrong things, but also to believe that they can be whatever they want to be.

I know it's hard when you're working harder for less, when you're under great stress to do these things. A lot of our people don't have the time or the emotional strength they think to do the work of citizenship.

Most of us in politics haven't helped very much. For years, we've mostly treated citizens like they were consumers or spectators, sort of political couch potatoes who were supposed to watch the TV ads, either promise them something for nothing or play on their fears and frustrations. And more and more of our citizens now get most of their information in very negative and aggressive ways that are hardly conducive to honest and open conversations. But the truth is, we have got to stop seeing each other as enemies, just because we have different views.

If you go back to the beginning of this country, the great strength of America, as [Alexis] de Tocqueville pointed out when he came here a long time ago, has always been our ability to associate with people who were different from ourselves and to work together to find common ground. And in this day, everybody has a responsibility to do more of that. We simply cannot wait for a tornado, a fire, or a flood to behave like Americans ought to behave in dealing with one another.

I want to finish up here by pointing out some folks that are up with the first lady that represent what I'm trying to talk about—citizens. I have no idea what their party affiliation is or who they voted for in the last election. But they represent what we ought to be doing.

Cindy Perry teaches second-graders to read in Americorps in rural Kentucky. She gains when she gives. She's a mother of four. She says that her service inspired her to get her high school equivalency last year. She was married when she was a teenager. She had four children, but she had time to serve other people, to get her high school equivalency. And she's going to use her Americorps money to go back to college.

Chief Stephen Bishop is the police chief of Kansas City. He's been a national leader in using more police in community policing, and he's worked with Americorps to do it. And the crime rate in Kansas City has gone down as a result of what he did.

Cpl. Gregory Depestre went to Haiti as part of his adopted country's force to help secure democracy in his native land. And I might add, we must be the only country in the world that could have gone to Haiti and taken Haitian-

Americans there who could speak the language and talk to the people. And he was one of them, and we're proud of him.

The next two folks I've had the honor of meeting and getting to know a little bit, the Rev. John and the Rev. Diana Cherry of the AME Zion Church in Temple Hills, Md. I'd like to ask them to stand. I want to tell you about them. In the early '80s, they left government service and formed a church in a small living room in a small house. Today that church has 17,000 members. It is one of the three or four biggest churches in the entire United States. It grows by 200 a month. They do it together. And the special focus of their ministry is keeping families together.

Two things they did make a big impression on me. I visited their church once, and I learned they were building a new sanctuary closer to the Washington, D.C., line in a higher crime, higher drug rate area because they thought it was part of their ministry to change the lives of the people who needed them.

The second thing I want to say is, that once Rev. Cherry was at a meeting at the White House with some other religious leaders, and he left early to go back to his church to minister to 150 couples that he had brought back to his church from all over America to convince them to come back together, to save their marriages, and to raise their kids. This is the kind of work that citizens are doing in America. We need more of it, and it ought to be lifted up and supported.

The last person I want to introduce is Jack Lucas from Hattiesburg, Miss. Jack, would you stand up? Fifty years ago, in the sands of Iwo Jima, Jack Lucas taught and learned the lessons of citizenship. On Feb. 20, 1945, he and three of his buddies encountered the enemy and two grenades at their feet. Jack Lucas threw himself on both of them.

In that moment, he saved the lives of his companions, and miraculously in the next instant, a medic saved his life. He gained a foothold for freedom, and at the age of 17, Jack Lucas became the youngest Marine in history and the youngest soldier in this century to win the Congressional Medal of Honor.

All these years later, yesterday, here's what he said about that day: "It didn't matter where you were from or who you were, you relied on one another. You did it for your country."

We all gain when we give, and we reap what we sow. That's at the heart of this New Covenant—responsibility, opportunity and citizenship. More than stale chapters in some remote civics book; they're still the virtue by which we can fulfill ourselves and reach our God-given potential and be like them; and also to fulfill the eternal promise of this country—the enduring dream from that first and most sacred covenant.

I believe every person in this country still believes that we are created equal, and given by our Creator, the right to life, liberty and the pursuit of happiness. This is a very, very great country. And our best days are still to come.

Thank you, and God bless you all.

WHITMAN'S REPUBLICAN RESPONSE

Good evening. Good evening. Before I begin, let me assure you, I am not going to ask for equal time.

I'm Christie Whitman, governor of New Jersey, and I am addressing you tonight from the historic legislative chamber in Trenton, one of the oldest in the nation. Speaking to you this evening is a tremendous honor for all of us here in New Jersey.

It is appropriate that we have come together tonight in Trenton. On Christmas morning in 1776, George Washington crossed the icy Delaware River and surprised King George's mercenaries in their barracks here on these grounds. The Battle of Trenton was a turning point in the American Revolution.

Just as that revolution two centuries ago began in the Colonies, there is a revolution sweeping America today, begun not in Washington, D.C., but in the states; in Wisconsin, in Ohio, in Massachusetts, in South Carolina, in California. The American people are seeking freedom in a new revolution that began before I ever came to office. It is a revolution of ideas, one in which the voters are given a clear choice between bigger or smaller government, higher or lower taxes, more or less spending. It is a revolution about a free and sovereign people saying they want power to return to them from their statehouses, from their county governments, their city halls.

[Choosing Smaller Government]

In elections all across America, the voters have chosen smaller government, lower taxes, and less spending. They rejected the tyranny of expanding welfare-state policies, the arrogance of bigger and bigger government, the frustration of "one size fits all" answers. In a word, they have chosen freedom. They elected leaders like Gov. [William F.] Weld of Massachusetts [R], who in his first month in office cut state spending by $1.7 billion. Since then, he's cut taxes five times and brought Massachusetts the third-lowest unemployment rate in the nation.

And Gov. Pete Wilson [R], who has already reformed health care in California using market forces to guarantee access for millions of uninsured and made health care more affordable for small businesses.

They elected governors who said we should have smaller, more efficient government, and meant it, like Gov. Tommy [G.] Thompson in Wisconsin [R]—he's cut spending, cut taxes, and led the most comprehensive welfare reform movement in the country; and Gov. Fife Symington of Arizona, who became one of several Republican governors to cut taxes every year they were in office and see their economies boom. In state after state, the revolution of ideas took hold. . . .

Here in New Jersey like so many other governors I was told that tax-cutting policies were a gimmick. I heard we couldn't do it, that it was impossible, that it would hurt the economy. But I had given the people of New Jersey my word that we would cut their taxes, and we did.

In the first year, with the help of the New Jersey Legislature, we cut business taxes. We reduced income taxes not once, but twice. We lowered state spending, not recklessly, but carefully and fairly. Just yesterday I announced a third wave of income tax cuts, another 15 percent, taking us to a 30-percent reduction, to put more money in the hands of families like yours. The results have been solid. State revenues are up, even from the income tax. And 60,000 more New Jerseyans are at work today than were a year ago, making this year our best year for job creation since 1988. And we did it all under a balanced-budget requirement to our state's Constitution.

In November, the revolution came to Washington. Now people want less government, lower taxes, and less spending from their federal government. People want results. In both houses of Congress, the Republican party has been elected like many of us in the states were, on an agenda of change.

We're committed to reforming welfare, to encourage people to work and to stop children from having children. We want to force the government to live within its means by stopping runaway spending and balancing the federal budget. We want to lower taxes for families and make it easier to achieve the American dream, to save money, buy a home and send the kids to college.

We're going to stop violent criminals in their tracks with real prison time for repeat offenders and a workable death penalty. We must send a message to our young people that crime doesn't pay.

And we're going to slash those unnecessary regulations that strangle small business in America, to make it easier to create more jobs and pay better wages and become more competitive in the global marketplace. We intend to create a new era of hope and opportunity for all Americans. Many of these ideas are the same ones governors have been enacting here in the states.

Time after time, Republicans and Democrats have found that things work better when states and communities set their own priorities rather than being bossed around by bureaucrats in Washington. Our colleagues on Capitol Hill are facing the same opposition we did, the same cries of, "It can't be done," from the Washington-knows-best crowd, people who think government can't be too big and that there's a virtue in raising taxes. Well, there is nothing virtuous about raising taxes. There is nothing heroic about preserving a welfare system that entraps people, and there's nothing high-minded about wasting other people's money on big government spending sprees.

We overcame the same objections, the same stalling and distortion, the same foot-dragging. We've heard it all. And in the end, we have won the battle of ideas in our states. Now it's time to win the battle of ideas in Washington. If the people's agenda is to succeed in Congress, everyone needs to work together. And while at times tonight some of the president's ideas sounded pretty Republican the fact remains that he has been opposed to the balanced-budget requirement, he proposed even more government spending, and he imposed the biggest tax increase in American history.

[A Call to the President]

It's clear that your votes in November sounded a warning to the president. If he has truly changed his big-government agenda, we say, "Great. Join us as we change America. Republicans welcome your ideas for making government not bigger, but smaller." As we have moved forward and as we move forward in the next two years, the president and Congress should be reminded that success is not measured in the number of laws passed, but in the results. Is government serving the people better? Are neighborhoods safer? Are families stronger? Are children learning more? Are we better prepared to meet the future? Do we have more freedom?

The election in November was a beginning, not an end. And we are committed to fulfilling the verdict of the voters and enacting our agenda of hope for the families of America. Change is hard, but we are going to work hard. We will keep faith with America. We will keep our word. We will do what you elected us to do. We will give you results. On Election Day, you gave us your trust. We accept your mandate. President Clinton, you must accept it as well. Put the principles of smaller, more effective government into action. Reduce spending and cut taxes.

Two weeks ago, in my State of the State address to the people of New Jersey, I made them a pledge which, in closing, I would now like to make to the American people on behalf of the Republican party. By the time President Clinton makes his next State of the Union address, we will have lower taxes. We will have more efficient government. We will have a stronger America. We will have more faith in our politics, more pride in our states and communities and more confidence in ourselves. We will go forward together as one family with many faces, building a future with opportunity, a future with security, a future based on mutual respect and responsibility, and, most of all, a future filled with hope for our children and our children's children.

Thank you very much, and God bless America.

STATE DEPARTMENT ON THE WORLDWIDE LAND MINE CRISIS
January 27, 1995

According to a State Department report prepared in 1994 by the Office of International Security and Peacekeeping Operations and made public January 27, an estimated 500 people—many of them innocent civilians— are killed or maimed each week by some of the estimated 80–110 million antipersonnel land mines scattered throughout sixty-four countries. In addition, new mines are being laid faster than old ones are being cleared. The report, "Hidden Killers: The Global Landmine Crisis," laid out the problems of uncleared land mines and the U.S. government's strategy for "demining" and controlling the use of land mines.

Although the report received little public debate when it was issued, the problem of land mines was likely to receive renewed attention as 20,000 American troops joined peacekeeping forces in Bosnia in late 1995 and early 1996. Factions in that civil war have reportedly laid hundreds of thousands of land mines, which were considered among the worst threats to American lives there.

In a statement issued when the report was released, Secretary of State Warren Christopher noted that the millions of land mines strewn through-out the world are not self-deactivating, which means "that they don't cease their killing when peace treaties are signed or other weapons of war fall silent." Nor do land mines distinguish between civilians and combatants. "Indeed," Christopher said, "they probably kill more children than they do soldiers."

In addition to the physical damage they inflict, uncleared mine fields impede repairs to basic infrastructure, such as roads and railroads; disrupt humanitarian aid shipments; make arable land untillable; and prevent refugee populations from returning home. In some countries entire communities have been made uninhabitable. "The burden imposed by the proliferation and indiscriminate use of these weapons is beyond calculation," the report said. "The world must take stronger steps to address this problem. . . ."

The Devastating Effects of Land Mines

According to the report, Africa was plagued the most by land mines, which had been laid extensively during wars for independence and in subsequent civil wars. The State Department estimated that land mines killed more than 12,000 Africans every year. It was also noted that in Cambodia 1 of every 236 people was an amputee as a result of a mine blast.

Land mines were cheap to purchase but expensive to clear. A mine that might cost as little as $3 to buy on the open market cost up to $1,000 to clear. The costs of not clearing the mines were even greater. Health care and rehabilitation costs for survivors of mine blasts were substantial; for example, in Afghanistan it cost an estimated $5,000 to treat and rehabilitate each survivor. Such costs were more than most mine-plagued countries in the developing world could support.

Land mines, the report noted, also pose obstacles to economic growth and political stability. Roads made impassable by land mines restrict the transportation of goods and services, thereby disrupting internal markets and causing shortages of food and other goods. "Even in an otherwise health economy," the report said, "landmines can artificially limit supplies of critical products, producing an inflationary spiral that is politically destabilizing."

The U.S. Government's Response to the Problem

In addition to a self-imposed unilateral moratorium on exporting land mines that was enacted in 1992 and extended for three years in 1993, the Clinton administration was working to strengthen existing international laws governing their use. To that end, President Bill Clinton in May 1994 asked the Senate to ratify the Convention on Conventional Weapons, which included a protocol on the use of land mines. The United States has proposed improvements in that protocol that would extend the protocol to civil wars and prohibit the use of land mines unless they were self-deactivating or were placed in marked and monitored areas. The treaty cleared the Foreign Relations Committee but languished in the Senate.

In a speech to the United Nations General Assembly on September 26, 1994, Clinton proposed a multilateral control regime aimed at the eventual elimination of land mines as a weapon of war. That regime would ask countries to reduce the number of mines that do not self-destruct. It would also allow the export of land mines only to countries that had ratified the Convention on Conventional Weapons and would expressly prohibit exports to countries whose actions had been condemned by the UN Security Council or who had provided mines to ineligible recipients.

In addition, the U.S. government in 1993 established the Demining Assistance Program to provide mine awareness and mine clearance training in affected countries. In fiscal 1994, the report said, the United States spent $17.9 million on demining efforts in Afghanistan, Cambodia, Eritrea, Ethiopia, Mozambique, Namibia, and Nicaragua. That amount

47

*was expected to increase to $25 million in fiscal 1995. Several other coun-
tries, international organizations, and nongovernmental organizations
were also involved in mine-clearing activities around the world.*

*Following are excerpts from "Hidden Killers: The Global Land-
mine Crisis," a report to Congress prepared in 1994 by the State
Department's Office of International Security and Peacekeeping
Operations and released to the public January 27, 1995:*

Worldwide Nature and Scope of the Problem

Antipersonnel (A/P) landmines are devastating weapons of war, but they
are equally devastating weapons after a war. The vast majority of landmines
stockpiled and in use today around the world have no means of self-neutral-
ization or self-destruction. These mines remain active and deadly long after
conflicts cease, killing and maiming an estimated 26,000 people, mostly innocent civilians, every year. . . .

According to the United Nations, ongoing and new mine clearance efforts
managed to extract 80,000 mines worldwide in 1993. However, another estimated 2.5 million mines were implanted. These facts, combined with the latest U.S. global survey, bring the worldwide estimate to 80 to 110 million landmines. To quote UN demining expert Brigadier General (Ret.) Patrick Blag-
den, "we're losing the battle."

Many of the 110 million mines are each capable of wounding or killing
several people, and efforts to destroy the mines are slow, painstaking, and
expensive. But the human costs of not destroying them are proving even
more expensive. Thousands of lives are lost to explosions; entire regions are
denied basic services because repairs to infrastructure are impeded; humanitarian aid shipments are disrupted; and societies are thrown into chaos.

The problem is greatest in Africa, where mines have been used extensively in wars for independence, and also in the subsequent power struggles.
Approximately 20 million landmines are strewn in nearly one half of Africa's
countries, killing over 12,000 people per year.

Landmines are a continuous impediment to the world economy. Mines
which cost as little as $3 each on the open market cost up to $1,000 each to
clear. If not cleared, mines will continue to inflict injuries. In Afghanistan, it
is estimated that $5,000 is required for treatment and rehabilitation for every
survivor. The fragile economies of many mine-plagued countries cannot support the cost of either mine clearance or victim rehabilitation.

The three nations with the largest landmine problem are Afghanistan,
Angola, and Cambodia. Collectively, they are besieged by an estimated 28
million mines and suffer 22,000 casualties every year (85 percent of the
world's total). The efforts to demine just those three countries will require
decades of work and vast amounts of resources. UN-initiated mine clearance
programs are making progress in Afghanistan and Cambodia, but no interna-

tional effort can commence in Angola until a lasting peace settlement is reached. Meanwhile, more mines will be deployed.

Other countries with more than 1 million landmines include Iraq, Sudan, Mozambique, Somalia, Ethiopia, and Eritrea. The United States is currently providing demining assistance to Eritrea, Ethiopia, and Mozambique. Many other countries are polluted with over 500,000 mines.

Landmines affect every aspect of a nation's reconstruction after combat. Refugees cannot return home. Those who do cannot work the fields to grow crops. Relief shipments cannot be delivered. Infrastructure cannot be repaired. Herd animals cannot approach watering holes. Peacekeeping forces cannot deploy as effectively. Every task required to rebuild a war-shattered society is put on hold until the mines are cleared, a process that can take years. Or reconstruction begins despite the mines, because social pressure demands that it begin, and lives are lost to landmine explosions. It truly is a no-win situation for fragile new governments.

The need for assistance around the world is growing. Except in those few areas where the international community has been able to mount successful mine clearance efforts, the mines lie waiting. The 1993 State Department report indicated that landmines kill or wound 150 people per week. Further investigation, more accurate field reporting, and increased awareness and attention to the problem now suggest that number was greatly understated. Landmines maim or kill an estimated 500 people per week worldwide.

The economic implications alone of these casualties in rural and agricultural areas is daunting. Those who survive a landmine blast are usually incapable of the strenuous, mobile labor required to make a living, and they also require extended medical attention and rehabilitation. The lost labor productivity and resources required for treatment of landmine injuries can further cripple an economy already weakened by war.

The world must recognize the landmine problem for what it is: a global crisis. . . .

Military History of Landmines

Mine warfare began as the practice of digging underneath fixed military fortifications to cause their collapse. The destructiveness of such mining increased with the invention of gunpowder, which was used in tunnels dug during the American Civil War and World War I. Technological advancement shifted mine warfare from attacking fixed targets to stopping moving troops and vehicles, particularly the tank. Mines were first used this way on a broad scale in World War I. . . .

Mine warfare became firmly established in World War II, when the landmine in its common form—encased explosives fitted with fuses or firing devices for actuation by the user or by the target itself—was used by all World War II combatants. Mines initially were used in North Africa to protect strongpoints in fighting between British and Italian forces on the Egyptian-Libyan border. . . .

The conventional nature of World War II, the dominance of armored warfare in many campaigns, and environmental factors made for similarities in mine warfare as practiced by the various belligerents. In all armies, as an economy-of-force measure, the landmine, or "silent soldier," was used to release men for combat. While wartime experience confirmed the importance of marking, recording, and removing mines, application of these doctrinal tenets became lax as operations became more mobile and during retreats. For all combatants, the unrecorded minefield was the equivalent of an enemy minefield, a hazard to the troops that emplaced it and to the civilian population.

The postwar division of Europe into Eastern and Western Blocs, accompanied by a buildup of American ground forces in the West, prompted the construction of barrier minefields across likely invasion routes. These minefields were designed to deter and, if necessary, delay an aggressor by channelizing and concentrating forces in target areas where they would be attacked by air and artillery fire. Communist powers in Europe laid defensive mine belts along their borders with the West for the same purposes. These elaborate arrays of barrier minefields became a feature of the West's cold war scenarios of containment and deterrence in Europe.

At the same time, mine warfare was developing in Korea differently from World War II both in scale and in tactics. Korea's predominantly mountainous terrain tended to channel movement along a few restricted corridors. Mines were most often used to block roads, passes, and other avenues of movement. Compared to North Africa, where approximately 2,000 A/T [antitank] mines were used per tank casualty, in Korea's restrictive terrain the rate was about 80 mines per tank casualty. . . .

The Vietnam War marked a change in mine warfare tactics from previous wars fought by the United States, in that the VC [Viet Cong] used mines as instruments of terror to intimidate selected local populations. The insurgents mined roads nightly, making mine clearing by combined infantry, armor, and engineer road-clearing teams a daily task. In addition to mine detectors, Americans used specially equipped tanks, plows, and bulldozers to detonate mines, cut tripwires, and clear vegetation to better detect mines and prevent ambushes. Plastic and other nonmetallic mines were virtually impossible to detect, except by manually probing for them.

Used in a manner and on a scale never before encountered by American forces, landmines emerged as a major weapons system for the VC/PA [People's Army of Vietnam] in South Vietnam. Of approximately 41,840 American ground soldiers killed in battle in the Vietnam War, slightly more than 7,400 were killed by mines or grenades, or approximately 16 percent; some estimates approach 30 percent. . . .

Insurgent and counterinsurgent use of mines characterized mine warfare in Vietnam. Insurgents and terrorists find mines plentiful, cheap, and simple to use. Lacking stronger firepower, mines often have been used in an offensive role as a substitute for artillery. In African anticolonial insurgencies, such as those in Angola, Guinea, Mozambique, and Zambia, mines were widely used as retaliatory weapons, for road interdiction, and in ambushes. The conflict in Angola against Portugal, for example, was characterized as one of "mines versus helicopters," and 50 percent of Portugal's casualties in 1970 were attributed to mines.

Two wars, Israel's Six-Day War in 1967 and the Yom Kippur War of 1973, offered an approximation of mature conventional mine warfare in the Cold War era against modern armored forces. In each war, Israel and the opposing Arab forces used mines extensively. In the Sinai, Egypt and Israel sowed landmines to form antitank barriers similar to those encountered in World War II desert fighting. Mines were also sown along the Israeli-Syrian border in the Golan Heights, which Israel had occupied since 1967. However, neither in 1967 nor in 1973 were mine defenses capable of stopping armored forces, suggesting that mine defenses, no matter how strong, whether based on natural or artificial barriers, could be penetrated by surprise, ingenuity, and determination.

Scatterable mines, deliverable by air, artillery, or tank weapons, enhanced the traditional defensive roles of mines. Speed and remote delivery greatly increased the offensive potential of mine warfare. Such mines could be deployed in front of a fleeing enemy or on alternate defense positions to impair withdrawal. They would often be seeded amid an enemy's assembly areas, artillery positions, and airfields. Fitted with a self-destruct feature (which has not always proved to be reliable), mines could be activated, detonated, or deactivated at prescribed times so as not to interfere with friendly maneuvers. With scatterable mines, impromptu minefields could be provided on demand at particular points.

These features, however, have modified certain aspects of mine warfare doctrine. Scrupulous marking and recording of minefields became more difficult. With the advent of new dispensing systems, responsibility for the employment of mines has been decentralized to other branches and to lower unit echelons, eroding the once predominant role of engineers. The smaller size and lethality of scatterable mines have increased the density of minefields, making clearing by opposing military forces more difficult, and thereby increasing the danger to civilians.

Until the early 1970s, modern mine warfare evolved largely in tandem with the development of armored forces. As better armor protection and antitank missiles were developed, the value of mines for defense against tanks decreased while the role of antipersonnel mines has grown. This shift in emphasis reflects both advances in mine technology and the proliferation of small wars, largely in the developing world, in which inexpensive and easily acquired and manufactured A/P mines fulfill a doctrinal and tactical need for a weapon of intimidation and destruction.

Landmine Control

The United States is pursuing a multifaceted effort aimed at preventing the continuation and spread of the human and economic tragedy caused by the presence of uncleared landmines. First, the United States is leading the effort to strengthen the existing international laws regulating the use of antipersonnel (A/P) landmines in times of armed conflict. Second, in an effort to slow the proliferation of A/P mines until a more permanent international control mechanism can be negotiated and implemented, the United States has imposed a unilateral moratorium on the export of these weapons and is encouraging other countries to do the same. Finally, in his speech at the United Nations on September 26, 1994, President Clinton announced the U.S. proposal for a multilateral control regime to govern A/P landmines.

Convention on Conventional Weapons

Landmines are an established weapon of war long used by many belligerents in ways that minimize the threat to civilian life. The landmine problem arises largely from the willingness of some warring parties to ignore these established practices and deliberately use landmines in irresponsible or cruel ways. The international community must respond by tightening and vigorously enforcing the existing legal requirements and constraints. The legal vehicle for codifying these rules is the 1980 Convention on Conventional Weapons (CCW) and its Protocol 11 on the use of landmines.

The United States is a signatory to the CCW, but is not yet a party. In May 1994 President Clinton submitted the CCW to the Senate for its advice and consent to ratification, which will help the United States take the lead in pressing for improvements to Protocol II. In order for the United States to participate as more than an observer in the September 1995 conference to review and update the convention, the United States must formally submit the instruments of ratification to the United Nations by March 1995.

The United States is helping to lead efforts to improve the landmines Protocol in a series of international experts meetings that will culminate in a review conference of the CCW in September 1995. Among the improvements the United States is seeking are: an extension of the scope of Protocol II to cover armed internal conflict; a system of stricter use controls that would prohibit the use of A/P mines which do not incorporate self-destruct devices, unless they are placed in a marked and monitored area; the establishment of the principle that the party that lays a minefield is responsible for maintaining the minefield in accordance with CCW rules until the minefield is cleared or turned over to a party who accepts responsibility for the minefield; a ban on the use of undetectable mines; a requirement for marking minefields; and the establishment of a practical verification system for the CCW.

Such changes would be broad and far-reaching. Extending the rules of the landmines Protocol to cover civil wars has enormous significance. Indeed, most conflicts since 1980 have not been subject to the landmines Protocol because the conflicts have been internal, usually in the developing world. An absolute ban on nondetectable mines would be of tremendous benefit to mine-clearing operations. Improving minefield marking and recording and providing for more rigorous verification both amount to real and substantial improvements. Finally, an effective ban on remotely deployed mines that are not self-destructing would reduce post-combat civilian mine casualties.

The United States is also promoting wider adherence to the CCW. With only 41 parties, even the most far-reaching changes will have limited real-world impact. The United States is actively encouraging more states, particularly the worst offenders, to become party to the CCW. . . .

Export Moratorium

In late 1992 the United States imposed a unilateral, 1-year moratorium on the transfer of A/P landmines to other countries. In 1993, it was extended for another 3 years (now to expire in 1996). Also, in December 1993, the United States proposed to the UN General Assembly (UNGA) a resolution calling for all countries to adopt a moratorium on the export of A/P mines that pose a grave risk to civilians. UNGA adopted that resolution unanimously. Since its adoption, the United States has repeatedly urged other countries, especially those which produce landmines, to adopt such a moratorium. A number of countries have done so, while others have imposed export controls equivalent to a moratorium. The United States continues to ask all nations that produce or export landmines to declare their own moratoria, and the United States is introducing an export moratorium resolution in the UNGA again this year. By adopting a moratorium, a nation is helping impose a pause in the spread of landmines, a pause that provides time to negotiate and implement a more permanent international control mechanism.

Multilateral Control Regime

President Clinton unveiled the U.S. proposal for a multilateral control regime during his speech to the UN General Assembly on September 26, 1994. As a first step toward the eventual elimination of antipersonnel landmines, the President called on all nations to join the United States in concluding an agreement to reduce the number and availability of A/P landmines.

This proposal is designed to address the two fundamental sources of the humanitarian problem associated with A/P landmines. The first is that these weapons too often find their way into the wrong hands. The landmine threat to civilians in the recent past has been caused almost exclusively by those who use landmines in violation of existing laws of armed conflict, sometimes even targeting civilians specifically. Second, most casualties are caused by landmines that, once deployed, remain lethal indefinitely rather than [those that are] self-destructing or self-deactivating.

The United States recognizes that A/P landmines are a legitimate weapon of war when used in accordance with the laws of armed conflict. However, the United States also recognizes that their proliferation coupled with widespread indiscriminate and irresponsible use causes unnecessary human suffering. For that reason, the ultimate goal of the United States is the eventual elimination of A/P landmines. Regime members can move most effectively toward that goal as viable and humane alternatives are developed.

As a first step toward this ultimate goal, the proposed regime lays downs restrictions governing A/P landmine production and stockpiling as well as export. It addresses the humanitarian problem in three basic ways. The regime will:

Reduce reliance on those types of A/P landmines that cause the greatest danger to civilians. Most civilian casualties occur in post-combat situations and are attributable to those A/P landmines with a long lifespan, i.e., those that do not self-destruct or self-deactivate. The U.S. proposal calls on countries to modify their stockpiles so that only a small percentage will consist of these long-lived mines. It also calls for a future conference to consider the feasibility of eliminating these types of mines entirely.

Restrict the availability of A/P landmines. The regime is designed to keep A/P landmines out of the hands of irresponsible users. It would allow the export of A/P landmines only to those countries which have ratified CCW/Protocol II. It would prohibit exports to any state whose actions have been condemned by the UN Security Council or any state found to have provided landmines to an ineligible recipient.

Reinforce the landmine use restrictions contained in CCW. As noted above, the United States is pressing for improvements in CCW in order to increase the protection afforded civilians. In parallel with that effort, the regime would prohibit the production, stockpiling, and export of any mine that is illegal to use under the terms of a strengthened CCW.

In the interest of establishing a regime as quickly as possible, the United States will seek an agreement based on political commitments as opposed to legally binding obligations.

Taken together, the United States believes these efforts constitute a pragmatic, effective approach to reducing the threat to civilians being caused by the proliferation and irresponsible use of A/P landmines. They are also an important first step toward the ultimate U.S. goal of the eventual elimination of all A/P landmines. . . .

SMITHSONIAN ANNOUNCEMENT ON *ENOLA GAY* EXHIBIT
JANUARY 30, 1995

The Smithsonian Institution announced on January 30 that it would drastically scale back its planned exhibit commemorating the fiftieth anniversary of the use of atomic bombs against Japan to end World War II. The secretary of the Smithsonian, I. Michael Heyman, made the announcement at a press conference in Washington, D.C., following a meeting with his Board of Regents.

The Smithsonian was responding to bitter protests by veterans groups and members of Congress against its original plans for exhibiting part of the fuselage of the Enola Gay, *the B-29 Superfortress bomber that dropped the first atomic bomb on Hiroshima on August 6, 1945. The veterans objected in particular to a narrative, which was to have been included in the exhibit, raising questions about the morality of and rationale for the use of atomic bombs against Japan.*

Spokesmen for veterans groups expressed satisfaction with the Smithsonian's decision to scale back the exhibit, which they said was misguided in the first place. "The institution has been badly damaged by its own mismanagement and zeal for revisionist history," said William M. Detwiler, national commander of the American Legion.

Japanese officials, and groups representing survivors of the atomic bomb attacks, reacted with dismay. "The government cannot intervene, but this is regrettable," Prime Minister Timichi Murayama was quoted as saying.

One casualty of the controversy was Martin O. Harwit, director of the Smithsonian's National Air and Space Museum, which had planned the exhibit. Harwit resigned on May 2 after eight years on the job, citing the damage done to his museum's reputation.

The scaled-back exhibit opened at the Air and Space Museum on June 28. That exhibit brought renewed criticism from the Japanese media, which portrayed it as an effort to justify the use of atomic bombs against Hiroshima and Nagasaki and to play down the price that was paid in human lives.

The Disputed Plan

The Smithsonian's original plan was to produce a huge, 10,000-square-foot exhibit called "The Final Act: The Atomic Bomb and the End of World War II." Along with sections of the Enola Gay, which the Smithsonian had restored, the exhibit was to have included photographs, videos, and a controversial 500-page narrative reviewing how the bombing ended the war.

Veterans groups and their supporters in Congress were incensed by what they viewed as the narrative's pro-Japanese slant. The most controversial item was in an early version, which reportedly said of World War II: "For most Americans, it was a war of vengeance [for the Japanese attack on Pearl Harbor]. For most Japanese, it was a war to defend their unique culture against Western imperialism."

Under political pressure, the Smithsonian repeatedly revised plans for the exhibit, but each revision failed to satisfy the critics. Republican leaders, after taking control of Congress in January, announced plans for hearings on the management of the Smithsonian.

Broader Controversy over First Atomic Bombs

The Enola Gay dispute also brought into the public spotlight a recurring debate among scholars over the wisdom of President Truman's decision to use the atomic bomb. Some historians have questioned the president's contention that the use of atomic bombs was necessary to avoid a massive U.S. invasion of Japan that might have caused hundreds of thousands of casualties on both sides.

In fact, one of the most controversial aspects of the Smithsonian exhibit was the last item added: a new estimate, offered by one historian, that about 60,000 Americans would have died in an invasion, about one-fourth the estimated number accepted by many other historians. Harwit's decision to use the lower figure in the Enola Gay exhibit enraged leaders of veterans groups and led to a call by eighty-one members of Congress for his dismissal.

The political pressure proved too much for the Smithsonian, which is normally one of the least controversial of the national institutions based in Washington, D.C. In his announcement that the Smithsonian was effectively scrapping the controversial parts of the exhibit, Secretary Heyman said the original plans for the exhibit were flawed, and he acknowledged that the dispute was "consuming me and the institution."

Heyman's announcement failed to quell criticism of the Smithsonian, especially by Republicans. Rep. Samuel Johnson of Texas, one of four Republicans appointed to the Smithsonian's Board of Regents in January, later complained about other exhibits at the National Portrait Gallery and the National Museum of American History. Smithsonian officials reportedly were prepared for further congressional inquiries.

Following is the text of the January 30, 1995, announcement by I. Michael Heyman, secretary of the Smithsonian Institution, of the scaling back of a planned exhibit commemorating the dropping of the first atomic bombs on Japan at the end of World War II:

This morning I shared with the Board of Regents my decision to replace "The Last Act: The Atomic Bomb and the End of World War II" (the *Enola Gay* exhibition) scheduled to open in May at the National Air and Space Museum. I have taken this action for one overriding reason: I have concluded that we made a basic error in attempting to couple an historical treatment of the use of atomic weapons with the 50th anniversary commemoration of the end of the war. Exhibitions have many purposes, equally worthwhile. But we need to know which of many goals is paramount, and not to confuse them.

In this important anniversary year, veterans and their families were expecting, and rightly so, that the nation would honor and commemorate their valor and sacrifice. They were not looking for analysis, and, frankly, we did not give enough thought to the intense feelings such an analysis would evoke.

Once the controversy was upon us, our staff made a sincere effort to create a more balanced exhibition. Within a month of my becoming Secretary of the Smithsonian last Fall, plans for the exhibition were substantially revamped. They included a new 4,000-square-foot section on the War in the Pacific and extensive revisions to the script throughout. In all, I believe we eventually succeeded in creating plans for a more balanced presentation. However, the problem was more than one of balance. There was, in fact, a fundamental flaw in the concept of the exhibition. In retrospect, I now feel strongly that despite our sincere efforts to address everyone's concerns, we were bound to fail. No amount of re-balancing could change the confusing nature of the exhibition.

Therefore, I intend to take several actions. Let me just say that it is rare for the Secretary of the Institution to step in and take direct charge of an exhibition, but I have concluded that given the complexity of the circumstances, it is the best course of action. As a first step, I intend to replace the exhibition to eliminate the fundamental inconsistency of purpose. I think the new exhibition should be a much simpler one, essentially a display, permitting the *Enola Gay* and its crew to speak for themselves. The focal point of the display would be the *Enola Gay*. Along with the plane would be a video about its crew. It is particularly important in this commemorative year that veterans and other Americans have the opportunity to see the restored portion of the fuselage of the *Enola Gay*.

Although there will be no formal consultation process for this undertaking, I will work with whomever I believe necessary to produce it.

Secondly, the Institution has much to learn from this experience. To that end, the University of Michigan has agreed to co-sponsor a forum with the Smithsonian this spring on the subject of the appropriate ways for museums to handle controversial subjects. In particular we will discuss the Smithsonian's role and responsibilities as a national museum.

Thirdly, I believe that the issue of atomic weapons is one which the Institution, in its role as a public forum on important issues, can address well in the future, but not necessarily in an exhibition. Therefore, I am considering a series of public symposia to be held at a later date. It is a serious and difficult undertaking, and I intend to enlist the assistance of national experts, curators, military historians, representatives of veterans groups, representatives of peace groups and others to consider what happened.

Finally, sometime in the future the *Enola Gay* will be displayed at the Air and Space Museum's extension at Dulles International Airport in Virginia. That extension will, for the first time, allow the Smithsonian to display this important icon in its entirety.

I have a number of regrets about this sad situation. One is that it has gotten in the way of the commemoration of our nation's victory over aggression 50 years ago. We at the Smithsonian do not want to have this controversy overshadow the recognition that our veterans so richly deserve.

I also regret that the *Enola Gay* controversy has led some to doubt the value of historical inquiry by museums. I believe that important artifacts of American history ought to be exhibited in an historical context. However, I do intend to conduct an extensive management review of the National Air and Space Museum.

And finally, I regret that this action will be seen by some as a criticism of those responsible for this exhibition. The central problem was not their lack of skill or hard work, but rather our collective inability to anticipate the difficulty of presenting this complex subject in conflicting contexts.

Just over four months ago, I came to the Smithsonian Institution imbued with great hopes I still feel. This Institution is a splendid array of museums and research centers with an extraordinary staff. But I also came in the midst of a controversy that is now consuming me and the Institution and is interfering with the important work our nation asks us to do. It is time to move forward. On this, the eve of our 150th anniversary in 1996, we can work to achieve our fundamental goal of making the Smithsonian, the nation's museum, representative of and accessible to greater and greater numbers of Americans. The public's trust is sacred, and we intend to do all in our power to be worthy of that trust.

February

CONTROVERSY OVER
SURGEON GENERAL NOMINATION
February 10 and June 22, 1995

The politics of abortion and the 1996 presidential race combined to doom the nomination of Dr. Henry W. Foster Jr. to be surgeon general of the United States. In the course of events Foster's credibility and medical ethics were challenged. The White House was sharply criticized by opponents and supporters alike for again having failed to perform an adequate background investigation of a nominee.

It was the second time in President Bill Clinton's term that the surgeon generalship had stirred controversy. Joycelyn Elders, Clinton's first surgeon general, had been forced to resign December 9, 1994, after making blunt remarks about sex education, drugs, and abortion. (Elders resignation, Historic Documents of 1994, p. 592)

Foster, born in Pine Bluff, Arkansas, in 1933, was the only African-American in his medical school class at the University of Arkansas, from which he graduated in 1958. He served a stint in the Air Force and practiced medicine in Tuskegee, Alabama, until 1973, when he took a position at the Meharry Medical College, a historically black college in Nashville, Tennessee. At Meharry he served as chairman of the department of obstetrics and gynecology, dean of the medical school, and acting president of the university. At the time of his nomination he was on sabbatical leave as a health policy fellow at the Association of Academic Health Centers in Washington, D.C.

During the course of his career, Foster delivered more than ten thousand babies and was founder of a program in Nashville called "I Have a Future." That program, which was aimed at preventing teenage pregnancy, was designated one of President George Bush's "1,000 Points of Light" in 1991. However, from the moment of his nomination on February 2, attention centered on how many abortions Foster had performed.

The Abortion Issue

Initially, the administration said Foster had performed only one abortion. In a formal statement issued February 3, Foster said he had per-

formed "fewer than a dozen." Within a week, however, Foster, in an appearance on the ABC News program Nightline, revealed that he had been the physician of record for thirty-nine abortions.

That he had performed any abortions made Foster highly suspect to pro-life organizations. The changing number also damaged his credibility. Foster claimed that his erroneous statement of February 3 was an "honest mistake" and that he had not intended any deception.

The controversy over the abortions also led to charges that the White House was once again mishandling a nomination. "I am not going to vote for a nominee where no deep thought was given before the nomination went up," Sen. Joseph R. Biden, Jr. (D-Del.) said February 10. (Biden later said he would withhold final judgment until the confirmation vote.) Several of Clinton's earlier nominations, including his first two for attorney general, were scuttled by revelations about the nominees' backgrounds that came out during the confirmation process. The White House was blamed for not having investigated the nominees thoroughly enough. (Nominations for attorney general, Historic Documents of 1993, p. 135)

On February 10, Foster sought to take a more aggressive stance against his opponents. "I have dedicated my medical career to taking all appropriate medical steps to meet the health needs of my patients, and that includes performing legal abortions," he said in a speech at George Washington University's School of Public Health. "I believe in the right of a woman to choose. And I also support the president's belief that abortions should be safe, legal, and rare."

Even as Foster and the administration were hoping to defuse the abortion issue, new doubts were raised about the nomination. The most damaging was an allegation concerning the Tuskegee Syphilis Study, in which the Public Health Service deliberately left four hundred black men untreated so that it could study the progress of the disease. Nearly all the men were sharecroppers from the Tuskegee area. The experiment began in 1932 and continued for decades, even after penicillin had been found to be an effective remedy for syphilis. The experiment did not end until 1972, when its existence was made public. According to allegations released by the Family Research Council, a conservative organization opposed to the Foster nomination, Foster had known about the experiment in 1969 but had done nothing to stop it. Foster vehemently denied the allegation. "I was outraged in 1972 when, as president of the Macon County medical society, I first learned the facts of the study," he said February 24. "Had I learned the facts of the study any sooner, I would have been equally outraged then and I would have insisted on appropriate treatment."

Presidential Politics

The approaching 1996 presidential race intruded itself into the debate when Sen. Phil Gramm of Texas, a candidate for the Republican presidential nomination and a staunch abortion foe, announced that he was opposed to Foster's nomination and would filibuster it on the Senate floor.

Majority Leader Bob Dole of Kansas, the leading contender for the Republican nomination, was under intense pressure to prove to conservative Republicans that he could block Foster, whom they vehemently opposed.

Dole initially hinted that he might not schedule a vote on the nomination. Democrats responded by threatening to slow down action on other legislation, and even some Republicans opposed to Foster's confirmation said that the Senate should vote on the issue. After meeting with Foster on June 19, Dole scheduled two votes to cut off Gramm's threatened filibuster. If those votes failed, Dole said, Foster's nomination would be returned to the Senate calendar to languish.

Although Foster appeared to have the simple majority needed for confirmation, his supporters were unable to muster the sixty votes needed to cut off debate. The first vote, on June 21, failed 57–43; the second vote, on June 22, failed by the same margin. Foster then withdrew. Dole could take credit both for putting the issue to a vote and for rounding up the votes to block Foster, as conservative activists had demanded. Gramm also claimed victory for blocking the nomination. "I believe that if I had not said I'd filibuster that Dr. Foster would be at the tailors today getting his uniform fitted," he said at a news conference after the vote.

Although Clinton lost the nomination, his support for Foster highlighted his differences with his rivals on the potent abortion rights issue. These votes, Clinton said June 22, were not "about my right to choose a surgeon general," but "about the right of every woman to choose." The president had not yet nominated a surgeon general by year's end.

Following are excerpts from remarks made before the School of Public Health at George Washington University by Dr. Henry W. Foster Jr. on February 10, 1995, defending his nomination to be surgeon general and from remarks made by President Bill Clinton on June 22, 1995, after the Senate failed for a second time to cut off debate on Foster's nomination:

FOSTER ON NOMINATION

Thank you . . . for that gracious introduction. It is a pleasure to be here at this prestigious university. . . .

. . . [E]ver since February the second—when President Clinton and Secretary Shalala publicly called me to service, the descriptions of myself and my work that I have read in the papers and seen on TV have cast an unrecognizable shadow of the man I really am. . . .

In his announcement of my nomination, the President thanked me for taking on the difficult task of public service at a time when public service sometimes has a high price.

I thought I knew what he meant at the time. But after the past week—I really know what he meant. So you might be wondering, why do I want this job? Let me tell you.

If you've been listening to the news lately, you may have gotten the wrong idea about my professional career.

I have been a doctor for 38 years.

I have run a major health sciences center, comprised of four schools: medicine, dentistry, allied health, and graduate studies.

In 1972, I became one of the youngest people ever inducted into the Institute of Medicine of the National Academy of Sciences.

I am the founder of the award-winning "I Have a Future Program," which was recognized as one of this nation's "Thousand Points of Light" in 1991 by President George Bush.

I am also a husband of 35 years and the father of a daughter and a son.

For the past 38 years, as a teacher, a university leader, and a practicing obstetrician/gynecologist, I have dedicated my entire professional life to bringing healthy lives into this world—and helping people reach their full potential.

I have personally delivered thousands and thousands of babies.

While chair of the Department of OB-GYN at Meharry Medical College, I taught more than 1,500 students. Founded 119 years ago, Meharry is among the nation's finest teaching institutions.

And I have worked tirelessly to improve the health of newborns, unborns, and their mothers.

When you've had the good fortune to participate in the miracle of birth as many times as I have, it is difficult to stand on the sidelines and watch so many people wasting the precious gift of life.

It is difficult to look around America today and see so much needless suffering because of a lack of knowledge about prevention . . . or a lack of access and utilization of quality health care . . . or the lack of those basic values that prevent violence or abuse from taking root.

But all is not lost.

America is moving forward to confront both our health care crisis and the crisis of values that has led to too much irresponsible behavior.

As your Surgeon General—working with you and all Americans—I believe that I can turn the small ripples of success that we have produced into great waves of progress.

I believe that I can help empower more people to reclaim the power over their own health. . . .

That I can help inspire people in communities all across this nation to put a stop to dangerous and destructive behaviors. That I can help draw more attention to the tragic public health problems confronting us from the epidemic of violence to the spread of AIDS to the terrible problem of substance abuse.

The biggest tragedy is that these conditions are largely preventable and the deaths they cause are so often unnecessary.

Take violence, for example.

I believe we have the power to eradicate this scourge and prevent its recurrence.

At least 2.2 million Americans are victims of violent injury each year.

In 1992, there were more than 37,000 firearm-related deaths in this country.

Escalating violence in America causes not only unnecessary injury and death;

It is also a major cause of the disintegration and the hopelessness that pervade so many of our communities.

We can dig at the root causes of this epidemic and we can weed it out of existence.

I know we can—but it's going to take entire communities, working together.

Then there's drug and alcohol abuse.

A growing number of our young people are using illicit drugs and ruining their chances to grow into healthy and productive adulthood.

Recent surveys by the Department of Health and Human Services confirm that for three years in a row, the use of marijuana and other drugs by 8th, 10th, and 12th graders has actually risen.

At the same time, we see an increase in the number of older drug users who are showing up in emergency rooms.

We've got to do a better job at drug prevention—sending clear, consistent anti-drug messages, listening to our young people, helping them form positive goals and giving them the support they need to achieve them. And then there's AIDS.

The Centers for Disease Control and Prevention has revealed that in 1993 AIDS overtook accidents as the number one killer of men, aged 25 to 44 in the United States.

And just this week, the World Health Organization reported that HIV cases are rising fastest among women—and especially young girls and adolescents.

While we are still searching for a cure—we know how to prevent the spread of HIV. And we must not be timid in sharing what we know.

The knowledge we have about preventing AIDS has the power to save millions of lives: the key is to commit ourselves not only to talking the talk—but walking the walk—of prevention.

Which brings me to the issue that the President asked me to place at the top of my agenda—teen pregnancy. . . .

All of the afflictions that I've just mentioned: violence, drug use, AIDS . . . all of them are linked to the unacceptably high teen pregnancy rate in this country.

Early sex and early pregnancy so often are linked—either as a cause or a consequence—of violence, drug use, AIDS, poverty, and so many other negative outcomes.

Every day 8,400 teenagers become sexually active.

And every day, 2,781 teenagers get pregnant: this translates into 116 pregnancies per hour.

This is bad for the teens and even worse for their children.

We know that children born to teenagers are more likely to have serious health problems, and are more likely to be poor.

We know that about 80 percent of children born to teenage parents who dropped out of high school now live in poverty.

If we want to prevent teen pregnancy, we must offer young people more than slogans and dependency.

We must offer them something that's worth more than gold—we must offer them a quality education, a full array of health services, and enhanced self-esteem and life-options.

Too many children today believe their only hope is having babies.

That's a dead-end dream and we've got to replace it with a dream of hope and unlimited achievement.

That's the philosophy that embodies the "I Have a Future" program we started at Meharry Medical College back in 1987.

Our approach is to expand adolescent health care programs beyond the schools, and bring them to the community, where they can become a part of the fabric of everyday life.

Our program is anchored in Nashville's public housing projects. With respect to sexuality the emphasis first and foremost is always placed on abstinence.

The program involves entire families and the total social matrix of the surrounding community.

Everybody from parents, grandparents to politicians, volunteers, and from the clergy to business leaders has a role to play.

There are three parts to the program:

First, we equip adolescents with the basic information they need about health, human sexuality, and drug and alcohol use so they understand the benefits of abstinence and the consequences of early sexual activity and other risky behaviors.

Second, we provide a comprehensive array of adolescent health services, with a focus on abstinence. In some cases, that means access to birth control—with a very strong emphasis on parental and community involvement.

And third, and most important, we help young people enhance their life-options through activities that improve their job skills, self-reliance, values and self-esteem.

For example, the youth entrepreneurial component of our program helps teenagers learn more about themselves and about the world of work by empowering them to start businesses in their communities.

This kind of skills-development and character-building is not only important for girls and young women—but, as research is showing us, it is also critically important for boys and young men.

We have to take the time to understand all the unique aspects of young peoples' lives: building up their self-esteem, telling them we believe in them, but not simply treating them as collections of problems.

That is what we have done in "I Have a Future"—and it works.

We know of only one of the program's participants from 1988 to 1991 who became pregnant—compared to 59 teenage pregnancies in the two other demographically similar Nashville housing projects where "I Have a Future" is not offered.

And just last year, 16 of the 24 program participants who graduated from high school went on to college. Eight of them were male and 8 were female.

It has not been easy—and results don't happen overnight.

In fact, it's a difficult process, and requires great dedication by many people—but it is working.

This shows you what one community can do when it makes teenage well-being a real priority—and I believe this kind of success is possible in every community. . . .

My opponents say that this nomination is about abortion. I have dedicated my medical career to taking all appropriate medical steps to meet the health needs of my patients, and that includes performing legal abortions.

I believe in the right of a woman to choose. And I also support the President's belief that abortions should be safe, legal and rare.

But my life's work has been dedicated to making sure that young people don't have to face the choice of having abortions.

To do this, we have to put life's possibilities within reach of all our young people.

One of the reasons I have hope is because there are so many positive trends out there: like the steady decline in smoking over the past 20 years, the steep decline in the numbers of people drinking and driving, and the steady increase in the use of seat belts.

Americans are demonstrating that, with quality leadership, we can make headway on major public health problems if we put our minds to it.

Since the President asked me to take on the job of Surgeon General, I have been in the fight of my life.

I am standing strong—and I appreciate the strong support of the President. And I appreciate your support.

One thing I know—my fight is no tougher than the one I'm asking all of you to join: that's the fight to improve the health of all Americans and to prevent teen pregnancy. . . .

CLINTON'S REMARKS

Good afternoon. Today 43 Republicans in the Senate failed the fundamental test of fairness. By choosing to side with extremists who would do anything to block a woman's right to choose, those senators have done a disservice to a good man, done a disservice to the nominating process, and sent a chilling message to the rest of the country.

The American people are smart enough to see through what just happened. They know this is not about my right to choose a surgeon general, this is about the right of every woman to choose. The committee recommended Dr. Foster to the Senate. A clear and substantial majority of senators were prepared to vote for his nomination. But a determined minority succumbed to political pressure and abused the filibuster rule.

It's wrong for a man as qualified and committed as Dr. Foster to be denied this chance to serve our country. He has gone where too few of us have ever dared to go. He has ridden the rickety elevators in high-rise projects to talk to young people about the importance of abstinence and avoiding teen pregnancy. He has traveled the back roads of rural Alabama, bringing health care and hope to women and children who would otherwise have never seen a doctor. He has been a father figure to many children who do not see their own fathers.

He has actually done something, in short, about the problems a lot of people in Washington just talk about. He's done something about teen pregnancy. He's done something to convince young people to abstain from sex. He's done something about women's health and crime prevention and giving young people hope for the future. One of his former patients even talked about how he talked her out of having an abortion.

Now, you would think that those who deplore teen pregnancy, advocate abstinence and oppose abortion would want to support a man who has actually done something to advance the aims they say they share, instead of just use them as political weapons. But no, in their brave new world, raw political power and political correctness—pure political correctness—are all that matter. They are determined to call the tune to which the Republican Party in Congress and in their presidential process march.

Well, they won a victory today, but America lost. And all those young people who come up here from Tennessee, what about them? What about those young people that came here believing in the congressional process and told the members of Congress that Dr. Foster had encouraged them to avoid sex, to stay away from teen pregnancy, not to do drugs, to stay in school? They had a role model and they saw their role model turned into a political football. In 1995, Henry Foster was denied even the right to [a] vote.

A minority in the Senate may have denied him this job, but I am confident that he will go on to serve our country. I think more of Henry Foster today than the first day I met him. This is not a good day for the United States Senate. But it is a good day for Henry Foster. He didn't get what he deserved, but he is still deserving. Those who denied him the right to a vote may have pleased their political bosses, but they have shown a lack of leadership that will surely be remembered.

Thank you very much.

PRESIDENT'S ECONOMIC REPORT, ECONOMIC ADVISERS' REPORT
February 13, 1995

In his second annual economic report, President Bill Clinton said February 13 that his economic strategy "to restore the American dream" had begun to pay off, with increased employment, stable inflation rates, a shrinking federal bureaucracy, and a decreasing federal deficit. He also acknowledged that many Americans were not sharing in the economic expansion. At a White House ceremony releasing both his report and the accompanying report by the Council of Economic Advisers (CEA), the president noted that "too many of our people are still working harder for less, with less security."

The performance of the economy in 1994 was "outstanding," the CEA stated, noting that the economy grew at a rate of 4 percent a year, while inflation remained stable at 2.7 percent. Some 3.5 million nonfarm payroll jobs were added to the economy in 1994, and the unemployment rate fell to 5.4 percent—a full percentage point lower than the 1993 rate. Real disposable income rose 4.3 percent.

Moreover, the federal budget deficit in fiscal 1994 was $50 billion less than it had been in fiscal 1993 and about $100 million lower than had been forecast before passage of the Omnibus Budget Reconciliation Act of 1993, which embodied much of Clinton's five-year economic plan. The ratio of federal discretionary spending to the gross domestic product fell to its lowest point in thirty years. (Clinton's five-year economic plan, Historic Documents of 1993, p. 181)

Those encouraging statistics were tempered by what the CEA was calling "disturbing" long-term trends. Throughout the past twenty years, productivity growth has slowed, real median family incomes have stagnated, and real compensation levels have declined for many American workers. At the same time income inequality has increased. Between 1973 and 1993, income declined for the lowest 80 percent of all families, while it increased substantially for the wealthiest 20 percent. In 1993, 39.3 million

Americans were living in poverty, a thirty-year high. Forty percent of those Americans were children.

In his report, Clinton offered no new initiatives to deal with these problems, but instead urged Congress to approve the middle-class tax relief package that he proposed in December 1994, to consolidate several dozen job-training programs into a single grant program, and to approve welfare and health reform. These efforts, he said, would boost the economy and give all Americans opportunity to achieve the American dream. At the White House ceremony, he also announced that he was sending legislation to Congress to raise the minimum wage ninety cents an hour, to $5.15. (Middle-Class Bill of Rights, Historic Documents of 1994, p. 610)

By year's end, however, action had not been completed on any of these proposals. The Republican-led Congress took no action on the minimum wage or comprehensive health reform, and tax cuts, welfare reform, and cuts in health spending were at the core of the budget impasse between Capitol Hill and the White House.

The CEA Report

The Council of Economic Advisers went further than the president in defending Clinton's economic program against attack from Republicans, who said he had not done enough to cut spending and reduce the budget deficit. In a February 13 speech to the Center for National Policy, a public policy think tank in Washington, D.C., CEA chairman Laura D'Andrea Tyson said that in fiscal 1994 federal revenues were "nearly sufficient" to cover all federal spending, not counting the interest on debt incurred in previous administrations (primarily those of Republican presidents Ronald Reagan and George Bush). She predicted that revenues would actually exceed expenditures, again not counting interest payments on federal debt, for the next three fiscal years. That, she said, would make "the Clinton administration the first . . . since the Johnson administration to run a non-interest surplus over the course of four fiscal years—and that is real progress on the deficit."

The CEA also challenged several of the economic planks in the Republican Contract with America. "Continued progress on reducing the Federal budget deficit is sound economics; a constitutional amendment requiring annual balance of the Federal budget is not," the CEA report said. Such a requirement would eliminate the automatic stabilizers that cushion economic downturns, the report said, removing "one of the great discoveries of modern economics" from the "macroeconomic policy arsenal."

The House Republican pledge to cut capital gains taxes "is problematic and ultimately ill-advised," the CEA said. Its direct effects on private saving and investment "are likely to be small" and the cut "is likely to encourage more-aggressive tax-sheltering activities."

On other matters, the CEA proposed eliminating several costly agricultural commodity support programs initially enacted to help farmers weather the Great Depression. Many of the original motivations for those

programs have disappeared, the advisers said. Most recipients are wealth-
ier than the average American and "the farm sector no longer looms large
in the macroeconomy."

The president's economic advisers also stressed that health reform must
be comprehensive, even if it is enacted step by step. "Limited reforms
designed to eliminate the most glaring shortcomings of private insurance
markets, although desirable, would not solve either the problem of provid-
ing health security for all Americans or the problem of escalating public
health care bills," they wrote.

Economic Projections

The economic advisers projected continued growth of the economy
through the year 2000, but at a slower pace, largely because of several
increases in interest rates engineered by the Federal Reserve Board in
1994. The advisers estimated that the real gross domestic product would
grow by 2.4 percent in 1996 and by 2.5 percent for each of the following
five years. Inflation was expected to hold steady at slightly more than 3
percent, while unemployment was expected to remain somewhere 5.5 per-
cent and 5.8 percent. Employment was expected to continue to grow, as an
additional 12 million jobs were expected to be created between 1994 and
2000.

Following is the text of the Economic Report of the President and
excerpts from chapter 1, "Implementing a National Economic
Strategy," of the Annual Report of the Council of Economic
Advisers, both issued by the White House February 13, 1995:

ECONOMIC REPORT OF THE PRESIDENT

To the Congress of the United States:

Two years ago I took office determined to improve the lives of average
American families. I proposed, and the Congress enacted, a new economic
strategy to restore the American dream. Two years later, that strategy has
begun to pay off.

Together we have created an environment in which America's private sector has been able to produce more than 5 million new jobs. Manufacturing
employment grew during each month of 1994—the first time that has happened since 1978. We have cut the deficit in the Federal budget for 3 years
running, we have kept inflation in check, and, based on actions I have already
taken, the Federal bureaucracy will soon be the smallest it has been in more
than 3 decades. We have opened up more new trade opportunities in just 2
years than in any similar period in a generation. And we have embarked on a
new partnership with American industry to prepare the American people to
compete and win in the new global economy.

In short, America's economic prospects have improved considerably in the last 2 years. And the economy will continue to move forward in 1995, with rising output, falling deficits, and increasing employment. Today there is no country in the world with an economy as strong as ours, as full of opportunity, as full of hope.

Still, living standards for many Americans have not improved as the economy has expanded. For the last 15 years, those Americans with the most education and the greatest flexibility to seek new opportunities have seen their incomes grow. But the rest of our workforce have seen their incomes either stagnate or fall. An America that, in our finest moments, has always grown together, now grows apart.

I am resolved to keep the American dream alive in this new economy. We must make it possible for the American people to invest in the education of their children and in their own training and skills. This is the essence of the New Covenant I have called for—economic opportunity provided in return for people assuming personal responsibility. This is the commitment my Administration made to the American people 2 years ago, and it remains our commitment to them today.

The Administration's Economic Strategy

Our economic strategy has been straightforward. First, we have pursued deficit reduction to increase the share of the Nation's economic resources available for private investment. At the same time we have reoriented the government's public investment portfolio with an eye toward preparing our people and our economy for the 21st century. We have cut yesterday's government to help solve tomorrow's problems, shrinking departments, cutting unnecessary regulations, and ending programs that have outlived their usefulness. We have also worked to expand trade and to boost American sales to foreign markets, so that the American people can enjoy the better jobs and higher wages that should result from their own high-quality, high-productivity labor. Having fixed the fundamentals, we are now proposing what I call the Middle Class Bill of Rights, an effort to build on the progress we have made in controlling the deficit while providing tax relief that is focused on the people who need it most.

Putting Our Own House in Order

The first task my Administration faced upon taking office in January 1993 was to put our own economic house in order. For more than a decade, the Federal Government had spent much more than it took in, borrowing the difference. As a consequence, by 1992 the Federal deficit had increased to 4.9 percent of gross domestic product—and our country had gone from being the world's largest creditor Nation to being its largest debtor.

As a result of my Administration's deficit reduction package, passed and signed into law in August 1993, the deficit in fiscal 1994 was $50 billion lower than it had been the previous year. In fact, it was about $100 billion lower than had been forecast before our budget plan was enacted. Between fiscal 1993 and fiscal 1998, our budget plan will reduce the deficit by $616 billion.

Our fiscal 1996 budget proposal includes an additional $81 billion in deficit reduction through fiscal 2000.

Preparing the American People to Compete and Win

As we were taking the necessary steps to restore fiscal discipline to the Federal Government, we were also working to reorient the government's investment portfolio to prepare our people and our economy for 21st-century competition.

Training and Education

In our new information-age economy, learning must become a way of life. Learning begins in childhood, and the opportunity to learn must be available to every American child—that is why we have worked hard to expand Head Start.

With the enactment of Goals 2000 we have established world-class standards for our Nation's schools. Through the School-to-Work Opportunities Act we have created new partnerships with schools and businesses to make sure that young people make a successful transition to the world of work. We have also dramatically reformed the college loan program. Americans who aspire to a college degree need no longer fear that taking out a student loan will one day leave them overburdened by debt.

Finally, we are proposing to take the billions of dollars that the government now spends on dozens of training programs and make that money directly available to working Americans. We want to leave it up to *them* to decide what new skills they need to learn—and when—to get a new or better job.

New Technology

Technological innovation is the engine driving the new global economy. This Administration is committed to fostering innovation in the private sector. We have reoriented the Federal Government's investment portfolio to support fundamental science and industry-led technology partnerships, the rapid deployment and commercialization of civilian technologies, and funding for technology infrastructure in transportation, communications, and manufacturing.

A Middle Class Bill of Rights

Fifty years ago the GI Bill of Rights helped transform an economy geared for war into one of the most successful peacetime economies in history. Today, after a peaceful resolution of the cold war, middle-class Americans have a right to move into the 21st century with the same opportunity to achieve the American dream.

People ought to be able to deduct the cost of education and training after high school from their taxable incomes. If a family makes less than $120,000 a year, the tuition that family pays for college, community college, graduate school, professional school, vocational education, or worker training should be fully deductible, up to $10,000 a year. If a family makes $75,000 a year or less, that family should receive a tax cut, up to $500, for every child under the age of 13. If a family makes less than $100,000 a year, that family should be able to put $2,000 a year, tax free, into an individual retirement account from which it can withdraw, tax free, money to pay for education, health care, a first home, or the care of an elderly parent.

Expanding Opportunity at Home
Through Free and Fair Trade

Our efforts to prepare the American people to compete and win in the new global economy cannot succeed unless we succeed in expanding trade and boosting exports of American products and services to the rest of the world. That is why we have worked so hard to create the global opportunities that will lead to more and better jobs at home. We won the fight for the North American Free Trade Agreement (NAFTA) and the Uruguay Round of the General Agreement on Tariffs and Trade (GATT).

Our commitment to free and fair trade goes beyond NAFTA and the GATT. Last December's Summit of the Americas set the stage for open markets throughout the Western Hemisphere. The Asia-Pacific Economic Cooperation (APEC) group is working to expand investment and sales opportunities in the Far East. We firmly believe that economic expansion and a rising standard of living will result in both regions, and the United States is well positioned both economically and geographically to participate in those benefits.

This Administration has also worked to promote American products and services to overseas customers. When foreign government contracts have been at stake, we have made sure that our exporters had an equal chance. Billions of dollars in new export sales have been the result, from Latin America to Asia. And these sales have created and safeguarded tens of thousands of American jobs.

Health Care and Welfare Reform:
The Unfinished Agenda

In this era of rapid change, Americans must be able to embrace new economic opportunities without sacrificing their personal economic security. My Administration remains committed to providing health insurance coverage for every American and containing health care costs for families, businesses, and governments. The Congress can and should take the first steps toward achieving these goals. I have asked the Congress to work with me to reform the health insurance market, to make coverage affordable for and available to children, to help workers who lose their jobs keep their health insurance, to level the playing field for the self-employed by giving them the same tax treatment as other businesses, and to help families provide long-term care for a sick parent or a disabled child. We simply must make health care coverage more secure and more affordable for America's working families and their children.

This should also be the year that we work together to end welfare as we know it. We have already helped to boost the earning power of 15 million low-income families who work by expanding the earned income tax credit. With a more robust economy, many more American families should also be able to escape dependence on welfare. Indeed, we want to make sure that people can move from welfare to work by giving them the tools they need to return to the economic mainstream. Reform must include steps to prevent the conditions that lead to welfare dependency, such as teen pregnancy and poor education, while also helping low-income parents find jobs with wages high enough to lift their families out of poverty. At the same time, we must ensure that welfare reform does not increase the Federal deficit, and that the States retain the flexibility they need to experiment with innovative programs that aim to increase self-sufficiency. But we must also ensure that our reform does not punish people for being poor and does not punish children for the mistakes of their parents.

Reinventing Government

Taking power away from Federal bureaucracies and giving it back to communities and individuals is something everyone should be able to support. We need to get government closer to the people it is meant to serve. But as we continue to reinvent the Federal Government by cutting regulations and departments, and moving programs to the States and communities where citizens in the private sector can do a better job, let us not overlook the benefits that have come from national action in the national interest: safer foods for our families, safer toys for our children, safer nursing homes for our elderly parents, safer cars and highways, and safer workplaces, cleaner air and cleaner water. We can provide more flexibility to the States while continuing to protect the national interest and to give relief where it is needed.

The New Covenant approach to governing unites us behind a common vision of what is best for our country. It seeks to shift resources and decisionmaking from bureaucrats to citizens, injecting choice and competition and individual responsibility into national policy. In the second round of reinventing government, we propose to cut $130 billion in spending by streamlining departments, extending our freeze on domestic spending, cutting 60 public housing programs down to 3, and getting rid of over 100 programs we do not need. Our job here is to expand opportunity, not bureaucracy—to empower people to make the most of their own lives. Government should be leaner, not meaner.

The Economic Outlook

As 1995 begins, our economy is in many ways as strong as it has ever been. Growth in 1994 was robust, powered by strong investment spending, and the unemployment rate fell by more than a full percentage point. Exports soared, consumer confidence rebounded, and Federal discretionary spending as a percentage of gross domestic product hit a 30-year low. Consumer spending should remain healthy and investment spending will remain strong through

1995. The Administration forecasts that the economy will continue to grow in 1995 and that we will remain on track to create 8 million jobs over 4 years.

We know, nevertheless, that there is a lot more to be done. More than half the adult work force in America is working harder today for lower wages than they were making 10 years ago. Millions of Americans worry about their health insurance and whether their retirement is still secure. While maintaining our momentum toward deficit reduction, increased exports, essential public investments, and a government that works better and costs less, we are committed to providing tax relief for the middle-class Americans who need it the most, for the investments they most need to make.

We live in an increasingly global economy in which people, products, ideas, and money travel across national borders at lightning speed. During the last 2 years, we have worked hard to help our workers take advantage of this new economy. We have worked to put our own economic house in order, to expand opportunities for education and training, and to expand the frontiers of free and fair trade. Our goal is to create an economy in which all Americans have a chance to develop their talents, have access to better jobs and higher incomes, and have the capacity to build the kind of life for themselves and their children that is the heart of the American dream.

THE ANNUAL REPORT OF THE COUNCIL OF ECONOMIC ADVISERS

Implementing a National Economic Strategy

By most standard macroeconomic indicators, the performance of the U.S. economy in 1994 was, in a word, outstanding. The economy has not enjoyed such a healthy expansion of strong growth and modest inflation in more than a generation.

Growth in 1994 was robust, fueled by strong investment spending. Nonfarm payroll employment grew by 3.5 million jobs, the largest annual increase in a decade, and the unemployment rate fell by more than a full percentage point, to 5.4 percent. Buoyed by improving job prospects and growing incomes, consumer sentiment hit a 5-year high, and retail sales expanded at their fastest pace in a decade. Yet despite growing demand both at home and abroad, inflation remained modest and stable. The core rate of consumer price inflation (which removes the effects of volatile food and energy prices) registered its smallest increase in 28 years. And the Federal deficit declined by more than $50 billion, as the ratio of Federal discretionary spending to gross domestic product (GDP) fell to its lowest level in 30 years.

The economy's performance in 1994 is even more remarkable when viewed against the backdrop of the economic challenges confronting the Nation around the time this Administration took office. Then the economy seemed mired in a slow and erratic recovery from the 1990–91 recession, business and consumer confidence was low, and the unemployment rate was over 7 percent. Between 1989 and 1992 the Federal deficit had jumped by $137.9 billion, to 4.9 percent of GDP, and even larger deficits were looming on the horizon. To make matters worse, the problems of anemic recovery and mounting deficits were superimposed on some disturbing long-term trends: a 20-year slowdown in productivity growth, a 20-year stagnation in real median family incomes, and a 20-year decline in real compensation levels for many American workers. For an increasing number of these workers and their families, the dream of rising incomes and prosperity appeared to be fading away under the pressures of rapid technological shifts and a changing global economy.

This Administration moved quickly and decisively to improve the economic situation, and the turnaround in macroeconomic performance has been dramatic. The deficit has declined sharply, the economy has grown at a more rapid and even pace, and more and more Americans are participating in the Nation's economic expansion. At the same time, the Administration has acted to help reverse the long-term trends that continue to depress the incomes of many Americans. That, however, will take time: problems that were 20 years in the making cannot be solved in the course of 2 years. But the Administration's economic policies have begun to move the Nation in the direction necessary to again place the American dream within the grasp of all Americans. . . .

The Administration's Economic Strategy: A Midterm Report

This Administration entered office at a time of sluggish economic recovery, mounting fiscal deficits, disappointing income growth, and growing income inequality and poverty. The first challenge was to get the Nation's fiscal house in order after more than a decade of fiscal profligacy. One of the most fundamental lessons of economic history is that sustained economic expansion depends on sound fiscal foundations. Therefore the linchpin of the Administration's economic strategy was and remains a deficit reduction plan that is balanced and gradual, yet large enough to be credible and to have a significant and sustained effect on the course of the deficit over time.

A second defining component of the strategy is a set of policies to help American workers and businesses realize the opportunities that flow from rapid changes in technology and an increasingly global economy. The common theme of these policies is investment, public and private: on the public side, a shift in government spending away from current consumption and toward investment in children, education and training, science and technology, and infrastructure; on the private side, tax incentives to encourage investment by businesses and individuals in physical, scientific, and human resources. A logical implication of these policies is that government must not only spend less—it must also spend better, by focusing more of its resources on the Nation's future.

A third component of the Administration's economic strategy is tax relief for working families who have seen their incomes stagnate or decline over the past 15 to 20 years. The dimensions of the family income problem are compelling. The real median family income in 1993, the last year for which complete data are available, was virtually unchanged from what it had been in 1973, despite the fact that during the intervening 20 years real output had increased by 57 percent.

The stagnation of real median family income has been accompanied by an equally disturbing trend of increasing income inequality. In contrast to the years from 1950 to 1973, when average real family incomes increased across the entire income distribution, between 1973 and 1993 the share of total family income declined for the lower 80 percent of the income distribution. Meanwhile, at the bottom of the income distribution, the number of Americans living in poverty hit a 30-year high in 1993 of 39.3 million, 40 percent of them children.

Although not all of the forces behind the rise in income inequality are understood, most economists agree that changes in technology that have reduced the demand for workers with relatively low levels of skill and education have played a major role. This insight lies behind the Administration's efforts to help Americans attain the skills and training they need for today's high-paying jobs through changes in both government spending priorities and tax policies.

The Administration's first response to the dwindling income prospects of many working Americans took the form of a substantial expansion of the earned income tax credit (EITC). The EITC expansion, included in the Omnibus Budget Reconciliation Act of 1993 (OBRA93), increased the after-tax incomes of over 15 million American workers and their families. The EITC is a refundable tax credit that provides a bonus to eligible low-income workers—a bonus that can amount to over $3,000 a year for a family with two children. Through the EITC these workers may realize after-tax incomes well in excess of their wages.

At the end of 1994 the President proposed a package of additional tax cuts that will extend tax relief to middle-class American families, to help them meet the costs of raising their children, acquire more education and training, and save for a variety of purposes. These proposed tax cuts reflect the much-improved outlook for the fiscal deficit, which allows the President to deliver on his campaign promise of tax relief for the middle class.

The Federal Government, too, must respond to the demands of economic change. That is why a fourth component of the Administration's economic strategy is to reinvent the Federal Government itself, so that it works better, costs less, and sheds functions that are no longer needed in today's economy or are better performed by either State and local governments or the private sector. The savings that can be realized by eliminating some existing programs and rationalizing and improving others are essential to achieving the goals of deficit reduction, tax relief to working families, and a shift in the balance of Federal spending toward more investment.

Finally, the Administration has linked its ambitious domestic economic strategy to an equally ambitious foreign economic strategy based on promoting global trade liberalization. During the last decade trade has become an increasingly important source of high-wage jobs for American workers. Recognizing this reality, the Administration has wedded policies to make Americans more productive with policies to improve their access to expanding international markets on more equitable terms.

Toward Full Employment with Fiscal Responsibility

In early 1993, the Administration faced the challenge of ensuring that the economic recovery from the 1990-91 recession would gain strength and return the economy to full utilization of its resources. At the same time it was vital that this be accomplished in a sound and balanced way, to avoid an acceleration of inflationary pressures. As the preceding discussion indicates . . . , this challenge was met in 1994.

In part as a result of the Administration's 1993 budget package, the Nation's fiscal environment today is sounder than it was during the preceding 14 years. Federal Government purchases of goods and services declined in real terms, and the Federal deficit in fiscal 1994 was more than $50 billion lower than in fiscal 1993 and about $100 billion lower than what had been forecast before the enactment of OBRA93. Excluding interest payments on the debt incurred by previous Administrations, the Federal budget in fiscal 1994 was essentially balanced, and the Federal debt outstanding, which had nearly quadrupled between 1981 and 1992, had begun to stabilize relative to the size of the economy. Moreover, . . . the Administration's deficit reduction measures—along with welcome slowdowns in projected Medicare and Medicaid spending—have significantly improved the long-run deficit and debt outlook. . . .

The actual deficit in 1993 was only 4.1 percent of GDP, thanks to the stronger than expected economic recovery and lower than expected interest rates. In 1994 the deficit fell to $203.2 billion, or 3.1 percent of GDP, and in 1998 it is slated to fall to 2.4 percent of GDP, the lowest level since 1979. Over the entire 1994–2000 period the deficit is forecast to average about 2.5 percent of GDP, well below the levels that would have been reached in the absence of OBRA93 and nearly 2 percentage points less than the 1982–93 average of 4.4 percent. . . . [T]he debt-GDP ratio is also expected to be stable through the end of the decade.

The effects of the Administration's budget plan on economic performance were in line with its predictions—and completely at odds with the gloomy prognostications of its critics. A dramatic decline in long-term interest rates in 1993, occasioned in part by market expectations of a significant long-term reduction in government borrowing needs, fostered strong growth in interest-sensitive investment and consumption spending. As business expectations improved, new job creation picked up pace, and the growth in incomes in turn reinforced consumer spending, creating the kind of virtuous cycle of employment, income, and spending growth that is the hallmark of periods of robust expansion. The acceleration of growth around the world, coupled with the Administration's strong leadership in expanding world trade, added to the momentum by encouraging American companies to invest in greater capacity to serve growing global markets.

As the economy expanded, the Federal Reserve raised interest rates several times, tightening the stance of monetary policy in an effort to prevent inflation from accelerating. The increase in short-term interest rates resulting from Federal Reserve actions was substantial. Long-term rates also increased significantly during the year, and the flattening of the yield curve (which plots rates of interest for debt of all maturities prevailing at a given time) that most economic forecasters had predicted failed to materialize. Although the causes of the rise in long-term rates continue to be debated, . . . it was largely the result of a strong economy and reflected an increase in the demand for capital, as businesses and households increased their borrowing to invest in durable goods and structures both at home and around the world. Despite this increase, however, long-term interest rates remained lower than they would have been if the government's voracious borrowing needs had not been curbed by the enactment of the Administration's deficit reduction program.

Enhancing the Economy's Long-Run Growth Potential

. . . [T]he rate of growth of productivity is the most important determinant of how fast the economy can grow and how much living standards can rise over time. What happens when productivity growth slows? . . . [G]rowth in both real compensation per hour and real median family income slowed markedly in the early 1970s. This is precisely the period when productivity growth also slowed, from an annual average rate of 3.1 percent between 1947 and 1973 to an average of just 1.1 percent in the two decades since. This slowdown shows up not only in the economic statistics, but also in the lives of many Americans who know that they are working harder for less. . . .

Although economists do not completely understand all the determinants of productivity growth, it is known that increases in physical, human, and technological capital play a key role. This insight has shaped the Administration's economic strategy from the beginning. The link between real productivity growth and the rate of investment in the Nation's capital stock is straightforward: investment in physical capital and new technology equips workers with more and better capital; workers so equipped are more productive. Investment in skills and training also adds to productivity by allowing workers to utilize physical capital more effectively. And more-productive workers tend to earn higher real wages. Few propositions in economics are as well documented as these or command as much support among professional economists, whatever their political persuasion.

Deficit Reduction and Investment

A primary economic reason for reducing the Federal deficit is to increase national saving, in the expectation that increased saving will in turn increase national investment in physical capital. . . . [I]nvestment rates and productivity growth rates correlate highly across countries. National saving rates and national investment rates also correlate highly across countries, despite the increasing globalization of world financial markets. The implication is that increased national saving should be associated with increased productivity.

According to this reasoning, deficit reduction is not an end in itself but a means to the end of greater national investment and higher living standards. This logic has three important corollaries.

First, bringing the Federal deficit down is only one step toward a more productive and prosperous future. That is why, in addition to measures to reduce the deficit, the Administration's 1993 budget package contained several new proposals to encourage private investment, including an increase in the amount of equipment that small businesses may deduct immediately in computing their income tax liability, a targeted reduction in capital gains tax rates on long-term equity investments in certain small businesses, and needed public investments. The President's 1996 budget plan builds on these priorities, holding the line on the deficit, cutting outdated government programs while investing in new and existing ones, and offering a package of new middle-class tax incentives.

Second, squeezing worthwhile public investments out of the budget is the wrong way to reduce the deficit. America needs more of both public and private investment, not a swap of one for the other. That is why the Administration seeks not only to constrain total government spending but also to reorient it more toward the future. Between fiscal 1993 and fiscal 1996, overall discretionary government spending is expected to remain nearly unchanged in nominal terms (and fall by more than 6 percent in real terms). At the same time, discretionary spending on the Administration's public investment programs in such vital areas as education and training, technology support, public health, and infrastructure increases by over $24 billion. Over this short time period, investment programs will increase from 11.5 percent to 15.5 percent of total discretionary spending.

Third, because deficit reduction—whether accomplished through increases in revenues or decreases in spending—has a direct contractionary effect on aggregate spending, there are limits to the amount of deficit reduction the economy can be expected to withstand within a short period without endangering economic growth. Over the long run, deficit reduction makes room for additional private investment, but in the short run it depresses aggregate demand and as a result can actually depress private investment. If long-term interest rates do not decline sufficiently fast and far to replace the aggregate demand lost through deficit reduction, economic growth will slow, and this will discourage private investment. The policy challenge is to bring the deficit down gradually and credibly, so as to increase national saving and investment, but not so rapidly as to threaten continued economic expansion. This challenge was met in 1994, and the Administration's economic forecast indicates that it will continue to be met through the remainder of this decade. The success to date in meeting this challenge is one reason why the Administration opposes a balanced budget amendment to the Constitution. . . .

Investing in Skills and Education

Education and training—investments in human capital—are a wellspring of human progress, a basic foundation of the country's long-run growth potential and its long-run viability as a democracy, and the ladder of opportunity for all of its citizens. . . . As already noted . . . , today's high-paying job opportunities demand increasing levels of education and training. In part as a result of rapid changes in technology and the global economy, the real average annual earnings of male high school graduates declined by 15 percent between 1979 and 1992. In 1992 the annual average earnings of a male college graduate were 64 percent higher than the average annual earnings of a male high school graduate; in 1979 the difference had been only 43 percent. . . .

The Administration is embarked on an ambitious agenda to improve the education and training prospects for all Americans, and with support in the Congress it has achieved considerable success on this agenda during the last 2 years. The Administration is committed to ensuring that at every stage of life—preschool, elementary school, secondary school, college, and in the work force—all Americans have the opportunity to acquire the skills they need to participate fully in today's economy. . . .

Expanded support for Head Start—funding for which increased by 45 percent between the fiscal 1993 and fiscal 1995 budgets—has ensured that fewer disadvantaged children will have their opportunities shut off even before they reach kindergarten. Goals 2000 has put in place a national framework for school assessments to help citizens throughout the country evaluate how well their local schools are achieving basic educational goals. The School-to-Work transition program has provided support to States to develop partnerships between schools and businesses, to facilitate the process of moving high school graduates into promising job opportunities or further training and education.

Two innovative education programs developed by the Administration during its first 2 years are AmeriCorps (the national service program) and the income contingent student loan program. The former provides Americans with the opportunity to participate in community service projects while earning funds that can be used to pay for college or other postsecondary education. The income contingent student loan program both reduces the cost of student loans, by making them directly available from the Federal Government at more attractive rates than those offered by private sector lenders, and makes loan repayment after college less burdensome by allowing repayments to vary with the borrower's postcollege income. This program addresses one of the major capital market imperfections that discourages many Americans from attending college at a time when the returns to higher education have increased dramatically.

Investing in Science and Technology

. . . [A]dvances in scientific and technological knowledge are another important determinant of long-run productivity growth. Moreover, as the history of this and other nations demonstrates, public investment has long played a vital role in promoting scientific discovery and technological change. At the heart of the dramatic improvements in agricultural productivity in the United States over the last century have been the research efforts conducted at federally supported land-grant colleges and the rapid dissemination of their results to millions of American farmers through the agricultural extension services supported by the Department of Agriculture. Similarly, Federal investments to promote research in public health, primarily through the National Institutes of Health, have produced many commercially successful new drugs, new treatment regimes, and innovative medical equipment, which are the foundations of America's premier position in the global biotechnology and medical equipment industries.

Federally supported research during World War II and the cold war promoted or accelerated the development of many new technologies for defense purposes—such as jet engines, computers, and advanced materials—that eventually found widespread success in commercial markets. One of the most successful computer-based innovations created by the Defense Department and adopted by the private sector is the Internet, which began life as ARPANET, a geographically distributed computer communications system designed to link researchers located at universities around the country. Today tens of millions of people around the world are communicating via the Internet for business, educational, and recreational purposes.

Most Federal investments in science and technology support the realization of a particular national mission—for example, increasing national security or enhancing public health. But economists have long recognized that there is a powerful rationale for Federal support to increase the general level of scientific investigation and technological innovation. Markets shape the behavior of private participants through incentives, but individuals and companies may invest too little in research and development, because market incentives do not reflect the full value to society of such investment. Significant economic gains from scientific discovery and technological innovation may remain unexploited because markets alone cannot guarantee that the innovator will capture all or even most of the economic returns to innovation. This is particularly true of basic research, which increases the store of fundamental knowledge that underlies most technological innovation. But it is also true of many generic technologies, the benefits of which flow quickly and in some cases automatically beyond the laboratory or the factory floor where they were invented. . . .

Reinventing Government

Through the Vice President's National Performance Review (NPR), the Administration has, from its inception, taken on the difficult but critical task of reinventing government.

When an organization in the private sector becomes unresponsive to customers, encumbered by inflexible internal rules, saddled with ineffective management, or unwilling to buy inputs or produce goods and services at lowest cost, it will lose customers to rivals offering lower prices, superior products, or better service. If the firm's customers do not force an improvement in organizational behavior, its shareholders may replace senior management directly or do so indirectly by selling the company, or the company may simply go out of business.

Public sector organizations, on the other hand, often lack a clear and indisputable bottom line for their performance and are not subject to the same remorseless pressures that force private firms to function efficiently. The Office of Management and Budget, along with relevant congressional committees, attempts to monitor organizational performance within the Federal Government. But systematic and thoroughgoing organizational improvement of how the government functions requires strong leadership and the commitment of the most senior executive branch officials—as has been provided in this Administration through the NPR.

The NPR analyzed the characteristics of successful organizations in both the public and the private sector. Four principles emerged from this analysis as key to success: cutting red tape, putting customers first, empowering employees to get results, and getting back to basics, which in the context of the Federal Government means producing a government that "works better and costs less." To implement these principles throughout the Federal Government, the NPR has sought ways to decentralize decisionmaking power within agencies, to give Federal workers the tools they need to do their jobs and hold them accountable for results, to replace regulation with incentives and market solutions, to expose Federal operations to competition, to eliminate unnecessary or duplicative government functions and rules, and to establish concrete measures of success, one of which is customer satisfaction with government services.

Through the end of 1994 the Administration's reinventing government reforms had reduced the Federal work force by about 100,000 employees, out of a total reduction of 272,000 planned by 1999, and essentially shredded the 10,000-page Federal personnel manual. . . .

At the end of 1994 the Administration announced a second round of NPR reforms, beginning with the restructuring of three cabinet departments and two major government agencies. The reform plan proposes to consolidate 60 existing programs in the Department of Housing and Urban Development (HUD) into three performance-based funds. This will enable HUD to focus its mission more sharply on promoting economic development for communities and facilitating transitions to economic independence for needy families. The Department of Transportation will collapse its 10 operating agencies into 3 and consolidate over 30 separate grant programs to States and cities into one flexible transportation infrastructure program, emphasizing capital investment assistance. And the Department of Energy will privatize some of its oil and gas reserves, sell its excess uranium, reduce costs in its research programs and laboratories, and substantially reorganize its nuclear waste cleanup program.

Taken together, the NPR reforms announced at the end of 1994 will cut $26 billion from government spending over 5 years. Yet another phase of the NPR will propose additional agency restructuring in the coming months. The savings from these and other reforms will be used to finance the President's proposed middle-class tax cuts and to continue progress on reducing the Federal deficit.

Opening Foreign Markets

The expansion of international trade is integral to raising American incomes, and exports play an increasingly important role in providing a livelihood for American workers. Between 1986 and 1993 increased exports were responsible for 37 percent of U.S. output growth. The jobs of more than 10 million American workers now depend on exports, and export-related jobs pay wages significantly above the average. In addition, the reduction of barriers to trade raises standards of living by providing a wider variety of goods at lower prices. And foreign competition leads to greater efficiency and higher quality in U.S. production, spurring the productivity growth that is essential for real income growth.

This Administration came to office committed to opening foreign markets to U.S. exports and bringing down barriers to trade, and it has achieved remarkable success. . . . [T]he Uruguay Round agreement of the General Agreement on Tariffs and Trade (GATT) will bring down foreign tariffs facing U.S. exporters by about a third on average, open foreign markets in agricultural products and services for the first time, and do much to establish a single rulebook for all trading countries. The North American Free Trade Agreement (NAFTA) with Mexico and Canada is a pathbreaking accord with two of our three largest trading partners, achieving a degree of liberalization well beyond that of similar international agreements. In its bilateral negotiations, the Administration has been forceful in seeking market-opening measures in Japan, China, and other countries and in advancing the interests of U.S. exports through its National Export Strategy. Finally, during the second half of 1994 the Administration helped launch negotiations that will lead to the creation of open and free trade areas among the countries of the Western Hemisphere by 2005 and among the countries of the Asia-Pacific Economic Cooperation forum by 2020. . . .

The Administration's Economic Strategy:
The Unfinished Agenda

For all of its remarkable accomplishments, the American economy continued to suffer from some persistent long-term difficulties in 1994. Although improvement was seen in the quality of new jobs created, the real earnings of American workers continued to stagnate. Long-term unemployment rates remained stubbornly high, especially when viewed against the backdrop of more than 3 years of economic recovery. The unemployment rates of black Americans remained more than double that for whites. More children lived in poverty in 1993 than in any year since 1965, despite the doubling of real GDP over the same period.

In light of such disturbing trends, it is not surprising that so many Americans feel increasingly cut off from the prosperity of an expanding economy. The experience of 1994 confirms that even though a strong and sustainable economic expansion is a necessary condition for improving the living standards of all Americans, it is not sufficient. Still other policies are required to help Americans obtain the skills and the education demanded by today's technologies and international markets, and to cope with the often significant dislocations that are a natural feature of today's economy.

Over the next 2 years the Administration plans several major policy initiatives, including tax relief for middle-class families, welfare reform, health care reform, and continued restructuring or reinvention of the Federal Government. In addition, the President recently announced a proposal to increase the minimum wage from its current level of $4.25 per hour. This proposal reflects a determination to ensure that working families can lift themselves out of poverty, as well as a recognition that inflation has reduced substantially the real value of the minimum wage. . . . Every one of these policy initiatives is designed to keep the economic expansion and deficit reduction on track while enabling all Americans to enjoy the benefits of a healthy American economy.

Middle-Class Tax Relief

. . . At the end of 1994 the President announced a new Middle Class Bill of Rights, which like the GI Bill of Rights from which it draws its inspiration, is designed to help average Americans cope with the demands of today's economy.

The Middle Class Bill of Rights includes a three-part tax package: a $500 per-child tax credit, a tax deduction for up to $10,000 for annual expenses on postsecondary training and education, and an expansion of individual retirement accounts (IRAs) to all middle-class families. An estimated 87 percent of the benefits of the proposed tax cuts would go to families with annual incomes under $100,000. In addition, the Middle Class Bill of Rights contains a plan to consolidate over 50 government training programs into a single training voucher system that would allow eligible workers to finance the training they need to obtain employment. What ties the package together is the belief that appropriately structured tax relief and support for training can help middle-class Americans invest in their own future earning power and that of their children.

The Administration proposes a $500 nonrefundable tax credit for children under 13 in middle-class families. The credit would be phased out between $60,000 and $75,000 of annual adjusted gross income (AGI). . . .

The proposed credit reflects the fact that the existing tax allowance for children—the dependent exemption—has not kept pace with inflation and income growth. In 1948 the real value of each child's personal exemption—$3,700 as measured in 1994 dollars—was nearly half again as large as today's $2,500 exemption. Meanwhile many of the costs of raising children—especially medical care and education—have increased far more rapidly than the overall price level. And child-rearing costs are often more burdensome for younger families, who are generally at a stage in their lives when incomes are relatively low. For all these reasons, taxpayers with children may have a substantially reduced ability to pay income taxes.

In addition to the child-based tax credit, the Administration has proposed a tax deduction for postsecondary education and training expenses. . . . Each year of postsecondary education or training has been shown to boost future earnings between 6 and 10 percent on average. Meanwhile the costs of a college education have increased much faster than the overall consumer price index. Middle-class families have become less able to afford higher education just at the time when it is becoming an increasingly critical determinant of future earnings.

Businesses have long been allowed to deduct the costs of providing education and training for their employees. Yet despite the high returns and the high costs of postsecondary training and education, the current tax code provides only limited preferences to individual taxpayers making such investments. The Administration's proposal will help ensure that the income tax deductibility of training and education expenses does not depend on one's employer paying for it. But more important, it will provide a financial incentive for Americans to get the education and training necessary to thrive in a changing economy. The Administration's proposed deduction recognizes that investment in human capital, like investment in physical capital, is a major determinant of growth in productivity and living standards.

The third component of the Administration's proposed tax package is an expansion of individual retirement accounts, aimed at encouraging households to save more and increase the Nation's worrisomely low private saving rate. . . . The proposal doubles the existing thresholds, making IRAs completely deductible for married couples filing joint returns with incomes below $80,000, regardless of pension coverage, and allowing partial deductions for those with incomes up to $100,000. In addition, the income thresholds and the $2,000 contribution limit (both set in 1986) would be indexed for inflation. Finally, withdrawals from IRAs would be allowed without penalty to buy a first home, to pay for postsecondary education, to defray large medical expenses, or to cover long-term unemployment expenses. . . .

Welfare Reform

The President entered office with a promise to reform the welfare system so that it would function as an effective safety net promoting work and family, rather than as a snare enmeshing poor families in long-term dependence. Under the current system some people have become long-term welfare recipients—although more than one-third of all women who ever receive AFDC do so for less than 2 years, almost one-fourth end up receiving AFDC for over 10 years during their lifetime. And, as currently structured, the welfare system in effect imposes a high marginal tax rate on paid employment, because low-income mothers lose their AFDC and food stamp benefits and eventually their Medicaid health insurance for themselves and their children when they take a job. In short, for many the current system contains powerful disincentives against work and in favor of continued welfare. . . .

The Administration's proposed welfare reform legislation, the Work and Responsibility Act, will help make work pay, by ensuring that welfare recipients obtain the skills they need to find employment, and by eliminating long-term welfare dependency as an option for those able to work. Under the Administration's plan, welfare recipients who are job-ready will begin a job search immediately, and anyone offered a job will be required to take it. Support for child care will be provided to help people move from dependence to independence. For those not ready for work, the Administration's proposed reforms will provide support, job training, and assistance in finding a job when they are ready. Each adult recipient of AFDC will be required to create an employability plan, to ensure that he or she will move into the work force as quickly as possible. Time limits on receipt of welfare benefits will require that anyone who can work, must work—in the private sector if possible, in a temporary, subsidized job if necessary.

The proposed program will strongly discourage children from bearing children. Parents under the age of 18, if they apply for welfare payments, generally will not be allowed to set up independent households; instead they will receive assistance to stay in school. The Administration's proposal also includes funding for grants to schools and communities to prevent teen pregnancy, and it toughens efforts to collect child support from all absent fathers—a provision that is expected to double Federal collections of child support payments, from $9 billion to an estimated $20 billion by 2000. These proposals to discourage teen pregnancy and to foster parental responsibility will help prevent the need for welfare in the first place. . . .

Health Care Reform

The President entered office with a pledge to reform the Nation's health care system, and he will continue to work with the Congress to realize this objective during the coming year. Reform is essential to address four separate but interrelated problems of the current system, which if left unsolved will result in an increasingly heavy financial burden on governments and individuals. . . .

First, millions of Americans, both insured and uninsured, do not have health security. Those who are insured face the risk of losing their coverage, at least temporarily, if they lose or change their jobs. Meanwhile the number of uninsured Americans continues to grow at an alarming rate.

Second, the current health insurance system has a number of shortcomings. One is that insurers know that a small proportion of the population incurs the bulk of medical expenditures, making it profitable to screen prospective purchasers to determine their risk characteristics; those who are sick—who have so-called pre-existing conditions—may be unable to purchase insurance altogether, or may only be able to purchase it at exorbitant prices. Another shortcoming is that people unable to obtain health insurance through their employers may be offered coverage only at prices unaffordable for many Americans. Still another is that many insurance policies do not cover a variety of large financial risks (e.g., high-cost illnesses), although these are exactly the kinds of risks for which insurance is most needed.

Third, the current health care system imposes a large and unsustainable burden on public sector budgets. Governments account for nearly half of all health care spending in the United States, primarily in the form of payments for Medicaid and Medicare. Since 1980 the share of health care spending in the Federal budget has doubled; the budgets of State and local governments also saw larger shares going toward health expenditures.

Fourth, the current health care system suffers from numerous structural features that may keep costs high. For instance, fee-for-service providers may have an incentive to overprovide care, and provide some care that is inappropriate or of equivocal value, because they are generally reimbursed for each additional test or procedure they perform. For their part, consumers often do not have the information they need to evaluate the differences among providers or to determine whether or not the care prescribed for them is necessary. Moreover, in a system dominated by third-party payers (insurers), consumers seldom have a strong reason to be directly concerned about the cost-effectiveness of their care. Third-party payers have responded by establishing programs to review diagnoses and suggested treatments. Competition among insurers may help offset some of the effects of informational asymmetries.

Over the past few years, under the pressure of rapidly escalating costs, the private health care system has begun a process of dramatic structural change. In 1988, for example, only about 29 percent of health insurance enrollees were in some form of managed care plan, in most cases either a health maintenance organization (HMO) or a preferred provider organization (PPO). By 1993 this figure had increased to 51 percent. Much of this migration toward managed care has occurred in larger firms, where nearly 60 percent of covered employees are now in managed care plans. Many analysts credit managed care with keeping health care costs down. In the Far West, where HMO penetration is higher than elsewhere in the country, real spending on health care grew more slowly over the 1980–91 period than in any other region in the country (3.4 percent per year versus a national average of more than 4.5 percent). In part as a result of these changes, there is some promising evidence that growth in health care costs in the private sector may be slowing somewhat. For instance, medical price inflation slowed to a 5.4 percent annual rate in 1993 and slowed still further to 4.9 percent in 1994. Even the 1994 rate, however, was still well above the overall rate of inflation. . . .

The Administration believes that any successful reform must ultimately be comprehensive in scope, even if it proceeds step by step. This belief rests on the reality that none of the four major problems of the current health care system identified above can be solved in isolation. For example, any attempt to impose arbitrary caps on Federal health care spending without more-fundamental reforms would simply shift more government program costs onto either State and local governments or the private sector. According to one recent estimate, uncompensated care and government programs that reimbursed hospitals below market prices shifted about $26 billion in costs onto the private sector in 1991. Similarly, any attempt to provide universal coverage without complementary measures to improve competition and sharpen the incentives for more cost-conscious decisions by both providers and consumers would mean even more dramatic increases in systemwide costs. Limited reforms designed to eliminate the most glaring shortcomings of private insurance markets, although desirable, would not solve either the problem of providing health security for all Americans or the problem of escalating public health care bills. Finally, efforts by the private sector to control costs might well increase the number of Americans without health insurance, especially children and those most in need of medical attention.

Ultimately, meaningful reform of the Nation's health care system will do more than just unburden public sector budgets and provide health security. It will also improve living standards. For years, the rising cost of health care has forced a shift in the composition of the typical compensation package away from take-home wages and salaries and toward fringe benefits, especially health insurance. Between 1966 and 1994 the share of health benefits in total labor compensation increased from 2.0 percent to 7.2 percent, while the share of cash compensation correspondingly fell. In absolute terms average real take-home pay barely increased: most of the gains in total compensation were realized as fringe benefits. In short, working men and women, for the most part, paid for escalating health costs by taking home lower pay than they would have otherwise. On the assumption that the future will look much like the past, the Administration expects that any benefits of a reduction in health care costs resulting from meaningful reforms will show up in higher take-home pay for working Americans.

Conclusion

Nineteen ninety-four was a very good year for the American economy. Indeed, robust growth, a dramatic decline in the unemployment rate, low inflation, and a much improved outlook for the Federal budget combined to yield the best overall economic performance in at least a generation. In addition, last year's economic performance ranks as the best among the advanced industrial countries with which the United States is usually compared.

But the economic successes of the past year must not obscure the long-term economic challenges facing the Nation. Some of these, like the dramatic growth in entitlement spending projected for the first few decades of the next century, or the disturbing increase in the number of Americans without health insurance, result in large part from the interaction of national economic policy choices with the changing demographics of the American population. Others, such as the persistent decline in real compensation for many groups and overall increasing income inequality, may in large part result from worldwide changes in technology and other areas. These changes are creating a new world economy and a new American economy, which hold both the promise of a more prosperous future and the threat of more dislocation and adjustment for many American workers and their families.

As the Nation enters the last half-decade of this century, this Administration has already put in place some important foundations for greater prosperity. Over the coming year we look forward to working with the Congress, with the States, and, most important, with the American people, to address the Nation's long-term economic challenges and to make the most of the Nation's long-term economic opportunities.

RUSSIAN PRESIDENT YELTSIN
ON STATE OF THE NATION
February 16, 1995

Russian president Boris Yeltsin, in his annual state of the nation address to parliament on February 16, pledged to continue economic and political reforms despite virulent opposition from both the right and left and the continuing turmoil in the country's economy. Yeltsin also appeared to be trying to assuage concerns that he would postpone forthcoming elections rather than face the discontent of voters. Parliamentary elections were held, as scheduled, on December 17, producing a strong showing for the former Communist party. At year's end maneuvering was under way for the upcoming presidential elections, which were set for June 1996.

Yeltsin's annual speech was widely viewed as an effort to reassure supporters, both at home and overseas, that he would not backslide on reforms and would not resort to authoritarian methods to contend with the nation's severe problems. By speaking for about an hour, Yeltsin also appeared to be hoping to put to rest concerns about his physical health. (Yeltsin later suffered a heart attack in July and was again hospitalized in October with another heart ailment.)

Reaction was predictable, with supporters saying Yeltsin had once again seized the initiative and demonstrated his political prowess and detractors insisting that the Russian leader was ignoring the extent of the nation's troubles. Communist party leader Gennady Zyuganov sounded the latter theme, saying of Yeltsin's speech that "there is not even an honest recognition of the tragic state of affairs in the country."

Yeltsin's Defense of His Government

Yeltsin acknowledged a few important lapses and failures, but in general he sought to put his critics on the defensive. He said the transition from the communist dictatorship to democracy and economic pluralism had put the country in a "complicated situation." He noted that the collapse of the communist system had allowed many bureaucrats in state enterprises to indulge their "selfish interests"—a reference to the tendency by some officials to give themselves large stockholdings in the companies they used to run for the government.

Yeltsin also admitted that the "social price" of economic reform was high, especially in the creation of a new class of people in Russia: the "new poor, the people who are employed but receive humiliating low wages. And often irregularly."

On general economic issues, the president admitted that some reforms had not been carried out as promised in 1994, especially the stabilization of the ruble. He insisted that the government had workable programs to reduce inflation (then running at nearly 25 percent a month) and to control the ballooning budget deficit. In a balancing act typical of his presidency, Yeltsin promised communist functionaries that he would not cut back state spending on defense and agriculture, two of the largest sectors of the economy.

Yeltsin insisted that he had a "principled position" of commitment to democracy and would not yield to demands by some for a postponement of the scheduled elections. Holding elections as promised was "our common duty before the voters," he told the parliament. The president also said he had refused calls to "straitjacket" the media.

Referring to the sharp upsurge in crime in recent years, Yeltsin said "criminal communities," or what many Russians call the "mafia," had begun to "act with impunity and with growing impudence. Law enforcement bodies have actually occupied the position of non-interference." As a result, he said, the country had no higher priority than to "establish the authority of law."

On foreign affairs, Yeltsin repeated earlier warnings against the prospect of an incorporation of Eastern Europe into the North Atlantic Treaty Organization (NATO). Several Eastern European nations have asked to join NATO. Such a step would be "detrimental to the joint efforts in creating a new model of genuine pan-European security. We do not conceal what does not suit us in this scenario and why Russia is against it," he said. While unequivocal, those words were considerably less sharp than Yeltsin's earlier comments that an expansion of NATO would create a "cold peace" in place of the cold war.

Yeltsin held two summit meetings during the year with President Clinton. They met in May at the Kremlin to celebrate the fiftieth anniversary of the end of World War II and again in November at Franklin Roosevelt's home in Hyde Park, New York. At the latter meeting, Yeltsin agreed that NATO peacekeeping forces could manage a peace agreement in Bosnia. Russian troops ultimately participated in the NATO mission in Bosnia, beginning in December, but Yeltsin refused to have them under direct NATO command. (NATO mission to Bosnia, p. 717)

The War in Chechnya

Yeltsin offered parliament a detailed defense of the single most controversial issue of his presidency: the bloody war against rebels in the

province of Chechnya, in southern Russia. The province had declared inde-
pendence from Russia in 1994, and in December of that year Yeltsin
ordered a massive assault on the Chechen capital, Grozny. The army drove
the rebels out of Grozny and occupied most of the region, but at a cost of
20,000 to 30,000 lives and the near total destruction of the capital. An esti-
mated 200,000 people were left homeless by the war.

Yeltsin's decision to launch the war raised serious concerns, both with-
in Russia and in foreign capitals, about his judgment and the extent of his
control over the military. Yeltsin and his military commanders, especially
defense minister Pavel Grachev, came under intense criticism for their
planning and management of the war.

In his speech, Yeltsin acknowledged the criticism, saying the "hackneyed
system of planning military operations" was the reason for "big losses" on
the battlefield, and that reforms would be needed. However, Yeltsin refused
demands that he sack Grachev.

Yeltsin defended his decision to attack Chechnya, saying that the rebel
regime there had established a "real dictatorship" in conjunction with the
"criminal world." Many Russians for years have believed that Chechens are
behind much of the criminal "mafia" gangs that preyed on the citizenry.

The rebellion in Chechnya, Yeltsin told parliament, was "a test ground
for preparation and spread of criminal power to other Russian regions. If
we do not want the Chechen developments to repeat, we must not allow the
establishment in any part of Russia of regional dictatorships, the usurp-
ing of power and so on."

Political Maneuvering

If Yeltsin expected his speech to end political bickering in Russia, he
had to be sorely disappointed by the events of the succeeding months. On
June 21, anti-Yeltsin factions in parliament took a preliminary vote of no
confidence in the government—a step that could have forced Yeltsin to
replace his entire cabinet or call early elections. Yeltsin fired three contro-
versial cabinet ministers but refused other demands by his critics. A fol-
low-up vote on July 1 fell short of the two-thirds majority needed to put the
no-confidence motion into force.

The critics got their revenge at the polls nearly six months later. In par-
liamentary elections on December 17, various anti-Yeltsin forces won a
combined 60 percent of the vote. The Communist party, on the rebound
after the collapse of the Soviet Union at the end of 1991, finished first with
22.3 percent of the vote. An ultranationalist party, headed by Vladimir
Zhironovsky, which had finished first in elections for the lower house of
parliament in 1993, captured 11.2 percent.

Various pro-reform parties won a combined tally of nearly 40 percent of
the vote, but they were so disorganized and distrustful of one another that
few analysts gave them much chance of uniting. Prime Minister Victor
Chernomyrdin, a former Communist party functionary who took over the
day-to-day management of Yeltsin's reform program, headed his own

reform party, but his poor showing at the polls raised doubts about his effectiveness as a possible presidential candidate in 1996 should Yeltsin chose not to run again.

Following are excerpts from the annual state of the nation speech delivered February 16, 1995, to the Russian parliament by President Boris Yeltsin. The text was provided by the Russian embassy in Washington, D.C.:

Esteemed deputies,

A year ago the annual message of the president to the Federal Assembly began our joint work. It was necessary at the time to find the basis for promoting cooperation and interaction. Now, a year later, we can say: We succeeded to do that. The central idea of the first message of the president to the Federal Assembly was the strengthening of the state and won a wide support in parliament, in Russian society.

In 1994 we managed to refrain from turning the Constitution into an object of political struggle. Traditions which were new for Russian politics began to appear. The mechanisms of interaction between the president, the Federation Council, the State Duma and the government began to work.

Russian society did not embark on the path of political extremism. The major part of the political forces of the country, of their leaders distanced themselves from extremist slogans and preferred lawful, peaceful means of political struggle.

In 1994 the support to slogans about secession of that or another territory from the Russian Federation considerably weakened. Illusions that it is possible to solve the problems of that or another region in such a way disappeared.

Thanks to joint efforts, the stand-off between the legislative and executive authorities in Russia, which has been the main threat to the country in the first years of reforms, has ceased to exist in general.

However, forces remain in the country which strive to provoke the dissolution of the Duma. I believe it necessary to resolutely state today that once harnessed into one cart you have to pull it together. We all have to work as long as it is fixed by the constitution and be ready to hold new elections of the State Duma and the president in time. Such is my principled position. Such is our common duty before the voters.

Esteemed deputies,

Several years ago Russia made its choice towards democracy and market reforms. The path, which took other countries centuries to traverse, we want to pass in a short time.

History put us in a complicated situation. On the one hand, there is the eternal love of the Russians to the motherland, on the other hand, there is non-acceptance of the yoke of the callous state machine. The gap has not been overcome so far. On the contrary, after having got rid of the so-called "guiding role of the CPSU" [Communist Party of the Soviet Union], the bureaucratic staff felt itself uncontrolled and tried to subordinate state institutions to its selfish interests. This is the root of many mishaps which we faced in recent years.

Most Russians were brought up in a different epoch. Many still believe that it is possible to ensure order by rude force. That means that a tricky demagogue can make Russia rear like a horse in a proper moment. The state bears the maximum of responsibility for not allowing that to happen.

No matter what goals face society, their implementation depends on efficient state authority. The past year showed that the efficiency of its work remains low. The old technique of authority based on political and ideological coercion still remains strong. The role of happenstance, of subjectivism in adopting state decisions still remains great. All this makes state authority fall behind the flow of new problems. . . .

[Establishing the Authority of Law]

Esteemed deputies, there is no other more important task than to establish the authority of law in our country. Many Russians still do not know how to protect their lawful interests in new conditions—where to go, who to ask for help, what is risky and what is reliable, what can be done and what not. They do not know what are the obligations of various state bodies in the protection of human rights. Many experience a deep psychological shock. To help people adapt to the quickly changing conditions is the task not less important than the change of the conditions proper.

In decades and even centuries the practice of disrespect to law by authorities was formed in Russia. And today its representatives sometimes ignore the law. That is why it is necessary to begin creating and enhancing in all ways the mechanisms of exercising powers in the framework of law. . . .

And the problem is not only in the lack of finances. It is no secret that they sometimes get into unworthy hands. Corruption in law enforcement agencies becomes an ever bigger obstacle for normal work. As long as the evil remains, there can be no talk about any successes.

Major criminal communities, the so-called authorities of the criminal world, act with impunity and with growing impudence. Law enforcement bodies have actually occupied the position of non-interference. I view such position as inadmissible and shall proceed from it in assessing the work of the law enforcement system. I hope deputies of the federal assembly will support such an approach. . . .

[Economic Picture]

In 1994 the economy has passed a certain part of the road marked in the first message of the president. The annual inflation was three times lower than in 1993 and nearly seven times lower than in 1992. Financial preconditions for increased investment activities appeared.

The first stage of the large-scale privatisation has been carried out in a short time. The non-state sector, having produced 62 per cent of the gross domestic product, began to dominate.

Market economy infrastructure (banks, trade, financial, insurance companies) vigorously progressed. The securities market developed intensively. The economy became more open.

In the first message to the federal assembly I intentionally and acutely raised the issue about the social price of economic reforms. A year has passed. The social price of the economic policy remains high. A proof to that are the new poor, the people who are employed, but receive humiliating low wages. And often irregularly.

I believe that the main reasons of 1994 failures are:

Firstly. The state authority poorly felt the pulse of market economy processes. It often either fell behind them or, on the contrary, was slow when it was necessary to speed up the transformations.

Secondly. The low efficiency of the state authority. This did not allow [us] to fulfill a number of important decisions and use the reserves of reforms to the maximum.

Thirdly. We miscalculated the receipts of the budget and the government was in the grip of an acute deficit of finances.

1994 results are contradictory. But in general, I believe that the year was not lost for economic reform. The task of 1995 is to form the starting conditions and the potential of future economic growth. We have to build a bridge between the inflationary past and the investment future. . . .

The main starting condition is the financial stabilisation and the strengthening of the rouble. If we fulfill it, the creation of the potential of economic growth will become a reality. Two serious attempts were made to curb inflation in the years of reforms—in the first half of 1992 and in the end of 1993, the beginning of 1994. For various reasons the job was not implemented in full. The third attempt must be a success. That is what the Russians expect from us, as well as foreign partners, including international financial organisations. . . .

In 1995, we shall continue our policy of integrating our economy into the world economy. The main thing now is to secure reliable protection of the domestic market primarily with the help of economic methods. This will be a tactical manoeuvre. It will not contradict the strategic policy of gradually reducing the customs tariff rates for imported goods. . . .

Much will have to be done in 1995 to ensure in real terms the right to adequate remuneration for work and to protection from unemployment. The forecasted explosive growth of unemployment failed to materialize again. But the time given the government for taking preventive measures against unemployment is coming to an end.

The present situation is clearly abnormal—the prices of goods are close to those on the world market, while the price of labour is much lower than that on the world market. Cheap labour cannot be effective. No new restrictions should be imposed on earnings, and those that exist will be gradually reduced.

The constitutional provision for minimal wages must be honoured at enterprises regardless of the form of ownership, including those financed from the local budget. Of course, decisions on raising minimal wages must be made responsibly, proceeding from the budget capacity.

One of the ills of the first reform years was mass-scale practice of delaying the payment of wages. That was a gross violation of man's inalienable rights. The recent strikes of miners reminded us again that tough legislative measures are needed in this sphere. . . .

[The Russian Media]

The Russian media are a question apart. Over the past few years, they have become a powerful mechanism of defence of democracy, which is not an honorary title but a heavy burden to carry. Only those will cope who are able to realise the huge responsibility which evolves to journalists at present.

Naturally, the Russian Government is only learning to exist in conditions of freedom of expression. Its patience sometimes runs short. Some people prefer to issue commands and bring direct pressure to bear on journalists. But I would point to the other side and speak about what the media sometimes feel free to do. This is also a reality of today's Russia.

The media sometimes violate the legal framework. It is impossible to agree to the attempts made by some publications to turn the freedom of mass information into a freedom from obligations before society. To my deep regret, words which in the past hit the eye only if scribbled on walls can now be used in headlines in national newspapers.

The constitutional principle of the freedom of the mass media is inviolable. Democratic society and Russia's state cannot exist without it. Openness of information must form the core of the state policy in the field of the mass media.

At the same time, the government information policy must promote creative principles and lay bare the true aims and motives of the activity of all branches of power. I believe that this is the position shared by most Russian journalists. Their vocation is to serve Russia's spiritual and moral renaissance and to support all useful and progressive initiatives. As it is, journalists seem to be oblivious of the whole of Russia from the Baltics to the Pacific, with the exception of Moscow and Chechnya.

I want to air my personal opinion. I am prepared to put up with the most rigorous criticism of statesmen and establishments. But I cannot put up with boorishness and insults. Criticism should not turn into mockery of the state. I am prepared to put up with the most rigorous criticism of our policy. But it must not call into question the country's integrity and cross the line behind which Russia's disintegration begins.

And another thing. It has become fashionable lately to picture the president as someone who persecutes the press. I shall say this frankly: Attempts have been made to use the president to put the press into a straitjacket. Those attempts failed. And new ones will fail. Although it is not easy to counteract such actions. If we really want to preserve the shoots of freedom which have already sprouted in Russia's severe climate, let us act together. . . .

[The Chechen Problem]

The latest events in Chechnya reflect all problems of modern Russia like a drop of water. . . .

The merging of the criminal world and authorities, which politicians and journalists constantly qualified as the main threat to Russia, became a reality in Chechnya. It was a test ground for preparation and spread of criminal power to other Russian regions. If we do not want the Chechen developments to repeat, we must not allow the establishment in any part of Russia of regional dictatorships, the usurping of power and so on.

We have been for too long cherishing the hope that the situation will be settled by itself, that a compromise was possible. This was a fatal mistake. Such abscesses like the Medellin cartel in Colombia, the "Golden Triangle" in South-East Asia and the criminal dictatorship in Chechnya do not resolve by themselves.

To preserve its sovereignty, independence and integrity the state can and must use the force of authority. But our state turned out to be unprepared for efficient power actions. At the initial stage the hackneyed system of planning military operations of such a scope, uncoordinated activities of ministries made themselves felt. This is the reason for big losses. This is the root of human rights violations in the course of combat activities.

We all have to learn lessons from the dramatic developments. And if we seriously intend to do that, we should not do it straight from the shoulder. We have to analyse all aspects of the Chechen anomaly together, to analyse the activities of all bodies of authority in restoring the constitutional lawfulness in Chechnya. Only on that basis should decisions be adopted. . . .

Another thing is also important. Russia is getting rid of the cancer tumour of the Groznyc regime during the beginning of the creation of its new statehood, while the civic society has not matured and democratic traditions are weak. In these conditions society refrained from chauvinistic and military hysteria. Authorities had enough patience not to cut short the wave of criticisms, to remain open both to the country and to the outside world. All these are signs of the emergence of a normal democratic statehood. It has passed the first and very severe test. . . .

It is to be admitted that the Armed Forces are not well prepared for settling conflicts of local character.

Inefficient is the interaction of the Armed Forces, the interior troops, frontier troops, the Federal Counterintelligence Service and other power structures in such conflicts. The legal and organisational mechanism of the use of the Armed Forces and other power structures in case of an armed mutiny on the territory of the Russian Federation has not been created.

The general conclusion which I make as the supreme commander-in-chief is that reform of the Armed Forces is carried out unsatisfactorily.

All this became a big burden on the shoulders of soldiers and officers participating in the settling of the Chechen crisis.

They do not shoot from behind the backs of women and children.

They do not use them as a live shield.

It is not the Russian servicemen who set up combat strongholds in settlements under the cover of residential buildings and hospitals. . . .

[Foreign Policy]

The new democratic Russia has advanced to the international arena three years ago. A lot of changes have taken place since then. Russia, which was unanimously recognised as the state-inheritor of the USSR, became a mighty factor of stability in the world, an active participant in the efforts of the international community to support peace in various hot spots of the planet. . . .

Sometimes we can hear that partnership with the new Russia is premature. As a rule, behind such statements there is the wish to eliminate a potential competitor. If such ambitions dominate in the West, then the efforts to create a new, more just and safer world order would be undermined. Then the humanity will not step into the 21st Century, but will be thrown back into the 19th Century.

Characteristic in this respect is the intention to push NATO towards a speedy expansion to the East which is detrimental to the joint efforts in creating a new model of genuine pan-European security. We do not conceal what does not suit us in this scenario and why Russia is against it. . . .

Partnership with the United States on the basis of mutually accepted balance of interests is a major direction of the Russian foreign policy. Firmly defending our positions, we shall continue to try and enhance the solid potential accumulated in the last years. Russia and, I hope, the USA will continue this year to learn to actively interact on all major issues. . . .

[Yeltsin's Priorities for 1995]

I think it necessary to point out the most important things which will be the focus of my concern in 1995. I shall work to:

First. Upgrade the efficiency of the Russian Government on the basis of law and democratic principles. Consolidating guarantees of human rights and freedoms.

Second. Restore peace and quiet in the Chechen Republic. We must transform the destructive energy of the Chechen crisis into potential for forthcoming changes in the institutes of power, in the army, and in political and government practice.

Third. Make deeper the country's public accord.

Fourth. Continue economic reform and fill it with social substance.

Fifth. Accomplish court reform.

Sixth. Prepare and hold the elections to the State Duma in December 1995 and the presidential elections in June 1996.

And finally. This year marks the 50th anniversary of the great victory. It is our duty to celebrate this anniversary in an appropriate manner and dedicate this year to the veterans of the Great Patriotic War.

I hope that these efforts will be supported by yourselves, esteemed deputies, by the government, parties and public movements, as well as by all those who hold Russia's future dear. . . .

MANDELA'S REMARKS
OPENING PARLIAMENT
February 17, 1995

Reviewing the initial months of South Africa's first freely elected, multiracial government, President Nelson Mandela on February 17 warned against an upsurge in domestic violence and sought to dampen expectations that the government could readily transform the lives of the nation's impoverished black majority. Mandela spoke to the opening of the second session of the South African Parliament, meeting in Cape Town. Mandela and members of the parliament had been elected nine months earlier in the country's first voting open to all races. (Mandela inauguration, Historic Documents of 1994, p. 247)

Mandela's speech was as much that of a stern father addressing an unruly family as it was that of a national political leader offering hope and promises. He spent more time explaining why his government's progress was slow on many fronts than he did advancing an agenda for change. Various commentators noted that one of Mandela's principle tasks, as South Africa's first black leader, was to restrain the expectation among many blacks that the end of apartheid would immediately improve their standard of living.

Budget Realities

Mandela affirmed that his government was committed to improving the lives of South Africans of all races, but, he said, the "actual reality" was that "the government has extremely limited resources to address the many and urgent needs of our people. . . . All of us, especially the leadership of political organizations and civil society, must rid ourselves of the wrong notion that the government has a big bag full of money. The government does not have such riches."

The government had many budgetary responsibilities, including contractual obligations carried over from the white-led regime of former president F. W. DeKlerk, Mandela said. For that reason, he warned, South Africans must avoid "a world of false hopes leading to unrealistic actions based on the wrong assumption that the government can be coerced to meet demands that it cannot meet, however justified and legitimate these demands might be."

Campaigning for office in 1994, Mandela had promised to improve the lives of South Africans of all races and had made specific pledges, such as building more than one million housing units in five years. In his first state of the union address, Mandela avoided a detailed discussion of those promises, except to say that "progress has been made." Government departments were still drawing up specific plans, he said, and would soon announce "realistic targets" on such needs as housing, clean water, primary health care, and jobs.

In another concession to the reality of governing a modern state, Mandela said one of his highest priorities was creating an "investor-friendly climate" in South Africa. Outside investment was essential to stimulate the economy and create jobs and would be encouraged, he said. This statement was an apparent effort to reassure international corporations and financiers who had been wary of Mandela's government because of the presence of numerous communists and socialists in senior posts.

Caution Against Extremism

Mandela had another audience in mind as he spoke to parliament: extremists of all races who were fomenting domestic violence in hopes of forcing the government to bend to their will. Those people, he said, were trying to "introduce anarchy" into South Africa, which had known two decades of racial strife that had lead to the collapse of the former white-minority regime.

"I speak to those who engage in such totally unacceptable practices as the murder of police officers, the taking of hostages, riots, looting, the forcible occupation of public building, blocking of public highways, vandalization of public and private property, and so on," he said. Some who had engaged in such activities "have misread freedom to mean license" and have wrongly concluded that an elected government is "open to compulsion through acts of anarchy."

The minority that foments violence, he warned, "will meet its match in the government we lead and the masses of the people who put that government in office." Mandela said he and other leaders had struggled for years to defeat apartheid and were not afraid to fight once more against those seeking to undermine the government.

Mandela treaded gingerly in addressing the sensitive issue of political violence in KwaZulu/Natal province, the nation's most populous sector and the power base of his longtime political rival, Inkatha Freedom Party leader Mongosuthu Buthelezi. Thousands of blacks in that province were killed during the 1980s and early 1990s in factional fighting between partisans of Inkatha and Mandela's African National Congress. The fighting diminished sharply after the 1994 elections, but the government was unable to stop it entirely.

In denouncing the continued violence, Mandela named no names but said that those who "claim to be genuine leaders of our people" must end the killings, both to save lives and to create the "climate of peace and stability" necessary for the economic development of KwaZulu/Natal.

The president also took note of several items of unfinished business in the transformation from an authoritarian regime to a democratic one. One priority was the creation of a new, multiracial police service. Another was the establishment of a "Truth and Reconciliation Commission" to review crimes committed by all sides during the previous two decades of civil strife. Mandela said the purpose of this commission was to uncover the truth of what happened during those years, not to seek vengeance.

Following are excerpts from the speech February 17, 1995, by President Nelson Mandela to the opening of the second session of the South African Parliament:

We have gathered in this hallowed chamber to begin the work of the second session of our democratic parliament, nine months after its first members were sworn in. Let me say this from the beginning that challenges ahead of us require that we move away from spectacle and rhetoric and bend our backs to the serious work ahead of us. . . .

All of us, precisely because we had never sat in any democratic parliament before, had to begin the continuing process of learning how to carry out our functions as people's deputies. We had to educate ourselves in an atmosphere characterised by a critical public focus which did not necessarily allow for the reality of that inexperience. Undoubtedly, many of us, both in the legislature and in the executive, have made mistakes. But mistakes are an inevitable element of any process of learning.

It is always the case that the spectators are better than the players on the field. None of us should therefore feel ashamed for having committed errors. We must, however, learn from these mistakes so that we do indeed improve our performance. Whatever it is that our critics might have to say, we can take pride in the fact that not only did we succeed to establish our two houses of parliament, as required by the Constitution, but we also ensured that they play their role in the governance of our country. . . .

In the recent past, much has been said about corruption among some members of this parliament and other leading political figures in the country. Many within and without this chamber and among the mass media have been very keen to condemn and to propel us into precipitate action on the basis of mere allegations. We have resisted this and will continue to do so. We have a responsibility to act on the basis of fact and not allegations, however strident the voice that makes those allegations.

Furthermore, we firmly believe that it is important that we build a society based on justice and fairness. At all times we must guarantee the right of the accused to be heard, without making any concession to a primeval instinct to pillory and burn people at the stake. As South Africans, with our particular history, we must be extremely careful not to reintroduce the McCarthyist atmosphere which resulted in people being herded into unthinking hordes that sought the blood of anybody who was labelled a communist.

We must also make this clear that we need no educators with regard to the matter of rooting out corruption, which we will deal with firmly and unequivocally, whoever may be involved.

We are conscious of the reality that corruption in many forms has deeply infected the fibre of our society. It is not possible to have a society based on a lie and patent injustice, as apartheid society was, without this spawning corrupt practices. Precisely because we face the challenge of dealing with systematic corruption we need a dispassionate and systematic approach to this question and not allow ourselves to be stampeded by responses which are not very different from a witchhunt.

[Importance of Local Government]

To address another important matter of the day, later this year we will be holding our local government elections to complete the process of establishing the democratic structures which we need to ensure that the people are able to take their destiny into their own hands. The importance of these popularly elected structures at the local level cannot be overestimated. It is at this level that we must deliver change. It is at this level that the people can most directly participate in making decisions about important matters that affect their daily lives.

It is also at this level that we must confront the divisions created by the system of apartheid and grapple with the problems that arise out of the racial and territorial maldistribution of resources and infrastructure that was imposed on the country by this system.

In reality, it is impossible to enter this next and critical stage of the dismantling of the system of apartheid until we have democratically elected structures of government which enjoy a popular mandate to bring about the non-racial, non-sexist and democratic society demanded of us by the constitution. I would therefore like to take this opportunity to call on all our people in their millions to take the forthcoming local government elections very seriously. . . .

I am also pleased to report that whatever the teething problems, the concept and vision of a government of national unity has proved its correctness and viability. It has succeeded in its intentions of ensuring cooperation among our people as a whole, the development of a national consensus around a whole range of important matters, enabling important minority parties to have a real voice in the government of the country and contributing to peace, stability and confidence in the future of our country. . . .

A few days ago, we were honoured to participate in the moving and historic opening of our Constitutional Court. This is yet another giant step in the transformation of our judicial system and the building of a law-governed society which will protect the fundamental human rights of all our citizens and ensure that the people are not threatened by arbitrary and oppressive rule. The process of the transformation of the judiciary will continue, among other things to ensure that it is representative of our society and to enable even the poor to have the ability to obtain legal redress where need arises. . . .

The public service will never be fully acceptable to the people as a whole and can never be truly responsive to the needs of the people unless it is composed in all its ranks in a manner that reflects the composition of our population.

To speed up this process, the government will continue to implement measures and programmes aiming at ensuring that those who were disadvantaged by apartheid in the past are given the capacity to catch up with those who were given the possibility to develop and advance themselves in terms of management and other skills. This is what we mean when we talk of affirmative action programmes. We speak of a human resource development programme which will ensure that all our people, and not merely some, are given the possibility to develop their talents and to contribute to the reconstruction and development of society to the best of their ability. I therefore call on all our people to refuse to listen to the false prophets who seek to perpetuate the apartheid divisions and imbalances of the past by presenting affirmative action as a programme intended to advantage some and disadvantage others on the basis of race and colour.

It is also appropriate that on this occasion we draw the attention of the country to the actual reality that the government has extremely limited resources to address the many and urgent needs of our people. We are very keen that this real situation should be communicated to the people as a whole. All of us, especially the leadership of political organisations and civil society, must rid ourselves of the wrong notion that the government has a big bag full of money. The government does not have such riches.

Because we have started the process of changing spending priorities, we do realise that the process of restructuring the budget so that it is directed towards addressing the needs of the people is no easy matter. This is especially so in the light of the contractual obligations that bind the state as well as carry-over expenditure which cannot be avoided. We must all absorb this reality into our thinking in a cold and dispassionate manner and not allow ourselves to be seduced into a world of false hopes leading to unrealistic actions based on the wrong assumption that the government can be coerced to meet demands that it cannot meet, however justified and legitimate these demands might be.

It is important that we rid ourselves of the culture of entitlement which leads to the expectation that the government must promptly deliver whatever it is that we demand, and results in some people refusing to meet their obligations such as rent and service payments or engaging in other unacceptable actions such as the forcible occupation of houses. . . .

[Warning Against Anarchy]

I must also address the question of the attempt by some in our country to introduce anarchy into our society. I speak of those who engage in such totally unacceptable practices as the murder of police officers, the taking of hostages, riots, looting, the forcible occupation of public buildings, blocking of public highways, vandalisation of public and private property and so on. Some of those who have initiated and participated in such activities have misread freedom to mean license. They have misinterpreted popular partici- pation to mean their ability to impose chaos on society. They have wrongly concluded that an elected government of the people is a government that is open to compulsion through acts of anarchy.

Let me therefore make this abundantly clear that the small minority in our midst which wears the mask of anarchy will meet its match in the govern- ment we lead and the masses of the people who put that government into office. This they must know that we are not afraid of struggle. We are, after all, a product of confrontation and struggle. In the past we were not defeat- ed by forces more powerful than they. In this instance, we will not be defeat- ed by those whose actions have nothing to do with defending or advancing the cause of the people.

We are certain that the democratic trade union movement will also join hands with us to isolate and defeat the minority which seeks to discredit the trade union movement by engaging in violent activities during the course of strike actions. Let it therefore be clear to all that the battle against the forces of anarchy and chaos has been joined. Let no one say they have not been warned.

In the same vein we must address the question of crime. The situation can- not be tolerated in which our country continues to be engulfed by the crime wave which includes murder, crime against women and children, drug traf- ficking, armed robbery, fraud and theft. We must take the war to the crimi- nals and no longer allow the situation in which we are mere sitting ducks of those in our society who, for whatever reason, are bent to engage in criminal and anti-social activities.

Instructions have therefore already gone out to the Minister for Safety and Security, the National Commissioner of the Police Service and the security organs as a whole to take all necessary measures to bring down the levels of crime. . . .

The Government is determined to do everything in its power to move speedily towards the formation of the new Police Service. We are very inter- ested to address the matter of the earnings and working conditions of all members of the Police Service and to give this Service the necessary means to enable it to discharge its responsibilities as effectively as possible.

In this regard, we must also make it clear that the Government is opposed to and has no intention to conduct a witchhunt against the police as a result of activities arising from orders given to the police by the apartheid regime. We therefore urge every member of the Police Service to get down to the urgent and pressing matter of enhancing the safety and security of the peo- ple as a whole.

When we opened parliament last year, we addressed the issue of racism in the workplace and in our society at large. We continue to be confronted by this problem. People have continued to die as a result of the continuing practice of racism—the latest being a victim of racist resistance to the use of a former white school by black children. Those who are responsible for these crimes of racism must be brought to book without delay. It is clear that insufficient progress has been made in many workplaces and elsewhere in our society to deal with this cancer. We trust that the Human Rights Commission will help us to deal with this matter firmly and continuously by encouraging the public to report all instances of racism so that these can be brought to light.

The Government has discussed this matter and is committed to carry out its constitutional obligation of transforming our country into a non-racial society. The situation cannot be allowed in which anyone acts in a manner which perpetuates the practice of apartheid. Both the government and the people as a whole share a common obligation to live up to the very purpose of the struggle that millions of people waged, of ending racism in our country and ensuring the equality of all our people.

One of the most sensitive matters we must address this year is the establishment of the Truth and Reconciliation Commission. We must move towards this as speedily as possible so as to remove all the uncertainties that have been created through the protracted discussion of this issue. The legislature is currently discussing the bill dealing with this matter and is receiving public submissions. I would like to urge that we achieve speedy progress in this regard.

I would also like to draw the attention of the legislature and the country as a whole, that our purpose in establishing the Truth and Reconciliation Commission is both to obtain the truth and to reinforce the process of reconciliation which our country needs. Nothing we do should lead to the heightening of tensions and the rekindling of the violent political conflicts which we have succeeded so well in bringing under reasonable control. This must also be borne in mind that many of us, who suffered quite significantly as a result of apartheid repression, are making no demand which would result in vengeance against or persecution of those who might have harmed us or those close to us.

Urgent steps are also required to end the continuing political violence in the province of KwaZulu/Natal. This is both a law-enforcement issue and a matter for the political parties and leaders in the province to address. If we claim to be genuine leaders of our people, it must surely be one of our principal tasks to end the killing both to save lives and to create the climate of peace and stability which we need to develop the province which is among the poorest areas in the country.

[The Government's Priorities]

Progress has been made with regard to the basic challenge of building a better life for all our people. Some of the projects which we announced last year, including the feeding of school children and the provision of free health services to certain sections of our population, have been implemented.

It is necessary that we draw the necessary lessons from our experience in this effort to meet the basic needs of the people. One of these, as we have stated already, is that the Government has very limited resources to address the multiple and urgent needs of our people. It is therefore critical that we determine a proper set of priorities on which we should focus to effect a visible and sustainable improvement in the lives of the people. It is also important that we implement any projects in this regard not in an ad-hoc manner, but within the context of 5-year and other medium- and long-term plans and projections.

The Cabinet has discussed this matter and decided on our priorities, which will include rural and urban development, human resource development, job creation and health.

Detailed inter-departmental work is now going on to elaborate plans reflecting this focus, to ensure that the Government uses in a rational and effective manner the limited resources at its disposal. In this regard, government will not make any commitments which it cannot meet on a continuous basis.

As compared to the time last year when we had to announce programmes for transformation without detailed preparation of implementable and affordable plans, we are now in the fortunate situation that we are well on the way to finalising detailed plans to meet our firm commitment to build a better life for all South Africans. Once they are ready, and after the necessary consultation with the elected representatives at both national and provincial levels, the local community structures and the public at large, we are determined, this year, to move speedily to expedite the process of social transformation and the improvement of the quality of life of our people, which is required of us in the context of our programme for reconstruction and development. This will be one of the high points in our national life, this year, when we announce realistic targets with regard to such needs as houses, clean water, primary health care and jobs.

I must repeat that it is our firm intention that we set these targets within the parameters of what the budget can carry, consistent with our objective of ensuring fiscal discipline. . . .

As the year begins, there are signs that our economy is beginning to pick up. The Government considers it a matter of critical importance that everything should be done to encourage a climate conducive to sustained and high levels of economic growth.

We are therefore ready to deal and have been dealing with all matters that are relevant to this goal, in particular to ensure the creation of an investor-friendly climate. Everything must be done to encourage a significant upward movement in the rate of investment to increase the productive capacity of the economy, to modernise and restructure the economy, to create jobs and to increase our international competitiveness.

With regard to these economic issues, I would also like to emphasise our continuing commitment to fiscal discipline, including the reduction of the budget deficit, the reduction of the share of the national income that accrues to government and the reorientation of government expenditure away from recurrent disbursements towards investment. The relevant authorities, including the Reserve Bank, remain seized of the issue of the two-tier exchange rate and the general question of foreign exchange controls. These matters will be addressed with the necessary speed and the equally necessary sense of responsibility towards the economy as a whole. . . .

I have the honour to declare the second session of our democratic parliament open.

Thank you.

March

GAO REPORT ON NUCLEAR CLEANUP PRIORITIES
March 3, 1995

Unrealistic schedules at individual sites and the lack of an overall priority list were primary factors impeding efforts by the Department of Energy (DOE) to clean up contamination at the nation's nuclear weapons plants. So concluded the General Accounting Office (GAO), the investigative arm of Congress, in a report dated March 3.

Throughout the cold war era, the DOE and its predecessors concentrated on manufacturing nuclear weapons and paid little attention to the environmental hazards created in the process. As a result some seven thousand sites at fifteen major weapons facilities and more than one hundred smaller sites suffered from hazardous or radioactive contamination or both, according to a DOE estimate. The department estimated that the cleanup would cost at least $300 billion (and perhaps as much as $1 trillion) and take thirty or more years to complete.

In making the materials and components of nuclear weapons, the DOE and its predecessors operated largely without environmental guidelines. When states and the federal government began enacting environmental protection laws in the 1970s, these agencies claimed exemption on national security grounds. It was not until a court ruling in 1984 that the DOE acknowledged that it should comply with federal environmental regulations, particularly the Resource Conservation and Recovery Act, which regulated the cleanup and disposal of hazardous (but not radioactive) waste, and the Comprehensive Environmental Response, Compensation, and Liability Act of 1980, better known as the Superfund, which established a procedure for cleaning up inactive waste sites. Most of the DOE's major facilities were on the Superfund's National Priorities List, which meant those sites were on an accelerated schedule for cleanup.

Both laws were administered by the Environmental Protection Agency, which used agreements negotiated with the DOE to stipulate what would be cleaned up, and how and when it would be done. It also established "milestones" to measure incremental progress on the agreements. These agreements were legally binding. (The DOE must also comply with some state environmental regulations.)

The GAO report stated that many of the agreements and milestones were unrealistic. In some cases, the schedules were too optimistic; in others, the technology to clean up the specific contamination did not exist. When the DOE sought to renegotiate some of these agreements, the regulators were reluctant to do so, the GAO said, seeing the proposed renegotiation as another sign of the DOE's mismanagement and historical resistance to environmental regulation. In a few instances, the report noted, the DOE decided not to seek renegotiation and instead proceeded with expensive cleanup activities that, although once deemed adequate, were now consid- ered ineffective. (Report on cleanup of nuclear weapons plants, Historic Documents of 1994, p. 339)

The GAO went on to state that the DOE has sometimes focused more on complying with the milestones than on cleanup, spending "scarce resources to demonstrate its willingness to meet its legal commitments even when its expenditures have not advanced its environmental goals." For example, the report said, when the DOE realized it did not have enough money to meet a high-priority milestone at its Rocky Flats facility in Col- orado, it completed several less expensive, low priority milestones instead.

This focus on meeting milestones at individual plants impeded the department from setting priorities for cleaning up the highest priority sites throughout the system. Previous efforts to set priorities and renegoti- ate agreements and milestones failed, the GAO report said, "largely because regulators have distrusted DOE's commitment to environmental remediation and have questioned DOE's analytical methods."

The GAO report concluded that the DOE should set national priorities to clean up those sites that pose the greatest risks to public health and safety and that it should undertake discussions with regulators to renegotiate milestones that do not reflect those priorities. If "infeasible" milestones cannot be renegotiated, the report said, "alternatives to the current cleanup program, such as establishing a separate federal or private entity to man- age the cleanup may have to be considered."

Hanford Cleanup Agreement Challenged

One alternative to the planned cleanup at a specific site was proposed on March 15 by Republican Frank H. Murkowski of Alaska, chairman of the Senate Energy Committee, and J. Bennett Johnston of Louisiana, the committee's ranking Democrat. After releasing a report by two former DOE officials concluding that the agreement to clean up the Hanford Nuclear Reservation in Washington was unachievable, the two senators suggested that the agreement be rewritten. They also proposed that Congress revoke a rule allowing the state to sue to force a federal cleanup of the site. Plutoni- um for bombs had been produced at the Hanford site for nearly fifty years, leaving behind extensive soil and water contamination and large amounts of waste stored in metal containers that have since rusted and leaked.

Although the two senators said they would work with state officials and residents to revise the agreement, their proposal drew immediate opposition from state officials, environmentalists, and concerned citizens. The state's assistant director for waste management said state officials "vehemently disagree" with the report's conclusion that the cleanup agreement was fatally flawed. What was needed, he said, was better management by the DOE and its contractors.

Revised Cleanup Costs

In another development, the Department of Energy in March updated its cleanup cost estimates, projecting that the federal government would have to spend between $200 billion and $350 billion through the year 2070 to clean up the nation's nuclear weapons complex and dispose of other radioactive waste. The mid-range estimate was $230 billion, of which $172 billion was for cleanup of the nuclear weapons plants.

The estimates were based on several assumptions that could be difficult to achieve, such as obtaining significant savings through improved efficiency and productivity in cleanup activities. The estimates were based on the use of existing technology and did not include estimates for contamination, such as most groundwater contamination, for which no feasible technology currently existed. Decisions about the level of cleanup at individual sites would also affect the costs significantly, the department said. Even if the assumptions turned out to be true, the report noted that projected costs would still significantly exceed the projected federal budget for the cleanup. The department said that changes in the laws and the compliance agreements would be necessary to bridge the budget gap.

Following is the executive summary of a report to the secretary of energy entitled "National Priorities Needed for Meeting Environmental Agreements," released March 3, 1995, by the General Accounting Office:

Purpose

From the 1940s, when the nation began to develop nuclear weapons, until the late 1980s, the Department of Energy's (DOE) predecessors and DOE gave little attention to the environmental consequences of their activities. As a result, many DOE sites are now contaminated with radioactive and hazardous wastes, and DOE faces the largest, most complex cleanup task in the country—estimated to cost at least $300 billion and perhaps as much as $1 trillion.

As part of a general management review, GAO [General Accounting Office] evaluated the progress made by DOE in cleaning up its nuclear weapons complex and identified impediments to the task. This report examines DOE's use of environmental agreements with state and federal regulators, many of which are legally binding, and recommends changes in DOE's current approach to cleanup.

Background

By generating radioactive and hazardous wastes at its facilities across the nation, DOE contaminated billions of cubic meters of soil and sediment. Starting in the 1970s, federal and state laws were enacted to regulate the disposal of such wastes. In general, the Environmental Protection Agency (EPA) oversees and enforces DOE's compliance with federal laws while the states where DOE's facilities are located oversee and enforce DOE's compliance with state laws.

To bring its weapons complex into environmental compliance, DOE has negotiated major cleanup agreements for sites on EPA's Superfund National Priorities List. DOE has also signed agreements with EPA and state regulators to correct violations at other sites. These agreements identify activities—generally called "milestones"—and schedules for achieving compliance, many of which are legally binding and enforceable. About $1.8 billion of DOE's annual $6 billion environmental budget is directed at environmental remediation, or "cleanup."

Results in Brief

DOE has prepared reports, investigated sites, and submitted decision documents to regulators, but it has put only a small part of its effort into physically cleaning up its nuclear weapons complex and has yet to complete the cleanup of a major facility. Although its recent performance has been more timely, DOE missed more than 20 percent of all milestones through 1994.

DOE has had difficulty meeting some milestones because it signed unrealistic agreements with regulators. To continue producing nuclear weapons and avoid prosecution for environmental violations, DOE made commitments it could not meet, given both budgetary and technical limitations. Delays in meeting these commitments led regulators to declare deficiencies and to doubt DOE's credibility. Adversarial relationships developed, making it hard for both parties to renegotiate milestones in response to fiscal constraints or new evidence suggesting that previously negotiated remedies would do little to reduce risks.

Future progress in cleaning up the weapons complex largely depends on how effectively DOE and its regulators can set national priorities and negotiate realistic agreements and milestones under increasingly restrictive budgets. The current practice of negotiating agreements for individual sites without considering other agreements or available resources does not ensure that limited resources will be allocated to reducing the greatest environmental risks. To its credit, DOE has begun to identify milestones that may require revision and to gather data on risks to workers, the public, and the environment. DOE should be able to use these data to set priorities across as well as within sites and to further develop a strategy that will maximize the impact of the resources available for cleanup.

Principal Findings

DOE Has Completed Few Cleanups

DOE has thus far focused largely on activities in the "characterization" phase of the cleanup process—collecting data and investigating sites. These activities, while necessary as part of the agreements between DOE and its regulators, are often lengthy and can delay "remediation," or the actual cleanup of sites, for years. About 16 percent of DOE's 856 cleanup projects are now in the remediation phase. Physical cleanup has been completed for about 13 percent of the projects (or for about 17 percent if projects that required no action beyond characterization are counted). The remainder are undergoing characterization. Increasingly, DOE is also performing "interim actions," or activities related to cleanups that are not required under agreements with regulators. Such actions range from posting signs and putting up a fence to removing contaminated soils. According to DOE, 118 interim actions were completed in fiscal year 1994 and another 100 are planned to be completed in fiscal year 1995.

Although DOE is improving its timeliness, it missed more than 20 percent of the milestones it agreed to complete through 1994. Most of the milestones that it did complete were studies or reports rather than cleanups, and some were low-priority activities. At the Rocky Flats facility in Colorado, for example, where DOE officials said they had tried to maximize the number of milestones they could meet within budgetary constraints, EPA assessed a penalty against DOE in 1993 for choosing to complete several low-priority documentary milestones rather than one high-priority cleanup milestone.

Despite recent data showing some improvement in DOE's performance, the Congress is increasingly questioning the Department's progress. Furthermore, as limits on funding tighten, as the costs of required activities increase, and as growing numbers of milestones come due, DOE is likely to fall farther behind. In 1994, 433 milestones came due, compared with 23 in 1989.

Unrealistic Agreements Have Impeded Progress

After claiming for years that its Cold War military mission exempted it from environmental regulation, DOE was, during the late 1980s, "prodded or dragged to the conclusion" that it would have to consider the environment "to stay in business to produce [nuclear weapons]," according to the former undersecretary who presided over the signing of many early agreements with regulators. However, the agreements that DOE reached were often unrealistic—that is, they were not based on adequate assessments of conditions at sites or of the Department's technical capabilities. For example, officials at Rocky Flats, who feared they would be jailed for environmental violations, signed an agreement to clean up the facility over a 10-year period even though, as one of them later told GAO, "any technical person would have known that we couldn't meet the milestones." Similarly, for the Hanford

Reservation's cleanup in Washington State, a DOE official said, "There was not [then]—and still is not—[any] technology to accomplish this task. . . ."

In negotiating agreements with aggressive schedules, DOE assumed that if milestones could not be achieved, changes would be made. However, DOE has since had difficulty renegotiating some agreements. Given the Department's history of resistance to environmental regulation, many regulators have been reluctant to renegotiate, seeing such requests as evidence of mismanagement rather than as legitimate responses to new information about conditions at sites or new understanding of environmental technologies. In light of regulators' reluctance to renegotiate, DOE has not sought to revise its commitments to remediate groundwater at 22 sites through "pump and treat" actions whose estimated life-cycle costs exceed $500 million, even though DOE now believes most of these actions will do little or nothing to reduce risks to public health and safety.

DOE has, however, negotiated some more realistic agreements that promote progress. For example, despite a history of vigorous conflict with regulators, DOE reached an agreement with the state of Idaho and EPA that has enabled DOE's Idaho National Engineering Laboratory to complete more remediation milestones than any other site in the weapons complex. This agreement establishes a single regulatory framework for complying with all applicable laws, creates opportunities for communication between DOE and the regulators, and supports a "bias for action" that encourages the use of the most cost-effective methods to remediate the greatest risks.

Future Progress Depends on Adopting a National Risk-Based Strategy

To date, DOE's cleanup strategy has been shaped by site-specific environmental agreements whose priorities and requirements have not always been consistent with technical or fiscal realities. Furthermore, although these agreements may have been designed to allocate resources efficiently at individual sites, under severe budgetary constraints the use of many separately negotiated agreements is not well suited to setting priorities among sites. To establish a baseline for a more comprehensive, risk-based cleanup strategy, DOE is now evaluating the risks and public concerns addressed by agreements at individual sites and identifying milestones that may require revision because they are not technically feasible or do not address immediate threats to health or the environment. DOE could use the results of this effort, which are due to the Congress in June 1995, to set priorities across as well as within sites and to further develop a national cleanup strategy that will target the available resources to the highest priorities.

DOE's past efforts to establish priorities and use them to renegotiate milestones have not been successful—largely because regulators have distrusted DOE's commitment to environmental remediation and have questioned DOE's analytical methods. Consequently, alternatives to the current cleanup program, such as establishing a separate federal or private entity to manage the cleanup, may have to be considered if DOE cannot successfully renegotiate infeasible milestones. Both the Office of Technology Assessment and the former chief of DOE's cleanup program have argued for alternatives to the current program. In 1989, GAO testified before the Congress that a national commission could help DOE develop a process for establishing a more comprehensive cleanup approach.

Recommendation

To enable DOE to target its resources to the sites that present the greatest risks, GAO recommends that the Secretary of Energy (1) set national priorities for cleaning up the Department's contaminated sites using data gathered during DOE's ongoing risk evaluation as a starting point and (2) initiate discussions with regulators to renegotiate milestones that no longer reflect national priorities. . . .

GAO TESTIMONY ON
THE PARK SERVICE
March 7, 1995

In testimony March 7 before two House and Senate subcommittees, an official of the General Accounting Office (GAO) warned that funding constraints were threatening the viability of the National Park Service and that difficult choices would have to be made to ensure that the service could "preserve these treasures for the enjoyment of future generations. . . ." In short, "the future of the parks is at a crossroads," said James Duffus III, director of Natural Resources Management Issues in the GAO's Resources, Community, and Economic Development Division.

Since 1872, when Yellowstone became the first national park, the national park system has grown to encompass 368 parks, historic sites, monuments, and recreation areas covering some 80 million acres. Thirty-one sites have been added since 1984. The National Park Service's operating budget was about $1.1 billion in fiscal 1995. Although that represented a 30 percent increase over ten years, it was not enough to cover the additional costs associated with increased visitation and with complying with regulations imposed by federal agencies, such as the Environmental Protection Agency and the Occupational Safety and Health Administration. Some 270 million visitors were expected in the park system in 1995, and that number was expected to increase to 300 million by the turn of the century.

A survey of twelve sites, including national parks, historic parks, a seashore, and a civil war battlefield, revealed that, while public satisfaction with the park service remained high, the overall level of visitor services was deteriorating. Deferred maintenance of roads, campgrounds, trails, and other facilities had more than doubled since 1988, totaling more than $4 billion, while park managers did not have the information necessary to assess whether the overall condition of the parks' natural and cultural resources were deteriorating, improving, or staying the same, Duffus said.

Neither Duffus nor a GAO report, released August 30, on the future of the national parks made any recommendations to cure this situation. They outlined three alternatives: raising entrance fees, concession fees, and other service fees; limiting additions to, or perhaps decreasing the number of units in, the park system; and reducing the level of visitor services, perhaps by cutting back the hours or days individual sites were open or even temporarily closing some sites.

All three alternatives were embodied in bills that came before Congress in 1995. The most extreme would have directed the Interior Department to assess all the sites in the national park system, excluding the fifty-four national parks, and determine which were "nationally significant." A specially created independent commission would then recommend to Congress which sites should be retained in the system and which should be turned over to other operators or closed.

The bill's sponsor, Rep. Joel Hefley (R-Colo.), said his legislation would rid the system of "pork parks," those sites of minimal natural, cultural, or historical value that were added to the system primarily to benefit a local economy. Opponents called it a "park-closing bill," and it was defeated on the House floor in September by an overwhelming margin. A subsequent attempt to include the bill in the House budget-reconciliation legislation also failed.

Two other measures appeared to have a better chance of success. One would raise entrance fees at some parks to a maximum of $6 a person and institute fees at several sites that currently do not have them, including many of the sites in Washington, D.C. The other would reform the way the park service managed privately run concessions, such as restaurants, lodges, and souvenir shops. In 1993 those concessions generated revenues in excess of $650 million but returned less than $19 million to the federal Treasury. The reform would open some concessions to competitive bidding, raising needed revenue for the park service. Both measures were incorporated in the budget-reconciliation bill, which was still pending at the end of the year, caught in the impasse over the federal budget between President Clinton and the Republican-led Congress.

Heavy usage and "inappropriate new units" were also cited as serious problems for the park service in 1992, by a committee of park service officials, conservationists, and university professors. The report, known as the "Vail Agenda," concluded that the park service had "lost the ability to exercise leadership in determining the fate of the resources and programs it manages. . . .[T]he Park Service is variously seen as run and overrun by Congress, the White House, the Secretary of the Interior, private interest groups, or public interest groups." (Vail Agenda, Historic Documents of 1992, p. 329)

> *Following are excerpts from testimony, entitled "Difficult Choices Need to Be Made on the Future of the Parks," presented March 7, 1995, by James Duffus III, director of Natural Resources Management Issues in the General Accounting Office's Resources, Community, and Economic Development*

Division, before a joint meeting of the Senate Energy and Natural Resources Subcommittee on Parks, Historic Preservation, and Recreation and the House Resources Subcommittee on National Parks, Forests, and Lands:

We are pleased to be here today to discuss conditions in the national parks. Our comments are based primarily on our work to date for the Chairman, Senate Committee on Energy and Natural Resources at 12 geographically dispersed sites within the national park system, including four national parks, two historic parks and one historic site, two national monuments, a civil war battlefield, a recreation area, and a seashore: Our remarks also draw on the 28 reports and testimonies that we have issued over the last 8 years on the Park Service's activities and programs.

As requested, our work focused on efforts of the National Park Service to meet its mission of serving visitors and managing park resources. Our specific objectives were to (1) determine what, if any, degradation in visitor services or park resources is occurring; (2) identify factors contributing to any degradation of visitor services or park resources; and (3) identify choices available to help deal with identified problems.

In summary . . . we found the following:

- The overall level of visitor services is deteriorating. While public satisfaction with the parks is very high, visitor services are being cut back and the condition of many trails, campgrounds, exhibits, and other facilities is declining. Since 1988, the Park Service estimates that the backlog of deferred maintenance has more than doubled to over $4 billion. In managing resources, most parks do not have the data needed to determine whether the overall condition of the natural and cultural resources is deteriorating, improving, or staying the same.
- There are many factors that influence the level of visitor services and resource management activities. Our work identified two factors that were common to most of the parks we visited and had substantial impact on the level of visitor services and resource management activities. These factors were (1) additional operating requirements resulting primarily from over 20 federal laws affecting the parks and (2) increased visitation which drives up routine operating costs for many items that support visitor activities.
- Since substantial increases in appropriations are very unlikely in today's tight budget climate, difficult choices need to be made on the future of the national parks. These choices involve: (1) generating more revenue within the parks, (2) limiting the number of parks in the system, and (3) reducing the level of visitor services and expectations. Regardless of which of these choices are made, the Park Service needs to look for ways to operate more efficiently and improve accountability to ensure that the limited dollars are used most effectively.

Background

The National Park Service is the caretaker of many of the nation's most precious natural and cultural resources. Today, more than 100 years after the first national park was created, the national park system has grown to include 368 units. These units cover over 80 million acres of land and include an increasingly diverse mix of sites, such as Yellowstone, Yosemite, and Grand Canyon National Parks; Independence National Historical Park; national battlefields; national historic sites; national monuments; national preserves; and national recreation areas.

The Park Service's mission has dual objectives. On one hand, the Park Service is to provide for the public's enjoyment of the lands that have been entrusted to its care. This objective involves promoting the use of the parks by providing appropriate visitor services and the infrastructure (such as roads and facilities) that support these services. On the other hand, the Park Service is to protect its lands so that they will be unimpaired for the enjoyment of future generations. Balancing these objectives has long shaped the debate about how best to manage the national park system.

The debate has also been shaped by a number of other developments. Despite the fiscal constraints facing all federal agencies, the number of parks continues to expand—31 parks have been added to the system in the last 10 years. In addition, the backlog of maintenance at national parks has increased substantially. In 1988, we reported that the amount of the backlog of deferred maintenance stood at about $1.9 billion. Currently, while agency officials acknowledge that they do not have reliable data on this backlog, they estimate that it will cost over $4 billion.

Visitor Services Declining; Condition of Park Resources Largely Unknown

The natural beauty and historical settings of the parks make visits by most people a pleasurable and often inspiring experience. Park Service surveys show that in general, visitors are very pleased with their experience at national parks. Nonetheless, our findings show cause for concern about the health of the parks.

Condition of Visitor Services

Of the 12 parks included in our review, 11 had recently cut back on the level of visitor services. This reduction is particularly significant considering that managers at most of the parks told us that meeting visitors' needs gets top priority, often at the expense of other park activities. For example:

- At Padre Island National Seashore in Texas, last summer for the first time in 20 years no lifeguards were on duty along the beach to help ensure the safety of swimmers. The beach is one of the primary attractions of the park.
- At Shenandoah National Park in Virginia, interpretive programs to assist visitors in understanding and appreciating the natural and scenic

aspects of the park were cut by over 80 percent from 1987 to 1993, and one of the park's most popular campgrounds has been closed. In addition, because of other park priorities, park staff have been unable to remove numerous trees that hang precariously over roads and popular hiking trails, posing a hazard to visitors.

- At Bandelier National Monument in New Mexico, the park museum—one of the most popular stops at the park—was closed for more than a year because of problems caused by a leaky roof and an improperly installed security system.

- At the Statue of Liberty and Ellis Island, the extended hours of operation to meet visitor demand during the peak summer season have been reduced by 3.5 hours each day—a reduction of more than 25 percent. Furthermore, the duration of the season in which hours are extended was reduced from 3 months to 2 months.

- At Lake Mead National Recreation Area in Nevada, during the summer months, park law enforcement personnel are often faced with a backlog of up to 12 calls in responding to health and safety needs of visitors.

As these examples illustrate, the cutbacks in services not only adversely affect visitors' convenience and enjoyment, but also reveal significant gaps in the Park Service's ability to meet visitors' safety needs.

Condition of Cultural and Natural Resources

Knowing the condition of the resources within the national park system is key to the ability of the Park Service to preserve and protect its cultural and natural resources. The Park Service's policy directs that parks be managed on the basis of a knowledge of the resources and their conditions. However, our review indicated that, by and large, the condition and trend of many park resources is largely unknown—particularly for parks featuring natural resources, such as Glacier and Yosemite.

Park Service officials at both headquarters and in the field emphasized to us that effective management of park resources depends heavily upon scientifically collected data that enables park managers to detect damaging changes to the parks' resources and guide the mitigation of those changes. Essentially, this approach involves collecting baseline data about the key park resources and monitoring their condition over time to detect any changes. One park official told us that without such information, damage to key resources could go undetected until it is obvious, at which point mitigation may be impossible or extremely expensive. However, while park officials emphasized the need for this kind of information, they also acknowledged that information is lacking for many of the parks' resources. . . .

Managers at the culturally oriented parks we visited—much as Statue of Liberty/Ellis Island and Hopewell Furnace National Historic Site—generally have greater knowledge about their resources than do those at parks that emphasize natural resources. Even at the cultural parks, however, we found instances where (1) the condition of cultural resources was declining or (2) the location and status of cultural resources in many portions of the park remains largely unknown. For example:

- Ellis Island was reopened in 1990 as the country's only museum devoted exclusively to immigration. While a portion of the Island's structures has been restored, 32 of 36 historic buildings have seriously deteriorated. According to park officials, about two-thirds of these buildings could be lost within 5 years if they are not properly stabilized. The structures are currently not available for public access. They include the former hospital, quarantine area, and morgue. In addition, although some new storage space is being built, much of Ellis Island's large collection of cultural artifacts is stored in deteriorating facilities. As a result, in one building, much of the collection is covered with dirt and debris from crumbling walls and peeling paint, and leaky roofs have damaged many artifacts.
- Hopewell Furnace National Historic Site is an 850-acre park in Pennsylvania that depicts a portion of the nation's early industrial development. The main features of the site are a charcoal-fueled blast furnace, an ironmaster's mansion, and auxiliary structures. Although Hopewell Furnace has been a national historical site since 1938, the Park Service has not performed an archeological survey of the site. Also, the Park Service has not developed a general management plan—which would outline an overall approach for protecting and managing the site's resources—even though having such a plan is a key component of effective resource management.

These conditions at cultural sites raise questions about the Park Service's ability to meet its responsibilities to preserve and protect cultural resources. . . .

The Park Service began efforts several years ago to gather better information about the condition of the parks' resources. However, progress has been limited, and the completion of much of the work is many years away. In the meantime, park managers often make decisions about the parks' operations without knowing the impact of these decisions on the resources. For example, at Yosemite National Park, after 70 years of stocking nonnative fish in various lakes and waterways, park officials realized that indiscriminate stocking had done more harm than good. As a result, according to park officials, the park's waterways have been compromised. Nonnative fish introduced into the park now outnumber native rainbow trout by a 4 to 1 margin. According to park officials, this stocking policy, which continued until 1990, has also resulted in a decline of at least one federally protected species.

Major Factors Contributing to the Current Situation

Since 1985, the Park Service's operating budget has risen from about $627 million to about $972 million—or by about 55 percent. After allowing for inflation, the increase still amounts to about 18 percent. At 11 of the 12 parks we visited, funding increases outpaced inflation from 1985 to 1993. Increases ranged from 5 percent to about 200 percent. However, despite these increases, additional demands on the parks are eroding the Park Service's ability to keep up with the needs for visitor services and resource management.

Many factors influence the level of visitor services and resource management activities. While these factors are not necessarily the same at all parks, our work identified two factors that were common to most of the parks we visited and had a substantial impact on the level of visitor services and resource management activities. These factors were (1) additional operating requirements and (2) increased visitation.

Additional Operating Requirements

Many additional operating requirements are passed on to the parks through federal laws. In many cases, funds are not made available to the parks to cover the entire costs of these requirements. Park managers cited numerous requirements from such laws as the Clean Air Act and the National Environmental Policy Act and from the implementing regulations of the Environmental Protection Agency and the Occupational Safety and Health Administration. Overall, at the 12 parks we visited, park managers cited over 20 different federal laws affecting the parks' operations.

Park managers told us that meeting these requirements meant diverting money from day-to-day park activities. In 1994, for example, Yosemite National Park spent about $100,000 to address the Occupational Safety and Health Administration's regulations and $80,000 to identify and remove hazardous waste. At Glacier National Park, federal requirements for lead paint abatement, asbestos removal, surface water treatment, waste water treatment systems, and accessibility for disabled visitors required park managers to divert operating funds from other park activities. While Glacier's records do not track the total costs associated with meeting these requirements, park officials told us these costs were substantial and significantly eroded the amount of operating funds available for day-to-day park activities. Each park we visited had similar examples. These costs are significant since only about 25 percent of a park's operating budget remains to meet day-to-day park needs after paying salaries and benefits.

Furthermore, because salaries and benefits are such a large portion of the parks' budgets, even small increases in these costs can diminish a park's ability to meet its needs for visitor services and resource management. These costs include expenditures for new law enforcement certification and training requirements for park rangers, increased compensation for rangers, full background checks on law enforcement personnel, cost-of-living increases, and retirement costs. For example, last year at Yosemite National Park the cost of doing routine background checks for park rangers was about $200,000. At Lake Mead, less than half of the cost of the increased compensation for park rangers was met through budget increases, leaving an additional $200,000 to be paid from the park's operating funds.

Increased Visitation

The second factor eroding the parks' operating budgets is the increase in visitation. Eight of the 12 parks showed increases in the number of visitors; the average increase was 27 percent since 1985. The four parks where decreases occurred were small historical parks where visitation averaged less than 200,000 in 1993. These substantial increases in visitation drive up costs for many items that directly support visitor activities, such as waste disposal, general maintenance, road and trail repair, employees' overtime, and utilities. For example, at Lake Mead National Recreation Area, the costs of trash disposal have more than tripled from $47,000 in 1990 to $152,000 last year. As a result, a portion of the increased funding that the parks have received has been spent to cover the costs associated with meeting the needs generated by increased visitation.

Choices Will Be Difficult

... [M]any of the problems we have told you about today are not new. At the same time that visitor services are being cut back and parks are operating without sufficient information on many of their resources, the Park Service faces a multibillion dollar maintenance backlog and, like all federal agencies, increasingly tight budgets. In addition, infrastructure and development needs on the system continue to grow as new units are added—31 since 1984.

Under these circumstances, it is difficult to envision a turnaround in the short term. Dealing with this situation calls for making difficult choices about how parks are funded and managed, some of which may require legislative changes. Our work indicates that these choices, or a combination of them, need to address three areas: (1) the amount of revenue going to the parks, (2) the number of units in the park system, and (3) the extent to which current park operating standards and visitor expectations can or should be revised. In addition, the Park Service needs to look for ways to operate more efficiently and improve accountability to assure that the limited dollars are used most effectively.

While substantial increases in appropriations are not likely in today's tight budget environment, other sources of revenues need to be considered. These could include (1) increasing park fees, such as entrance fees, concession fees, and fees for other in-park services, and allowing parks to retain more of these revenues to address their needs, and (2) encouraging park managers to be more entrepreneurial in addressing their park's needs by entering into partnership arrangements with the private sector or other parties. However, any increase in revenues must be accompanied by improvements in the Park Service's accountability. The need for improved accountability is critical in light of the broad discretion given to individual park managers in determining how to spend operating funds. Park Service officials indicated to us that they plan to improve accountability.

A second choice would be to limit additions to, or perhaps decrease the number of units in the national park system. To the extent that the system is permitted to grow, associated infrastructure and development needs will also grow. As this growth occurs, more park units will be competing for limited federal funding. While certainly not an easy decision, limiting the number of parks, or perhaps even reducing the number until the parks' current conditions can be adequately addressed will help ease the financial pressures now facing the park system. In both the last and current Congress, proposals have been offered that would address this alternative.

A third choice would be to reduce the level of visitor services, as well as visitors' expectations, to more closely match the level of services that can realistically be provided with available resources. The Park Service could, for example, limit operations to fewer hours per day or fewer days per year, limit the number of visitors, or perhaps temporarily close some facilities to public use. We believe that the Park Service should make the choice to provide the public with a lower-quality experience only after developing a carefully thought-out strategy and consulting with the Congress.

Regardless of which of these choices or combination of choices are made, the Park Service needs to look for ways to stretch its limited resources by operating more efficiently. Toward this end, the Park Service has developed a restructuring plan to meet the goals of the first phase of the administration's National Performance Review. However, this restructuring plan is limited primarily to changes that can be accomplished within the Park Service's existing structure. The plan does not address the potential to improve operations through a collaborative approach to land management involving other federal land management agencies. The current fiscal climate demands that federal land management agencies look beyond existing jurisdictional boundaries in their search to reduce costs, increase efficiency, and improve service to the public. Park Service officials told us they are currently working with other land management agencies to improve operations and will continue to do so.

In summary, . . . our work reveals that the future of the parks is at a crossroads. While more people are visiting parks, the services available to these visitors are deteriorating. The Park Service, as the steward for many of the nation's natural and cultural treasures, has a myriad of problems to address ranging from insufficient data on the conditions of resources to an ever increasing maintenance backlog. While the Park Service has recognized its problems and has taken some actions to address them, we believe that because of their magnitude, difficult choices must be made. Unless these choices are made, the Park Service's ability to preserve these treasures for the enjoyment of future generations may be in jeopardy. . . .

EXECUTIVE ORDER ON STRIKING WORKERS
March 8, 1995

In a move that pleased organized labor, President Bill Clinton issued Executive Order 12954 March 8 barring federal contracts worth $100,000 or more with companies that hired permanent replacements for striking workers. At year's end that order was still under attack both in Congress and the federal courts.

Under the executive order, the secretary of labor had two options for dealing with federal contractors found to have hired permanent replacements for strikers. The secretary could terminate the contract. However, if the head of the contracting agency objected to the termination, the contract would continue in force. Alternatively, the labor secretary could debar the contractor, making the company ineligible for future government contracts. The debarment would end once the labor dispute that had caused the initial strike was resolved.

A Top Labor Priority

The ban on the use of permanent replacement workers by federal contractors was a top political priority for organized labor, which had tried unsuccessfully in 1994 to win enactment of legislation that would have barred private companies from permanently replacing striking workers.

Under the National Labor Relations Act of 1935, workers have the right to strike and employers have the option to hire replacements during the walkout. The law did not clearly address the issue of permanent replacements. In 1938 the Supreme Court ruled in the case of National Labor Relations Board v. Mackay Radio and Telegraph *that employees could be replaced permanently if they were striking for economic benefits, such as higher pay, but not if they had walked out over unfair labor practices. The 1994 legislation would have effectively overturned that decision.*

Many labor leaders complained that the Clinton administration had not worked hard enough on passing the ban in 1994. The legislation passed in the House but was killed in the Senate. Organized labor was also angered by the Clinton administration's support for the North America Free Trade Agreement and the extensive revision of the General Agreement on Tariff and Trade. In what was widely seen as an effort by the Democratic administration to mend its political fences with a traditional ally, Vice President Al Gore announced the imminent signing of the executive order at the annual meeting of the AFL-CIO executive committee in Bal Harbour, Florida, on February 20.

The administration said the order was necessary to protect the collective bargaining process by preventing management from firing legally striking workers. In addition, because replacement workers were typically not as well trained as the striking employees, both productivity and quality suffered, the administration said. The order would affect only about 10 percent of all federal procurement contracts, but these contracts—many of them for defense and aerospace needs—accounted for about 90 percent of the funds the government spent on contracts.

Congressional Attempts to Block Order

Although the order did not apply to strikes that did not involve federal contracts, congressional Republicans expressed outrage at the president's action. "Frankly, I'm surprised that the president would attempt to circumvent Congress and impose an executive order that undermines federal labor law," said Sen. Nancy Landon Kassebaum (R-Kan.), chairman of the Labor and Human Resources Committee. "In my view this is a direct challenge to congressional authority."

Kassebaum introduced an amendment in the Senate March 8 that would prohibit the Labor Department from spending any money to enforce the order. Democrats began a filibuster of her measure on March 9, however. On March 15 the Senate fell two votes short of the sixty needed to end the filibuster. Although Senate Majority Leader Bob Dole threatened to hold additional votes on shutting off debate, he changed his mind when it became apparent that those votes also would lose.

In September the Senate Appropriations Committee added a similar amendment to the fiscal 1996 spending bill for the Labor Department. That bill stalled when Senate Democrats again threatened a filibuster over the replacement striker provision and the bill's proposed cuts in numerous social programs. The president had threatened to veto any legislation that overturned his executive order.

Challenge in Federal Court

Separately, a coalition of pro-business groups, including the U.S. Chamber of Commerce and the National Association of Manufacturers, announced March 15 that they had filed suit in U.S. District Court for the District of Columbia to block the directive. The president left "us no alternative but to file this lawsuit," said Jeffrey C. McGuinness, president of the Labor Policy Association. The order "takes away from management the right to defend itself against long-term strikes."

On July 31 U.S. District Judge Gladys Kessler upheld the legality of Clinton's order, but she blocked its enforcement until the issue was resolved by higher courts. She said that she expected the case to be reviewed by the Supreme Court.

Kessler said the president had the authority to issue the order "in his capacity as manager of the federal government's property" but that the government would not sustain great harm if the order were not enforced while her ruling was appealed. In contrast, she said, contractors could suffer significant economic losses if they were forced to choose between hiring replacement workers and getting federal contracts. "Not only will the ability to hire permanent striker replacements have an enduring effect upon the relative bargaining power of employers and the unions representing their workers, but the executive order constitutes a radical departure from long-established prior policy," Kessler wrote. "Preservation of the status quo" for the time being, she said, is in "the public interest."

Following is the text of Executive Order 12954, signed by President Bill Clinton March 8, 1995, barring federal contractors from hiring permanent replacements for striking workers:

Ensuring the Economical and Efficient Administration and Completion of Federal Government Contracts

Efficient economic performance and productivity are directly related to the existence of cooperative working relationships between employers and employees. When Federal contractors become involved in prolonged labor disputes with their employees, the Federal Government's economy, efficiency, and cost of operations are adversely affected. In order to operate as effectively as possible, by receiving timely goods and quality services, the Federal Government must assist the entities with which it has contractual relations to develop stable relationships with their employees.

An important aspect of a stable collective bargaining relationship is the balance between allowing businesses to operate during a strike and preserving worker rights. This balance is disrupted when permanent replacement employees are hired. It has been found that strikes involving permanent replacement workers are longer in duration than other strikes. In addition, the use of permanent replacements can change a limited dispute into a broader, more contentious struggle, thereby exacerbating the problems that initially led to the strike. By permanently replacing its workers, an employer loses the accumulated knowledge, experience, skill, and expertise of its incumbent employees. These circumstances then adversely affect the businesses and entities, such as the Federal Government, which rely on that employer to provide high quality and reliable goods or services.

NOW, THEREFORE, to ensure the economical and efficient administration and completion of Federal Government contracts, and by the authority vested in me as President by the Constitution and the laws of the United States of America, including 40 U.S.C. 486(a) and 3 U.S.C. 301, it is hereby ordered as follows:

Section 1. It is the policy of the executive branch in procuring goods and services that, to ensure the economical and efficient administration and completion of Federal Government contracts, contracting agencies shall not contract with employers that permanently replace lawfully striking employees. All discretion under this Executive order shall be exercised consistent with this policy.

Sec. 2. (a) The Secretary of Labor ("Secretary") may investigate an organizational unit of a Federal contractor to determine whether the unit has permanently replaced lawfully striking workers. Such investigation shall be conducted in accordance with procedures established by the Secretary.

(b) The Secretary shall receive and may investigate complaints by employees of any entity covered under section 2(a) of this order where such complaints allege lawfully striking employees have been permanently replaced.

(c) The Secretary may hold such hearings, public or private, as he or she deems advisable, to determine whether an entity covered under section 2(a) has permanently replaced lawfully striking employees.

Sec. 3. (a) When the Secretary determines that a contractor has permanently replaced lawfully striking employees, the Secretary may make a finding that it is appropriate to terminate the contract for convenience. The Secretary shall transmit that finding to the head of any department or agency that contracts with the contractor.

(b) The head of the contracting department or agency may object to the termination for convenience of a contract or contracts of a contractor determined to have permanently replaced legally striking employees. If the head of the agency so objects, he or she shall set forth the reasons for not terminating the contract or contracts in a response in writing to the Secretary. In such case, the termination for convenience shall not be issued. The head of the contracting agency or department shall report to the Secretary those contracts that have been terminated for convenience under this section.

Sec. 4. (a) When the Secretary determines that a contractor has permanently replaced lawfully striking employees, the Secretary may debar the contractor, thereby making the contractor ineligible to receive government contracts. The Secretary shall notify the Administrator of the General Services Administration of the debarment, and the Administrator shall include the contractor on the consolidated list of debarred contractors. Departments and agencies shall not solicit offers from, award contracts to, or consent to subcontracts with these contractors unless the head of the agency or his or her designee determines, in writing, that there is a compelling reason for such action, in accordance with the Federal Acquisition Regulation.

(b) The scope of the debarment normally will be limited to those organizational units of a Federal contractor that the Secretary finds to have permanently replaced lawfully striking workers.

(c) The period of the debarment may not extend beyond the date when the labor dispute precipitating the permanent replacement of lawfully striking workers has been resolved, as determined by the Secretary.

Sec. 5. The Secretary shall publish or cause to be published, in the *Federal Register,* the names of contractors that have, in the judgment of the Secretary, permanently replaced lawfully striking employees and have been the subject of debarment.

Sec. 6. The Secretary shall be responsible for the administration and enforcement of this order. The Secretary, after consultation with the Secretary of Defense, the Administrator of the General Services, the Administrator of the National Aeronautics and Space Administration, and the Administrator of the Office of Federal Procurement Policy, may adopt such rules and regulations and issue such orders as may be deemed necessary and appropriate to achieve the purposes of this order.

Sec. 7. Each contracting department and agency shall cooperate with the Secretary and provide such information and assistance as the Secretary may require in the performance of the Secretary's functions under this order.

Sec. 8. The Secretary may delegate any function or duty of the Secretary under this order to any officer in the Department of Labor or to any other officer in the executive branch of the Government, with the consent of the head of the department or agency in which that officer serves.

Sec. 9. The Secretary of Defense, the Administrator of the General Services, and the Administrator of the National Aeronautics and Space Administration, after consultation with the Administrator of the Office of Federal Procurement Policy, shall take whatever action is appropriate to implement the provisions of this order and of any related rules, regulations, or orders of the Secretary issued pursuant to this order.

Sec. 10. This order is not intended, and should not be construed, to create any right or benefit, substantive or procedural, enforceable at law by a party against the United States, its agencies, its officers, or its employees. This order is not intended, however, to preclude judicial review of final agency decisions in accordance with the Administrative Procedure Act, 5 U.S.C. 701 *et seq.*

Sec. 11. The meaning of the term "organizational unit of a Federal contractor" as used in this order shall be defined in regulations that shall be issued by the Secretary of Labor, in consultation with affected agencies. This order shall apply only to contracts in excess of the Simplified Acquisition Threshold.

Sec. 12. (a) The provisions of section 3 of this order shall only apply to situations in which contractors have permanently replaced lawfully striking employees after the effective date of this order.

(b) This order is effective immediately.

WILLIAM J. CLINTON
The White House,
March 8, 1995.

UN SUMMIT ON POVERTY
March 12, 1995

In what was thought to be the largest gathering of its type in history, some 120 world leaders and 13,000 other delegates met in Copenhagen, Denmark, for six days in March at a United Nations summit on eliminating poverty worldwide. Although the aims of the World Summit for Social Development were lofty, the final declaration, endorsed by the world leaders on March 12, was short on specific actions. "There is a lot of good language but very little substance," one participant told the Washington Post.

No one disagreed on the extent of the problem. Some 1.3 billion people—one-fifth of the world's population—are impoverished. Nearly three-quarters of those people are women. One of every ten people cannot find work at a living wage; two-fifths of all women living in rural areas are not paid at all for the work they do. Between 13 million and 18 million people die every year of causes related to poverty. Two million children die annually of preventable infectious diseases. Eight million children in the world do not attend primary school. Civil wars, overpopulation, and other factors have driven people to migrate both within and between countries, displacing them from their land and their jobs.

Few Specifics on Aid

The summit produced little agreement on specific actions to alleviate these global problems. One of the most promising proposals was the "20/20" plan, in which countries that donated aid would earmark 20 percent of those funds for education, health, and other human welfare programs, while recipient countries would target 20 percent of their budgets on the same programs. Most developing nations now spend far less than that amount on such programs.

Donor countries, which have seen a great deal of past aid squandered on corruption and ineffective programs, wanted recipient governments to make visible strides toward ending corruption and giving their people basic human rights before embarking on new aid programs. They insisted on retaining control over how any aid is used. Developing countries said those conditions are an intrusion into their internal affairs, and they asked for outright cancellation of debt and more aid with few or no strings attached. Thus, the final declaration urged, but did not compel, countries to adopt the 20/20 plan.

The declaration urged lender countries to consider writing off or reducing debt owed them by the poorest countries, and asked international lending organizations such as the World Bank and the International Monetary Fund to look for ways to reduce debt and "develop techniques of debt conversion applied to social development" programs. During the conference, Denmark announced that it was canceling about $200 million in debt owed it by six poor nations—Angola, Egypt, Ghana, and Zimbabwe in Africa and Bolivia and Nicaragua in Latin America. Austria subsequently announced that it would forgive $100 million owed it by several poor countries.

While a consensus seemed to be developing that some debt held by very poor countries should be forgiven, questions remained about how much to cancel and whether poor countries should be required to do anything in exchange. Mahbub-ul Haq, a special adviser to the administrator of the United Nations Development Program, told the New York Times *that countries should be required to spend every dollar of canceled debt on social programs and to reduce spending on defense by the same amount. "It would be tragic if debts are canceled in the name of the poor and the resources saved were then wasted on the military or on irrelevant projects," he said.*

Although the declaration repeatedly referred to the need for increased aid, simply maintaining current levels of aid was likely to be difficult for some industrial nations, including the United States, that were experiencing not only constrained budgets but also strong political pressure to reduce aid levels. Speaking to the assembly on March 12, the final day of the conference, Vice President Al Gore said he thought the Republicans would fail in their efforts to force the United States to "step back from the front ranks of nations that recognize a bond of shared responsibility toward men and women elsewhere in the world." He stressed that recipient nations must not waste their aid money but use it to help generate their own development through free market economies. "In our view," the vice president said, "only the market system unlocks a higher fraction of the human potential than any other form of economic organization and has the demonstrated potential to create broadly distributed new wealth."

One proposal for raising funds to help alleviate poverty, offered by American economist James Tobin and supported by President François Mitterrand of France, would tax speculative international currency transactions. According to UN officials, a tax of 0.05 percent on short-term currency transactions could generate $150 billion a year.

Weak Outcome Decried

Few expected the conference to produce much more than the general statement it came up with. At the opening speeches on March 6, UN Gen-

*eral Secretary Boutros Boutros-Ghali warned that "you will not have pro-
found change here because the international community will not be ready
for it." Some participants put an optimistic gloss on the conference, suggesting that if no concrete actions had been taken, at least some attitudes
were beginning to change and to move in the right direction. "We have
everybody now thinking about doing a better job with existing resources
rather than always talking about adding more money to the pot," said Timothy Wirth, U.S. undersecretary of state for global affairs.*

*Such sentiments were not enough for many representatives of private
aid groups, charities, and other nongovernmental organizations who met
simultaneously in Copenhagen and believed that governments needed to
take more concrete steps to alleviate poverty. "The poor can't eat promises," Earthaction, a coalition of hundreds of citizens groups in 129 countries, said in a statement. "If the world's governments can't even agree on
the most modest proposals for meeting the basic needs of the citizens, then
why are they here at all?" Others criticized the conference, which was
three years in the making and cost $30 million, as a waste of both time
and money.*

*The poverty conference was the first of two world gatherings the United
Nations hosted in 1995 aimed at improving social welfare throughout the
world; the second was a summit on women's rights, held in Beijing in September. In 1994 the UN sponsored a conference in Cairo on stabilizing the
world's population, and in 1990 it held a conference in Rio de Janeiro to
find cures for world environmental ills.* (Women's rights, p. 581; world population, Historic Documents of 1994, p. 351; earth summit, Historic Documents of 1992, p. 499)

> *Following are excerpts of the "Declaration and Programme of
> Action" endorsed March 12, 1995, by world leaders attending
> the UN World Summit for Social Development in Copenhagen,
> Denmark:*

[Introduction and Part A omitted]

B. Principles and goals

25. We Heads of State and Government are committed to a political, economic, ethical and spiritual vision for social development based on human
dignity, human rights, equality, respect, peace, democracy, mutual responsibility and cooperation, and full respect for the various religious and ethical
values and cultural backgrounds of people. Accordingly, we will give the
highest priority in national, regional and international policies and actions to
the promotion of social progress, justice and the betterment of the human
condition, based on full participation by all.

26. To this end we will create a framework for action to:

(a) Place people at the centre of development and direct our economies to
meet human needs more effectively;

(b) Fulfil our responsibility for present and future generations by ensuring equity among generations, and protecting the integrity and sustainable use of our environment;

(c) Recognize that, while social development is a national responsibility, it cannot be successfully achieved without the collective commitment and efforts of the international community;

(d) Integrate economic, cultural and social policies so that they become mutually supportive, and acknowledge the interdependence of public and private spheres of activity;

(e) Recognize that the achievement of sustained social development requires sound, broadly based economic policies;

(f) Promote democracy, human dignity, social justice and solidarity at the national, regional and international levels; ensure tolerance, non-violence, pluralism and non-discrimination in full respect of diversity within and among societies;

(g) Promote the equitable distribution of income and greater access to resources through equity and equality of opportunity for all;

(h) Recognize the family as the basic unit of society and acknowledge that it plays a key role in social development and as such should be strengthened, with attention to the rights, capabilities and responsibilities of its members. In different cultural, political and social systems various forms of family exist. It is entitled to receive comprehensive protection and support;

(i) Ensure that disadvantaged and vulnerable persons and groups are included in social development, and that society acknowledges and responds to the consequences of disability by securing the legal rights of the individual and by making the physical and social environment accessible;

(j) Promote universal respect for, and observance and protection of, all human rights and fundamental freedoms for all, including the right to development; promote the effective exercise of rights and the discharge of responsibilities at all levels of society; promote equality and equity between women and men; protect the rights of children and youth; and promote the strengthening of social integration and civil society;

(k) Reaffirm the right of self-determination of all peoples under colonial or other forms of alien domination or foreign occupation, and the importance of the effective realization of this right, as enunciated, inter alia, in the Vienna Declaration and Programme of Action adopted at the World Conference on Human Rights;

(l) Support progress and security for people and communities whereby every member of society is enabled to satisfy basic human needs and to realize his or her personal dignity, safety and creativity;

(m) Recognize and support indigenous people in their pursuit of economic and social development with full respect for their identity, traditions, forms of social organization and cultural values;

(n) Underline the importance of transparent and accountable governance and administration in all public and private national and international institutions;

(o) Recognize that empowering people, particularly women, to strengthen their own capacities is a main objective of development and its principal resource. Empowerment requires the full participation of people in the formulation, implementation and evaluation of decisions determining the functioning and well-being of our societies;

(p) Assert the universality of social development, and outline a new and strengthened approach to social development, with a renewed impetus for international cooperation and partnership;

(q) Improve the possibility of older persons achieving a better life;

(r) Recognize that the new information technologies and new approaches to the access to and use of technologies by people living in poverty can help in fulfilling social development goals; and therefore recognize the need to facilitate access to such technologies;

(s) Strengthen policies and programmes that improve, ensure and broaden the participation of women in all spheres of political, economic, social and cultural life, as equal partners, and improve their access to all resources needed for the full exercise of their fundamental rights;

(t) Create the political, legal, material and social conditions that allow for the voluntary repatriation of refugees in safety and dignity to their countries of origin, and the voluntary and safe return of internally displaced persons to their places of origin and their smooth reintegration into their societies;

(u) Emphasize the importance of the return of all prisoners of war, persons missing in action and hostages to their families, in accordance with international conventions, in order to reach full social development.

27. We acknowledge that it is the primary responsibility of States to attain these goals. We also acknowledge that these goals cannot be achieved by States alone. The international community, the United Nations, the multilateral financial institutions, all regional organizations and local authorities, and all actors of civil society need to positively contribute their own share of efforts and resources in order to reduce inequalities among people and narrow the gap between developed and developing countries in a global effort to reduce social tensions, and to create greater social and economic stability and security. Radical political, social and economic changes in the countries with economies in transition have been accompanied by a deterioration in their economic and social situation. We invite all people to express their personal commitment to enhancing the human condition through concrete actions in their own fields of activities and through assuming specific civic responsibilities.

C. Commitments

28. Our global drive for social development and the recommendations for action contained in the Programme of Action are made in a spirit of consensus and international cooperation, in full conformity with the purposes and principles of the Charter of the United Nations, recognizing that the formulation and implementation of strategies, policies, programmes and actions for social development are the responsibility of each country and should take

into account the economic, environmental and social diversity of conditions in each country, with full respect for the various religious and ethical values, cultural backgrounds and philosophical convictions of its people, and in conformity with all human rights and fundamental freedoms. In this context, international cooperation is essential for the full implementation of the social development programmes and actions.

29. On the basis of our common pursuit of social development, which aims at social justice, solidarity, harmony and equality within and among countries, in full respect for national sovereignty and territorial integrity, as well as policy objectives, development priorities and religious and cultural diversity, and full respect for all human rights and fundamental freedoms, we launch a global drive for social progress and development embodied in the following commitments.

Commitment 1

We commit ourselves to create an economic, political, social, cultural and legal environment that will enable people to achieve social development. . . .

Commitment 2

We commit ourselves to the goal of eradicating poverty in the world, through decisive national actions and international cooperation, as an ethical, social, political and economic imperative of humankind. . . .

Commitment 3

We commit ourselves to promoting the goal of full employment as a basic priority of our economic and social policies, and to enabling all men and women to attain secure and sustainable livelihoods through freely chosen productive employment and work. . . .

Commitment 4

We commit ourselves to promoting social integration by fostering societies that are stable, safe and just and based on the promotion and protection of all human rights, and on non-discrimination, tolerance, respect for diversity, equality of opportunity, solidarity, security and participation of all people, including disadvantaged and vulnerable groups and persons. . . .

Commitment 5

We commit ourselves to promoting full respect for human dignity and to achieving equality and equity between women and men, and to recognizing and enhancing the participation and leadership roles of women in political, civil, economic, social and cultural life and in development. . . .

Commitment 6

We commit ourselves to promoting and attaining the goals of universal and equitable access to quality education, the highest attainable standard of physical and mental health and the access of all to primary health care, making particular efforts to rectify inequalities relating to social conditions and without distinction as to race, national origin, gender, age or disability; respecting and promoting our common and particular cultures; striving to strengthen the role of culture in development; preserving the essential bases of people-centered sustainable development and contributing to the full development of human resources and to social development. The purpose of these activities is to eradicate poverty, promote full and productive employment and foster social integration. . . .

Commitment 7

We commit ourselves to accelerating the economic, social and human resource development of Africa and the least developed countries. . . .

Commitment 8

We commit ourselves to ensuring that when structural adjustment programmes are agreed to, they include social development goals, in particular eradicating poverty, promoting full and productive employment and enhancing social integration. . . .

Commitment 9

We commit ourselves to increase significantly and/or utilize more efficiently the resources allocated to social development in order to achieve the goals of the Summit through national action and regional and international cooperation. . . .

Commitment 10

We commit ourselves to an improved and strengthened framework for international, regional and subregional cooperation for social development, in a spirit of partnership, through the United Nations and other multilateral institutions. . . .

CLINTON ON UNFUNDED
MANDATES LEGISLATION
March 22, 1995

President Bill Clinton on March 22 signed into law legislation that would curb Congress's ability to impose costly new regulatory programs on state and local governments without providing federal funds to carry them out. The measure was a key victory for congressional Republicans, who hailed it as a first important step toward shifting power from Washington to state and local governments. It was also welcomed by governors and mayors, who had long complained that Congress's penchant for telling the states and local governments what to do without paying for it cost them billions of dollars and diverted money from other high-priority programs.

"This bill is another acknowledgement that Washington doesn't necessarily have all the answers, that we have to continue to push decision-making down to the local level, and we shouldn't make the work of governing at the local level any harder than the circumstances of the time already ensure that it will be," the president told legislators, governors, and mayors attending the bill-signing ceremony at the White House.

As budget constraints grew tighter and tighter during the 1980s, the Democratic Congress pushed more of the costs of complying with federal programs onto to states and localities. The Congressional Budget Office (CBO) estimated that these so-called unfunded federal mandates cost between $8.9 billion and $12.7 billion from 1983 to 1990. Programs imposing costs on local governments and businesses ranged from making voting registration easier to requiring a waiting period for purchasing handguns to removing asbestos from schools. Governors particularly complained about expanded eligibility and new requirements for Medicaid, which is funded in part by the federal government and in part by the states, while local governments complained about costly water pollution regulations.

During the 1994 election campaign, House Republican candidates pledged in the Contract with America to push for an outright ban on unfunded mandates. "This bill will restore state and local governments to their true places as partners in our federal system," Rep. William F. Clinger (R-Pa.) said.

The New Procedure

Under the new legislation, the CBO would be required to estimate the costs of bills, amendments, and conference reports that would impose regulations without providing the funds to pay for them. For those unfunded mandates that would cost state and local governments more than $50 million or the private sector more than $100 million, any member in either chamber could try to block consideration of the bill by raising a point of order. Supporters of the unfunded mandate would then have to win a majority vote to waive the point of order before any further action could be taken on the bill. Sponsors of the point-of-order procedure were betting that most committees would not draft legislation that did not pay for itself and that most legislators, wary of political backlash, would not vote for such unfunded mandates.

The point-of-order procedure had some built-in limitations. It applied only to new mandates. Laws dealing with antidiscrimination, national security, and emergency relief were exempt, as were requirements states and localities must meet as a condition of receiving federal funding. To reach already enacted mandates, the new law directed the Advisory Commission on Intergovernmental Relations (ACIR), an independent executive agency that deals with federalism issues, to make recommendations on paring back existing mandates.

Delayed Passage

The unfunded mandates legislation was one of the first measures considered by the new 104th Congress, as Republicans took over leadership in both chambers in January 1995. The bill had wide bipartisan support—60 cosponsors in the Senate and 168 in the House from both parties—and had been expected to pass quickly. However, debate stalled in both chambers as Democrats used the legislation as a vehicle to show the Republicans that they could not be ignored in the legislative process. Both chambers eventually passed the measure by overwhelming margins, but the political posturing set the tone of the congressional debate for much of the rest of the year.

Liberal Democrats in both chambers charged that the mandates legislation was really an indirect assault on laws that protected the environment, fair labor practices, children, and welfare recipients. Their efforts to exempt such laws from coverage under the legislation failed. For their part, conservatives said the final bill did not go far enough. Sen. Phil Gramm of Texas, a candidate for the Republican presidential nomination, said he might try to amend the bill in the future so that a three-fifths majority of Congress, rather than a simply majority, would be required to impose an unfunded mandate.

Conservatives were also concerned that the terms of the exemptions contained in the law would still allow Congress to impose unfunded mandates.

According to the ACIR, only nine of twenty-seven mandates that Congress enacted between 1981 and 1990, most of them environmental laws, would have been covered under the unfunded mandate law. The eighteen others either prohibited discrimination, such as the Americans with Disabilities Act, or set certain requirements as a condition for receiving federal funding. "I do not think any of us know what the effects [of the legislation] ultimately will be," said former Democratic majority leader Sen. Robert C. Byrd of West Virginia, who opposed the bill.

Following are excerpts of the text of President Bill Clinton's remarks as he signed the unfunded mandates legislation (S 1–PL 104–2) on March 22, 1995, at the White House:

... I had the privilege in 1989—he may not remember this—of having dinner in Chicago with Mayor [Richard] Daley, just a couple of weeks after he took office. I learned that night somewhere between salad and the main course, just how much Mayor Daley hated unfunded mandates. (Laughter.)...

I share these concerns, having served as a governor for a dozen years and witnessed the growth of many of the unfair burdens that unfunded mandates impose. Shortly after I became president I signed an executive order to prohibit federal agencies from imposing non-statutory unfunded mandates on state and local governments without full consultations first....

This bill today extends that discipline to Congress, and I applaud Congress for passing it. It for the first time limits the ability of Congress to pass laws which impose unfunded mandates on state, county, local governments and tribal governments. Having been there as a governor, I know this bill will make a big difference in the lives of our people.

We've made important progress this year in reforming government already. The Congress passed a bill which I was proud to sign which requires Congress to live by the laws it imposes on the private sector. Now, this unfunded mandates law will be another model for how we have to continue to change the way Washington does business. The best ideas and the most important work that affect the public interest are often done a long way away from Washington. This bill is another acknowledgment that Washington doesn't necessarily have all the answers, that we have to continue to push decision-making down to the local level, and we shouldn't make the work of governing at the local level any harder than the circumstances of the time already ensure that it will be.

The other thing that this bill shows is that Republicans and Democrats can come together and break gridlock and do what the American people expect us to do. For all of you who are part of that cooperative effort and especially for the members of the Congress, I thank you.

This is spring and the roses are about to bloom here in the Rose Garden. This is a new beginning and a time for a new spirit of cooperation. I hope the Congress will move on from this to first pass the line-item veto so we can bring more real discipline to our spending process, and then to pass welfare reform that promotes work and responsible parenting and tough child support enforcement. We have got to build a true partnership with the American people, with a government that gets rid of what's unnecessary for today and tomorrow, and does what we have to do in a limited but effective way. We're trying to do that in reducing the deficit, the size of the federal government, reducing the burden of unnecessary regulation. This bill will make a real start.

Listen to this: Before 1964 the number of explicit mandates from the Congress on state and local governments was zero; but according to the National Performance Review, on the day I took office there were at least 172 separate pieces of legislation that imposed requirements on state and local government. The Congressional Budget Office estimates the cost to states and localities of all the regulations imposed just between 1983 and 1990 is between $8.9 and $12.7 billion.

After today, this should stop. This bill requires Congress to show how much mandates over $50 million per year will cost state and local governments, to require Congress to identify a specific funding source for these mandates, and if it does not meet these criteria, Congress must explicitly waive the requirement that there be no unfunded mandate, something which I think will become increasingly rare with the passage of this law.

You know our founders gave us strong guiding principles about how our governments ought to work, and they trusted us in every generation to reinvigorate the partnership they created with such wisdom so long ago. For 200 years we've had to do that over and over and over, and about once a generation we have to make some really big changes in the way we work together as a people—citizens in their private lives, local governments, state governments, and our government here in Washington.

Today we are making history. We are working to find the right balance for the 21st century. We are recognizing that the pendulum had swung too far and that we have to rely on the initiative, the creativity, the determination and the decision-making of people at the state and local level to carry much of the load for America as we move into the 21st century.

This bill will help to keep the American dream alive and help to keep our country strong. Every member of Congress here who voted for it, and every one who is not here, deserves the thanks of the American people. And all of you from all over America who are here, from the cities, from the county operations, from the state legislatures, the state governments, we are all in your debt, I thank you, and I am honored to sign this bill.

Thank you.

PAPAL ENCYCLICAL ON
A 'CULTURE OF DEATH'
MARCH 30, 1995

In a papal encyclical released to the public on March 30, Pope John Paul II warned against a "culture of death" that he said was gripping modern society, making it "increasingly difficult" for individuals "to distinguish between good and evil in what concerns the basic value of human life." Entitled Evangelium Vitae, *or* Gospel of Life, *the papal message painted a grim picture of a sinister world, where a multiplicity of social problems combine with hedonism, technology, and a desire for efficiency to unleash a "conspiracy against life."*

This conspiracy is fostered, the pope wrote, at the political and governmental levels where the will of the majority can deny "the inalienable right to life" through laws permitting abortion, euthanasia, experimentation with human embryos, capital punishment, and other kinds of death. "In this way," John Paul wrote, "democracy, contradicting its own principles, effectively moves toward a form of totalitarianism."

In espousing a "culture of life," the pontiff reaffirmed the Roman Catholic Church's opposition to contraception; condemned abortion and euthanasia in the strongest terms, calling them "crimes which no human law can claim to legitimize"; and said that capital punishment was permissible only in rare instances.

The Gospel of Life, *the eleventh encyclical of John Paul's pontificate, was written at the request of the church's cardinals at a meeting in Rome in 1991. An encyclical is a pope's most authoritative form of doctrinal instruction. The pope's last encyclical, on moral theology, was issued in 1993.* (Papal encyclical, Historic Documents of 1993, p. 843)

The papal message was expected to create even more pressure and controversy among the world's nearly one billion Catholics, many of whom questioned or disregarded the church's teachings on such issues as contraception and abortion. "The Pope is affirming that this is the teaching of the church and that means it binds all Catholics," Bishop James T. McHugh of Camden, New Jersey, said. "It makes it increasingly impossible for public citizens or public officials or theologians to say, 'I have some reservations about this teaching.'"

Condemnation of Abortion

No reservations were apparent in the Pope's message to heed in virtually all ways the commandment "thou shalt not kill." "I declare that direct abortion, that is, abortion willed as an end or a means, always constitutes a grave moral disorder, since it is the deliberate killing of an innocent human being," the pope said. Responsibility for the crime of abortion lies with the mother, the pope said, even when she terminates the pregnancy "to protect certain important values such as her own health or a decent standard of living for the other members of her family." Also at fault are those who have directly or indirectly encouraged the abortion or assisted with it, including the father, doctors, nurses, legislators who voted to make the procedure legal, those who have helped spread an "attitude of sexual permissiveness," and international organizations that "systematically campaign for legalization and spread of abortion in the world."

The same rationale also extended to experimentation with human embryos and in vitro fertilization, John Paul said, because those procedures resulted in the death of at least some embryos. The pope said that certain prenatal diagnostic techniques, such as amniocentesis, were permissible if they did not involve undue risk to the child and mother and were not used to advance "selective abortion" of fetuses shown to have birth defects.

Euthanasia: A False Mercy

The pope defined euthanasia as "an action or omission which of itself and by intention causes death, with the purpose of eliminating all suffering" and declared that it was not a humane act but "one of the more alarming symptoms of the 'culture of death.'" This culture, which was gaining ground in the more advanced industrial countries, was "marked by an attitude of excessive preoccupation with efficiency, . . . which sees the growing number of elderly and disabled people as intolerable and too burdensome." True compassion, the pope said, "leads to sharing another's pain; it does not kill the person whose suffering we cannot bear."

It was permissible, the pontiff said, to refuse "extraordinary or disproportionate" medical treatment in the face of imminent and inevitable death. Such a refusal was neither euthanasia nor suicide but "an acceptance of the human condition in the face of death."

The Death Penalty and Unjust Laws

In the only significant shift in Catholic doctrine, the pope took a firmer stand against capital punishment, declaring that execution should be used only in "cases of absolute necessity," which, the pope said, "are very rare." The church formerly had held that capital punishment was permissible in some cases to protect society. Joseph Cardinal Ratzinger, head of the Vati-

can Congregation for the Doctrine of Faith, told a news conference that the pope's statements on the death penalty were "a real development" of Catholic teaching.

The pope asked Roman Catholics and others to resist laws that violated what he called the fundamental right to human life. "No circumstance, no purpose, no law whatsoever can ever make licit an act which is intrinsically illicit. . . . Christians, like all people of good will, are called upon under grave obligation of conscience not to cooperate formally in practices which, even if permitted by civil legislation, are contrary to God's law," he wrote. Doctors, other health care personnel, and the directors of hospitals, clinics, and convalescent care facilities should be protected against legal and financial retaliation for refusing to take part in abortions or euthanasia, the pope said.

The pope also explicitly sanctioned legislators publicly opposed to abortion to vote for measures that restricted abortion without banning it outright. Such a vote would "not represent an illicit cooperation with an unjust law," the pope said, "but rather a legitimate and proper attempt to limit its evil aspects."

Following are excerpts from Pope John Paul II's papal encyclical, Evangelium Vitae (Gospel of Life), released by the Vatican March 30, 1995, and provided in English translation by the Catholic News Service in Washington, D.C.:

. . . Every individual, precisely by reason of the mystery of the Word of God who was made of flesh, is entrusted to the maternal care of the church. Therefore every threat to human dignity and life must necessarily be felt in the church's very heart; it cannot but affect her at the core of her faith in the redemptive incarnation of the Son of God, and engage her in her mission of proclaiming the Gospel of life in all the world and to every creature.

Today this proclamation is especially pressing because of the extraordinary increase and gravity of threats to the life of individuals and peoples, especially where life is weak and defenseless. In addition to the ancient scourges of poverty, hunger, endemic diseases, violence and war, new threats are emerging on an alarmingly vast scale.

The Second Vatican Council, in a passage which retains all its relevance today, forcefully condemned a number of crimes and attacks against human life. Thirty years later, taking up the words of the council and with the same forcefulness, I repeat that condemnation in the name of the whole church, certain that I am interpreting the genuine sentiment of every upright conscience:

"Whatever is opposed to life itself such as any type of murder, genocide, abortion, euthanasia or willful self-destruction; whatever violates the integrity of the human person such as mutilation, torments inflicted on body or mind, attempts to coerce the will itself; whatever insults human dignity such as subhuman living conditions, arbitrary imprisonment, deportation, slavery, prostitution, the selling of women and children, as well as disgraceful working conditions, where people are treated as mere instruments of gain rather than as free and responsible persons: All these things and others like them are infamies indeed. They poison human society, and they do more harm to those who practice them than to those who suffer from the injury. Moreover, they are a supreme dishonor to the Creator."

Unfortunately, this disturbing state of affairs, far from decreasing, is expanding: With the new prospects opened up by scientific and technological progress there arise new forms of attacks on the dignity of the human being. At the same time a new cultural climate is developing and taking hold which gives crimes against life a new and—if possible—even more sinister character, giving rise to further grave concern: Broad sectors of public opinion justify certain crimes against life in the name of the rights of individual freedom, and on this basis they claim not only exemption from punishment but even authorization by the state, so that these things can be done with total freedom and indeed with the free assistance of health-care systems.

All this is causing a profound change in the way in which life and relationships between people are considered. The fact that legislation in many countries, perhaps even departing from basic principles of their constitutions, has determined not to punish these practices against life, and even to make them altogether legal, is both a disturbing symptom and a significant cause of grave moral decline. Choices once unanimously considered criminal and rejected by the common moral sense are gradually becoming socially acceptable. Even certain sectors of the medical profession, which by its calling is directed to the defense and care of human life, are increasingly willing to carry out these acts against the person. In this way the very nature of the medical profession is distorted and contradicted, and the dignity of those who practice it is degraded. In such a cultural and legislative situation, the serious demographic, social and family problems which weigh upon many of the world's peoples and which require responsible and effective attention from national and international bodies are left open to false and deceptive solutions opposed to the truth and the good of persons and nations.

The end result of this is tragic: Not only is the fact of the destruction of so many human lives still to be born or in their final stage extremely grave and disturbing, but no less grave and disturbing is the fact that conscience itself, darkened as it were by such widespread conditioning, is finding it increasingly difficult to distinguish between good and evil in what concerns the basic value of human life. . . .

[Strong Against Weak]

Here . . . we shall concentrate particular attention on another category of attacks affecting life in its earliest and in its final stages, attacks which present new characteristics with respect to the past and which raise questions of extraordinary seriousness. It is not only that in generalized opinion these attacks tend no longer to be considered as "crimes"; paradoxically they assume the nature of "rights," to the point that the state is called upon to give them legal recognition and to make them available through the free services of health-care personnel. Such attacks strike human life at the time of its greatest frailty, when it lacks any means of self-defense. Even more serious is the fact that most often those attacks are carried out in the very heart of and with the complicity of the family—the family, which by its nature is called to be the "sanctuary of life.". . .

. . . [W]hile the climate of widespread moral uncertainty can in some way be explained by the multiplicity and gravity of today's social problems, and these can sometimes mitigate the subjective responsibility of individuals, it is no less true that we are confronted by an even larger reality, which can be described as a veritable structure of sin. This reality is characterized by the emergence of a culture which denies solidarity and in many cases takes the form of a veritable "culture of death." This culture is actively fostered by powerful cultural, economic and political currents which encourage an idea of society excessively concerned with efficiency. Looking at the situation from this point of view, it is possible to speak in a certain sense of a war of the powerful against the weak: A life which would require greater acceptance, love and care is considered useless or held to be an intolerable burden, and is therefore rejected in one way or another. A person who, because of illness, handicap or, more simply, just by existing, compromises the well-being or lifestyle of those who are more favored tends to be looked upon as an enemy to be resisted or eliminated. In this way a kind of "conspiracy against life" is unleashed. This conspiracy involves not only group relationships, but goes far beyond, to the point of damaging and distorting at the international level relations between peoples and states. . . .

. . . [D]espite their differences of nature and moral gravity, contraception and abortion are often closely connected, as fruits of the same tree. It is true that in many cases contraception and even abortion are practiced under the pressure of real-life difficulties, which nonetheless can never exonerate from striving to observe God's law fully. Still, in very many other instances such practices are rooted in a hedonistic mentality unwilling to accept responsibility in matters of sexuality, and they imply a self-centered concept of freedom, which regards procreation as an obstacle to personal fulfillment. The life which could result from a sexual encounter thus becomes an enemy to be avoided at all costs, and abortion becomes the only possible decisive response to failed contraception.

The close connection which exists in mentality between the practice of contraception and that of abortion is becoming increasingly obvious. It is being demonstrated in an alarming way by the development of chemical products, intrauterine devices and vaccines which, distributed with the same ease as contraceptives, really act as abortifacients in the very early stages of the development of the life of the new human being.

The various techniques of artificial reproduction, which would seem to be at the service of life and which are frequently used with this intention, actually open the door to new threats against life. Apart from the fact that they are morally unacceptable since they separate procreation from the fully human context of the conjugal act, these techniques have a high rate of failure: not just failure in relation to fertilization, but with regard to the subsequent development of the embryo, which is exposed to the risk of death, generally within a very short space of time. Furthermore, the number of embryos produced is often greater than that needed for implantation in the woman's womb, and these so-called "spare embryos" are then destroyed or used for research which, under the pretext of scientific or medical progress, in fact reduces human life to the level of simple "biological material" to be freely disposed of.

Prenatal diagnosis, which presents no moral objections if carried out in order to identify the medical treatment which may be needed by the child in the womb, all too often becomes an opportunity for proposing and procuring an abortion. This is eugenic abortion, justified in public opinion on the basis of a mentality—mistakenly held to be consistent with the demands of "therapeutic interventions"—which accepts life only under certain conditions and rejects it when it is affected by any limitation, handicap or illness.

Following this same logic, the point has been reached where the most basic care, even nourishment, is denied to babies born with serious handicaps or illnesses. The contemporary scene, moreover, is becoming even more alarming by reason of the proposals advanced here and there to justify even infanticide, following the same arguments used to justify the right to abortion. In this way we revert to a state of barbarism which one hoped had been left behind forever.

Threats which are no less serious hang over the incurably ill and the dying. In a social and cultural context which makes it more difficult to face and accept suffering, the temptation becomes all the greater to resolve the problem of suffering by eliminating it at the root, by hastening death so that it occurs at the moment considered most suitable.

Various considerations usually contribute to such a decision, all of which converge in the same terrible outcome. In the sick person the sense of anguish, of severe discomfort and even of desperation brought on by intense and prolonged suffering can be a decisive factor. Such a situation can threaten the already fragile equilibrium of an individual's personal and family life, with the result that, on the one hand, the sick person, despite the help of increasingly effective medical and social assistance, risks feeling overwhelmed by his or her own frailty; and on the other hand, those close to the sick person can be moved by an understandable, even if misplaced, compassion. All this is aggravated by a cultural climate which fails to perceive any meaning or value in suffering, but rather considers suffering the epitome of evil, to be eliminated at all costs. This is especially the case in the absence of a religious outlook which could help to provide a positive understanding of the mystery of suffering.

On a more general level, there exists in contemporary culture a certain Promethean attitude which leads people to think that they can control life and death by taking the decisions about them into their own hands. What really happens in this case is that the individual is overcome and crushed by a death deprived of any prospect of meaning or hope. We see a tragic expression of all this in the spread of euthanasia—disguised and surreptitious or practiced openly and even legally. As well as for reasons of a misguided pity at the sight of the patient's suffering, euthanasia is sometimes justified by the utilitarian motive of avoiding costs which bring no return and which weigh heavily on society. Thus it is proposed to eliminate malformed babies, the severely handicapped, the disabled, the elderly, especially when they are not self-sufficient, and the terminally ill. Nor can we remain silent in the face of other more furtive, but no less serious and real forms of euthanasia. These could occur, for example, when, in order to increase the availability of organs for transplants, organs are removed without respecting objective and adequate criteria which verify the death of the donor.

Another present-day phenomenon, frequently used to justify threats and attacks against life, is the demographic question. This question arises in different ways in different parts of the world. In the rich and developed countries there is a disturbing decline or collapse of the birthrate. The poorer countries, on the other hand, generally have a high rate of population growth, difficult to sustain in the context of low economic and social development, and especially where there is extreme underdevelopment. In the face of overpopulation in the poorer countries, instead of forms of global intervention at the international level—serious family and social policies, programs of cultural development and of fair production and distribution of resources—anti-birth policies continue to be enacted.

Contraception, sterilization and abortion are certainly part of the reason why in some cases there is a sharp decline in the birthrate. It is not difficult to be tempted to use the same methods and attacks against life also where there is a situation of "demographic explosion.". . .

Decisions that go against life sometimes arise from difficult or even tragic situations of profound suffering, loneliness, a total lack of economic prospects, depression and anxiety about the future. Such circumstances can mitigate even to a notable degree subjective responsibility and the consequent culpability of those who make these choices, which in themselves are evil. But today the problem goes far beyond the necessary recognition of these personal situations. It is a problem which exists at the cultural, social and political level, where it reveals its more sinister and disturbing aspect in the tendency, ever more widely shared, to interpret the above crimes against life as legitimate expressions of individual freedom, to be acknowledged and protected as actual rights.

In this way, and with tragic consequences, a long historical process is reaching a turning point. The process which once led to discovering the idea of "human rights"—rights inherent in every person and prior to any constitution and state legislation—is today marked by a surprising contradiction. Precisely in an age when the inviolable rights of the person are solemnly proclaimed and the value of life is publicly affirmed, the very right to life is being denied or trampled upon, especially at the more significant moments of existence: the moment of birth and the moment of death. . . .

In seeking the deepest roots of the struggle between the "culture of life" and the "culture of death," we cannot restrict ourselves to the perverse idea of freedom mentioned above. We have to go to the heart of the tragedy being experienced by modern man: the eclipse of the sense of God and of man, typical of a social and cultural climate dominated by secularism, which with its ubiquitous tentacles succeeds at times in putting Christian communities themselves to the test. Those who allow themselves to be influenced by this climate easily fall into a sad, vicious circle: When the sense of God is lost, there is also a tendency to lose the sense of man, of his dignity and his life; in turn, the systematic violation of the moral law, especially in the serious matter of respect for human life and its dignity, produces a kind of progressive darkening of the capacity to discern God's living and saving presence. . . .

God's Holy Law

"And behold, one came up to him, saying, 'Teacher, what good deed must I do, to have eternal life?' " Jesus replied, "If you would enter life, keep the commandments." The Teacher is speaking about eternal life, that is, a sharing in the life of God himself. This life is attained through the observance of the Lord's commandments, including the commandment "you shall not kill." This is the first precept from the Decalogue, which Jesus quotes to the young man who asks him what commandments he should observe: "Jesus said, 'You shall not kill, you shall not commit adultery, you shall not steal.' "

[Capital Punishment]

. . . To kill a human being, in whom the image of God is present, is a particularly serious sin. Only God is the master of life! Yet from the beginning, faced with the many and often tragic cases which occur in the life of individuals and society, Christian reflection has sought a fuller and deeper understanding of what God's commandment prohibits and prescribes. There are in fact situations in which values proposed by God's law seem to involve a genuine paradox. This happens, for example, in the case of legitimate defense, in which the right to protect one's own life and the duty not to harm someone else's life are difficult to reconcile in practice. Certainly, the intrinsic value of life and the duty to love oneself no less than others are the basis of a true right to self-defense. . . . Unfortunately, it happens that the need to render the aggressor incapable of causing harm sometimes involves taking his life. In this case, the fatal outcome is attributable to the aggressor whose action brought it about, even though he may not be morally responsible because of a lack of the use of reason.

This is the context in which to place the problem of the death penalty. On this matter there is a growing tendency, both in the church and in civil society, to demand that it be applied in a very limited way or even that it be abolished completely. The problem must be viewed in the context of a system of penal justice ever more in line with human dignity and thus, in the end, with God's plan for man and society. The primary purpose of the punishment which society inflicts is "to redress the disorder caused by the offense." Public authority must redress the violation of personal and social rights by imposing on the offender an adequate punishment for the crime, as a condition for the offender to regain the exercise of his or her freedom. In this way authority also fulfills the purpose of defending public order and ensuring people's safety, while at the same time offering the offender an incentive and help to change his or her behavior and be rehabilitated.

It is clear that for these purposes to be achieved, the nature and extent of the punishment must be carefully evaluated and decided upon, and ought not go to the extreme of executing the offender except in cases of absolute necessity: In other words, when it would not be possible otherwise to defend society. Today, however, as a result of steady improvements in the organization of the penal system, such cases are very rare if not practically nonexistent. . . .

If such great care must be taken to respect every life, even that of criminals and unjust aggressors, the commandment "you shall not kill" has absolute value when it refers to the innocent person. And all the more so in the case of weak and defenseless human beings, who find their ultimate defense against the arrogance and caprice of others only in the absolute binding force of God's commandment. . . .

Faced with the progressive weakening in individual consciences and in society of the sense of the absolute and grave moral illicitness of the direct taking of all innocent human life, especially at its beginning and at its end, the church's magisterium has spoken out with increasing frequency in defense of the sacredness and inviolability of human life. The papal magisterium, particularly insistent in this regard, has always been seconded by that of the bishops, with numerous and comprehensive doctrinal and pastoral documents issued either by episcopal conferences or by individual bishops. The Second Vatican Council also addressed the matter forcefully in a brief but incisive passage.

Therefore, by the authority which Christ conferred upon Peter and his successors, and in communion with the bishops of the Catholic Church, *I confirm that the direct and voluntary killing of an innocent human being is always gravely immoral.* . . .

[Abortion]

Among all the crimes which can be committed against life, procured abortion has characteristics making it particularly serious and deplorable. The Second Vatican Council defines abortion, together with infanticide, as an "unspeakable crime."

But today in many people's consciences the perception of its gravity has become progressively obscured. The acceptance of abortion in the popular mind, in behavior and even in law itself, is a telling sign of an extremely dangerous crisis of the moral sense, which is becoming more and more incapable of distinguishing between good and evil when the fundamental right to life is at stake. . . .

Procured abortion is the deliberate and direct killing, by whatever means it is carried out, of a human being in the initial phase of his or her existence, extending from conception to birth.

The moral gravity of procured abortion is apparent in all its truth if we recognize that we are dealing with murder and, in particular, when we consider the specific elements involved. The one eliminated is a human being at the very beginning of life. No one more absolutely innocent could be imagined. In no way could this human being ever be considered an aggressor, much less an unjust aggressor! He or she is weak, defenseless, even to the point of lacking that minimal form of defense consisting in the poignant power of a newborn baby's cries and tears. The unborn child is totally entrusted to the protection and care of the woman carrying him or her in the womb. And yet sometimes it is precisely the mother herself who makes the decision and asks for the child to be eliminated, and who then goes about having it done.

It is true that the decision to have an abortion is often tragic and painful for the mother insofar as the decision to rid herself of the fruit of conception is not made for purely selfish reasons or out of convenience, but out of a desire to protect certain important values such as her own health or a decent standard of living for the other members of the family. Sometimes it is feared that the child to be born would live in such conditions that it would be better if the birth did not take place. Nevertheless, these reasons and others like them, however serious and tragic, can never justify the deliberate killing of an innocent human being.

As well as the mother, there are often other people too who decide upon the death of the child in the womb. In the first place, the father of the child may be to blame, not only when he directly pressures the woman to have an abortion, but also when he indirectly encourages such a decision on her part by leaving her alone to face the problems of pregnancy: In this way the family is thus mortally wounded and profaned in its nature as a community of love and in its vocation to be the "sanctuary of life." Nor can one overlook the pressures which sometimes come from the wider family circle and from friends. Sometimes the woman is subjected to such strong pressure that she feels psychologically forced to have an abortion: Certainly in this case moral responsibility lies particularly with those who have directly or indirectly obliged her to have an abortion. Doctors and nurses are also responsible when they place at the service of death skills which were acquired for promoting life.

But responsibility likewise falls on the legislators who have promoted and approved abortion laws and, to the extent that they have a say in the matter, on the administrators of the health care centers where abortions are performed. A general and no less serious responsibility lies with those who have encouraged the spread of an attitude of sexual permissiveness and a lack of esteem for motherhood, and with those who should have ensured—but did not—effective family and social policies in support of families, especially larger families and those with particular financial and educational needs. Finally, one cannot overlook the network of complicity which reaches out to include international institutions, foundations and associations which systematically campaign for the legalization and spread of abortion in the world. In this sense abortion goes beyond the responsibility of individuals and beyond the harm done to them, and takes on a distinctly social dimension. It is a most serious wound inflicted on society and its culture by the very people who ought to be society's promoters and defenders. . . .

Therefore, by the authority which Christ conferred upon Peter and his successors, in communion with the bishops . . . *I declare that direct abortion, that is, abortion willed as an end or as a means, always constitutes a grave moral disorder*, since it is the deliberate killing of an innocent human being. . . .

[Fetal Research]

This evaluation of the morality of abortion is to be applied also to the recent forms of intervention on human embryos which, although carried out for purposes legitimate in themselves, inevitably involve the killing of those embryos. This is the case with experimentation on embryos, which is becoming increasingly widespread in the field of biomedical research and is legally permitted in some countries. . . . [I]t must nonetheless be stated that the use of human embryos or fetuses as an object of experimentation constitutes a crime against their dignity as human beings who have a right to the same respect owed to a child once born, just as to every person.

This moral condemnation also regards procedures that exploit living human embryos and fetuses—sometimes specifically "produced" for this purpose by in vitro fertilization—either to be used as "biological material" or as providers of organs or tissue for transplants in the treatment of certain diseases. The killing of innocent human creatures, even if carried out to help others, constitutes an absolutely unacceptable act.

Special attention must be given to evaluating the morality of prenatal diagnostic techniques which enable the early detection of possible anomalies in the unborn child. In view of the complexity of these techniques, an accurate and systematic moral judgment is necessary. When they do not involve disproportionate risks for the child and the mother, and are meant to make possible early therapy or even to favor a serene and informed acceptance of the child not yet born, these techniques are morally licit. But since the possibilities of prenatal therapy are today still limited, it not infrequently happens that these techniques are used with a eugenic intention which accepts selective abortion in order to prevent the birth of children affected by various types of anomalies. Such an attitude is shameful and utterly reprehensible, since it presumes to measure the value of a human life only within the parameters of "normality" and physical well-being, thus opening the way to legitimizing infanticide and euthanasia as well. . . .

[Euthanasia]

At the other end of life's spectrum, men and women find themselves facing the mystery of death. Today, as a result of advances in medicine and in a cultural context frequently closed to the transcendent, the experience of dying is marked by new features. When the prevailing tendency is to value life only to the extent that it brings pleasure and well-being, suffering seems like an unbearable setback, something from which one must be freed at all costs. Death is considered "senseless" if it suddenly interrupts a life still open to a future of new and interesting experiences. But it becomes a "rightful liberation" once life is held to be no longer meaningful because it is filled with pain and inexorably doomed to even greater suffering.

Furthermore, when he denies or neglects his fundamental relationship to God, man thinks he is his own rule and measure, with the right to demand that society should guarantee him the ways and means of deciding what to do with his life in full and complete autonomy. It is especially people in the developed countries who act in this way: They feel encouraged to do so also by the constant progress of medicine and its ever more advanced techniques. By using highly sophisticated systems and equipment, science and medical practice today are able not only to attend to cases formerly considered untreatable and to reduce or eliminate pain, but also to sustain and prolong life even in situations of extreme frailty, to resuscitate artificially patients whose basic biological functions have undergone sudden collapse and to use special procedures to make organs available for transplanting.

In this context the temptation grows to have recourse to euthanasia, that is, to take control of death and bring it about before its time, "gently" ending one's own life or the life of others. In reality what might seem logical and humane, when looked at more closely is seen to be senseless and inhumane. Here we are faced with one of the more alarming symptoms of the "culture of death," which is advancing above all in prosperous societies, marked by an attitude of excessive preoccupation with efficiency, and which sees the growing number of elderly and disabled people as intolerable and too burdensome. These people are very often isolated by their families and by society, which are organized almost exclusively on the basis of criteria of productive efficiency, according to which a hopelessly impaired life no longer has any value. . . .

Euthanasia must be distinguished from the decision to forgo so-called "aggressive medical treatment," in other words, medical procedures which no longer correspond to the real situation of the patient either because they are by now disproportionate to any expected results or because they impose an excessive burden on the patient and his family. In such situations, when death is clearly imminent and inevitable, one can in conscience "refuse forms of treatment that would only secure a precarious and burdensome prolongation of life, so long as the normal care due to the sick similar cases is not interrupted.". . .

To forgo extraordinary or disproportionate means is not the equivalent of suicide or euthanasia; it rather expresses acceptance of the human condition in the face of death. . . .

Taking into account these distinctions, in harmony with the magisterium of my predecessors and in communion with the bishops of the Catholic

Church, *I confirm that euthanasia is a grave violation of the law of God*, since it is the deliberate killing of a human person. . . .

Suicide is always as morally objectionable as murder. The church's position has always rejected it as a gravely evil choice. . . . [S]uicide, when viewed objectively, is a gravely immoral act. In fact, it involves the rejection of love of self and the renunciation of the obligation of justice and charity toward one's neighbor, toward the communities to which one belongs and toward society as a whole. In its deepest reality, suicide represents a rejection of God's absolute sovereignty over life and death. . . .

To concur with the intention of another person to commit suicide and to help in carrying it out through so-called "assisted suicide" means to cooperate in and at times to be the actual perpetrator of an injustice which can never be excused even if it is requested. . . . Even when not motivated by a selfish refusal to be burdened with the life of someone who is suffering, euthanasia must be called a false mercy and indeed a disturbing "perversion" of mercy. True "compassion" leads to sharing another's pain; it does not kill the person whose suffering we cannot bear. Moreover, the act of euthanasia appears all the more perverse if it is carried out by those like relatives, who are supposed to treat a family member with patience and love, or by those such as doctors, who by virtue of their specific profession are supposed to care for the sick person even in the most painful terminal stages.

The choice of euthanasia becomes more serious when it takes the form of a murder committed by others on a person who has in no way requested it and who has never consented to it. The height of arbitrariness and injustice is reached when certain people such as physicians or legislators arrogate to themselves the power to decide who ought to live and who ought to die. . . .

[Unjust Laws]

. . . [L]aws which legitimize the direct killing of innocent human beings through abortion or euthanasia are in complete opposition to the inviolable right to life proper to every individual; they thus deny the equality of everyone before the law. It might be objected that such is not the case in euthanasia, when it is requested with full awareness by the person involved. But any state which made such a request legitimate and authorized it to be carried out would be legalizing a case of suicide-murder, contrary to the fundamental principles of absolute respect for life and of the protection of every innocent life. In this way the state contributes to lessening respect for life and opens the door to ways of acting which are destructive of trust in relations between people. Laws which authorize and promote abortion and euthanasia are therefore radically opposed not only to the good of the individual but also to the common good; as such they are completely lacking in authentic juridical validity. Disregard for the right to life, precisely because it leads to the killing of the person whom society exists to serve, is what most directly conflicts with the possibility of achieving the common good. Consequently, a civil law authorizing abortion or euthanasia ceases by that very fact to be a true, morally binding civil law.

Abortion and euthanasia are thus crimes which no human law can claim to legitimize. There is no obligation in conscience to obey such laws; instead there is a grave and clear obligation to oppose them by conscientious objection. . . .

A particular problem of conscience can arise in cases where a legislative vote would be decisive for the passage of a more restrictive law, aimed at limiting the number of authorized abortions, in place of a more permissive law already passed or ready to be voted on. Such cases are not infrequent. It is a fact that while in some parts of the world there continue to be campaigns to introduce laws favoring abortion, often supported by powerful international organizations, in other nations—particularly those which have already experienced the bitter fruits of such permissive legislation—there are growing signs of a rethinking in this matter. In a case like the one just mentioned, when it is not possible to overturn or completely abrogate a pro-abortion law, an elected official whose absolute personal opposition to procured abortion was well known could licitly support proposals aimed at limiting the harm done by such a law and at lessening its negative consequences at the level of general opinion and public morality. This does not in fact represent an illicit cooperation with an unjust law, but rather a legitimate and proper attempt to limit its evil aspects.

The passing of unjust laws often raises difficult problems of conscience for morally upright people with regard to the issue of cooperation, since they have a right to demand not to be forced to take part in morally evil actions. Sometimes the choices which have to be made are difficult; they may require the sacrifice of prestigious professional positions or the relinquishing of reasonable hopes of career advancement. . . .

. . . [T]he opportunity to refuse to take part in the phases of consultation, preparation and execution of these acts against life should be guaranteed to physicians, health care personnel and directors of hospitals, clinics and convalescent facilities. Those who have recourse to conscientious objection must be protected not only from legal penalties, but also from any negative effects on the legal, disciplinary, financial and professional plane. . . .

[The Culture of Life]

. . . [T]here is an everyday heroism made up of gestures of sharing, big or small, which build up an authentic culture of life. A particularly praiseworthy example of such gestures is the donation of organs, performed in an ethically acceptable manner, with a view to offering a chance of health and even of life itself to the sick who sometimes have no other hope.

Part of this daily heroism is also the silent but effective and eloquent witness of all those "brave mothers who devote themselves to their own family without reserve, who suffer in giving birth to their children and who are ready to make any effort, to face any sacrifice, in order to pass on to them the best of themselves." In living out their mission "these heroic women do not always find support in the world around them." On the contrary, the cultural models frequently promoted and broadcast by the media do not encourage motherhood. In the name of progress and modernity the values of fidelity, chastity, sacrifice, to which a host of Christian wives and mothers have borne and continue to bear outstanding witness, are presented as obsolete. . . .

By virtue of our sharing in Christ's royal mission, our support and promotion of human life must be accomplished through the service of charity, which finds expression in personal witness, various forms of volunteer work, social activity and political commitment. This is a particularly pressing need at the present time, when the "culture of death" so forcefully opposes the "culture of life" and often seems to have the upper hand. . . .

Where life is involved, the service of charity must be profoundly consistent. It cannot tolerate bias and discrimination, for human life is sacred and inviolable at every stage and in every situation; it is an indivisible good. We need then to "show care" for all life and for the life of everyone. Indeed, at an even deeper level, we need to go to the very roots of life and love.

It is this deep love for every man and woman which has given rise down the centuries to an outstanding history of charity, a history which has brought into being in the church and society many forms of service to life which evoke admiration from all unbiased observers. Every Christian community, with a renewed sense of responsibility, must continue to write this history through various kinds of pastoral and social activity. To this end, appropriate and effective programs of support for new life must be implemented, with special closeness to mothers who, even without the help of the father, are not afraid to bring their child into the world and to raise it. Similar care must be shown for the life of the marginalized or suffering, especially in its final phases.

All of this involves a patient and fearless work of education aimed at encouraging one and all to bear each other's burdens. It requires a continuous promotion of vocations to service, particularly among the young. It involves the implementation of long-term practical projects and initiatives inspired by the Gospel.

Many are the means toward this end which need to be developed with skill and serious commitment. At the first stage of life, centers for natural methods of regulating fertility should be promoted as a valuable help to responsible parenthood, in which all individuals, and in the first place the child, are recognized and respected in their own right and where every decision is guided by the ideal of the sincere gift of self. Marriage and family counseling agencies by their specific work of guidance and prevention, carried out in accordance with an anthropology consistent with the Christian vision of the person, of the couple and of sexuality, also offer valuable help in rediscovering the meaning of love and life, and in supporting and accompanying every family in its mission as the "sanctuary of life." Newborn life is also served by centers of assistance and homes or centers where new life receives a welcome. Thanks to the work of such centers, many unmarried mothers and couples in difficulty discover new hope and find assistance and support in overcoming hardship and the fear of accepting a newly conceived life or life which has just come into the world.

When life is challenged by conditions of hardship, maladjustment, sickness or rejection, other programs—such as communities for treating drug addiction, residential communities for minors or the mentally ill, care and relief centers for AIDS patients, associations for solidarity especially toward the disabled—are eloquent expressions of what charity is able to devise in order to give everyone new reasons for hope and practical possibilities for life.

And when earthly existence draws to a close, it is again charity which finds the most appropriate means for enabling the elderly, especially those who can no longer look after themselves, and the terminally ill to enjoy genuinely humane assistance and to receive an adequate response to their needs, in particular their anxiety and their loneliness. In these cases the role of families is indispensable; yet families can receive much help from social welfare agencies and, if necessary, from recourse to palliative care, taking advantage of suitable medical and social services available in public institutions or in the home. . . .

A unique responsibility belongs to health care personnel: doctors, pharmacists, nurses, chaplains, men and women religious, administrators and volunteers. Their profession calls for them to be guardians and servants of human life. In today's cultural and social context, in which science and the practice of medicine risk losing sight of their inherent ethical dimension, health care professionals can be strongly tempted at times to become manipulators of life or even agents of death. In the face of this temptation their responsibility today is greatly increased. Its deepest inspiration and strongest support lie in the intrinsic and undeniable ethical dimension of the health care profession, something already recognized by the ancient and still relevant Hippocratic oath, which requires every doctor to commit himself to absolute respect for human life and its sacredness.

Absolute respect for every innocent human life also requires the exercise of conscientious objection in relation to procured abortion and euthanasia. "Causing death" can never be considered a form of medical treatment, even when the intention is solely to comply with the patient's request. Rather, it runs completely counter to the health care profession, which is meant to be an impassioned and unflinching affirmation of life. Biomedical research too, a field which promises great benefits for humanity, must always reject experimentation, research or applications which disregard the inviolable dignity of the human being and thus cease to be at the service of people and become instead means which, under the guise of helping people, actually harm them. . . .

Closely connected with the formation of conscience is the work of education, which helps individuals to be ever more human, leads them ever more fully to the truth, instills in them growing respect for life and trains them in right interpersonal relationships.

In particular, there is a need for education about the value of life from its very origins. It is an illusion to think that we can build a true culture of human life if we do not help the young to accept and experience sexuality and love and the whole of life according to their true meaning and in their close interconnection. Sexuality, which enriches the whole person, "manifests its inmost meaning in leading the person to the gift of self in love." The trivialization of sexuality is among the principal factors which have led to contempt for new life. Only a true love is able to protect life. There can be no avoiding the duty to offer, especially to adolescents and young adults, an authentic education in sexuality and in love, an education which involves training in chastity as a virtue which fosters personal maturity and makes one capable of respecting the "spousal" meaning of the body. . . .

I would now like to say a special word to women who have had an abortion. The church is aware of the many factors which may have influenced your decision, and she does not doubt that in many cases it was a painful and even shattering decision. The wound in your heart may not yet have healed. Certainly what happened was and remains terribly wrong. But do not give in to discouragement and do not lose hope. Try rather to understand what happened and face it honestly. If you have not already done so, give yourselves over with humility and trust to repentance. The Father of mercies is ready to give you his forgiveness and his peace in the sacrament of reconciliation. You will come to understand that nothing is definitively lost, and you will also be able to ask forgiveness from your child, who is now living in the Lord. . . .

April

HOUSE LEADERS ON CONGRESS'S FIRST ONE HUNDRED DAYS
April 7, 1995

House Speaker Newt Gingrich (R-Ga.) claimed a tentative victory in fulfilling the Contract with America at the end of the first one hundred days in power for House Republicans. Addressing a nationally televised audience on April 7, Gingrich said he and fellow Republicans had accomplished their initial goals in getting major pieces of legislation, including a constitutional amendment requiring a balanced budget, passed by the House during the first one hundred days of the 104th Congress.

Gingrich said he and his party would not be satisfied with that significant achievement. He predicted hard work would be needed to get the proposed legislation enacted into law, and then to follow through on other aspects of the Republican agenda to reshape the federal government. The contract, a set of election-year pledges, had been signed in September 1994 by more than three hundred Republican House candidates. (Contract with America, Historic Documents of 1994, p. 374)

In setting the ambitious agenda, Gingrich said in his April 7 speech, "we wanted to prove to you, and I think to us that democracy still has the vitality and the will to do something about the problems facing our nation."

House Minority Leader Richard Gephardt (D-Mo.) and Senate Minority Leader Tom Daschle (D-S.D.) responded to Gingrich's address by denouncing the Republican-planned cutbacks in social programs. Their response was taped at the Long Branch Elementary School in Arlington, Virginia, just outside Washington, D.C. Gephardt said the Republicans were paying for tax cuts for the wealthy by cutting spending on school lunches and college aid—"the programs that work for people who are working hard."

Obstacles to House Plans

The House Republican agenda faced two obstacles. The first was the Republican-controlled Senate. Many senators, even Republicans, were less dedicated than their House counterparts to the Contract with America's call for radical changes in the federal government. President Bill Clinton promised to veto most of the House-passed legislation if it reached his desk unchanged. Clinton did not have to exercise his veto pen on the balanced budget amendment, by far the most contentious of the Republican proposals. The amendment had already stalled in the Senate in March and was generally given only a modest chance of passage before the 1996 congressional and presidential elections.

At year's end, Clinton and the Republican Congress had agreed, in principle, to balance the budget by 2002, but they were battling over the specifics of how to do it. Their disagreements led to two partial shutdowns of the federal government. (Budget impasse, p. 737)

All other major elements of the Republican agenda were also on the table at year's end, most of them pending in the Senate or awaiting negotiations between Congress and the administration. The House itself rejected only one of the key contract proposals: a constitutional amendment limiting congressional service to twelve years. This term-limit proposal fell short of the required two-thirds majority vote in the House on March 29.

The Contract Agenda

The heart of the Contract with America was a series of legislative proposals on ten broad issues, ranging from congressional procedures to welfare reform. Enactment of all the proposals would constitute the most sweeping change in national governance since the New Deal in the 1930s. In the contract, Republicans had pledged to get all ten proposals passed by the House within the first one hundred days. Except for the term-limit proposal, that deadline was met, giving Gingrich and his colleagues the chance to boast that they were delivering on their ambitious campaign promises.

Only one set of proposals had gone into effect by the end of the one hundred days, however: a package of congressional reforms. One bill (S 2—PL 104–1) ended the congressional exemption from eleven laws governing the workplace, ranging from civil rights to safety requirements. Two other House resolutions (H Res 6 and H Res 107) revised the operations of House committees by setting limits on the number of terms committee chairmen could serve, reducing the size of committee staffs, and eliminating proxy voting in committees. The House resolutions did not require approval by the Senate or the president.

Other major issues in the Contract with America, still pending in Congress at year's end, were:

- *The balanced budget amendment, and presidential veto power over line items in appropriations bills. Both chambers approved the veto power, but with different procedures. The issue was pending in conference committee at year's end.*
- *A series of anticrime measures on such issues as victim restitution, rules of evidence, prison construction, and procedures for appealing*

death sentences. Tied to these items was a repeal of a 1994 ban on certain semiautomatic assault weapons, a repeal that Clinton vowed to veto. Most of these items were pending in the Senate Judiciary Committee at year's end.

- A "welfare reform" package that gave states broad new authority to craft their own welfare programs. The Senate cleared a major welfare reform package (HR 4) on December 22, but President Clinton said he would veto it.
- A series of proposals to "strengthen families," including tax credits for families that adopted children, tougher penalties for sex crimes against children, and stronger child-support enforcement laws.
- Several tax cuts, packaged as "middle class" tax cuts, even though some provisions would benefit those earning as much as $200,000 annually. Several of these proposals were included in the budget legislation that was under negotiation between Congress and the administration at year's end.
- Several "national security" measures, including restrictions on U.S. participation in international peacekeeping efforts by the United Nations. Many of these provisions found their way into pieces of legislation, but all were pending at year's end. One of the most controversial, a statement of support for an antimissile defense of U.S. territory, was rejected in the House.
- Legislation to reduce Social Security taxes, allow some senior citizens to earn more income without losing Social Security benefits, and slow the rise in Medicaid costs. Several of these items were in the pending "budget reconciliation" bill under negotiation at year's end.
- A series of proposals bundled together as a cut in capital gains taxes and a gutting of numerous federal regulatoins. After approval in the House, the capital gains tax cut never reached the Senate floor. The Senate took up a package of regulatory changes, but suspended debate on July 20.
- The constitutional amendment limiting congressional term limits, which failed in the House and faced a difficult future in the Senate.

Following are excerpts from an April 7 address by House Speaker Newt Gingrich (R-Ga.), on the first one hundred days in power for Republicans, and a Democratic response by House Minority Leader Richard Gephardt (D-Mo.) and Sen. Tom Daschle (D-S.D.):

SPEAKER GINGRICH'S SPEECH

Thank you for joining me tonight and for this chance to give you, the American people, a report on the new Congress, what we've been doing, what we hope to do, and how we're working to keep faith with what you sent us here to do. But first, let me thank the hundreds of thousands of Americans who've written me over the past few months. Your letters, nearly 400,000, are full of good ideas and often moving words of encouragement. This letter, addressed to "Dear Mr. Newt," included a portrait of George Washington. It was sent to me by first grader Steven Frankoviak from Georgia, and I thank Steven and everyone else who wrote me, even if you didn't include a picture of George Washington.

Last September the House Republicans signed a Contract with America. We signed this Contract and made some promises to you and to ourselves. You elected us, and for the last 93 days we have been keeping our word. With your help, we're bringing about real change. We made Congress subject to the same laws as everyone else. We cut congressional committee staffs and budgets by 30 percent. And we voted on every item in the Contract. And I can tell you tonight we're going to sell one congressional building and privatize at least one congressional parking lot.

While we've done a lot, this Contract has never been about curing all the ills of the nation. One hundred days can't overturn the neglect of decades. The Contract's purpose has been to show that change is possible, that even in Washington you can do what you say you're going to do. In short, we wanted to prove to you, and I think to us, that democracy still has the vitality and the will to do something about the problems facing our nation. And it seems to me that whether you're a conservative or a liberal, that is a very positive thing. And so I want to talk about the Contract tonight, our successes and our failures, but I also want to talk about something much larger, because although I've spent the last six months of my life living and breathing and fighting for what's written in this Contract, I know the American people want more than these 10 items.

So what I want to talk with you about tonight is not just what a new political majority on Capitol Hill has accomplished in one hundred days, but how all of us together, Republicans and Democrats alike, must totally remake the federal government, to change the very way it thinks, the way it does business, the way it treats its citizens. After all, the purpose of changing government is to improve the lives of our citizens, to strengthen the future of our children, to make our neighborhoods safe and to build a better country. Government is not the end. It is the means.

We Americans wake up every morning, go to work, take our kids to school, fix dinner, do all the things we expect of ourselves, and yet something isn't quite right. There's no confidence that government understands the values and realities of our lives. The government is out of touch and out of control. It is in need of deep and deliberate change. . . .

We sincerely believe we can reduce spending and at the same time make government better. You know, virtually every institution in America except government has re-engineered itself to become more efficient over the last decade. They cut spending, provided better products, better education and better service for less. But I believe we must remake government for reasons much larger than saving money or improving services. The fact is, no civilization can survive with 12-year-olds having babies, with 15-year-olds killing each other, with 17-year-olds dying of AIDS, with 18-year-olds getting diplomas they can't even read.

Every night on every local news we see the human tragedies that have grown out of the current welfare state. As a father of two daughters, I can't ignore the terror and worry parents in our inner cities must feel for their children. Within a half-mile of this Capitol, your Capitol, drugs, violence and despair threaten the lives of our citizens. We cannot ignore our fellow Americans in such desperate straits by thinking that huge amounts of tax dollars release us from our moral responsibility to help these parents and their children. There is no reason the federal government must keep an allegiance to failure. You know, with good will, with common sense, with the courage to change, we can do better for all Americans.

Another fact we cannot turn our head away from is this: No truly moral civilization would burden its children with the economic excesses of the parents and grandparents. Now, this talk of burdening future generations is not just rhetoric. We're talking about hard economic consequences that will limit our children and grandchildren's standard of living. Yet that is what we are doing for the children trapped in poverty, for the children whose futures are trapped by a government debt they're going to have to pay. We have an obligation tonight to talk about the legacy we are leaving our children and our grandchildren, an obligation to talk about the deliberate remaking of our government.

This change will not be accomplished in the next one hundred days. But we must start by recognizing the moral and economic failure of the current methods of government. In these last one hundred days, we have begun to change those failed methods. We outlined 10 major proposals in the Contract that begin to break the logjam of the past. The House passed nine out of 10.

First, we passed the Shays Act, which makes the Congress obey all the laws that other Americans have to obey. The House passed it, the Senate passed it and the president signed it. So that's one law signed, sealed and delivered.

We passed the balanced budget amendment in the House with bipartisan support. It has been temporarily defeated in the Senate by one vote. Although constitutional amendments are harder to get through Congress because they require a two-thirds vote rather than a simple majority, don't be discouraged. Senator Dole has said he will call it up for another vote. The momentum is with us. And with your help and your voice, I believe it is possible this amendment will pass later in this Congress.

As promised, we introduced a constitutional amendment on term limits, but we failed, even though 85 percent of House Republicans voted for it; again, that two-thirds vote. There have been 180 bills introduced to limit congressional terms over America's history, but not one of them ever made it to the House floor until last week, when we brought term limits to a vote. I pledge to you that term limits will be the first vote of the next Congress. So keep the pressure on. Keep your hopes up.

In both the House and the Senate, we passed the line-item veto, just as you asked. It's remarkable that a Republican House and a Republican Senate are giving such a strong tool to the president of the other party. I believe it shows our good-faith determination to cut spending.

Other Contract proposals have passed the House and are being worked on in the Senate. We passed regulatory reform, legal reform and welfare reform. We passed a $500 tax credit per child. We passed an increase in the earning limit for senior citizens so they won't have their Social Security checks cut if they earn extra money. We passed a capital gains tax cut and indexed those gains to spur the savings and investment that creates jobs.

[Contract Only a Beginning]

Even with all these successes and others, the Contract with America is only a beginning. It is the preliminary skirmish to the big battles yet to come. The big battles will deal with how we remake the government of the United States. The measure of everything we do will be whether we are creating a better future with more opportunities for our children. New ideas, new ways and old-fashioned common sense can improve government while reducing its costs. . . .

The purpose of all this change is not simply a better government. It is a better America. A truly compassionate government would replace the welfare state with opportunity, because the welfare system's greatest cost is the human cost to the poor. In the name of compassion, we have funded a system that is cruel and destroys families. Its failure is reflected by the violence, brutality, child abuse and drug addiction in every local TV news broadcast. Poor Americans are trapped in unsafe government housing, saddled with rules that are anti-work, anti-family and anti-property. . . .

I believe we have to do a number of things to become an opportunity society. We must restore freedom by ending bureaucratic micromanagement here in Washington. As any good business leader will tell you, decisions should be made as closely as possible to the source of the problem. This country is too big and too diverse for Washington to have the knowledge to make the right decisions on local matters. We've got to return power back to you, to your families, your neighborhoods, your local and state governments.

We need to promote economic growth by reducing regulation, reducing taxation and reducing frivolous lawsuits. And everywhere I go, Americans complain about an overly complicated tax code and an arrogant, unpredictable and unfair Internal Revenue Service. This summer we will begin hearings on bold, decisive reform of the income tax system. We're looking at a simplified flat tax and other ways to bring some sense to the disorder and inequity of our tax system. . . .

[Balancing the Budget]

It was once an American tradition to pay off the mortgage and leave the children the farm. Now we seem to be selling the farm and leaving our children the mortgage. By 1997 we will pay more for interest on the debt than for the national defense. That's right, more of our tax money will be spent to pay interest on government bonds than will pay for the Army, the Navy, the Air Force, the Marine Corps, the intelligence agencies and the defense bureaucracy combined.

Okay, let's go beyond interest on the debt and discuss Social Security. I want to reassure all of you who are on Social Security or who will soon retire that your Social Security is fine. No one will touch your Social Security, period. But we must make sure that the baby boomers' retirements, which are coming up in the next century, are as secure as their parents'. Unfortunately, the money the government supposedly has been putting aside for the baby boomers' Social Security is not there. The government has been borrowing that money to pay for the budget deficit. So when the baby boomers get set to retire, where's the money to pay them going to come from? "Well," you might ask, "can't the government just borrow more money?" The honest answer is no. No system, no country is wealthy enough to have unlimited borrowing.

The answer is clear. The key to protecting the baby boomers' Social Security is to balance the budget. That way, by the time the baby boomers retire, the government will be financially sound. It'll have the money to pay them. The problem is not Social Security, after all. Social Security would be fine if the federal government would stop borrowing the money. The government can stop borrowing the money when we balance the budget. It is just that simple.

Our goals are simple. We don't want our children to drown in debt. We want baby boomers to be able to retire with the same security as their parents. We want our senior Americans to be able to rely on Medicare without fear. These are the reasons why, as President Franklin Delano Roosevelt said, our generation has a rendezvous with destiny. This is the year we rendezvous with our destiny to establish a clear plan to balance the budget. It can no longer be put off. That's why I'm speaking to you so frankly.

Next month we will propose a budget that is balanced over seven years. The budget can be balanced even with the problems of the federal government. It can be balanced without touching a penny of Social Security and without raising taxes. In fact, spending overall can go up every year. We simply have to limit annual spending increases to about 3 percent between now and 2002. The key is the willingness to change, to set priorities, to redesign the government, to recognize that this is not the '60s or the '70s. This is the 1990s, and we need a government to match the times.

As I said, Social Security is off the table. But, you know, that leaves a lot on the table—corporate welfare, subsidies of every special interest. Defense is on the table. I'm a hawk, but I'm a cheap hawk. As the budget battle rages over the coming months, you'll hear screams from the special-interest groups. I'm sure you've already heard the dire cries that we're going to take food out of the mouths of school children, that we're going to feed them ketchup. The fact of the matter is, all we did was vote to increase school lunch four and a half percent every year for five years and give the money to the states to spend because we thought they would do a better job than the federal government of managing the children's meals and the school lunch program. . . .

If I had one message for this country on this day, when we celebrate the act of keeping our word, it would be a simple message. Idealism is American. To be romantic is American. It's okay to be a skeptic, but don't be a cynic. It's okay to raise good questions, but don't assume the worst. It's okay to report difficulties, but it's equally good to report victories.

Yes, we have problems, and of course it's going to be difficult to enact these things. That's the American way. And of course we're going to have to work hard, and of course we're going to have to negotiate with the president, and of course the American people are going to have to let their will be known. But why should we be afraid of that? That is freedom.

I'm here tonight to say that we're going to open a dialogue because we want to create a new partnership with the American people, a plan to remake the government and balance the budget that is the American people's plan— not the House Republican plan, not the Gingrich plan, but the plan of the American people. And it is in that spirit of committing ourselves idealistically, committing ourselves romantically, believing in America, that we celebrate having kept our word. And we promise to begin a new partnership so that together we and all of the American people can give our children and our country a new birth of freedom.

Thank you and good night.

GEPHARDT'S DEMOCRATIC RESPONSE

Good evening, I'm [House Minority Leader] Dick Gephardt. I'm speaking to you tonight from Long Branch Elementary School in Arlington, Virginia. And, to me, there's no better place to talk about the first one hundred days of the Republican Congress, because while the Republicans are celebrating the end of their Contract with America, for the children here at Long Branch the contract is only just beginning.

Next year, there are children here who won't have school lunches; the Republicans cut them to pay for tax breaks for the wealthiest Americans. Next summer, there are children all across America who won't have summer jobs, because the Republicans wiped out the whole program. They abolished jobs for kids at the same time they were abolishing all the income taxes for some of the largest and wealthiest corporations. And unless we reverse the policy of these hundred days, when it comes time for students here to go to college, many of them, and many of your children, will find the door slammed in their face. The Republicans in the House want to cut student loans for millions of young men and women from middle-class families.

The Republicans have even tried to classify school lunches and college loans as welfare. How dare they? Those are the programs that work for people who are working hard. Is this what you voted for last November? The wrong kind of budget cuts that will hurt your families in order to pay for the wrong kind of tax cuts that will help the few?

Under the Republican capital gains tax cut, if you earn $350,000 a year, you will reap a $13,000 tax deduction. But if you earn $30,000 a year, you'll just get 50 cents a week. Speaker Gingrich says this tax cut is the crown jewel of the Republican agenda. I think that's the right phrase for it, because it goes mostly to the most privileged Americans. But don't take it from me; take it from today's *Wall Street Journal*, which announced in a headline, and I quote, that this tax bill could mean a "windfall for the well-off." And they go on to tell their readers, don't do anything yet, but start salivating.

We've seen a hundred days of tax cuts for the wealthy and budget cuts for the middle class. Of course there has been some progress. Republicans and Democrats have joined together to make honest changes in the way we do the public's business. We stood together to make sure the laws Congress applies to you are also applied to the Congress. We voted together for the line-item veto so a president can cut spending by literally crossing it out of the budget line by line. We will work with Republicans wherever we can. But we cannot agree to policies that hurt the middle-class and working families who need someone to stand up and fight for them.

For more than a decade and a half, wages and income have declined for all but the wealthiest Americans. You have had to work longer and harder just to keep from falling behind. How can you raise a strong family when you are working day and night, and barely have time to spend with your children? What matters is not the bills the Republicans passed, but the bills you have to pay. The truth is nothing in these hundred days addresses the fundamental challenge of an America that has fallen to seventh in the world in standard of living. Never has so much been done in so little time to help so few at the expense of so many.

The speaker's rhetoric cannot conceal the reality. Franklin Roosevelt's hundred days were for the people; these hundred days have been for the privileged.

So now that the headlines have been written and the bows have been taken, let's get down to the real work of changing this nation. Let's sit down, Republicans and Democrats together, and do something about jobs and incomes, health care and education. Let's worry about the hard-working majority of our people, and not try to trick you into supporting legislation that just lavishes more on those who have the most. Let's recognize that if we don't begin to protect, preserve and defend the middle class, we may not have one in 20 years. If you ask me, that's a fight worth making.

We can start with health care. Just because it became a problem for the politicians doesn't mean it stopped being a problem for you. Tonight I asked Speaker Gingrich to sit down with me in the days ahead on a bipartisan basis to negotiate a solution to America's health care crisis. We can do it step by step. But let's take the first step now, and let's do it together.

Then let's move on to strengthen education, not cut it; to fight for America's standard of living, not wring our hands while it erodes; let's raise the minimum wage to make it a living wage. Let's encourage corporations to put a little more money in the pockets of workers who are more productive, and not just a lot more money in the bank accounts of a few executives who don't deserve to reap all the rewards.

We as Democrats are ready, and I know the President is ready, to work with the Republicans, and do the real work of change. And let's measure our success not by bills passed, or popularity scores, or a checklist of contract clauses, but by a more fundamental test: Let's ask what every decision means to the children here at Long Branch, and to the families that send them to school each day—families that work and save and hope for their future. That should be our new bipartisan contract with America.

Now let me turn this over to my friend Tom Daschle, our Senate Democratic leader.

DASCHLE'S REMARKS

The question before us at the end of these hundred days isn't who stands for change—clearly both parties do. The issue is: What kind of change is it going to be? In these past one hundred days, Democrats and Republicans have joined together to make changes in how the government works. Where we have divided, and sharply, is over the question of who the government should be working for. On that question, day after day, the differences between the two parties have become clearer and clearer.

While claiming to place government on the side of working Americans, over the past one hundred days the Republicans have shown their true loyalties to the forces of privilege and power who need no help and deserve no special favors. We all know that we can never balance the federal budget, create new jobs, raise our standard of living, without attacking obsolete and wasteful government spending. But that's not what the Republicans in Congress have been doing. Instead they've hammered programs that provide opportunities for our children—school lunches, college scholarships, educational reform, student loans—while sparing, and even increasing, government subsidies and tax breaks for the very wealthy and the largest corporations.

And for all the tough talk at the end of these hundred days, none of the cutting that has been done by the Republican Congress has moved us to a balanced federal budget—not even close. Instead, the Republicans have passed bills to slash taxes for the rich, and allow many large corporations to stop paying income taxes altogether. They bowed to special interest demands that weaken the laws that protect our health and safety. They have given lobbyists unprecedented access and influence. No wonder the legislation emerging from the Republican Congress favors powerful interests. Their lobbyists are actually sitting in the committee rooms writing it.

There have been changes, all right, but by and large it isn't the change you voted for. Instead it is America's middle-class families that are getting short-changed again. What the Republican Congress has produced is not a contract with America, but a plan that has lost contact with the real America, with middle-class families who are struggling harder and harder to stay even, and even who have less and less time to spend with their kids.

Democrats want to work with Republicans where we can. But most of all we are committed to standing on your side. So when Republicans pick the powerful and special interests over you, we're going to fight them every step of the way. And it isn't just Democrats who are troubled by this. Many of Speaker Gingrich's ideas are so extreme, so unfair, so wrong, that even Republicans in the Senate will refuse to pass them. When Republicans tried to stop new health and safety rules, rules to set safety standards for mammograms and drinking water, the Senate said no. The Senate has rejected House Republican cuts in education programs. And many Senate Republicans have joined Democrats in questioning Speaker Gingrich's tax plan. And I believe that Democrats will have Republican help in rejecting his proposals to eliminate 100,000 new police, and to end college scholarships for young people ready to serve their country.

In these hundred days the House has passed many bills, but, as Dick said, nothing—nothing has been done to help you pay your bills, the bills you pay each month—your credit cards, your mortgage, your car and loan payments.

In the next hundred days we ask Republicans to work with us to change this country and make government work for you. Tonight we call on Republicans to join us on at least three specific challenges in the days ahead. First, let's work together to make health insurance affordable and available to all Americans, and let's make sure a family doesn't lose its coverage when parents change jobs or find themselves out of work. Second, let's work together, in reducing college costs and making them more affordable—let's expand opportunities, not shrink them. For parents who are trying to send their kids to school, and for adults who are trying on top of everything else to go back to school and improve their skills. And, third, let's pass a plan that replaces the current welfare system, one that helps people work their way out of poverty without punishing young children. That was President Clinton's goal in 1992, and the time for Congress to act is now.

We are ready to sit down with Republican leaders right away to begin working on these priorities. I believe if Republicans and Democrats do what is right for you, we can make the second hundred days truly historic—a time when we can finally begin to make this a government both of and for the people. That would be a real cause for celebration—not for politicians and their campaign strategists, or for lobbyists who are cashing in their IOUs, but for hard-working middle-class families. They are the true strength of this nation, and our real purpose for being here. Thank you, and good night.

REMARKS AT PRAYER SERVICE FOR BOMBING VICTIMS
April 23, 1995

The United States, which for many years seemed almost invulnerable to the kinds of terrorist attack that plagued other countries, lost its sense of security on the morning of April 19, when a truck bomb was detonated outside the Alfred P. Murrah Federal Building in Oklahoma City. The explosion killed 168 people, several of them children attending a daycare center on the second floor of the building. Most of the remaining victims were federal workers and visitors who had business with federal offices, including a Social Security office.

The bombing was not the first terrorist action directed at American targets. An explosion at the World Trade Center Building in New York City on February 26, 1993, and the bomb that exploded December 21, 1988, aboard Pan America Flight 103 over Lockerbie, Scotland, killing all 259 people aboard, were two chilling reminders that the United States and its citizens were a target for extremist groups in other parts of the world. This attack on a city in America's heartland was allegedly perpetrated, it turned out, by Americans.

For the first hours and days, firefighters, rescue crews, medical teams, police, and volunteers risked their lives as they searched for survivors and bodies in the still crumbling building. Through the medium of television the nation watched—horrified and fascinated—as the city struggled heroically to deal with its collective pain, grief, and anger. Amid all the images, those emotions were perhaps most eloquently captured in a photograph of a firefighter who had just been handed the bloody body of tiny child, Baylee Almon, who had celebrated her first birthday the previous day.

More than 10,000 people gathered at the state fairgrounds on April 23 for a prayer service for the victims of the bombing and their families. They listened as Gov. Frank Keating paid honor to the dead, the survivors, and all those who had helped in the aftermath of the tragedy. "Our pain is vast. Our loss is beyond measure," he said. "We cannot fathom this act, but we can reach beyond its horrible consequences." President Bill Clinton, accom-

panied by his wife, also addressed the assembly, pledging "to do all we can to help you heal the injured, to rebuild this city, and to bring to justice those who did this evil."

Two Suspects Quickly Arrested

Initially, it was widely assumed that the bombing was the work of foreign terrorists. A piece of the blown-apart truck with a vehicle identification number allowed law enforcement officials to trace the truck to a Ryder rental agency in Junction City, Kansas, about 270 miles north of Oklahoma City. The clerk at the rental agency was able to describe two men who rented the truck, and agents of the Federal Bureau of Investigation (FBI) soon tracked one of them to a motel where he had used his real name, Timothy McVeigh.

Ironically, the twenty-seven-year-old McVeigh had been arrested in Perry, Oklahoma, about ninety minutes after the explosion. A state trooper had pulled McVeigh over for driving without a license plate and then arrested him after discovering he had a knife and a loaded semiautomatic handgun. McVeigh was about to be released on $500 bond on April 21, when his jailers realized that he was the "John Doe No. 1" the FBI had been searching for.

A second man, forty-year-old Terry L. Nichols, of Herington, Kansas, surrendered to authorities that same day after the FBI had declared him to be a suspect. An army friend of McVeigh's, Nichols was thought to have bought the ammonium nitrate fertilizer and fuel oil that were the key ingredients of the bomb. Nichols' brother, James, was also being held as a material witness.

On August 10, a federal grand jury in Oklahoma City indicted McVeigh and Terry Nichols on eleven counts of conspiring to use a weapon of mass destruction to kill people and destroy federal property, destroying federal property, using a truck bomb to kill people, and murdering eight federal law enforcement officials; the Secret Service, the Bureau of Alcohol, Tobacco and Firearms (ATF), and the Drug Enforcement Administration all had offices in the federal building. If convicted, the two men could receive the death penalty.

A third man, Michael J. Fortier, pleaded guilty on August 10 to a lesser indictment charging him with knowing about but not informing law enforcement officials of the bombing plan. Fortier, who had been in the same infantry company at Fort Riley, Kansas, as McVeigh and Nichols, was expected to be the prosecution's lead witness. An earlier indictment brought against James Nichols was dropped.

The motive for the bombing was unclear, but both men were thought to have a deep-seated hatred of the federal government. The FBI said that McVeigh held "extreme right-wing views" and was "particularly agitated" about the government's handling of the Waco, Texas, incident in 1993, in which seventy-two members of a religious cult led by David Koresh died in a fire that swept their compound, while it was under siege by the FBI. The

177

Oklahoma bombing occurred on the second anniversary of the Waco disaster. (Waco disaster, Historic Documents of 1993, p. 293)

The connection to the Waco incident, which had been the subject of numerous congressional hearings, led to speculation that McVeigh and Nichols might have been part of a larger conspiracy, perhaps organized by an extremist paramilitary group. No evidence to that effect had been revealed by year's end, however.

The bombing focused public attention on the numerous paramilitary organizations or militias that had sprung up around the country in recent years. Many of these groups were extremely distrustful of the federal government, believing that it was intent on taking away their individual rights, including the right to bear arms. The FBI and ATF were particular targets of these groups' animosity, in large part because of their role in both the Waco tragedy and an August 1992 incident known as "Ruby Ridge." In that episode, government agents seeking to arrest white separatist Randy Weaver at his cabin in a remote area in the Idaho mountains were involved in a shootout that resulted in the deaths of a federal marshal and Weaver's wife and son. Both internal and congressional reports had found fault with the law enforcement agencies' planning and execution of those operations.

The Waco and Ruby Ridge incidents figured in the sabotage of an Amtrak train in the Arizona desert on October 9. One person was killed and some seventy-five were injured when the train derailed as it was crossing a trestle; four cars fell into a thirty-foot gulch. Investigators found that the bolts holding a bar joining two sections of track had been deliberately removed. They also found a letter, headed "indictment of the ATF and FBI," which castigated the two agencies for abuse of their powers. The letter was signed "Sons of the Gestapo," a group federal authorities said was unfamiliar to them. The authorities cautioned that the sabotage might be the work of a disgruntled railroad employee, who used the letter as a subterfuge. By year's end, no suspects had been charged in the case.

Stepped-Up Security Measures

On April 20 President Clinton asked Attorney General Janet Reno to review security measures at all federal buildings and to recommend improvements. On June 28, the president ordered all federal agencies to begin to implement the fifty-two minimum security standards the Justice Department recommended. These included tighter identification systems for clearing employees into buildings, better lighting, shatterproof windows, and greater television monitoring and security at entrances and exists. Clinton on May 20 also ordered the two-block stretch of Pennsylvania Avenue in front of the White House to be closed to vehicular traffic. (Closing of Pennsylvania Avenue, p. 254)

Within days of the bombing, the president also pledged to ask Congress to grant federal law enforcement agencies new authorities to deal with both domestic and foreign terrorism. The Senate passed an antiterrorism bill (S 735) on June 7 by a vote of 91–8. The legislation would make international terrorism a federal crime, bar terrorist groups from raising funds in the United States, and enhance wiretap authority in terrorism cases.

Over the objections of their leaders, however, conservative Republicans in the House blocked similar legislation from coming to the House floor for debate. "I think people are just psychologically against giving more resources to law enforcement," said Judiciary Committee Chairman Henry J. Hyde (R-Ill.), the bill's sponsor in the House. Others said the conservative Republicans were unwilling to support the measure unless they were guaranteed a vote on repealing a 1994 ban on certain types of assault weapons.

Following are texts of remarks by Gov. Frank Keating of Oklahoma and President Bill Clinton made April 23, 1995, at a prayer service at the Oklahoma State Fair Arena in Oklahoma City, honoring the victims of the April 19 bombing of the Alfred P. Murrah Federal Building:

GOV. KEATING'S REMARKS

The tragedy of April 19th shocked America. Its unspeakable evil sickened the world. Never in the history of our country have Americans witnessed such senseless barbarism. It has been suggested that those who committed this act of mass murder chose us as their victims because we were supposedly immune—the heartland of America.

Well, we are the heartland of America. Today we stand before the world, and before our God, together—our hearts and hands linked in a solidarity these criminals can never understand. We stand together in love.

We have seen the terrifying images and read the heart-touching stories. Some of us have lived them.

- The firefighter clutching the body of a sweet, innocent child.
- The policeman reaching through rubble to grasp an outstretched hand.
- The volunteer stretcher bearers—some black, some white, some brown, all linked in courage and compassion—rushing aid to the wounded.
- The healers embracing life . . . the mourners lamenting death.
- The endless lines of donors and helpers and givers—giving their labor, their hopes, their treasure, their very blood.

Through all of this—through the tears, the righteous anger, the soul-rending sorrow of immeasurable loss—we have sometimes felt alone. But we are never truly alone. We have God, and we have each other.

Today we have our neighbors—more than 3 million Oklahomans, and never have we drawn so close. There is something special about Oklahoma. We have always known that; now, so does America, and the world.

Today, we have our fellow Americans—from the power of our federal relief and investigative agencies to the prayers of millions. They will bring us justice as they have already brought us hope, and we will be forever grateful for this wonderful outpouring of love and support.

Today we have our families—so many of them torn by sorrow and hurt, but families still, strong through the generations, stronger yet through this terrible ordeal.

Today we have our heroes and heroines—saints in gray and blue and white and khaki—the rescuers and the healers. They have labored long and nobly. And they have cried with us.

Today we have our leaders: Mister President, Reverend Graham, we are moved by your presence. The warmth of our welcome may be dimmed by tears, but it is one of deep gratitude. Thank you for coming to touch our lives.

Today we have our children—Oklahoma is still a young state, and our young people are very special to us. We have been brutally reminded of how precious they are by the events of the last few days. For them we reserve our warmest hugs and gentlest touch.

Today we have our God. He is not a God of your religion or mine, but of all people, in all times. He is a God of love, but He is also a God of justice. Today He assures us once again that good is stronger than evil, that love is greater than hate, that each of us is His special child, embraced by the Father's love.

Our pain is vast. Our loss is beyond measure. We cannot fathom this act, but we can reach beyond its horrible consequences.

The thousands of us gathered here today are multiplied by God's love, anointed by His gentle mercy. Today we are one with Him, and with one another.

It is right for us to grieve. We have all been touched by an immense tragedy, and our sorrow is part of the healing process. For some of us stricken with intense personal losses, it will be a long and tortured path. For all of us it is a journey through darkness.

But darkness ends in morning light. That is God's promise, and it is our hope.

There is a lovely parable of a man who looked back on his life and saw it as an endless series of footprints in the sand. At times there were two sets of footprints, side by side, and he remembered these times as happy. At others there was but one set of prints—the times of sadness and pain.

He confronted God and asked why He had ceased to walk beside him when he most needed that support. Why, he wondered, had God abandoned him?

And God answered: BUT MY SON, THOSE WERE THE TIMES I WAS CARRYING YOU.

He carries us today, cupped gently in His loving hands.

CLINTON'S REMARKS

Thank you very much. Governor Keating and Mrs. Keating, Reverend Graham, to the families of those who have been lost and wounded, to the people of Oklahoma City, who have endured so much, and the people of this wonderful state, to all of you who are here as our fellow Americans.

I am honored to be here today to represent the American people. But I have to tell you that Hillary and I also come as parents, as husband and wife, as people who were your neighbors for some of the best years of our lives.

Today our Nation joins with you in grief. We mourn with you. We share your hope against hope that some may still survive. We thank all those who have worked so heroically to save lives and to solve this crime, those here in Oklahoma and those who are all across this great land and many who left their own lives to come here to work hand in hand with you.

We pledge to do all we can to help you heal the injured, to rebuild this city, and to bring to justice those who did this evil.

This terrible sin took the lives of our American family, innocent children in that building, only because their parents were trying to be good parents as well as good workers; citizens in the building going about their daily business; and many there who served the rest of us—who worked to help the elderly and the disabled, who worked to support our farmers and our veterans, who worked to enforce our laws and to protect us. Let us say clearly, they served us well, and we are grateful.

But for so many of you they were also neighbors and friends. You saw them at church or the PTA meetings, at the civic clubs, at the ball park. You know them in ways that all the rest of America could not.

And to all the members of the families here present who have suffered loss, though we share your grief, your pain is unimaginable, and we know that. We cannot undo it. That is God's work.

Our words seem small beside the loss you have endured. But I found a few I wanted to share today. I've received a lot of letters in these last terrible days. One stood out because it came from a young widow and a mother of three whose own husband was murdered with over 200 other Americans when Pan Am 103 was shot down. Here is what that woman said I should say to you today: "The anger you feel is valid, but you must not allow yourselves to be consumed by it. The hurt you feel must not be allowed to turn into hate, but instead into the search for justice. The loss you feel must not paralyze your own lives. Instead, you must try to pay tribute to your loved ones by continuing to do all the things they left undone, thus ensuring they did not die in vain."

Wise words from one who also knows.

You have lost too much, but you have not lost everything. And you have certainly not lost America, for we will stand with you for as many tomorrows as it takes.

If ever we needed evidence of that, I could only recall the words of Governor and Mrs. Keating. If anybody thinks that Americans are mostly mean and selfish, they ought to come to Oklahoma. If anybody thinks Americans have lost the capacity for love and caring and courage, they ought to come to Oklahoma.

To all my fellow Americans beyond this hall, I say, one thing we owe those who have sacrificed is the duty to purge ourselves of the dark forces which gave rise to this evil. They are forces that threaten our common peace, our freedom, our way of life.

Let us teach our children that the God of comfort is also the God of righteousness. Those who trouble their own house will inherit the wind. Justice will prevail. Let us let our own children know that we will stand against the forces of fear. When there is talk of hatred, let us stand up and talk against it. When there is talk of violence, let us stand up and talk against it. In the face of death, let us honor life. As St. Paul admonished us, let us not be overcome by evil, but overcome evil with good.

Yesterday Hillary and I had the privilege of speaking with some children of other Federal employees—children like those who were lost here. And one little girl said something we will never forget. She said, we should all plant a tree in memory of the children. So this morning before we got on the plane to come here, at the White House, we planted that tree in honor of the children of Oklahoma. It was a dogwood with its wonderful spring flower and its deep, enduring roots. It embodies the lesson of the Psalms: that the life of a good person is like a tree whose leaf does not wither.

My fellow Americans, a tree takes a long time to grow, and wounds take a long time to heal. But we must begin. Those who are lost now belong to God. Some day we will be with them. But until that happens, their legacy must be our lives.

Thank you all, and God bless you.

SUPREME COURT ON GUN-FREE SCHOOL ZONES
April 26, 1995

Departing from nearly sixty years of a broad interpretation of Congress's power to regulate interstate commerce, the Supreme Court ruled April 26 that Congress had exceeded its authority in 1990 when it made the possession of firearms within 1,000 feet of a school a federal crime. The 5–4 decision was certain to contribute to the swirling controversy over the limits of federal power, particularly in areas such as law enforcement traditionally governed by the states.

That controversy had been heightened by the terrorist bombing just weeks earlier that destroyed a federal office building in Oklahoma City and killed 168 people. In the wake of that tragedy several federal legislators were pushing for new laws to give federal law enforcement officials greater authority to investigate domestic terrorist groups. (Oklahoma City bombing, p. 176)

Since 1937 the Supreme Court has interpreted the congressional commerce power expansively, endorsing the legislature's authority to regulate intrastate matters so long as they "substantially affect" interstate commerce. That rationale has been used not only to justify ever more detailed regulation of commercial activity, but also to prohibit racial discrimination in public accommodations, to remove restrictions on interstate travel, and to regulate environmental pollutants. In recent years, Congress has also used its authority under the commerce clause to define several activities as federal crimes, including carjackings, drive-by shootings, and violent demonstrations at abortion clinics.

Infringement on State Police Power

This case, United States v. Lopez, *arose when Alfonso Lopez Jr., a high school senior, was caught carrying a .38–caliber handgun and five bullets to his San Antonio school in 1992. He was charged under the federal gun-free school zone law and convicted in U.S. District Court. The Fifth Circuit Court of Appeals reversed the conviction, saying Congress had not ade-*

quately justified the legislation under the commerce clause. The Supreme Court affirmed the appeals court ruling. Chief Justice William H. Rehnquist wrote the opinion.

Rehnquist rejected the government's argument that the possession of a gun in a school zone substantially affects interstate commerce because it leads to violence, which interferes with learning, which makes students less productive workers. The federal gun ban, Rehnquist wrote, was "a criminal statute that by its terms has nothing to do with 'commerce' or any sort of economic enterprise, however broadly one might define these terms." Under the government's reasoning, Rehnquist said, "Congress could regulate any activity that it found was related to the economic productivity of individual citizens: family law (including marriage, divorce, and child custody), for example. . . . To uphold the Government's contentions here . . . would bid fair to convert congressional authority under the Commerce Clause to a general police power of the sort retained by the States."

Joining Rehnquist were Justices Antonin Scalia, Sandra Day O'Connor, Anthony M. Kennedy, and Clarence Thomas. Kennedy, for himself and O'Connor, and Thomas wrote concurring opinions.

Writing for the four dissenters, Justice Stephen G. Breyer said that the majority's ruling "threatens legal uncertainty in an area of law that, until this case, seemed reasonably well settled. . . . [T]he legal uncertainty now created will restrict Congress' ability to enact criminal laws aimed at criminal behavior that . . . seriously threatens the economic, as well as social, well-being of Americans." Breyer underscored his dissent by reading part of it from the bench. David H. Souter, Ruth Bader Ginsburg, and John Paul Stevens joined Breyer's dissent; Souter and Stevens also wrote separate dissents.

In his dissent, Souter chided the majority for failing to exercise judicial restraint and to defer to the judgment of Congress. "The modern respect for the competence and primacy of Congress in matters affecting commerce developed only after one of this Court's most chastening experiences," Souter reminded the majority. He was referring to President Franklin Delano Roosevelt's threat to pack the Court in 1937, after the Court had struck down several laws Congress had enacted to deal with the Great Depression on the grounds that Congress was misusing its powers, including its interstate commerce powers. The crisis was resolved only after one of the justices reversed his vote in a series of crucial rulings that upheld several New Deal measures. The Court's expansive interpretation of the commerce clause began with those decisions.

The Court's decision in Lopez *was unlikely to have much effect on guns in and around schools; more than forty states had laws on the books banning guns in school zones. Furthermore, President Bill Clinton sent Congress proposed legislation May 6 that would make it illegal for anyone to bring a firearm "that has moved in or that otherwise affects interstate commerce" within a school zone.*

Uncertain Effect on Congressional Powers

The decision's broader effect on Congress's power under the commerce clause was less clear. "It's capable of undoing a lot of law," said Henry P. Monaghan, a constitutional law professor at Columbia University.

Barbara McDowell, a Washington attorney who represented gun control groups in the case, said the ruling did not appear to threaten other federal gun control laws, such as the ban on some kinds of assault weapons or the waiting period for purchasing handguns. Those laws set terms for buying and selling guns and were more readily understood as "commerce," she said. Other federal laws, including criminal statutes that often lacked a clear commercial link, could be in jeopardy.

Harvard Law School professor Laurence H. Tribe said the decision was a "dramatic move" by the Court, but that if a federal law ever exceeded congressional authority under the commerce clause, the school zone gun ban was it. Noting that Congress had not explicitly made findings linking guns in schools with interstate commerce, Tribe said that the majority revealed that it "takes structural limits [to Congress's legislative powers] more seriously than people had thought . . . which liberals and pragmatists find dismaying."

Monaghan and other legal analysts said it would take more rulings to determine whether the Court was in fact narrowing its interpretation of Congress's legislative power.

Following are excerpts from the majority, concurring, and dissenting opinions in the Supreme Court's ruling April 26, 1995, in the case of United States v. Lopez, *in which the Court ruled that Congress had exceeded its power under the commerce clause of the Constitution when it banned guns within 1,000 feet of a school:*

<u>No. 93–1260</u>

United States, Petitioner

v.

Alfonso Lopez, Jr.

} On writ of certiorari to the United States Court of Appeals for the Fifth Circuit

[April 26, 1995]

CHIEF JUSTICE REHNQUIST delivered the opinion of the Court.

In the Gun-Free School Zones Act of 1990, Congress made it a federal offense "for any individual knowingly to possess a firearm at a place that the individual knows, or has reasonable cause to believe, is a school zone." 18 U.S.C. §922 (q)(1)(A). The Act neither regulates a commercial activity nor contains a requirement that the possession be connected in any way to interstate commerce. We hold that the Act exceeds the authority of Congress "[t]o regulate Commerce . . . among the several States. . . ." U.S. Const., Art. I, §8, cl. 3.

On March 10, 1992, respondent, who was then a 12th-grade student, arrived at Edison High School in San Antonio, Texas, carrying a concealed .38 caliber handgun and five bullets. Acting upon an anonymous tip, school authorities confronted respondent, who admitted that he was carrying the weapon. He was arrested and charged under Texas law with firearm possession on school premises. The next day, the state charges were dismissed after federal agents charged respondent by complaint with violating the Gun-Free School Zones Act of 1990.

A federal grand jury indicted respondent on one count of knowing possession of a firearm at a school zone, in violation of §922(q). Respondent moved to dismiss his federal indictment on the ground that §922(q) "is unconstitutional as it is beyond the power of Congress to legislate control over our public schools." The District Court denied the motion, concluding that §922(q) "is a constitutional exercise of Congress' well-defined power to regulate activities in and affecting commerce, and the 'business' of elementary, middle and high schools . . . affects interstate commerce." Respondent waived his right to a jury trial. The District Court conducted a bench trial, found him guilty of violating §922(q), and sentenced him to six months' imprisonment and two years' supervised release.

On appeal, respondent challenged his conviction based on his claim that §922(q) exceeded Congress' power to legislate under the Commerce Clause. The Court of Appeals for the Fifth Circuit agreed and reversed respondent's conviction. It held that, in light of what it characterized as insufficient congressional findings and legislative history, "section 922(q), in the full reach of its terms, is invalid as beyond the power of Congress under the Commerce Clause." Because of the importance of the issue, we granted certiorari (1994), and we now affirm.

We start with first principles. The Constitution creates a Federal Government of enumerated powers. See U.S. Const., Art. I, §8. As James Madison wrote, "the powers delegated by the proposed Constitution to the federal government are few and defined. Those which are to remain in the State governments are numerous and indefinite." *The Federalist No. 45*. This constitutionally mandated division of authority "was adopted by the Framers to ensure protection of our fundamental liberties." *Gregory* v. *Ashcroft* (1991). "Just as the separation and independence of the coordinate branches of the Federal Government serves to prevent the accumulation of excessive power in any one branch, a healthy balance of power between the States and the Federal Government will reduce the risk of tyranny and abuse from either front."

The Constitution delegates to Congress the power "[t]o regulate Commerce with foreign Nations, and among the several States, and with the Indian Tribes." The Court, through Chief Justice Marshall, first defined the nature of Congress' commerce power in *Gibbons* v. *Ogden* (1824):

"Commerce, undoubtedly, is traffic, but it is something more: it is intercourse. It describes the commercial intercourse between nations, and parts of nations, in all its branches, and is regulated by prescribing rules for carrying on that intercourse."

The commerce power "is the power to regulate; that is, to prescribe the rule by which commerce is to be governed. This power, like all others vested in Congress, is complete in itself, may be exercised to its utmost extent, and acknowledges no limitations, other than are prescribed in the constitution." The *Gibbons* Court, however, acknowledged that limitations on the commerce power are inherent in the very language of the Commerce Clause.

"It is not intended to say that these words comprehend that commerce, which is completely internal, which is carried on between man and man in a State, or between different parts of the same State, and which does not extend to or affect other States. Such a power would be inconvenient, and is certainly unnecessary.". . .

For nearly a century thereafter, the Court's Commerce Clause decisions dealt but rarely with the extent of Congress' power, and almost entirely with the Commerce Clause as a limit on state legislation that discriminated against interstate commerce. . . . Under this line of precedent, the Court held that certain categories of activity such as "production," "manufacturing," and "mining" were within the province of state governments, and thus were beyond the power of Congress under the Commerce Clause.

In 1887, Congress enacted the Interstate Commerce Act, and in 1890, Congress enacted the Sherman Antitrust Act. These laws ushered in a new era of federal regulation under the commerce power. When cases involving these laws first reached this Court, we imported from our negative Commerce Clause cases the approach that Congress could not regulate activities such as "production," "manufacturing," and "mining.". . . Simultaneously, however, the Court held that, where the interstate and intrastate aspects of commerce were so mingled together that full regulation of interstate commerce required incidental regulation of intrastate commerce, the Commerce Clause authorized such regulation.

In *A. L. A. Schechter Poultry Corp.* v. *United States* (1935), the Court struck down regulations that fixed the hours and wages of individuals employed by an intrastate business because the activity being regulated related to interstate commerce only indirectly. In doing so, the Court characterized the distinction between direct and indirect effects of intrastate transactions upon interstate commerce as "a fundamental one, essential to the maintenance of our constitutional system." Activities that affected interstate commerce directly were within Congress' power; activities that affected interstate commerce indirectly were beyond Congress' reach. The justification for this formal distinction was rooted in the fear that otherwise "there would be virtually no limit to the federal power and for all practical purposes we should have a completely centralized government."

Two years later, in the watershed case of *NLRB* v. *Jones & Laughlin Steel Corp.* (1937), the Court upheld the National Labor Relations Act against a Commerce Clause challenge, and in the process, departed from the distinction between "direct" and "indirect" effects on interstate commerce.... The Court held that intrastate activities that "have such a close and substantial relation to interstate commerce that their control is essential or appropriate to protect that commerce from burdens and obstructions" are within Congress' power to regulate.

In *United States* v. *Darby* (1941), the Court upheld the Fair Labor Standards Act, stating:

> "The power of Congress over interstate commerce is not confined to the regulation of commerce among the states. It extends to those activities intrastate which so affect interstate commerce or the exercise of the power of Congress over it as to make regulation of them appropriate means to the attainment of a legitimate end, the exercise of the granted power of Congress to regulate interstate commerce."...

In *Wickard* v. *Filburn* [1942], the Court upheld the application of amendments to the Agricultural Adjustment Act of 1938 to the production and consumption of home-grown wheat. The *Wickard* Court explicitly rejected earlier distinctions between direct and indirect effects on interstate commerce, stating:

> "[E]ven if appellee's activity be local and though it may not be regarded as commerce, it may still, whatever its nature, be reached by Congress if it exerts a substantial economic effect on interstate commerce, and this irrespective of whether such effect is what might at some earlier time have been defined as 'direct' or 'indirect'"

The *Wickard* Court emphasized that although Filburn's own contribution to the demand for wheat may have been trivial by itself, that was not "enough to remove him from the scope of federal regulation where, as here, his contribution, taken together with that of many others similarly situated, is far from trivial."

Jones & Laughlin Steel, *Darby*, and *Wickard* ushered in an era of Commerce Clause jurisprudence that greatly expanded the previously defined authority of Congress under that Clause. In part, this was a recognition of the great changes that had occurred in the way business was carried on in this country. Enterprises that had once been local or at most regional in nature had become national in scope. But the doctrinal change also reflected a view that earlier Commerce Clause cases artificially had constrained the authority of Congress to regulate interstate commerce.

But even these modern-era precedents which have expanded congressional power under the Commerce Clause confirm that this power is subject to outer limits....

Consistent with this structure, we have identified three broad categories of activity that Congress may regulate under its commerce power. First, Congress may regulate the use of the channels of interstate commerce.... Second, Congress is empowered to regulate and protect the instrumentalities of interstate commerce, or persons or things in interstate commerce, even though the threat may come only from intrastate activities. . . . Finally, Congress' commerce authority includes the power to regulate those activities having a substantial relation to interstate commerce, *i.e.*, those activities that substantially affect interstate commerce.

Within this final category, admittedly, our case law has not been clear whether an activity must "affect" or "substantially affect" interstate commerce in order to be within Congress' power to regulate it under the Commerce Clause. . . . We conclude, consistent with the great weight of our case law, that the proper test requires an analysis of whether the regulated activity "substantially affects" interstate commerce.

We now turn to consider the power of Congress, in the light of this framework, to enact §922(q). The first two categories of authority may be quickly disposed of: §922(q) is not a regulation of the use of the channels of interstate commerce, nor is it an attempt to prohibit the interstate transportation of a commodity through the channels of commerce; nor can §922(q) be justified as a regulation by which Congress has sought to protect an instrumentality of interstate commerce or a thing in interstate commerce. Thus, if §922(q) is to be sustained, it must be under the third category as a regulation of an activity that substantially affects interstate commerce.

First, we have upheld a wide variety of congressional Acts regulating intrastate economic activity where we have concluded that the activity substantially affected interstate commerce. . . .

Section 922(q) is a criminal statute that by its terms has nothing to do with "commerce" or any sort of economic enterprise, however broadly one might define those terms. Section 922(q) is not an essential part of a larger regulation of economic activity, in which the regulatory scheme could be undercut unless the intrastate activity were regulated. It cannot, therefore, be sustained under our cases upholding regulations of activities that arise out of or are connected with a commercial transaction, which viewed in the aggregate, substantially affects interstate commerce.

Second, §922(q) contains no jurisdictional element which would ensure, through case-by-case inquiry, that the firearm possession in question affects interstate commerce. For example, in *United States* v. *Bass* (1971), the Court interpreted former 18 U.S.C. §1202(a), which made it a crime for a felon to "receive, possess, or transport in commerce or affecting commerce . . . any firearm." The Court interpreted the possession component of §1202(a) to require an additional nexus to interstate commerce. . . . Unlike the statute in *Bass*, §922(q) has no express jurisdictional element which might limit its reach to a discrete set of firearm possessions that additionally have an explicit connection with or effect on interstate commerce.

Although as part of our independent evaluation of constitutionality under the Commerce Clause we of course consider legislative findings, and indeed even congressional committee findings, regarding effect on interstate commerce, the Government concedes that "[n]either the statute nor its legislative history contain[s] express congressional findings regarding the effects upon interstate commerce of gun possession in a school zone." We agree with the Government that Congress normally is not required to make formal findings as to the substantial burdens that an activity has on interstate commerce. . . . But to the extent that congressional findings would enable us to evaluate the legislative judgment that the activity in question substantially affected interstate commerce, even though no such substantial effect was visible to the naked eye, they are lacking here.

The Government argues that Congress has accumulated institutional expertise regarding the regulation of firearms through previous enactments. We agree, however, with the Fifth Circuit that importation of previous findings to justify §922(q) is especially inappropriate here because the "prior federal enactments or Congressional findings [do not] speak to the subject matter of section 922(q) or its relationship to interstate commerce. Indeed, section 922(q) plows thoroughly new ground and represents a sharp break with the long-standing pattern of federal firearms legislation."

The Government's essential contention, *in fine*, is that we may determine here that §922(q) is valid because possession of a firearm in a local school zone does indeed substantially affect interstate commerce. The Government argues that possession of a firearm in a school zone may result in violent crime and that violent crime can be expected to affect the functioning of the national economy in two ways. First, the costs of violent crime are substantial, and, through the mechanism of insurance, those costs are spread throughout the population. Second, violent crime reduces the willingness of individuals to travel to areas within the country that are perceived to be unsafe. The Government also argues that the presence of guns in schools poses a substantial threat to the educational process by threatening the learning environment. A handicapped educational process, in turn, will result in a less productive citizenry. That, in turn, would have an adverse effect on the Nation's economic well-being. As a result, the Government argues that Congress could rationally have concluded that §922(q) substantially affects interstate commerce.

We pause to consider the implications of the Government's arguments. The Government admits, under its "costs of crime" reasoning, that Congress could regulate not only all violent crime, but all activities that might lead to violent crime, regardless of how tenuously they relate to interstate commerce. Similarly, under the Government's "national productivity" reasoning, Congress could regulate any activity that it found was related to the economic productivity of individual citizens: family law (including marriage, divorce, and child custody), for example. Under the theories that the Government presents in support of §922(q), it is difficult to perceive any limitation on federal power, even in areas such as criminal law enforcement or education where States historically have been sovereign. Thus, if we were to accept the Government's arguments, we are hard-pressed to posit any activity by an individual that Congress is without power to regulate.

Although JUSTICE BREYER argues that acceptance of the Government's rationales would not authorize a general federal police power, he is unable to identify any activity that the States may regulate but Congress may not. JUSTICE BREYER posits that there might be some limitations on Congress' commerce power such as family law or certain aspects of education. These suggested limitations, when viewed in light of the dissent's expansive analysis, are devoid of substance.

JUSTICE BREYER focuses, for the most part, on the threat that firearm possession in and near schools poses to the educational process and the potential economic consequences flowing from that threat. Specifically, the dissent reasons that (1) gun-related violence is a serious problem; (2) that problem, in turn, has an adverse effect on classroom learning; and (3) that adverse effect on classroom learning, in turn, represents a substantial threat to trade and commerce. This analysis would be equally applicable, if not more so, to subjects such as family law and direct regulation of education.

For instance, if Congress can, pursuant to its Commerce Clause power, regulate activities that adversely affect the learning environment, then, *a fortiori*, it also can regulate the educational process directly. Congress could determine that a school's curriculum has a "significant" effect on the extent of classroom learning. As a result, Congress could mandate a federal curriculum for local elementary and secondary schools because what is taught in local schools has a significant "effect on classroom learning" and that, in turn, has a substantial effect on interstate commerce.

JUSTICE BREYER rejects our reading of precedent and argues that "Congress . . . could rationally conclude that schools fall on the commercial side of the line." Again, JUSTICE BREYER's rationale lacks any real limits because, depending on the level of generality, any activity can be looked upon as commercial. Under the dissent's rationale, Congress could just as easily look at child rearing as "fall[ing] on the commercial side of the line" because it provides a "valuable service—namely, to equip [children] with the skills they need to survive in life and, more specifically, in the workplace." We do not doubt that Congress has authority under the Commerce Clause to regulate numerous commercial activities that substantially affect interstate commerce and also affect the educational process. That authority, though broad, does not include the authority to regulate each and every aspect of local schools.

Admittedly, a determination whether an intrastate activity is commercial or noncommercial may in some cases result in legal uncertainty. But, so long as Congress' authority is limited to those powers enumerated in the Constitution, and so long as those enumerated powers are interpreted as having judicially enforceable outer limits, congressional legislation under the Commerce Clause always will engender "legal uncertainty.". . . The Constitution mandates this uncertainty by withholding from Congress a plenary police power that would authorize enactment of every type of legislation. Any possible benefit from eliminating this "legal uncertainty" would be at the expense of the Constitution's system of enumerated powers.

In *Jones & Laughlin Steel*, we held that the question of congressional power under the Commerce Clause "is necessarily one of degree." To the same effect is the concurring opinion of Justice Cardozo in *Schechter Poultry*:

> "There is a view of causation that would obliterate the distinction of what is national and what is local in the activities of commerce. Motion at the outer rim is communicated perceptibly, though minutely, to recording instruments at the center. A society such as ours 'is an elastic medium which transmits all tremors throughout its territory; the only question is of their size' "

These are not precise formulations, and in the nature of things they cannot be. But we think they point the way to a correct decision of this case. The possession of a gun in a local school zone is in no sense an economic activity that might, through repetition elsewhere, substantially affect any sort of interstate commerce. Respondent was a local student at a local school; there is no indication that he had recently moved in interstate commerce, and there is no requirement that his possession of the firearm have any concrete tie to interstate commerce.

To uphold the Government's contentions here, we would have to pile inference upon inference in a manner that would bid fair to convert congressional authority under the Commerce Clause to a general police power of the sort retained by the States. Admittedly, some of our prior cases have taken long steps down that road, giving great deference to congressional action. The broad language in these opinions has suggested the possibility of additional expansion, but we decline here to proceed any further. To do so would require us to conclude that the Constitution's enumeration of powers does not presuppose something not enumerated and that there never will be a distinction between what is truly national and what is truly local. This we are unwilling to do.

For the foregoing reasons the judgment of the Court of Appeals is

Affirmed.

JUSTICE KENNEDY, with whom JUSTICE O'CONNOR joins, concurring.

The history of the judicial struggle to interpret the Commerce Clause during the transition from the economic system the Founders knew to the single, national market still emergent in our own era counsels great restraint before the Court determines that the Clause is insufficient to support an exercise of the national power. That history gives me some pause about today's decision, but I join the Court's opinion with these observations on what I conceive to be its necessary though limited holding. . . .

The history of our Commerce Clause decisions contains at least two lessons of relevance to this case. The first, as stated at the outset, is the imprecision of content-based boundaries used without more to define the limits of the Commerce Clause. The second, related to the first but of even greater consequence, is that the Court as an institution and the legal system as a whole have an immense stake in the stability of our Commerce Clause jurisprudence as it has evolved to this point. *Stare decisis* operates with great force in counseling us not to call in question the essential principles now in place respecting the congressional power to regulate transactions of a commercial nature. That fundamental restraint on our power forecloses us from reverting to an understanding of commerce that would serve only an 18th-century economy, dependent then upon production and trading practices that had changed but little over the preceding centuries; it also mandates against returning to the time when congressional authority to regulate undoubted commercial activities was limited by a judicial determination that those matters had an insufficient connection to an interstate system. Congress can regulate in the commercial sphere on the assumption that we have a single market and a unified purpose to build a stable national economy. . . .

The statute before us upsets the federal balance to a degree that renders it an unconstitutional assertion of the commerce power, and our intervention is required. As the CHIEF JUSTICE explains, unlike the earlier cases to come before the Court here neither the actors nor their conduct have a commercial character, and neither the purposes nor the design of the statute have an evident commercial nexus. The statute makes the simple possession of a gun within 1,000 feet of the grounds of the school a criminal offense. In a sense any conduct in this interdependent world of ours has an ultimate commercial origin or consequence, but we have not yet said the commerce power may reach so far. If Congress attempts that extension, then at the least we must inquire whether the exercise of national power seeks to intrude upon an area of traditional state concern.

An interference of these dimensions occurs here, for it is well established that education is a traditional concern of the States. The proximity to schools, including of course schools owned and operated by the States or their subdivisions, is the very premise for making the conduct criminal. In these circumstances, we have a particular duty to insure that the federal-state balance is not destroyed. . . .

While it is doubtful that any State, or indeed any reasonable person, would argue that it is wise policy to allow students to carry guns on school premises, considerable disagreement exists about how best to accomplish that goal. In this circumstance, the theory and utility of our federalism are revealed, for the States may perform their role as laboratories for experimentation to devise various solutions where the best solution is far from clear.

If a State or municipality determines that harsh criminal sanctions are necessary and wise to deter students from carrying guns on school premises, the reserved powers of the States are sufficient to enact those measures. Indeed, over 40 States already have criminal laws outlawing the possession of firearms on or near school grounds.

Other, more practicable means to rid the schools of guns may be thought by the citizens of some States to be preferable for the safety and welfare of the schools those States are charged with maintaining. . . . These might include inducements to inform on violators where the information leads to arrests or confiscation of the guns, programs to encourage the voluntary surrender of guns with some provision for amnesty, penalties imposed on parents or guardians for failure to supervise the child, laws providing for suspension or expulsion of gun-toting students, or programs for expulsion with assignment to special facilities.

The statute now before us forecloses the States from experimenting and exercising their own judgment in an area to which States lay claim by right of history and expertise, and it does so by regulating an activity beyond the realm of commerce in the ordinary and usual sense of that term. The tendency of this statute to displace state regulation in areas of traditional state concern is evident from its territorial operation. There are over 100,000 elementary and secondary schools in the United States. Each of these now has an invisible federal zone extending 1,000 feet beyond the (often irregular) boundaries of the school property. In some communities no doubt it would be difficult to navigate without infringing on those zones. Yet throughout these areas, school officials would find their own programs for the prohibition of guns in danger of displacement by the federal authority unless the State chooses to enact a parallel rule. . . .

For these reasons, I join in the opinion and judgment of the Court.

JUSTICE THOMAS, concurring.

The Court today properly concludes that the Commerce Clause does not grant Congress the authority to prohibit gun possession within 1,000 feet of a school, as it attempted to do in the Gun-Free School Zones Act of 1990. Although I join the majority, I write separately to observe that our case law has drifted far from the original understanding of the Commerce Clause. In a future case, we ought to temper our Commerce Clause jurisprudence in a manner that both makes sense of our more recent case law and is more faithful to the original understanding of that Clause.

We have said that Congress may regulate not only "Commerce . . . among the several states," but also anything that has a "substantial effect" on such commerce. This test, if taken to its logical extreme, would give Congress a "police power" over all aspects of American life. Unfortunately, we have never come to grips with this implication of our substantial effects formula. Although we have supposedly applied the substantial effects test for the past 60 years, we *always* have rejected readings of the Commerce Clause and the scope of federal power that would permit Congress to exercise a police power; our cases are quite clear that there are real limits to federal power. . . .

While the principal dissent concedes that there are limits to federal power, the sweeping nature of our current test enables the dissent to argue that Congress can regulate gun possession. But it seems to me that the power to regulate "commerce" can by no means encompass authority over mere gun possession, any more than it empowers the Federal Government to regulate marriage, littering, or cruelty to animals, throughout the 50 States. Our Constitution quite properly leaves such matters to the individual States, notwithstanding these activities' effects on interstate commerce. Any interpretation of the Commerce Clause that even suggests that Congress could regulate such matters is in need of reexamination.

In an appropriate case, I believe that we must further reconsider our "substantial effects" test with an eye toward constructing a standard that reflects the text and history of the Commerce Clause without totally rejecting our more recent Commerce Clause jurisprudence. . . .

JUSTICE STEVENS, dissenting.

The welfare of our future "Commerce with foreign Nations, and among the several States" is vitally dependent on the character of the education of our children. I therefore agree entirely with JUSTICE BREYER's explanation of why Congress has ample power to prohibit the possession of firearms in or near schools—just as it may protect the school environment from harms posed by controlled substances such as asbestos or alcohol. I also agree with JUSTICE SOUTER's exposition of the radical character of the Court's holding and its kinship with the discredited, pre-Depression version of substantive due process. I believe, however, that the Court's extraordinary decision merits this additional comment.

Guns are both articles of commerce and articles that can be used to restrain commerce. Their possession is the consequence, either directly or indirectly, of commercial activity. In my judgment, Congress' power to regulate commerce in firearms includes the power to prohibit possession of guns at any location because of their potentially harmful use; it necessarily follows that Congress may also prohibit their possession in particular markets. The market for the possession of handguns by school-age children is, distressingly, substantial. Whether or not the national interest in eliminating that market would have justified federal legislation in 1789, it surely does today.

JUSTICE SOUTER, dissenting.

In reviewing congressional legislation under the Commerce Clause, we defer to what is often a merely implicit congressional judgment that its regulation addresses a subject substantially affecting interstate commerce "if there is any rational basis for such a finding." If that congressional determination is within the realm of reason, "the only remaining question for judicial inquiry is whether 'the means chosen by Congress [are] reasonably adapted to the end permitted by the Constitution.' "

The practice of deferring to rationally based legislative judgments "is a paradigm of judicial restraint." In judicial review under the Commerce Clause, it reflects our respect for the institutional competence of the Congress on a subject expressly assigned to it by the Constitution and our appreciation of the legitimacy that comes from Congress's political accountability in dealing with matters open to a wide range of possible choices.

It was not ever thus, however, as even a brief overview of Commerce Clause history during the past century reminds us. The modern respect for the competence and primacy of Congress in matters affecting commerce developed only after one of this Court's most chastening experiences, when it perforce repudiated an earlier and untenably expansive conception of judicial review in derogation of congressional commerce power. . . . [T]oday's decision tugs the Court off course, leading it to suggest opportunities for further developments that would be at odds with the rule of restraint to which the Court still wisely states adherence. . . .

JUSTICE BREYER, with whom JUSTICE STEVENS, JUSTICE SOUTER, and JUSTICE GINSBURG join, dissenting.

The issue in this case is whether the Commerce Clause authorizes Congress to enact a statute that makes it a crime to possess a gun in, or near, a school. 18 U.S.C. §922(q)(1)(A). In my view, the statute falls well within the scope of the commerce power as this Court has understood that power over the last half-century.

I

In reaching this conclusion, I apply three basic principles of Commerce Clause interpretation. First, the power to "regulate Commerce . . . among the several States," U.S. Const., Art. I, §8, cl. 3, encompasses the power to regulate local activities insofar as they significantly affect interstate commerce. . . . I use the word "significant" because the word "substantial" implies a somewhat narrower power than recent precedent suggests. But, to speak of "substantial effect" rather than "significant effect" would make no difference in this case.

Second, in determining whether a local activity will likely have a significant effect upon interstate commerce, a court must consider, not the effect of an individual act (a single instance of gun possession), but rather the cumulative effect of all similar instances (*i.e.*, the effect of all guns possessed in or near schools). . . .

Third, the Constitution requires us to judge the connection between a regulated activity and interstate commerce, not directly, but at one remove. Courts must give Congress a degree of leeway in determining the existence of a significant factual connection between the regulated activity and interstate commerce—both because the Constitution delegates the commerce power directly to Congress and because the determination requires an empirical judgment of a kind that a legislature is more likely than a court to make with accuracy. The traditional words "rational basis" capture this leeway. Thus, the specific question before us, as the Court recognizes, is not whether the "regulated activity sufficiently affected interstate commerce," but, rather, whether Congress could have had "*a rational basis*" for so concluding (emphasis added). . . .

II

Applying these principles to the case at hand, we must ask whether Congress could have had a *rational basis* for finding a significant (or substantial) connection between gun-related school violence and interstate commerce. Or, to put the question in the language of the explicit finding that Congress made when it amended this law in 1994: Could Congress rationally have found that "violent crime in school zones," through its effect on the "quality of education," significantly (or substantially) affects "interstate" or "foreign commerce"? As long as one views the commerce connection, not as a "technical legal conception," but as "a practical one," the answer to this question must be yes. Numerous reports and studies—generated both inside and outside government—make clear that Congress could reasonably have found the empirical connection that its law, implicitly or explicitly, asserts. (See Appendix for a sample of the documentation. . . .) [omitted]

For one thing, reports, hearings, and other readily available literature make clear that the problem of guns in and around schools is widespread and extremely serious. These materials report, for example, that four percent of American high school students (and six percent of inner-city high school students) carry a gun to school at least occasionally; that 12 percent of urban high school students have had guns fired at them; that 20 percent of those students have been threatened with guns; and that, in any 6-month period, several hundred thousand schoolchildren are victims of violent crimes in or near their schools. And, they report that this widespread violence in schools throughout the Nation significantly interferes with the quality of education in those schools. . . . Based on reports such as these, Congress obviously could have thought that guns and learning are mutually exclusive. And, Congress could therefore have found a substantial educational problem-teachers unable to teach, students unable to learn-and concluded that guns near schools contribute substantially to the size and scope of that problem.

Having found that guns in schools significantly undermine the quality of education in our Nation's classrooms, Congress could also have found, given the effect of education upon interstate and foreign commerce, that gun-related violence in and around schools is a commercial, as well as a human, problem. Education, although far more than a matter of economics, has long been inextricably intertwined with the Nation's economy. . . . Scholars estimate that nearly a quarter of America's economic growth in the early years of this century is traceable directly to increased schooling; that investment in "human capital" (through spending on education) exceeded investment in "physical capital" by a ratio of almost two to one; and that the economic returns to this investment in education exceeded the returns to conventional capital investment.

In recent years the link between secondary education and business has strengthened, becoming both more direct and more important. Scholars on the subject report that technological changes and innovations in management techniques have altered the nature of the workplace so that more jobs now demand greater educational skills. . . .

Increasing global competition also has made primary and secondary education economically more important. . . .

Finally, there is evidence that, today more than ever, many firms base their location decisions upon the presence, or absence, of a work force with a basic education. . . . In light of this increased importance of education to individual firms, it is no surprise that half of the Nation's manufacturers have become involved with setting standards and shaping curricula for local schools, that 88 percent think this kind of involvement is important, that more than 20 States have recently passed educational reforms to attract new business, and that business magazines have begun to rank cities according to the quality of their schools.

The economic links I have just sketched seem fairly obvious. Why then is it not equally obvious, in light of those links, that a widespread, serious, and substantial physical threat to teaching and learning *also* substantially threatens the commerce to which that teaching and learning is inextricably tied? That is to say, guns in the hands of six percent of inner-city high school students and gun-related violence throughout a city's schools must threaten the trade and commerce that those schools support. The only question, then, is whether the latter threat is (to use the majority's terminology) "substantial." And, the evidence of (1) the *extent* of the gun-related violence problem, (2) the *extent* of the resulting negative effect on classroom learning, and (3) the *extent* of the consequent negative commercial effects, when taken together, indicate a threat to trade and commerce that is "substantial." At the very least, Congress could rationally have concluded that the links are "substantial."

Specifically, Congress could have found that gun-related violence near the classroom poses a serious economic threat (1) to consequently inadequately educated workers who must endure low-paying jobs, and (2) to communities and businesses that might (in today's "information society") otherwise gain, from a well-educated work force, an important commercial advantage.... Congress might also have found these threats to be no different in kind from other threats that this Court has found within the commerce power, such as the threat that loan sharking poses to the "funds" of "numerous localities," *Perez* v. *United States* [1971], and that unfair labor practices pose to instrumentalities of commerce, see *Consolidated Edison Co.* v. *NLRB* (1938). As I have pointed out, Congress has written that "the occurrence of violent crime in school zones" has brought about a "decline in the quality of education" that "has an adverse impact on interstate commerce and the foreign commerce of the United States." 18 U.S.C.A. §§922 (q)(1)(F), (G) (Nov. 1994 Supp.). The violence-related facts, the educational facts, and the economic facts, taken together, make this conclusion rational. And, because under our case law, the sufficiency of the constitutionally necessary Commerce Clause link between a crime of violence and interstate commerce turns simply upon size or degree, those same facts make the statute constitutional.

To hold this statute constitutional is not to "obliterate" the "distinction of what is national and what is local"; nor is it to hold that the Commerce Clause permits the Federal Government to "regulate any activity that it found was related to the economic productivity of individual citizens," to regulate "marriage, divorce, and child custody," or to regulate any and all aspects of education. For one thing, this statute is aimed at curbing a particularly acute threat to the educational process—the possession (and use) of life-threatening firearms in, or near, the classroom. The empirical evidence that I have discussed above unmistakably documents the special way in which guns and education are incompatible. This Court has previously recognized the singularly disruptive potential on interstate commerce that acts of violence may have. For another thing, the immediacy of the connection between education and the national economic well-being is documented by scholars and accepted by society at large in a way and to a degree that may not hold true for other social institutions. It must surely be the rare case, then, that a statute strikes at conduct that (when considered in the abstract) seems so removed from commerce, but which (practically speaking) has so significant an impact upon commerce.

In sum, a holding that the particular statute before us falls within the commerce power would not expand the scope of that Clause. Rather, it simply would apply pre-existing law to changing economic circumstances. It would recognize that, in today's economic world, gun-related violence near the classroom makes a significant difference to our economic, as well as our social, well-being. . . .

III

The majority's holding—that §922 falls outside the scope of the Commerce Clause-creates three serious legal problems. First, the majority's holding runs contrary to modern Supreme Court cases that have upheld congressional actions despite connections to interstate or foreign commerce that are less significant than the effect of school violence. . . .

The second legal problem the Court creates comes from its apparent belief that it can reconcile its holding with earlier cases by making a critical distinction between "commercial" and noncommercial "transactions." That is to say, the Court believes the Constitution would distinguish between two local activities, each of which has an identical effect upon interstate commerce, if one, but not the other, is "commercial" in nature. As a general matter, this approach fails to heed this Court's earlier warning not to turn "questions of the power of Congress" upon "formula[s]" that would give

> "controlling force to nomenclature such as 'production' and 'indirect' and foreclose consideration of the actual effects of the activity in question upon interstate commerce." *Wickard* [v. *Filburn* (1942)].

. . . Moreover, the majority's test is not consistent with what the Court saw as the point of the cases that the majority now characterizes. . . . In fact, the *Wickard* Court expressly held that Wickard's consumption of home grown wheat, "*though it may not be regarded as commerce*," could nevertheless be regulated—"*whatever its nature*"—so long as "it exerts a substantial economic effect on interstate commerce." (emphasis added).

The third legal problem created by the Court's holding is that it threatens legal uncertainty in an area of law that, until this case, seemed reasonably well settled. Congress has enacted many statutes (more than 100 sections of the United States Code), including criminal statutes (at least 25 sections), that use the words "affecting commerce" to define their scope, see, *e.g.*, 18 U.S.C. §844(i) (destruction of buildings used in activity affecting interstate commerce), and other statutes that contain no jurisdictional language at all, see, *e.g.*, 18 U.S.C. §922(o)(1) (possession of machine guns). Do these, or similar, statutes regulate noncommercial activities? If so, would that alter the meaning of "affecting commerce" in a jurisdictional element? . . . More importantly, in the absence of a jurisdictional element, are the courts nevertheless to take *Wickard* (and later similar cases) as inapplicable, and to judge the effect of a single noncommercial activity on interstate commerce without considering similar instances of the forbidden conduct? However these questions are eventually resolved, the legal uncertainty now created will restrict Congress' ability to enact criminal laws aimed at criminal behavior that, considered problem by problem rather than instance by instance, seriously threatens the economic, as well as social, well-being of Americans.

IV

In sum, to find this legislation within the scope of the Commerce Clause would permit "Congress . . . to act in terms of economic . . . realities." It would interpret the Clause as this Court has traditionally interpreted it. . . . Upholding this legislation would do no more than simply recognize that Congress had a "rational basis" for finding a significant connection between guns in or near schools and (through their effect on education) the interstate and foreign commerce they threaten. For these reasons, I would reverse the judgment of the Court of Appeals. Respectfully, I dissent.

May

JOINT STATEMENT
ON CUBAN BOAT PEOPLE
May 2, 1995

The Clinton administration on May 2 reversed long-standing U.S. poli-cy that gave preferential treatment to Cubans seeking to emigrate to the United States. In an agreement with the Cuban government, the adminis-tration announced that the United States would return to Cuba any "boat people" seeking to flee to the United States. In the past, the United States had automatically accepted most Cuban émigrés or held them at detention centers, including one at the U.S. Naval Station at Guantanamo Bay in Cuba.

In the same agreement, the administration said it would admit a final group of about 20,000 Cuban migrants being detained at Guantanamo Bay. They were to be admitted to the United States gradually over a period of a year or more.

The U.S.-Cuban agreement, announced at the White House, was a land-mark step in the constantly evolving relations between the two countries. It received mixed reactions. Officials in Florida, who had feared a new upsurge in illegal immigration by Cubans fleeing the regime of President Fidel Castro, hailed the agreement; it was denounced by conservative Cuban-American groups that wanted Washington to maintain a rigidly hard-line stance against Castro.

Later in 1995, President Bill Clinton relaxed some travel restrictions on Cuba and took steps to ease the flow of humanitarian relief to the belea-guered island nation. These actions by the president proved unpopular on Capitol Hill, where anti-Castro forces promoted legislation aimed at dis-couraging foreign investment in Cuba.

Agreement on Cuban Boat People

The May 2 agreement, negotiated secretly by high-level U.S. and Cuban officials, was widely seen as an effort by both countries to deal with two difficult problems: the presence at Guantanamo Bay of some 20,000 angry and frustrated Cubans who were picked up trying to flee their country on rafts and makeshift boats in August and September 1994, and the prospect of a new flood of boat people in the summer of 1995.

Housing and feeding the Cubans at the Guantanamo Bay base was expensive (the Pentagon put the cost at $1 million a day), and U.S. officials were concerned about the potential for rioting there. Cuba reportedly saw the presence of the angry would-be emigrants as a security threat. U.S. officials also said they had reason to believe that thousands more Cubans were preparing to try to flee in 1995.

The agreement attempted to resolve both problems. First, the Clinton administration agreed to allow nearly all the 20,000 Cubans at Guantanamo Bay to enter the United States over a period of twelve months or more. Cubans convicted of criminal offenses would be excluded. Second, the two countries agreed on a procedure for the United States to return to Cuba anyone caught trying to flee to the United States. The Cuban government promised not to retaliate against those people, and the United States agreed to consider political refugee status, on a case-by-case basis, for anyone claiming the threat of persecution once returned.

For the United States, this agreement ended a policy, dating from the 1960s, that essentially treated most Cuban refugees as victims of political persecution. Under that policy, tens of thousands of Cubans were allowed into the United States, even while most refugees from other dictatorial regimes were turned away.

Administration officials insisted the new policy did not represent a concession to Castro and was not a step toward weakening tough economic sanctions against Cuba, which had been in effect for most of Castro's thirty-five years in power. Maintaining a hard-line stance toward Castro was the chief priority of many Cubans who had emigrated to the United States since the late 1950s. Most of them had settled in South Florida, where they have become a potent political force.

Representatives of several Cuban-American groups denounced the new policy of forcibly repatriating boat people, although they praised the agreement to admit the Cubans at Guantanamo Bay. Gov. Lawton Chiles of Florida welcomed it as an effort to "insure that Florida should never again confront a massive wave of uncontrolled immigration from Cuba."

The agreement was the administration's second major step on Cuban refugee policy in a little more than six months. On September 9, 1994, the administration had agreed to admit at least 20,000 Cubans a year, in return for a promise by the Cuban government to try to stop the exodus of boat people. The number of boat people surged in August 1994 after a series of riots in Cuba led Castro to announce that he would not try to prevent people from leaving.

The May 2 agreement provided that Cubans at Guantanamo Bay would be counted toward the 20,000 annual admissions, at the rate of 5,000 a year, regardless of when they were actually admitted to the United States.

Easing Travel Restrictions

Five months later, on October 3, President Clinton acted to ease restrictions on travel to Cuba by Cuban-Americans. Under his order, Cuban-Americans could travel to their homeland once a year to visit sick relatives; in the past they could make such a visit only after a relative had died. The order also allowed U.S. human rights groups to expand their efforts in Cuba by cooperating with agencies independent of the Cuban government. Further, Clinton authorized U.S. news organizations to establish permanent bureaus in Cuba. All these steps would require the cooperation of the Cuban government—something that was not assured.

Administration officials said the new order was intended to promote the flow of democratic ideas into Cuba, thus weakening Castro's grip on power. White House Press Secretary Mike McCurry said new administrative procedures ordered by Clinton would make it easier for the Treasury Department to enforce the economic embargo against Cuba. Representatives of several Cuban-American organizations denounced the policy as a misguided effort that would strengthen Castro, not weaken him.

The U.S. actions came at a time when Castro was moving to open his tightly controlled country to outside influences in hopes of gaining foreign investment to shore up the feeble economy. In September, the Cuban National Assembly adopted legislation allowing foreigners to own businesses and property in most major sectors of the economy. In the past, Cuba had allowed foreign investment in tourism, mining, and a limited number of other sectors, but only as part of joint ventures in which the government held the controlling interest. Cuba also had banned foreign investment in sugar production, once the underpinning of the economy.

Congressional Action

While the Clinton administration was set on a path of encouraging openness in Cuba, many in Congress continued to take the opposite approach: punishing the Castro government and anyone seen as cooperating with it.

The House on September 21 overwhelmingly adopted, 294–130, legislation (HR 927) aimed at curtailing foreign investment in Cuba. The bill's major provision would allow U.S. nationals whose properties were confiscated by the Cuban government to seek legal redress in U.S. courts against foreign companies that knowingly "traffic" in those properties. That would allow Cuban-Americans to file suit against companies that purchased or leased expropriated property in Cuba. The bill also would bar officials of those companies and their families from obtaining U.S. visas.

The Senate passed the bill on October 19, but only after eliminating the key provision that would have allowed U.S. legal action by Cuban-Americans against foreign companies using expropriated property in Cuba. The Senate weakened the bill because it faced a determined filibuster by oppo-

nents and a veto threat from the Clinton administration. At year's end, the
bill was still in conference committee between the House and Senate.

Following is the text of the joint statement by the governments
of the United States and Cuba, released by the White House May
2, 1995, under which the United States agreed to admit some
20,000 Cubans being detained at Guantanamo Bay Naval Sta-
tion, and the two countries agreed on procedures for returning
Cubans caught attempting to flee to the United States:

The United States of America and the Republic of Cuba have reached
agreement on steps to normalize further their migration relationship. These
steps build upon the September 9, 1994, agreement and seek to address safety and humanitarian concerns and to ensure that migration between the
countries is safe, legal, and orderly.

Humanitarian Parole

The United States and the Republic of Cuba recognize the special circumstances of Cuban migrants currently at Guantanamo Bay. Accordingly, the
two governments have agreed that the process of humanitarian parole into
the United States should continue beyond those eligible for parole under
existing criteria. The two governments agree that if the United States carries
out such paroles, it may count them towards meeting the minimum number
of Cubans it is committed to admit every year pursuant to the September 9,
1994, agreement. Up to 5,000 such paroles may be counted towards meeting
the minimum number in any one year period beginning September 9, 1995,
regardless of when the migrants are paroled into the United States.

Safety of Life at Sea

The United States and the Republic of Cuba reaffirm their common interest in preventing unsafe departures from Cuba. Effective immediately, Cuban
migrants intercepted at sea by the United States and attempting to enter the
United States will be taken to Cuba. Similarly, migrants found to have
entered Guantanamo illegally will also be returned to Cuba. The United
States and the Republic of Cuba will cooperate jointly in this effort. All
actions taken will be consistent with the parties' international obligations.
Migrants taken to Cuba will be informed by United States officials about procedures to apply for legal admission to the United States at the U.S. Interests
Section in Havana.

The United States and the Republic of Cuba will ensure that no action is
taken against those migrants returned to Cuba as a consequence of their
attempt to immigrate illegally. Both parties will work together to facilitate the
procedures necessary to implement these measures. The United States and
the Republic of Cuba agree to the return to Cuba of Cuban nationals currently at Guantanamo who are ineligible for admission to the United States.

September 9, 1994, Agreement

The United States and the Republic of Cuba agree that the provisions of the September 9, 1994, agreement remain in effect, except as modified by the present Joint Statement. In particular, both sides reaffirm their joint commitment to take steps to prevent unsafe departures from Cuba which risk loss of human life and to oppose acts of violence associated with illegal immigration.

BUSH RESIGNATION FROM THE NATIONAL RIFLE ASSOCIATION
May 3 and 20, 1995

Criticism of the National Rifle Association (NRA) reached new levels of intensity when, just weeks after the Oklahoma City bombing, former president George Bush resigned his membership in the organization. In his resignation letter, dated May 3 but not made public until May 10, Bush said he was "outraged" by an NRA fundraising letter that referred to federal law enforcement officers as "jack-booted thugs" who wanted to "attack law abiding citizens."

NRA officials denied that the organization in any way condoned violence or terrorism, but they refused to back down from their position that some agents of the Federal Bureau of Investigation (FBI) and Bureau of Alcohol, Tobacco and Firearms (ATF) had abused their powers. "We respect and support our many heroes out there doing their jobs every day under impossible circumstances," Wayne LaPierre, the executive vice president of the gun lobby and the target of Bush's resignation letter, said May 20 in a speech to the NRA's annual convention in Phoenix. "But I have also repeatedly said that if a handful of them behave like bullies, we're gonna call them bullies."

The NRA was originally a sports association that promoted hunting, target shooting, and gun safety, but since the mid-1960s, when Congress began to consider gun control legislation, it has become one of the most powerful lobbying forces in Washington and in state capitals. It opposes any regulation of any type of gun; it argued, for example, against the successful 1994 legislation banning certain kinds of assault weapons on the grounds that the ban was the first step in the government's campaign to disarm its citizens.

Since 1991, however, when a group of conservative hardliners won control of the NRA's board of directors, the organization's antigovernment rhetoric has grown increasingly strident. Although it criticizes the FBI and the Secret Service for alleged excesses, the NRA's main target has been the Treasury Department's Bureau of Alcohol, Tobacco, and Firearms, the agency responsible for enforcing federal gun laws. NRA literature routinely called these agents "armed terrorists" who use "Gestapo" tactics to harass and intimidate honest citizens.

The NRA was especially critical of the ATF's role in the botched raid on a cult compound in Waco, Texas, in 1993, in which nearly eighty people were killed. When it was reported that the two men arrested in connection with the Oklahoma City bombing may have been motivated by their intense hatred for FBI and ATF agents, critics of the NRA said it must share some of the blame because of its disparaging comments on federal agents.

An Escalating Controversy

Bush's resignation came in reaction to a fundraising letter that the NRA sent out in March and that LaPierre defended after the Oklahoma City bombing. The letter read in part that "in Clinton's administration, if you have a badge, you have the government's go-ahead to harass, intimidate, even murder law-abiding citizens." This attack on federal agents "deeply offends my own sense of decency and honor," Bush wrote in a letter to NRA president Thomas L. Washington dated May 3. "It indirectly slanders a wide array of government law enforcement officials, who are out there, day and night, laying their lives on the line for all of us."

President Clinton praised Bush for resigning, adding that anyone who denigrated federal agents "ought to be ashamed." NRA president Washington sent a five-page reply to Bush, asking him to withhold his resignation until Congress completed its investigation of the Waco disaster and other incidents where the NRA said there had been ATF abuses. "I'm sorry that you have chosen to unequivocally condemn NRA's words without first seeking an explanation," Washington wrote. "Have you forgotten . . . your previous passion for justice and fairness for all law-abiding citizens," he asked, referring to constraints that the Reagan-Bush administration had placed on the ATF after NRA complaints in the early 1980s.

Similar sentiments were contained in an open letter to the former president that the NRA ran in several major newspapers. On May 18, the eve of the NRA's annual convention, LaPierre offered a tepid apology. "If anyone thought the intention was to paint all federal law enforcement officials with the same broad brush, I'm sorry and I apologize," he said.

President Clinton May 19 challenged the NRA to back up its apology by donating the money the fundraising letter brought in to the families of slain police officers. "I am glad the NRA apologized for the cruel attack on law enforcement officers," Clinton said. "However, I note . . . that yesterday they seemed to be bragging about how much money they made." The NRA had estimated that the letter would raise more than $1 million. If the NRA was sincere about its apology, Clinton continued, "they ought to put their money where their mouth is."

In his May 20 speech LaPierre showed that he would not be intimidated. "There is not, nor has there ever been, any room at NRA for anyone who supports—or even fantasizes about—terrorism, sedition, insurrection, treason, conspiracy or any other unlawful activity . . . ," he declared. He added that there was also "no room in America for a "double standard of justice" that permitted serious abuses by federal agents acting in the name of the law and he vowed that the NRA would work to defeat Clinton in the 1996 elections.

Repercussions Assessed

It was unclear what repercussions, if any, the NRA would feel as a result of the controversy over its fundraising letter. Polls have shown a steady waning of public support for the organization's causes in recent years. It lost major legislative battles in 1993, when Congress passed the Brady Bill (which mandated a waiting period for purchasing handguns) and in 1994, when Congress banned certain types of assault weapons. Its aggressive drive for new members reportedly eroded the NRA's finances, and serious rifts are said to have developed between the NRA's board and more moderate staff members.

Still, the NRA was a major factor in the Republican takeover of the House of Representatives in the 1994 elections, and some of the gun lobby's most prominent allies were in powerful positions in Congress.

Following are the texts of a letter, dated May 3, 1995, in which former president George Bush resigned from the National Rifle Association and of a speech by Wayne LaPierre, executive vice president of the NRA, delivered on May 20, 1995, to the organization's annual convention in Phoenix:

BUSH RESIGNATION LETTER

Dear Mr. Washington:

I was outraged when, even in the wake of the Oklahoma City tragedy, Mr. Wayne LaPierre, Executive Vice President of NRA, defended his attack on federal agents as "jack-booted thugs." To attack Secret Service Agents or ATF people or any government law enforcement people as "wearing Nazi bucket helmets and black storm trooper uniforms" wanting to "attack law abiding citizens" is a vicious slander on good people.

Al Whicher, who served on my USSS [U.S. Secret Service] detail when I was Vice President and President, was killed in Oklahoma City. He was no Nazi. He was a kind man, a loving parent, a man dedicated to serving his country—and serve it well he did.

In 1993, I attended the wake for ATF agent Steve Willis, another dedicated officer who did his duty. I can assure you that this honorable man, killed by weird cultists, was no Nazi.

John Magaw, who used to head the USSS and now heads ATF, is one of the most principled, decent men I have ever known. He would be the last to condone the kind of illegal behavior your ugly letter charges. The same is true for the FBI's able Director Louis Freeh. I appointed Mr. Freeh to the Federal Bench. His integrity and honor are beyond question.

Both John Magaw and Judge Freeh were in office when I was President. They both now serve in the current administration. They both have badges. Neither of them would ever give the government's "go ahead to harass, intimidate, *even murder* law abiding citizens." (Your words)

I am a gun owner and an avid hunter. Over the years I have agreed with most of NRA's objectives, particularly your educational and training efforts, and your fundamental stance in favor of owning guns.

However, your broadside against Federal agents deeply offends my own sense of decency and honor; and it offends my concept of service to country. It indirectly slanders a wide array of government law enforcement officials, who are out there, day and night, laying their lives on the line for all of us.

You have not repudiated Mr. La Pierre's unwarranted attack. Therefore, I resign as a Life Member of NRA, said resignation to be effective upon your receipt of this letter. Please remove my name from your membership list.

Sincerely,
George Bush

LaPIERRE SPEECH

We . . . are being watched.

The eyes of the nation, the eyes of history, are upon us. Our every word is being scrutinized, our every action studied. And we should be grateful. Let me tell you why.

A few weeks ago I decided what I wanted to say here today. I wanted to give America a clear definition of our mission at NRA: That at the end of this century we want to leave the Second Amendment in the same condition as it was at the beginning of this century. But since April 19, that day of terrible, cowardly cruelty in Oklahoma City, I've realized that job will be harder than I thought.

As we gather here today, our mission is in jeopardy. Because too many Americans are increasingly confused about who we are. I don't know. You could blame it on tragic events, or on poor reporting, or on political opportunists, or even on our adversaries. But all of a sudden, N-R-A patriots are being confused with Grade-A terrorists. Well . . . to those in the national media, I hope you're listening, because I'm going to put a stop to the confusion right here and now.

I will not sit idly by while the media, or the President, or anyone else, tries to disgrace the members of this great Association by blurring the distinction between heroism, and terrorism!

There is a difference between democracy, and anarchy. There is a difference between criticism, and insurrection. There is a difference between sound reason, and sheer treason. There is a difference between acting within the law, and acting above the law. And believe me, there is a difference between 3.5 million united NRA members, and some scattered band of paranoid hatemongers!

And if someone in this room doesn't know the difference, THEN THERE'S THE DOOR!

For 124 years the National Rifle Association of America has been promoting liberty. Not mutiny. Our fight is for the minds of men. Never against the lives of children. We do not do battle with bullets. We fight with ballots.

We don't train for revolt in the woods. We train for safety—in grade schools and shooting ranges and police departments. We don't break laws. We help make the laws.

We don't sit home and complain about bad government. We vote for and elect good government.

If there is anyone within the sound of my voice who still doesn't get it . . . get it and get it now: There is not, nor has there ever been, any room at NRA for anyone who supports—or even fantasizes about—terrorism, sedition, insurrection, treason, conspiracy or any other unlawful activity. Period! End of story!

And you know what? If you do support any of that stuff, you'd better not let the Americans in this room find out about it.

At the same time, there is no room in America for those who support a double standard of justice. And at NRA, we've been saying so—for years.

I'm talking about the double standard that says if someone wants to profiteer from rap music about killing cops, those rights are defended. But if a shotgun barrel is a quarter-inch below the legal minimum, they can surround a Ruby Ridge home and shoot a 14-year-old boy in the back and kill a mother holding a baby. Then promote the guy in charge of it all.

I'm talking about the double standard that says, if a drugged-up ex-con speeds through L.A., resists arrest and gets beat up, he can sue for a few million bucks and win. While the cop in charge gets ruined.

But if a religious cult is suspected of a gun law violation, it can be assaulted with bullets, tanks and tear gas. Everyone dies . . . and the cop in charge gets promoted.

I'm talking about the double standard that says, it's okay to call gun owners "gun nuts" and call the NRA "an evil empire of lying, stupid, rednecks, zealots and extremists."

But if we engage in some impassioned name-calling about abuses by a few federal police, we are suddenly indicted, tried and found guilty-by-association with America's most despicable criminals.

Nonetheless, for some of my words, an apology was due. And I apologized.

I have repeatedly said it, and our actions back it up: The NRA is pro-law-enforcement. We respect and support our many heroes out there doing their jobs every day under impossible circumstances. We're proud of them—hundreds of thousands are NRA members.

But I have also repeatedly said that if a handful of them behave like bullies, we're gonna call them bullies. If some of them act like thugs . . . then that's what we'll call them.

That's why the NRA and ACLU and several other civil rights groups joined together 18 months ago to ask President Clinton to create a commission to investigate serious abuses by federal law enforcement agencies, in order to reduce many reported violations of constitutional and human rights.

And what do we have to show for our repeated requests? Nothing. No fact-finding action that could settle the issue once and for all. No hearings. No investigations. No answers.

Just hypocrisy and arrogance.

While he appealed for "toning down the rhetoric," Mr. Clinton criticized NRA for our language by using this language! Let me quote him from a few days ago, quote: "We must stand up against these people who say they love their country but not this government. Who do these people think they are?" End quote.

I'll tell you who we are. We are the people who helped clean out Congress in 1994, and who are going to help clean your clock in 1996!

Mr. President, there is nothing un-American about questioning our leaders. As citizens, it's our job.

There is nothing unpatriotic about being skeptical of our government. As citizens, it's our job.

In fact, our very system of self-government requires us to question our officials and candidates with each election cycle. The more zeal and passion we bring to the process, the better government we get.

So why do they so readily attack the NRA? I'll tell you why. They're attacking the messenger, instead of the message, because most Americans agree with the message!

Most Americans think that government has grown so big it can't keep its hands out of our pockets or off of our rights. In fact, just eight days after the bombing in Oklahoma City, a 52% majority of Americans said they think the federal government has become so powerful that it poses a threat to the rights and freedoms of its citizens.

That's not an NRA poll—that's a *Time*/CNN poll April 27, 1995. That's the message, and Mr. Clinton doesn't get it.

Think about it: Over half of your countrymen think the federal government has become so powerful that it poses a threat to the rights and freedoms of its citizens.

Surely you've felt that invasion bit by bit, year after year. More and more you've got to scoot-your-butt-over-and-make-room-for-a-bureaucrat-and-his-book-of-rules.

I know you've felt it. Especially if you own land, if you own a small business, if you own a home, if you drive a car, or heaven forbid, if you want to own a gun.

But it's not just about your gun freedoms. It's about plans for a federal multi-agency super-police force called the "Directorate of Central Law

Enforcement" that Bill Clinton and Janet Reno wanted to put together.

It's about HR 97, a bill that would allow Reno to establish a 2,500-member "Rapid Deployment Strike Force" that could be deployed to enforce federal, state and local anti-gun laws.

It's about special micro-chips that the government wanted to put in every phone, fax and computer so it could tap into people's communications at will.

It's about saddling the states with unfunded federal mandates, paperwork, red tape and regulations that deny private property rights and civil rights.

It's about that California farmer whose tractor was seized and who faced a year in jail plus a $200,000 find for allegedly running over an "endangered" kangaroo rat while plowing his own land.

It's about federal agencies like HUD threatening to prosecute citizens for exercising their first Amendment right by opposing criminal halfway houses in their neighborhoods.

It's about why 300 Marines, on a written test at Twentynine Palms Combat Center in California, were asked whether they would, quote "fire upon U.S. citizens who refuse or resist confiscation of firearms banned by the U.S. government," end quote.

In the end, it's about all these creeping cancers feeding on all the freedoms we once took for granted. So it'll be tough to leave this century with the Second Amendment in the same condition as it was at the beginning of this century. But with courage and character, we will.

Today, as 95 years ago, there is no room at NRA for any people that support violence against government. But there is also no room in America for government that supports violence against the people, and a double standard of justice.

We will continue our important work of gun safety, hunting and wildlife conservation, crime prevention, judicial reform and protecting the cherished Second Amendment. But we will meet the millennium with our more difficult—and perhaps more unpopular—duty: of living on the leading edge of defining what patriotism means in modern America . . . of making government put our freedom where its mouth is.

I began today by telling you that, like never before, we are being watched. And we will be judged not by what we say, but what we do.

So I ask those in the media who observe this Association to do so closely, with fairness and balance. But I also ask those who participate in this Association to be worthy of scrutiny, by living up to a promise you made . . . when you were a kid: "I pledge allegiance to the flag of the United States of America, and to the Republic for which it stands, one nation, under God, indivisible, with liberty and justice for all."

In spite of the diversity of opinion that comes with 3.5 million members, we are all still united by that promise. Don't let the chaos of current events tarnish the majesty of its meaning: We don't promise to try when it's convenient, we pledge our allegiance. Not to who's powerful or popular, but to the flag of the United States of America.

And not just to its stars and stripes, but to the republic for which it stands. Which isn't one faction, but one nation. Not under tyranny, but under God. Not divided, but indivisible. With liberty and with justice, not for a few, but for all.

Let's tell it, teach it, live it, and breathe it. To give the kids of this country a running start at another glorious century of being the envy . . . of the world.

God bless you all and thank you.

COMMEMORATION OF THE FIFTIETH ANNIVERSARY OF WWII
May 8, 1995

Participating in one of many ceremonies in 1995 marking the fiftieth anniversary of the end of World War II, President Bill Clinton paid tribute May 8 to the "extraordinary generation" of Americans who helped defeat fascism and then worked to keep the peace during the Cold War.

The president spoke to a large gathering of veterans and others at a ceremony at Summerall Field in Fort Myer, Virginia, just outside Washington, D.C. The ceremony was held on the fiftieth anniversary of the day the German military surrender took effect—known in the West as Victory in Europe Day, or VE-Day. President Clinton then immediately flew to Moscow for another celebration on May 9 marking the day the German high command officially ratified the surrender documents. The former Soviet Union, and now the Russian government, have celebrated May 9 as Victory Day.

Four months later, on September 2, President Clinton took part in a ceremony at the National Cemetery of the Pacific, in Honolulu, marking the fiftieth anniversary of the Japanese surrender that finally ended World War II.

Clinton was the first American president born after World War II, and he was one of the few postwar presidents never to have served in the military. Several of his predecessors fought in the war, most notably Dwight Eisenhower, who commanded all Allied forces in Europe.

All the ceremonies were generally harmonious and focused on the heroism of those who fought in the war. The thousands of veterans who attended those ceremonies were nearly all in their seventies and eighties; for many of them the fiftieth anniversary of the end of the war may have been the last opportunity to bask in the glory of what many considered the most monumental achievement of the twentieth century.

Despite the air of mutual congratulation in the world's capitals, a few disputes arose over some of the issues still lingering from the end of the war. In Europe, for example, Chancellor Helmet Kohl of German stirred

216

some complaints when he appeared to equate the plight of ethnic Germans who were expelled from eastern Europe at the war's end with the deaths of combat troops and the estimated 6 million Jews who perished in the Holocaust.

Clinton Recalls Unity of Purpose

Speaking at the VE-Day ceremony in Virginia, President Clinton noted that an estimated 40 million people were killed during World War II, and untold millions more were wounded or forced from their homes. He recalled in particular the "unique sacrifice" of the Soviet Union, where estimates of the war dead have ranged as high as 27 million people. "At almost every table in every home [in the Soviet Union] there was an empty place," Clinton said. He also spoke of the "brave and defiant people" of Great Britain, who "had stood alone through the war's darkest hours."

The president devoted the bulk of his speech to the American role in defeating Nazi Germany, noting that it became an "all-consuming effort" for a country that at first had resisted entering the war. Clinton said that "millions were heroes here on the home front," accepting sacrifices, such as rationing, and working ceaselessly to produce the tanks, planes, and other necessities of America's military machine. Overseas, he said, millions of fighters and support personnel "gave the best years of their lives to the terrible business of war."

The president described to his audience the individual accomplishments of seven Americans who had served overseas in the various branches of military service. Among them was Frederick McIntosh, of Leesburg, Virginia, who as a second lieutenant in the Eighth Air Force flew 104 combat missions over Europe. McIntosh was given the honor of introducing the president to the VE-Day audience.

Of those veterans, and the millions of others they represented, Clinton said: "In their bravery, and that of all their brothers and sisters in arms, America found the will to defeat the forces of fascism. And today we, the sons and daughters of their sacrifice, say thank you and well done."

Postwar Challenges

In paying tribute to the "extraordinary generation" that won World War II, the president also noted the American response to the postwar challenges of aiding the defeated foes and standing firm against the advance of communism. It was a generation, he said, "that won the war and then made sure we would not lose the peace."

Once the war was over, he said, that generation established the North Atlantic Treaty Organization and the United Nations and funded the Marshall Plan. These were the institutions and programs "that brought half a century of security and prosperity to the West and brought our former enemies back to life and to true partnership with us," he said.

The president warned that the world remained a dangerous place, both overseas and at home. It will be up to future generations to follow the example of those who demonstrated in World War II "that we can prevail over the forces of darkness, that we must prevail," he said.

Following is the text, as released by the White House Press Office, of the speech by President Bill Clinton at VE-Day ceremonies in Fort Myer, Virginia, on May 8, 1995:

Thank you, Colonel McIntosh, for those remarkable words and your remarkable service. General Shalikashvili, Secretary Perry, Secretary Brown, Father Sampson, members of Congress, members of the Armed Forces, distinguished guests, American veterans all, and especially to our most honored guests, the veterans of the second world war:

Fifty years ago on this day the guns of war in Europe fell silent. A long shadow that had been cast on the entire continent was lifted. Freedom's warriors rejoiced. We come today, 50 years later, to recall their triumph, to remember their sacrifice, and to rededicate ourselves to the ideals for which they fought and for which so many of them died.

By Victory Day in Europe, from the beaches of Normandy to the gates of Moscow, some 40 million people lost their lives in World War II. These enormous but faceless numbers hid millions upon millions of personal tragedies—soldiers shot and shattered by weapons of war; prisoners cut down by disease and starvation; children buried in the rubble of bombed out buildings; and entire families exterminated solely because of the blood that ran in their vein. And for every death so many more fell wounded, physically and emotionally. They would survive, but their lives would be changed forever.

At war's end, an eight-year-old boy, already a veteran of air raids and bomb shelters, was asked what he wanted to be when he grew up. He answered with one word: "Alive."

The American people, secure on our continent, sobered by memories of the last war, were not eager to enter into the struggle. But they were stirred by the extraordinary courage of the British, all alone and carrying liberty's flickering torch into Europe's darkening night. Pushed by their passion for freedom, prodded by the wise leadership of President Roosevelt, and provoked, finally, by the infamy at Pearl Harbor, Americans went to war.

It became an all-consuming effort. Millions were heroes here on the home front. They built the planes, the ships, the tanks, the trucks that carried the Allied armies into battle. They bought victory bonds to pay for the war. The collected scrap metal for weapons, worn-out rubber for tires, left-over fat for explosives. And they planted 20 million victory gardens to help feed the nation.

With good cheer they sacrificed, rationing food and clothing, holding themselves to three gallons of gas a week. And President Roosevelt willed them onward. "There is one front and one battle," he said, "where everyone in the United States, every man, woman, and child, is in action. That front is right here at home."

Across the ocean, their fathers and brothers, sisters and mothers, friends and neighbors gave the best years of their lives to the terrible business of war. Some of them were among the greatest leaders our country and the world have ever known: Eisenhower, Marshall, Bradley, Patton. But no matter their rank, every soldier, airman, Marine, sailor, every Merchant Marine, every nurse, every doctor was a hero who carried the banner of justice into the battle for freedom.

Some of them are here with us today. The gentleman who introduced me, Frederick McIntosh, was then an Air Force lieutenant. He flew, as has been said, 104 missions. His daring dive-bomb raids on D-Day helped clear the way for the Allied landing.

Another veteran behind me, Robert Katayama, a private with the Japanese American 442nd Regimental Combat Team, that finally broke through the formidable Gothic line in Italy after five months of ferocious assault.

Another, Anna Connelly Wilson, a nurse who tended American soldiers moving gasoline and munitions across the deserts of Iran into the hands of our Russian allies.

Another, Abben MaGuire, a Navy demolition expert who landed on Omaha Beach ahead of the Allied assault, clearing mines, barbed wire, and booby traps, under heavy fire from the enemy. Another, George Ellers, a seaman on Coast Guard boats, charged with protecting the Merchant Marine armadas that ferried food and supplies from America to Europe and beyond.

Joseph Kahoe, a lieutenant with the all-African American 761st tank battalion, who braved the deadening cold of the Ardennes and the brutal Nazi counterattacks to help win the Battle of the Bulge.

And Father Francis Sampson, an Army chaplain who parachuted into Normandy, then into Holland; was wounded, captured, but managed to escape.

In their bravery, and that of all their brothers and sisters in arms, America found the will to defeat the forces of fascism. And today we, the sons and daughters of their sacrifice, say thank you and well done.

I ask all the veterans of World War II now to stand and be recognized.

During the war's final weeks, America's fighting forces thundered across Europe, liberating small villages and great cities from a long nightmare. Many witnessed an outpouring of love and gratitude they would remember for the rest of their lives.

Deep in the Bavarian countryside, Corporal Bill Ellington piloted his armored vehicle into a battle against retreating enemy troops. As a firefight raged, a rail-thin teenage boy ran, shouting toward the tank. He was a young Polish Jew. Samuel Pisar, who had survived four years at Auschwitz and other concentration camps, but along the way had lost his entire family. Samuel Pisar had seen the tank and its glorious five-point white star from his hideaway in a barn.

As Ellington looked down at him, the boy dropped to his knees and repeated over and over the few words of English his mother had taught him: "God bless America. God bless America." And Ellington, the son of a slave, lifted the boy through the hatch and into the warm embrace of freedom.

Bill Ellington died a few years ago. But Samuel Pisar, now an American citizen, is here with us today. And I'd like to ask him to stand as a reminder of what that war was all about.

The saga of hope emerged from the ashes of a horror that defies comprehension still—the Nazi death camps. In the gas chambers and crematoriums was proof of man's infinite capacity for evil. In the empty eyes of the skeletal survivors was a question that to this day has never been answered: How could this happen?

But at 2:40 a.m. on May 7th, in a small red-brick schoolhouse in France, the Germans signed their unconditional surrender. The armistice took effect the next day—this day 50 years ago.

News of the victory spread and grew from a ripple of excitement to a river of joy. The liberated capitals of Western Europe were awash in relief and jubilation. The boulevards burst with flag-waving, teary-eyed thanksgiving celebrants. Everywhere people tore down their black-out curtains and let the light of peace shine out.

In the sky over Moscow, gigantic white rays of light from huge projectors slashed the darkness of night and a 1,000-gun salute shook the city. There, too, millions teemed into the street. But their joy was dulled by the pain of their nation's unique sacrifice, for one out of every eight Soviet citizens was killed in World War II. Twenty-seven million people. At almost every table in every home there was an empty place.

In London, where a brave and defiant people had stood alone through the war's darkest hours, great bonfires ringed the city. And on the balcony of Buckingham Palace, Prime Minister Churchill stilled the delirious crowd with his own silence. Then he took one, deep, all-embracing bow, and the crowd exploded into a roar of triumph. "This is your victory," Churchill declared. And the people of the United Kingdom answered back as one: "No, it is yours." Of course, both were right.

Here at home, the Washington Monument, the Capitol Dome, the Statue of Liberty were bathed in floodlights for the very first time since Pearl Harbor. New York was New Year's Day and the 4th of July rolled into one. Millions cheered, shouted, sang, danced in the streets. And in an image that traveled all around the world, a sailor took a nurse in his arms and kissed her, with all the pent-up youthful enthusiasm of a people forgetting for an instant the new burdens of adulthood.

Less than a month in office, President Truman addressed the nation, and said, "This is a solemn, but glorious hour. I only wish FDR had lived to witness this day." Millions of Americans shared that conviction, for in their darkest hour, President Roosevelt refused to let us give up in despair. He rallied the Americans to defeat depression, and triumph in war. And so it was his victory, too.

It was America's victory, but the job for us was not yet complete. In the Pacific, war raged on. During the three months between V-E and V-J Day, many thousands more of our fighting men and women would lose their lives. After Japan surrendered, who could have blamed the American people for wanting to turn from the front lines abroad to the home front? But after winning the most difficult and crucial victory in our nation's history, our leaders were determined not to repeat the mistakes of the past.

Instead, they took to new challenges with a newfound confidence. And this remarkable generation of Americans, then through NATO, the United Nations, and the Marshall Plan, created the institutions and provided the resources and the vision that brought half a century of security and prosperity to the West, and brought our former enemies back to life and to true partnership with us.

And their special resolve and military strength held totalitarianism in check until the power of democracy, the failure of communism, and the heroic determination of people to be free prevailed in the Cold War.

Today we must draw inspiration from the extraordinary generation we come here to honor. A generation that won the war, and then made sure we would not lose the peace. A generation that understood our destiny is inexorably linked to that of other nations. A generation that believed that with our great wealth, great power, and great blessings of democratic freedom come great responsibilities to stand for and work for the common good.

So let me say again to the generation that won the Second World War, on this 50th anniversary, on behalf of the American people, we say, thank you. Thank you, and God bless you. Because of all you did we live in a moment of hope, in a nation at peace. For the first time since the dawn of the nuclear age, no Russian missiles are pointed at our children. Our economy is sound. And because free markets and democracy now are on the march throughout the world, more people than ever before have the opportunity to reach their God-given potential. All because of what you did 50 years ago.

But there is one thing that even you could not do; that no generation can ever do. You could not banish the forces of darkness from the future. We confront them now in different forms all around the world, and, painfully, here at home. But you taught us the most important lesson—that we can prevail over the forces of darkness; that we must prevail. That is what we owe to you, and the incomparable legacy you have given us—and what we all owe to the generations of remarkable Americans yet to come.

Thank you for teaching us that lesson. God bless you, and God bless America.

REPORT ON U.S.-RUSSIAN SPACE COOPERATION
May 15, 1995

The United States can gain significant benefits by expanding its cooperation with Russia in space programs, but steps must be taken to minimize the risks that could jeopardize some of those programs.

Those were the underlying findings of an extensive study, "U.S.-Russian Cooperation in Space," published May 15, 1995, by the congressional Office of Technology Assessment (OTA). The 130-page study was based, in large part, on discussions at a November 9, 1994, OTA-sponsored conference of sixteen U.S. scientists, academics, corporate representatives, and government officials.

The Office of Technology Assessment was an arm of Congress that conducted studies and issued reports on highly technical issues faced by the legislative branch. The report on U.S.-Russian space cooperation was one of its last; Congress voted to eliminate the OTA in September 1995.

The report was intended to provide guidance to Congress and the administration on how to manage future space projects involving the Russian government and newly developed Russian companies. Although it suggested many specific steps for the United States and U.S.-based private companies, the report avoided a conclusive bottom-line recommendation on whether, and to what extent, the United States should proceed with cooperative space programs with Russia. However, the report appeared to be based on the assumption that space cooperation will continue at some level in the future.

Much of the report was devoted to the planned International Space Station, a cooperative project involving the United States, Japan, Canada, and the multinational European Space Agency. In 1993 the United States and Russia signed an agreement to cooperate on the space station, in effect adding Russia to the list of partners. Plans called for the station to be assembled in orbit by 2002; the station would conduct scientific experiments for ten years.

Shortly after the release of the OTA report, the most important U.S.-Russian space cooperative project so far occurred 245 miles above the earth. The space shuttle Atlantis *and the Russian space station* Mir *docked together on June 29 and conducted joint experiments for five days. The two spaceships docked again on November 15 for three days. (Atlantis-Mir press conference, p. 222)*

Benefits of Cooperating with Russia

The OTA report cited numerous technical, budgetary, and political benefits to the United States and its Western partners in expanding cooperation with Russia on space programs. Past cooperative efforts involving the former Soviet Union, especially the French-Soviet space programs dating from 1966, had been quite successful.

On a technical level, the OTA report said, the most important reason to cooperate with Russia was that its space program was very advanced and sophisticated in many areas. In particular, the report cited Russian capabilities in launching space vehicles. It was possible that the space station could be built sooner, and more efficiently, if Russian vehicles were used to transport bulky equipment into space, the report said. Cooperating with Russia also could reduce duplication of effort, thereby lowering costs and enabling all the nations involved to concentrate their efforts on the most useful programs.

*From the U.S. point of view, cooperating with Russia would have several important benefits, the report said. Foremost among these would be helping to stabilize the Russian economy, which remained in a state of near collapse in the years following the dissolution of the Soviet Union. As of 1995 U.S. purchases of Russian space equipment and services constituted one of the most significant sources of Western currency in Russia. For example, the OTA report noted that over a four-year period the United States planned to buy at least $400 million worth of Russian goods and services for the shuttle-*Mir *program. Cooperating with Russia also would help keep the Russian space program intact, thus providing jobs for thousands of scientists and technicians. The report said it would be better to keep those people working in Russia on a peaceful space program than looking for work outside Russia, possibly on military programs in countries such as Iran or North Korea that had foreign policy agendas opposed to U.S. interests. The report noted that many Russian space agency employees already had lost their jobs to cutbacks.*

Nearly every U.S.-based company involved in the space industry already had signed contracts with the Russian government or private interests in Russia. Some of those U.S. firms could reap enormous financial and technical benefits from their Russian ventures, the OTA report said.

Risks and Uncertainties in U.S.-Russian Cooperation

The benefits of cooperating with Russia were at least partly offset by potential risks, the OTA report said, which could make Russia an unreliable partner.

On a management level, the Russian space agency, like its predecessor Soviet agency, had trouble keeping within its schedules and budgets in developing new spacecraft and components, the report said. Relying on Russia to help complete the space station, for example, could pose serious risks to the station and even prevent it from becoming a reality.

Political instability was another factor that could jeopardize Russia's ability to sustain a cooperative space program. The OTA report noted that Russian democratic political institutions remain fragile, so that "legal and political instability is great and appears likely to remain so for some time." The stability of the Russian military also was uncertain, the report said. As a result, cooperation on expensive and politically sensitive space programs could easily fall victim to a major upheaval in Russia.

Further, the report warned that U.S. government agencies and companies might find it difficult to carry out normal, Western-style arrangements with their Russian counterparts because of widespread corruption and cultural differences.

Despite those risks, the OTA report said the United States could act to minimize, or at least anticipate, the drawbacks. Among the steps recommended were working to increase U.S. understanding of the political and economic forces in Russia and their potential impact on that country's space industry; fostering "open and frank communications" with Russians; being prepared for delays and reverses, and having fallback plans in hand; and understanding the cultural differences between the American and Russian ways of doing things.

Following is the executive summary of the report, "U.S.-Russian Cooperation in Space," issued May 15, 1995, by the congressional Office of Technology Assessment:

The end of the Cold War, the collapse of the Soviet Union, and the changing world order have provided new opportunities and new incentives for the United States and other countries to cooperate with Russia in space science, space applications, and human spaceflight. Although U.S. attempts to cooperate on space activities with the Soviet Union began more than 30 years ago, intense political and military competition between the two countries severely limited the scope and duration of such activities. Today, the United States government is actively pursuing cooperation with Russia on a wide range of space activities, including the International Space Station. In addition, U.S. aerospace firms have entered into joint ventures, licensing agreements, and cooperative technical agreements with a variety of newly organized Russian counterparts.

The emergence of Russia as a major cooperative partner for the United States and other spacefaring nations offers the potential for a significant increase in the world's collective space capabilities. Expanding U.S.-Russian cooperation in space since 1991 has begun to return scientific, technological, political, and economic benefits to the United States. Yet, Russia is experiencing severe economic hardship and its space program has undergone major structural changes. The future success of U.S.-Russian cooperative projects in space will depend on:

- successful management of complex, large-scale bilateral and multilateral cooperative projects;
- progress in stabilizing Russia's political and economic institutions;
- preservation of the viability of Russian space enterprises;
- flexibility in managing cultural and institutional differences;
- continued Russian adherence to missile-technology-proliferation controls; and
- additional progress in liberalizing U.S. and Russian laws and regulations in export control, customs, and finance.

Foreign Policy Benefits and Risks

Russia's technical contributions to the International Space Station offer a substantial increase in planned space station capabilities. Just as important to the United States are the foreign policy gains from this and other human spaceflight projects, such as the Shuttle-Mir dockings. U.S. officials expect cooperative activities to help promote economic and political stability in Russia. For example, the National Aeronautics and Space Administration's (NASA's) purchase of nearly $650 million in goods and services from Russia during fiscal years 1994–97, by far the largest transfer of U.S. public funds to the Russian government and private organizations, is an important signal of U.S. support for Russia's transition to a market economy. These purchases should help preserve employment for Russian engineers and technicians in at least some of Russia's major space-industrial centers, thereby inhibiting proliferation through "brain drain" and helping to sustain Russian adherence to the Missile Technology Control Regime. Moreover, NASA's purchases improve the chances that Russia will be able to meet its obligations to the space station project, thereby enhancing prospects for success.

Nevertheless, such purchases entail some political risk in the United States, as well as the risk to the space station if the Russian government and enterprises are not able to perform. Some U.S. observers question the wisdom of supporting any part of the Russian aerospace industry, which provided much of the technological substance for the Soviet threat to the United States; others believe that U.S. officials have made adequate provision to ensure that U.S. funds remain in the civil space sector.

Other Benefits and Risks

NASA is exploring cooperative space research and development with Russia in virtually every programmatic area. Aside from the space station, activities include flights of instruments on each other's spacecraft and joint missions using Russian launch capabilities with U.S.-built spacecraft. Public sector cooperation in space science and Earth observations is developing well

225

for the most part. The political, technical, and administrative risks involved are somewhat higher than they are in NASA's traditional cooperative relationships, but—except for the space station—Russian contributions are not in the "critical path" to completion of key projects; program managers understand the risks involved and have made contingency plans to minimize long-term risks.

Cooperation on projects involving human spaceflight involves both potentially greater programmatic benefits and higher risks than it does in space science and applications. The United States stands to gain new experience in long-duration spaceflight and a better understanding of Russia's technology and methods. On the other hand, the United States risks possible project failure if Russia proves unable to perform as promised.

Placing the Russian contribution in the critical path to completion of the space station poses unprecedented programmatic and political risks. The Russian elements must be delivered on time and within budget; failure to do so could cause serious difficulties, both programmatically and in NASA's relations with its other partners and with Congress. Knowledgeable observers express concern about the stability and staying power of the Russian aerospace sector, about the Russian track record in delivering new spacecraft, and about the condition of the Baikonur launch complex (used to launch Proton and Soyuz vehicles). On another level, observers worry that political and/or military events within Russia or between Russia and other countries could cause either party to seek to amend the space station program or withdraw from it.

Given the significance of the Russian contribution to the space station, the U.S. ability to make up for delays or failure to deliver is severely limited by available U.S. resources. However, participants in current cooperative ventures suggest some other precautions that could be taken, both in the space station project and in space robotic cooperation:

- Seek better understanding of the larger political and economic forces that could affect Russian ability to deliver on commitments, perhaps through further systematic analysis of Russian aerospace industry developments.
- Maximize open and frank communication. To avoid as many technical and managerial surprises as possible, seek (and be willing to allow) a high degree of communication and interpenetration between the U.S. and Russian programs.
- Be prepared for delays and reverses.
- Be aware of and manage cultural differences effectively.

Commercial Cooperation

Because of the potential for diverting civilian space technologies to enhance Soviet military capabilities, during the Cold War, the federal government effectively precluded U.S. aerospace firms from entering into cooperative business agreements with Russian entities. Now, most large U.S. aerospace companies are pursuing some form of joint venture or partnership with Russian concerns, especially in launch services and propulsion technologies. Although several of these emerging commercial partnerships show promise, and some could result in large revenues, none of them yet appear to be profitable, and it is too early to tell how successful they will be. Here, too, the risks are larger than they are in cooperative ventures with Japanese and Western aerospace firms because of unstable Russian political, economic, and legal conditions and potential linkage to U.S.-Russian political relations. The U.S. government could assist U.S. industry by further liberalizing U.S. export-control laws and regulations.

Russia, Third Parties, and the United States

The French experience in cooperating with the Soviet Union and Russia since 1966 largely parallels and confirms that of the United States. The European Space Agency has budgeted over $320 million for space cooperation with Russia, largely for European-built hardware that will be installed in the Russian portion of the International Space Station.

The U.S. decision to bring Russia into the space station partnership initially caused considerable strain in relations with the existing partners, already frayed by years of U.S. design changes and cost increases and aggravated by a general cooling of public enthusiasm for human spaceflight. Challenging negotiations remain to complete the realignment of the agreements covering the station's construction and utilization, but the working relationships now appear to be developing more smoothly.

Domestic Economic Impact

Experts disagree over the nature and extent of the effect that expanded cooperation with Russia will have on the U.S. aerospace industry, and particularly on the retention of U.S. jobs. Some industry officials have expressed concern that U.S. aerospace employment could be lost and the technological base adversely affected by use of Russian technology in the U.S. space program. Others have argued that skillful incorporation of Russian technologies into U.S. projects could save taxpayer dollars in publicly funded programs such as the space station and could boost U.S. international competitiveness in commercial programs. Both could happen and have to be weighed against each other.

Russian launch vehicles and related systems have the most obvious potential for U.S. commercial use, but using them could adversely affect the U.S. launch industry. This industry is the subject of upcoming OTA [Office of Technology Assessment] reports.

INAUGURAL ADDRESS BY
FRENCH PRESIDENT CHIRAC
May 17, 1995

As he began a seven-year term as the fifth president of France's Fifth Republic, Jacques Chirac promised to make curing unemployment the nation's highest priority. Chirac was inaugurated in a ceremony ten days after he won the presidency on his third try.

Just seven months later, France was gripped by its most serious labor unrest in years, as public employees protested the Chirac government's plans for budget cutbacks and reductions in worker benefits.

Chirac succeeded François Mitterrand, who had served two terms. The transfer of power was the culmination of a political shift that began several years before when conservative forces, under Chirac, wrested control of the National Assembly from leftist parties under Mitterrand's leadership. The two men for years had been the dominant political figures in France, at opposite ends of the political spectrum.

Mitterrand, leader of the Socialist party, had swept to power in 1981 on a wave of popular dissatisfaction with high unemployment and increasing social strife. He led a coalition government with the Communists that easily dominated the National Assembly. Mitterrand's grip on political power dwindled, especially in his second term, starting in 1988. Mitterrand was forced to participate in a series of what the French called "cohabitation" arrangements, in which he served as the country's overall political leader but the reins of day-to-day government were held by a conservative cabinet. One of the prime ministers with whom Mitterrand had to cohabit was Jacques Chirac.

The long-time mayor of Paris, Chirac had sought the presidency twice before. In 1981 he was knocked out of the first round of voting by centrist leader Valéry Giscard d'Estang. In 1988 he lost the final round to Mitterrand.

At the start of campaigning in 1995, Chirac was given little chance of succeeding against either of his major rivals, fellow conservative Edouard Balladur or the Socialist candidate, Lionel Jospin. After a bitter campaign,

Chirac managed to edge out Balladur in the April 23 first round voting. Jospin finished first with 23 percent of the vote; Chirac finished second with 20 percent, just one point above Balladur.

The remarkable aspect of the first round was the strong showing of several extremist candidates, who combined to attract nearly 40 percent of the vote. Analysts said the strong showing for these candidates demonstrated the extent of French dissatisfaction with the inability of the country's political system and mainstream politicians to deal with the same economic and social problems that helped put Mitterrand in power in 1981.

Communist party candidate Robert Hue won 17 percent in the first round, and Arlette Laguiller, head of a Trotskyite party, polled 5 percent. At the opposite end of the political spectrum, National Front leader Jean-Marie Le Pen finished with 15 percent. Le Pen's movement advocated limiting immigration and expelling thousands of Arabs, Turks, and other non-French from the country. Le Pen finished first in several areas of the country where anti-immigrant sentiment was especially strong.

In the final round of voting, held May 7, Chirac defeated Jospin by a margin of 52 percent to 48 percent. Chirac won solid support from his own Rally for the Republic party and that of centrist leader Giscard d'Estang. Chirac's party represented the political legacy of France's most important postwar leader, Charles de Gaulle.

Chirac's Political Support

Chirac entered office in a strong political position, comparable to that enjoyed by Mitterrand when he first took office in 1981. Chirac's alliance with the centrist Giscardists gave his government about 80 percent of the 577 National Assembly seats and control of all but two of the twenty-two provinces. Chirac immediately appointed his loyal lieutenant, Alain Juppé, as prime minister. Juppé on May 18 unveiled a forty-two-member cabinet, about equally divided between representatives of Chirac's conservative party and Giscard's centrist movement.

The cabinet reflected both the political necessity of representation from the two elements that controlled the National Assembly and Chirac's tendency to make whatever compromises were necessary to gain political power. Never known for the strength of his ideological convictions, Chirac often was accused of bending to prevailing winds. Although Chirac was nominally a conservative, many of his policy prescriptions, especially on economic matters, differed only in degree from those of the moderate left.

Of all the challenges faced by Chirac and his new government, without doubt the most difficult was unemployment, which stood at 12.2 percent when he took office. According to some estimates, one in four young adults was without a job. During his campaign, Chirac had promised a package of incentives for companies to hire the long-term unemployed, even at the risk of increasing the nation's huge budget deficit.

In his inaugural address, Chirac avoided specifics on any subject. He said of employment only that it "will be my constant concern."

The program outlined by Juppé on May 23 followed the general outlines of what Chirac had promised during the election campaign. Generally aimed at encouraging businesses to create jobs and hire the unemployed, the program included a reduction in payroll taxes, government subsidies for companies that hired people who had been out of work for more than a year, an increase in the already high minimum wage, and increases in pensions and child care subsidies. To reduce homelessness, which had become one of the country's most visible social problems, Juppé planned a massive home-building program.

Socialist leaders, reduced to an insignificant minority in parliament, could find little to criticize in these aspects of the conservative economic program.

Other elements of the government program proved decidedly less popular, however. Juppé's government proposed sharp cutbacks in the state-owned railway system and reductions in social security protections, wages, and retirement benefits for public employees. Led by railway workers, thousands of public workers went on strike November 24, shutting down much of the nation's public transportation system. The strike lasted nearly a month, disabling much of the economy and forcing millions of people to spend hours on clogged highways commuting to work in Paris and other major cities.

Just before Christmas, Juppé withdrew his plan to curtail pensions for railway workers, an action that convinced the railway union to return to work and led to the eventual collapse of the strike. Most of the government's austerity measures remained intact, representing at least a temporary victory for Juppé and his boss, President Chirac.

The French Role in Europe

Although the heir to de Gaulle's legacy, Chirac did not necessarily imitate his mentor's approach of emphasizing French greatness at every possible opportunity. In his inaugural speech, Chirac avoided bombastic references to French glory and the superiority of French culture and instead talked about the need for change. While calling for the nation to become more confident, unified, and patriotic, Chirac said it should be "more European" as well.

One of Chirac's first official acts as president was to have lunch on May 18 with Chancellor Helmut Kohl of Germany, in Strasbourg, at the border between the two countries. Chirac reportedly sought to assure Kohl that his government would not backtrack on the move toward European integration. France and Germany had been the strongest proponents for a unified European monetary system by 1999, followed by political unity early in the twenty-first century. Chirac also went beyond symbolic meetings by forming a cabinet whose leaders were considered proponents of faster European integration.

In trying to address his country's social problems, Chirac faced a dilemma: it would be difficult to create jobs without increasing the budget deficit, thereby undermining the strength of the franc. A strong franc, backed by a healthy French economy, would be essential as Europe took important steps down the road toward unity. In a speech to parliament on December 7, Juppé acknowledged that his planned budget cutbacks were motivated largely by the need to defend the franc and reduce government spending so France would be eligible to join Germany in the unified European monetary system.

Following is the text of the inaugural address by President Jacques Chirac of France, delivered May 17, 1995:

On this day when I am assuming the responsibility of the highest office of the State, I feel that I am the depository of a hope.

The presidential election was not the victory of one France against another, of one ideology against another. It was the victory of a France who wants to give herself the means to enter the third millennium strong and united.

On 7 May the French people expressed their desire for change.

I am determined to place the seven-year term now beginning under the sign of dignity, simplicity, and fidelity to the essential values of our republic.

My only ambition will be to make the French people more united and more equal and to give greater momentum to a France fortified by her history and her assets.

I shall do everything so that an impartial State, assuming to the full its missions of sovereignty and solidarity, will be the guarantor of the citizens' rights and the protector of their liberties.

I shall do everything so that our democracy will be stronger and better balanced, through a fair sharing of powers between the executive and the legislative, as General de Gaulle, founder of the Fifth Republic, wished. The President will arbitrate, will set the overall guidelines, will guarantee the unity of the nation, will preserve its independence. The Government will conduct the nation's policy. Parliament will make the laws and will monitor the action of the Government. These are the paths to follow.

I shall see that an independent judiciary is given the additional means necessary for carrying out its task.

Above all, I shall commit all my strength to restoring France's cohesion and to renewing the republican pact among the people of France. Employment will be my constant concern. The campaign which is over has enabled our country to get to know itself as it is, with its scars, its fractures, its inequalities, those who are excluded, but also with its ardour, its generosity, its desire to dream and to transform dreams into reality.

France is an old country, but she is also a young nation, enthusiastic, ready to free the best of herself if only she is shown the horizon, and not the narrow confines of closed walls.

President François Mitterrand has marked with his imprint the 14 years which have just ended.

A new seven-year term is beginning. When I leave office I would like the French people to see that the hoped-for change has been achieved.

I would like all our fellow citizens, more assured of their personal future, to feel that they are participants in a collective undertaking. I hope that in these years, when much is at stake but all possibilities are open, they will become more confident, more [united], more patriotic, and at the same time more European, for internal strength is always the source of an impetus toward the exterior.

With the help of the men and women of good will, consistent with the spirit and the letter of our institutions and also with the idea I hold of my mission, I shall be beside the people of France, guarantor of public welfare, in charge of France's higher interests in the world and of the universality of her message.

Long live the Republic!

Long live France!

EXTENSION OF THE NUCLEAR NONPROLIFERATION TREATY
May 17, 1995

The Clinton administration scored one of its most important diplomatic victories on May 11 when a special United Nations conference agreed to extend indefinitely, and without conditions, an international treaty that sought to curb the spread of nuclear weapons. After four weeks of intense negotiations in New York City, the Review and Extension Conference of 175 nations agreed to continue adhering to the Treaty on Non-Proliferation of Nuclear Weapons.

Speaking at the Woodrow Wilson Center in Washington, D.C., on May 17, Ambassador Thomas Graham Jr., the chief U.S. negotiator at the conference, said the decision to extend the treaty "established a permanent landmark on the arms control horizon that we will be blessed to have in years to come." The treaty, which was negotiated in the late 1960s and went into effect in 1970, was a landmark achievement of international arms control efforts during the Cold War era. The treaty effectively legitimized the holding of nuclear weapons by only five countries (the United States, the Soviet Union, China, Britain, and France) and mandated steps to prevent the development of such weapons by all other countries. At the core of the treaty was a set of UN-enforced international "safeguards" and inspections to prevent countries from diverting nuclear facilities and materials into weapons production. It also set limits on international trade in items that could be used to produce nuclear weapons.

The treaty was due to expire in 1995 unless extended. The special UN conference called to review the treaty began work on April 17 but quickly became bogged down in disputes between nations that possessed nuclear weapons and those that did not. A fundamental issue was a demand by some of the nuclear "have-not" states that the five "have" nations allow a freer exchange of technology for peaceful nuclear uses. Several Arab nations also sought to use the treaty review conference to protest Israel's nuclear arsenal.

The Clinton administration made extending the nonproliferation treaty one of its highest foreign policy priorities. For months before the review conference began, and then during conference negotiations, U.S. ambassadors pressed other governments to support the treaty extension. President Bill Clinton and Vice Al President Gore both joined the lobbying effort at key points. The administration reportedly had to apply especially intense pressure on Egypt and Mexico, two of the most important nations resisting indefinite extension of the treaty.

Outline of Agreement

The result was a series of compromise documents pledging accelerated negotiations toward worldwide nuclear disarmament and stronger monitoring of international compliance with the nonproliferation treaty. In a Statement of Principles, the five nuclear powers agreed to pursue "systematic and progressive efforts to reduce nuclear weapons globally, with the ultimate goal of eliminating those weapons." The conference also agreed on yearly assessments of compliance with the nonproliferation treaty; these assessments would begin in 1997 and continue for five years. The yearly assessments were demanded by several nonnuclear states as a means of maintaining pressure on the five nuclear powers to reduce their arsenals.

These agreements were adopted by "consensus," a diplomatic procedure that avoided a direct on-the-record vote by the 175 nations participating in the conference. Representatives of eight nations (Egypt, Iran, Iraq, Jordan, Libya, Malaysia, Nigeria, and Syria) made speeches dissenting from all or part of the final agreements. The United States and its allies worried that a less-than-unanimous vote would have undermined the effectiveness of the treaty.

During the negotiations, the Clinton administration promised that it would redouble efforts to win Senate approval of the second Strategic Arms Reduction Treaty (START II), which had been stymied in the Foreign Relations Committee. The committee reported the treaty favorably on December 12, but the Senate was still considering it at the year's end. (START II Treaty, Historic Documents of 1993, p. 17)

Ambassador Points to Achievements

In his speech marking the extension of the treaty, Ambassador Graham declared that the outcome "was not a victory for any country or region but rather was a significant achievement for all parties" to the treaty. Graham noted that many nonnuclear countries had been skeptical of the treaty when it was negotiated in the 1960s, a skepticism that led to the initial twenty-five-year limit. With the agreement to extend the treaty, he said, there now was "confidence that nuclear nonproliferation should be an enduring norm and that the ultimate goal of a world without nuclear weapons . . . is what all nations support."

In one important step to gain support for extension of the nonproliferation treaty, the five nuclear powers agreed to conclude a Comprehensive

Nuclear Test Ban Treaty "no later than 1996." Graham noted that such a treaty had been under discussion since the 1950s, but had always proven elusive because of opposition by one or more of the five nuclear powers. Many of the nonnuclear states had been demanding a test ban treaty, and some made it an issue during the conference on the nonproliferation treaty. On August 11, President Clinton announced that the United States would support such a treaty. (Comprehensive test ban treaty, p. 553)

Graham said the United States "is prepared to conclude that we have already conducted our last nuclear test." As a result of the New York conference, he said, the Clinton administration "is committed to delivering this [test ban] treaty."

France appeared to threaten progress toward a test ban in September, when it resumed testing in the South Pacific after a three-year moratorium. In December the French defense ministry announced that it would conduct its last test in February 1996. The French government stated that France would sign a comprehensive test ban treaty once that last test was conducted.

The nations at the review conference also agreed to begin negotiations toward a treaty banning production of fissile material for nuclear weapons, such as separated plutonium and highly enriched uranium. Graham said this treaty "would cap the amount of material available for nuclear explosives. . . ."

> *Following is the text, provided by the U.S. Arms Control and Disarmament Agency, of a May 17, 1995, speech at the Woodrow Wilson Center in Washington, D.C., by Ambassador Thomas Graham Jr., special representative of the president for arms control, nonproliferation, and disarmament, in which he praised an international agreement to extend indefinitely the Treaty on Non-Proliferation of Nuclear Weapons:*

The Trinity test, almost fifty years ago, changed the world forever, affirming for the first time our potential capacity to extinguish life on Earth. The most important—and in many respects the most difficult—challenge that emerged was not how to design and build more and better nuclear weapons, but how to control them. Most importantly, how to stop them from spreading. It became clear that this could be achieved only through an effective common, that is multilateral, effort.

I am pleased to report that multilateral arms control works, and while we still have a long way to go, we have reason to hope for a world free of nuclear weapons.

The consensus decision to extend the Nuclear Non-Proliferation Treaty (NPT) indefinitely and without conditions demonstrates that the international community's skepticism that gave the NPT an initially limited duration has given way to confidence that nuclear nonproliferation should be an enduring norm and that the ultimate goal of a world without nuclear weapons as contemplated by the NPT is what all nations support.

The consensus decision to extend the NPT indefinitely and without conditions was a collaborative victory, not a competitive one. The NPT Review and Extension Conference was not similar to a football game with winners and losers. Rather it was a debate over how best to make this Treaty, the centerpiece of international peace and security, strong and durable. All the nations and peoples of the world are winners as a result of the decision in New York.

The 1995 Review and Extension Conference did more than extend the NPT indefinitely. It adopted a set of principles and objectives on nonproliferation and a framework for a strengthened review process. These decisions give us the framework for our future efforts and guiding principles by which we can judge our success. The United States is fully committed to the effective implementation of these documents. It is particularly satisfying that the impetus for two of these decisions—the principles and the strengthened review—came from a recent adherent to the NPT, South Africa.

The United States Government is resolutely committed to do its part to support the decisions taken in New York and the terms and obligations of all the articles of the NPT. In the short run, this will mean redoubling our efforts to achieve a Comprehensive Test Ban Treaty (CTBT) and a fissile material cutoff agreement, but at the same time we will be exploring ways to move beyond the significant reductions to which we have committed ourselves in the START I and START II Treaties. We will not—we cannot—walk away from this process.

While the review of the Treaty did not produce a final review document, it did reveal large areas of agreement. NPT parties agreed to give Conference endorsement to the "93 + 2" plan for strengthened and cost-effective safeguards. They also endorsed the value of increased cooperation in the peaceful uses of nuclear energy, including particularly the safe and efficient utilization of nuclear energy. NPT Parties agreed to pursue the creation of more nuclear weapon free zones (such as the emerging African Nuclear Weapon Free Zone Treaty) and have agreed on the importance of nuclear weapon state support for such zones through their implementing protocols, the universal adherence to the NPT, and the early attainment of a Comprehensive Test Ban Treaty.

Let me again stress that the outcome of the Review and Extension Conference was not a victory for any country or region but rather was a significant achievement for all the parties to the NPT, indeed for the whole world. On March 1, 1995, President Clinton noted that the United States believes that nothing is more important to international security than the achievement of the indefinite extension, without conditions, of this Treaty. In that view, the United States associated itself with an overwhelming majority of the parties to the Treaty. Every sovereign nation at the 1995 NPT Conference rendered an historic judgement; the United States is hopeful that all parties will now work together toward the Treaty's ultimate goal: a world without nuclear weapons.

Let me turn to some specific disarmament issues. Through the agreed enhanced review process, the nuclear weapon states have given their commitment for nuclear arms control and disarmament progress in the future. The United States intends to keep its pledge.

A Comprehensive Nuclear Test Ban Treaty [CNTBT] has been the central objective of nuclear arms control since the late 1950s. All five of the declared nuclear weapon states are committed to achieving a CNTBT by 1996. The United States is prepared to conclude that we have already conducted our last nuclear test. President Clinton is committed to delivering this Treaty, which has been the elusive principal object of the arms control quest for over forty years. Achievement of this all-important goal will close and double lock the tomb of the Cold War forever.

The United States will continue exercising global leadership toward the conclusion of a treaty banning the production of fissile material for nuclear weapons purposes. The United States no longer produces fissile material for nuclear weapons purposes and is working to help Russia obtain alternative power sources for its three remaining military production reactors. Last year, the United States placed a substantial quantity of nuclear material under IAEA [International Atomic Energy Agency] safeguards, including 10 tons of highly enriched uranium from the Department of Energy's Y-12 facility, and this effort is expanding. A fissile material cutoff treaty would cap the amount of material available for nuclear explosives and it would bring the unsafeguarded nuclear programs of certain non-NPT states under some measure of international restraint for the first time. Perhaps most importantly, it would prevent any further production of separated plutonium and highly-enriched uranium for weapons or other explosive purposes.

The United States is committed to the establishment and strengthening of nuclear weapon free zones. South Africa's unprecedented dismantlement of its nuclear weapon program, as indicated earlier, has cleared the way for an African Nuclear Weapon Free Zone Treaty. The United States Government has been on record since 1964 in support of the denuclearization of Africa and supports the concept of this being achieved through a nuclear weapon free zone treaty. The text of this treaty is not yet final, but we hope to be in a position to become a protocol party to the final treaty soon, assuming it meets longstanding U.S. criteria for such zones, as we are with the Latin American Nuclear Weapon Free Zone Treaty, the Treaty of Tlatelolco. We recognize the great importance attached to U.S. adherence as a protocol party to the South Pacific Nuclear Free Zone by our negotiating partners from that region and we are actively studying that course of action. The United States supports the establishment of regional nuclear weapon free zones that meet our longstanding criteria for such zones, and encourages progress toward this goal in the different regions of the world. President Clinton has informed President Soeharto of Indonesia that, in principle, the United States would support the creation of a Southeast Asia Nuclear Weapon Free Zone, assuming it meets longstanding U.S. criteria for such zones. We understand that global solutions can start with regional approaches.

If there is one lesson of the NPT Review and Extension Conference, it is that the Treaty and the nonproliferation regime it supports become stronger and better with each new adherence. Each new member brings the Treaty one step closer to universality and makes the danger of nuclear proliferation more improbable. The United States supports universality for the NPT and looks forward to the day when this goal is achieved.

The consensus decision to extend the NPT indefinitely and without conditions was a team effort that required numerous contributions that could only be made by partners from diverse perspectives. Vice President Gore demonstrated United States leadership by reaffirming that complete nuclear disarmament remains the ultimate goal of the United States. South African Foreign Minister Nzo played an indispensable role in bridging the gap between the developed and the developing world and providing the basis for the discussion of principles and objectives on nonproliferation and of beneficial enhancements to the NPT Review Process. Indonesian Foreign Minister Alatas demonstrated great diplomatic leadership through his proposal to establish a direct relationship between the arms control and nonproliferation principles and objectives and strengthened review process which empowered the conference to reach the consensus which will be beneficial to all. Above all, the farsighted leadership and steady hand of Conference President Ambassador Jayantha Dhanapala guided the Review and Extension Conference to the best outcome, locking in a larger area of general agreement among the parties than almost anyone thought possible on the eve of the Conference. As I said, the United States is committed to all three documents of the Conference, the Extension Decision, the Principles and Objectives for Non-Proliferation, and the Strengthened Review Process, and to seeing that they are carried out. We are very grateful to all of our partners around the world who helped us arrive at these historic decisions and look forward to continuing to work with these partners, and all NPT parties, to ensure that their concerns are addressed.

The victory on May 11 was a common victory. It established a permanent landmark on the arms control horizon that we will be blessed to have in years to come. In the last twelve months alone, the headlines and attention of the world have been drawn repeatedly to the grim specter of nuclear proliferation. North Korea's nuclear program, the smuggling of fissile materials out of the former Soviet Union, and the apparent Iranian decision to seek nuclear weapons capability have each reinforced the gravity of the problem. The international community will have to continue to work together to keep nuclear proliferation in check and, to this end, it is important to the United States that all states parties to the NPT feel a part of our common victory.

Reflecting on this month's historic decision to make the NPT permanent, it is important for us to ask ourselves what the essential elements of this decision are, what made it possible and what will make it work. The answers include peace, cooperation, and the conscious decision to establish the permanent basis for efforts to achieve a world free from nuclear weapons.

REPORT ON SEGREGATION IN COLLEGES AND UNIVERSITIES
May 17, 1995

Four decades after the U.S. Supreme Court struck down school segregation, not one of twelve states that formerly maintained segregated university and college systems could "demonstrate an acceptable level of success in desegregating its higher education system." That was the conclusion of "Redeeming the American Promise," a report published by the Southern Education Foundation on May 17, the forty-first anniversary of the Supreme Court's ruling in Brown v. Board of Education *finding "separate but equal" school facilities to be unconstitutional. The foundation was created in 1937 from the merger of four philanthropic funds aimed at promoting equity and quality in education in the South; it has been actively involved in efforts to desegregate higher education.*

The foundation's report grew out of another case, U.S. v. Fordice, decided in 1992, in which the Supreme Court was asked to rule whether a state had met its constitutional obligation to dismantle a formerly segregated system of higher education. In holding that the adoption of race-neutral policies alone was not enough, the court ruled that states must eradicate the remnants of official segregation from their higher education systems and must do so by adopting "sound educational practices." (Court on Desegregation at Mississippi Colleges, Historic Documents of 1992, p. 575)

In the wake of the Fordice *decision, the foundation established the Panel on Educational Opportunity and Postsecondary Desegregation, a twenty-six member panel comprised of educators, elected officials, activists, and members of the business community. The panel was asked "to consider what sound educational practices might best promote minority access to and success in higher education" in an overall system not limited by race. It studied twelve of the nineteen states that set up segregated higher education systems after the Civil War (Alabama, Florida, Georgia, Kentucky, Louisiana, Maryland, Mississippi, North Carolina, Pennsylvania, Tennessee, Texas, and Virginia) and found that for minority students "the promise of equal opportunity for a high-quality education has not been kept."*

According to the panel, black and Hispanic students were underrepresented in most four-year universities, in virtually every field of study, and, with three exceptions, in the number of bachelor's degrees awarded. Blacks accounted for 25 percent of the college-age population in the twelve states, but represented only 16 percent of full-time freshmen and 10 percent of bachelor's degree recipients. Minority faculty members were also in short supply.

A major factor limiting access was money. The availability of need-based grants, the type of financial aid that most benefits minority families, has decreased significantly even as the costs of attending college have been climbing. In the 1970s more students received need-based Pell grants from the federal government than borrowed through federal student loan programs. In 1995 the number of borrowers was expected to be 70 percent higher than the number of grant recipients, and more than four times as much federal money was expected to be spent on loans as on grants. As a consequence, the panel wrote, federal financial aid is now geared more toward the needs of the middle- and upper-middle-income families than it is to lower-income families, where minorities are heavily represented.

Beyond issues of financial aid, the panel also found that minority students were often poorly prepared for college work. One of the most "pernicious" practices facing black students in the South, the report said, was "tracking them into dead-end curricula" and away from college preparatory courses. Moreover, the panel said, college admission officials often misused tests and test scores. "Too often, test scores are used to fulfill institutional needs for prestige rather than as a genuine assessment of student potential."

The panel outlined ten recommendations that it said would help establish higher education systems "where choice of institution is unfettered, and success is realizable for everyone, regardless of race." These recommendations were based on three principles. First, education should be student-centered, organized to advance the needs of the student and not the preferences of the institution. Second, states must promote desegregation and equal opportunity for all students at every level of schooling so that all students are prepared for the demands of a postsecondary education. As part of that reform, the panel called on states and local communities to find a fairer way to fund public elementary and secondary schools than the traditional local property tax. Third, the panel urged that education be performance-based and that school systems be held accountable for results.

Following is the text of the executive summary from "Redeeming the American Promise," a report on the status of college desegregation in twelve states, issued May 17, 1995, by the Southern Education Foundation:

Forty-one years after the United States Supreme Court's historic decision in *Brown v. Board of Education,* not one of the 12 formerly segregated states examined by the Southern Education Foundations Panel on Educational

Opportunity and Postsecondary Desegregation can demonstrate an acceptable level of success in desegregating its higher education system. Substantial remnants of segregation continue to shape higher education in these states, and consequently opportunity for minority students is limited, fragmented, and uneven. For them, the promise of equal opportunity for a high-quality education has not been kept. As a result:

- Minority college students have limited access to predominantly white four-year institutions; in all but two of the states that were analyzed, more than three of every five black first-time freshmen attended either historically black colleges and universities (HBCUs) or community colleges; in eight of these states, fewer than 10 percent of black first-time freshmen were enrolled in the state's flagship institution; only three of all public HBCUs report that 10 percent or more of their first-year class is white.
- In Florida and Texas, two states with significant Hispanic populations, Hispanic students are severely underrepresented in four-year institutions. In Florida, 15 percent of the states 17- to 21-year-old population is Hispanic, but only 11 percent of the first-year, full-time students in the four-year institutions are. In Texas the figures are 32 percent and 19 percent, respectively.
- Blacks and Hispanics are underrepresented among bachelor's degree recipients in every state and in every field of study, with the following exceptions: In Louisiana, the proportion of bachelor's degrees awarded to blacks in engineering and physical sciences exceeds their share of the state's population, and in Florida, the percentage of bachelor's degrees conferred to Hispanics in foreign languages surpasses their representation among the state's population.
- In the 12 states, blacks account for an average of 25 percent of the college-age population, yet they represent only 16 percent of full-time freshmen and 10 percent of bachelor's degree recipients.
- The percentage of white adults who hold bachelor's degrees in all 12 states is approximately twice as high as the proportion of black adults who are college graduates.

Minorities are also denied full participation as faculty in institutions of higher education:

- The shortage of minority faculty—black and Hispanic—is acute in every institution and in every state. Across the board, the higher the faculty rank, the lower the representation of black and Hispanic faculty.
- In the states that we studied, on average blacks earn fewer than 4 percent of total doctorates awarded, although they account for 20 percent of the population.

Increasingly, minority students tell of feeling unwelcome at majority institutions and that the environments at these institutions negatively affect what and how they learn.

- Recent poll results report that only one-quarter of academic administrators believe that their campuses provide a "very good" or "excellent" climate for black students; even fewer believe that their campus climates are supportive of Hispanic students.
- Another national survey revealed that almost one-third (32 percent) of black students had experienced racial harassment; 51 percent had heard faculty make inappropriate remarks regarding minority students.

To change this situation—and to make real the promise of equal opportunity—race must finally be disentangled from education. Desegregation remains a powerful way to effect this transformation. The Southern Education Foundation's Panel on Educational Opportunity and Postsecondary Desegregation has concluded that the United States Supreme Court's decision in *U.S. v. Fordice* presents a compelling opportunity to eliminate race as an impediment to student access and achievement in higher education. Fordice, the first full application of the principles set forth in *Brown v. Board of Education* to higher education, emphasizes "sound educational practices"—ones that are rooted in the interests of students—as the means by which to effect desegregation. *Fordice* presents an approach to transforming education so that it focuses on opportunity and no longer disadvantages individuals and institutions on the basis of race. It also provides a chance for the South to lead the way in designing effective and lasting solutions to issues of minority access and success in higher education.

Recommendations

The Panel's ultimate goal is higher education that is student-centered, where choice of institutions is unfettered and success is realizable for everyone, regardless of race. Each institution has a defined and separate mission, but each is linked to the others and to elementary and high schools. The institutions and people in this system are all accountable for their performance and rewarded for results. To attain this goal, the Panel makes 10 recommendations. These were shaped by core beliefs that the Panel came to share during its investigation. The Panel believes that:

- Higher education is central to opportunity. While a college degree is increasingly essential to success, race remains a barrier to full participation in higher education for too many minority students.
- Effective higher education desegregation requires comprehensive reform. All sectors must collaborate—including elementary and secondary education and community colleges—to develop and implement strategies that will lead to better results for students.
- The Supreme Court's decision in *U.S. v. Fordice* provides a framework for fundamental reform in higher education because it enables us to approach desegregation by focusing on the needs of students. A comprehensive, student-centered approach to desegregation emphasizes results and requires accountability.

- Achieving a fully desegregated system—one that promotes choice and offers opportunity—requires the vision, commitment, and will of government, courts, educators, and private citizens, including students and their families. Opportunity cannot be defined and driven by the law alone.

The Panel's recommendations are related parts of a coherent whole. Each is connected to the others and, to work effectively, each must be implemented in conjunction with the others. To desegregate higher education and promote opportunity, we must:

1. Address the systemic nature of the problem: Create comprehensive state plans
   - Every state which formerly operated a dual system of higher education should develop a long-term plan containing comprehensive and coordinated remedies that effectively treat public schools and higher education as one system.
   - As the first step in this effort, governors should convene every state agency and instrumentality responsible for the development, funding, and implementation of public policies in education and related areas to determine how best to eliminate the vestiges of segregation and advance educational opportunity.
2. Make campuses responsible: Develop institutional plans
   - Each public institution of higher education should be required to develop its own plan outlining how it proposes to promote minority access and success.
3. Provide a fair start: Make access an institutional mission
   - All colleges and universities in the state system should adopt policies and practices that will expand access to high-quality education for more minority students and promote opportunity.
4. Level the playing field: Make success a core institutional responsibility
   - States and institutions should declare their commitment to success for all students and then work relentlessly to ensure it.
5. Strengthen the system: Make community colleges full partners in higher education
   - State and institutional plans should promote easy transfer between two- and four-year institutions.
6. Be clear about accomplishments: Measure success and failure
   - States should develop accountability measures keyed to the missions of individual institutions as well as to indicators of progress toward institutional and statewide desegregation goals.
   - All elements of higher education governance—from state boards to faculty and administrations at individual institutions—must be accountable for promoting real progress in desegregation.
7. Advance access and enhance success: Support historically black institutions

- States should take advantage of the capacity of historically black institutions to advance access and equity.
- States should enhance these institutions to promote desegregation.

8. Build on strength: Restructure systems rather than close or merge institutions
   - In creating nonracial systems, states should transform institutions through new mission statements, creative program assignments, and enhanced institutional cooperation, avoiding the closure of HBCUs and merging or consolidating institutions only as a last resort.

9. Share responsibility for effective desegregation: Promote leadership from both the public and private sectors
   - Desegregation and the provision of opportunity are not exclusively the province of educators—they require collaborative leadership from all sectors.

10. Make promises real: Invest in reform
   - States and the federal government must make good on their commitments to students and families by financing the promises they have made.

Implementing these recommendations is the first step toward redeeming the American promise of equal educational opportunity.

Miles to Go

Despite the progress resulting from the civil rights revolution of the last generation, large remnants of America's fixation with race continue to disadvantage too many Americans. These remnants are powerfully present within the nation's colleges and universities—nowhere more so than in the southern states that at one time operated dual systems of higher education—one for whites, the other for blacks.

Yet much has changed in the region. The duty to desegregate elementary and secondary education has, in many ways, begun to liberate the South from its past. In the 1980s, the region took the lead in promoting public school reform. A similar opportunity now presents itself with regard to higher education. The South's unique history gives it a special chance to find effective and lasting solutions for problems that affect the entire nation.

The future of the nation and the future of minority children and youth are one. And it is in our nation's schools, colleges, and universities that this future can be determined. It will be shaped by our success in developing and utilizing the talents of an increasingly diverse population. Our educational institutions must prepare students to live and work in a new environment and, in so doing, strengthen both the fabric of our society and our connections to each other.

Desegregation enables the nation to embrace one of its defining values— equality of opportunity. Democracy is strengthened when students of different races are educated together in institutions that are dedicated to the development of the full social and intellectual capacities of each of them.

A new chance to desegregate higher education is provided by the Supreme Court's 1992 decision in *U.S. v. Fordice*. If we seize the initiative we can transform higher education so that it focuses on opportunity for students and no longer disadvantages individuals and institutions because of race.

The transforming challenge facing the United States today is to keep the promise it has made to all of its citizens and to put behind it the shame, anger, and pain of the nation's racial history. The nation has promises to keep. Although miles stretch out ahead before rest is earned, the passage has been paid and the nation's people must, together, go forward and redeem the American promise of opportunity for all.

The Legal Context

In the century after the Civil War, 19 states established segregated colleges and universities, primarily to keep blacks out of white institutions and to limit their entry to all but the most menial occupations. States found numerous ways to keep their institutions segregated and to keep graduate and professional education beyond the reach of blacks.

For blacks in the South, segregation was strictly enforced and there was never a pretense of equality. Despite state-imposed restrictions, historically black colleges evolved into full-fledged college-level institutions—many offering graduate-level degrees. These institutions took primary responsibility for educating black students in the South and had remarkable success in doing so.

Yet, even their best efforts have not been able to compensate fully for the harm inflicted on black students by official policies. The vestiges of these policies remain, and black students continue to suffer from more limited access to and lower rates of success in higher education than do their white peers.

From 1954 to 1992, the Supreme Court heard numerous elementary and secondary education cases, but no significant higher education desegregation cases. States argued that if they were not using their powers to require segregation in higher education, they were doing all that the law required. The federal government and many private citizens disagreed with this interpretation, and in 1978, with the approval of the federal courts in *Adams v. Richardson*, the government developed criteria for desegregating higher education. By the mid-1980s, however, the federal government de-emphasized the pursuit of these criteria and limited the collection of relevant data to monitor states' progress in implementing these plans.

Many states, including Mississippi, continued to argue that nondiscriminatory admissions policies were all that were required in higher education. In 1975, a group of Mississippi blacks, led by Jake Ayers, sued the state in federal court to demand a more equitable system of higher education—requesting, among other things, enhanced funding for the states three historically black colleges. The Mississippi case went to trial in 1987 and the district court concluded that state officials were not violating federal law because the state's duty to desegregate only extended to ensuring that its policies are racially neutral. The United States Court of Appeals affirmed the court's decision.

In 1992, the Supreme Court agreed to review the rulings by the lower courts in Mississippi and, in *U.S. v. Fordice*, concluded that the lower courts had failed to apply the correct legal standard to the state's public university system. The Supreme Court said that discriminatory policies and practices could exist even if there are race-neutral admissions. According to the Court, "if policies traceable to the *de jure* system are still enforced and have discriminatory effects, these policies too [in addition to segregative admissions policies] must be reformed to the extent practicable and consistent with sound educational practices." The Court identified four areas in which Mississippi's policies appeared problematic: admissions policies, program duplication, mission statements, and the number of institutions.

The Court ordered the state to remove or correct these vestiges and to consider, among other things, closing or merging some of the eight extant institutions. *Fordice* thus raised the possibility that historically black colleges and universities—the very institutions that have provided opportunities for blacks—might be sacrificed in the name of desegregation.

The Supreme Court decision in *Fordice* appeared to resolve several important questions. First, it recognized the continuing legacy of segregation in the persistence of racial inequity in public higher education. Second, the Court confirmed that its decision in *Brown* applies to public higher education. Third, the Court rejected the argument that the adoption of race-neutral policies was a sufficient remedy in states that had previously mandated racial segregation in higher education. The correct standard, said the Supreme Court, is whether any "policies traceable to the *de jure* system" are still in force and have discriminatory effects. Fourth, the Court, in saying that such policies should be remedied "consistent with *sound educational practices*," indicated that the lower courts should defer, to some degree, to educators. Finally, the Supreme Court affirmed that vestiges of segregation must be eliminated systemwide in higher education.

Fordice also left several important issues to be resolved by the lower courts, including how to determine whether a policy or practice is traceable to past segregation and what types of remedial measures are appropriate. Several lower court rulings since the Supreme Court decision in *Fordice*—in Alabama, Louisiana, and Mississippi offer some guidance on these issues. Some of the remedial measures—including enhancement of HBCUs, linkages to community colleges, and an avoidance of closure and merger—are encouraging. They do not, however, take a comprehensive, student-centered, and accountability-driven approach to ensuring greater access to and success in higher education for minority students.

The legal history is the starting point of a journey that will end only when real educational opportunity is available to all students. The courts are a necessary, but ultimately imperfect, means of resolving issues of equity in higher education. Our goal must be educational systems that provide all students with equal access to high-quality educational institutions and equal opportunity to succeed once they have been admitted. A powerful way to reach that goal is by understanding and applying the sound educational practices to which *Fordice* gave special prominence. The Panel believes that *"sound educational practices"* are those that promote the interests of students, and that *Fordice* enables state and education leaders to emphasize these interests. It is individual students who have been harmed by the legacy of segregation and who must be provided with the choice and opportunity called for by *Fordice*. This means that states must attack the systemic underlying failures of public education, from pre-kindergarten through postgraduate education, and create, in effect, a comprehensive education system that provides all students with an education of high quality.

Building a New System

Higher education can be transformed and nonracial systems created if state and academic leaders adopt three principles. They are:

- Student-centered: Education must become student-centered; systems must be organized to advance the interests and respond to the needs of students rather than the preferences of the institutions created to meet those needs.
- Comprehensive: States must concentrate on systemwide approaches to desegregation and equal opportunity and promote the principle that each sector of education—kindergarten through grade 12 (K-12), community colleges, four-year colleges, and graduate schools—is linked to the others. The states cannot use their failure to provide an education of high quality to all students in public schools as a rationale for their failure to desegregate higher education. They must treat all of education as one system in shaping remedies that will eliminate the vestiges of segregation.
- Accountable and Performance-Driven: Education must be performance based and accountable for results.

In a nonracial system of higher education, traditionally white institutions will demonstrate convincingly that they no longer restrict or exclude minority students, and that they provide them with an education of high quality. In this system, HBCUs will not be relegated by state policy to second-tier status.

The Panel emphatically rejects closing HBCUs to promote desegregation. Both traditionally white and historically black institutions are vestiges of purposeful, state-imposed segregation. No set of institutions has any more right than another to survive. The burden of desegregation should not fall exclusively or disproportionately on HBCUs.

Furthermore, it is not educationally sound to desegregate systems by eliminating institutions which are the primary providers of effective minority access to higher education. When given the opportunity, HBCUs consistently demonstrate their capacity to provide high-quality programs that can attract white students.

A good-faith, comprehensive response to the challenge presented by *Fordice* will put a human face on the idea of desegregation. *Fordice* enables us to develop comprehensive new approaches and more meaningful measures of success. By emphasizing the interests of students, it allows us to concentrate on education at all levels and to promote opportunity for all by adopting a systemic, results-oriented approach to desegregation.

Access

Access for minority students must be the very first consideration in building a desegregated system that provides all students with both choice and opportunity. Students who never enter the nation's colleges and universities will never graduate from them.

The standard that the Panel recommends to measure access is similar to the one adopted by the federal government almost two decades ago: Minority student representation in public institutions of higher learning should equal their representation among high school graduates. We have a long way to go to meet that standard. To do so, we must deal with three problems:

Inadequate Preparation for College Work

Tracking and Curricular Exposure

To get to college, black students in the South must depend on some of the worst public schools in the United States in terms of facilities and course offerings. Among the most pernicious of the practices facing them is that of tracking them into dead-end curricula. Recent studies demonstrate that minority students disproportionately suffer this fate. For example, a College Board examination of nationwide course-taking patterns by race, ethnicity, and secondary schools revealed that minority students are directed away from courses designed to prepare them for college—algebra, geometry, foreign languages, and laboratory sciences—and into undemanding "general" tracks, in which mathematics is likely to be consumer arithmetic and the study of other languages and science is nowhere to be found.

School Finance

An equally severe problem is inadequate funding of schools in low-income areas, predominantly in minority communities. Testimony in a 1993 Alabama school finance suit described Black Belt schools where sewage leaked onto playgrounds, the libraries and classrooms were termite-infested, hallways crawled with ants, and tables had to be propped up with milk crates. Reliance on local property taxes to fund public schools accounts for most of the school finance inequities within states. One of the bedrock values of the United States is fairness, a commitment to the proposition that all children deserve a level playing field, that they all are entitled to a fair chance as they start out in life. Funding disparities of nearly 3 to 1 call into question the commitment of state and local officials to that basic value.

Inappropriate Admissions Practices

Many minority students, having successfully negotiated the hurdles placed before them in public schools, are denied access to higher education through the misuse of tests and test scores.

It is hardly surprising—given the dead-end curricula into which minority students are tracked—that average scores for black and Hispanic students are frequently lower than average scores for white students. What is not taught is not learned.

Testing has a legitimate role to play in admissions policy, but some states and institutions rely too heavily and too rigidly upon tests. Too often, test scores are used to fulfill institutional needs for prestige rather than as genuine assessments of student potential.

Expert opinion on this issue is unanimous: The combination of multiple admissions criteria—high school grade point average, the rigor of the high school course sequence completed, teacher recommendations, extracurricular activities and community service, and standardized test scores—is a much better predictor of college success than test scores alone.

Access via Community Colleges

Many states—including those which formerly operated dual systems of higher education—have consigned a major part of the responsibility for access on the part of black and Hispanic students to community colleges. Enrollment patterns in the 12 states studied make this abundantly clear.

Community colleges are less expensive, they are more accessible geographically, they offer a variety of programs, and their admissions requirements are generally lower than those of four-year colleges. These and other attributes make them attractive to low-income students, including minorities.

For the most part, however, community colleges have not been able to fulfill their potential to provide genuine access to further higher education. In concept, community colleges appear to be access channels to four-year higher education. All too often, community colleges become an extension of the tracking students have been subject to since entering kindergarten.

Access via Historically Black Colleges and Universities

Historically black institutions are major points of entry for black students in each of the 12 states. Among other things, they continue to provide opportunities for inadequately prepared students who would not otherwise be able to go to college. HBCUs remain central to efforts to ensure access for black students; without them, the limited access to higher education for black students would be drastically reduced. Consequently, it is important for states to ensure that HBCUs have the capacity and capability to provide disadvantaged students whom they accept with an appropriate, high-quality education. HBCUs should also be provided with high-profile, high-demand programs that can attract more other-race students.

Recruitment Strategies

At the same time, equitable access means that flagship and other traditionally white institutions must accept many more minority students. "Creaming" a few minority students does not compensate for insufficient access. Effective recruitment strategies must promote diversity, be tied to the university's regular academic programs, and involve collaboration with other sectors of education.

Insufficient Student Financial Aid

Finally, students who cannot afford to pay for college are much less likely to attend. College costs are going up and the real value of student aid is going down. The "affordability" crisis in American higher education is real, and it must be addressed by institutions and policymakers. Minority families in the South are among the least likely of those in any region to afford the cost of higher education and students from these families must rely heavily on student aid if they are to attend at all.

Opinion polls, even amidst current budget problems of federal and state governments, demonstrate conclusively that the general public is convinced that no deserving student—majority or minority—should be denied the opportunity to attend college simply because he or she cannot afford it. Adequate financial aid should be available to any student who needs it. The Panel believes that minority scholarships, appropriately designed to remedy past discrimination and encourage diversity, are an important means to desegregation and will result in expanded access.

Success

No student enters a four-year college or university expecting to drop out or leave without graduating. Each aspires to a degree along with the sense of satisfaction and accomplishment, and the income potential that accompanies it. Students' expectations and hopes are universal; their success is not.

In the South, the gap between where higher education is and where it should be in promoting minority success can be measured by the failure of states to meet the graduation and graduate school enrollment goals developed by the federal government 17 years ago. None of the 12 states studied by the Panel has come close to attaining these goals. In fact, in each of the 12, the success of minority students, as measured by persistence to the degree and graduate and postgraduate enrollment rates, is static or falling, despite litigation and a decade of school reform efforts. Today minority students' pattern of attainment is almost exactly the opposite of that of white students, who are overrepresented at almost every degree level; in none of the states we looked at does black bachelor's degree attainment approach that of whites.

If state officials and higher education leaders in southern and border states are to succeed in reversing this situation, they must attend to three issues:

Creating a More Hospitable Environment
for Minority Students

While many colleges and universities are recognized for their tolerance, the evidence the Panel received of race-baiting on some campuses, faculty indifference to the concerns of minority students, inappropriate curricula, and lack of minority role models and mentors cannot be dismissed.

Institutions need to take the lead and structure situations in which white students and minority students—most raised and educated in racially isolated communities and schools—can come to know and understand each other. Such a climate is not something that can be created by serendipity or by fragmented efforts. The approach must be systematic and comprehensive and begin in the classroom. Institutions will create a truly supportive learning environment only if they are unequivocal in their embrace of diversity and if they infuse campus policies and practices with that value.

Developing More Appropriate Academic Programs and Support Strategies

It is clear that poorly prepared first-year students need academic and other support if they are to survive. Many experts believe that opportunities to work in small groups, to take advantage of small classes, and to receive intensive faculty attention and extensive academic assistance are essential to minority success on campus. The most effective strategies appear to have several things in common. First is an early warning system to alert faculty and counselors to students who are getting into academic difficulty. Second is regular interaction with faculty members. Third is sustained and comprehensive faculty leadership.

The nurturing environment that is a key to success is often present at Hispanic-serving and historically black institutions. On traditionally white campuses student polarization is sometimes related not only to how students are taught but to what they are taught. All institutions should recognize the different cultural identities of those who are part of the university community and ensure that their experiences are reflected in the curriculum.

Recruiting More Minority Faculty and Staff and Providing More Incentives for Graduate and Professional Study

Historic discrimination against minority students has left the nation's colleges and universities with a desperate shortage of minority Ph.D.s. In the 12 states examined by the Panel, blacks make up between 2 and 3 percent of faculty at leading universities. Hispanics account for just 2 percent of tenured full professors at the University of Texas.

Increasing the numbers of minority faculty and administrators begins with the production of more doctoral candidates. However, even if every institution were to make a commitment today to equalize minority representation on its faculty and staff tomorrow, given the shortage of minority Ph.D. recipients, the commitment could not be kept.

Data from the National Academy of Sciences indicate that American universities produced only 1,641 black and Hispanic doctorates in 1991, the last year for which such data are available. The assumption that all of these degree recipients hope for an academic career is unrealistic—their education opens opportunities across the economic spectrum.

Some states are beginning to attack the problem through comprehensive partnerships with the private sector. The situation cannot be reversed quickly or easily—but it will never be improved until state and academic leaders make its resolution a priority.

Promoting Success at All Institutions

Black retention and graduation rates are far below those of their white and Hispanic counterparts, both statewide and within the same institutions. The most selective colleges and universities appear to have the highest retention, progression, and graduation rates for both white and minority students, while historically black institutions have retention, progression, and graduation rates for blacks that often lag behind other institutions in the same states.

The need to increase significantly the success rates for minority students confronts all institutions. At predominantly white institutions, part of this challenge can be met by making the campus a more hospitable and welcoming place for minority students and targeting programs to enhance their success. HBCUs serve substantial numbers of underprepared students, and these institutions must develop comprehensive strategies to increase success for these students. States must provide public HBCUs with sufficient resources to meet the extraordinary challenge of serving underprepared students. At the same time, if the states relieve HBCUs from bearing a disproportionate share of the burden of serving as opportunity institutions and provide them with resources to develop and implement high-profile programs to attract highly qualified students of all races, success rates at HBCUs are sure to improve.

What is central to increased success rates at all institutions is a system of accountability that is tied to the comprehensive approaches discussed in this report. Rewards and sanctions must be established that recognize the obligations of institutions to invest in students' success.

Promoting Opportunity

Education continues to be the most powerful vehicle for achieving the American promise and preserving our common ideals. The nation's schools, colleges, and universities are among the few places where the artificial barriers of race, religion, class, and language can be transcended.

As we approach the twenty-first century, the national imperative to develop the talents of all of our citizens has been reinforced by a constitutional mandate to desegregate higher education. In the past, litigation was often the only way to resolve questions of desegregation and opportunity. We believe that the South, along with the rest of the nation, is open to new ways to resolve abiding issues. The comprehensive solutions that we urge here depend upon leadership and voluntary cooperation among many sectors.

Implementing these solutions will require increased investment in education. Without sufficient investment, opportunity will be lost and more lives wasted. It is far more prudent to invest now in our future rather than to pay a higher price, at some later date, for our neglect.

The recommendations in this report are strategic elements of a comprehensive approach to desegregating higher education that emphasizes student interests. The approach stresses the importance of accountability for engendering real reform, and it underscores the need for sustained involvement by federal and state governments, the courts, educators, and private citizens in fostering comprehensive change. The recommendations are but a beginning, a new starting point on the continuing quest for equity in education. Realization of equity requires commitment from all those who would embrace a vision of America defined by possibility rather than limited by the past.

The promise of desegregation without a commitment to expanded opportunity is an empty one. In this document, we have detailed what is required to keep the promise of equality of opportunity. That promise cannot be kept until the issues examined in this document have been addressed—not as a matter of expedience, or even of law, but as a matter of fidelity to America's definition of itself.

CLINTON ON THE CLOSING
OF PENNSYLVANIA AVENUE
May 20, 1995

President Bill Clinton announced May 20 that the two blocks of Pennsylvania Avenue that ran in front of the White House were being closed immediately to vehicular traffic to deter a potential car- or truck-bomb attack on the president and the building. The closure came just a month after a bomb destroyed a federal office building in Oklahoma City, killing 168 people. (Oklahoma bombing, p. 176)

By all accounts, the president was reluctant to close that section of Pennsylvania Avenue, which was known as "America's Main Street." Like other presidents before him, he wanted to maintain the White House as a symbol of an open democracy. Security analysts, however, convinced the president that detonation of a large bomb in a truck parked 150 feet from the White House could inflict lethal damage, injuring or killing not only the president and his family but also White House personnel, visitors, and tourists.

"Pennsylvania Avenue has been routinely open to traffic for the entire history of our Republic," Clinton said, announcing the closing in his weekly radio address to the nation. "Through four Presidential assassinations and eight unsuccessful attempts on the lives of Presidents, it's been open; through a civil war, two world wars and the Gulf War, it was open. And now it must be closed. . . . Clearly, this closing is necessary because of the changing nature and scope of the threat of terrorist actions." Clinton said the two-block area would remain open to foot traffic and would eventually become part of a pedestrian mall joined with Lafayette Park, which is located across Pennsylvania Avenue, facing the White House. Government vehicles would be permitted to use the closed portion of the street for certain important events, including presidential inaugurations and state dinners.

Commuters who normally used the street found the stretch barricaded early May 20, first by sawhorses and then by concrete barriers. Pennsylvania Avenue was blocked between 15th and 17th streets, as were portions

254

of State Place and South Executive Avenue behind the Old Executive Office Building, which is adjacent to the White House. An estimated 26,000 vehicles had driven past the White House daily. Within hours, the once busy street was filled with tourists on foot, joggers, and rollerbladers.

Lengthy Review

The decision to close the street was one of eleven recommendations Clinton accepted to strengthen security around the White House. Five of the recommendations were not made public. The recommendations grew out of a review of White House security, conducted by a panel of experts both in and out of government. That review was begun in the fall of 1994 after Frank Eugene Corder, an unlicensed pilot with a history of mental illness, stole a small airplane from a Maryland airport and crashed it onto the White House lawn just before 2:00 a.m. on September 12. Corder was killed in the crash, and the plane itself hit a corner of the White House. One of the accepted recommendations was a new system of coordination between the Federal Aviation Administration and the Secret Service to deter air attacks.

The Secret Service had long sought the closing of the street in front of the White House, but Clinton and his predecessors had resisted. According to a Washington Post *report, however, after Clinton and Treasury Secretary Robert E. Rubin reviewed the devastation caused by the Oklahoma City bombing, "their doubts about the closing were eclipsed by their sense of how easy it would be to assemble a car bomb and set it off near" the presidential mansion.*

Several alternatives to deter potential car bombs were studied, and all were rejected as being unworkable, ineffective, or too militaristic for a democratic society. These included establishing checkpoints at 15th and 17th Streets to search vehicles and installing bomb detectors that vehicles would drive through. William Webster, former head of the Federal Bureau of Investigation and the Central Intelligence Agency and a member of the panel that reviewed the recommendations, said that he had resisted closing the street until after the Oklahoma City bombing. "I don't really like to see concessions to terrorists," Webster said, "but I came to see this [closing] as drawing a sensible line."

Pledge to Remain Accessible

In his radio address, the president characterized the closure not as a concession to terrorists but "a responsible security step necessary to preserve our freedom." He called on Congress to pass his antiterrorism legislation and pledged that he would not "allow the fight against domestic and foreign terrorism to build a wall between me and the American people."

Despite that promise, a wall of security literally surrounds the White House. Electronic and seismic sensors and video equipment monitor the grounds, as do guards on the roofs of the White House and the nearby Treasury Building. The grounds are patrolled. Tourists must pass through metal detectors and are watched on closed-circuit television monitors as they tour the house. All handbags, packages, and newspapers are inspected, and the movements of all White House personnel are also monitored. Bullet-proof shields cover the windows of the Oval Office, and the president has a "panic button" located at knee-level under his Oval Office desk. Precautions are taken with food, and the White House is also equipped with highly sensitive water and air filtration systems for detecting poisonous gas and bacteria.

All these precautions—which were taken before Pennsylvania Avenue was closed—have not prevented the occasional attempt to reach the president. On October 19, 1994, for example, Francisco Martin Duran fired twenty-nine rounds from a semiautomatic rifle at the White House before he was tackled by two bystanders. Duran was subsequently convicted of attempted assassination. Two months later, on December 17, 1994, bullets were fired at the White House from the Ellipse, in what officials said might have been a drive-by shooting. Three days later National Park police shot and killed a homeless man who was brandishing a knife on Pennsylvania Avenue in front of the White House. On May 23, 1995, just three days after the street was closed, Leland William Modjeski jumped the White House fence and ran toward the mansion with what turned out to be an unloaded gun. He was shot in the arm and apprehended by the Secret Service.

Closing Pennsylvania Avenue was unlikely to stop similar incidents, but others of the recommendations were expected to help minimize the threat. "We looked at what did occur and what might occur and what practically could occur, and took the steps against those threats," one official told the Washington Post.

> *Following is the text of President Bill Clinton's radio address on May 20, 1995, announcing the immediate closing to vehicular traffic of two blocks of Pennsylvania Avenue in front of the White House:*

Today, the Secretary of the Treasury, who oversees the Secret Service, will announce that from now on the two blocks of Pennsylvania Avenue in front of the White House will be closed to motor vehicle traffic.

Pennsylvania Avenue has been routinely open to traffic for the entire history of our Republic. Through four Presidential assassinations and eight unsuccessful attempts on the lives of Presidents, it's been open; through a civil war, two world wars and the Gulf War, it was open.

And now, it must be closed. This decision follows a lengthy review by the Treasury Department, the Secret Service and independent experts, including distinguished Americans who served in past administrations of both Democratic and Republican Presidents.

This step is necessary in the view of the Director of the Secret Service and the panel of experts to protect the President and his family, the White House itself, all the staff and others who work here, and the visitors and distinguished foreign and domestic guests who come here every day.

The Secret Service risk their lives to protect the President and his family. For 130 years they have stood watch over the people and the institutions of our Democracy. They are the best in the world at what they do. Though I am reluctant to accept any decision that might inconvenience the people who work or visit our nation's capital, I believe it would be irresponsible to ignore their considered opinion, or to obstruct their decisions about the safety of our public officials, especially given the strong supporting voice of the expert panel.

Clearly, this closing is necessary because of the changing nature and scope of the threat of terrorist actions. It should be seen as a responsible security step necessary to preserve our freedom, not part of a long-term restriction of our freedom.

First, let me make it clear that I will not in any way allow the fight against domestic and foreign terrorism to build a wall between me and the American people. I will be every bit as active and in touch with ordinary American citizens as I have been since I took office.

Pennsylvania Avenue may be closed to cars and trucks but it will remain open to the people of America. If you want to visit the White House you can still do that just as you always could, and I hope you will. If you want to have your picture taken out in front of the White House, please do so. If you want to come here and protest our country's policies, you are still welcome to do that as well. And now you will be more secure in all these activities because it will be less likely that you could become an innocent victim of those who would do violence against symbols of our Democracy.

Closing Pennsylvania Avenue to motor vehicles is a practical step to protect against the kind of attack we saw in Oklahoma City, but I won't allow the people's access to the White House and their President to be curtailed.

The two blocks of Pennsylvania Avenue in front of the White House will be converted into a pedestrian mall. Free and public tours will continue as they always have. For most Americans this won't change much beyond the traffic patterns here in Washington.

For people who work in Washington, D.C., we will work hard to reroute the traffic in cooperation with local officials in the least burdensome way possible.

Now let's think for a minute about what this action says about the danger terrorism poses to the openness of our society, or to any free society. The fact that the Secret Service feels compelled to close Pennsylvania Avenue is an important reminder that we have to come together as a people and hold fast against the divisive tactics of violent extremists.

We saw in the awful tragedy of Oklahoma City and the bombing of the World Trade Center that America, as an open and free society, is not immune from terrorists from within and beyond our borders who believe they have a right to kill innocent civilians to pursue their own political ends, or to protest other policies. Such people seek to instill fear in our citizens, in our whole people. But when we are all afraid to get on a bus, or drive to work, or open an envelope or send our children off to school; when our children are fixated on the possibility of terrorist action against them, or other innocent children, we give terrorists a victory. That kind of corrosive fear could rust our national spirit, drain our will and wear away our freedom.

These are the true stakes in our war against terrorism. We cannot allow ourselves to be frightened or intimidated into a bunker mentality. We cannot allow our sacred freedoms to wither or diminish. We cannot allow the paranoia and conspiracy theories of extreme militants to dominate our society.

What we do today is a practical step to preserve freedom and peace of mind. It should be seen as a step in a long line of efforts to improve security in the modern world, that began with the installation of airport metal detectors. I remember when that started, and a lot of people thought that it might be seen as a restriction on our freedom, but most of us take it for granted now and after all, highjackings have gone way down. The airport metal detectors increased the freedom of the American people and so can this.

But more must be done to reduce the threat of terrorism—to deter terrorism. First, Congress must pass my anti-terrorism legislation. We mustn't let our country fight the war against terrorism ill-armed or ill-prepared. I want us to be armed with 1,000 more FBI agents. I want the ability to monitor high-tech communications among far-flung terrorists. I want to be able to have our people learn their plans before they strike. That's the key. Congress can give us these tools by passing the anti-terrorism bill before them. And they should do it now. Congressional leaders pledged to pass this bill by Memorial Day, in the wake of the terrible bombing in Oklahoma City. This is a commitment Congress must keep.

On a deeper level, we must all fight terrorism by fighting the fear that terrorists sow. Today, the Secret Service is taking a necessary precaution, but let no one mistake, we will not relinquish our fundamental freedoms. We will secure the personal safety of all Americans to live and move about as they please; to think and to speak as they please; to follow their beliefs and their conscience, as our founding fathers intended.

Thanks for listening.

SUPREME COURT ON
CONGRESSIONAL TERM LIMITS
May 22, 1995

By a 5–4 vote, the Supreme Court May 22 struck down state laws that limit the number of terms members of Congress could serve, holding that such laws violated the constitutional prescription that "the people should choose whom they please to govern them." Noting that the Constitution listed only three qualifications for those seeking election to the U.S. Congress, the majority said that if those qualifications were to be changed, the Constitution itself would have to be amended, just as the Twenty-second amendment, ratified in 1951, limited presidents to two terms.

Although the case involved an amendment to the Arkansas state constitution, the ruling struck down federal term limits measures in twenty-two other states. None of the measures had gone into effect. Senate Majority Leader Robert Dole (R-Kan.) promised a quick Senate vote on a term limit amendment, but the House earlier in the year had fallen far short of the two-thirds majority needed to send a constitutional amendment to the states, and it seemed unlikely that any further substantive action would take place in Congress until after the 1996 elections. Several groups advocating term limits vowed to make the issue a focal point of those elections.

Perhaps more important than the political ramifications of the decision was the revelation of the extent of the division among the justices about the proper role of the federal government. Since the Supreme Court agreed to hear the term limit case in June 1994, it had been widely anticipated that the state laws would be declared unconstitutional. What surprised many observers was the closeness of the vote and the depth of disagreement among the justices on the role the federal government should have in the federal system.

As Linda Greenhouse, the long-time court reporter for the New York Times, *wrote two days after the decision, the dissenting opinion "would have deposed the Federal Government from its primary role in the constitutional system and resurrected the states as the authentic organs of demo-*

cratic government." Harvard law school professor Laurence H. Tribe told Greenhouse that "it is hard to overstate the importance of how close they came to something radically different from the modern understanding of the Constitution."

The term limits case was the second of the court's term to raise fundamental questions about federalism and federal power. On April 26, in the case of United States v. Lopez, *the court held, 5–4, that Congress had misused its authority under the Constitution's commerce clause when it made possession of a gun within 1,000 feet of a school a federal crime.* (Supreme Court on school zone gun ban, p. 183)

Justice Anthony M. Kennedy was the swing vote in the two cases, voting with the majority to limit congressional use of the commerce clause and again with the majority to limit state authority over federal elections.

The Opinions

The terms limits case revolved around the Constitution's qualifications clauses, which stipulate that candidates for the U.S. House and Senate must meet specific age and citizenship requirements and be a resident of the state in which they are seeking election.

Writing the dissenting opinion for himself, Chief Justice William H. Rehnquist, and Justices Sandra Day O'Connor and Antonin Scalia, Justice Clarence Thomas argued that the qualifications clauses set a floor, rather than a ceiling, for candidate requirements and that states are empowered under the Tenth Amendment to set additional conditions. The Tenth Amendment reserves to the states powers not specifically granted to the federal government.

"Nothing in the Constitution deprives the people of each state of the power to prescribe eligibility requirements. . . . The Constitution is simply silent on this question" of additional qualifications, Thomas wrote. "And where the Constitution is silent, it raises no bar to action by the States or the people. . . . The ultimate source of the Constitution's authority is the consent of the people of each individual state, not the consent of the undifferentiated people of the Nation as a whole."

The Court majority took a dramatically different view, asserting that the qualifications clauses were exclusive and that neither Congress nor the states could impose new requirements by statute. "Permitting individual States to formulate diverse qualifications for their representatives would result in a patchwork of state qualifications, undermining the uniformity and the national character that the Framers envisioned and sought to ensure," Justice John Paul Stevens wrote for the majority. In 1969, in the case of Powell v. McCormack, *the Court had ruled that Congress could not look beyond the qualifications clause when deciding whether to seat a newly elected member.*

Stevens was joined by Justices Ruth Bader Ginsburg, David H. Souter, Stephen G. Breyer, and Kennedy, who filed a concurring opinion elaborat-

ing Stevens's arguments. "There can be no doubt," Kennedy wrote, "if we are to respect the Republican origins of the Nation and preserve its federal character, that there exists a federal right of citizenship, a relationship between the people of the Nation and their National Government, with which the States may not interfere."

The majority justices were not persuaded by the arguments of term limit proponents that the Arkansas law did not impose a new eligibility requirement because incumbents would remain free to run as write-in candidates. "In our view," Stevens wrote, the state law "is an indirect attempt to accomplish what the Constitution prohibits Arkansas from accomplishing directly."

Political Fallout

In the aftermath of the Court ruling, passage of a constitutional amendment limiting the number of terms members of Congress could serve appeared uncertain. On March 29 the House had failed to pass a term limits amendment, when a proposal to impose a twelve-year limit on members of both chambers fell sixty-one votes short of the two-thirds majority required for passage. Three alternative proposals did not even garner a simple majority. The amendment's failure represented the first outright defeat of a plank in the House Republican Contract with America. (House leaders on the 104th Congress's first one hundred days, p. 165; House Republican Contract with America, Historic Documents of 1994, p. 374)

With the amendment dead in the House for the remainder of the congressional session, it seemed unlikely that the Senate would take a stand on the issue during the current term, despite Dole's promise. Despite some pressure, few lawmakers had signed voluntary pledges to step down after a fixed number of terms; many said it would be unfair to constituents to limit their own terms when colleagues did not face similar restrictions.

That seemed to leave matters up to the voters. Polls showed that voters supported term limits. The question was whether voters wanted term limits enough to make resistant politicians fight for them. "I think people are going to lose their enthusiasm for it," said Sen. Dale Bumpers (D-Ark.), who opposed limits. But, he added, "that may be more a wish than a fact."

Following are excerpts from the majority, concurring, and dissenting opinions in the Supreme Court's ruling May 22, 1995, in U.S. Term Limits, Inc., v. Thornton, *striking down state laws imposing term limits on members of Congress:*

Nos. 93–1456 and 93–1828

U.S. Term Limits, Inc., et al.,
Petitioners
v.
Ray Thornton et al.

Winston Bryant, Attorney General
of Arkansas, Petitioner
v.
Bobbie E. Hill et al.

On writs of certiorari to the
Supreme Court of Arkansas

[May 22, 1995]

JUSTICE STEVENS delivered the opinion of the Court.

The Constitution sets forth qualifications for membership in the Congress of the United States. Article I, §2, cl. 2, which applies to the House of Representatives, provides:

> "No Person shall be a Representative who shall not have attained to the Age of twenty five Years, and been seven Years a Citizen of the United States, and who shall not, when elected, be an Inhabitant of that State in which he shall be chosen."

Article I, §3, cl. 3, which applies to the Senate, similarly provides:

> "No Person shall be a Senator who shall not have attained to the Age of thirty Years, and been nine Years a Citizen of the United States, and who shall not, when elected, be an Inhabitant of that State for which he shall be chosen."

Today's cases present a challenge to an amendment to the Arkansas State Constitution that prohibits the name of an otherwise-eligible candidate for Congress from appearing on the general election ballot if that candidate has already served three terms in the House of Representatives or two terms in the Senate. The Arkansas Supreme Court held that the amendment violates the Federal Constitution. We agree with that holding. Such a state-imposed restriction is contrary to the "fundamental principle of our representative democracy," embodied in the Constitution, that "the people should choose whom they please to govern them." *Powell* v. *McCormack* (1969). Allowing individual States to adopt their own qualifications for congressional service would be inconsistent with the Framers' vision of a uniform National Legislature representing the people of the United States. If the qualifications set forth in the text of the Constitution are to be changed, that text must be amended.

I

At the general election on November 3, 1992, the voters of Arkansas adopted Amendment 73 to their State Constitution. Proposed as a "Term Limitation Amendment," its preamble stated:

"The people of Arkansas find and declare that elected officials who remain in office too long become preoccupied with reelection and ignore their duties as representatives of the people. Entrenched incumbency has reduced voter participation and has led to an electoral system that is less free, less competitive, and less representative than the system established by the Founding Fathers. Therefore, the people of Arkansas, exercising their reserved powers, herein limit the terms of the elected officials."

The limitations in Amendment 73 apply to three categories of elected officials. . . . Section 3, the provision at issue in these cases, applies to the Arkansas Congressional Delegation. It provides:

"(a) Any person having been elected to three or more terms as a member of the United States House of Representatives from Arkansas shall not be certified as a candidate and shall not be eligible to have his/her name placed on the ballot for election to the United States House of Representatives from Arkansas.

(b) Any person having been elected to two or more terms as a member of the United States Senate from Arkansas shall not be certified as a candidate and shall not be eligible to have his/her name placed on the ballot for election to the United States Senate from Arkansas."

Amendment 73 states that it is self-executing and shall apply to all persons seeking election after January 1, 1993.

On November 13, 1992, respondent Bobbie Hill, on behalf of herself, similarly situated Arkansas "citizens, residents, taxpayers and registered voters," and the League of Women Voters of Arkansas, filed a complaint in the Circuit Court for Pulaski County, Arkansas, seeking a declaratory judgment that §3 of Amendment 73 is "unconstitutional and void." Her complaint named as defendants then-Governor Clinton, other state officers, the Republican Party of Arkansas, and the Democratic Party of Arkansas. The State of Arkansas, through its Attorney General, petitioner Winston Bryant, intervened as a party defendant in support of the amendment. Several proponents of the amendment also intervened, including petitioner U.S. Term Limits, Inc.

On cross-motions for summary judgment, the Circuit Court held that §3 of Amendment 73 violated Article I of the Federal Constitution.

With respect to that holding, in a 5-to-2 decision, the Arkansas Supreme Court affirmed. *U.S. Term Limits, Inc.* v. *Hill* (1994). Writing for a plurality of three justices, Justice Robert L. Brown concluded that the congressional restrictions in Amendment 73 are unconstitutional because the States have no authority "to change, add to, or diminish" the requirements for congressional service enumerated in the Qualifications Clauses. . . .

The State of Arkansas, by its Attorney General, and the intervenors petitioned for writs of certiorari. Because of the importance of the issues, we granted both petitions and consolidated the cases for argument. We now affirm.

II

As the opinions of the Arkansas Supreme Court suggest, the constitutionality of Amendment 73 depends critically on the resolution of two distinct issues. The first is whether the Constitution forbids States from adding to or altering the qualifications specifically enumerated in the Constitution. The second is, if the Constitution does so forbid, whether the fact that Amendment 73 is formulated as a ballot access restriction rather than as an outright disqualification is of constitutional significance. Our resolution of these issues draws upon our prior resolution of a related but distinct issue: whether Congress has the power to add to or alter the qualifications of its Members.

Twenty-six years ago, in *Powell v. McCormack* (1969), we reviewed the history and text of the Qualifications Clauses in a case involving an attempted exclusion of a duly elected Member of Congress. The principal issue was whether the power granted to each House in Art. I, §5, to judge the "Qualifications of its own Members" includes the power to impose qualifications other than those set forth in the text of the Constitution. In an opinion by Chief Justice Warren for eight Members of the Court, we held that it does not. Because of the obvious importance of the issue, the Court's review of the history and meaning of the relevant constitutional text was especially thorough. . . .

[Stevens discussed the Court's ruling in *Powell* at length. He said the Court conducted a "detailed and persuasive" historical analysis before concluding that the Framers intended the Constitution to establish "fixed qualifications" for serving in Congress. He said that *Powell* relied on two "democratic principles." The first was "the egalitarian concept that the opportunity to be elected was open to all." The second, Stevens continued, was "the critical postulate that sovereignty is vested in the people, and that sovereignty confers on the people the right to choose freely their representatives to the National Government."]

In sum, after examining *Powell*'s historical analysis and its articulation of the "basic principles of our democratic system," we reaffirm that the qualifications for service in Congress set forth in the text of the Constitution are "fixed," at least in the sense that they may not be supplemented by Congress.

III

Our reaffirmation of *Powell* does not necessarily resolve the specific questions presented in these cases. For petitioners argue that whatever the constitutionality of additional qualifications for membership imposed by Congress, the historical and textual materials discussed in *Powell* do not support the conclusion that the Constitution prohibits additional qualifications imposed by States. In the absence of such a constitutional prohibition, petitioners argue, the Tenth Amendment and the principle of reserved powers require that States be allowed to add such qualifications.

Before addressing these arguments, we find it appropriate to take note of the striking unanimity among the courts that have considered the issue. None of the overwhelming array of briefs submitted by the parties and amici has called to our attention even a single case in which a state court or federal court has approved of a State's addition of qualifications for a member of Congress. To the contrary, an impressive number of courts have determined that States lack the authority to add qualifications. [Citations omitted.] This impressive and uniform body of judicial decisions and learned commentary indicates that the obstacles confronting petitioners are formidable indeed.

Petitioners argue that the Constitution contains no express prohibition against state-added qualifications, and that Amendment 73 is therefore an appropriate exercise of a State's reserved power to place additional restrictions on the choices that its own voters may make. We disagree for two independent reasons. First, we conclude that the power to add qualifications is not within the "original powers" of the States, and thus is not reserved to the States by the Tenth Amendment. Second, even if States possessed some original power in this area, we conclude that the Framers intended the Constitution to be the exclusive source of qualifications for members of Congress, and that the Framers thereby "divested" States of any power to add qualifications. . . .

As we have frequently noted, "[t]he States unquestionably do retain a significant measure of sovereign authority. They do so, however, *only to the extent that the Constitution has not divested them of their original powers* and transferred those powers to the Federal Government." *Garcia* v. *San Antonio Metropolitan Transit Authority* (1985) (emphasis added).

Source of the Power

Contrary to petitioners' assertions, the power to add qualifications is not part of the original powers of sovereignty that the Tenth Amendment reserved to the States. Petitioners' Tenth Amendment argument misconceives the nature of the right at issue because that Amendment could only "reserve" that which existed before. . . .

With respect to setting qualifications for service in Congress, no such right existed before the Constitution was ratified. The contrary argument overlooks the revolutionary character of the government that the Framers conceived. Prior to the adoption of the Constitution, the States had joined together under the Articles of Confederation. In that system, "the States retained most of their sovereignty, like independent nations bound together only by treaties." *Wesberry* v. *Sanders* (1964). After the Constitutional Convention convened, the Framers were presented with, and eventually adopted a variation of, "a plan not merely to amend the Articles of Confederation but to create an entirely new National Government with a National Executive, National Judiciary, and a National Legislature." In adopting that plan, the Framers envisioned a uniform national system, rejecting the notion that the Nation was a collection of States, and instead creating a direct link between the National Government and the people of the United States. . . . In that National Government, representatives owe primary allegiance not to the people of a State, but to the people of the Nation. As Justice Story observed, each Member of Congress is "an officer of the union, deriving his powers and qualifications from the constitution, and neither created by, dependent upon, nor controllable by, the states.". . .

We believe that the Constitution reflects the Framers' general agreement with the approach later articulated by Justice Story. For example, Art. I, §5, cl. 1 provides: "Each House shall be the Judge of the Elections, Returns and Qualifications of its own Members." The text of the Constitution thus gives the representatives of all the people the final say in judging the qualifications of the representatives of any one State. For this reason, the dissent falters when it states that "the people of Georgia have no say over whom the people of Massachusetts select to represent them in Congress."

Two other sections of the Constitution further support our view of the Framers' vision. First, consistent with Story's view, the Constitution provides that the salaries of representatives should "be ascertained by Law, and paid out of the Treasury of the United States," Art. I, §6, rather than by individual States. The salary provisions reflect the view that representatives owe their allegiance to the people, and not to States. Second, the provisions governing elections reveal the Framers' understanding that powers over the election of federal officers had to be delegated to, rather than reserved by, the States. It is surely no coincidence that the context of federal elections provides one of the few areas in which the Constitution expressly requires action by the States, namely that "[t]he Times, Places and Manner of holding Elections for Senators and Representatives, shall be prescribed in each State by the legislature thereof." This duty parallels the duty under Article II that "Each State shall appoint, in such Manner as the Legislature thereof may direct, a Number of Electors." Art II., §1, cl. 2. These Clauses are express delegations of power to the States to act with respect to federal elections. . . .

In short, as the Framers recognized, electing representatives to the National Legislature was a new right, arising from the Constitution itself. The Tenth Amendment thus provides no basis for concluding that the States possess reserved power to add qualifications to those that are fixed in the Constitution. Instead, any state power to set the qualifications for membership in Congress must derive not from the reserved powers of state sovereignty, but rather from the delegated powers of national sovereignty. In the absence of any constitutional delegation to the States of power to add qualifications to those enumerated in the Constitution, such a power does not exist.

The Preclusion of State Power

Even if we believed that States possessed as part of their original powers some control over congressional qualifications, the text and structure of the Constitution, the relevant historical materials, and, most importantly, the "basic principles of our democratic system" all demonstrate that the Qualifications Clauses were intended to preclude the States from exercising any such power and to fix as exclusive the qualifications in the Constitution. . . .

Democratic Principles

Our conclusion that States lack the power to impose qualifications vindicates the same "fundamental principle of our representative democracy" that we recognized in *Powell*, namely that "the people should choose whom they please to govern them."

As we noted earlier, the *Powell* Court recognized that an egalitarian ideal—that election to the National Legislature should be open to all people of merit—provided a critical foundation for the Constitutional structure. This egalitarian theme echoes throughout the constitutional debates. In *The Federalist No. 57*, for example, Madison wrote:

> "Who are to be the objects of popular choice? Every citizen whose merit may recommend him to the esteem and confidence of his country. No qualification of wealth, of birth, of religious faith, or of civil profession is permitted to fetter the judgment or disappoint the inclination of the people."

. . . Additional qualifications pose the same obstacle to open elections whatever their source. The egalitarian ideal, so valued by the Framers, is thus compromised to the same degree by additional qualifications imposed by States as by those imposed by Congress.

Similarly, we believe that state-imposed qualifications, as much as congressionally imposed qualifications, would undermine the second critical idea recognized in *Powell:* that an aspect of sovereignty is the right of the people to vote for whom they wish. Again, the source of the qualification is of little moment in assessing the qualification's restrictive impact.

Finally, state-imposed restrictions, unlike the congressionally imposed restrictions at issue in *Powell*, violate a third idea central to this basic principle: that the right to choose representatives belongs not to the States, but to the people. From the start, the Framers recognized that the "great and radical vice" of the Articles of Confederation was "the principle of LEGISLATION for STATES or GOVERNMENTS, in their CORPORATE or COLLECTIVE CAPACITIES, and as contradistinguished from the INDIVIDUALS of whom they consist." *The Federalist No. 15*, (Hamilton). Thus the Framers, in perhaps their most important contribution, conceived of a Federal Government directly responsible to the people, possessed of direct power over the people, and chosen directly, not by States, but by the people. . . .

Consistent with these views, the constitutional structure provides for a uniform salary to be paid from the national treasury, allows the States but a limited role in federal elections, and maintains strict checks on state interference with the federal election process. The Constitution also provides that the qualifications of the representatives of each State will be judged by the representatives of the entire Nation. The Constitution thus creates a uniform national body representing the interests of a single people.

Permitting individual States to formulate diverse qualifications for their representatives would result in a patchwork of state qualifications, undermining the uniformity and the national character that the Framers envisioned and sought to ensure. . . . Such a patchwork would also sever the direct link that the Framers found so critical between the National Government and the people of the United States. . . .

IV

Petitioners argue that, even if States may not add qualifications, Amendment 73 is constitutional because it is not such a qualification, and because Amendment 73 is a permissible exercise of state power to regulate the "Times, Places and Manner of Holding Elections." We reject these contentions.

Unlike §§1 and 2 of Amendment 73, which create absolute bars to service for long-term incumbents running for state office, §3 merely provides that certain Senators and Representatives shall not be certified as candidates and shall not have their names appear on the ballot. They may run as write-in candidates and, if elected, they may serve. Petitioners contend that only a legal bar to service creates an impermissible qualification, and that Amendment 73 is therefore consistent with the Constitution. . . .

We need not decide whether petitioners' narrow understanding of qualifications is correct because, even if it is, Amendment 73 may not stand. . . .

In our view, Amendment 73 is an indirect attempt to accomplish what the Constitution prohibits Arkansas from accomplishing directly. As the plurality opinion of the Arkansas Supreme Court recognized, Amendment 73 is an "effort to dress eligibility to stand for Congress in ballot access clothing," because the "intent and the effect of Amendment 73 are to disqualify congressional incumbents from further service." We must, of course, accept the State Court's view of the purpose of its own law: we are thus authoritatively informed that the sole purpose of §3 of Amendment 73 was to attempt to achieve a result that is forbidden by the Federal Constitution. Indeed, it cannot be seriously contended that the intent behind Amendment 73 is other than to prevent the election of incumbents. The preamble of Amendment 73 states explicitly: "[T]he people of Arkansas . . . herein limit the terms of elected officials." Sections 1 and 2 create absolute limits on the number of terms that may be served. There is no hint that §3 was intended to have any other purpose.

Petitioners do, however, contest the Arkansas Supreme Court's conclusion that the Amendment has the same practical effect as an absolute bar. They argue that the possibility of a write-in campaign creates a real possibility for victory, especially for an entrenched incumbent. One may reasonably question the merits of that contention. Indeed, we are advised by the state court that there is nothing more than a faint glimmer of possibility that the excluded candidate will win. Our prior cases, too, have suggested that write-in candidates have only a slight chance of victory. But even if petitioners are correct that incumbents may occasionally win reelection as write-in candidates, there is no denying that the ballot restrictions will make it significantly more difficult for the barred candidate to win the election. In our view, an amendment with the avowed purpose and obvious effect of evading the requirements of the Qualifications Clauses by handicapping a class of candidates cannot stand. . . .

We do not understand the dissent to contest our primary thesis, namely that if the qualifications for Congress are fixed in the Constitution, then a State-passed measure with the avowed purpose of imposing indirectly such an additional qualification violates the Constitution. The dissent, instead, raises two objections, challenging the assertion that the Arkansas amendment has the likely effect of creating a qualification, and suggesting that the true intent of Amendment 73 was not to evade the Qualifications Clause but rather to simply "level the playing field." Neither of these objections has merit.

As to the first, it is simply irrelevant to our holding today. . . . [O]ur prior cases strongly suggest that write-in candidates will have only a slim chance of success, and the Arkansas plurality agreed. However, we expressly do not rest on this Court's prior observations regarding write-in candidates. Instead, we hold that a state amendment is unconstitutional when it has the likely effect of handicapping a class of candidates and has the sole purpose of creating additional qualifications indirectly. Thus, the dissent's discussion of the evidence concerning the possibility that a popular incumbent will win a write-in election is simply beside the point.

As to the second argument, we find wholly unpersuasive the dissent's suggestion that Amendment 73 was designed merely to "level the playing field.". . . [I]t is obvious that the sole purpose of Amendment 73 was to limit the terms of elected officials, both State and federal, and that Amendment 73, therefore, may not stand.

V

The merits of term limits, or "rotation," have been the subject of debate since the formation of our Constitution, when the Framers unanimously rejected a proposal to add such limits to the Constitution. The cogent arguments on both sides of the question that were articulated during the process of ratification largely retain their force today. Over half the States have adopted measures that impose such limits on some offices either directly or indirectly, and the Nation as a whole, notably by constitutional amendment, has imposed a limit on the number of terms that the President may serve. Term limits, like any other qualification for office, unquestionably restrict the ability of voters to vote for whom they wish. On the other hand, such limits may provide for the infusion of fresh ideas and new perspectives, and may decrease the likelihood that representatives will lose touch with their constituents. It is not our province to resolve this longstanding debate.

We are, however, firmly convinced that allowing the several States to adopt term limits for congressional service would effect a fundamental change in the constitutional framework. Any such change must come not by legislation adopted either by Congress or by an individual State, but rather— as have other important changes in the electoral process—through the Amendment procedures set forth in Article V. The Framers decided that the qualifications for service in the Congress of the United States be fixed in the Constitution and be uniform throughout the Nation. That decision reflects the Framers' understanding that Members of Congress are chosen by separate constituencies, but that they become, when elected, servants of the people of the United States. They are not merely delegates appointed by separate, sovereign States; they occupy offices that are integral and essential components of a single National Government. In the absence of a properly passed constitutional amendment, allowing individual States to craft their own qualifications for Congress would thus erode the structure envisioned by the Framers, a structure that was designed, in the words of the Preamble to our Constitution, to form a "more perfect Union."

The judgment is affirmed.

It is so ordered.

JUSTICE KENNEDY, concurring.

I join the opinion of the Court.

The majority and dissenting opinions demonstrate the intricacy of the question whether or not the Qualifications Clauses are exclusive. In my view, however, it is well settled that the whole people of the United States asserted their political identity and unity of purpose when they created the federal system. The dissent's course of reasoning suggesting otherwise might be construed to disparage the republican character of the National Government, and it seems appropriate to add these few remarks to explain why that course of argumentation runs counter to fundamental principles of federalism.

Federalism was our Nation's own discovery. The Framers split the atom of sovereignty. It was the genius of their idea that our citizens would have two political capacities, one state and one federal, each protected from incursion by the other. The resulting Constitution created a legal system unprecedented in form and design, establishing two orders of government, each with its own direct relationship, its own privity, its own set of mutual rights and obligations to the people who sustain it and are governed by it. . . .

In one sense it is true that "the people of each State retained their separate political identities," for the Constitution takes care both to preserve the States and to make use of their identities and structures at various points in organizing the federal union. It does not at all follow from this that the sole political identity of an American is with the State of his or her residence. It denies the dual character of the Federal Government which is its very foundation to assert that the people of the United States do not have a political identity as well, one independent of, though consistent with, their identity as citizens of the State of their residence. . . .

It is maintained by our dissenting colleagues that the State of Arkansas seeks nothing more than to grant its people surer control over the National Government, a control, it is said, that will be enhanced by the law at issue here. The arguments for term limitations (or ballot restrictions having the same effect) are not lacking in force; but the issue, as all of us must acknowledge, is not the efficacy of those measures but whether they have a legitimate source, given their origin in the enactments of a single State. There can be no doubt, if we are to respect the republican origins of the Nation and preserve its federal character, that there exists a federal right of citizenship, a relationship between the people of the Nation and their National Government, with which the States may not interfere. Because the Arkansas enactment intrudes upon this federal domain, it exceeds the boundaries of the Constitution.

JUSTICE THOMAS, with whom THE CHIEF JUSTICE, JUSTICE O'CON-NOR, and JUSTICE SCALIA join, dissenting.

It is ironic that the Court bases today's decision on the right of the people to "choose whom they please to govern them." Under our Constitution, there is only one State whose people have the right to "choose whom they please" to represent Arkansas in Congress. The Court holds, however, that neither the elected legislature of that State nor the people themselves (acting by ballot initiative) may prescribe any qualifications for those representatives. The majority therefore defends the right of the people of Arkansas to "choose whom they please to govern them" by invalidating a provision that won nearly 60% of the votes cast in a direct election and that carried every congressional district in the State.

I dissent. Nothing in the Constitution deprives the people of each State of the power to prescribe eligibility requirements for the candidates who seek to represent them in Congress. The Constitution is simply silent on this question. And where the Constitution is silent, it raises no bar to action by the States or the people.

I

Because the majority fundamentally misunderstands the notion of "reserved" powers, I start with some first principles. Contrary to the majority's suggestion, the people of the States need not point to any affirmative grant of power in the Constitution in order to prescribe qualifications for their representatives in Congress, or to authorize their elected state legislators to do so.

A

Our system of government rests on one overriding principle: all power stems from the consent of the people. To phrase the principle in this way, however, is to be imprecise about something important to the notion of "reserved" powers. The ultimate source of the Constitution's authority is the consent of the people of each individual State, not the consent of the undifferentiated people of the Nation as a whole. . . .

When they adopted the Federal Constitution, of course, the people of each State surrendered some of their authority to the United States (and hence to entities accountable to the people of other States as well as to themselves). . . . Because the people of the several States are the only true source of power, however, the Federal Government enjoys no authority beyond what the Constitution confers: the Federal Government's powers are limited and enumerated. . . .

In each State, the remainder of the people's powers—"[t]he powers not delegated to the United States by the Constitution, nor prohibited by it to the States," Amdt. 10—are either delegated to the state government or retained by the people. The Federal Constitution does not specify which of these two possibilities obtains; it is up to the various state constitutions to declare which powers the people of each State have delegated to their state government. As far as the Federal Constitution is concerned, then, the States can exercise all powers that the Constitution does not withhold from them. . . .

II

I take it to be established, then, that the people of Arkansas do enjoy "reserved" powers over the selection of their representatives in Congress. Purporting to exercise those reserved powers, they have agreed among themselves that the candidates covered by §3 of Amendment 73—those whom they have already elected to three or more terms in the House of Representatives or to two or more terms in the Senate—should not be eligible to appear on the ballot for reelection, but should nonetheless be returned to Congress if enough voters are sufficiently enthusiastic about their candidacy to write in their names. Whatever one might think of the wisdom of this arrangement, we may not override the decision of the people of Arkansas unless something in the Federal Constitution deprives them of the power to enact such measures.

The majority settles on "the Qualifications Clauses" as the constitutional provisions that Amendment 73 violates. Because I do not read those provisions to impose any unstated prohibitions on the States, it is unnecessary for me to decide whether the majority is correct to identify Arkansas' ballot-access restriction with laws fixing true term limits or otherwise prescribing "qualifications" for congressional office. As I discuss in Part A below, the Qualifications Clauses are merely straightforward recitations of the minimum eligibility requirements that the Framers thought it essential for every Member of Congress to meet. They restrict state power only in that they prevent the States from *abolishing* all eligibility requirements for membership in Congress.

Because the text of the Qualifications Clauses does not support its position, the majority turns instead to its vision of the democratic principles that animated the Framers. But the majority's analysis goes to a question that is not before us: whether Congress has the power to prescribe qualifications for its own members. As I discuss in Part B, the democratic principles that contributed to the Framers' decision to withhold this power from Congress do not prove that the Framers also deprived the people of the States of their reserved authority to set eligibility requirements for their own representatives.

In Part C, I review the majority's more specific historical evidence. . . . [T]he records of the Philadelphia Convention affirmatively support my unwillingness to find hidden meaning in the Qualifications Clauses, while the surviving records from the ratification debates help neither side. As for the postratification period, five States supplemented the constitutional disqualifications in their very first election laws. The historical evidence thus refutes any notion that the Qualifications Clauses were generally understood to be exclusive. Yet the majority must establish just such an understanding in order to justify its position that the Clauses impose unstated prohibitions on the States and the people. In my view, the historical evidence is simply inadequate to warrant the majority's conclusion that the Qualifications Clauses mean anything more than what they say. [Remainder of section omitted.]

III

It is radical enough for the majority to hold that the Constitution implicitly precludes the people of the States from prescribing any eligibility requirements for the congressional candidates who seek their votes. This holding, after all, does not stop with negating the term limits that many States have seen fit to impose on their Senators and Representatives. Today's decision also means that no State may disqualify congressional candidates whom a court has found to be mentally incompetent, who are currently in prison, or who have past vote-fraud convictions. Likewise, after today's decision, the people of each State must leave open the possibility that they will trust someone with their vote in Congress even though they do not trust him with a vote in the election for Congress.

In order to invalidate §3 of Amendment 73, however, the majority must go farther. The bulk of the majority's analysis—like Part II of my dissent—addresses the issues that would be raised if Arkansas had prescribed "genuine, unadulterated, undiluted term limits." But as the parties have agreed, Amendment 73 does not actually create this kind of disqualification. It does not say that covered candidates may not serve any more terms in Congress if reelected, and it does not indirectly achieve the same result by barring those candidates from seeking reelection. It says only that if they are to win reelection, they must do so by write-in votes.

One might think that this is a distinction without a difference. As the majority notes, "[t]he uncontested data submitted to the Arkansas Supreme Court" show that write-in candidates have won only six congressional elections in this century. But while the data's accuracy is indeed "uncontested," petitioners filed an equally uncontested affidavit challenging the data's relevance. As political science professor James S. Fay swore to the Arkansas Supreme Court, "[m]ost write-in candidacies in the past have been waged by fringe candidates, with little public support and extremely low name identification." To the best of Professor Fay's knowledge, in modern times only two incumbent Congressmen have ever sought reelection as write-in candidates. One of them was Dale Alford of Arkansas, who had first entered the House of Representatives by winning 51% of the vote as a write-in candidate in 1958; Alford then waged a write-in campaign for reelection in 1960, winning a landslide 83% of the vote against an opponent who enjoyed a place on the ballot. The other incumbent write-in candidate was Philip J. Philbin of Massachusetts, who—despite losing his party primary and thus his spot on the ballot—won 27% of the vote in his unsuccessful write-in candidacy. According to Professor Fay, these results ... "demonstrate that when a write-in candidate is well-known and well-funded, it is quite possible for him or her to win an election."

The majority responds that whether "the Arkansas amendment has the likely effect of creating a qualification" is "simply irrelevant to our holding today." But the majority . . . never adequately explains how it can take this position and still reach its conclusion. . . .

. . . One of petitioners' central arguments is that congressionally conferred advantages have artificially inflated the pre-existing electoral chances of the covered candidates, and that Amendment 73 is merely designed to level the playing field on which challengers compete with them.

To understand this argument requires some background. Current federal law (enacted, of course, by congressional incumbents) confers numerous advantages on incumbents, and these advantages are widely thought to make it "significantly more difficult" for challengers to defeat them. For instance, federal law gives incumbents enormous advantages in building name recognition and good will in their home districts. . . . At the same time that incumbent Members of Congress enjoy these in-kind benefits, Congress imposes spending and contribution limits in congressional campaigns that "can prevent challengers from spending more . . . to overcome their disadvantage in name recognition." Many observers believe that the campaign-finance laws also give incumbents an "enormous fund-raising edge" over their challengers by giving a large financing role to entities with incentives to curry favor with incumbents. In addition, the internal rules of Congress put a substantial premium on seniority, with the result that each Member's already plentiful opportunities to distribute benefits to his constituents increase with the length of his tenure. In this manner, Congress effectively "fines" the electorate for voting against incumbents. . . .

At the same time that incumbents enjoy the electoral advantages that they have conferred upon themselves, they also enjoy astonishingly high reelection rates. . . .

The voters of Arkansas evidently believe that incumbents would not enjoy such overwhelming success if electoral contests were truly fair—that is, if the government did not put its thumb on either side of the scale. The majority offers no reason to question the accuracy of this belief. Given this context, petitioners portray §3 of Amendment 73 as an effort at the state level to offset the electoral advantages that congressional incumbents have conferred upon themselves at the federal level.

To be sure, the offset is only rough and approximate; no one knows exactly how large an electoral benefit comes with having been a long-term Member of Congress, and no one knows exactly how large an electoral disadvantage comes from forcing a well-funded candidate with high name recognition to run a write-in campaign. But the majority does not base its holding on the premise that Arkansas has struck the wrong balance. Instead, the majority holds that the Qualifications Clauses preclude Arkansas from trying to strike any balance at all; the majority simply says that "an amendment with the avowed purpose and obvious effect of evading the requirements of the Qualifications Clauses by handicapping a class of candidates cannot stand." Thus, the majority apparently would reach the same result even if one could demonstrate at trial that the electoral advantage conferred by Amendment 73 upon challengers precisely counterbalances the electoral advantages conferred by federal law upon long-term Members of Congress.

For me, this suggests only two possibilities. Either the majority's holding is wrong and Amendment 73 does not violate the Qualifications Clauses, or (assuming the accuracy of petitioners' factual claims) the electoral system that exists without Amendment 73 is no less unconstitutional than the electoral system that exists with Amendment 73.

I do not mean to suggest that States have unbridled power to handicap particular classes of candidates, even when those candidates enjoy federally conferred advantages that may threaten to skew the electoral process. But laws that allegedly have the purpose and effect of handicapping a particular class of candidates traditionally are reviewed under the First and Fourteenth Amendments rather than the Qualifications Clauses. . . . Term-limit measures have tended to survive such review without difficulty. See, e.g., *Moore* v. *McCartney* (1976) (dismissing an appeal on the ground that limits on the terms of state officeholders do not even raise a substantial federal question under the First and Fourteenth Amendments).

To analyze such laws under the Qualifications Clauses may open up whole new vistas for courts. If it is true that "the current congressional campaign finance system . . . has created an electoral system so stacked against challengers that in many elections voters have no real choices," are the Federal Election Campaign Act Amendments of 1974 unconstitutional under (of all things) the Qualifications Clauses? . . . If it can be shown that nonminorities are at a significant disadvantage when they seek election in districts dominated by minority voters, would the intentional creation of "majority-minority districts" violate the Qualifications Clauses even if it were to survive scrutiny under the Fourteenth Amendment? . . . More generally, if "[d]istrict lines are rarely neutral phenomena" and if "districting inevitably has and is intended to have substantial political consequences," will plausible Qualifications Clause challenges greet virtually every redistricting decision? . . .

The majority's opinion may not go so far, although it does not itself suggest any principled stopping point. No matter how narrowly construed, however, today's decision reads the Qualifications Clauses to impose substantial implicit prohibitions on the States and the people of the States. I would not draw such an expansive negative inference from the fact that the Constitution requires Members of Congress to be a certain age, to be inhabitants of the States that they represent, and to have been United States citizens for a specified period. Rather, I would read the Qualifications Clauses to do no more than what they say. I respectfully dissent.

NEW U.S. RULES ON ASYLUM FOR WOMEN
May 26, 1995

The Immigration and Naturalization Service (INS) issued new guidelines May 26 to help INS agents determine when sexual violence against a woman might qualify her for refugee status in the United States. The United States thus joined Canada in formally recognizing that some instances of sexual violence against women are tantamount to political persecution.

"These new standards do not change the standard that must be met by women seeking refugee status," INS commissioner Doris Meissner said in a news release. "What they do is educate Asylum Officers about gender-based discrimination and provide them with procedures and methods for evaluating whether individual claims meet the refugee standard."

To qualify for refugee status, applicants must show that they cannot return home and cannot avail themselves of the protection of their home country because of "persecution or a well-founded fear of persecution on account of race, religion, nationality, membership in a particular social group, or political opinion."

Political, Not Personal, Violence

*In the past the INS and immigration courts had usually regarded rape and other forms of sexual violence against women as personal matters, even when such acts were committed by soldiers or government officials or to "punish" a woman for her political beliefs. In recent years more attention had been paid to claims of gender-based abuses of human rights, prompted in part by the mass rape of women in Bosnia and Haiti during political conflicts in both countries. "Human rights violations against women are not a new phenomenon, but the issue has recently risen to the forefront of the international agenda," Meissner said. (Amnesty Inter-*national Report on Human Rights, Historic Documents of 1993, p. 561)

The United Nations High Commissioner for Refugees issued a set of guidelines regarding gender-based political persecution in 1991. In 1993 Canada became the first country to adopt gender-based standards for asylum. The INS guidelines grew out of both of those sets of guidelines, as well as a set of rules proposed by Harvard Law School's Women Refugee Project.

The new rules were the latest in a series of developments shifting U.S. policy on the treatment of gender-based asylum claims. In September 1994 Congress enacted the Violence Against Women Act, which allowed immigrant women in the United States to leave abusive husbands without risking deportation. In December 1994 an immigration judge granted political asylum to a Jordanian woman on the grounds that the Jordanian government had failed to protect her from years of physical and mental abuse by her husband.

In May the Board of Immigration Appeals, overturning a ruling by an immigration judge, granted asylum to a Haitian woman who had been gang-raped by soldiers because of her support for exiled Haitian president Jean-Bertrand Aristide. The appeals board ruling recognizing rape as a form of political persecution has become a controlling decision for immigration judges.

The INS emphasized that its gender guidelines do not enlarge the grounds on which women may be granted asylum. Domestic violence cannot be "purely personal," the fact sheet accompanying the guidelines said, but must be related to one of the grounds already established for granting asylum, such as fear of persecution for religious or political beliefs. A woman must also show that her fear of persecution extends to the entire country; in other words, a woman might be denied asylum in the United States because she could have found safety from an abusive husband in her own country. "National protection should take precedence over international protection," the fact sheet said.

The INS said it would also issue "alerts" and country profiles providing information on the legal and cultural situation of women in their countries of origin, on the incidence of domestic and sexual violence, and on the adequacy of protection for women.

Reaction to the Guidelines

Michele Beasley, a member of the Women's Commission for Refugee Women and Children, hailed the guidelines as "a major shift in both the commitment of the agency and in its understanding of the way that the asylum claims of refugee women differ from those of men." The Federation for American Immigration Reform, which supports reduced levels of immigration into the United States, warned that the guidelines would encourage women to apply for asylum. "We cannot bring people here simply because they are suffering under cultural forms of oppression," the organization's president, Dan Stein, told the Washington Post.

Noting that Canada had received only about two hundred gender-based claims for asylum since it issued its rules in 1993, the INS said it did not expect any increase in claims. "While the guidelines will help enhance the ability of Asylum Officers to more sensitively deal with the procedural and substantive aspects of gender-related claims, they are not anticipated to create an upsurge" in new claims, the fact sheet said.

Harvard Law School instructor Nancy Kelly, the coordinator of the Women Refugees Project, and Harvard lecturer Deborah Anker acknowledged that the new rules would affect only a small number of women, but said they were nonetheless important "because they establish the principle that human rights instruments cannot exclude women and that the harms women face because of their gender must be recognized and taken seriously."

Following is the text of "INS Asylum Gender Guidelines," a fact sheet issued May 26, 1995, by the U.S. Immigration and Naturalization Service:

Background

- Human rights violations against women are not a new phenomenon in the world. Yet, only recently have they risen to the forefront of the international agenda.
  - In 1979, the Convention on the Elimination of All Forms of Discrimination Against Women (CEDAW) recommended the eradication of violations Against women.
  - In June 1993, the United Nations World Conference on Human Rights emphasized the need to incorporate the rights of women, and called upon the General Assembly to adopt the Declaration on the Elimination of Violence against Women. On December 20, 1993, the United Nations General Assembly adopted the Declaration.
  - There have also been Conclusions from the United Nations High Commissioner for Refugees (UNHCR). For example, in 1985 the UNHCR Executive Committee adopted Conclusion No. 39, noting that refugee women and girls constitute the majority of the world population and that many of them are exposed to special problems.

All of these international initiatives underscored and contributed to the development of guidance related to women refugee claimants.

- The Canadian Immigration and Refugee Board (IRB) issued its asylum gender guidelines over two years ago, in March 1993. The UNHCR issued a set of guidelines in 1991, and faculty members at Harvard Law School also submitted a proposed set of guidelines in 1994. Despite the increased attention to gender-based asylum claims, they are still relatively new developments in refugee protection.

INS Implementation

- Because gender issues are novel, and adjudicators of asylum claims are guided by recent (and still developing) U.S. case law, INS felt that guidance to all Asylum Officers would be appropriate to ensure uniformity in adjudications, and would allow Asylum Officers to be more responsive to bona fide asylum claims.

- Women asylum applicants, like all applicants, must satisfy the refugee definition provided for by statute. Under U.S. law, the term *refugee* means "... any person who is outside any country of such person's nationality," and who is "unable or unwilling to return to ... that country because of persecution or a well-founded fear of persecution on account of race, religion, nationality, membership in a particular social group, or political opinion. ..."
- The U.S. refugee definition is a narrow one. Individuals cannot qualify for asylum in the United States unless the persecution is on account of one of the protected grounds specified by Congress. There must also be a favorable credibility finding by an Asylum Officer. The INS Guidelines summarize recent decisions from the courts and the Board of Immigration Appeals which provide appropriate analysis for gender-related and other asylum claims. The INS Gender Guidelines do not enlarge or expand on the grounds that were specified by Congress and the understandings the courts have reached about those grounds.
- Not all women who apply for asylum under this new guidance will be granted asylum. INS asylum decisions are individualized, case-by-case determinations. For example, INS sometimes encounters women asylum applicants who come from countries where domestic or sexual abuse is tolerated. However, to qualify for asylum these women must show, for example, that:
  - The domestic violence cannot be purely "personal." It must relate to one of the grounds enumerated in the statute.
  - The harm feared must rise to the level of "persecution." The courts have uniformly held that "persecution" denotes extreme conduct and does not include every sort of treatment our society regards as offensive, unfair, unjust, or even unlawful or unconstitutional.
  - Also, both U.S. law and the UN Protocol require that the fear of persecution must normally extend to the entire country of origin; that is, in order for an applicant to meet the definition of a refugee she must do more than show a well-founded fear of persecution in a particular place or abode within a "country"—she must show that the threat of persecution exists for her countrywide. For example, some battered women may be denied asylum because they could have sought safety from the batterer simply by moving to another town or province in their country of origin. National protection should take precedence over international protection.

In sum, every asylum applicant is carefully interviewed. No applicant can be approved unless all the definitional elements of the statute are satisfied.

- INS does not expect the rate of asylum applications to increase because of the Gender Guidelines. That was not the experience of the Canadians who issued their guidelines more than 2 years ago.
- Asylum Interviews/Officers: All INS Asylum Officers—men and women—will be expected to conduct interviews of women with gender-

based claims. To the extent that personnel resources permit, however, Asylum Offices may allow women Asylum Officers to interview these cases. An interview will not generally be canceled because of the unavailability of a woman Asylum Officer. But INS also recognizes that, because of the very delicate and personal issues arising from sexual abuse, some women claimants may understandably have inhibitions about disclosing past experiences to male interviewers.

- Interpreters/Presence of Family Members: Testimony on sensitive issues such as sexual abuse can be diluted when received through the filter of a male interpreter. While INS encourages the use of female interpreters, interviews will not generally be canceled and rescheduled because women with gender-based asylum claims have brought male interpreters.

  Interviewing Asylum Officers will provide women with the opportunity to be interviewed outside the hearing of other members of their family, especially male family members and children. There is a greater likelihood that a woman applicant may more freely communicate a claim involving sexual abuse when family members are not present.

- Generally, the new Guidelines will assist Asylum Officers in the attentive examination of cases, and the approval of legitimate claimants.

June

SOUTH AFRICAN COURT ON THE DEATH PENALTY
June 6, 1995

South Africa's new supreme court issued its first major decision on June 6, declaring the death penalty to be unconstitutional. The unanimous decision by the multiracial Constitutional Court was important not only for its stance on a controversial public issue but also because it had the potential to establish the court—and the rule of law—as important factors in a troubled country under new black leadership.

The court took office in February 1995 under the interim constitution that had provided for South Africa's first multiracial elections. While seven of its eleven justices were white, the remaining four members represented the country's major ethnic and racial groups. The new court replaced the white-only court that functioned under the previous white minority government.

In an editorial praising the decision, the New York Times *compared its importance to the historic* Marbury v. Madison *decision of 1803, in which the U.S. Supreme Court asserted its power to determine the constitutionality of legislation. The South African justices themselves referred repeatedly, in their opinions, to precedents in the United States, Great Britain, Canada, and other countries.*

In South Africa, the court's decision won general praise from black leaders. President Nelson Mandela said the decision "is in line with contemporary civilized norms." Mandela's government had argued in court against the death penalty. Anglican archbishop Desmond Tutu was quoted as saying the decision helped make South Africa a "civilized society."

Many whites, especially those who opposed the transition to black rule, criticized the ruling as subverting law and order. F. W. DeKlerk, who as the country's last white president was the chief architect of the transition, said his National party would support reinstatement of the death penalty.

A History of Executions and Violence

During the 1980s, as the then-ruling National party sought to deal with black unrest and an upsurge in violent crime, South Africa became a world leader in executions. According to the current government, 1,123 people—the overwhelming majority of them black—were hanged during the decade. The National party government used the death penalty to fight common crime and punish blacks who used violence as a political means to fight the apartheid system of minority rule.

DeKlerk had declared a moratorium on executions in 1990, when he also took the historic step of freeing Mandela from prison. Mandela in 1994 became the country's first black president, and DeKlerk became one of his deputies.

Despite the 1990 moratorium, South African judges continued to impose the death sentence. By the time of the decision, 453 prisoners were awaiting execution. With the new ruling, those death sentences were replaced with life terms.

The court's decision came at a time when South Africa was again facing an explosive increase in violent crime. Murders, robberies, rapes, and other crimes were becoming commonplace not only in big cities but also in rural areas. Mandela, in his annual state of the union address on February 17, denounced the violence and said it endangered the country's fragile new democracy. In his reaction to the death penalty decision, Mandela reiterated that the government would fight violent crime "with all the resources and determination it can muster." (Mandela speech, p. 101)

The Court's Decision

The Constitutional Court chose the death penalty issue for its first major case apparently to signal its determination to deal decisively with matters of major national importance. In another symbolically important step, each of the eleven justices issued a written opinion in the case.

The death penalty case arose from the convictions of two black men for killing four people, including two policemen, during a payroll hijacking attempt in August 1990. The men were given the death sentence, and their appeal was denied at the appellate court level. Their case reached the Constitutional Court just as it took office and was ready to tackle a major issue.

The main opinion was written by the court's presiding officer, Arthur Chaskalson. A white, Chaskalson had represented Mandela in 1964 in the court case that led to Mandela's long imprisonment. Mandela and his codefendants were convicted of sabotage and plotting to overthrow the government; they could have been given the death penalty but were spared. Instead, Mandela spent more than twenty-five years in prison.

In his decision, Chaskalson sought to demonstrate that the death penalty was unconstitutional on two grounds, even though the constitution itself was silent on the matter. First, he said, capital punishment violated broad constitutional guarantees of the right to life and human dignity. "Everyone, including the most abominable of human beings, has a right to life, and capital punishment is therefore unconstitutional," he wrote. Second, Chaskalson wrote, capital punishment violated a section of the constitution prohibiting "cruel, inhuman or degrading treatment or pun-

ishment." His opinion declared that capital punishment was each of those things.

Chaskalson also rejected the argument that potential criminals are deterred by the threat of capital punishment. "The greatest deterrent to crime is the likelihood that offenders will be apprehended, convicted and punished," his opinion said. That likelihood "is presently lacking in our criminal justice system," he said. To combat lawlessness, he added, the government must address the causes of crime and convince criminals that they are likely to be caught.

Following are excerpts from the June 6, 1995, opinion by presiding judge Arthur Chaskalson of the South African Constitutional Court in which the court declared the death penalty to be unconstitutional:

. . . The differences that exist between rich and poor, between good and bad prosecutions, between good and bad defence, between severe and lenient judges, between judges who favour capital punishment and those who do not, and the subjective attitudes that might be brought into play by factors such as race and class, may in similar ways affect any case that comes before the courts, and is almost certainly present to some degree in all court systems. Such factors can be mitigated, but not totally avoided, by allowing convicted persons to appeal to a higher court. Appeals are decided on the record of the case and on findings made by the trial court. If the evidence on record and the findings made have been influenced by these factors, there may be nothing that can be done about that on appeal. Imperfection inherent in criminal trials means that error cannot be excluded; it also means that persons similarly placed may not necessarily receive similar punishment. This needs to be acknowledged. What also needs to be acknowledged is that the possibility of error will be present in any system of justice and that there cannot be perfect equality as between accused persons in the conduct and outcome of criminal trials. We have to accept these differences in the ordinary criminal cases that come before the courts, even to the extent that some may go to gaol [jail] when others similarly placed may be acquitted or receive non-custodial sentences. But death is different, and the question is, whether this is acceptable when the difference is between life and death. Unjust imprisonment is a great wrong, but if it is discovered, the prisoner can be released and compensated; but the killing of an innocent person is irremediable. . . .

[Cruel, Inhuman, and Degrading Punishment]

. . . The carrying out of the death sentence destroys life, which is protected without reservation under section 9 of our Constitution, it annihilates human dignity which is protected under section 10, elements of arbitrariness are present in its enforcement and it is irremediable. Taking these factors into account, as well as the assumption that I have made in regard to public opinion in South Africa, and giving the words of section 11(2) the broader meaning to which they are entitled at this stage of the enquiry, rather than a narrow meaning, I am satisfied that in the context of our Constitution the death penalty is indeed a cruel, inhuman and degrading punishment. . . .

[Deterrent Effect of the Death Penalty]

. . . The greatest deterrent to crime is the likelihood that offenders will be apprehended, convicted and punished. It is that which is presently lacking in our criminal justice system; and it is at this level and through addressing the causes of crime that the State must seek to combat lawlessness.

In the debate as to the deterrent effect of the death sentence, the issue is sometimes dealt with as if the choice to be made is between the death sentence and the murder going unpunished. That is of course not so. The choice to be made is between putting the criminal to death and subjecting the criminal to the severe punishment of a long term of imprisonment which, in an appropriate case, could be a sentence of life imprisonment. Both are deterrents, and the question is whether the possibility of being sentenced to death, rather than being sentenced to life imprisonment, has a marginally greater deterrent effect, and whether the Constitution sanctions the limitation of rights affected thereby.

In the course of his argument the Attorney General contended that if sentences imposed by the Courts on convicted criminals are too lenient, the law will be brought into disrepute, and members of society will then take the law into their own hands. Law is brought into disrepute if the justice system is ineffective and criminals are not punished. But if the justice system is effective and criminals are apprehended, brought to trial and in serious cases subjected to severe sentences, the law will not fall into disrepute. We have made the commitment to "a future founded on the recognition of human rights, democracy and peaceful co-existence . . . for all South Africans." Respect for life and dignity lies at the heart of that commitment. One of the reasons for the prohibition of capital punishment is "that allowing the State to kill will cheapen the value of human life and thus [through not doing so] the State will serve in a sense as a role model for individuals in society." Our country needs such role models. . . .

Conclusion

The rights to life and dignity are the most important of all human rights, and the source of all other personal rights . . . . By committing ourselves to a society founded on the recognition of human rights we are required to value these two rights above all others. And this must be demonstrated by the State in everything that it does, including the way it punishes criminals. This is not achieved by objectifying murderers and putting them to death to serve as an example to others in the expectation that they might possibly be deterred thereby.

In the balancing process the principal factors that have to be weighed are on the one hand the destruction of life and dignity that is a consequence of the implementation of the death sentence, the elements of arbitrariness and the possibility of error in the enforcement of capital punishment, and the existence of a severe alternative punishment (life imprisonment) and, on the other, the claim that the death sentence is a greater deterrent to murder, and will more effectively prevent its commission, than would a sentence of life imprisonment, and that there is a public demand for retributive justice to be imposed on murderers, which only the death sentence can meet.

Retribution cannot be accorded the same weight under our Constitution as the rights to life and dignity, which are the most important of all the rights in Chapter Three [of the constitution]. It has not been shown that the death sentence would be materially more effective to deter or prevent murder than the alternative sentence of life imprisonment would be. Taking these factors into account, as well as the elements of arbitrariness and the possibility of error in enforcing the death penalty, the clear and convincing case that is required to justify the death sentence as a penalty for murder has not been made out. The requirements of section 33(1) have accordingly not been satisfied, and it follows that the provisions of section 277(1)(a) of the Criminal Procedure Act, 1977 must be held to be inconsistent with section 11(2) of the Constitution. . . .

HUBBLE FINDINGS ON THE BIRTH OF STARS
June 6 and November 2, 1995

The Hubble Space Telescope, a $1.5 billion optical instrument, transmitted a series of detailed reports in 1995 that gave researchers their closest look ever at how stars are formed. On June 6 the National Aeronautics and Space Administration (NASA) released photographs showing five stars in different stages of evolution. Five months later, on November 2, NASA released another set of images showing how some stars emerge from massive pockets of interstellar gas.

Astronomers were delighted with the new information from the Hubble telescope, which provided much clearer images, from above Earth's atmosphere, than are possible from Earth-bound telescopes. Hubble researcher Jeff Hester, of Arizona State University in Tempe, said the photographs would allow scientists to "look so close to a star that many details of star birth become clear immediately."

Also in 1995, the Hubble confirmed the existence, long theorized by scientists, of a huge ring of comets beyond the orbit of Pluto, at the edge of the solar system. The comets are believed to be debris remaining from the formation of the solar system about 4.5 billion years ago. Based on data from Hubble, scientists speculated that at least 200 million comets are in the ring, which has a diameter of about 90 billion miles.

The Hubble, the largest and most complex scientific instrument ever put into orbit, had a shaky beginning. Almost immediately after its release from the space shuttle Discovery *in April 1990, critical flaws were found in one of its mirrors. In December 1993 astronauts from the space shuttle* Endeavor *were able to grab the telescope, repair the mirror, and return the Hubble to its orbit. Since then, the Hubble has astounded scientists with its findings, including measurements taken in 1994 that indicated that the universe may not be as old as scientists had previously thought.* (Hubble telescope flaws, NASA's future direction, Historic Documents of 1990, p. 753; Findings on age of the universe, Historic Documents of 1994, p. 458)

June 6 Report

NASA's June 6 report provided detailed pictures of how five stars in different parts of the Milky Way galaxy are in the process of development—or, rather, were in the process of developing some several hundred years ago. It took that long for the light produced by those stellar births to reach the Hubble's camera. What has happened to those stars since then will not be known for a comparable period of time. Scientists said it would take tens of thousands of years for those stars to emerge full-developed like the Sun, fueled by hydrogen fusion. The developing stars themselves are invisible in the Hubble photographs, obscured by the clouds of gas and dust from which they are being formed.

Hester called the Hubble images "a bit of a time machine" showing what happened about five billion years ago "when our own Sun and solar system were forming." Scientists theorize that the Sun was created in much the same fashion as the new stars photographed by the Hubble. In the Sun's case, Earth and other planets were formed before the Sun ignited its hydrogen explosion and blew away the remaining bits of matter in what became the solar system.

The Hubble photographs showed what scientists call "accretion disks" of hydrogen, helium, and dust. These bowl-shaped objects are gradually collapsing in on themselves, because of gravity, in some cases to form stars, in others to form giant objects known as black holes. From deep within these disks, what NASA described as "blowtorch-like jets of hot gas" are shooting out in narrow beams several billion miles long. NASA said it was not known why these gaseous jets are concentrated into beams, but one possibility was that magnetic fields keep them focused.

The Hubble camera also photographed how the emerging stars shoot out "clumps of gas" at speeds of up to a half-million miles an hour. These clumps apparently are caused when bits of material fall into the star and explode. According to NASA, the resulting jets of gas follow the star's rotation axis, much like an axle through a wheel. NASA's report compared the photographs of these gaseous clumps to a "ticker tape" that allows scientists to trace the history of these events.

Hester said that, although the Hubble photographed only five stars, the process involved appears to be "a critical part of star formation, and not just the peculiarities of a few oddball objects." The NASA report also said the Hubble's photographs confirmed most generally accepted theories of how stars are formed but would force scientists to develop new theories to explain some things, such as the gaseous jets being ejected from the stars.

November 2 Report

NASA on November 2 released a related series of images from the Hubble telescope showing how some stars emerge on the edges of giant columns of gas. The photographs were taken of the Eagle nebula, about seven thousand light-years away.

In those photographs, the columns of hydrogen are rising from a much larger cloud of gas and dust, almost like columns of smoke from a chimney. On the edges of those columns are denser masses of gas, some of them looking like bumps and others like fingers. NASA scientists called these latter structures Evaporating Gaseous Globules, or EGGs. These EGGs contain stars in the process of development. Intense ultraviolet radiation from nearby stars constantly bombard the EGGs, thus stripping away the gas that surrounds the new stars. That process also exposed the new stars to the Hubble telescope.

Scientists said some of the embryonic stars in those EGGs will never develop into full-scale stars fueled by hydrogen fusion—as is the Sun— because the ultraviolet radiation has cut them off from the gaseous cloud that helps them form. The same process also may determine how large these stars will become and whether planets can be formed around them.

Following are the texts of two announcements from the National Aeronautics and Space Administration, dated June 6, 1995, and November 2, 1995, on discoveries about the birth of stars, based on photographs taken by the Hubble Space Telescope:

JUNE 6 STATEMENT

NASA's Hubble Space Telescope has provided a detailed look at the fitful, eruptive, and dynamic processes accompanying the final stages of a star's "construction."

Images from the orbiting observatory reveal new details that will require further refinement of star formation theories, according to several independent teams of astronomers who have used Hubble to observe different embryonic stars. The Hubble observations shed new light on one of modern astronomy's central questions: how do tenuous clouds of interstellar gas and dust make stars like our Sun?

"For the first time we are seeing a newborn star close up—at the scale of our solar system—and probing the inner workings," said Chris Burrows of the Space Telescope Science Institute, Baltimore, MD, and the European Space Agency. "In doing so we will be able to create detailed models of star birth and gain a much better understanding of the formation of our Sun and planets."

The Hubble images provide a dramatically clear look at a collapsing circumstellar disk of dust and gas that builds the star and provides the ingredients for a planetary system, blowtorch—like jets of hot gas funneled from deep within several embryonic systems, and machine-gun like bursts of material fired from the stars at speeds of a half-million miles per hour.

The images offer clues to events that occurred in our solar system when the Sun was born 4.5 billion years ago. Astronomers commonly believe that Earth and the other eight planets condensed out of a circumstellar disk because they lie in the same plane and orbit the Sun in the same direction. According to this theory, when the Sun ignited it blew away the remaining disk, but not before the planets had formed.

"The Hubble images are opening up a whole new field of stellar research for astronomers and clearing up a decade's worth of uncertainty," added Jeff Hester of Arizona State University, Tempe, AZ. "Now we can look so close to a star that many details of star birth become clear immediately."

The key new details revealed by the Hubble pictures:

- Jets originate from the star and the inner parts of the disk and become confined to a narrow beam within a few billion miles of their source. It's not known how the jets are focused, or collimated. One theory is that magnetic fields, generated by the star or disk, might constrain the jets.
- Stars shoot out clumps of gas that might provide insights into the nature of the disk collapsing onto the star. The beaded jet structure is a "ticker tape" recording of how clumps of material have, episodically, fallen onto the star. In one case, Hubble allowed astronomers to follow the motion of the blobs and measure their velocity.
- Jets "wiggle" along their multi-trillion-mile long paths, suggesting the gaseous fountains change their position and direction. The wiggles may result from the gravitational influence of one or more unseen proto-stellar companions.

More generally, Hester emphasizes: "Disks and jets are ubiquitous in the universe. They occur over a vast range of energies and physical scales, in a variety of phenomena." Gaining an understanding of these young circum-stellar structures might shed light on similar activity in a wide array of astro-nomical phenomena: novae, black holes, radio galaxies and quasars.

"The Hubble pictures appear to exclude whole classes of models regard-ing jet formation and evolution," said Jon Morse of the Space Telescope Sci-ence Institute.

A disk appears to be a natural outcome when a slowly rotating cloud of gas collapses under the force of gravity—whether the gas is collapsing to form a star, or is falling onto a massive black hole.

Material falling onto the star creates a jet when some of it is heated and blasted along a path that follows the star's rotation axis, like an axle through a wheel.

Jets may assist star formation by carrying away excess angular momen-tum that otherwise would prevent material from reaching the star. Jets also provide astronomers with a unique glimpse of the inner workings of the star and disk. "Not even the Hubble Telescope can watch as material makes its final plunge onto the surface of the forming star, but the new observations are still telling us much about that process," said Hester.

Burrows, Hester, Morse and their co-investigators independently observed several star birth sites in our galactic neighborhood. "All of these objects tell much the same story," Hester emphasized. "We are clearly seeing a process that is a crucial part of star formation, and not just the peculiarities of a few oddball objects."

The researchers all agree that the Hubble pictures generally confirm models of star formation but will send theorists back to the drawing board to explain the details. The researchers emphasize that future models of star formation will have to take into account why jets are ejected from such a well-defined region in the disk, why jets are collimated a few billion miles out from the star, and why gas in the jets is ejected quasi-periodically.

NOVEMBER 2 STATEMENT

Eerie, dramatic new pictures from NASA's Hubble Space Telescope show newborn stars emerging from "eggs"—not the barnyard variety—but rather dense, compact pockets of interstellar gas called evaporating gaseous globules (EGGs). Hubble found the "EGGs," appropriately enough, in the Eagle nebula, a nearby star-forming region 7,000 light-years away in the constellation Serpens.

"For a long time astronomers have speculated about what processes control the sizes of stars—about why stars are the sizes that they are," said Jeff Hester of Arizona State University, Tempe, AZ. "Now in M16 we seem to be watching at least one such process at work right in front of our eyes."

Striking pictures taken by Hester and co-investigators with Hubble's Wide Field and Planetary Camera 2 (WFPC2) resolve the EGGs at the tip of finger-like features protruding from monstrous columns of cold gas and dust in the Eagle nebula (also called M16—16th object in the Messier catalog). The columns—dubbed "elephant trunks"—protrude from the wall of a vast cloud of molecular hydrogen, like stalagmites rising above the floor of a cavern. Inside the gaseous towers, which are light-years long, the interstellar gas is dense enough to collapse under its own weight, forming young stars that continue to grow as they accumulate more and more mass from their surroundings.

Hubble gives a clear look at what happens as a torrent of ultraviolet light from nearby young, hot stars heats the gas along the surface of the pillars, "boiling it away" into interstellar space—a process called "photoevaporation." The Hubble pictures show photoevaporating gas as ghostly streamers flowing away from the columns. But not all of the gas boils off at the same rate. The EGGs, which are denser than their surroundings, are left behind after the gas around them is gone.

"It's a bit like a wind storm in the desert," said Hester. "As the wind blows away the lighter sand, heavier rocks buried in the sand are uncovered. But in M16, instead of rocks, the ultraviolet light is uncovering the denser egg-like globules of gas that surround stars that were forming inside the gigantic gas columns."

Some EGGs appear as nothing but tiny bumps on the surface of the columns. Others have been uncovered more completely, and now resemble "fingers" of gas protruding from the larger cloud. (The fingers are gas that has been protected from photoevaporation by the shadows of the EGGs). Some EGGs have pinched off completely from the larger column from which they emerged, and now look like teardrops in space.

By stringing together these pictures of EGGs caught at different stages of being uncovered, Hester and his colleagues from the Wide Field and Planetary Camera Investigation Definition Team are getting an unprecedented look at what stars and their surroundings look like before they are truly stars.

"This is the first time that we have actually seen the process of forming stars being uncovered by photoevaporation," Hester emphasized. "In some ways it seems more like archaeology than astronomy. The ultraviolet light from nearby stars does the digging for us, and we study what is unearthed."

"In a few cases we can see the stars in the EGGs directly in the WFPC2 images," says Hester. "As soon as the star in an EGG is exposed, the object looks something like an ice cream cone, with a newly uncovered star playing the role of the cherry on top."

Ultimately, photoevaporation inhibits the further growth of the embryonic stars by dispersing the cloud of gas they were "feeding" from. "We believe that the stars in M16 were continuing to grow as more and more gas fell onto them, right up until the moment that they were cut off from that surrounding material by photoevaporation," said Hester.

This process is markedly different from the process that governs the sizes of stars forming in isolation. Some astronomers believe that, left to its own devices, a star will continue to grow until it nears the point where nuclear fusion begins in its interior. When this happens, the star begins to blow a strong "wind" that clears away the residual material. Hubble has imaged this process in detail in so-called Herbig-Haro objects.

Hester also speculated that photoevaporation might actually inhibit the formation of planets around such stars. "It is not at all clear from the new data that the stars in M16 have reached the point where they have formed the disks that go on to become solar systems," said Hester, "and if these disks haven't formed yet, they never will."

Hester plans to use Hubble's high resolution to probe other nearby star-forming regions to look for similar structures. "Discoveries about the nature of the M16 EGGs might lead astronomers to rethink some of their ideas about the environments of stars forming in other regions, such as the Orion Nebula," he predicted.

TAKEOVER OF CHICAGO HOUSING AUTHORITY
June 7, 1995

The federal Department of Housing and Urban Development (HUD) on May 30, 1995, took over the management of the Chicago Housing Authority, one of the nation's largest and most troubled public housing systems. HUD officials cited chronic management problems and dreadful living conditions in many of the city's public housing units as the main reasons for the takeover.

In congressional testimony on May 30, the General Accounting Office (GAO) supported the takeover, saying that "the long-run benefits of taking such a drastic action outweigh the costs of continued troubled status" for the Chicago public housing system. However, the GAO expressed concern about HUD's ability, over the long term, to sustain its commitment to addressing the problems of troubled housing authorities in Chicago and other cities.

With nearly 90,000 tenants living in 40,000 units, the Chicago Housing Authority was the nation's third largest, behind New York, with 180,000 units, and Puerto Rico, with nearly 58,000 units. HUD had ranked the Chicago authority as a "troubled" one since 1979, when it began a system of evaluating local public housing systems. HUD defines a local public housing authority as troubled if it fails to score at least 60 on a 0–100 scale measuring various factors, such as vacancy rates, housing conditions, and use of modernization funds.

As of January 1995, the Chicago authority scored 46.38 on this scale. The two lowest ratings among major cities were held by Philadelphia's housing authority, with 22,766 units, which rated at 28.86, and the Washington, D.C., authority, with 11,786 units, which rated 22.38. Before the Chicago takeover, Philadelphia's authority was the largest to be taken over by HUD. The Washington, D.C., authority was taken over by a court-appointed receiver in 1995. Other large systems with low ratings were in Atlanta, Detroit, New Orleans, and Pittsburgh, none of which have been taken over by HUD.

While troubled housing authorities get plenty of media attention and require huge infusions of tax dollars, they represent a small minority of all public housing agencies, the GAO reported. Judy A. England-Joseph, director of housing and community development issues for the GAO, testified that only 92 of the nation's 3,300 public housing authorities were classified as troubled. Because they tended to be in large cities, those authorities ran a disproportionate share of public housing units, 14 percent, she said.

The Chicago Takeover

HUD's takeover of the Chicago authority came after years of discussion, both in Chicago and Washington, about how best to address the enormous problems of that system. The Chicago regional office of HUD in 1987 recommended a federal takeover of the authority, but then-mayor Harold Washington blocked the move. Starting in 1988, the Chicago authority was headed by Vince Lane, who developed a national reputation for creativity but reportedly was unable to solve the agency's persistent management problems.

In mid-May 1995, HUD executives and Chicago officials, including Mayor Richard M. Daley, finally agreed that the time had come for the federal government to take over the Chicago housing system. Lane and other members of the authority's board resigned on May 27, and HUD officially took charge three days later.

On June 7, England-Joseph testified about the Chicago takeover to the Subcommittee on Housing and Community Opportunity of the House Banking and Financial Services Committee. She presented a litany of bad news about the Chicago Housing Authority. Perhaps the worst news was that most of the problems that led HUD to take over the Chicago authority had existed for at least fifteen years.

Using HUD statistics, reports by consultants, and other information, England-Joseph pointed to several reasons for the poor state of the Chicago authority. Among them were:

- *An unusually high percentage of residents in the Chicago housing projects were on welfare (69 percent, compared with 25 percent in New York), and an increasing number of households in Chicago's projects had incomes of less than 10 percent of the local area median income.*
- *Serious management flaws were evident throughout the agency, especially at the middle levels, reducing program accountability and causing inefficiencies.*
- *Despite an infusion of about $100 million a year in special federal aid, the authority was unable to control or improve living conditions at many units.*
- *The authority had a high vacancy rate of about 17 percent, which was costing it more than $14 million annually in lost rental income.*

Follow-up Testimony

On September 5, England-Joseph presented follow-up testimony on the Chicago takeover to the Subcommittee on Human Resources and Intergovernmental Relations of the House Government Reform and Oversight Committee. She told the panel that HUD's decision to take over direct management of the Chicago authority was the best of the available options, but that the department faced major financial and management obstacles in Chicago that would take years to resolve.

Among those obstacles, she said, were the need to demolish or rehabilitate some 15,000 high-rise units, at an estimated cost of $1 billion; the Chicago authority's "top-heavy" and inefficient management structure; gang violence in the projects; reduced federal funding for public housing; skepticism and even hostility by tenants toward the housing authority; and counterproductive federal laws and regulations, such as rent rules that discouraged tenants from working.

England-Joseph said the new HUD team supervising the Chicago authority was making good progress toward short-term goals, such as streamlining the management structure and revising tenant admission and eviction policies. HUD was still working on its long-term plan for such needs as rehabilitating the housing stock and improving the quality of services to tenants. Over the longer haul, she said, HUD must also develop a plan to turn over responsibility for Chicago public housing, either back to a new housing authority or to one or more private agencies.

An even bigger challenge in Chicago, England-Joseph testified, will be to develop a broader community development plan to provide jobs and improved social services, along with housing. "Because of the magnitude and persistence of the problems," she said, "improvements at the [housing] authority will take years to accomplish and short-term gains will be difficult to achieve or sustain. Thus, it is important that HUD officials do not raise expectations of tenants or the public of immediate solutions to difficult and chronic problems."

> *Following are excerpts from the June 6, 1995, testimony by Judy A. England-Joseph, director of housing and community development issues for the General Accounting Office, to the Subcommittee on Housing and Community Opportunity of the House Banking and Financial Services Committee, in which she detailed the troubled history of the Chicago Housing Authority:*

We are pleased to be here today to discuss troubled public housing, in particular the takeover by the Department of Housing and Urban Development (HUD) of the Chicago Housing Authority (CHA). Over a dozen large public housing authorities (PHA) are "troubled" because they do not score high enough against HUD's management assessment criteria. These low performances are generally due to a combination of factors at the PHAs, including ineffective management, inability to productively use federal funding assistance, and deteriorated housing stock.

As a result, HUD recently has focused highly structured "recovery" efforts at several large troubled authorities to upgrade them from troubled status. When recovery fails, however, more drastic actions can occur, such as the court-appointed receivership in the District of Columbia or the HUD takeover 2 weeks ago in Chicago. However, these kinds of actions are rare. During the past 16 years, many large authorities have remained troubled for 10 years or more without HUD taking strong corrective actions. Although these chronically troubled authorities manage 14 percent of all public housing and account for most of the distressed developments, troubled authorities represent only 92 out of the nation's 3,300 housing authorities.

Today we will discuss the long-standing problems at the Chicago Housing Authority, our view of the HUD's capacity to take over troubled authorities, and several administration proposals to enhance a housing authority's ability to overcome its distressed housing. Our statement is based on our ongoing work for this Subcommittee as well as reports that we have issued and testimony that we have given over the past several years.

In summary,

- the Chicago Housing Authority has a long history of troubled management and distressed housing conditions that stem, in part, from deficient management systems; aging, deteriorated, and poorly designed stock; and the very low income levels of residents;
- HUD's ability to effectively take over the operations of a troubled housing authority has been hampered in the past, in part because of limited resources and staff expertise; however, key officials with housing management expertise have joined HUD in the past 2 years and the long-run benefits of taking such a drastic action outweigh the costs of continued troubled status; and
- proposed statutory changes, such as repealing the one-for-one replacement requirement, reforming rent calculation rules, and changing public housing eligibility criteria could result in better use of available federal funds for assisted housing.

Background

Troubled large public housing authorities have been persistent problems for HUD's assisted housing program for many years. While a relatively small number—13 of the nearly 100 large PHAs—account for about 14 percent of the 1.4 million units of public housing nationwide, these authorities account for most of the distressed, dilapidated, and boarded up housing stock. Even though some distressed housing can be found in even a high-performing PHA's inventory, a troubled authority is much less able to remedy the distressed conditions than one in good shape.

In 1979, HUD began to focus on low-performing PHAs and classified 23 large (those with more than 1,250 units) PHAs as troubled at that time, and five of these authorities still remain on the current list. They are in Philadelphia, Detroit, New Orleans, Chicago, and Washington, D.C. To measure a PHA's performance, HUD developed the Public Housing Management Assessment Program (PHMAP) that scores PHAs on a series of performance indicators—including vacancy rates, use of modernization funds, and housing conditions. An authority is designated as troubled if it achieves a score of 60 or below. In 1994, HUD substantially revised its oversight approach by creating an office of Distressed and Troubled Housing Recovery that focuses on proactive outreach to troubled authorities. The office provides troubled authorities with direct, on-site assistance from experienced teams of housing professionals and major funding to rehabilitate distressed housing.

HUD provides all PHAs with operating subsidies and funds to build and modernize public housing. In return, the PHAs agree to provide housing that meets HUD's standards. If a housing authority does not meet the standards, HUD can take corrective action and, if necessary, take over the assets and management of the authority. Since 1979, HUD has initiated takeovers at large housing authorities in Chester, PA; Philadelphia; East St. Louis; and Chicago; court-appointed receivers have taken over authorities in Kansas City, Boston, and the District of Columbia.

Chicago Housing Authority: A Long History of Mismanagement and Poor Housing Conditions

With over 40,000 units, the Chicago Housing Authority is the third largest PHA after New York and Puerto Rico. Yet in contrast to the well-run New York authority, HUD ranked CHA among the worst.... In 1989, we reported that CHA had had long-standing management problems in virtually all operating areas. Our analysis of 48 reports issued by various sources and covering the period 1979 to 1987 showed material weaknesses in CHA's internal control systems, poor fiscal responsibility, and frequent turnover of top management. We said that CHA operated for years without reasonable assurance that federal funds were adequately safeguarded against waste, loss, or misuse.

In 1989, we reported that deteriorating buildings, damaged heating and water systems, broken elevators, and roach and rodent infestation were commonplace at many projects. Abusive tenants had also contributed to this situation. At that time, CHA estimated that it would need about $1 billion over a 5-year period to upgrade its projects. After receiving modernization grants of over $100 million each year from 1991 through 1995, CHA's estimate of its funding needs to modernize its stock is still over $1 billion.

Additional insight into CHA's problems, especially its recent conditions, is available from a consultant report completed for HUD. This report highlighted the following conditions at CHA:

- CHA's high-rise family projects were built in excessively large concentrations. For example, Robert Taylor Homes and Stateway form one continuous 6,059-unit development. In contrast, the average size of New York's public housing high-rises is 1,000 units.

- CHA's high operating costs are due in part to the relatively high percentage of its residents being on welfare: 68 percent compared to New York's 25 percent.
- CHA has experienced an especially marked increase in the number of public housing households with incomes below 10 percent of the local area median income, indicating extreme economic disadvantage.

The consultant report also noted many organizational issues that impede CHA's ability to effectively manage its total program. Among the problems noted were the following:

- large and loosely structured middle management that impedes program accountability and causes operational inefficiencies;
- inability to consistently set and enforce performance standards throughout the agency; and
- inability, despite extraordinary efforts, to control the general living environment—management rules, security, and physical conditions—at certain housing developments.

HUD Has Been Reluctant to Take Over Troubled PHAs

According to HUD's OIG [Office of Inspector General] and an official [in] its District of Columbia field offices, HUD is reluctant to take over troubled authorities because the Department lacks the resources and confidence that it can succeed in turning around the authority. On the other hand, HUD top management told us that the Department is staffed with key officials who have experience in operating large and troubled PHAs. These officials are now learning how to marshal that expertise to effectively take over a troubled authority. Still, when key officials are deployed to a takeover, it creates a need to backfill their posts with other staff. HUD field office and headquarters officials told us that when HUD field staff are temporarily assigned to take over the operations or participate in the recovery of all or part of an authority, they are unavailable to perform their primary duties overseeing PHAs in their home jurisdiction.

In May 1987, HUD's Chicago field office recommended that HUD place CHA in the hands of private management. In addition, the Philadelphia Regional Office recommended that HUD take over the District's housing authority. In both instances, HUD headquarters decided not to follow the field or Regional office's recommendation, and in both cases the authorities have ultimately been taken over—one by HUD and one by a receiver.

The cost of taking over this authority may be high because of the need to rehabilitate much of its 40,000 units of public housing and the associated costs of administration. We believe that estimating the takeover cost will be difficult because of the large but undetermined balance of unspent federal funding accumulated by CHA. We reported in 1994 that CHA's public housing program has $472 million in approved funds, and, according to a HUD official in HUD's recovery office, most of this funding is still available for CHA's use. HUD officials believe that other funds granted to CHA but not yet spent may also be available. With CHA officials estimating that about $1 billion will be needed to rehabilitate CHA's distressed housing and address its unmet housing modernization needs, the unexpended balance of earlier grants may be available to offset the needed funds for rehabilitation. However, competent management will be needed to ensure these funds are employed productively.

Notwithstanding the possible availability of federal funds already allocated to CHA, the total cost of turning around the authority is high. However, these costs could be outweighed by the costs of not taking over CHA. CHA's current vacancy rate is 17 percent, or over nearly 7,000 units. At an average rental of about $2,000 per year, CHA has been losing over $14 million per year in rental income due to vacancies. This income must be made up with federal funding to subsidize CHA's operating costs. Moreover, as we have testified in the past, housing authorities spend millions of dollars on vacant properties and more money to rehabilitate aging buildings than it would cost them to construct new ones. In addition, backlogged modernization funds mean that rehabilitation is not being done and deterioration is escalating along with the crime and vandalism associated with vacant buildings.

Proposed Statutory Changes Could Help PHAs to Provide Better Housing Assistance

Several statutory changes proposed as part of HUD's American Community Partnerships Act have the potential for helping housing authorities provide better assistance to low-income families. These changes include repealing the requirement that PHAs must replace on a one-for-one basis any nonviable housing units they tear down or sell or at least provide certificates for equivalent rental assistance. Two other important proposals include (1) reforming current rules for rent calculations for tenants of public housing so working families are not penalized and (2) relaxing federal preference rules that force PHAs to favor the lowest income families when filling vacancies in public housing so PHAs can attract higher-income families. HUD believes that adopting this proposal would not only raise rent collections but also provide role models for other tenants.

According to officials at several large PHAs, constraints related to the "one-for-one" requirement either make it difficult for PHAs to tear down housing that costs more to maintain than replace or, in some cases, prevent them from doing so. These constraints include insufficient federal funding for new housing or other replacement assistance and a lack of suitable sites for replacement housing. Not tearing down nonviable housing leads to excessive operating costs, inefficient use of federal subsidies, and the costly crime and vandalism associated with vacant public housing.

Reforming rent calculations and federal preference rules could raise the average income of tenants in public housing. Raising average income could, in turn, reduce the operating subsidies HUD pays to housing authorities. Currently, working families pay 30 percent of their adjusted income as rent in public housing. Moreover, 30 percent of any increases in the incomes of family members must also be paid as rent. This presents a significant disincentive to work. Also, current law requires housing authorities to offer vacant units to the lowest-income families first. These two requirements contribute to the decline of average public housing incomes from 34 percent of area median in 1982 to 16 percent in 1995, and [account] for operating subsidies increasing from $1.9 billion in 1990 to $2.9 billion in 1995 (both amounts in nominal dollars).

Conclusion

. . . [W]e believe that HUD's recovery efforts at large troubled housing authorities—and its more drastic move to take over housing authorities such as CHA—are important first steps. These steps signal that the federal government will not tolerate poorly managed, federally funded assisted housing. Essential to this leadership is the capacity and sustained commitment to resolve the management problems that threaten the viability of low-income housing. Legislative proposals, such as those suggested by HUD to help working families, can provide housing authorities with greater flexibility to make public housing viable and promote economic self-sufficiency.

We believe that the focused nature of HUD's recovery teams and the exercising of takeover rights are essential actions. However, even with the recent addition of key officials with housing management expertise, we are concerned about HUD's capacity, particularly in the long term, to maintain the sustained commitment necessary to address the problems of chronically troubled housing. The critical next steps to ensure that HUD's intervention at CHA and other troubled authorities results in sorely needed improvement will be the most telling.

JAPANESE APOLOGY FOR WORLD WAR II SUFFERING
June 9 and August 15, 1995

Speaking on the fiftieth anniversary of the Japanese surrender ending World War II, Prime Minister Tomichi Murayama on August 15 expressed his "heartfelt apology" to the millions of people, especially in Asia, who suffered as a result of the aggression of his country. The statement was the first formal apology by a prime minister for Japanese aggression. It followed by two months a much weaker statement of "remorse" that Murayama had forced through a reluctant House of Representatives.

The prime minister's statement was welcomed by representatives of several Asian countries that were occupied by Japan, including China and South Korea. However, those spokesmen made it clear they did not regard the apology as a particularly sincere expression of deep regret by the Japanese people as a whole. The House of Representatives on June 9 had adopted a much more restrained resolution expressing "remorse" at the suffering caused by World War II.

Murayama's overall apology to Asia came just a month after he offered "profound apologies" to the thousands of women in Asia who were forced to be sex slaves for the Japanese military during the war. The Japanese referred to them as "comfort women," and by some reports there were as many as 200,000 of them. Murayama promised support for private efforts to compensate survivors, and he pledged that the Japanese government would provide medical and welfare payments for them. That apology failed to satisfy many of the women, who faulted the government for its reluctance to fully compensate them.

The Road to an Apology

Confronting the legacy of World War II has been difficult for Japan. Even fifty years after the war, many nationalists and Japanese veterans refused to acknowledge their country's aggression in Asia. For them, Japan was seeking merely to free Asia from domination by Britain, France, and other Western powers. Some in Japan cited the U.S. atomic bombing of Hiroshi-

ma and Nagasaki as the worst atrocity of the war, one that mitigated Japan's guilt for having initiated the fighting.

Still others in Japan drew a distinction between the two aspects of the war. They argued that Japan had no right to conduct war against other Asian nations, beginning with the invasion of Manchuria in 1931, but that Japan had legitimate anti-imperialist reasons to conduct war against the United States and its allies. Very few Japanese suggested apologizing to the United States for the surprise attack on Pearl Harbor.

Even so, millions of Japanese, among them Murayama, were confirmed pacifists as a result of the war, and public opinion polls showed that most Japanese wanted their government to apologize to other Asian nations.

With 1995 being celebrated worldwide as the fiftieth anniversary of the war's end, many Asian leaders made it clear they expected the Japanese government finally to apologize for its conduct in the 1930s and 1940s. Murayama, a Socialist, began maneuvering for an apology as soon as he took office in mid-1994 at the head of a fragile coalition government.

During a period of several months, Murayama negotiated with his coalition partners about the wording of a parliamentary resolution expressing regret about the war. Those negotiations sparked heated debate and quickly bogged down in wrangling over semantics.

By early June Murayama had to threaten to resign before he could win agreement on language for the resolution. Ultimately, the coalition backed a mild resolution that sought to put Japanese actions in the broader context of world events. It noted the "many instances of colonial rule and acts of aggression in the modern history of the world" and acknowledged that Japan itself "carried out those acts in the past, inflicting pain and suffering upon the peoples of other countries, especially in Asia." Because of that, the resolution said, members of the House of Representatives "express a sense of deep remorse." The resolution pointedly did not use the word apology.

A half-empty chamber of the House of Representatives approved the resolution on June 9; dozens of coalition party members boycotted the session, as did most members of the opposition Liberal Democratic party, which had ruled Japan for most of the half century since the end of the war.

As controversial as it was in Japan, that resolution failed to satisfy other Asian countries, which viewed it as the latest demonstration of Japan's refusal to recognize the harm it caused during the war.

Murayama's Apology

Two weeks later, on July 23, Murayama's party and some of his coalition partners suffered a stinging setback in partial parliamentary elections, weakening his grip on power. Most observers said the outcome of those elections was determined largely by popular dissatisfaction with the government's pace of economic and political reform.

Despite his weakened position, Murayama appeared determined to stake out a stronger position on the wartime apology issue than he had been able to get through parliament. On August 15, the fiftieth anniversary of the Japanese surrender, Murayama read a statement directly apologizing for the pain and suffering that Japan caused during the war.

Citing a "mistaken national policy," Murayama said Japan "through its colonial rule and aggression, caused tremendous damage and suffering to the people of many countries, particularly to those of Asian nations." That was one of the "irrefutable facts of history," he said, and for those actions he expressed "my feelings of deep remorse and . . . my heartfelt apology." Murayama used the word owabi, *which translates as "apology," as opposed to the milder terms most Japanese politicians had used in the past.*

Asian reaction was mixed. Some countries reacted positively to Japan's willingness to apologize. Philippine president Fidel Ramos said the step "will be welcomed by the entire world." Others took note of the widespread reluctance in Japan to look deeply into what had happened a half-century earlier. The Chinese Foreign Ministry, for example, welcomed the statement as "positive," but noted that many Japanese "are still unable to adopt a correct attitude toward the history of that period."

Following are texts provided by the Japanese Embassy in Washington, D.C., of the Resolution to Renew the Determination for Peace on the Basis of Lessons Learned from History, adopted by the House of Representatives of the National Diet of Japan on June 9, 1995, expressing "deep remorse" over the events of World War II, and the August 15, 1995, statement by Prime Minister Tomichi Murayama offering a "heartfelt apology" for the suffering caused by Japanese aggression before and during the war:

RESOLUTION BY NATIONAL DIET

The House of Representatives resolves as follows:

On the occasion of the 50th anniversary of the end of World War II, this House offers its sincere condolences to those who fell in action and victims of wars and similar actions all over the world.

Solemnly reflecting upon many instances of colonial rule and acts of aggression in the modern history of the world, and recognizing that Japan carried out those acts in the past, inflicting pain and suffering upon the peoples of other countries, especially in Asia, the Members of this House express a sense of deep remorse.

We must transcend the differences over historical views of the past war and learn humbly the lessons of history so as to build a peaceful international society.

This House expresses its resolve, under the banner of eternal peace enshrined in the Constitution of Japan, to join hands with other nations of the world and to pave the way to a future that allows all human beings to live together.

PRIME MINISTER'S STATEMENT

The world has seen fifty years elapse since the war came to an end. Now, when I remember the many people both at home and abroad who fell victim to war, my heart is overwhelmed by a flood of emotions.

The peace and prosperity of today were built as Japan overcame great difficulty to arise from a devastated land after defeat in the war. That achievement is something of which we are proud, and let me herein express my heartfelt admiration for the wisdom and untiring effort of each and every one of our citizens. Let me also express once again my profound gratitude for the indispensable support and assistance extended to Japan by the countries of the world, beginning with the United States of America. I am also delighted that we have been able to build the friendly relations which we enjoy today with the neighboring countries of the Asia-Pacific region, the United States and the countries of Europe.

Now that Japan has come to enjoy peace and abundance, we tend to overlook the pricelessness and blessings of peace. Our task is to convey to younger generations the horrors of war, so that we never repeat the errors in our history. I believe that, as we join hands, especially with the peoples of neighboring countries, to ensure true peace in the Asia-Pacific region—indeed, in the entire world—it is necessary, more than anything else, that we foster relations with all countries based on deep understanding and trust. Guided by this conviction, the Government has launched the Peace, Friendship and Exchange Initiative, which consists of two parts promoting: support for historical research into relations in the modern era between Japan and the neighboring countries of Asia and elsewhere; and rapid expansion of exchanges with those countries. Furthermore, I will continue in all sincerity to do my utmost in efforts being made on the issues arisen from the war, in order to further strengthen the relations of trust between Japan and those countries.

Now, upon this historic occasion of the 50th anniversary of the war's end, we should bear in mind that we must look into the past to learn from the lessons of history, and ensure that we do not stray from the path to the peace and prosperity of human society in the future.

During a certain period in the not too distant past, Japan, following a mistaken national policy, advanced along the road to war, only to ensnare the Japanese people in a fateful crisis, and, through its colonial rule and aggression, caused tremendous damage and suffering to the people of many countries, particularly to those of Asian nations. In the hope that no such mistake be made in the future, I regard, in a spirit of humility, these irrefutable facts of history, and express here once again my feelings of deep remorse and state my heartfelt apology. Allow me also to express my feelings of profound mourning for all victims, both at home and abroad, of that history.

Building from our deep remorse on this occasion of the 50th anniversary of the end of the war, Japan must eliminate self-righteous nationalism, promote international coordination as a responsible member of the international community and, thereby, advance the principles of peace and democracy. At the same time, as the only country to have experienced the devastation of atomic bombing, Japan, with a view to the ultimate elimination of nuclear weapons, must actively strive to further global disarmament in areas such as the strengthening of the nuclear non-proliferation regime. It is my conviction that in this way alone can Japan atone for its past and lay to rest the spirits of those who perished.

It is said that one can rely on good faith. And so, at this time of remembrance, I declare to the people of Japan and abroad my intention to make good faith the foundation of our Government policy, and this is my vow.

SUPREME COURT ON FEDERAL AFFIRMATIVE ACTION PLANS
June 12, 1995

*The Supreme Court ruled June 12 that the federal government's affir-
mative action plans designed to help racial minorities overcome past discrimination must meet the Court's "strict scrutiny" standard if they are to
be found constitutional. That test, the most difficult for a race-based program to pass, required that the program serve a "compelling governmental
interest" and be narrowly tailored to address past discrimination. Before
the June 12 ruling, federal affirmative action plans were required to meet
a less rigorous standard.*

*The 5–4 ruling represented the first time that the Supreme Court had
refused to uphold a federal affirmative action plan and came at a time
when the moral justification for such plans was being challenged by both
the general public and in Congress. Many whites had complained that hiring preferences were unfairly displacing qualified whites, particularly
males. Republicans in Congress were preparing legislation to outlaw federal preferences based on race and gender. The Clinton administration was
in the midst of a major review of the government's affirmative action
plans.* (Clinton speech on affirmative action, p. 483)

The case of Adarand Constructors v. Peña *concerned a Department of
Transportation policy that gave contractors a bonus if they hired minority subcontractors. Under the program, the bonus applied to any "disadvantaged business enterprise." Racial minorities were presumed to meet
the "disadvantaged" criterion, subject to a challenge showing otherwise.
Others could become eligible for the program if they could show how they
were socially and economically disadvantaged. After losing a contract to
build guardrails to a minority firm, despite offering the lowest bid, a white
contractor challenged the program in court, claiming that it violated the
Constitution's guarantees of equal protection and due process.*

*Two lower courts upheld the program, but the Supreme Court ruled that
those courts had used too lenient a standard to test its constitutionality.
Justice Sandra Day O'Connor wrote the Court's opinion. She said that the*

*Fifth and Fourteenth amendments to the Constitution guarantee equal pro-
tection to individuals rather than groups. "It follows from that principle all
governmental action based on race—a group classification long recognized
as 'in most circumstances irrelevant and therefore prohibited' . . . should
be subjected to detailed judicial inquiry to ensure that the personal right to
equal protection of the laws has not been infringed."*

*The Court has applied the strict scrutiny test to state and local affirma-
tive action plans since 1989, when it held in the case of* Richmond v. J. A.
Croson *that such plans could be justified only if they served a "compelling
state interest" of redressing "identified discrimination." Until the* Adarand
*case, the federal government had operated under a somewhat looser stan-
dard that gave it more leeway in implementing affirmative action plans.
This intermediate standard required that a policy serve important goals
and be "substantially related" to those ends.*

As recently as 1990, in the case of Metro Broadcasting, Inc. v. Federal
Communications Commission, *the high court upheld a program to grant
minority broadcasters a preference in obtaining federal licenses. In that
case, the majority said that when the federal government made racial distinctions for a benign or remedial purpose, the race-based program need
only survive intermediate-level scrutiny by the federal courts. That opinion was explicitly overruled in the* Adarand *case. (*Metro Broadcasting v.
FCC, Historic Documents of 1990, p. 419)

In Adarand, *O'Connor did not specify whether the Transportation
Department would meet the new test. "Because our decision today alters
the playing field in some important respects," she wrote, the Court thought
it best to remand the case to the lower courts for further consideration
under the strict scrutiny test. Chief Justice William H. Rehnquist and Justices Antonin Scalia, Anthony M. Kennedy, and Clarence Thomas joined
O'Connor in the majority.*

*In two separate opinions, Thomas and Scalia said they would have gone
further and outlawed any use of racial preferences. "There can be no doubt
that the paternalism that appears to lie at the heart of this [Transportation
Department] program is at war with the principle of inherent equality that
underlies and infuses our Constitution," Thomas wrote. Scalia wrote that
"government can never have a compelling interest in discriminating on
the basis of race in order to 'make up' for past racial discrimination in the
opposite direction."*

*The four dissenting justices said the main opinion went too far. Justice
John Paul Stevens wrote a lengthy dissent, taking issue with almost every
step in the majority's reasoning. Stevens said Congress should have more
leeway than state or local governments in fashioning remedies against
past discrimination. He noted that the Fourteenth Amendments, while prohibiting the states from discriminating against racial minorities, explicitly empowered Congress to take action to make equal protection meaningful. "There is no moral or constitutional equivalence between a policy that
is designed to perpetuate a caste system and one that seeks to eradicate*

racial subordination," he said. Justices Stephen G. Breyer, Ruth Bader Ginsburg, and David H. Souter also dissented.

The likely effect of the Adarand decision was unclear. At a minimum, the ruling seemed certain to invite legal challenges to other federal affirmative action programs. The Clinton administration moved quickly to respond to the case. On June 28, the Justice Department issued new guidelines for federal agencies, directing, for example, that affirmative action programs respond to specific discrimination rather than to general racism.

There was considerable debate about which federal preferences would survive the strict scrutiny test. Some analysts, such as conservative activist Clint Bolick, predicted that few programs would pass muster. Judith Lichtman, president of the Women's Legal Defense Fund, noted, however, that dozens of state and local affirmative action programs have been upheld under the strict scrutiny standard.

Advocates of affirmative action were quick to observe that all but two of the justices, Thomas and Scalia, indicated that such programs are sometimes appropriate to address ongoing problems of discrimination and that the Adarand decision did not touch on gender-based preference programs. By fencing out race-conscious programs that cannot meet the strict test, many supporters said, the Court simultaneously has drawn a protective line around a permissible zone for affirmative action. "The Supreme Court has boxed some of my colleagues in," said Rep. Melvin Watt (D-N.C.), referring to those who wanted to abolish all preference laws.

Following are excerpts from the majority, concurring, and dissenting opinions in the case of Adarand Constructors, Inc. v. Peña, in which the Supreme Court ruled June 12, 1995, that federal affirmative action plans would be held to be constitutional only if they showed that they met a compelling government interest and were narrowly tailored to meet that interest:

No. 93–1841

Adarand Constructors, Inc.,
Petitioner
v.
Federico Peña,
Secretary of Transportation, et al.

On writ of certiorari to the United States Court of Appeals for the Tenth Circuit

[June 12, 1995]

JUSTICE O'CONNOR announced the judgment of the Court and delivered an opinion with respect to Parts I, II, III-A, III-B, III-D, and IV, which is for the

Court except insofar as it might be inconsistent with the views expressed in JUSTICE SCALIA's concurrence, and an opinion with respect to Part III-C in which JUSTICE KENNEDY joins.

Petitioner Adarand Constructors, Inc., claims that the Federal Government's practice of giving general contractors on government projects a financial incentive to hire subcontractors controlled by "socially and economically disadvantaged individuals," and in particular, the Government's use of race-based presumptions in identifying such individuals, violates the equal protection component of the Fifth Amendment's Due Process Clause. The Court of Appeals rejected Adarand's claim. We conclude, however, that courts should analyze cases of this kind under a different standard of review than the one the Court of Appeals applied. We therefore vacate the Court of Appeals' judgment and remand the case for further proceedings.

I

In 1989, the Central Federal Lands Highway Division (CFLHD), which is part of the United States Department of Transportation (DOT), awarded the prime contract for a highway construction project in Colorado to Mountain Gravel & Construction Company. Mountain Gravel then solicited bids from subcontractors for the guardrail portion of the contract. Adarand, a Colorado-based highway construction company specializing in guardrail work, submitted the low bid. Gonzales Construction Company also submitted a bid.

The prime contract's terms provide that Mountain Gravel would receive additional compensation if it hired subcontractors certified as small businesses controlled by "socially and economically disadvantaged individuals." Gonzales is certified as such a business; Adarand is not. Mountain Gravel awarded the subcontract to Gonzales, despite Adarand's low bid, and Mountain Gravel's Chief Estimator has submitted an affidavit stating that Mountain Gravel would have accepted Adarand's bid, had it not been for the additional payment it received by hiring Gonzales instead. Federal law requires that a subcontracting clause similar to the one used here must appear in most federal agency contracts, and it also requires the clause to state that "the contractor shall presume that socially and economically disadvantaged individuals include Black Americans, Hispanic Americans, Native Americans, Asian Pacific Americans, and other minorities, or any other individual found to be disadvantaged by the [Small Business] Administration pursuant to section 8(a) of the Small Business Act." Adarand claims that the presumption set forth in that statute discriminates on the basis of race in violation of the Federal Government's Fifth Amendment obligation not to deny anyone equal protection of the laws.

These fairly straightforward facts implicate a complex scheme of federal statutes and regulations. . . . The Small Business Act, as amended, 15 U.S.C. §631 *et seq.* (Act), declares it to be "the policy of the United States that small business concerns, [and] small business concerns owned and controlled by socially and economically disadvantaged individuals, . . . shall have the maximum practicable opportunity to participate in the performance of contracts let by any Federal agency." §8(d)(1). The Act defines "socially disadvantaged individuals" as "those who have been subjected to racial or ethnic prejudice or cultural bias because of their identity as a member of a group without regard to their individual qualities," and it defines "economically disadvantaged individuals" as "those socially disadvantaged individuals whose ability to compete in the free enterprise system has been impaired due to diminished capital and credit opportunities as compared to others in the same business area who are not socially disadvantaged. . . .

The Small Business Administration (SBA) has implemented these statutory directives in a variety of ways, two of which are relevant here. One is the "8(a) program," which is available to small businesses controlled by socially and economically disadvantaged individuals as the SBA has defined those terms. The 8(a) program confers a wide range of benefits on participating businesses. . . . To participate in the 8(a) program, a business must be "small," and it must be 51% owned by individuals who qualify as "socially and economically disadvantaged." The SBA presumes that Black, Hispanic, Asian Pacific, Subcontinent Asian, and Native Americans, as well as "members of other groups designated from time to time by SBA," are "socially disadvantaged." It also allows any individual not a member of a listed group to prove social disadvantage "on the basis of clear and convincing evidence." Social disadvantage is not enough to establish eligibility, however; SBA also requires each 8(a) program participant to prove "economic disadvantage.". . .

The other SBA program relevant to this case is the "8(d) subcontracting program," which unlike the 8(a) program is limited to eligibility for subcontracting provisions like the one at issue here. In determining eligibility, the SBA presumes social disadvantage based on membership in certain minority groups, just as in the 8(a) program, and again appears to require an individualized, although "less restrictive," showing of economic disadvantage. A different set of regulations, however, says that members of minority groups wishing to participate in the 8(d) subcontracting program are entitled to a race-based presumption of social *and* economic disadvantage. . . . [I]n both the 8(a) and the 8(d) programs, the presumptions of disadvantage are rebuttable if a third party comes forward with evidence suggesting that the participant is not, in fact, either economically or socially disadvantaged.

The contract giving rise to the dispute in this case came about as a result of the Surface Transportation and Uniform Relocation Assistance Act of 1987 (STURAA), a DOT appropriations measure. Section 106(c)(1) of STURAA provides that "not less than 10 percent" of the appropriated funds "shall be expended with small business concerns owned and controlled by socially and economically disadvantaged individuals." STURAA adopts the Small Business Act's definition of "socially and economically disadvantaged individual," including the applicable race-based presumptions, and adds that "women shall be presumed to be socially and economically disadvantaged individuals for purposes of this subsection." STURAA also requires the Secretary of Transportation to establish "minimum uniform criteria for State governments to use in certifying whether a concern qualifies for purposes of this subsection.". . . . Those regulations say that the certifying authority should presume both social and economic disadvantage (*i.e.*, eligibility to participate) if the applicant belongs to certain racial groups, or is a woman. As with the SBA programs, third parties may come forward with evidence in an effort to rebut the presumption of disadvantage for a particular business.

[The Court quoted the operative clause of the contract in the case. It provides "monetary compensation" to a contractor that awards a subcontract to a "Disadvantaged Business Enterprise (DBE)" in the amount of 10 percent of the subcontract, not to exceed 1.5 percent of the original contract.] To benefit from this clause, Mountain Gravel had to hire a subcontractor who had been certified as a small disadvantaged business by the SBA, a state highway agency, or some other certifying authority acceptable to the Contracting Officer. . . .

After losing the guardrail subcontract to Gonzales, Adarand filed suit against various federal officials in the United States District Court for the District of Colorado, claiming that the race-based presumptions involved in the use of subcontracting compensation clauses violate Adarand's right to equal protection. The District Court granted the Government's motion for summary judgment. The Court of Appeals for the Tenth Circuit affirmed. It understood our decision in *Fullilove* v. *Klutznick* (1980) to have adopted "a lenient standard, resembling intermediate scrutiny, in assessing" the constitutionality of federal race-based action. Applying that "lenient standard," as further developed in *Metro Broadcasting Inc.* v. *FCC* (1990), the Court of Appeals upheld the use of subcontractor compensation clauses. We granted certiorari. (1994).

[II omitted]

III

The Government urges that "the Subcontracting Compensation Clause program is . . . a program based on *disadvantage*, not on race," and thus that it is subject only to "the most relaxed judicial scrutiny." To the extent that the statutes and regulations involved in this case are race neutral, we agree. The Government concedes, however, that "the race-based rebuttable presumption used in some certification determinations under the Subcontracting Compensation Clause" is subject to some heightened level of scrutiny. The parties disagree as to what that level should be. . . .

Adarand's claim arises under the Fifth Amendment to the Constitution, which provides that "No person shall . . . be deprived of life, liberty, or property, without due process of law." Although this Court has always understood that Clause to provide some measure of protection against *arbitrary* treatment by the Federal Government, it is not as explicit a guarantee of *equal* treatment as the Fourteenth Amendment, which provides that "No *State* shall . . . deny to any person within its jurisdiction the equal protection of the laws" (emphasis added). Our cases have accorded varying degrees of significance to the difference in the language of those two Clauses. We think it necessary to revisit the issue here.

A

Through the 1940s, this Court had routinely taken the view in non-race-related cases that, "unlike the Fourteenth Amendment, the Fifth contains no equal protection clause and it provides no guaranty against discriminatory legislation by Congress." *Detroit Bank* v. *United States* (1943). . . . When the Court first faced a Fifth Amendment equal protection challenge to a federal racial classification, it adopted a similar approach, with most unfortunate results. [The Court summarized the two World War II decisions, *Hirabayashi* v. *United States* (1943), and *Korematsu* v. *United States* (1944), that rejected equal protection challenges to the curfew and wartime relocation of Japanese-Americans.]

In *Bolling* v. *Sharpe* (1954), the Court for the first time explicitly questioned the existence of any difference between the obligations of the Federal Government and the States to avoid racial classifications. . . .

Later cases in contexts other than school desegregation did not distinguish between the duties of the States and the Federal Government to avoid racial classifications. [The Court noted that its opinion in *McLaughlin* v. *Florida*, a 1964 case that struck down a race-based state law, cited passages from *Bolling*, *Korematsu*, and *Hirabayashi* to show that racial classifications are "constitutionally suspect."] *McLaughlin*'s reliance on cases involving federal action for the standards applicable to a case involving state legislation suggests that the Court understood the standards for federal and state racial classifications to be the same.

Cases decided after *McLaughlin* continued to treat the equal protection obligations imposed by the Fifth and the Fourteenth Amendments as indistinguishable. *Loving* v. *Virginia* [1967], which struck down a race-based state law [prohibiting interracial marriage], cited *Korematsu* for the proposition that "the Equal Protection Clause demands that racial classifications . . . be subjected to the 'most rigid scrutiny.' " The various opinions in *Frontiero* v. *Richardson*, (1973), which concerned sex discrimination by the Federal Government, took their equal protection standard of review from *Reed* v. *Reed*, (1971), a case that invalidated sex discrimination by a State, without mentioning any possibility of a difference between the standards applicable to state and federal action. Thus, in 1975, the Court stated explicitly that "[t]his Court's approach to Fifth Amendment equal protection claims has always been precisely the same as to equal protection claims under the Fourteenth Amendment." *Weinberger* v. *Wiesenfeld* (1975). . . .

B

Most of the cases discussed above involved classifications burdening groups that have suffered discrimination in our society. In 1978, the Court confronted the question whether race-based governmental action designed to *benefit* such groups should also be subject to "the most rigid scrutiny." *Regents of Univ. of California* v. *Bakke* involved an equal protection challenge to a state-run medical school's practice of reserving a number of spaces in its entering class for minority students. The petitioners argued that "strict scrutiny" should apply only to "classifications that disadvantage 'discrete and insular minorities.' " *Bakke* did not produce an opinion for the Court, but Justice Powell's opinion announcing the Court's judgment rejected the argument. In a passage joined by Justice White, Justice Powell wrote that "[t]he guarantee of equal protection cannot mean one thing when applied to one individual and something else when applied to a person of another color." He concluded that "[r]acial and ethnic distinctions of any sort are inherently suspect and thus call for the most exacting judicial examination.". . .

Two years after *Bakke*, the Court faced another challenge to remedial race-based action, this time involving action undertaken by the Federal Government. In *Fullilove* v. *Klutznick* (1980), the Court upheld Congress' inclusion of a 10% set-aside for minority-owned businesses in the Public Works Employment Act of 1977. As in *Bakke*, there was no opinion for the Court. Chief Justice Burger, in an opinion joined by Justices White and Powell, observed that "[a]ny preference based on racial or ethnic criteria must necessarily receive a most searching examination to make sure that it does not conflict with constitutional guarantees." That opinion, however, "d[id] not adopt, either expressly or implicitly, the formulas of analysis articulated in such cases as [*Bakke*]." It employed instead a two-part test which asked, first, "whether the *objectives* of th[e] legislation are within the power of Congress, and second, "whether the limited use of racial and ethnic criteria, in the context presented, is a constitutionally permissible *means* for achieving the congressional objectives." It then upheld the program under that test. . . . Justice Powell wrote separately to express his view that the plurality opinion had essentially applied "strict scrutiny" as described in his *Bakke* opinion . . . and had so done correctly. Justice Stewart (joined by then-JUSTICE REHNQUIST) dissented, arguing that the Constitution required the Federal Government to meet the same strict standard as the States when enacting racial classifications, and that the program before the Court failed that standard. JUSTICE STEVENS also dissented, arguing that "[r]acial classifications are simply too pernicious to permit any but the most exact connection between justification and classification," and that the program before the Court could not be characterized "as a 'narrowly tailored' remedial measure." Justice Marshall (joined by Justices Brennan and Blackmun) concurred in the judgment, reiterating the view of four Justices in *Bakke* that any race-based governmental action designed to "remed[y] the present effects of past racial discrimination" should be upheld if it was "substantially related" to the achievement of an "important governmental objective"—*i.e.*, such action should be subjected only to what we now call "intermediate scrutiny."

In *Wygant* v. *Jackson Board of Ed.* (1986), the Court considered a Fourteenth Amendment challenge to another form of remedial racial classification. The issue in *Wygant* was whether a school board could adopt race-based preferences in determining which teachers to lay off. Justice Powell's plurality opinion observed that "the level of scrutiny does not change merely because the challenged classification operates against a group that historically has not been subject to governmental discrimination" and stated the two-part inquiry as "whether the layoff provision is supported by a compelling state purpose and whether the means chosen to accomplish that purpose are narrowly tailored.". . . The plurality then concluded that the school board's interest in "providing minority role models for its minority students, as an attempt to alleviate the effects of societal discrimination," was not a compelling interest that could justify the use of a racial classification. It added that "[s]ocietal discrimination, without more, is too amorphous a basis for imposing a racially classified remedy," and insisted instead that "a public employer . . . must ensure that, before it embarks on an affirmative-action program, it has convincing evidence that remedial action is warranted. That is, it must have sufficient evidence to justify the conclusion that there has been prior discrimination." Justice White concurred only in the judgment, although he agreed that the school board's asserted interests could not, "singly or together, justify this racially discriminatory layoff policy.". . .

The Court's failure to produce a majority opinion in *Bakke, Fullilove,* and *Wygant* left unresolved the proper analysis for remedial race-based governmental action. . . .

The Court resolved the issue, at least in part, in 1989. *Richmond* v. *J. A. Croson* Co. concerned a city's determination that 30% of its contracting work should go to minority-owned businesses. A majority of the Court in *Croson* held that "the standard of review under the Equal Protection Clause is not dependent on the race of those burdened or benefited by a particular classification," and that the single standard of review for racial classifications should be "strict scrutiny." (opinion of O'CONNOR, J., joined by REHNQUIST, C. J., White, and KENNEDY, J.); (SCALIA, J., concurring in judgment) ("I agree . . . with JUSTICE O'CONNOR's conclusion that strict scrutiny must be applied to all governmental classification by race"). As to the classification before the Court, the plurality agreed that "a state or local subdivision . . . has the authority to eradicate the effects of private discrimination within its own legislative jurisdiction," but the Court thought that the city had not acted with "a 'strong basis in evidence for its conclusion that remedial action was necessary.' " The Court also thought it "obvious that [the] program is not narrowly tailored to remedy the effects of prior discrimination."

With *Croson,* the Court finally agreed that the Fourteenth Amendment requires strict scrutiny of all race-based action by state and local governments. But *Croson* of course had no occasion to declare what standard of review the Fifth Amendment requires for such action taken by the Federal Government. . . . On the other hand, the Court subsequently indicated that *Croson* had at least some bearing on federal race-based action when it vacated a decision upholding such action and remanded for further consideration in light of *Croson. H. K. Porter Co.* v. *Metropolitan Dade County* (1989). . . .

Despite lingering uncertainty in the details, however, the Court's cases through *Croson* had established three general propositions with respect to governmental racial classifications. First, skepticism: " '[a]ny preference based on racial or ethnic criteria must necessarily receive a most searching examination' " [citations omitted]. Second, consistency: "the standard of review under the Equal Protection Clause is not dependent on the race of those burdened or benefited by a particular classification," [citing *Croson* and *Bakke*] *i.e.*, all racial classifications reviewable under the Equal Protection Clause must be strictly scrutinized. And third, congruence: "[e]qual protection analysis in the Fifth Amendment area is the same as that under the Fourteenth Amendment" [citations omitted]. Taken together, these three propositions lead to the conclusion that any person, of whatever race, has the right to demand that any governmental actor subject to the Constitution justify any racial classification subjecting that person to unequal treatment under the strictest judicial scrutiny. . . .

A year later, however, the Court took a surprising turn. *Metro Broadcasting, Inc.* v. *FCC* (1990) involved a Fifth Amendment challenge to two race-based policies of the Federal Communications Commission. In *Metro Broadcasting*, the Court repudiated the long-held notion that "it would be unthinkable that the same Constitution would impose a lesser duty on the Federal Government" than it does on a State to afford equal protection of the laws. It did so by holding that "benign" federal racial classifications need only satisfy intermediate scrutiny, even though *Croson* had recently concluded that such classifications enacted by a State must satisfy strict scrutiny. "[B]enign" federal racial classifications, the Court said, "—even if those measures are not 'remedial' in the sense of being designed to compensate victims of past governmental or societal discrimination—are constitutionally permissible to the extent that they serve *important* governmental objectives within the power of Congress and are *substantially related* to achievement of those objectives." (Emphasis added.) The Court did not explain how to tell whether a racial classification should be deemed "benign," other than to express "confiden[ce] that an 'examination of the legislative scheme and its history' will separate benign measures from other types of racial classifications."

Applying this test, the Court first noted that the FCC policies at issue did not serve as a remedy for past discrimination. Proceeding on the assumption that the policies were nonetheless "benign," it concluded that they served the "important governmental objective" of "enhancing broadcast diversity" and that they were "substantially related" to that objective. It therefore upheld the policies.

By adopting intermediate scrutiny as the standard of review for congressionally mandated "benign" racial classifications, *Metro Broadcasting* departed from prior cases in two significant respects. First, it turned its back on *Croson*'s explanation of why strict scrutiny of all governmental racial classifications is essential:

> "Absent searching judicial inquiry into the justification for such race-based measures, there is simply no way of determining what classifications are 'benign' or 'remedial' and what classifications are in fact motivated by illegitimate notions of racial inferiority or simple racial politics. . . ." *Croson* (plurality opinion of O'CONNOR, J.).

We adhere to that view today, despite the surface appeal of holding "benign" racial classifications to a lower standard, because "it may not always be clear that a so-called preference is in fact benign." *Bakke* (opinion of Powell, J.). . . .

Second, *Metro Broadcasting* squarely rejected one of the three propositions established by the Court's earlier equal protection cases, namely, congruence between the standards applicable to federal and state racial classifications, and in so doing also undermined the other two—skepticism of all racial classifications, and consistency of treatment irrespective of the race of the burdened or benefited group. Under *Metro Broadcasting*, certain racial classifications ("benign" ones enacted by the Federal Government) should be treated less skeptically than others; and the race of the benefited group is critical to the determination of which standard of review to apply. *Metro Broadcasting* was thus a significant departure from much of what had come before it.

The three propositions undermined by *Metro Broadcasting* all derive from the basic principle that the Fifth and Fourteenth Amendments to the Constitution protect *persons*, not *groups*. It follows from that principle that all governmental action based on race . . . should be subjected to detailed judicial inquiry to ensure that the *personal* right to equal protection of the laws has not been infringed. These ideas have long been central to this Court's understanding of equal protection, and holding "benign" state and federal racial classifications to different standards does not square with them. . . . Accordingly, we hold today that all racial classifications, imposed by whatever federal, state, or local governmental actor, must be analyzed by a reviewing court under strict scrutiny. In other words, such classifications are constitutional only if they are narrowly tailored measures that further compelling governmental interests. To the extent that *Metro Broadcasting* is inconsistent with that holding, it is overruled.

In dissent, JUSTICE STEVENS criticizes us for "delivering a disconcerting lecture about the evils of governmental racial classifications." With respect, we believe his criticisms reflect a serious misunderstanding of our opinion.

JUSTICE STEVENS concurs in our view that courts should take a skeptical view of all governmental racial classifications. He also allows that "nothing is inherently wrong with applying a single standard to fundamentally different situations, as long as that standard takes relevant differences into account." What he fails to recognize is that strict scrutiny *does* take "relevant differences" into account—indeed, that is its fundamental purpose. The point of carefully examining the interest asserted by the government in support of a racial classification, and the evidence offered to show that the classification is needed, is precisely to distinguish legitimate from illegitimate uses of race in governmental decisionmaking. And JUSTICE STEVENS concedes that "some cases may be difficult to classify," all the more reason, in our view, to examine all racial classifications carefully. Strict scrutiny does not "trea[t] dissimilar race-based decisions as though they were equally objectionable"; to the contrary, it evaluates carefully all governmental race-based decisions *in order to decide* which are constitutionally objectionable and which are not. . . .

JUSTICE STEVENS chides us for our "supposed inability to differentiate between 'invidious' and 'benign' discrimination," because it is in his view sufficient that "people understand the difference between good intentions and bad." But, as we have just explained, the point of strict scrutiny is to "differentiate between" permissible and impermissible governmental use of race. . . .

Perhaps it is not the standard of strict scrutiny itself, but our use of the concepts of "consistency" and "congruence" in conjunction with it, that leads JUSTICE STEVENS to dissent. According to JUSTICE STEVENS, our view of consistency "equates remedial preferences with invidious discrimination" and ignores the difference between "an engine of oppression" and an effort "to foster equality in society," or, more colorfully, "between a 'No Trespassing' sign and a welcome mat." It does nothing of the kind. The principle of consistency simply means that whenever the government treats any person unequally because of his or her race, that person has suffered an injury that falls squarely within the language and spirit of the Constitution's guarantee of equal protection. It says nothing about the ultimate validity of any particular law; that determination is the job of the court applying strict scrutiny. The principle of consistency explains the circumstances in which the injury requiring strict scrutiny occurs. The application of strict scrutiny, in turn, determines whether a compelling governmental interest justifies the infliction of that injury.

Consistency *does* recognize that any individual suffers an injury when he or she is disadvantaged by the government because of his or her race, whatever that race may be. This Court clearly stated that principle in *Croson*. JUSTICE STEVENS does not explain how his views square with *Croson*, or with the long line of cases understanding equal protection as a personal right.

JUSTICE STEVENS also claims that we have ignored any difference between federal and state legislatures. But requiring that Congress, like the States, enact racial classifications only when doing so is necessary to further a "compelling interest" does not contravene any principle of appropriate respect for a co-equal Branch of the Government. It is true that various Members of this Court have taken different views of the authority §5 of the Fourteenth Amendment confers upon Congress to deal with the problem of racial discrimination, and the extent to which courts should defer to Congress' exercise of that authority. We need not, and do not, address these differences today. For now, it is enough to observe that JUSTICE STEVENS' suggestion that any Member of this Court has repudiated in this case his or her previously expressed views on the subject is incorrect.

[C and D omitted]

IV

Because our decision today alters the playing field in some important respects, we think it best to remand the case to the lower courts for further consideration in light of the principles we have announced. The Court of Appeals, following *Metro Broadcasting* and *Fullilove*, analyzed the case in terms of intermediate scrutiny. It upheld the challenged statutes and regulations because it found them to be "narrowly tailored to achieve [their] *significant governmental purpose* of providing subcontracting opportunities for small disadvantaged business enterprises" (emphasis added). The Court of Appeals did not decide the question whether the interests served by the use of subcontractor compensation clauses are properly described as "compelling." It also did not address the question of narrow tailoring in terms of our strict scrutiny cases, by asking, for example, whether there was "any consideration of the use of race-neutral means to increase minority business participation" in government contracting or whether the program was appropriately limited such that it "will not last longer than the discriminatory effects it is designed to eliminate."

Moreover, unresolved questions remain concerning the details of the complex regulatory regimes implicated by the use of subcontractor compensation clauses. For example, the SBA's 8(a) program requires an individualized inquiry into the economic disadvantage of every participant, whereas the DOT's regulations do not require certifying authorities to make such individualized inquiries. And the regulations seem unclear as to whether 8(d) subcontractors must make individualized showings, or instead whether the race-based presumption applies both to social *and* economic disadvantage. . . . We also note an apparent discrepancy between the definitions of which socially disadvantaged individuals qualify as economically disadvantaged for the 8(a) and 8(d) programs; the former requires a showing that such individuals' ability to compete has been impaired "as compared to others in the same or similar line of business *who are not socially disadvantaged*" (emphasis added), while the latter requires that showing only "as compared to others in the same or similar line of business." The question whether any of the ways in which the Government uses subcontractor compensation clauses can survive strict scrutiny, and any relevance distinctions such as these may have to that question, should be addressed in the first instance by the lower courts.

Accordingly, the judgment of the Court of Appeals is vacated, and the case is remanded for further proceedings consistent with this opinion.

It is so ordered.

JUSTICE SCALIA, concurring in part and concurring in the judgment.

I join the opinion of the Court, except Part III-C, and except insofar as it may be inconsistent with the following: In my view, government can never have a "compelling interest" in discriminating on the basis of race in order to "make up" for past racial discrimination in the opposite direction. Individuals who have been wronged by unlawful racial discrimination should be made whole; but under our Constitution there can be no such thing as either a creditor or a debtor race. . . . To pursue the concept of racial entitlement—even for the most admirable and benign of purposes—is to reinforce and preserve for future mischief the way of thinking that produced race slavery, race privilege and race hatred. In the eyes of government, we are just one race here. It is American.

It is unlikely, if not impossible, that the challenged program would survive under this understanding of strict scrutiny, but I am content to leave that to be decided on remand.

JUSTICE THOMAS, concurring in part and concurring in the judgment.

I agree with the majority's conclusion that strict scrutiny applies to all government classifications based on race. I write separately, however, to express my disagreement with the premise underlying JUSTICE STEVENS' and JUSTICE GINSBURG's dissents: that there is a racial paternalism exception to the principle of equal protection. I believe that there is a "moral [and] constitutional equivalence" (STEVENS, J., dissenting), between laws designed to subjugate a race and those that distribute benefits on the basis of race in order to foster some current notion of equality. Government cannot make us equal; it can only recognize, respect, and protect us as equal before the law.

That these programs may have been motivated, in part, by good intentions cannot provide refuge from the principle that under our Constitution, the government may not make distinctions on the basis of race. As far as the Constitution is concerned, it is irrelevant whether a government's racial classifications are drawn by those who wish to oppress a race or by those who have a sincere desire to help those thought to be disadvantaged. There can be no doubt that the paternalism that appears to lie at the heart of this program is at war with the principle of inherent equality that underlies and infuses our Constitution. . . .

. . . [T]here can be no doubt that racial paternalism and its unintended consequences can be as poisonous and pernicious as any other form of discrimination. So-called "benign" discrimination teaches many that because of chronic and apparently immutable handicaps, minorities cannot compete with them without their patronizing indulgence. Inevitably, such programs engender attitudes of superiority or, alternatively, provoke resentment among those who believe that they have been wronged by the government's use of race. These programs stamp minorities with a badge of inferiority and may cause them to develop dependencies or to adopt an attitude that they are "entitled" to preferences. . . .

In my mind, government-sponsored racial discrimination based on benign prejudice is just as noxious as discrimination inspired by malicious prejudice. In each instance, it is racial discrimination, plain and simple.

JUSTICE STEVENS, with whom JUSTICE GINSBURG joins, dissenting.

Instead of deciding this case in accordance with controlling precedent, the Court today delivers a disconcerting lecture about the evils of governmental racial classifications. For its text the Court has selected three propositions, represented by the bywords "skepticism," "consistency," and "congruence." I shall comment on each of these propositions, then add a few words about *stare decisis*, and finally explain why I believe this Court has a duty to affirm the judgment of the Court of Appeals.

I

The Court's concept of skepticism is, at least in principle, a good statement of law and of common sense. Undoubtedly, a court should be wary of a governmental decision that relies upon a racial classification. "Because racial characteristics so seldom provide a relevant basis for disparate treatment, and because classifications based on race are potentially so harmful to the entire body politic," a reviewing court must satisfy itself that the reasons for any such classification are "clearly identified and unquestionably legitimate." *Fullilove* v. *Klutznick* (1980) (STEVENS, J., dissenting). This principle is explicit in Chief Justice Burger's opinion, in Justice Powell's concurrence, and in my dissent in *Fullilove*. I welcome its renewed endorsement by the Court today. But, as the opinions in *Fullilove* demonstrate, substantial agreement on the standard to be applied in deciding difficult cases does not necessarily lead to agreement on how those cases actually should or will be resolved. In my judgment, because uniform standards are often anything but uniform, we should evaluate the Court's comments on "consistency," "congruence," and *stare decisis* with the same type of skepticism that the Court advocates for the underlying issue.

II

The Court's concept of "consistency" assumes that there is no significant difference between a decision by the majority to impose a special burden on the members of a minority race and a decision by the majority to provide a benefit to certain members of that minority notwithstanding its incidental burden on some members of the majority. In my opinion that assumption is untenable. There is no moral or constitutional equivalence between a policy that is designed to perpetuate a caste system and one that seeks to eradicate racial subordination. Invidious discrimination is an engine of oppression, subjugating a disfavored group to enhance or maintain the power of the majority. Remedial race-based preferences reflect the opposite impulse: a desire to foster equality in society. No sensible conception of the Government's constitutional obligation to "govern impartially" should ignore this distinction. . . .

The consistency that the Court espouses would disregard the difference between a "No Trespassing" sign and a welcome mat. It would treat a Dixiecrat Senator's decision to vote against Thurgood Marshall's confirmation in order to keep African Americans off the Supreme Court as on a par with President Johnson's evaluation of his nominee's race as a positive factor. It would equate a law that made black citizens ineligible for military service with a program aimed at recruiting black soldiers. An attempt by the majority to exclude members of a minority race from a regulated market is fundamentally different from a subsidy that enables a relatively small group of newcomers to enter that market. An interest in "consistency" does not justify treating differences as though they were similarities.

The Court's explanation for treating dissimilar race-based decisions as though they were equally objectionable is a supposed inability to differentiate between "invidious" and "benign" discrimination. But the term "affirmative action" is common and well understood. Its presence in everyday parlance shows that people understand the difference between good intentions and bad. As with any legal concept, some cases may be difficult to classify, but our equal protection jurisprudence has identified a critical difference between state action that imposes burdens on a disfavored few and state action that benefits the few "in spite of" its adverse effects on the many. . . .

As a matter of constitutional and democratic principle, a decision by representatives of the majority to discriminate against the members of a minority race is fundamentally different from those same representatives' decision to impose incidental costs on the majority of their constituents in order to provide a benefit to a disadvantaged minority. Indeed, as I have previously argued, the former is virtually always repugnant to the principles of a free and democratic society, whereas the latter is, in some circumstances, entirely consistent with the ideal of equality. By insisting on a doctrinaire notion of "consistency" in the standard applicable to all race-based governmental actions, the Court obscures this essential dichotomy.

III

The Court's concept of "congruence" assumes that there is no significant difference between a decision by the Congress of the United States to adopt an affirmative-action program and such a decision by a State or a municipality. In my opinion that assumption is untenable. It ignores important practical and legal differences between federal and state or local decisionmakers.

These differences have been identified repeatedly and consistently both in opinions of the Court and in separate opinions authored by members of today's majority. Thus, in *Metro Broadcasting, Inc.* v. *FCC* (1990), in which we upheld a federal program designed to foster racial diversity in broadcasting, we identified the special "institutional competence" of our National Legislature. "It is of overriding significance in these cases," we were careful to emphasize, "that the FCC's minority ownership programs have been specifically approved—indeed, mandated—by Congress.". . .

The majority in *Metro Broadcasting* and the plurality in *Fullilove* were not alone in relying upon a critical distinction between federal and state programs. In his separate opinion in *Richmond* v. *J. A. Croson Co.* (1989), JUSTICE SCALIA discussed the basis for this distinction. He observed that "it is one thing to permit racially based conduct by the Federal Government—whose legislative powers concerning matters of race were explicitly enhanced by the Fourteenth Amendment—and quite another to permit it by the precise entities against whose conduct in matters of race that Amendment was specifically directed.". . .

Our opinion in *Metro Broadcasting* relied on several constitutional provisions to justify the greater deference we owe to Congress when it acts with respect to private individuals. In the programs challenged in this case, Congress has acted both with respect to private individuals and, as in

Fullilove, with respect to the States themselves. . . . One of the "provisions of this article" that Congress is thus empowered to enforce reads: "No State shall make or enforce any law which shall abridge the privileges or immunities of citizens of the United States; nor shall any State deprive any person of life, liberty, or property, without due process of law; nor deny to any person within its jurisdiction the equal protection of the laws." U.S. Const., Amdt. 14, §1. The Fourteenth Amendment directly empowers Congress at the same time it expressly limits the States. This is no accident. It represents our Nation's consensus, achieved after hard experience throughout our sorry history of race relations, that the Federal Government must be the primary defender of racial minorities against the States, some of which may be inclined to oppress such minorities. A rule of "congruence" that ignores a purposeful "incongruity" so fundamental to our system of government is unacceptable.

In my judgment, the Court's novel doctrine of "congruence" is seriously misguided. Congressional deliberations about a matter as important as affirmative action should be accorded far greater deference than those of a State or municipality.

[The remaining sections omitted.]

JUSTICE SOUTER, with whom JUSTICE GINSBURG and JUSTICE BREYER join, dissenting.

As this case worked its way through the federal courts prior to the grant of certiorari that brought it here, petitioner Adarand Constructors, Inc. was understood to have raised only one significant claim: that before a federal agency may exceed the goals adopted by Congress in implementing a race-based remedial program, the Fifth and Fourteenth Amendments require the agency to make specific findings of discrimination, as under *Richmond* v. *J. A. Croson Co.*. (1989), sufficient to justify surpassing the congressional objective. . . .

Although the petition for certiorari added an antecedent question challenging the use, under the Fifth and Fourteenth Amendments, of any standard below strict scrutiny to judge the constitutionality of the statutes under which the respondents acted, I would not have entertained that question in this case. The statutory scheme must be treated as constitutional if *Fullilove* v. *Klutznick* (1980) is applied, and petitioners did not identify any of the factual premises on which *Fullilove* rested as having disappeared since that case was decided.

As the Court's opinion explains in detail, the scheme in question provides financial incentives to general contractors to hire subcontractors who have been certified as disadvantaged business enterprises on the basis of certain race-based presumptions. These statutes (or the originals, of which the current ones are reenactments) have previously been justified as providing remedies for the continuing effects of past discrimination, and the Government has so defended them in this case. Since petitioner has not claimed the obsolescence of any particular fact on which the *Fullilove* Court upheld the statute, no issue has come up to us that might be resolved in a way that would render *Fullilove* inapposite. . . .

In these circumstances, I agree with JUSTICE STEVENS's conclusion that *stare decisis* compels the application of *Fullilove*. Although *Fullilove* did not reflect doctrinal consistency, its several opinions produced a result on shared grounds that petitioner does not attack: that discrimination in the construction industry had been subject to government acquiescence, with effects that remain and that may be addressed by some preferential treatment falling within the congressional power under §5 of the Fourteenth Amendment. Once *Fullilove* is applied, as JUSTICE STEVENS points out, it follows that the statutes in question here (which are substantially better tailored to the harm being remedied than the statute endorsed in *Fullilove*) pass muster under Fifth Amendment due process and Fourteenth Amendment equal protection.

The Court today, however, does not reach the application of *Fullilove* to the facts of this case. . . . Be that as it may, it seems fair to ask whether the statutes will meet a different fate from what *Fullilove* would have decreed. The answer is, quite probably not, though of course there will be some interpretive forks in the road before the significance of strict scrutiny for congressional remedial statutes becomes entirely clear. . . .

JUSTICE GINSBURG, with whom JUSTICE BREYER joins, dissenting.

For the reasons stated by JUSTICE SOUTER, and in view of the attention the political branches are currently giving the matter of affirmative action, I see no compelling cause for the intervention the Court has made in this case. I further agree with JUSTICE STEVENS that, in this area, large deference is owed by the Judiciary to "Congress' institutional competence and constitutional authority to overcome historic racial subjugation." I write separately to underscore not the differences the several opinions in this case display, but the considerable field of agreement—the common understandings and concerns—revealed in opinions that together speak for a majority of the Court.

I

The statutes and regulations at issue, as the Court indicates, were adopted by the political branches in response to an "unfortunate reality": "[t]he unhappy persistence of both the practice and the lingering effects of racial discrimination against minority groups in this country." The United States suffers from those lingering effects because, for most of our Nation's history, the idea that "we are just one race," (SCALIA, J., concurring in part and concurring in judgment), was not embraced. For generations, our lawmakers and judges were unprepared to say that there is in this land no superior race, no race inferior to any other. . . .

The divisions in this difficult case should not obscure the Court's recognition of the persistence of racial inequality and a majority's acknowledgement of Congress' authority to act affirmatively, not only to end discrimination, but also to counteract discrimination's lingering effects. Those effects, reflective of a system of racial caste only recently ended, are evident in our workplaces, markets, and neighborhoods. Job applicants with identical resumes, qualifications, and interview styles still experience different receptions, depending on their race. White and African-American consumers still encounter different deals. People of color looking for housing still face discriminatory treatment by landlords, real estate agents, and mortgage lenders. Minority entrepreneurs sometimes fail to gain contracts though they are the low bidders, and they are sometimes refused work even after winning contracts. Bias both conscious and unconscious, reflecting traditional and unexamined habits of thought, keeps up barriers that must come down if equal opportunity and nondiscrimination are ever genuinely to become this country's law and practice.

Given this history and its practical consequences, Congress surely can conclude that a carefully designed affirmative action program may help to realize, finally, the "equal protection of the laws" the Fourteenth Amendment has promised since 1868.

II

The lead opinion uses one term, "strict scrutiny," to describe the standard of judicial review for all governmental classifications by race. But that opinion's elaboration strongly suggests that the strict standard announced is indeed "fatal" for classifications burdening groups that have suffered discrimination in our society. That seems to me, and, I believe, to the Court, the enduring lesson one should draw from *Korematsu* v. *United States* (1944); for in that case, scrutiny the Court described as "most rigid" nonetheless yielded a pass for an odious, gravely injurious racial classification. A *Korematsu*-type classification, as I read the opinions in this case, will never again survive scrutiny: such a classification, history and precedent instruct, properly ranks as prohibited.

For a classification made to hasten the day when "we are just one race," however, the lead opinion has dispelled the notion that "strict scrutiny" is " 'fatal in fact' " Properly, a majority of the Court calls for review that is searching, in order to ferret out classifications in reality malign, but masquerading as benign. The Court's once lax review of sex-based classifications demonstrates the need for such suspicion. [Citations omitted.] Today's decision thus usefully reiterates that the purpose of strict scrutiny "is precisely to distinguish legitimate from illegitimate uses of race in governmental decisionmaking," "to 'differentiate between' permissible and impermissible governmental use of race," to distinguish " 'between a "No Trespassing" sign and a welcome mat.' "

Close review also is in order for this further reason. As JUSTICE SOUTER points out, and as this very case shows, some members of the historically favored race can be hurt by catch-up mechanisms designed to cope with the lingering effects of entrenched racial subjugation. Court review can ensure that preferences are not so large as to trammel unduly upon the opportunities of others or interfere too harshly with legitimate expectations of persons in once-preferred groups.

* * *

While I would not disturb the programs challenged in this case, and would leave their improvement to the political branches, I see today's decision as one that allows our precedent to evolve, still to be informed by and responsive to changing conditions.

SUPREME COURT ON EXCLUDING GAY MARCHERS FROM PARADE
June 19, 1995

The Supreme Court ruled June 19 that private sponsors of a St. Patrick's Day Parade had the right under the First Amendment to exclude members of a gay rights organization from their parade. "The issue in this case is whether Massachusetts may require private citizens who organize a parade to include among the marchers a group imparting a message the organizers do not wish to convey," Justice David H. Souter wrote for the unanimous court. "We hold that such a mandate violates the First Amendment."

The decision means that "nobody can rain on anybody else's parade," Burt Neuborne, an attorney for the American Civil Liberties Union, told the Washington Post. *The ruling appeared to vindicate a federal district court in New York City, which had ruled in 1993 that it was unconstitutional for city officials to force the Ancient Order of Hibernians to allow a gay organization to march in its St. Patrick's Day parade.*

The decision in the Boston case, Hurley v. Irish-American Gay, Lesbian and Bisexual Group of Boston, *centered on free speech rather than gay rights and continued a long line of cases in which the Court had held that private speakers could not be forced to change the content of their speech to include sentiments with which they disagreed.*

The parade in question celebrated two events: St. Patrick's Day, and evacuation day, March 17, 1776, the day George Washington drove the British out of South Boston. Since 1947 the parade has been organized by the South Boston Allied War Veterans Council. Until 1992 the city of Boston allowed the veterans to use the city's seal and provided some funding for the parade. In some years, the parade has drawn 20,000 marchers and a million spectators.

In 1992 the Irish-American Gay, Lesbian and Bisexual Group of Boston, known as GLIB, formed specifically to march in the parade. The veterans council rejected their request to participate, but a state court ordered the council to allow GLIB to march.

That march was uneventful, and the following year GLIB again request-ed permission to join the parade and was again turned down by the veter-ans council. GLIB sued, and a state trial court ruled in the group's favor, holding that the parade was a "public accommodation" under the state's civil rights law and that, as such, its organizers could not discriminate on the basis of sexual orientation.

The Massachusetts supreme court upheld that ruling. The gay group marched in 1993, but organizers canceled the event in 1994 rather than be forced to let GLIB march. In the 1995 parade marchers carried black, rather than green, banners to protest the state court decisions. The gay group did not march.

In appealing the state supreme court's holding, the veterans' council argued that their parade conveyed a message and that it was a violation of their First Amendment rights to be forced to allow a group with a contra-dictory message to participate. The Supreme Court agreed. The word parade, *Souter wrote, means "marchers who are making some sort of col-lective point, not just to each other but to bystanders along the way. . . . Parades are thus a form of expression, not just motion."*

Moreover, Souter continued, participation of the GLIB marchers under a banner identifying them as gay Irish-Americans was "equally expres-sive." In refusing to allow the GLIB unit to parade, Souter said, the veter-ans' council "clearly decided to exclude a message it did not like from the communication it chose to make." Such exclusion, he said, was protected under the First Amendment: "Since all speech inherently involves choices of 'what to say and what to leave unsaid,' one important manifestation of the principle of free speech is that one who chooses to speak may also decide 'what not to say.' "

Souter rejected arguments that the parade was a "public accommoda-tion" and thus subject to state law barring discrimination, including dis-crimination against homosexuals. He added that the state is free to try to change discriminatory conduct, but it is not free to interfere with a speaker, in this instance the parade organizers, based on the content of the speech. "Disapproval of a private speaker's statement does not legitimize use of the [state's] power to compel the speaker to alter the message by including one more acceptable to others," Souter concluded. Souter also observed that the parade organizers did not attempt to exclude homosex-uals from other parade units carrying messages with which the organiz-ers agreed.

Following are excerpts from the opinion, written by Justice David H. Souter, in the case of Hurley v. Irish-American Gay, Les-bian and Bisexual Group of Boston, *in which the Supreme Court ruled, 9–0, on June 19, 1995, that a private group had a consti-tutional right under the First Amendment to exclude a gay rights group from its St. Patrick's Day parade:*

No. 94–749

John J. Hurley and South Boston Allied War Veterans Council, Petitioners *v.* Irish-American Gay, Lesbian and Bisexual Group of Boston, etc., et al.	On writ of certiorari to the Supreme Judicial Court of Massachusetts

[June 19, 1995]

JUSTICE SOUTER delivered the opinion of the Court.

The issue in this case is whether Massachusetts may require private citizens who organize a parade to include among the marchers a group imparting a message the organizers do not wish to convey. We hold that such a mandate violates the First Amendment.

I

March 17 is set aside for two celebrations in South Boston. As early as 1737, some people in Boston observed the feast of the apostle to Ireland, and since 1776 the day has marked the evacuation of royal troops and Loyalists from the city, prompted by the guns captured at Ticonderoga and set up on Dorchester Heights under General Washington's command. Washington himself reportedly drew on the earlier tradition in choosing "St. Patrick" as the response to "Boston," the password used in the colonial lines on evacuation day. Although the General Court of Massachusetts did not officially designate March 17 as Evacuation Day until 1938, the City Council of Boston had previously sponsored public celebrations of Evacuation Day. . . .

The tradition of formal sponsorship by the city came to an end in 1947, however, when Mayor James Michael Curley himself granted authority to organize and conduct the St. Patrick's Day–Evacuation Day Parade to the petitioner South Boston Allied War Veterans Council, an unincorporated association of individuals elected from various South Boston veterans groups. Every year since that time, the Council has applied for and received a permit for the parade, which at times has included as many as 20,000 marchers and drawn up to 1 million watchers. No other applicant has ever applied for that permit. Through 1992, the city allowed the Council to use the city's official seal, and provided printing services as well as direct funding.

1992 was the year that a number of gay, lesbian, and bisexual descendants of the Irish immigrants joined together with other supporters to form the respondent organization, GLIB, to march in the parade as a way to express pride in their Irish heritage as openly gay, lesbian, and bisexual individuals, to demonstrate that there are such men and women among those so descended, and to express their solidarity with like individuals who sought to march in New York's St. Patrick's Day Parade. Although the Council denied GLIB's application to take part in the 1992 parade, GLIB obtained a state-court order to include its contingent, which marched—uneventfully— among that year's 10,000 participants and 750,000 spectators.

In 1993, after the Council had again refused to admit GLIB to the upcoming parade, the organization and some of its members filed this suit against the Council, the individual petitioner John J. "Wacko" Hurley, and the City of Boston, alleging violations of the State and Federal Constitutions and of the state public accommodations law, which prohibits "any distinction, discrimination or restriction on account of . . . sexual orientation . . . relative to the admission of any person to, or treatment in any place of public accommodation, resort or amusement.". . . [T]he state trial court ruled that the parade fell within the statutory definition of a public accommodation, which includes "any place . . . which is open to and accepts or solicits the patronage of the general public and, without limiting the generality of this definition, whether or not it be . . . (6) a boardwalk or other public highway [or] . . . (8) a place of public amusement, recreation, sport, exercise or entertainment.". . . .

The Supreme Judicial Court of Massachusetts affirmed, seeing nothing clearly erroneous in the trial judge's findings that GLIB was excluded from the parade based on the sexual orientation of its members, that it was impossible to detect an expressive purpose in the parade, that there was no state action, and that the parade was a public accommodation within the meaning of [the state law]. . . .

We granted certiorari to determine whether the requirement to admit a parade contingent expressing a message not of the private organizers' own choosing violates the First Amendment. We hold that it does and reverse.

II [omitted]

III

A

If there were no reason for a group of people to march from here to there except to reach a destination, they could make the trip without expressing any message beyond the fact of the march itself. Some people might call such a procession a parade, but it would not be much of one. Real "[p]arades are public dramas of social relations, and in them performers define who can be a social actor and what subjects and ideas are available for communication and consideration." Hence, we use the word "parade" to indicate marchers who are making some sort of collective point, not just to each other but to bystanders along the way. Indeed a parade's dependence on watchers is so extreme that nowadays, as with Bishop Berkeley's celebrated tree, "if a parade or demonstration receives no media coverage, it may as well not have happened." Parades are thus a form of expression, not just motion, and the inherent expressiveness of marching to make a point explains our cases involving protest marches. In *Gregory* v. *Chicago* (1969), for example, petitioners had taken part in a procession to express their grievances to the city government, and we held that such a "march, if peaceful and orderly, falls well within the sphere of conduct protected by the First Amendment." Similarly, in *Edwards* v. *South Carolina* (1963), where petitioners had joined in a march of protest and pride, carrying placards and singing *The Star Spangled Banner*, we held that the activities "reflect an exercise of these basic constitutional rights in their most pristine and classic form."

The protected expression that inheres in a parade is not limited to its banners and songs, however, for the Constitution looks beyond written or spoken words as mediums of expression. Noting that "[s]ymbolism is a primitive but effective way of communicating ideas," *West Virginia Bd. of Ed.* v. *Barnette* (1943), our cases have recognized that the First Amendment shields such acts as saluting a flag (and refusing to do so), wearing an arm band to protest a war, *Tinker* v. *Des Moines Independent Community School Dist.* (1969), displaying a red flag, *Stromberg* v. *California* (1931), and even "[m]arching, walking or parading" in uniforms displaying the swastika, *National Socialist Party of America* v. *Skokie*. As some of these examples show, a narrow, succinctly articulable message is not a condition of constitutional protection, which if confined to expressions conveying a "particularized message," would never reach the unquestionably shielded painting of Jackson Pollock, music of Arnold Schoenberg, or Jabberwocky verse of Lewis Carroll.

Not many marches, then, are beyond the realm of expressive parades, and the South Boston celebration is not one of them. Spectators line the streets; people march in costumes and uniforms, carrying flags and banners with all sorts of messages (e.g., "England get out of Ireland," "Say no to drugs"); marching bands and pipers play, floats are pulled along, and the whole show is broadcast over Boston television. To be sure, we agree with the state courts that in spite of excluding some applicants, the Council is rather lenient in admitting participants. But a private speaker does not forfeit constitutional protection simply by combining multifarious voices, or by failing to edit their themes to isolate an exact message as the exclusive subject matter of the speech. Nor, under our precedent, does First Amendment protection require a speaker to generate, as an original matter, each item featured in the communication. Cable operators, for example, are engaged in protected speech activities even when they only select programming originally produced by others. . . .

Respondents' participation as a unit in the parade was equally expressive. GLIB was formed for the very purpose of marching in it, as the trial court found, in order to celebrate its members' identity as openly gay, lesbian, and bisexual descendants of the Irish immigrants, to show that there are such individuals in the community, and to support the like men and women who sought to march in the New York parade. The organization distributed a fact sheet describing the members' intentions, and the record otherwise corroborates the expressive nature of GLIB's participation. In 1993, members of GLIB marched behind a shamrock-strewn banner with the simple inscription "Irish American Gay, Lesbian and Bisexual Group of Boston." GLIB understandably seeks to communicate its ideas as part of the existing parade, rather than staging one of its own.

B

The Massachusetts public accommodations law under which respondents brought suit has a venerable history. At common law, innkeepers, smiths, and others who "made profession of a public employment," were prohibited from refusing, without good reason, to serve a customer. . . .

After the Civil War, the Commonwealth of Massachusetts was the first State to codify this principle to ensure access to public accommodations regardless of race. . . . In prohibiting discrimination "in any licensed inn, in any public place of amusement, public conveyance or public meeting," the original statute already expanded upon the common law, which had not conferred any right of access to places of public amusement. As with many public accommodations statutes across the Nation, the legislature continued to broaden the scope of legislation, to the point that the law today prohibits discrimination on the basis of "race, color, religious creed, national origin, sex, sexual orientation, . . . deafness, blindness or any physical or mental disability or ancestry" in "the admission of any person to, or treatment in any place of public accommodation, resort or amusement." Provisions like these are well within the State's usual power to enact when a legislature has reason to believe that a given group is the target of discrimination, and they do not, as a general matter, violate the First or Fourteenth Amendments. . . . Nor is this statute unusual in any obvious way, since it does not, on its face, target speech or discriminate on the basis of its content, the focal point of its prohibition being rather on the act of discriminating against individuals in the provision of publicly available goods, privileges, and services on the proscribed grounds.

C

In the case before us, however, the Massachusetts law has been applied in a peculiar way. Its enforcement does not address any dispute about the participation of openly gay, lesbian, or bisexual individuals in various units admitted to the parade. The petitioners disclaim any intent to exclude homosexuals as such, and no individual member of GLIB claims to have been excluded from parading as a member of any group that the Council has approved to march. Instead, the disagreement goes to the admission of GLIB as its own parade unit carrying its own banner. Since every participating unit affects the message conveyed by the private organizers, the state courts' application of the statute produced an order essentially requiring petitioners to alter the expressive content of their parade. Although the state courts spoke of the parade as a place of public accommodation, once the expressive character of both the parade and the marching GLIB contingent is understood, it becomes apparent that the state courts' application of the statute had the effect of declaring the sponsors' speech itself to be the public accommodation. Under this approach any contingent of protected individuals with a message would have the right to participate in petitioners' speech, so that the communication produced by the private organizers would be shaped by all those protected by the law who wished to join in with some expressive demonstration of their own. But this use of the State's power violates the fundamental rule of protection under the First Amendment, that a speaker has the autonomy to choose the content of his own message.

"Since all speech inherently involves choices of what to say and what to leave unsaid," *Pacific Gas & Electric Co.* v. *Public Utilities Comm'n of Cal.* (1986) (plurality opinion), one important manifestation of the principle of free speech is that one who chooses to speak may also decide "what not to say." Although the State may at times "prescribe what shall be orthodox in commercial advertising" by requiring the dissemination of "purely factual and uncontroversial information," *Zauderer* v. *Office of Disciplinary Counsel of Supreme Court of Ohio* (1985) outside that context it may not compel affirmance of a belief with which the speaker disagrees. Indeed this general rule, that the speaker has the right to tailor the speech, applies not only to expressions of value, opinion, or endorsement, but equally to statements of fact the speaker would rather avoid, subject, perhaps, to the permissive law of defamation. Nor is the rule's benefit restricted to the press, being enjoyed by business corporations generally and by ordinary people engaged in unsophisticated expression as well as by professional publishers. Its point is simply the point of all speech protection, which is to shield just those choices of content that in someone's eyes are misguided, or even hurtful.

Petitioners' claim to the benefit of this principle of autonomy to control one's own speech is as sound as the South Boston parade is expressive. Rather like a composer, the Council selects the expressive units of the parade from potential participants, and though the score may not produce a particularized message, each contingent's expression in the Council's eyes comports with what merits celebration on that day. Even if this view gives the Council credit for a more considered judgment than it actively made, the Council clearly decided to exclude a message it did not like from the communication it chose to make, and that is enough to invoke its right as a private speaker to shape its expression by speaking on one subject while remaining silent on another. The message it disfavored is not difficult to identify. Although GLIB's point (like the Council's) is not wholly articulate, a contingent marching behind the organization's banner would at least bear witness to the fact that some Irish are gay, lesbian, or bisexual, and the presence of the organized marchers would suggest their view that people of their sexual orientations have as much claim to unqualified social acceptance as heterosexuals and indeed as members of parade units organized around other identifying characteristics. The parade's organizers may not believe these facts about Irish sexuality to be so, or they may object to unqualified social acceptance of gays and lesbians or have some other reason for wishing to keep GLIB's message out of the parade. But whatever the reason, it boils down to the choice of a speaker not to propound a particular point of view, and that choice is presumed to lie beyond the government's power to control. . . .

The statute is a piece of protective legislation that announces no purpose beyond the object both expressed and apparent in its provisions, which is to prevent any denial of access to (or discriminatory treatment in) public accommodations on proscribed grounds, including sexual orientation. On its face, the object of the law is to ensure by statute for gays and lesbians desiring to make use of public accommodations what the old common law promised to any member of the public wanting a meal at the inn, that accepting the usual terms of service, they will not be turned away merely on the proprietor's exercise of personal preference. When the law is applied to expressive activity in the way it was done here, its apparent object is simply to require speakers to modify the content of their expression to whatever extent beneficiaries of the law choose to alter it with messages of their own. But in the absence of some further, legitimate end, this object is merely to allow exactly what the general rule of speaker's autonomy forbids.

It might, of course, have been argued that a broader objective is apparent: that the ultimate point of forbidding acts of discrimination toward certain classes is to produce a society free of the corresponding biases. Requiring access to a speaker's message would thus be not an end in itself, but a means to produce speakers free of the biases, whose expressive conduct would be at least neutral toward the particular classes, obviating any future need for correction. But if this indeed is the point of applying the state law to expressive conduct, it is a decidedly fatal objective. Having availed itself of the public thoroughfares "for purposes of assembly [and] communicating thoughts between citizens," the Council is engaged in a use of the streets that has "from ancient times, been a part of the privileges, immunities, rights, and liberties of citizens," *Hague* v. *Committee for Industrial Organization* (1939) (opinion of Roberts, J.) Our tradition of free speech commands that a speaker who takes to the street corner to express his views in this way should be free from interference by the State based on the content of what he says. The very idea that a noncommercial speech restriction be used to produce thoughts and statements acceptable to some groups or, indeed, all people, grates on the First Amendment, for it amounts to nothing less than a proposal to limit speech in the service of orthodox expression. The Speech Clause has no more certain antithesis. While the law is free to promote all sorts of conduct in place of harmful behavior, it is not free to interfere with speech for no better reason than promoting an approved message or discouraging a disfavored one, however enlightened either purpose may strike the government. . . .

IV

Our holding today rests not on any particular view about the Council's message but on the Nation's commitment to protect freedom of speech. Disapproval of a private speaker's statement does not legitimize use of the Commonwealth's power to compel the speaker to alter the message by including one more acceptable to others. Accordingly, the judgment of the Supreme Judicial Court is reversed and the case remanded for proceedings not inconsistent with this opinion.

It is so ordered.

SOUTHERN BAPTIST CONVENTION APOLOGY FOR RACISM
June 20, 1995

The Southern Baptist Convention, the largest Protestant denomination in the country and one born out of a defense of slavery, apologized to African-Americans for "condoning and perpetuating" racism and vowed to eradicate racism from the church and its people. The apology came in the form of a resolution that passed overwhelmingly June 20 by a show of hands among the 20,000 delegates to the convention's annual meeting in Atlanta.

Symbolically, the apology was approved on the one hundred fiftieth anniversary of the founding of the convention, which was created in 1845 by southern churchmen who split from the American Baptist Convention after that denomination refused to appoint a slaveholder as a missionary. Many Southern Baptist congregations were also adamantly opposed to the civil rights movement of the 1950s and 1960s, a fact the resolution acknowledged.

The apology came even as conservative leaders of the convention seemed to be adopting harder positions in opposition to abortion, homosexuality, and ordaining women as pastors. The decision to issue the resolution tacitly took account of the changing demographics of the denomination, which had 15.6 million members, the vast majority of them white southerners. Of the approximately 40,000 congregations, a church official said, nearly 1,900 were predominantly black, a figure that was growing by nearly 200 congregations a year. Hispanics predominated in another 3,000 congregations, Korean immigrants in 800, and American Indians in about 700.

In the resolution, the convention acknowledged its long history of racism, from "the significant role that slavery played in the formation" of the church through more modern times when the church "did not take bold initiatives to secure" the civil rights of blacks "and often tragically stood in the way of such initiatives taken by others." In offering its apology and asking forgiveness, the resolution stated that the convention's "own healing is at stake, that racism discredits the Gospel we proclaim, that racism hinders the reconciling works of Christ, and that racism impedes our own development as a denomination."

Gary L. Frost, a pastor from Youngstown, Ohio, and the only African-American in the convention's leadership, accepted the apology on behalf of all black Southern Baptists. "We pray that the genuineness of your repentance will be reflected in your attitude and your reactions," Frost told the delegates in Atlanta.

Other reaction ranged from enthusiastic to skeptical. The Rev. Calvin O. Butts III, pastor of the Abyssinian Baptist Church in Harlem, called it a "marvelous statement." The Rev. Arlee Griffin Jr., pastor of the Berean Missionary Baptist Church in Brooklyn and historian of the Progressive National Baptist Convention, called the resolution a first step. "It is only when one's request for forgiveness is reflected in a change of attitude and actions that the victim can then believe that the request for forgiveness is authentic," Griffin told the New York Times.

Following is the text of the "Resolution on Racial Reconciliation," adopted June 20, 1995, by the Southern Baptist Convention at its annual meeting, in which the church apologized to blacks for past racism:

Adopted by the Southern Baptist Convention Christian Life Commission May 22, 1995, Race Relations Consultation, to be presented to the Sesquicentennial Southern Baptist Convention meeting in Atlanta, Georgia, June 22, 1995.

WHEREAS, since its founding in 1845, the Southern Baptist Convention has been an effective instrument of God in missions, evangelism, and social ministry; and

WHEREAS, the Scriptures teach that "Eve is the mother of all living" (Genesis 3:20), and that "God shows no partiality, but in every nation whoever fears him and works righteousness is accepted by him" (Acts 10:34–35), and that God has "made from one blood every nation of men to dwell on the face of the earth" (Acts 17:26); and

WHEREAS our relationship to African-Americans has been crippled from the beginning by the significant role that slavery played in the formation of the Southern Baptist Convention; and

WHEREAS, many of our Southern Baptist forbears defended the "right" to own slaves, and either participated in, supported, or acquiesced in the particularly inhumane nature of American slavery; and

WHEREAS in later years Southern Baptists, though a dominant Christian denomination in the South, did not take bold initiatives to secure the civil rights of African-American people, and often tragically stood in the way of such initiatives taken by others; and

WHEREAS, racism has borne the dreadful fruit of discrimination, oppression, injustice, and violence, both in the Civil War and throughout the history of our nation; and

WHEREAS, racism has divided the body of Christ and Southern Baptists in particular, and separated us from our African-American brothers and sisters; and

WHEREAS, even since the end of slavery, many of our congregations have perpetuated racism by intentionally and/or unintentionally excluding African-Americans from worship, membership, and leadership; and

WHEREAS, racism profoundly distorts our understanding of Christian morality, leading many Southern Baptists to believe the lie that racial prejudice and discrimination are compatible with the Gospel; and

WHEREAS, Jesus performed the ministry of reconciliation to restore sinners to a right relationship with the Heavenly Father, and to restore right relations among all human beings, especially within the family of faith.

BE IT THEREFORE RESOLVED, that we, the messengers of the Sesquicentennial meeting, of the Southern Baptist Convention, assembling in Atlanta, Georgia, June 20–22, 1995, unwaveringly denounce racism, in all its forms, as deplorable sin; and

BE IT FURTHER RESOLVED, that we affirm the Bible's teaching that every human life is sacred, and is of equal and immeasurable worth, made in God's image, regardless of race or ethnicity (Genesis 1:27), and that, with respect to salvation through Christ, "There is neither Jew nor Greek, there is neither slave nor free, there is neither male nor female, for [we] are all one in Christ Jesus" (Galatians 3:28); and

BE IT FURTHER RESOLVED, that we lament and repudiate historic acts of evil such as slavery, from which we continue to reap a bitter harvest (Ezekiel 18:2), and we recognize that the racism which yet plagues our culture today is inextricably tied to the past; and

BE IT FURTHER RESOLVED, that we repent both of conscious and unconscious racism (Psalm 19:13), and apologize to all African-Americans for condoning and perpetuating individual and systemic racism in our lifetime; and

BE IT FURTHER RESOLVED, that we ask for forgiveness from our African-American brothers and sisters, acknowledging that our own healing is at stake, that racism discredits the Gospel we proclaim, that racism hinders the reconciling work of Christ, and that racism impedes our own development as a denomination; and

BE IT FURTHER RESOLVED, that we hereby commit ourselves to eradicate racism in all its forms from the Southern Baptist Convention and its people; and

BE IT FURTHER RESOLVED, that we commit ourselves to be "doers of the Word" (James 1:22) by pursuing racial reconciliation with our neighbors, co-workers, classmates, and brothers and sisters in Christ, to the end that our light would so shine before others, "that they may see [our] good works and glorify [our] Father in heaven" (Matthew 5:16); and

BE IT FINALLY RESOLVED, that we pledge our commitment to the Great Commission task of preaching the Gospel to all nations, confessing that in the church God is calling together one people from every tribe and nation (Revelation 5:9), and proclaiming that the Gospel of our Lord Jesus Christ is the only certain and sufficient ground upon which redeemed persons will stand together in restored brotherhood and sisterhood.

SUPREME COURT ON
RANDOM DRUG TESTING
June 26, 1995

The Supreme Court ruled, 6–3, June 26 that it was not an unreasonable search in violation of the Fourth Amendment to randomly perform drug tests on junior and senior high school athletes. It was the first time that the Court had upheld random drug testing of individuals without a showing that they were suspected of using drugs.

Writing for the majority, Justice Antonin Scalia said that, given the circumstances of the case, the school's interest in curbing drug use outweighed students' rights under the Fourth Amendment. "School years are the time when the physical, psychological, and addictive effects of drugs are most severe," Scalia wrote. "Deterring drug use by our nation's schoolchildren is at least as important as enhancing efficient enforcement of the nation's laws against the importation of drugs."

In dissent, Justice Sandra Day O'Connor said that the Court's ruling meant that millions of students, "an overwhelming majority of whom have given school officials no reason whatsoever to suspect they use drugs at school, are open to an intrusive bodily harm."

A Scheme to Curb Widespread Drug Abuse

The case, Vernonia School District 47J v. Acton, *began in a small logging town thirty-five miles northwest of Portland, Oregon, when school officials sought to control increasing drug and alcohol abuse among students. By 1989, despite drug education and other efforts, classroom disruption had worsened and disciplinary problems had reached "epidemic proportions." According to school administrators, many of the school athletes not only were drug users but were known to be leaders of the drug culture. In their petition to the Court, the administrators said they "feared that the corruption of the school's leading athletes would have a significant poisoning impact on the broader student population, including the younger and more impressionable elementary school students who emulated the older athletes."*

With the approval of the parents who attended a special meeting, school officials instituted a program under which all students who signed up for interscholastic sports would be tested at the beginning of the sport's season and then randomly throughout the year. Students were required to produce a urine sample, which was analyzed for cocaine, marijuana, and amphetamines. A positive result could result in suspension from sports.

The specific case arose when the school district refused to allow twelve-year-old James Acton to play football after he and his parents refused to sign the form consenting to the urinalysis tests. Acton's parent sued the school district.

A federal district court upheld the random testing policy, but the Ninth Circuit Court of Appeals declared the policy to be a violation of both the Fourth Amendment's protection against unreasonable searches and the Oregon constitution's privacy protection. "Children are compelled to attend school, but nothing suggests that they lose their right to privacy in their excretory functions when they do so," Judge Ferdinand F. Fernandez wrote for the appeals court.

The Majority and Dissenting Opinions

In his majority opinion, Scalia emphasized that children in the custody of the government, in this case the public school, do not have the same protection as free adults. When, as in this case, Scalia wrote, "the government acts as guardian and tutor the relevant question is whether the search is one that a reasonable guardian and tutor might undertake."

In answering that question, Scalia cited three reasons for finding the random testing program reasonable. First, he said, student athletes have lower expectations of privacy than others. "School sports are not for the bashful," Scalia said, describing the communal nature of locker rooms. Second, although the student athletes are monitored when they produce urine samples for testing, the conditions of that monitoring "are nearly identical to those typically encountered in public restrooms, which men, women, and especially school children use daily" and thus have a negligible effect on the students' privacy. Finally, Scalia said, the school district's concern about drug abuse was important enough to justify the random testing. Not only can drug use physically and psychologically harm the student athletes within the school's care, but the "effects of a drug-infested school are visited not just upon the users, but upon the entire school body and faculty," Scalia said.

Chief Justice William H. Rehnquist and Justices Stephen G. Breyer, Ruth Bader Ginsburg, Anthony M. Kennedy, and Clarence Thomas voted with Scalia.

Joining O'Connor in dissent were Justices David H. Souter and John Paul Stevens. "For most of our constitutional history," O'Connor wrote, "mass, suspicionless searches have been generally considered per se *unreasonable within the meaning of the Fourth Amendment." O'Connor argued that a random testing program that included individuals not suspected of using drugs would be permissible only if a suspicion-based program proved ineffectual. "Because that is not the case here, I dissent."*

Reaction to the Decision

The White House had filed a brief supporting the Oregon school district, and the White House adviser on drug control policy, Lee P. Brown, hailed the decision as a "victory for kids" that would help maintain drug-free schools. The contrasting opinion was voiced by Steven Shapiro, the legal director for the American Civil Liberties Union, which had argued the case in behalf of Acton and his family. The decision "makes students' rights the latest casualty of the 'War on Drugs,'" Shapiro said.

Although Brown predicted that schools everywhere would set up drug-testing programs for its athletes, other were not so sure. According to the National School Boards Association, very few schools had drug-testing programs, in large part because their constitutionality was suspect. The cost was another prohibitive factor. A lawyer for the association told the New York Times *that schools would consider setting up testing programs in light of the decision. "But it's not something you just jump into," she said, noting that schools districts would have to seek the support of their communities to institute such programs.*

Following are excerpts from the majority and dissenting opinions in the case of Vernonia School District 47J v. Acton, *in which the Supreme Court ruled on June 26, 1995, that random drug tests of students in junior and senior high school did not constitute an unreasonable search prohibited by the Fourth Amendment to the Constitution:*

No. 94–590

Vernonia School District 47J, Petitioner *v.* Wayne Acton	On writ of certiorari to the United States Court of Appeals for the Ninth Circuit

[June 26, 1995]

JUSTICE SCALIA delivered the opinion of the Court.

The Student Athlete Drug Policy adopted by School District 47J in the town of Vernonia, Oregon, authorizes random urinalysis drug testing of students who participate in the District's school athletics programs. We granted certiorari to decide whether this violates the Fourth and Fourteenth Amendments to the United States Constitution.

[I omitted]

II

The Fourth Amendment to the United States Constitution provides that the Federal Government shall not violate "[t]he right of the people to be secure in their persons, houses, papers, and effects, against unreasonable searches and seizures. . . ." We have held that the Fourteenth Amendment extends this constitutional guarantee to searches and seizures by state officers, including public school officials, *New Jersey* v. *T. L. O.* (1985). In *Skinner* v. *Railway Labor Executives' Assn.* (1989), we held that state-compelled collection and testing of urine, such as that required by the Student Athlete Drug Policy, constitutes a "search" subject to the demands of the Fourth Amendment. See also *Treasury Employees* v. *Von Raab* (1989).

As the text of the Fourth Amendment indicates, the ultimate measure of the constitutionality of a governmental search is "reasonableness." At least in a case such as this, where there was no clear practice, either approving or disapproving the type of search at issue, at the time the constitutional provision was enacted, whether a particular search meets the reasonableness standard " 'is judged by balancing its intrusion on the individual's Fourth Amendment interests against its promotion of legitimate governmental interests.' " Where a search is undertaken by law enforcement officials to discover evidence of criminal wrongdoing, this Court has said that reasonableness generally requires the obtaining of a judicial warrant. Warrants cannot be issued, of course, without the showing of probable cause required by the Warrant Clause. But a warrant is not required to establish the reasonableness of *all* government searches; and when a warrant is not required (and the Warrant Clause therefore not applicable), probable cause is not invariably required either. A search unsupported by probable cause can be constitutional, we have said, "when special needs, beyond the normal need for law enforcement, make the warrant and probable cause requirement impracticable." *Griffin* v. *Wisconsin* (1987).

We have found such "special needs" to exist in the public-school context. . . . The school search we approved in *T. L. O.*, while not based on probable cause, *was* based on individualized *suspicion* of wrongdoing. As we explicitly acknowledged, however, " 'the Fourth Amendment imposes no irreducible requirement of such suspicion.' " We have upheld suspicionless searches and seizures to conduct drug testing of railroad personnel involved in train accidents, [*Skinner*], to conduct random drug testing of federal customs officers who carry arms or are involved in drug interdiction [*Von Raab*], and to maintain automobile checkpoints looking for illegal immigrants and contraband, *United States* v. *Martinez-Fuerte* [1976], and drunk drivers, *Michigan Dept. of State Police* v. *Sitz* (1990).

III

The first factor to be considered is the nature of the privacy interest upon which the search here at issue intrudes. The Fourth Amendment does not protect all subjective expectations of privacy, but only those that society recognizes as "legitimate." What expectations are legitimate varies, of course, with context. . . . In addition, the legitimacy of certain privacy expectations vis-à-vis the State may depend upon the individual's legal relationship with the State. . . . Central, in our view, to the present case is the fact that the subjects of the Policy are (1) children, who (2) have been committed to the temporary custody of the State as schoolmaster. . . .

Fourth Amendment rights, no less than First and Fourteenth Amendment rights, are different in public schools than elsewhere; the "reasonableness" inquiry cannot disregard the schools' custodial and tutelary responsibility for children. For their own good and that of their classmates, public school children are routinely required to submit to various physical examinations, and to be vaccinated against various diseases. . . .

Legitimate privacy expectations are even less with regard to student athletes. School sports are not for the bashful. They require "suiting up" before each practice or event, and showering and changing afterwards. Public school locker rooms, the usual sites for these activities, are not notable for the privacy they afford. The locker rooms in Vernonia are typical: no individual dressing rooms are provided; shower heads are lined up along a wall, unseparated by any sort of partition or curtain; not even all the toilet stalls have doors. . . .

There is an additional respect in which school athletes have a reduced expectation of privacy. By choosing to "go out for the team," they voluntarily subject themselves to a degree of regulation even higher than that imposed on students generally. In Vernonia's public schools, they must submit to a preseason physical exam (James testified that his included the giving of a urine sample), they must acquire adequate insurance coverage or sign an insurance waiver, maintain a minimum grade point average, and comply with any "rules of conduct, dress, training hours and related matters as may be established for each sport by the head coach and athletic director with the principal's approval." Somewhat like adults who choose to participate in a "closely regulated industry," students who voluntarily participate in school athletics have reason to expect intrusions upon normal rights and privileges, including privacy.

IV

Having considered the scope of the legitimate expectation of privacy at issue here, we turn next to the character of the intrusion that is complained of. We recognized in *Skinner* that collecting the samples for urinalysis intrudes upon "an excretory function traditionally shielded by great privacy." We noted, however, that the degree of intrusion depends upon the manner in which production of the urine sample is monitored. Under the District's Policy, male students produce samples at a urinal along a wall. They remain fully clothed and are only observed from behind, if at all. Female students produce samples in an enclosed stall, with a female monitor standing outside listening only for sounds of tampering. These conditions are nearly identical to those typically encountered in public restrooms, which men, women, and especially school children use daily. Under such conditions, the privacy interests compromised by the process of obtaining the urine sample are in our view negligible.

The other privacy-invasive aspect of urinalysis is, of course, the information it discloses concerning the state of the subject's body, and the materials he has ingested. In this regard it is significant that the tests at issue here look only for drugs, and not for whether the student is, for example, epileptic, pregnant, or diabetic. Moreover, the drugs for which the samples are screened are standard, and do not vary according to the identity of the student. And finally, the results of the tests are disclosed only to a limited class of school personnel who have a need to know; and they are not turned over to law enforcement authorities or used for any internal disciplinary function. . . .

V

Finally, we turn to consider the nature and immediacy of the governmental concern at issue here, and the efficacy of this means for meeting it. In both *Skinner* and *Von Raab*, we characterized the government interest motivating the search as "compelling." *Skinner* (interest in preventing railway accidents); *Von Raab* (interest in insuring fitness of customs officials to interdict drugs and handle firearms). Relying on these cases, the District Court held that because the District's program also called for drug testing in the absence of individualized suspicion, the District "must demonstrate a 'compelling need' for the program." The Court of Appeals appears to have agreed with this view. It is a mistake, however, to think that the phrase "compelling state interest," in the Fourth Amendment context, describes a fixed, minimum quantum of governmental concern, so that one can dispose of a case by answering in isolation the question: Is there a compelling state interest here? Rather, the phrase describes an interest which appears *important enough* to justify the particular search at hand, in light of other factors which show the search to be relatively intrusive upon a genuine expectation of privacy. Whether that relatively high degree of government concern is necessary in this case or not, we think it is met.

That the nature of the concern is important—indeed, perhaps compelling—can hardly be doubted. Deterring drug use by our Nation's schoolchildren is at least as important as enhancing efficient enforcement of the Nation's laws against the importation of drugs . . . or deterring drug use by engineers and trainmen. . . . School years are the time when the physical, psychological, and addictive effects of drugs are most severe. . . . And of course the effects of a drug-infested school are visited not just upon the users, but upon the entire student body and faculty, as the educational process is disrupted. In the present case, moreover, the necessity for the State to act is magnified by the fact that this evil is being visited not just upon individuals at large, but upon children for whom it has undertaken a special responsibility of care and direction. Finally, it must not be lost sight of that this program is directed more narrowly to drug use by school athletes, where the risk of immediate physical harm to the drug user or those with whom he is playing his sport is particularly high. Apart from psychological effects, which include impairment of judgment, slow reaction time, and a lessening of the perception of pain, the particular drugs screened by the District's Policy have been demonstrated to pose substantial physical risks to athletes. . . .

As for the immediacy of the District's concerns: We are not inclined to question—indeed, we could not possibly find clearly erroneous —the District Court's conclusion that "a large segment of the student body, particularly those involved in interscholastic athletics, was in a state of rebellion," that "[d]isciplinary actions had reached 'epidemic proportions,' " and that "the rebellion was being fueled by alcohol and drug abuse as well as by the student's misperceptions about the drug culture." That is an immediate crisis of greater proportions than existed in *Skinner*, where we upheld the Government's drug testing program based on findings of drug use by railroad employees nationwide, without proof that a problem existed on the particular railroads whose employees were subject to the test. And of much greater proportions than existed in *Von Raab*, where there was no documented history of drug use by any customs officials.

As to the efficacy of this means for addressing the problem: It seems to us self-evident that a drug problem largely fueled by the "role model" effect of athletes' drug use, and of particular danger to athletes, is effectively addressed by making sure that athletes do not use drugs. Respondents argue that a "less intrusive means to the same end" was available, namely, "drug testing on suspicion of drug use." We have repeatedly refused to declare that only the "least intrusive" search practicable can be reasonable under the Fourth Amendment. Respondents' alternative entails substantial difficulties—if it is indeed practicable at all. . . .

VI

Taking into account all the factors we have considered above—the decreased expectation of privacy, the relative unobtrusiveness of the search, and the severity of the need met by the search—we conclude Vernonia's Policy is reasonable and hence constitutional.

We caution against the assumption that suspicionless drug testing will readily pass constitutional muster in other contexts. The most significant element in this case is the first we discussed: that the Policy was undertaken in furtherance of the government's responsibilities, under a public school system, as guardian and tutor of children entrusted to its care. Just as when the government conducts a search in its capacity as employer (a warrantless search of an absent employee's desk to obtain an urgently needed file, for example), the relevant question is whether that intrusion upon privacy is one that a reasonable employer might engage in; so also when the government acts as guardian and tutor the relevant question is whether the search is one that a reasonable guardian and tutor might undertake. Given the findings of need made by the District Court, we conclude that in the present case it is.

We may note that the primary guardians of Vernonia's schoolchildren appear to agree. The record shows no objection to this districtwide program by any parents other than the couple before us here—even though, as we have described, a public meeting was held to obtain parents' views. We find insufficient basis to contradict the judgment of Vernonia's parents, its school board, and the District Court, as to what was reasonably in the interest of these children under the circumstances.

* * *

The Ninth Circuit held that Vernonia's Policy not only violated the Fourth Amendment, but also, by reason of that violation, contravened Article I, ¶9 of the Oregon Constitution. Our conclusion that the former holding was in error means that the latter holding rested on a flawed premise. We therefore vacate the judgment, and remand the case to the Court of Appeals for further proceedings consistent with this opinion.

It is so ordered.

JUSTICE O'CONNOR, with whom JUSTICE STEVENS and JUSTICE SOUTER join, dissenting.

The population of our Nation's public schools, grades 7 through 12, numbers around 18 million. By the reasoning of today's decision, the millions of these students who participate in interscholastic sports, an overwhelming majority of whom have given school officials no reason whatsoever to suspect they use drugs at school, are open to an intrusive bodily search.

In justifying this result, the Court dispenses with a requirement of individualized suspicion on considered policy grounds. First, it explains that precisely because *every* student athlete is being tested, there is no concern that school officials might act arbitrarily in choosing who to test. Second, a broad-based search regime, the Court reasons, dilutes the accusatory nature of the search. In making these policy arguments, of course, the Court sidesteps powerful, countervailing privacy concerns. Blanket searches, because they can involve "thousands or millions" of searches, "pos[e] a greater threat to liberty" than do suspicion-based ones, which "affec[t] one person at a time," *Illinois* v. *Krull* (1987) (O'CONNOR, J., dissenting). Searches based on individualized suspicion also afford potential targets considerable control over whether they will, in fact, be searched because a person can avoid such a search by not acting in an objectively suspicious way. And given that the surest way to avoid acting suspiciously is to avoid the underlying wrongdoing, the costs of such a regime, one would think, are minimal.

But whether a blanket search is "better" than a regime based on individualized suspicion is not a debate in which we should engage. In my view, it is not open to judges or government officials to decide on policy grounds which is better and which is worse. For most of our constitutional history, mass, suspicionless searches have been generally considered *per se* unreasonable within the meaning of the Fourth Amendment. And we have allowed exceptions in recent years only where it has been clear that a suspicion-based regime would be ineffectual. Because that is not the case here, I dissent.

I

[A omitted]

B

. . . [W]hether the Court is right that the District reasonably weighed the lesser intrusion of a suspicion-based scheme against its policy concerns is beside the point. As stated, a suspicion-based search regime is not just any less intrusive alternative; the individualized suspicion requirement has a legal pedigree as old as the Fourth Amendment itself, and it may not be easily cast aside in the name of policy concerns. It may only be forsaken, our cases in the personal search context have established, if a suspicion-based regime would likely be ineffectual.

But having misconstrued the fundamental role of the individualized suspicion requirement in Fourth Amendment analysis, the Court never seriously engages the practicality of such a requirement in the instant case. And that failure is crucial because nowhere is it less clear that an individualized suspicion requirement would be ineffectual than in the school context. In most schools, the entire pool of potential search targets—students—is under constant supervision by teachers and administrators and coaches, be it in classrooms, hallways, or locker rooms.

The record here indicates that the Vernonia schools are no exception. The great irony of this case is that most (though not all) of the evidence the District introduced to justify its suspicionless drug-testing program consisted of first- or second-hand stories of particular, identifiable students acting in ways that plainly gave rise to reasonable suspicion of in-school drug use—and thus that would have justified a drug-related search under our *T. L. O.* decision. . . . Small groups of students, for example, were observed by a teacher "passing joints back and forth" across the street at a restaurant before school and during school hours. Another group was caught skipping school and using drugs at one of the students' houses. Several students actually *admitted* their drug use to school officials (some of them being caught with marijuana pipes). One student presented himself to his teacher as "clearly obviously inebriated" and had to be sent home. Still another was observed dancing and singing at the top of his voice in the back of the classroom; when the teacher asked what was going on, he replied, "Well, I'm just high on life." To take a final example, on a certain road trip, the school wrestling coach smelled marijuana smoke in a hotel room occupied by four wrestlers, an observation that (after some questioning) would probably have given him reasonable suspicion to test one or all of them. . . .

In light of all this evidence of drug use by particular students, there is a substantial basis for concluding that a vigorous regime of suspicion-based testing (for which the District appears already to have rules in place) would have gone a long way toward solving Vernonia's school drug problem while preserving the Fourth Amendment rights of James Acton and others like him. And were there any doubt about such a conclusion, it is removed by indications in the record that suspicion-based testing could have been supplemented by an equally vigorous campaign to have Vernonia's parents encourage their children to submit to the District's *voluntary* drug testing program. In these circumstances, the Fourth Amendment dictates that a mass, suspicionless search regime is categorically unreasonable.

I recognize that a suspicion-based scheme, even where reasonably effective in controlling in-school drug use, may not be *as* effective as a mass, suspicionless testing regime. In one sense, that is obviously true—just as it is obviously true that suspicion-based law enforcement is not as effective as mass, suspicionless enforcement might be. "But there is nothing new in the realization" that Fourth Amendment protections come with a price. Indeed, the price we pay is higher in the criminal context, given that police do not closely observe the entire class of potential search targets (all citizens in the area) and must ordinarily adhere to the rigid requirements of a warrant and probable cause.

The principal counterargument to all this, central to the Court's opinion, is that the Fourth Amendment is more lenient with respect to school searches. That is no doubt correct, for, as the Court explains, schools have traditionally had special guardian-like responsibilities for children that necessitate a degree of constitutional leeway. This principle explains the considerable Fourth Amendment leeway we gave school officials in *T. L. O.* In that case, we held that children at school do not enjoy two of the Fourth Amendment's traditional categorical protections against unreasonable searches and seizures: the warrant requirement and the probable cause requirement. . . .

The instant case, however, asks whether the Fourth Amendment is even more lenient than that, *i.e.,* whether it is *so* lenient that students may be deprived of the Fourth Amendment's only remaining, and most basic, categorical protection: its strong preference for an individualized suspicion requirement, with its accompanying antipathy toward personally intrusive, blanket searches of mostly innocent people. . . .

For the contrary position, the Court relies on cases such as *T. L. O., Ingraham* v. *Wright* (1977), and *Goss* v. *Lopez* (1975). But I find the Court's reliance on these cases ironic. If anything, they affirm that schools have substantial constitutional leeway in carrying out their traditional mission of responding to *particularized* wrongdoing. See *T. L. O.* (leeway in investigating particularized wrongdoing); *Ingraham* (leeway in punishing particularized wrongdoing); *Goss* (leeway in choosing procedures by which particularized wrongdoing is punished).

By contrast, intrusive, blanket searches of school children, most of whom are innocent, for evidence of serious wrongdoing are not part of any traditional school function of which I am aware. Indeed, many schools, like many parents, prefer to trust their children unless given reason to do otherwise. As James Acton's father said on the witness stand, "[suspicionless testing] sends a message to children that are trying to be responsible citizens . . . that they have to prove that they're innocent. . . , and I think that kind of sets a bad tone for citizenship.". . .

[II omitted]

III

It cannot be too often stated that the greatest threats to our constitutional freedoms come in times of crisis. But we must also stay mindful that not all government responses to such times are hysterical overreactions; some crises are quite real, and when they are, they serve precisely as the compelling state interest that we have said may justify a measured intrusion on constitutional rights. The only way for judges to mediate these conflicting impulses is to do what they should do anyway: stay close to the record in each case that appears before them, and make their judgments based on that alone. Having reviewed the record here, I cannot avoid the conclusion that the District's suspicionless policy of testing all student-athletes sweeps too broadly, and too imprecisely, to be reasonable under the Fourth Amendment.

CLINTON, BOUTROS-GHALI ON UNITED NATIONS ANNIVERSARY
June 26, 1995

At a ceremony in San Francisco commemorating the fiftieth anniversary of the signing of the United Nations charter, President Bill Clinton on June 26 defended the world body against its harshest American critics but called for reform of the organization's "bloated" bureaucracy. UN Secretary General Boutros Boutros-Ghali called on member nations to renew "the dream of global cooperation" that led to the UN's founding at the end of World War II. Boutros-Ghali skirted the many controversies surrounding the United Nations and instead focused on its role in keeping the peace, fostering global development, and promoting democracy.

Clinton and Boutros-Ghali were featured speakers at a ceremony at the War Memorial Opera House, where President Harry Truman spoke after delegates representing fifty-one nations signed the UN charter in the closing weeks of the war. The ceremony was one of many celebrations marking the half-century point after the end of the war. Leaders around the world used those occasions to recall the agony of the war years, the reasons the war was fought, and the changes the world has seen in the intervening years. (Commemoration of the fiftieth anniversary of World War II, p. 216; Japanese apology, p. 302; French apology, p. 478)

Clinton's Praise for the UN

In his address, President Clinton challenged critics of the United Nations, especially those in Congress, but also sought to sustain U.S. pressure on behalf of organizational and political reforms within the United Nations and its related organizations. Clinton spoke of the "new isolationists," who, he said, agree that the United States must play a strong role overseas but who "refuse to supply the nonmilitary resources our nation needs to carry out our responsibilities" or who believe that "America must act alone" in foreign affairs.

The president did not name individuals, but aides said he was referring to congressional critics, such as Sen. Jesse Helms (R-N.C.), chairman of the Foreign Relations Committee, who wanted to end U.S. participation in most United Nations programs. The Republican-controlled Congress in 1995 voted sharp cuts in U.S. contributions to the United Nations.

Clinton praised UN efforts to thwart aggression, from the Korean War to the Persian Gulf War, and to make or keep peace, in southern Africa, Central America, and Southeast Asia. Clinton also praised UN development and antipoverty programs, such as those run by UNICEF and the World Health Organization.

Reforming the UN

Despite the UN's successes, Clinton said, the world body "does not work as well as it should" and "must be reformed." The United Nations, he said, "has grown too bloated, too often encouraging duplication, and spending resources on meetings rather than results." The member states must create a UN "that is more flexible, that operates more rapidly, that wastes less and produces more, and most importantly, that inspires confidence among our governments and our people."

Public support for the United Nations has waxed and waned over the years, depending on world events and the level of political rhetoric about the UN within the United States. According to Gallup Poll figures reported by the New York Times, *American dissatisfaction with the United Nations was highest in the late 1970s and early 1980s, first when the Iranian hostage crisis demonstrated UN ineffectiveness and then when the Reagan administration made it a favorite target for criticism. American public support for the world body peaked in 1991, when the Bush administration used UN backing as the legal basis for the Persian Gulf War to drive Iraq out of Kuwait.*

Without mentioning specifics, Clinton said the UN must consider "major structural changes" because it does not need "a separate agency with its own acronym, stationary, and bureaucracy for every problem." In this remark, Clinton appeared to reflect the views of some congressional critics who have charged that the United Nations has too many agencies dealing with discrete issues, from agriculture to family planning. Since the mid-1980s, Congress had sharply curtailed U.S. funding for some of those agencies, and the United States pulled entirely out of the United Nations Educational, Scientific, and Cultural Organization, one of the largest agencies.

The president did not mention what was perhaps the single most controversial UN operation underway at the time of his speech—the UN peacekeeping effort in Bosnia. An undermanned and underarmed international force had been in Bosnia for several years, trying to protect the capital Sarajevo and several ethnic enclaves from aggression by Bosnian Serb forces. The UN's inability to protect those so-called safe havens, much less stop the fighting, became for many critics a symbol of the world body's failure in general. The UN's Bosnia mission ended in December, when a much better-equipped NATO force arrived to enforce a peace agree-

ment brokered by the Clinton administration in Dayton, Ohio. (Bosnia agreement, p. 717)

Clinton made no direct reference to the UN's chronic financial troubles, or the fact that the United States for years led the list of nations failing to pay their assessments to it. As of May 31, according to the secretary general's office, the United States was $1.18 billion in arrears on its UN payments; that represented nearly half of the $2.8 billion owed the United Nations and its agencies by all member countries. The United States disputed the $1.18 billion, claiming the shortfall was closer to $900 million.

Clinton offered a six-point agenda for UN priorities in the future, starting with the fight against terrorism and support for "those who continue to take risks for peace in the face of violence." Other items on his agenda included nuclear nonproliferation; combating "manmade and natural forces of disintegration," such as drug cartels and deforestation; UN peacekeeping programs; health and antipoverty programs; and UN efforts to promote "human dignity and human rights."

Following are the texts of speeches on June 26, 1995, by UN Secretary General Boutros Boutros-Ghali and President Bill Clinton at a ceremony in San Francisco commemorating the fiftieth anniversary of the signing of the United Nations charter:

BOUTROS-GHALI'S REMARKS

The United Nations expresses the age-old dream of universal cooperation. We are here to renew this dream.

The blueprint for the world Organization was drawn here in San Francisco 50 years ago. The Charter created here is more than a document of history; it is the foundation stone of international relations.

For five decades, the United Nations has permitted nations to join together to deal with challenges that no single nation can resolve. Universal membership offers a forum for expressing universal ideals. Through the United Nations, the world has enshrined the ideal of sovereign independence—to accommodate the emergence of new States and to secure the dignity of their peoples.

Fifty-one Member States ratified the Charter of the United Nations in 1945. Since then, millions of the world's citizens won the right to determine their destiny as independent nations. Today, the United Nations comprises 185 Member States. Decolonization utterly changed the international landscape, and could have led to chaos. But through the United Nations, the framework of international relations survived—and was strengthened by—this profound transformation.

At the United Nations, peoples took their first steps as States on the international stage. Within the United Nations, they could assume their rightful place and gain recognition as legitimate members of the world community.

Through the United Nations, the world has embraced the ideals of peace and security—to preserve the integrity of States and to protect the lives of their peoples. The concept of peace—keeping is not explicit in the Charter, but the Charter proved flexible enough to respond when the need for such missions arose.

Peace-keeping is a manifestation of the world's capacity to work together. For both troop-contributing countries and the lands that they serve, United Nations peace operations reinforce the ideal of international solidarity in the face of conflict.

Peace-keeping operations have proven their practical importance. They can monitor compliance with the terms of an agreement. They can give combatants the time and encouragement to pursue lasting peace. They can provide humanitarian relief. And, in the context of new forms of conflict, they can help to reconstruct entire societies.

Through the United Nations, the world has pledged itself to the ideal of development—to advance the prosperity of States and the welfare of their peoples. Working through the United Nations, the world's peoples have framed a vision for global development. They have forged a consensus about the rights that belong to all humanity.

Through the United Nations, strategies have been devised to realize this vision. An understanding of the common interest between North and South has grown. The advancement of women as the key to nearly every issue of development is becoming understood. Ways to approach the complex new problems of the planet are urgently being found.

Five decades are a brief moment in history. Yet, since 1945, a new reality of global cooperation has taken shape, based on the Charter that was framed here in San Francisco.

Today, the world is accepting the ideals of democracy. Democratization can balance the individual's need for identity with the need for a workable international system: it can help to prevent conflict; it is vital for development. The United Nations is helping States express the ideal of democracy, and find practical ways of attaining it.

We are the custodians of the dream of global cooperation. We will not let it perish. As long as people seek national identities; as long as people seek protection from aggression; and as long as people yearn for a better world for their children, the United Nations will endure, and it will succeed.

CLINTON'S REMARKS

Thank you very much. . . .

The 800 delegates from 50 nations who came here 50 years ago to lift the world from the ashes of war and bring life to the dreams of peacemakers included both giants of diplomacy and untested leaders of infant nations. They were separated by tradition, race and language, sharing only a vision of a better, safer future. On this day 50 years ago, the dream President Roosevelt did not live to see of a democratic organization of the world was launched.

The Charter the delegates signed reflected the harsh lessons of their experience; the experience of the '30s, in which the world watched and reacted too slowly to fascist aggression, bringing millions sacrificed on the battlefields and millions more murdered in the death chambers.

Those who had gone through this and the second world war knew that celebrating victory was not enough; that merely punishing the enemy was self-defeating; that instead the world needed an effective and permanent system to promote peace and freedom for everyone. Some of those who worked at that historic conference are still here today, including our own Sen. Claiborne Pell [D-R.I.], who to this very day, every day, carries a copy of the U.N. Charter in his pocket.

San Francisco gave the world renewed confidence and hope for the future. On that day President Truman said, "This is proof that nations, like men, can state their differences, can face them, and then can find common ground on which to stand." Five decades later, we see how very much the world has changed. The Cold War has given way to freedom and cooperation. On this very day, a Russian spacecraft and an American spacecraft are preparing to link in orbit some 240 miles above the Earth. From Jericho to Belfast, ancient enemies are searching together for peace. On every continent nations are struggling to embrace democracy, freedom and prosperity. New technologies move people and ideas around the world, creating vast new reservoirs of opportunity.

Yet we know that these new forces of integration also carry within them the seeds of disintegration and destruction. New technologies and greater openness make all our borders more vulnerable to terrorists, to dangerous weapons, to drug traffickers. Newly independent nations offer ripe targets for international criminals and nuclear smugglers. Fluid capital markets make it easier for nations to build up their economies, but also make it much easier for one nation's troubles first to be exaggerated, then to spread to other nations. . . .

Our generation's enemies are the terrorists and their outlaw nation sponsors—people who kill children or turn them into orphans; people who target innocent people in order to prevent peace; people who attack peacemakers, as our friend President [Hosni] Mubarak [of Egypt] was attacked just a few hours ago; people who in the name of nationalism slaughter those of different faiths or tribes, and drive their survivors from their own homelands. . . .

Today, the threat to our security is not in an enemy silo, but in the briefcase or the car bomb of a terrorist. Our enemies are also international criminals and drug traffickers who threaten the stability of new democracies and the future of our children. Our enemies are the forces of natural destruction—encroaching deserts that threaten the Earth's balance, famines that test the human spirit, deadly new diseases that endanger whole societies.

So, my friends, in this increasingly interdependent world, we have more common opportunities and more common enemies than ever before. It is, therefore, in our interest to face them together as partners, sharing the burdens and costs, and increasing our chances of success.

Just months before his death, President Roosevelt said, "We have learned that we cannot live alone at peace, that our own well-being is dependent on the well-being of other nations far away." Today, more than ever, those words ring true. Yet some here in our own country, where the United Nations was founded, dismissed Roosevelt's wisdom. Some of them acknowledge that the United States must play a strong role overseas, but refuse to supply the nonmilitary resources our nation needs to carry on its responsibilities. Others believe that outside our border America should only act alone.

Well, of course, the United States must be prepared to act alone when necessary, but we dare not ignore the benefits that coalitions bring to this nation. We dare not reject decades of bipartisan wisdom. We dare not reject decades of bipartisan support for international cooperation. Those who would do so, these new isolationists, dismiss 50 years of hard evidence.

['Remarkable Record of Progress']

In those years we've seen the United Nations compile a remarkable record of progress that advances our nation's interest and, indeed, the interest of people everywhere. From President Truman in Korea to President Bush in the Persian Gulf, America has built United Nations military coalitions to contain aggressors. U.N. forces also often pick up where United States troops have taken the lead.

As the Secretary of State said, we saw it just yesterday, when Haiti held parliamentary and local elections with the help of U.N. personnel. We saw the U.N. work in partnership with the United States and the people of Haiti, as they labor to create a democracy. And they have now been given a second chance to renew that promise.

On every continent the United Nations has played a vital role in making people more free and more secure. For decades, the U.N. fought to isolate South Africa, as that regime perpetuated apartheid. Last year, under the watchful eyes of U.N. observers, millions of South Africans who had been disenfranchised for life cast their first votes for freedom.

In Namibia, Mozambique, and soon we hope in Angola, the United Nations is helping people to bury decades of civil strife and turn their energies into building new democratic nations. In Cambodia, where a brutal regime left more than one million dead in the killing fields, the U.N. helped hundreds of thousands of refugees return to their native land and stood watch over democratic elections that brought 90 percent of the people to the polls. In El Salvador, the U.N. brokered an end to 12 years of bloody civil war and stayed on to help reform the army, bring justice to the citizens, and open the doors of democracy.

From the Persian Gulf to the Caribbean, U.N. economic and political sanctions have proved to be a valuable means short of military action to isolate regimes and to make aggressors and terrorists pay at least a price for their actions: In Iraq, to help stop that nation from developing weapons of mass destruction or threatening its neighbors again; in the Balkans, to isolate aggressors; in North Africa, to pressure Libya to turn over for trial those indicted in the bombing of Pan Am flight 103.

The record of the United Nations includes a proud battle for child survival and against human suffering and disease of all kinds. Every year UNICEF oral vaccines save the lives of three million children. Last year alone the World Food Program, using the contributions of many governments including our own, fed 57 million hungry people. The World Health Organization has eliminated smallpox from the face of the Earth and is making great strides in its campaign to eliminate polio by the year 2000. It has helped to contain fatal diseases like the Ebola virus that could have threatened an entire continent. . . .

[Call for Reform]

. . . The end of the Cold War, the strong trend toward democratic ideals among all nations, the emergence of so many problems that can best be met by collective action, all these things enable the United Nations at this 50-year point finally to fulfill the promise of its founders.

But if we want the U.N. to do so, we must face the fact that for all its successes and all its possibilities, it does not work as well as it should. The United Nations must be reformed. In this age of relentless change, successful governments and corporations are constantly reducing their bureaucracies, setting clearer priorities, focusing on targeted results.

In the United States we have eliminated hundreds of programs, thousands of regulations. We're reducing our government to its smallest size since President Kennedy served here, while increasing our efforts in areas most critical to our future. The U.N. must take similar steps.

Over the years it has grown too bloated, too often encouraging duplication, and spending resources on meetings rather than results. As its board of directors, all of us—we, the member states—must create a U.N. that is more flexible, that operates more rapidly, that wastes less and produces more, and most importantly, that inspires confidence among our governments and our people.

In the last few years we have seen some good reforms—a new oversight office to hold down costs, a new system to review personnel, a start toward modernization and privatization. But we must do more. . . .

We must consider major structural changes. The United Nations simply does not need a separate agency with its own acronym, stationery and bureaucracy for every problem. The new U.N. must peel off what doesn't work and get behind what will.

We must also realize, in particular, the limits to peacekeeping and not ask the Blue Helmets to undertake missions they cannot be expected to handle. Peacekeeping can only succeed when the parties to a conflict understand they cannot profit from war. We have too often asked our peacekeepers to work miracles while denying them the military and political support required and the modern command-and-control systems they need to do their job as safely and effectively as possible. Today's U.N. must be ready to handle tomorrow's challenges. Those of us who most respect the U.N. must lead the charge of reform.

Not all the critics of today's United Nations are isolationists. Many are supporters who gladly would pay for the U.N.'s essential work if they were convinced their money was being well-spent. But I pledge to all of you, as we work together to improve the United Nations, I will continue to work to see that the United States takes the lead in paying its fair share of our common load.

Meanwhile, we must all remember that the United Nations is a reflection of the world it represents. Therefore, it will remain far from perfect. It will not be able to solve all problems. But even those it cannot solve, it may well be able to limit in terms of the scope and reach of the problem, and it may well be able to limit the loss of human life until the time for solution comes.

So just as withdrawing from the world is impossible, turning our backs on the U.N. is no solution. It would be shortsighted and self-destructive. It would strengthen the forces of global disintegration. It would threaten the security, the interest and the values of the American people. So I say especially to the opponents of the United Nations here in the United States, turning our back on the U.N. and going it alone will lead to far more economic, political and military burdens on our people in the future and would ignore the lessons of our own history.

Instead, on this 50th anniversary of the charter signing, let us renew our vow to live together as good neighbors. And let us agree on a new United Nations agenda to increase confidence and ensure support for the United Nations, and to advance peace and prosperity for the next 50 years.

[A New Agenda]

First and foremost, the U.N. must strengthen its efforts to isolate states and people who traffic in terror and support those who continue to take risks for peace in the face of violence. The bombing in Oklahoma City, the deadly gas attack in Tokyo, the struggles to establish peace in the Middle East and in Northern Ireland—all of these things remind us that we must stand against terror and support those who move away from it. Recent discoveries of laboratories working to produce biological weapons for terrorists demonstrate the dangerous link between terrorism and the weapons of mass destruction. . . .

Where nations and groups honestly seek to reform, to change, to move away from the killing of innocents, we should support them. But when they are unrepentant in the delivery of death, we should stand tall against them. My friends, there is no easy way around the hard question: If nations and groups are not willing to move away from the delivery of death, we should put aside short-term profits for the people in our countries to stop, stop, stop their conduct.

Second, the U.N. must continue our efforts to stem the proliferation of weapons of mass destruction. There are some things nations can do on their own. The U.S. and Russia today are destroying our nuclear arsenals rapidly.

But the U.N. must also play a role. We were honored to help secure an indefinite extension of the Nuclear Non-Proliferation Treaty under U.N. auspices.

We rely on U.N. agencies to monitor nations bent on acquiring nuclear capabilities. We must work together on the Chemical Weapons Convention. We must strengthen our common efforts to fight biological weapons. We must do everything we can to limit the spread of fissile materials. We must work on conventional weapons like the land mines that are the curse of children the world over. And we must complete a comprehensive nuclear test ban treaty.

Third, we must support through the United Nations the fight against man-made and natural forces of disintegration, from crime syndicates and drug cartels, to new diseases and disappearing forests. These enemies are elusive; they cross borders at will. Nations can and must oppose them alone. But we know, and the Cairo Conference reaffirmed, that the most effective opposition requires strong international cooperation and mutual support.

Fourth, we must reaffirm our commitment to strengthen U.N. peacekeeping as an important tool for deterring, containing and ending violent conflict. The U.N. can never be an absolute guarantor of peace, but it can reduce human suffering and advance the odds of peace.

Fifth, . . . we must continue what is too often the least noticed of the U.N.'s missions, its unmatched efforts on the front lines of the battle for child survival and against disease and human suffering.

And finally, let us vow to make the United Nations an increasing strong voice for the protection of fundamental human dignity and human rights. After all, they were at the core of the founding of this great organization.

Today we honor the men and women who gave shape to the United Nations. We celebrate 50 years of achievement. We commit ourselves to real reforms. We reject the siren song of the new isolationists. We set a clear agenda worthy of the vision of our founders. The measure of our generation will be whether we give up because we cannot achieve a perfect world or strive on to build a better world. . . .

Let us not forget that each child saved, each refugee housed, each disease prevented, each barrier to justice brought down, each sword turned into a ploughshare, brings us closer to the vision of our founders—closer to peace, closer to freedom, closer to dignity.

So my fellow citizens of the world, let us not lose heart. Let us gain renewed strength and energy and vigor from the progress which has been made and the opportunities which are plainly before us. Let us say no to isolation; yes to reform; yes to a brave, ambitious new agenda; most of all, yes to the dream of the United Nations.

Thank you.

SUPREME COURT ON THE ENDANGERED SPECIES ACT
June 29, 1995

In an important victory for environmentalists, the Supreme Court June 29 upheld, 6–3, a federal regulation aimed at protecting the habitat of endangered species on private land. That regulation was still in jeopardy, however, as conservatives in Congress, backed by property rights advocates, sought to rewrite the Endangered Species Act itself in ways that would overturn the Court's ruling. "Today's decision will serve as a rallying cry for . . . reform from communities across the country that have been hurt by the current law," said Sen. Slade Gorton (R-Wash.), the author of a bill that would restrict the government's authority to place private lands off limits to development in order to protect the habitat of endangered or threatened species.

The Endangered Species Act of 1973 prohibits any activity "within the United States" that would "harm" an animal or plant species that faces an imminent or likely threat of extinction. An Interior Department regulation implementing the statute defined "harm" as "an act which actually kills or injures wildlife. Such act may include significant habitat modification or degradation where it actually kills or injures wildlife by significantly impairing essential behavioral patterns, including breeding, feeding, or sheltering."

Timber industry interests in the Northwest and Southeast brought the case, Babbitt v. Sweet Home Chapter of Communities for a Greater Oregon, *after the Clinton administration moved to protect the preferred habitat of the endangered red cockaded woodpecker and the threatened northern spotted owl by restricting logging of old growth timber on both federal and private land. The loggers and their supporters argued that the government had been too expansive and that the habitat restrictions prevented private property owners from using their land for what would otherwise be allowable activities. The restrictions, they argued, had cost many loggers their jobs and damaged property values.*

The U.S. District Court for the District of Columbia rejected these arguments in 1992, but, after first agreeing with the district court, the Court of

Appeals reversed itself in 1994 and in a split decision sided with the log-gers. "We find that the [agency's] definition of 'harm' was neither clearly authorized by Congress nor a reasonable interpretation of the statute, and . . . that no later action of Congress supplied the missing authority," the appeals court said. The Supreme Court decision reversed that ruling.

A Reasonable Definition of Harm

Writing for the majority, Justice John Paul Stevens wrote, "Given Con-gress' clear expression of the [Endangered Species Act's] broad purpose to protect endangered and threatened wildlife, the [Interior] Secretary's defi-nition of 'harm' is reasonable." Stevens also said the Court was not willing to second-guess the interior secretary. "The proper interpretation of a term such as 'harm' involves a complex policy choice," Stevens wrote. "When Congress has entrusted the Secretary with broad discretion, we are espe-cially reluctant to substitute our views of wise policy for his. In this case, that reluctance accords with our conclusion, based on the text, structure, and legislative history of the [act], that the Secretary reasonably construed the intent of Congress when he defined 'harm' to include 'significant habi-tat modification or degradation that actually kills or injures wildlife.' "

Voting with Stevens were Justices Anthony M. Kennedy, David H. Souter, Sandra Day O'Connor, Ruth Bader Ginsburg, and Stephen G. Breyer.

Justice Antonin Scalia, joined by Chief Justice William H. Rehnquist and Justice Clarence Thomas, dissented. The Court's decision " 'imposes unfairness to the point of financial ruin'—not just upon the rich, but upon the simplest farmer who finds his land conscripted to national zoological use," Scalia wrote.

Environmentalists in and out of Congress hailed the ruling. "This his-toric decision confirms what Congress has said for twenty years, that habi-tat protection is essential to species conservation," said Rodger Schlick-eisen, president of the Defenders of Wildlife. "If we can't protect the dinner tables that feed species or the nurseries where they shelter their young, we can't protect endangered species," said Rep. Gerry E. Studds (D-Mass.).

Interior Secretary Bruce Babbitt welcomed the Court's decision, saying that protecting the habitat of threatened and endangered species was the best way to preserve those species. He noted that the Interior Department was seeking to change the way the law was enforced to make it "less oner-ous" for private landowners. In particular, he said, the department was negotiating agreements that would allow developers to destroy some habi-tat in return for protecting other lands essential to endangered animals or plants.

Effort to Narrow the Endangered Species Act

Property rights activists in Congress pursued their efforts to overturn the Court's ruling, however. The House Resources Committee October 12 approved a bill (HR 2275) that would narrow the definition of "harm" to only those activities that directly kill or injure a member of an endangered or threatened species. To protect broad areas of habitat on private land, federal officials would have to enter into cooperative management agreements with landowners, provide compensation to landowners when a regulatory action caused a property to lose 20 percent or more of its value, or provide financial incentives such as grants or tax breaks to encourage individuals' participation in species protection activities. The bill was not taken up for a vote by the end of the year.

Following are excerpts from the majority and dissenting opinions in the Supreme Court's ruling July 29, 1995, in Babbitt v. Sweet Home Chapter of Communities for a Greater Oregon, *in which the Court upheld the Interior Department's authority under the Endangered Species Act to bar activities on private land that would destroy the habitat of endangered and threatened wildlife:*

No. 94–859

Bruce Babbitt, Secretary of the Interior, et al., Petitioners

v.

Sweet Home Chapter of Communities for a Great Oregon et al.

} On writ of certiorari to the United States Court of Appeals for the District of Columbia Circuit

[June 29, 1995]

JUSTICE STEVENS delivered the opinion of the Court.

The Endangered Species Act of 1973, 16 U.S.C. §1531 (ESA or Act), contains a variety of protections designed to save from extinction species that the Secretary of the Interior designates as endangered or threatened. Section 9 of the Act makes it unlawful for any person to "take" any endangered or threatened species. The Secretary has promulgated a regulation that defines the statute's prohibition on takings to include "significant habitat modification or degradation where it actually kills or injures wildlife." This case presents the question whether the Secretary exceeded his authority under the Act by promulgating that regulation.

I

Section §9(a)(1) of the Endangered Species Act provides the following protection for endangered species:

"Except as provided in sections 1535(g)(2) and 1539 of this title, with respect to any endangered species of fish or wildlife listed pursuant to section 1533 of this title it is unlawful for any person subject to the jurisdiction of the United States to—

"(B) take any such species within the United States or the territorial sea of the United States[.]" 16 U.S.C. §1538(a)(1)."

Section §3(19) of the Act defines the statutory term "take":

"The term 'take' means to harass, harm, pursue, hunt, shoot, wound, kill, trap, capture, or collect, or to attempt to engage in any such conduct." 16 U.S.C. §1532(19)."

The Act does not further define the terms it uses to define "take." The Interior Department regulations that implement the statute, however, define the statutory term "harm":

"*Harm* in the definition of 'take' in the Act means an act which actually kills or injures wildlife. Such act may include significant habitat modification or degradation where it actually kills or injures wildlife by significantly impairing essential behavioral patterns, including breeding, feeding, or sheltering." 50 CFR §17.3 (1994).

This regulation has been in place since 1975. . . .

Respondents in this action are small landowners, logging companies, and families dependent on the forest products industries in the Pacific Northwest and in the Southeast, and organizations that represent their interests. They brought this declaratory judgment action against petitioners, the Secretary of the Interior and the Director of the Fish and Wildlife Service, in the United States District Court for the District of Columbia to challenge the statutory validity of the Secretary's regulation defining "harm," particularly the inclusion of habitat modification and degradation in the definition. Respondents challenged the regulation on its face. Their complaint alleged that application of the "harm" regulation to the red-cockaded woodpecker, an endangered species, and the northern spotted owl, a threatened species, had injured them economically.

Respondents advanced three arguments to support their submission that Congress did not intend the word "take" in §9 to include habitat modification, as the Secretary's "harm" regulation provides. First, they correctly noted that language in the Senate's original version of the ESA would have defined "take" to include "destruction, modification, or curtailment of [the] habitat or range" of fish or wildlife, but the Senate deleted that language from the bill before enacting it. Second, respondents argued that Congress intended the Act's express authorization for the Federal Government to buy private land in order to prevent habitat degradation in §5 to be the exclusive check against habitat modification on private property. Third, because the Senate added the term "harm" to the definition of "take" in a floor amendment without debate, respondents argued that the court should not interpret the term so expansively as to include habitat modification.

The District Court considered and rejected each of respondents' arguments, finding "that Congress intended an expansive interpretation of the word 'take,' an interpretation that encompasses habitat modification." (1992). . . .

A divided panel of the Court of Appeals initially affirmed the judgment of the District Court. After granting a petition for rehearing, however, the panel reversed. . . .

The Court of Appeals' decision created a square conflict with a 1988 decision of the Ninth Circuit that had upheld the Secretary's definition of "harm.". . . We granted certiorari to resolve the conflict. (1995). Our consideration of the text and structure of the Act, its legislative history, and the significance of the 1982 amendment persuades us that the Court of Appeals' judgment should be reversed.

II

Because this case was decided on motions for summary judgment, we may appropriately make certain factual assumptions in order to frame the legal issue. First, we assume respondents have no desire to harm either the red-cockaded woodpecker or the spotted owl; they merely wish to continue logging activities that would be entirely proper if not prohibited by the ESA. On the other hand, we must assume *arguendo* that those activities will have the effect, even though unintended, of detrimentally changing the natural habitat of both listed species and that, as a consequence, members of those species will be killed or injured. Under respondents' view of the law, the Secretary's only means of forestalling that grave result—even when the actor knows it is certain to occur—is to use his §5 authority to purchase the lands on which the survival of the species depends. The Secretary, on the other hand, submits that the §9 prohibition on takings, which Congress defined to include "harm," places on respondents a duty to avoid harm that habitat alteration will cause the birds unless respondents first obtain a permit pursuant to §10.

The text of the Act provides three reasons for concluding that the Secretary's interpretation is reasonable. First, an ordinary understanding of the word "harm" supports it. The dictionary definition of the verb form of "harm" is "to cause hurt or damage to: injure." In the context of the ESA, that definition naturally encompasses habitat modification that results in actual injury or death to members of an endangered or threatened species. Respondents argue that the Secretary should have limited the purview of "harm" to direct applications of force against protected species, but the dictionary definition does not include the word "directly" or suggest in any way that only direct or willful action that leads to injury constitutes "harm." Moreover, unless the statutory term "harm" encompasses indirect as well as direct injuries, the word has no meaning that does not duplicate the meaning of other words that §3 uses to define "take." A reluctance to treat statutory terms as surplusage supports the reasonableness of the Secretary's interpretation.

Second, the broad purpose of the ESA supports the Secretary's decision to extend protection against activities that cause the precise harms Congress enacted the statute to avoid.

. . . "The plain intent of Congress in enacting this statute," we recognized [in *TVA* v. *Hill* (1978)], "was to halt and reverse the trend toward species extinction, whatever the cost. This is reflected not only in the stated policies of the Act, but in literally every section of the statute." Although the §9 "take" prohibition was not at issue in *Hill*, we took note of that prohibition, placing particular emphasis on the Secretary's inclusion of habitat modification in his definition of "harm." In light of that provision for habitat protection, we could "not understand how TVA intends to operate Tellico Dam without 'harming' the snail darter." Congress' intent to provide comprehensive protection for endangered and threatened species supports the permissibility of the Secretary's "harm" regulation.

Respondents advance strong arguments that activities that cause minimal or unforeseeable harm will not violate the Act as construed in the "harm" regulation. Respondents, however, present a facial challenge to the regulation. Thus, they ask us to invalidate the Secretary's understanding of "harm" in every circumstance, even when an actor knows that an activity, such as draining a pond, would actually result in the extinction of a listed species by destroying its habitat. Given Congress' clear expression of the ESA's broad purpose to protect endangered and threatened wildlife, the Secretary's definition of "harm" is reasonable.

Third, the fact that Congress in 1982 authorized the Secretary to issue permits for takings that §9(a)(1)(B) would otherwise prohibit, "if such taking is incidental to, and not the purpose of, the carrying out of an otherwise lawful activity," strongly suggests that Congress understood §9(a)(1)(B) to prohibit indirect as well as deliberate takings. The permit process requires the applicant to prepare a "conservation plan" that specifies how he intends to "minimize and mitigate" the "impact" of his activity on endangered and threatened species, making clear that Congress had in mind foreseeable rather than merely accidental effects on listed species. No one could seriously request an "incidental" take permit to avert §9 liability for direct, deliberate action against a member of an endangered or threatened species, but respondents would read "harm" so narrowly that the permit procedure would have little more than that absurd purpose. . . . Congress' addition of the §10 permit provision supports the Secretary's conclusion that activities not intended to harm an endangered species, such as habitat modification, may constitute unlawful takings under the ESA unless the Secretary permits them. . . .

We need not decide whether the statutory definition of "take" compels the Secretary's interpretation of "harm," because our conclusions that Congress did not unambiguously manifest its intent to adopt respondents' view and that the Secretary's interpretation is reasonable suffice to decide this case. The latitude the ESA gives the Secretary in enforcing the statute, together with the degree of regulatory expertise necessary to its enforcement, establishes that we owe some degree of deference to the Secretary's reasonable interpretation.

III

Our conclusion that the Secretary's definition of "harm" rests on a permissible construction of the ESA gains further support from the legislative history of the statute. The Committee Reports accompanying the bills that became the ESA do not specifically discuss the meaning of "harm," but they make clear that Congress intended "take" to apply broadly to cover indirect as well as purposeful actions. . . .

Two endangered species bills, S. 1592 and S. 1983, were introduced in the Senate and referred to the Commerce Committee. Neither bill included the word "harm" in its definition of "take," although the definitions otherwise closely resembled the one that appeared in the bill as ultimately enacted. Senator Tunney, the floor manager of the bill in the Senate, subsequently introduced a floor amendment that added "harm" to the definition, noting that this and accompanying amendments would "help to achieve the purposes of the bill." Respondents argue that the lack of debate about the amendment that added "harm" counsels in favor of a narrow interpretation. We disagree. An obviously broad word that the Senate went out of its way to add to an important statutory definition is precisely the sort of provision that deserves a respectful reading.

The definition of "take" that originally appeared in S. 1983 differed from the definition as ultimately enacted in one other significant respect: It included "the destruction, modification, or curtailment of [the] habitat or range" of fish and wildlife. Respondents make much of the fact that the Commerce Committee removed this phrase from the "take" definition before S. 1983 went to the floor. We do not find that fact especially significant. The legislative materials contain no indication why the habitat protection provision was deleted. That provision differed greatly from the regulation at issue today. Most notably, the habitat protection in S. 1983 would have applied far more broadly than the regulation does because it made adverse habitat modification a categorical violation of the "take" prohibition, unbounded by the regulation's limitation to habitat modifications that actually kill or injure wildlife. The S. 1983 language also failed to qualify "modification" with the regulation's limiting adjective "significant." We do not believe the Senate's unelaborated disavowal of the provision in S. 1983 undermines the reasonableness of the more moderate habitat protection in the Secretary's "harm" regulation. . . .

IV

When it enacted the ESA, Congress delegated broad administrative and interpretive power to the Secretary. The task of defining and listing endangered and threatened species requires an expertise and attention to detail that exceeds the normal province of Congress. Fashioning appropriate standards for issuing permits under §10 for takings that would otherwise violate §9 necessarily requires the exercise of broad discretion. The proper interpretation of a term such as "harm" involves a complex policy choice. When Congress has entrusted the Secretary with broad discretion, we are especially reluctant to substitute our views of wise policy for his. In this case, that reluctance accords with our conclusion, based on the text, structure, and legislative history of the ESA, that the Secretary reasonably construed the intent of Congress when he defined "harm" to include "significant habitat modification or degradation that actually kills or injures wildlife."

In the elaboration and enforcement of the ESA, the Secretary and all persons who must comply with the law will confront difficult questions of proximity and degree; for, as all recognize, the Act encompasses a vast range of economic and social enterprises and endeavors. These questions must be addressed in the usual course of the law, through case-by-case resolution and adjudication.

The judgment of the Court of Appeals is reversed.

It is so ordered.

JUSTICE O'CONNOR, concurring.

My agreement with the Court is founded on two understandings. First, the challenged regulation is limited to significant habitat modification that causes actual, as opposed to hypothetical or speculative, death or injury to identifiable protected animals. Second, even setting aside difficult questions of scienter, the regulation's application is limited by ordinary principles of proximate causation, which introduce notions of foreseeability. These limitations, in my view, call into question *Palila* v. *Hawaii Dept. of Land and Natural Resources* (CA9 1988) *(Palila II)*, and with it, many of the applications derided by the dissent. Because there is no need to strike a regulation on a facial challenge out of concern that it is susceptible of erroneous application, however, and because there are many habitat-related circumstances in which the regulation might validly apply, I join the opinion of the Court. . . .

JUSTICE SCALIA, with whom THE CHIEF JUSTICE and JUSTICE THOMAS join, dissenting.

I think it unmistakably clear that the legislation at issue here (1) forbade the hunting and killing of endangered animals, and (2) provided federal lands and federal funds *for the acquisition of private lands*, to preserve the habitat of endangered animals. The Court's holding that the hunting and killing prohibition incidentally preserves habitat on private lands imposes unfairness to the point of financial ruin—not just upon the rich, but upon the simplest farmer who finds his land conscripted to national zoological use. I respectfully dissent.

I

The [challenged] regulation has three features which do not comport with the statute. First, it interprets the statute to prohibit habitat modification that is no more than the cause-in-fact of death or injury to wildlife. Any "significant habitat modification" that in fact produces that result by "impairing essential behavioral patterns" is made unlawful, regardless of whether that result is intended or even foreseeable, and no matter how long the chain of causality between modification and injury. . . .

Second, the regulation does not require an "act": the Secretary's officially stated position is that an *omission* will do. . . .

The third and most important unlawful feature of the regulation is that it encompasses injury inflicted, not only upon individual animals, but upon populations of the protected species. "Injury" in the regulation includes "significantly impairing essential behavioral patterns, including *breeding*" (1994) (emphasis added). Impairment of breeding does not "injure" living creatures; it prevents them from propagating, thus "injuring" a *population* of animals which would otherwise have maintained or increased its numbers. . . .

None of these three features of the regulation can be found in the statutory provisions supposed to authorize it. The term "harm" in §1532(19) has no legal force of its own. An indictment or civil complaint that charged the defendant with "harming" an animal protected under the Act would be dismissed as defective, for the only operative term in the statute is to "take." If "take" were not elsewhere defined in the Act, none could dispute what it means, for the term is as old as the law itself. To "take," when applied to wild animals, means to reduce those animals, by killing or capturing, to human control. . . .

The Act's definition of "take" does expand the word slightly (and not unusually), so as to make clear that it includes not just a completed taking, but the process of taking, and all of the acts that are customarily identified with or accompany that process ("to harass, harm, pursue, hunt, shoot, wound, kill, trap, capture, or collect"); and so as to include attempts. The tempting fallacy—which the Court commits with abandon—is to assume that *once defined*, "take" loses any significance, and it is only the definition that matters. . . .

That is what has occurred here. The verb "harm" has a range of meaning: "to cause injury" at its broadest, "to do hurt or damage" in a narrower and more direct sense. . . . To define "harm" as an act or omission that, however remotely, "actually kills or injures" a population of wildlife through habitat modification, is to choose a meaning that makes nonsense of the word that "harm" defines—requiring us to accept that a farmer who tills his field and causes erosion that makes silt run into a nearby river which depletes oxygen and thereby "impairs [the] breeding" of protected fish, has "taken" or "attempted to take" the fish. . . .

Here the evidence shows the opposite. "Harm" is merely one of 10 prohibitory words in §1532(19), and the other 9 fit the ordinary meaning of "take" perfectly. To "harass, pursue, hunt, shoot, wound, kill, trap, capture, or collect" are all affirmative acts . . . which are directed immediately and intentionally against a particular animal—not acts or omissions that indirectly and accidentally cause injury to a population of animals. The Court points out that several of the words ("harass," "pursue," "wound," and "kill") "refer to actions or effects that do not require direct *applications of force*." That is true enough, but force is not the point. Even "taking" activities in the narrowest sense, activities traditionally engaged in by hunters and trappers, do not all consist of direct applications of force; pursuit and harassment are part of the business of "taking" the prey even before it has been touched. What the nine other words in §1532(19) have in common—and share with the narrower meaning of "harm" described above, but not with the Secretary's ruthless dilation of the word—is the sense of affirmative conduct intentionally directed against a particular animal or animals. . . .

The penalty provisions of the Act counsel this interpretation as well. Any person who "knowingly" violates §1538(a)(1)(B) is subject to criminal penalties under §1540(b)(1) and civil penalties under §1540(a)(1); moreover, under the latter section, any person "who otherwise violates" the taking prohibition (*i.e.*, violates it *un*knowingly) may be assessed a civil penalty of $500 for each violation, with the stricture that "[e]ach such violation shall be a separate offense." This last provision should be clear warning that the regulation is in error, for when combined with the regulation it produces a result that no legislature could reasonably be thought to have intended: A large number of routine private activities—farming, for example, ranching, roadbuilding, construction and logging—are subjected to strict-liability penalties when they fortuitously injure protected wildlife, no matter how remote the chain of causation and no matter how difficult to foresee (or to disprove) the "injury" may be (*e.g.*, an "impairment" of breeding). The Court says that "[the strict-liability provision] is potentially sweeping, but it would be so with or without the Secretary's 'harm' regulation." That is not correct. Without the regulation, the routine "habitat modifying" activities that people conduct to make a daily living would not carry exposure to strict penalties; only acts directed at animals, like those described by the other words in §1532(19), would risk liability. . . .

[II and III omitted]

The Endangered Species Act is a carefully considered piece of legislation that forbids all persons to hunt or harm endangered animals, but places upon the public at large, rather than upon fortuitously accountable individual landowners, the cost of preserving the habitat of endangered species. There is neither textual support for, nor even evidence of congressional consideration of, the radically different disposition contained in the regulation that the Court sustains. For these reasons, I respectfully dissent.

SUPREME COURT ON
RACE-BASED REDISTRICTING
June 29, 1995

Striking down the map of Georgia's 11th Congressional District as an unconstitutional racial gerrymandering, the Supreme Court ruled June 29 that any districting plan in which race was the "predominant factor" should be considered constitutionally suspect. A race-based districting plan may be justified only by showing that the plan was "narrowly tailored to achieving a compelling state interest," which Georgia failed to do, the Court said in the case of Miller v. Johnson.

The 5–4 ruling may have jeopardized the historic gains that blacks and Hispanics had made in Congress in recent years, in large part by winning in majority-minority districts that had been drawn in several states under the Voting Rights Act of 1965. Several of these districts could be vulnerable to legal challenge under the "strict scrutiny" test outlined in Miller v. Johnson.

At the same time, the Court's opinion, written by Justice Anthony M. Kennedy, left unanswered several important questions about when race can properly be a factor in a state's districting considerations. When, for example, is race not simply present but "predominant" in the districting process? What constitutes a "compelling interest" that would justify making race the predominant factor in drawing a particular district's boundaries?

These and other questions might be addressed in two cases that the Court, only hours after handing down its decision in Miller v. Johnson, *announced it had agreed to hear in its 1995–1996 term. The cases, from Texas and North Carolina, involved the proper scope of race-based districting.*

The Role of the Justice Department

The ruling was a clear slap at the Justice Department, which had pushed minority-dominated districts aggressively under both Presidents George Bush and Bill Clinton. The Voting Rights Act of 1965 required states with a history of racially discriminatory voting, including Georgia, to "preclear" new districting plans with the Justice Department or a federal dis-

trict court. The Supreme Court laid out many of the rules for race-conscious districting under the Voting Rights Act in the 1986 case of Thornburg v. Gingles. *Legislatures were generally required to draw a minority-dominant district when there was evidence that the minority voters were sufficiently compact, numerous, and politically cohesive and where there was evidence that white voters tended to vote along racial lines. The Justice Department interpreted these mandates fairly broadly in the redistricting that followed the 1990 census, often prodding states to draw additional districts in which minorities would make up a majority of the voting-age population.*

The Court voiced its concern with race-conscious districts in the 1993 case of Shaw v. Reno, *when it said that minority-dominated districts had the potential of violating constitutional guarantees of equal protection under the Fourteenth Amendment. In that case the majority was particularly concerned about the "bizarre" shape of the challenged district.* (Court on gerrymandering, Historic Documents of 1993, p. 459)

The Shaw *ruling was vague but provocative, and a string of challenges followed. Two of those cases reached the Supreme Court in the 1994–1995 term—the* Miller *case from Georgia and a Louisiana case called* United States v. Hays. *In both, lower federal courts had rejected congressional districting maps designed to provide new, black-majority districts.*

In Louisiana white voters challenged a newly drawn congressional district that in 1992 elected Democrat Cleo Fields, an African-American. The Supreme Court June 29 sidestepped the core of the Hays *case, instead ruling that the white plaintiffs had no grounds to sue because they lived outside the challenged district.*

Georgia initially had drawn a district map with two black-majority congressional districts. However, under pressure from the Justice Department during the Bush administration, Georgia redrew the map to provide three such districts (the 2nd, 5th, and 11th Districts). Democrat Cynthia A. McKinney, an African-American, was elected to the House from that additional black-majority district, the 11th District. Because McKinney's district had a more regular shape than the district at issue in Shaw *and because it was drawn to meet the Justice Department's view of the Voting Rights Act requirements, states officials and its defenders thought the 11th District could survive a court challenge.*

The Majority and Dissenting Opinions

In his majority opinion, Kennedy quashed both those lines of argument. A highly irregular shape is just a clue that race may have been the motivating factor in drawing a particular set of district lines, he wrote, not a necessary requirement to mount a legal challenge under the equal protection clause. Kennedy set forth a new standard for such challenges, namely a showing that race was the "predominant factor" in shaping the district.

To meet this standard, Kennedy said, "a plaintiff must prove that the legislature subordinated traditional race-neutral districting principles . . . to racial considerations." Some of those traditional principles recognized by the Court majority were compactness, contiguity, adherence to political subdivisions, and "actual shared interests." Kennedy added that, although shared racial identity may in some cases reflect shared interests, it cannot be assumed to do so.

Even where race was found to be the predominant factor in drawing the district boundaries, as the majority said it was in Miller v. Johnson, *Kennedy said that states could still defend their district lines if they could prove they were drawn to serve a "compelling interest." Kennedy did not specify what would meet this standard, but he made it clear that adhering to Justice Department directives did not suffice. In the Georgia case, Kennedy concluded that the Justice Department had overstepped the requirements of the Voting Rights Act when it pressed the state to create a third black-majority district.*

Joining in Kennedy's opinion were Chief Justice William H. Rehnquist and Justices Sandra Day O'Connor, Antonin Scalia, and Clarence Thomas. O'Connor also wrote a brief concurring opinion. These same five justices constituted the majority in a June 12, 1995, ruling that cast doubt on federal affirmative action programs. In that case, Adarand Constructors v. Peña, *the Court criticized the moral justification for affirmative action programs, saying that race-conscious programs could amount to unconstitutional reverse discrimination and even harm those they sought to help.* (Supreme Court on affirmative action plans, p. 307*)*

Justice Ruth Bader Ginsburg dissented, joined by Justice Stephen G. Breyer, David H. Souter, and John Paul Stevens. Ginsburg wrote that the Miller *ruling would create chaos in the redistricting process and involve federal judges in complex map drawing, which properly should be left to politicians. "The Court's disposition renders redistricting perilous work for state legislatures," she wrote.*

Ginsburg said the Court majority seemed to be placing a greater burden on districts drawn to promote racial, rather than ethnic, identity. "Until now, no constitutional infirmity has been seen in districting Irish or Italian voters together, for example, so long as the delineation does not abandon familiar apportionment practices," she wrote. Moreover, she continued, "special circumstances justify vigilant judicial inspection to protect minority voters—circumstances that do not apply to majority voters." In a separate dissent Justice Stevens said that he could "not see how a districting plan that favors a politically weak group can violate equal protection," and he found "especially unfortunate" the majority's "refusal to distinguish an enactment that helps a minority group from enactments that cause it harm."

Reaction

Reaction to the Court's ruling was immediate. President Clinton called the decision "a setback in the struggle to ensure that all Americans participate fully in the electoral process."

"Twenty, thirty years ago, we looked to the Supreme Court as a sympathetic referee in the struggle for civil rights and social justice," said Democrat John Lewis, another of the African-American representatives from Georgia and a civil rights activist who helped get the Voting Rights Act passed in 1965. "This court is not a friend of civil rights."

Other civil rights activists worried that, if states were required to redraw their minority-dominated districts, some legislators from those districts would lose their seats. The Court ruling might also limit creation of additional majority-minority districts, they said. That would be fine with Rep. Gary A. Franks (R-Conn.), an African-American who represents a white-majority district and is a long-time opponent of minority-dominated districts, which he considered "set-asides" for minorities. "You should not be looking at race as the prominent factor. . . . It's very sensible that we cannot allow districts to be race-driven," he said.

Others welcomed the ruling as an overdue check on the Justice Department's role in state map drawing. "The Justice Department has totally distorted the Voting Rights Act," said Abigail Thernstrom, the author of a book critical of race-conscious redistricting. The Justice Department denied that it was pursuing a policy of maximizing the number of minority-dominated districts. Pamela Karlan, a law professor at the University of Virginia agreed, but she predicted the department would have no choice but to ease up on its enforcement recommendations or leave states in an untenable position.

Perhaps the most indisputable observation came from Justice Ginsburg. After reading portions of her dissent from the bench, she cautioned that "the Court has not yet spoken a final word" on the difficult issues raised in the Miller *case.*

New District Lines Drawn

After the Court's edict, the Georgia legislature convened a twenty-day session that ended in early September to redraw the map. The state legislators were unable to agree on a new plan. The remapping was then remanded to a three-judge federal panel, which imposed new boundaries on December 13. In a 2–1 decision, the judges eliminated two of the three majority-minority districts and brought demographic changes to seven of the eleven districts in the state. With the new boundaries, the 2nd and 11th Districts would no longer be minority-dominated.

The new map was immediately criticized by civil rights groups and several House members. "I suppose they couldn't wait to toss us out of our districts, even before our constituents had a say in the matter," said McKinney. The American Civil Liberties Union and the NAACP Legal Defense Fund planned to appeal the decision to the Supreme Court.

> *Following are excerpts from the majority and dissenting opinions in the Supreme Court's ruling June 29, 1995, in* Miller v. Johnson, *in which the Court said that a congressional district drawn with race as the predominant factor violates the equal*

protection clause of the Constitution unless the district can be shown to serve a "compelling state interest":

Nos. 94–631, 94–797, and 94–929

Zell Miller,et al., Appellants
v.
Davida Johnson et al.

Lucious Abrams, Jr., et al., Appellants
v.
Davida Johnson et al.

United States, Appellant
v.
Davida Johnson et al.

On appeals from the United States District Court for the Southern District of Georgia

[June 29, 1995]

JUSTICE KENNEDY delivered the opinion of the Court.

The constitutionality of Georgia's congressional redistricting plan is at issue here. In *Shaw* v. *Reno* (1993), we held that a plaintiff states a claim under the Equal Protection Clause by alleging that a state redistricting plan, on its face, has no rational explanation save as an effort to separate voters on the basis of race. The question we now decide is whether Georgia's new Eleventh District gives rise to a valid equal protection claim under the principles announced in *Shaw*, and, if so, whether it can be sustained nonetheless as narrowly tailored to serve a compelling governmental interest.

I

A

The Equal Protection Clause of the Fourteenth Amendment provides that no State shall "deny to any person within its jurisdiction the equal protection of the laws." U.S. Const., Amdt. 14, §1. Its central mandate is racial neutrality in governmental decisionmaking. . . . Laws classifying citizens on the basis of race cannot be upheld unless they are narrowly tailored to achieving a compelling state interest.

In *Shaw* v. *Reno*, we recognized that these equal protection principles govern a State's drawing of congressional districts, though, as our cautious approach there discloses, application of these principles to electoral districting is a most delicate task. Our analysis began from the premise that "[l]aws that explicitly distinguish between individuals on racial grounds fall within the core of [the Equal Protection Clause's] prohibition." This prohibition extends not just to explicit racial classifications, but also to laws neutral on their face but " 'unexplainable on grounds other than race.' " Applying this basic Equal Protection analysis in the voting rights context, we held that "redistricting legislation that is so bizarre on its face that it is 'unexplainable on grounds other than race,' . . . demands the same close scrutiny that we give other state laws that classify citizens by race."

This case requires us to apply the principles articulated in *Shaw* to the most recent congressional redistricting plan enacted by the State of Georgia.

[B omitted]

II

A

Finding that the "evidence of the General Assembly's intent to racially gerrymander the Eleventh District is overwhelming, and practically stipulated by the parties involved," the District Court held that race was the predominant, overriding factor in drawing the Eleventh District. Appellants do not take issue with the court's factual finding of this racial motivation. Rather, they contend that evidence of a legislature's deliberate classification of voters on the basis of race cannot alone suffice to state a claim under *Shaw*. They argue that, regardless of the legislature's purposes, a plaintiff must demonstrate that a district's shape is so bizarre that it is unexplainable other than on the basis of race, and that appellees failed to make that showing here. Appellants' conception of the constitutional violation misapprehends our holding in *Shaw* and the Equal Protection precedent upon which *Shaw* relied.

Shaw recognized a claim "analytically distinct" from a vote dilution claim. Whereas a vote dilution claim alleges that the State has enacted a particular voting scheme as a purposeful device "to minimize or cancel out the voting potential of racial or ethnic minorities," an action disadvantaging voters of a particular race, the essence of the equal protection claim recognized in *Shaw* is that the State has used race as a basis for separating voters into districts. Just as the State may not, absent extraordinary justification, segregate citizens on the basis of race in its public parks, buses, golf courses, beaches, and schools, so did we recognize in *Shaw* that it may not separate its citizens into different voting districts on the basis of race. . . . When the State assigns voters on the basis of race, it engages in the offensive and demeaning assumption that voters of a particular race, because of their race, "think alike, share the same political interests, and will prefer the same candidates at the polls." Race-based assignments "embody stereotypes that treat individuals as the product of their race, evaluating their thoughts and efforts—their very worth as citizens—according to a criterion barred to the Government by history and the Constitution." . . . They also cause society serious harm. As we concluded in *Shaw*:

"Racial classifications with respect to voting carry particular dangers. Racial gerrymandering, even for remedial purposes, may balkanize us into competing racial factions; it threatens to carry us further from the goal of a political system in which race no longer matters—a goal that the Fourteenth and Fifteenth Amendments embody, and to which the Nation continues to aspire. It is for these reasons that race-based districting by our state legislatures demands close judicial scrutiny."

Our observation in *Shaw* of the consequences of racial stereotyping was not meant to suggest that a district must be bizarre on its face before there is a constitutional violation. Nor was our conclusion in *Shaw* that in certain instances a district's appearance (or, to be more precise, its appearance in combination with certain demographic evidence) can give rise to an equal protection claim, a holding that bizarreness was a threshold showing, as appellants believe it to be. Our circumspect approach and narrow holding in *Shaw* did not erect an artificial rule barring accepted equal protection analysis in other redistricting cases. Shape is relevant not because bizarreness is a necessary element of the constitutional wrong or a threshold requirement of proof, but because it may be persuasive circumstantial evidence that race for its own sake, and not other districting principles, was the legislature's dominant and controlling rationale in drawing its district lines. The logical implication, as courts applying *Shaw* have recognized, is that parties may rely on evidence other than bizarreness to establish race-based districting.

Our reasoning in *Shaw* compels this conclusion. We recognized in *Shaw* that, outside the districting context, statutes are subject to strict scrutiny under the Equal Protection Clause not just when they contain express racial classifications, but also when, though race neutral on their face, they are motivated by a racial purpose or object. . . .

Shaw applied these same principles to redistricting. "In some exceptional cases, a reapportionment plan may be so highly irregular that, on its face, it rationally cannot be understood as anything other than an effort to 'segregat[e] . . . voters' on the basis of race." In other cases, where the district is not so bizarre on its face that it discloses a racial design, the proof will be more "difficul[t]." Although it was not necessary in *Shaw* to consider further the proof required in these more difficult cases, the logical import of our reasoning is that evidence other than a district's bizarre shape can be used to support the claim.

Appellants and some of their *amici* argue that the Equal Protection Clause's general proscription on race-based decisionmaking does not obtain in the districting context because redistricting by definition involves racial considerations. Underlying their argument are the very stereotypical assumptions the Equal Protection Clause forbids. It is true that redistricting in most cases will implicate a political calculus in which various interests compete for recognition, but it does not follow from this that individuals of the same race share a single political interest. The view that they do is "based on the demeaning notion that members of the defined racial groups ascribe to certain 'minority views' that must be different from those of other citizens,"

Metro Broadcasting (KENNEDY, J., dissenting), the precise use of race as a proxy the Constitution prohibits. Nor can the argument that districting cases are excepted from standard equal protection precepts be resuscitated by *United Jewish Organizations of Williamsburgh, Inc.* v. *Carey* (1977), where the Court addressed a claim that New York violated the Constitution by splitting a Hasidic Jewish community in order to include additional majority-minority districts. As we explained in *Shaw*, a majority of the Justices in *UJO* construed the complaint as stating a vote dilution claim, so their analysis does not apply to a claim that the State has separated voters on the basis of race. To the extent any of the opinions in that "highly fractured decision" can be interpreted as suggesting that a State's assignment of voters on the basis of race would be subject to anything but our strictest scrutiny, those views ought not be deemed controlling.

In sum, we make clear that parties alleging that a State has assigned voters on the basis of race are neither confined in their proof to evidence regarding the district's geometry and makeup nor required to make a threshold showing of bizarreness. Today's case requires us further to consider the requirements of the proof necessary to sustain this equal protection challenge.

B

Federal court review of districting legislation represents a serious intrusion on the most vital of local functions. It is well settled that "reapportionment is primarily the duty and responsibility of the State." Electoral districting is a most difficult subject for legislatures, and so the States must have discretion to exercise the political judgment necessary to balance competing interests. Although race-based decisionmaking is inherently suspect, until a claimant makes a showing sufficient to support that allegation the good faith of a state legislature must be presumed. The courts, in assessing the sufficiency of a challenge to a districting plan, must be sensitive to the complex interplay of forces that enter a legislature's redistricting calculus. Redistricting legislatures will, for example, almost always be aware of racial demographics; but it does not follow that race predominates in the redistricting process. . . . The distinction between being aware of racial considerations and being motivated by them may be difficult to make. This evidentiary difficulty, together with the sensitive nature of redistricting and the presumption of good faith that must be accorded legislative enactments, requires courts to exercise extraordinary caution in adjudicating claims that a state has drawn district lines on the basis of race. The plaintiff's burden is to show, either through circumstantial evidence of a district's shape and demographics or more direct evidence going to legislative purpose, that race was the predominant factor motivating the legislature's decision to place a significant number of voters within or without a particular district. To make this showing, a plaintiff must prove that the legislature subordinated traditional race-neutral districting principles, including but not limited to compactness, contiguity, respect for political subdivisions or communities defined by actual shared interests, to racial considerations. Where these or other race-neutral considerations are the basis for redistricting legislation, and are not subordinated to race, a state can "defeat a claim that a district has been gerrymandered on racial lines." These principles inform the plaintiff's burden of proof. . . .

In our view, the District Court applied the correct analysis, and its finding that race was the predominant factor motivating the drawing of the Eleventh District was not clearly erroneous. The court found it was "exceedingly obvious" from the shape of the Eleventh District, together with the relevant racial demographics, that the drawing of narrow land bridges to incorporate within the District outlying appendages containing nearly 80% of the district's total black population was a deliberate attempt to bring black populations into the district. Although by comparison with other districts the geometric shape of the Eleventh District may not seem bizarre on its face, when its shape is considered in conjunction with its racial and population densities, the story of racial gerrymandering seen by the District Court becomes much clearer. Although this evidence is quite compelling, we need not determine whether it was, standing alone, sufficient to establish a *Shaw* claim that the Eleventh District is unexplainable other than by race. The District Court had before it considerable additional evidence showing that the General Assembly was motivated by a predominant, overriding desire to assign black populations to the Eleventh District and thereby permit the creation of a third majority-black district in the Second.

The court found that "it became obvious," both from the Justice Department's objection letters and the three preclearance rounds in general, "that [the Justice Department] would accept nothing less than abject surrender to its maximization agenda.". . . It further found that the General Assembly acquiesced and as a consequence was driven by its overriding desire to comply with the Department's maximization demands. . . . The State admitted that it " 'would not have added those portions of Effingham and Chatham Counties that are now in the [far southeastern extension of the] present Eleventh Congressional District but for the need to include additional black population in that district to offset the loss of black population caused by the shift of predominantly black portions of Bibb County in the Second Congressional District which occurred in response to the Department of Justice's March 20th, 1992, objection letter' " It conceded further that "[t]o the extent that precincts in the Eleventh Congressional District are split, a substantial reason for their being split was the objective of increasing the black population of that district." And in its brief to this Court, the State concedes that "[i]t is undisputed that Georgia's eleventh is the product of a desire by the General Assembly to create a majority black district." Hence the trial court had little difficulty concluding that the Justice Department "spent months demanding purely race-based revisions to Georgia's redistricting plans, and that Georgia spent months attempting to comply." On this record, we fail to see how the District Court could have reached any conclusion other than that race was the predominant factor in drawing Georgia's Eleventh District; and in any event we conclude the court's finding is not clearly erroneous. . . .

Race was, as the District Court found, the predominant, overriding factor explaining the General Assembly's decision to attach to the Eleventh District various appendages containing dense majority-black populations. As a result, Georgia's congressional redistricting plan cannot be upheld unless it satisfies strict scrutiny, our most rigorous and exacting standard of constitutional review.

III

To satisfy strict scrutiny, the State must demonstrate that its districting legislation is narrowly tailored to achieve a compelling interest. There is a "significant state interest in eradicating the effects of past racial discrimination." [Citing *Shaw*.] The State does not argue, however, that it created the Eleventh District to remedy past discrimination, and with good reason: there is little doubt that the State's true interest in designing the Eleventh District was creating a third majority-black district to satisfy the Justice Department's preclearance demands. . . . Whether or not in some cases compliance with the Voting Rights Act, standing alone, can provide a compelling interest independent of any interest in remedying past discrimination, it cannot do so here. As we suggested in *Shaw*, compliance with federal antidiscrimination laws cannot justify race-based districting where the challenged district was not reasonably necessary under a constitutional reading and application of those laws. The congressional plan challenged here was not required by the Voting Rights Act under a correct reading of the statute.

The Justice Department refused to preclear both of Georgia's first two submitted redistricting plans. The District Court found that the Justice Department had adopted a "black-maximization" policy under §5, and that it was clear from its objection letters that the Department would not grant preclearance until the State . . . created a third majority-black district. It is, therefore, safe to say that the congressional plan enacted in the end was required in order to obtain preclearance. It does not follow, however, that the plan was required by the substantive provisions of the Voting Rights Act.

We do not accept the contention that the State has a compelling interest in complying with whatever preclearance mandates the Justice Department issues. When a state governmental entity seeks to justify race-based remedies to cure the effects of past discrimination, we do not accept the government's mere assertion that the remedial action is required. Rather, we insist on a strong basis in evidence of the harm being remedied. . . . Our presumptive skepticism of all racial classifications prohibits us as well from accepting on its face the Justice Department's conclusion that racial districting is necessary under the Voting Rights Act. Where a State relies on the Department's determination that race-based districting is necessary to comply with the Voting Rights Act, the judiciary retains an independent obligation in adjudicating consequent equal protection challenges to ensure that the State's actions are narrowly tailored to achieve a compelling interest. . . .

For the same reasons, we think it inappropriate for a court engaged in constitutional scrutiny to accord deference to the Justice Department's interpretation of the Act. Although we have deferred to the Department's interpretation in certain statutory cases, we have rejected agency interpretations to which we would otherwise defer where they raise serious constitutional questions. When the Justice Department's interpretation of the Act compels race-based districting, it by definition raises a serious constitutional question, . . . and should not receive deference.

Georgia's drawing of the Eleventh District was not required under the Act because there was no reasonable basis to believe that Georgia's earlier enacted plans violated §5. Wherever a plan is "ameliorative," a term we have used to describe plans increasing the number of majority-minority districts, it "cannot violate §5 unless the new apportionment itself so discriminates on the basis of race or color as to violate the Constitution." Georgia's first and second proposed plans increased the number of majority-black districts from 1 out of 10 (10%) to 2 out of 11 (18.18%). These plans were "ameliorative" and could not have violated §5's non-retrogression principle. Acknowledging as much, the United States now relies on the fact that the Justice Department may object to a state proposal either on the ground that it has a prohibited purpose or a prohibited effect. The Government justifies its preclearance objections on the ground that the submitted plans violated §5's purpose element. The key to the Government's position . . . is and always has been that Georgia failed to proffer a nondiscriminatory purpose for its refusal in the first two submissions to take the steps necessary to create a third majority-minority district.

The Government's position is insupportable. . . . Although it is true we have held that the State has the burden to prove a nondiscriminatory purpose under §5, Georgia's Attorney General provided a detailed explanation for the State's initial decision not to enact the max-black plan. The District Court accepted this explanation and found an absence of any discriminatory intent. The State's policy of adhering to other districting principles instead of creating as many majority-minority districts as possible does not support an inference that the plan "so discriminates on the basis of race or color as to violate the Constitution," and thus cannot provide any basis under §5 for the Justice Department's objection.

Instead of grounding its objections on evidence of a discriminatory purpose, it would appear the Government was driven by its policy of maximizing majority-black districts. Although the Government now disavows having had that policy, and seems to concede its impropriety, the District Court's well-documented factual finding was that the Department did adopt a maximization policy and followed it in objecting to Georgia's first two plans. . . . In utilizing §5 to require States to create majority-minority districts wherever possible, the Department of Justice expanded its authority under the statute beyond what Congress intended and we have upheld. . . .

IV

The Voting Rights Act, and its grant of authority to the federal courts to uncover official efforts to abridge minorities' right to vote, has been of vital importance in eradicating invidious discrimination from the electoral process and enhancing the legitimacy of our political institutions. Only if our political system and our society cleanse themselves of that discrimination will all members of the polity share an equal opportunity to gain public office regardless of race. As a Nation we share both the obligation and the aspiration of working toward this end. The end is neither assured nor well served, however, by carving electorates into racial blocs. . . . It takes a shortsighted and unauthorized view of the Voting Rights Act to invoke that statute, which has played a decisive role in redressing some of our worst forms of discrimination, to demand the very racial stereotyping the Fourteenth Amendment forbids.

* * *

The judgment of the District Court is affirmed, and the case is remanded for further proceedings consistent with this decision.

It is so ordered.

JUSTICE GINSBURG, with whom JUSTICES STEVENS and BREYER join, and with whom JUSTICE SOUTER joins except as to Part III-B, dissenting.

Legislative districting is highly political business. This Court has generally respected the competence of state legislatures to attend to the task. When race is the issue, however, we have recognized the need for judicial intervention to prevent dilution of minority voting strength. Generations of rank discrimination against African-Americans, as citizens and voters, account for that surveillance.

Two Terms ago, in *Shaw* v. *Reno* (1993), this Court took up a claim "analytically distinct" from a vote dilution claim. *Shaw* authorized judicial intervention in "extremely irregular" apportionments, in which the legislature cast aside traditional districting practices to consider race alone—in the *Shaw* case, to create a district in North Carolina in which African-Americans would compose a majority of the voters.

Today the Court expands the judicial role, announcing that federal courts are to undertake searching review of any district with contours "predominantly motivated" by race: "strict scrutiny" will be triggered not only when traditional districting practices are abandoned, but also when those practices are "subordinated to"—given less weight than—race. Applying this new "race-as-predominant-factor" standard, the Court invalidates Georgia's districting plan even though Georgia's Eleventh District, the focus of today's dispute, bears the imprint of familiar districting practices. Because I do not endorse the Court's new standard and would not upset Georgia's plan, I dissent.

I

At the outset, it may be useful to note points on which the Court does not divide. First, we agree that federalism and the slim judicial competence to draw district lines weigh heavily against judicial intervention in apportionment decisions; as a rule, the task should remain within the domain of state legislatures. . . . Second, for most of our Nation's history, the franchise has not been enjoyed equally by black citizens and white voters. To redress past wrongs and to avert any recurrence of exclusion of blacks from political processes, federal courts now respond to Equal Protection Clause and Voting Rights Act complaints of state action that dilutes minority voting strength. Third, to meet statutory requirements, state legislatures must sometimes consider race as a factor highly relevant to the drawing of district lines . . . . Finally, state legislatures may recognize communities that have a particular racial or ethnic makeup, even in the absence of any compulsion to do so, in order to account for interests common to or shared by the persons grouped together. . . .

Therefore, the fact that the Georgia General Assembly took account of race in drawing district lines—a fact not in dispute—does not render the State's plan invalid. To offend the Equal Protection Clause, all agree, the legislature had to do more than consider race. How much more, is the issue that divides the Court today. . . .

[A and B omitted]

II

A

Before *Shaw* v. *Reno*, (1993), this Court invoked the Equal Protection Clause to justify intervention in the quintessentially political task of legislative districting in two circumstances: to enforce the one-person-one-vote requirement and to prevent dilution of a minority group's voting strength.

In *Shaw*, the Court recognized a third basis for an equal protection challenge to a State's apportionment plan. The Court wrote cautiously, emphasizing that judicial intervention is exceptional: "Strict [judicial] scrutiny" is in order, the Court declared, if a district is "so extremely irregular on its face that it rationally can be viewed only as an effort to segregate the races for purposes of voting.". . .

The problem in *Shaw* was not the plan architects' consideration of race as relevant in redistricting. Rather, in the Court's estimation, it was the virtual exclusion of other factors from the calculus. Traditional districting practices were cast aside, the Court concluded, with race alone steering placement of district lines.

B

The record before us does not show that race similarly overwhelmed traditional districting practices in Georgia. Although the Georgia General Assembly prominently considered race in shaping the Eleventh District, race did not crowd out all other factors. . . .

In contrast to the snake-like North Carolina district inspected in *Shaw*, Georgia's Eleventh District is hardly "bizarre," "extremely irregular," or "irrational on its face." Instead, the Eleventh District's design reflects significant consideration of "traditional districting factors (such as keeping political subdivisions intact) and the usual political process of compromise and trades for a variety of nonracial reasons.". . . The District covers a core area in central and eastern Georgia, and its total land area of 6,780 square miles is about average for the State. The border of the Eleventh District runs 1,184 miles, in line with Georgia's Second District, which has a 1,243-mile border, and the State's Eighth District, with a border running 1,155 miles.

Nor does the Eleventh District disrespect the boundaries of political subdivisions. Of the 22 counties in the District, 14 are intact and 8 are divided. That puts the Eleventh District at about the state average in divided counties. By contrast, of the Sixth District's 5 counties, none are intact, and of the Fourth District's 4 counties, just 1 is intact. Seventy-one percent of the Eleventh District's boundaries track the borders of political subdivisions. Of the State's 11 districts, 5 score worse than the Eleventh District on this criterion, and 5 score better. Eighty-three percent of the Eleventh District's geographic area is composed of intact counties, above average for the State's congressional districts. And notably, the Eleventh District's boundaries largely follow precinct lines.

Evidence at trial similarly shows that considerations other than race went into determining the Eleventh District's boundaries. For a "political reason"—to accommodate the request of an incumbent State Senator regarding the placement of the precinct in which his son lived—the DeKalb County portion of the Eleventh District was drawn to include a particular (largely white) precinct. The corridor through Effingham County was substantially narrowed at the request of a (white) State Representative. In Chatham County, the District was trimmed to exclude a heavily black community in Garden City because a State Representative wanted to keep the city intact inside the neighboring First District. The Savannah extension was configured by "the narrowest means possible" to avoid splitting the city of Port Wentworth.

Georgia's Eleventh District, in sum, is not an outlier district shaped without reference to familiar districting techniques. Tellingly, the District that the Court's decision today unsettles is not among those on a statistically calculated list of the 28 most bizarre districts in the United States, a study prepared in the wake of our decision in *Shaw*.

[C omitted]

D

Along with attention to size, shape, and political subdivisions, the Court recognizes as an appropriate districting principle, "respect for . . . communities defined by actual shared interests." The Court finds no community here, however, because a report in the record showed "fractured political, social, and economic interests within the Eleventh District's black population."

But ethnicity itself can tie people together, as volumes of social science literature have documented—even people with divergent economic interests. For this reason, ethnicity is a significant force in political life. . . .

To accommodate the reality of ethnic bonds, legislatures have long drawn voting districts along ethnic lines. Our Nation's cities are full of districts identified by their ethnic character—Chinese, Irish, Italian, Jewish, Polish, Russian, for example. . . . The creation of ethnic districts reflecting felt identity is not ordinarily viewed as offensive or demeaning to those included in the delineation.

III

To separate permissible and impermissible use of race in legislative apportionment, the Court orders strict scrutiny for districting plans "predominantly motivated" by race. No longer can a State avoid judicial oversight by giving—as in this case—genuine and measurable consideration to traditional districting practices. Instead, a federal case can be mounted whenever plaintiffs plausibly allege that other factors carried less weight than race. This invitation to litigate against the State seems to me neither necessary nor proper.

A

The Court derives its test from diverse opinions on the relevance of race in contexts distinctly unlike apportionment. The controlling idea, the Court says, is " 'the simple command [at the heart of the Constitution's guarantee of equal protection] that the Government must treat citizens as individuals, not as simply components of a racial, religious, sexual or national class.' ". . .

In adopting districting plans, however, States do not treat people as individuals. Apportionment schemes, by their very nature, assemble people in groups. . . .

That ethnicity defines some of these groups is a political reality. Until now, no constitutional infirmity has been seen in districting Irish or Italian voters together, for example, so long as the delineation does not abandon familiar apportionment practices. If Chinese-Americans and Russian-Americans may seek and secure group recognition in the delineation of voting districts, then African-Americans should not be dissimilarly treated. . . .

B

Under the Court's approach, judicial review of the same intensity, *i.e.*, strict scrutiny, is in order once it is determined that an apportionment is predominantly motivated by race. It matters not at all, in this new regime, whether the apportionment dilutes or enhances minority voting strength. . . .

Special circumstances justify vigilant judicial inspection to protect minority voters—circumstances that do not apply to majority voters. A history of exclusion from state politics left racial minorities without clout to extract provisions for fair representation in the lawmaking forum. The equal protection rights of minority voters thus could have remained unrealized absent the

Judiciary's close surveillance. . . . The majority, by definition, encounters no such blockage. White voters in Georgia do not lack means to exert strong pressure on their state legislators. The force of their numbers is itself a powerful determiner of what the legislature will do that does not coincide with perceived majority interests.

State legislatures like Georgia's today operate under federal constraints imposed by the Voting Rights Act—constraints justified by history and designed by Congress to make once-subordinated people free and equal citizens. But these federal constraints do not leave majority voters in need of extraordinary judicial solicitude. The Attorney General, who administers the Voting Rights Act's preclearance requirements, is herself a political actor. She has a duty to enforce the law Congress passed, and she is no doubt aware of the political cost of venturing too far to the detriment of majority voters. Majority voters, furthermore, can press the State to seek judicial review if the Attorney General refuses to preclear a plan that the voters favor. Finally, the Act is itself a political measure, subject to modification in the political process.

C

The Court's disposition renders redistricting perilous work for state legislatures. Statutory mandates and political realities may require States to consider race when drawing district lines. But today's decision is a counterforce; it opens the way for federal litigation if "traditional . . . districting principles" arguably were accorded less weight than race. Genuine attention to traditional districting practices and avoidance of bizarre configurations seemed, under *Shaw*, to provide a safe harbor. . . . In view of today's decision, that is no longer the case.

Only after litigation—under either the Voting Rights Act, the Court's new *Miller* standard, or both—will States now be assured that plans conscious of race are safe. Federal judges in large numbers may be drawn into the fray. This enlargement of the judicial role is unwarranted. The reapportionment plan that resulted from Georgia's political process merited this Court's approbation, not its condemnation. Accordingly, I dissent.

SUPREME COURT ON RELIGIOUS SYMBOLS AND PUBLICATIONS
June 29, 1995

In a pair of cases decided June 29, the Supreme Court handed down rulings that enlarged somewhat the support the government might give religious groups. The decisions, one involving a student religious publication, the other a religious symbol, did not set new legal precedents so much as refine those the Court had issued in the past.

In the more controversial of the two cases, Rosenberger v. Rector and Visitors of the University of Virginia, *the Court, by a 5–4 vote, ruled that the school violated the free speech rights of a student religious organization when it refused funding for publication of the group's religious magazine at the same time that it provided funding for other student publications. Writing for the Court, Justice Anthony M. Kennedy said states must treat student religious and nonreligious groups equally. "We have held that the guarantee of neutrality is respected, not offended, when the government, following neutral criteria and evenhanded policies, extends benefits to recipients whose ideologies and viewpoints, including religious ones, are broad and diverse," Kennedy said.*

Equal treatment was also at the core of the second case, Capital Square Review v. Pinette. *There the Court upheld the right of a private group to display a religious symbol in a public park that was open to a variety of private expressions, including other religious symbols. "Our precedent establishes that private religious speech, far from being a First Amendment orphan, is as fully protected under the Free Speech clause as secular private expression," Justice Antonin Scalia wrote for the majority.*

Free Speech and Religious Publications

The Rosenberger *case involved a student organization at the University of Virginia that published a magazine called* Wide Awake: A Christian Perspective, *which it distributed free on campus. The group was granted contracted independent organization (CIO) status by the university, a status that is denied to "religious organizations." University rules permitted use of a student activity fund to pay for some of the activities of CIOs, but the rules specifically excluded "religious activities," which were defined as "any activity that 'primarily promotes or manifests a particular belie[f] in or about a deity or an ultimate reality.' " When the university denied the organization's request that the student activity fund pay the printer for the costs of printing its magazine—on the ground that the magazine was religious activity—the organization sued, claiming that its right to free speech had been violated.*

In agreeing with the student organization, Kennedy argued that the university was discriminating against a point of view rather than a class of speech. "Religion may be a vast area of inquiry, but it also provides, as it did here, a specific premise, a perspective, a standpoint from which a variety of subjects may be discussed and considered," Kennedy wrote, in an opinion joined by Chief Justice William H. Rehnquist and Justices Sandra Day O'Connor, Clarence Thomas, and Scalia. "Having offered to pay the third-party contractors on behalf of private speakers who convey their own messages, the University may not silence the expression of selected viewpoints."

Kennedy also rejected the claim that the university would be violating the Establishment Clause, which prohibited government support of religion, by using the student activity fund to pay for printing the magazine. The money, Kennedy observed, came from students, not general taxpayers, and it would have been paid directly to the printer, not to the student organization. In these circumstances, he wrote, "any benefit to religion is incidental to the government's provision of secular services for secular purposes on a religious-neutral basis. Printing is a routine, secular, and recurring attribute of student life."

Justice David H. Souter wrote a sharply worded dissent, joined by Justices Stephen G. Breyer, Ruth Bader Ginsburg, and John Paul Stevens. "The Court is ordering an instrumentality of the State to support religious evangelism with direct funding. This is a flat violation of the Establishment Clause," Souter wrote.

The decision represented the first time that the Court had permitted government funding for a religious activity, but Kennedy warned that it was not an opening to more direct state funding of religion. "This is a far cry from a general public assessment designed and effected to provide financial support for a church," he wrote. Nonetheless, supporters of government-funded tuition vouchers for religious schools claimed a victory. "This settles the matter that if public benefits are distributed neutrally, it is irrelevant whether people choose to spend them for religious purposes," said Kevin J. Hasson, president and general counsel of the Becket Fund for Religious Liberty.

Those who believe in strong separation between church and state expressed dismay at the ruling. "This is a sad day for religious liberty," said J. Brent Walker, general counsel for the Baptist Joint Committee on Public Affairs. "For the first time in our nation's history, the Supreme

Court has sanctioned funding of religion with public funds. Our founders understood that, for religion to be meaningful it must be voluntary, free from government assistance and control."

The Establishment Clause and Religious Symbols

The second case arose when the state of Ohio sought to bar the Ku Klux Klan from displaying a cross on public property next to the state capitol building on the ground that to do otherwise would violate the Establishment Clause. The property had traditionally been used as a public forum for various sorts of private speech and expression, including the display of a state-sponsored Christmas tree and a menorah. In ruling against the state, the majority relied on precedent, which held that public schools must provide equal access to the school's facilities to both religious and nonreligious groups. "Religious expression cannot violate the Establishment Clause where it (1) is purely private and (2) occurs in a traditional or designated public forum, publicly announced and open to all on equal terms," Scalia wrote.

The majority split on the question of whether the display of the cross on state property implied state endorsement of a private religious message, which would contravene the Establishment Clause. Scalia, Rehnquist, Kennedy, and Thomas said that in this instance it did not. "Capitol Square is a genuinely public forum, is known to be a public forum, and has been widely used as a public forum for many, many years," Scalia wrote. "Private religious speech cannot be subject to veto by those who see favoritism where there is none." Although they concurred in the judgment, Justices Breyer, O'Connor, and Souter disagreed with the other four justices in the majority on the endorsement test.

Stevens and Ginsburg wrote separate dissents finding a clear violation of the Establishment Clause. "While this unattended, freestanding wooden cross was unquestionably a religious symbol, observers may well have received completely different messages from that symbol," Stevens wrote. "Some might have perceived it as a message of love, others as a message of hate, still others as a message of exclusion. . . . In any event, it was a message that the State of Ohio may not communicate to its citizens without violating the Establishment Clause."

> *Following are excerpts from the majority and dissenting opinions in two cases handed down by the Supreme Court on June 29, 1995. In* Rosenberger v. Rector and Visitors of the University of Virginia, *the Court held that it was constitutionally permissible for the university to use a student activity fee to pay for the printing costs of a student paper espousing a Christian viewpoint; in* Capitol Square Review v. Pinette, *the Court held that the state of Ohio could not bar the private display of a religious symbol in a traditionally public forum where it had permitted other similar displays:*

No. 94-329

Ronald W. Rosenberger, et al.,
Petitioners
v.
Rector and Visitors of the
University of Virginia et al.

On writ of certiorari to the United
States Court of Appeals for the
Fourth Circuit

[June 29, 1995]

JUSTICE KENNEDY delivered the opinion of the Court.

The University of Virginia, an instrumentality of the Commonwealth for which it is named and thus bound by the First and Fourteenth Amendments, authorizes the payment of outside contractors for the printing costs of a variety of student publications. It withheld any authorization for payments on behalf of petitioners for the sole reason that their student paper "primarily promotes or manifests a particular belie[f] in or about a deity or an ultimate reality." That the paper did promote or manifest views within the defined exclusion seems plain enough. The challenge is to the University's regulation and its denial of authorization, the case raising issues under the Speech and Establishment Clauses of the First Amendment.

I

. . . Before a student group is eligible to submit bills from its outside contractors for payment by the fund described below, it must become a "Contracted Independent Organization" (CIO). CIO status is available to any group the majority of whose members are students. . . .

All CIOs may exist and operate at the University, but some are also entitled to apply for funds from the Student Activities Fund (SAF). Established and Governed by University Guidelines, the purpose of the Saf is to support a broad range of extracurricular student activities that "are related to the educational purpose of the University.". . . The SAF receives its money from a mandatory fee of $14 per semester assessed to each full-time student. . . .

Some, but not all, CIOs may submit disbursement requests to the SAF. The Guidelines recognize 11 categories of student groups that may seek payment to third-party contractors because they "are related to the educational purpose of the University of Virginia." One of these is "student news, information, opinion, entertainment, or academic communications media groups." The Guidelines also specify, however, that the costs of certain activities of CIOs that are otherwise eligible for funding will not be reimbursed by the SAF. The students activities which are excluded from SAF support [include] religious activities. . . . A "religious activity" . . . is defined as an activity that "primarily promotes or manifests a particular belie[f] in or about a deity or an ultimate reality." . . .

Petitioners' organization, Wide Awake Productions (WAP), qualified as a CIO. Formed by petitioner Ronald Rosenberger and other undergraduates in 1990, WAP was established "[t]o provide a unifying focus for Christians of multicultural backgrounds." WAP publishes Wide Awake: A Christian Perspective at the University of Virginia. The paper's Christian viewpoint was evident from the first issue, in which its editors wrote that the journal "offers a Christian perspective on both personal and community issues, especially those relevant to college students at the University of Virginia." the editors committed the paper to a two-fold mission: "to challenge Christians to live, in word and deed, according to the faith they proclaim and to encourage students to consider what a personal relationship with Jesus Christ means.". . .

WAP had acquired CIO status soon after it was organized. This is an important consideration in this case, for had it been a "religious organization," WAP would not have been accorded CIO status. As defined by the Guidelines, a "religious organization" is "an organization whose purpose is to practice a devotion to an acknowledged ultimate reality or deity." At no stage in this controversy has the University contended that WAP is such an organization.

A few months after being given CIO status, WAP requested the SAF to pay its printer $5,862 for the costs of printing its newspaper. The Appropriations Committee of the Student Council denied WAP's request on the ground that Wide Awake was a "religious activity" within the meaning of the Guidelines, i.e., that the newspaper "promote[d] or manifest[ed] a particular belief in or about a deity or an ultimate reality." It made its determination after examining the first issue. WAP appealed the denial to the full Student Council. . . . The appeal was denied without further comments, and WAP appealed to the next level, the Student Activities Committee. In a letter signed by the Dean of Students, the committee sustained the denial of funding.

Having no further recourse within the University structure, WAP, Wide Awake, and three of its editors and members filed suit in the United States District Court for the Western District of Virginia. . . . They alleged that refusal to authorize payment of the printing costs of the publication, solely on the basis of its religious editorial viewpoint, violated their rights to freedom of speech and press, to the free exercise of religion, and to equal protection of the law. . . .

On cross-motions for summary judgment, the District Court ruled for the University, holding that denial of SAF support was not an impermissible content or viewpoint discrimination against petitioners' speech, and that the University's Establishment Clause concern over its "religious activities" was a sufficient justification for denying payment to third-party contractors. . . .

The United States Court of Appeals for the Fourth Circuit, in disagreement with the District Court, held that the Guidelines did discriminate on the basis of content. It ruled that, while the State need not underwrite speech, there was a presumptive violation of the Speech Clause when viewpoint discrimination was invoked to deny third-party payment otherwise available to CIOs.

(1994). The Court of Appeals affirmed the judgment of the District Court nonetheless, concluding that the discrimination by the University was justified by the "compelling interest in maintaining strict separation of church and state."

II

It is axiomatic that the government may not regulate speech based on its substantive content or the message it conveys. Other principles follow from this precept. In the realm of private speech or expression, government regulation may not favor one speaker over another. Discrimination against speech because of its message is presumed to be unconstitutional. These rules informed our determination that the government offends the First Amendment when it imposes financial burdens on certain speakers based on the content of their expression. When the government targets not subject matter but particular views taken by speakers on a subject, the violation of the First Amendment is all the more blatant. Viewpoint discrimination is thus an egregious form of content discrimination. The government must abstain from regulating speech when the specific motivating ideology or the opinion or perspective of the speaker is the rationale for the restriction.

These principles provide the framework forbidding the State from exercising viewpoint discrimination, even when the limited public forum is one of its own creation. In a case involving a school district's provision of school facilities for private uses, we declared that "[t]here is no question that the District, like the private owner of property, may legally preserve the property under its control for the use to which it is dedicated." *Lamb's Chapel* v. *Center Moriches Union Free School Dist.* (1993). The necessities of confining a forum to the limited and legitimate purposes for which it was created may justify the State in reserving it for certain groups or for the discussion of certain topics. Once it has opened a limited forum, however, the State must respect the lawful boundaries it has itself set. . . . Thus, in determining whether the State is acting to preserve the limits of the forum it has created so that the exclusion of a class of speech is legitimate, we have observed a distinction between, on the one hand, content discrimination, which may be permissible if it preserves the purposes of that limited forum, and, on the other hand, viewpoint discrimination, which is presumed impermissible when directed against speech otherwise within the forum's limitations. . . .

The University does acknowledge . . . that "ideologically driven attempts to suppress a particular point of view are presumptively unconstitutional in funding, as in other contexts," but insists that this case does not present that issue because the Guidelines draw lines based on content, not viewpoint. As we have noted, discrimination against one set of views or ideas is but a subset or particular instance of the more general phenomenon of content discrimination. And, it must be acknowledged, the distinction is not a precise one. It is, in a sense, something of an understatement to speak of religious thought and discussion as just a viewpoint, as distinct from a comprehensive body of thought. The nature of our origins and destiny and their dependence upon the existence of a divine being have been subjects of philosophic inquiry throughout human history. We conclude, nonetheless, that here, as in *Lamb's Chapel*, viewpoint discrimination is the proper way to interpret the University's objections to Wide Awake. By the very terms of the SAF prohibition, the University does not exclude religion as a subject matter but selects for disfavored treatment those student journalistic efforts with religious editorial viewpoints. Religion may be a vast area of inquiry, but it also provides, as it did here, a specific premise, a perspective, a standpoint from which a variety of subjects may be discussed and considered. The prohibited perspective, not the general subject matter, resulted in the refusal to make third-party payments, for the subjects discussed were otherwise within the approved category of publications. . . .

To this end the University relies on our assurance in *Widmar* v. *Vincent* [1981]. There, in the course of striking down a public university's exclusion of religious groups from use of school facilities made available to all other student groups, we stated: "Nor do we question the right of the University to make academic judgments as to how best to allocate scarce resources." The quoted language in *Widmar* was but a proper recognition of the principle that when the State is the speaker, it may make content-based choices. . . .

It does not follow, however, . . . that viewpoint-based restrictions are proper when the University does not itself speak or subsidize transmittal of a message it favors but instead expends funds to encourage a diversity of views from private speakers. A holding that the University may not discriminate based on the viewpoint of private persons whose speech it facilitates does not restrict the University's own speech, which is controlled by different principles. . . .

The distinction between the University's own favored message and the private speech of students is evident in the case before us. The University itself has taken steps to ensure the distinction in the agreement each CIO [Contracted Independent Organization] must sign. The University declares that the student groups eligible for SAF support are not the University's agents, are not subject to its control, and are not its responsibility. Having offered to pay the third-party contractors on behalf of private speakers who convey their own messages, the University may not silence the expression of selected viewpoints. . . .

III

. . . A central lesson of our decisions is that a significant factor in upholding governmental programs in the face of Establishment Clause attack is their neutrality towards religion. . . . We have held that the guarantee of neutrality is respected, not offended, when the government, following neutral criteria and evenhanded policies, extends benefits to recipients whose ideologies and viewpoints, including religious ones, are broad and diverse. . . .

The governmental program here is neutral toward religion. There is no suggestion that the University created it to advance religion or adopted some ingenious device with the purpose of aiding a religious cause. The object of the SAF is to open a forum for speech and to support various student enterprises, including the publication of newspapers, in recognition of the diversity and creativity of student life. The University's SAF Guidelines have a separate classification for, and do not make third-party payments on behalf of, "religious organizations," which are those "whose purpose is to practice a devotion to an acknowledged ultimate reality or deity." The category of support here is for "student news, information, opinion, entertainment, or academic communications media groups," of which Wide Awake was 1 of 15 in the 1990 school year. WAP did not seek a subsidy because of its Christian editorial viewpoint; it sought funding as a student journal, which it was.

The neutrality of the program distinguishes the student fees from a tax levied for the direct support of a church or group of churches. A tax of that sort, of course, would run contrary to Establishment Clause concerns dating from the earliest days of the Republic. The apprehensions of our predecessors involved the levying of taxes upon the public for the sole and exclusive purpose of establishing and supporting specific sects. The exaction here, by contrast, is a student activity fee designed to reflect the reality that student life in its many dimensions includes the necessity of wide-ranging speech and inquiry and that student expression is an integral part of the University's educational mission. The fee is mandatory, and we do not have before us the question whether an objecting student has the First Amendment right to demand a pro rata return to the extent the fee is expended for speech to which he or she does not subscribe. We must treat it, then, as an exaction upon the students. But the $14 paid each semester by the students is not a general tax designed to raise revenue for the University. . . . The SAF cannot be used for unlimited purposes, much less the illegitimate purpose of supporting one religion. Much like the arrangement in *Widmar*, the money goes to a special fund from which any group of students with CIO status can draw for purposes consistent with the University's educational mission; and to the extent the student is interested in speech, withdrawal is permitted to cover the whole spectrum of speech, whether it manifests a religious view, an antireligious view, or neither. Our decision, then, cannot be read as addressing an expenditure from a general tax fund. Here, the disbursements from the fund go to private contractors for the cost of printing that which is protected under the Speech Clause of the First Amendment. This is a far cry from a general public assessment designed and effected to provide financial support for a church. . . .

It does not violate the Establishment Clause for a public university to grant access to its facilities on a religion-neutral basis to a wide spectrum of student groups, including groups which use meeting rooms for sectarian activities, accompanied by some devotional exercises. See *Widmar; [Board of Ed. of Westside Community Schools (Dist. 66) v.] Mergens* (1990). This is so even where the upkeep, maintenance, and repair of the facilities attributed to those uses is paid from a student activities fund to which students are required to contribute. . . . If the expenditure of governmental funds is prohibited whenever those funds pay for a service that is, pursuant to a religion-neutral program, used by a group for sectarian purposes, then *Widmar, Mergens* and *Lamb's Chapel* would have to be overruled. Given our holdings in these cases, it follows that a public university may maintain its own computer facility and give student groups access to that facility, including the use of the printers, on a religion neutral, say first-come first-served, basis. If a religious student organization obtained access on that religion-neutral basis and used a computer to compose or a printer or copy machine to print speech with a religious content or viewpoint, the State's action in providing the group with access would no more violate the Establishment Clause than would giving those groups access to an assembly hall. There is no difference in logic or principle, and no difference of constitutional significance, between a school using its funds to operate a facility to which students have access, and a school paying a third-party contractor to operate the facility on its behalf. The latter occurs here. The University provides printing services to a broad spectrum of student newspapers qualified as CIOs by reason of their officers and membership. Any benefit to religion is incidental to the government's provision of secular services for secular purposes on a religion-neutral basis. Printing is a routine, secular, and recurring attribute of student life. . . .

To obey the Establishment Clause, it was not necessary for the University to deny eligibility to student publications because of their viewpoint. The neutrality commanded of the State by the separate Clauses of the First Amendment was compromised by the University's course of action. The viewpoint discrimination inherent in the University's regulation required public officials to scan and interpret student publications to discern their underlying philosophic assumptions respecting religious theory and belief. That course of action was a denial of the right of free speech and would risk fostering a pervasive bias or hostility to religion, which could undermine the very neutrality the Establishment Clause requires. There is no Establishment Clause violation in the University's honoring its duties under the Free Speech Clause.

The judgment of the Court of Appeals must be, and is, reversed.

It is so ordered.

JUSTICE SOUTER, with whom JUSTICE STEVENS, JUSTICE GINSBURG and JUSTICE BREYER join, dissenting.

The Court today, for the first time, approves direct funding of core religious activities by an arm of the State. It does so, however, only after erroneous treatment of some familiar principles of law implementing the First Amendment's Establishment and Speech Clauses, and by viewing the very funds in question beyond the reach of the Establishment Clause's funding restrictions as such. Because there is no warrant for distinguishing among

public funding sources for purposes of applying the First Amendment's prohibition of religious establishment, I would hold that the University's refusal
to support petitioners' religious activities is compelled by the Establishment
Clause. I would therefore affirm.

I

The central question in this case is whether a grant from the Student Activities Fund to pay Wide Awake's printing expenses would violate the Establishment Clause. Although the Court does not dwell on the details of Wide
Awake's message, it recognizes something sufficiently religious in the publication to demand Establishment Clause scrutiny. Although the Court places
great stress on the eligibility of secular as well as religious activities for
grants from the Student Activities Fund, it recognizes that such evenhanded
availability is not by itself enough to satisfy constitutional requirements for
any aid scheme that results in a benefit to religion. Something more is necessary to justify any religious aid. Some members of the Court, at least, may
think the funding permissible on a view that it is indirect, since the money
goes to Wide Awake's printer, not through Wide Awake's own checking
account. The Court's principal reliance, however, is on an argument that providing religion with economically valuable services is permissible on the theory that services are economically indistinguishable from religious access to
governmental speech forums, which sometimes is permissible. But this reasoning would commit the Court to approving direct religious aid beyond anything justifiable for the sake of access to speaking forums. The Court implicitly recognizes this in its further attempt to circumvent the clear bar to direct
governmental aid to religion. . . . The opinion of the Court makes the novel
assumption that only direct aid financed with tax revenue is barred, and
draws the erroneous conclusion that the involuntary Student Activities Fee
is not a tax. . . .

A

The Court's difficulties will be all the more clear after a closer look at Wide
Awake than the majority opinion affords. The character of the magazine is
candidly disclosed on the opening page of the first issue, where the editor-in-
chief announces Wide Awake's mission in a letter to the readership signed,
"Love in Christ": it is "to challenge Christians to live, in word and deed,
according to the faith they proclaim and to encourage students to consider
what a personal relationship with Jesus Christ means.". . .

This writing is no merely descriptive examination of religious doctrine or
even of ideal Christian practice in confronting life's social and personal problems. Nor is it merely the expression of editorial opinion that incidentally
coincides with Christian ethics and reflects a Christian view of human obligation. It is straightforward exhortation to enter into a relationship with God
as revealed in Jesus Christ, and to satisfy a series of moral obligations
derived from the teachings of Jesus Christ. These are not the words of "student news, information, opinion, entertainment, or academic communica-

tio[n]. . . ." (in the language of the University's funding), but the words of "challenge [to] Christians to live, in word and deed, according to the faith they proclaim and . . . to consider what a personal relationship with Jesus Christ means" (in the language of Wide Awake's founder). The subject is not the discourse of the scholar's study or the seminar room, but of the evangelist's mission station and the pulpit. It is nothing other than the preaching of the word, which (along with the sacraments) is what most branches of Christianity offer those called to the religious life.

Using public funds for the direct subsidization of preaching the word is categorically forbidden under the Establishment Clause, and if the Clause was meant to accomplish nothing else, it was meant to bar this use of public money. . . .

The principle against direct funding with public money is patently violated by the contested use of today's student activity fee. . . . The University exercises the power of the State to compel a student to pay it, and the use of any part of it for the direct support of religious activity thus strikes at what we have repeatedly held to be the heart of the prohibition on establishment. [Citation of cases omitted.]

The Court, accordingly, has never before upheld direct state funding of the sort of proselytizing published in Wide Awake and, in fact, has categorically condemned state programs directly aiding religious activity. [Citation of cases omitted.]

Even when the Court has upheld aid to an institution performing both secular and sectarian functions, it has always made a searching enquiry to ensure that the institution kept the secular activities separate from its sectarian ones, with any direct aid flowing only to the former and never the latter. [Citation of cases omitted.]

Reasonable minds may differ over whether the Court reached the correct result in each of these cases, but their common principle has never been questioned or repudiated. "Although Establishment Clause jurisprudence is characterized by few absolutes, the Clause does absolutely prohibit government-financed . . . indoctrination into the beliefs of a particular religious faith." *[Board of Ed. of Central] School Dist. [No. 1]* v. *Ball* [(1968)].

[B and C omitted]

D

Nothing in the Court's opinion would lead me to end this enquiry into the application of the Establishment Clause any differently from the way I began it. The Court is ordering an instrumentality of the State to support religious evangelism with direct funding. This is a flat violation of the Establishment Clause. . . .

No. 94–780

Capitol Square Review and
Advisory Board, et al., Petitioners
v.
Vincent J. Pinette, Donnie A. Carr
and Knights of the Ku Klux Klan

On writ of certiorari to the United
States Court of Appeals for the
Sixth Circuit

[June 29, 1995]

JUSTICE SCALIA announced the judgment of the Court and delivered the
opinion of the Court with respect to Parts I, II, and III, and an opinion with
respect to Part IV, in which the CHIEF JUSTICE, JUSTICE KENNEDY and
JUSTICE THOMAS join.

The Establishment Clause of the First Amendment, made binding upon
the States through the Fourteenth Amendment, provides that government
"shall make no law respecting an establishment of religion." The question in
this case is whether a State violates the Establishment Clause when, pursuant to a religiously neutral state policy, it permits a private party to display
an unattended religious symbol in a traditional public forum located next to
its seat of government.

I

Capitol Square is a 10-acre, state-owned plaza surrounding the Statehouse
in Columbus, Ohio. For over a century the square has been used for public
speeches, gatherings, and festivals advocating and celebrating a variety of
causes, both secular and religious. [The state] makes the square available
"for use by the public . . . for free discussion of public questions, or for activities of a broad public purpose," and . . . gives the Capitol Square Review and
Advisory Board responsibility for regulating public access. To use the square,
a group must simply fill out an official application form and meet several criteria, which concern primarily safety, sanitation, and non-interference with
other uses of the square, and which are neutral as to the speech content of
the proposed event.

It has been the Board's policy "to allow a broad range of speakers and
other gatherings of people to conduct events on the Capitol Square." Such
diverse groups as homosexual rights organizations, the Ku Klux Klan and
the United Way have held rallies. The Board has also permitted a variety of
unattended displays on Capitol Square: a State-sponsored lighted tree during the Christmas season, a privately-sponsored menorah during
Chanukah, a display showing the progress of a United Way fundraising
campaign, and booths and exhibits during an arts festival. Although there
was some dispute in this litigation regarding the frequency of unattended

displays, the District Court found, with ample justification, that there was no policy against them.

In November 1993, after reversing an initial decision to ban unattended holiday displays from the square during December 1993, the Board authorized the State to put up its annual Christmas tree. On November 29, 1993, the Board granted a rabbi's application to erect a menorah. That same day, the Board received an application from respondent Donnie Carr, an officer of the Ohio Ku Klux Klan, to place a cross on the square from December 8, 1993, to December 24, 1993. The Board denied that application on December 3, informing the Klan by letter that the decision to deny "was made upon the advice of counsel, in a good faith attempt to comply with the Ohio and United States Constitutions, as they have been interpreted in relevant decisions by the Federal and State Courts."

Two weeks later, having been unsuccessful in its effort to obtain administrative relief from the Board's decision, the Ohio Klan, through its leader Vincent Pinette, filed the present suit in the United States District Court for the Southern District of Ohio, seeking an injunction requiring the Board to issue the requested permit. The Board defended on the ground that the permit would violate the Establishment Clause. The District Court determined that Capitol Square was a traditional public forum open to all without any policy against free-standing displays; that the Klan's cross was entirely private expression entitled to full First Amendment protection; and that the Board had failed to show that the display of the cross could reasonably be construed as endorsement of Christianity by the State. The District Court issued the injunction and, after the Board's application for an emergency stay was denied (1993) (STEVENS, J., in chambers), the Board permitted the Klan to erect its cross. The Board then received, and granted, several additional applications to erect crosses on Capitol Square during December 1993 and January 1994.

On appeal by the Board, the United States Court of Appeals for the Sixth Circuit affirmed the District Court's judgment (1994). That decision agrees with a ruling by the Eleventh Circuit, *Chabad-Lubavitch* v. *Miller* (1993), but disagrees with decisions of the Second and Fourth Circuits, *Chabad-Lubavitch* v. *Burlington* (CA2 1991), cert. denied (1992), *Kaplan* v. *Burlington* (CA2 1989), cert. denied (1990), *Smith* v. *County of Albemarle* (CA4), cert. denied, (1990). We granted certiorari. (1995).

II

First, a preliminary matter: Respondents contend that we should treat this as a case in which freedom of speech (the Klan's right to present the message of the cross display) was denied because of the State's disagreement with that message's political content, rather than because of the State's desire to distance itself from sectarian religion. They suggest in their merits brief and in their oral argument that Ohio's genuine reason for disallowing the display was disapproval of the political views of the Ku Klux Klan. Whatever the fact may be, the case was not presented and decided that way. The record facts before us and the opinions below address only the Establishment Clause issue; that is the question upon which we granted certiorari; and that is the sole question before us to decide.

Respondents' religious display in Capitol Square was private expression. Our precedent establishes that private religious speech, far from being a First Amendment orphan, is as fully protected under the Free Speech Clause as secular private expression. *Lamb's Chapel* v. *Center Moriches Union Free School Dist.* (1993); *Board of Ed. of Westside Community Schools (Dist. 66)* v. *Mergens* (1990); *Widmar* v. *Vincent* (1981); *Heffron* v. *International Soc. for Krishna Consciousness, Inc.* (1981). Indeed, in Anglo-American history, at least, government suppression of speech has so commonly been directed precisely at religious speech that a free-speech clause without religion would be *Hamlet* without the prince. Accordingly, we have not excluded from free-speech protections religious proselytizing, *Heffron,* or even acts of worship, *Widmar.* Petitioners do not dispute that respondents, in displaying their cross, were engaging in constitutionally protected expression. They do contend that the constitutional protection does not extend to the length of permitting that expression to be made on Capitol Square.

It is undeniable, of course, that speech which is constitutionally protected against state suppression is not thereby accorded a guaranteed forum on all property owned by the State. The right to use government property for one's private expression depends upon whether the property has by law or tradition been given the status of a public forum, or rather has been reserved for specific official uses. If the former, a State's right to limit protected expressive activity is sharply circumscribed: it may impose reasonable, content-neutral time, place and manner restrictions (a ban on all unattended displays, which did not exist here, might be one such), but it may regulate expressive *content* only if such a restriction is necessary, and narrowly drawn, to serve a compelling state interest. These strict standards apply here, since the District Court and the Court of Appeals found that Capitol Square was a traditional public forum.

Petitioners do not claim that their denial of respondents' application was based upon a content-neutral time, place, or manner restriction. To the contrary, they concede—indeed it is the essence of their case—that the Board rejected the display precisely because its content was religious. Petitioners advance a single justification for closing Capitol Square to respondents' cross: the State's interest in avoiding official endorsement of Christianity, as required by the Establishment Clause.

III

There is no doubt that compliance with the Establishment Clause is a state interest sufficiently compelling to justify content-based restrictions on speech. Whether that interest is implicated here, however, is a different question. And we do not write on a blank slate in answering it. We have twice previously addressed the combination of private religious expression, a forum available for public use, content-based regulation, and a State's interest in complying with the Establishment Clause. Both times, we have struck down the restriction on religious content.

In *Lamb's Chapel*, a school district allowed private groups to use school facilities during off-hours for a variety of civic, social and recreational purposes, excluding, however, religious purposes. We held that even if school property during off-hours was not a public forum, the school district violated an applicant's free-speech rights by denying it use of the facilities solely because of the religious viewpoint of the program it wished to present. We rejected the district's compelling-state-interest Establishment Clause defense (the same made here) because the school property was open to a wide variety of uses, the district was not directly sponsoring the religious group's activity, and "any benefit to religion or to the Church would have been no more than incidental." The *Lamb's Chapel* reasoning applies *a fortiori* here, where the property at issue is not a school but a full-fledged public forum.

Lamb's Chapel followed naturally from our decision in *Widmar*, in which we examined a public university's exclusion of student religious groups from facilities available to other student groups. There also we addressed official discrimination against groups who wished to use a "generally open forum" for religious speech. And there also the State claimed that its compelling interest in complying with the Establishment Clause justified the content-based restriction. We rejected the defense because the forum created by the State was open to a broad spectrum of groups and would provide only incidental benefit to religion. We stated categorically that "an open forum in a public university does not confer any imprimatur of state approval on religious sects or practices."

Quite obviously, the factors that we considered determinative in *Lamb's Chapel* and *Widmar* exist here as well. The State did not sponsor respondents' expression, the expression was made on government property that had been opened to the public for speech, and permission was requested through the same application process and on the same terms required of other private groups.

IV

Petitioners argue that one feature of the present case distinguishes it from *Lamb's Chapel* and *Widmar*: the forum's proximity to the seat of government, which, they contend, may produce the perception that the cross bears the State's approval. They urge us to apply the so-called "endorsement test," see, *e.g.*, *Allegheny County* v. *American Civil Liberties Union, Greater Pittsburgh Chapter* (1989); *Lynch v. Donnelly* (1984), and to find that, because an observer might mistake private expression for officially endorsed religious expression, the State's content-based restriction is constitutional.

We must note, to begin with, that it is not really an "endorsement test" of any sort, much less the "endorsement test" which appears in our more recent Establishment Clause jurisprudence, that petitioners urge upon us. "Endorsement" connotes an expression or demonstration of approval or support. Our cases have accordingly equated "endorsement" with "promotion" or "favoritism." We find it peculiar to say that government "promotes" or "favors" a religious display by giving it the same access to a public forum that all other displays enjoy. And as a matter of Establishment Clause jurisprudence, we have consistently held that it is no violation for government to enact neutral policies that happen to benefit religion. . . . The test petitioners propose, which would attribute to a neutrally behaving government *private* religious expression, has no antecedent in our jurisprudence, and would better be called a "transferred endorsement" test. . . .

Of course, giving sectarian religious speech preferential access to a forum close to the seat of government (or anywhere else for that matter) would violate the Establishment Clause (as well as the Free Speech Clause, since it would involve content discrimination). And one can conceive of a case in which a governmental entity manipulates its administration of a public forum close to the seat of government (or within a government building) in such a manner that only certain religious groups take advantage of it, creating an impression of endorsement *that is in fact accurate.* But those situations, which involve governmental *favoritism,* do not exist here. Capitol Square is a genuinely public forum, is known to be a public forum, and has been widely used as a public forum for many, many years. Private religious speech cannot be subject to veto by those who see favoritism where there is none. . . .

If Ohio is concerned about misperceptions, nothing prevents it from requiring all private displays in the Square to be identified as such. That would be a content-neutral "manner" restriction which is assuredly constitutional. But the State may not, on the claim of misperception of official endorsement, ban all private religious speech from the public square, or discriminate against it by requiring religious speech alone to disclaim public sponsorship.

* * *

Religious expression cannot violate the Establishment Clause where it (1) is purely private and (2) occurs in a traditional or designated public forum, publicly announced and open to all on equal terms. Those conditions are satisfied here, and therefore the State may not bar respondents' cross from Capitol Square.

The judgment of the Court of Appeals is

affirmed.

JUSTICE O'CONNOR, with whom JUSTICE SOUTER and JUSTICE BREYER join, concurring in part and concurring in the judgment.

I join Parts I, II, and III of the Court's opinion and concur in the judgment. Despite the messages of bigotry and racism that may be conveyed along with religious connotations by the display of a Ku Klux Klan cross, at bottom this case must be understood as it has been presented to us—as a case about private religious expression and whether the State's relationship to it violates the Establishment Clause. In my view, "the endorsement test asks the right question about governmental practices challenged on Establishment Clause grounds, including challenged practices involving the display of religious symbols," *Allegheny County* v. *American Civil Liberties Union, Greater Pittsburgh Chapter* (1989) (O'CONNOR, J., concurring in part and concurring in judgment), even where a neutral state policy toward private religious speech in a public forum is at issue. Accordingly, I see no necessity to carve out, as the plurality opinion would today, an exception to the endorsement test for the public forum context. . . .

JUSTICE SOUTER, with whom JUSTICE O'CONNOR and JUSTICE BREYER join, concurring in part and concurring in the judgment.

I concur in Parts I, II, and III of the Court's opinion. I also want to note specifically my agreement with the Court's suggestion that the State of Ohio could ban all unattended private displays in Capitol Square if it so desired. The fact that the Capitol lawn has been the site of public protests and gatherings, and is the location of any number of the government's own unattended displays, such as statues, does not disable the State from closing the square to all privately owned, unattended structures. . . .

Otherwise, however, I limit my concurrence to the judgment. Although I agree in the end that, in the circumstances of this case, petitioners erred in denying the Klan's application for a permit to erect a cross on Capitol Square, my analysis of the Establishment Clause issue differs from JUSTICE SCALIA'S, and I vote to affirm in large part because of the possibility of affixing a sign to the cross adequately disclaiming any government sponsorship or endorsement of it.

The plurality's opinion declines to apply the endorsement test to the Board's action, in favor of a *per se* rule: religious expression cannot violate the Establishment Clause where it (1) is private and (2) occurs in a public forum, even if a reasonable observer would see the expression as indicating state endorsement. This *per se* rule would be an exception to the endorsement test, not previously recognized and out of square with our precedents. . . .

JUSTICE STEVENS, dissenting.

The Establishment Clause should be construed to create a strong presumption against the installation of unattended religious symbols on public property. Although the State of Ohio has allowed Capitol Square, the area around the seat of its government, to be used as a public forum, and although it has occasionally allowed private groups to erect other sectarian displays there, neither fact provides a sufficient basis for rebutting that presumption. On the contrary, the sequence of sectarian displays disclosed by the record in this case illustrates the importance of rebuilding the "wall of separation between church and State" that Jefferson envisioned.

I

At issue in this case is an unadorned Latin cross, which the Ku Klux Klan placed, and left unattended, on the lawn in front of the Ohio State Capitol. The Court decides this case on the assumption that the cross was a religious symbol. I agree with that assumption notwithstanding the hybrid character of this particular object. The record indicates that the "Grand Titan of the Knights of the Ku Klux Klan for the Realm of Ohio" applied for a permit to place a cross in front of the State Capitol because "the Jews" were placing a "symbol for the Jewish belief" in the Square. Some observers, unaware of who had sponsored the cross, or unfamiliar with the history of the Klan and its reaction to the menorah, might interpret the Klan's cross as an inspirational symbol of the crucifixion and resurrection of Jesus Christ. More knowledgeable observers might regard it, given the context, as an anti-semitic symbol of bigotry and disrespect for a particular religious sect. Under the first interpretation, the cross is plainly a religious symbol. Under the second, an icon of intolerance expressing an anti-clerical message should also be treated as a religious symbol because the Establishment Clause must prohibit official sponsorship of irreligious as well as religious messages. This principle is no less binding if the anti-religious message is also a bigoted message. . . .

Thus, while this unattended, freestanding wooden cross was unquestionably a religious symbol, observers may well have received completely different messages from that symbol. Some might have perceived it as a message of love, others as a message of hate, still others as a message of exclusion— a Statehouse sign calling powerfully to mind their outsider status. In any event, it was a message that the State of Ohio may not communicate to its citizens without violating the Establishment Clause.

II

The plurality does not disagree with the proposition that the State may not espouse a religious message. It concludes, however, that the State has not sent such a message; it has merely allowed others to do so on its property. Thus, the State has provided an "incidental benefit" to religion by allowing private parties access to a traditional public forum. In my judgment, neither precedent nor respect for the values protected by the Establishment Clause justifies that conclusion.

The Establishment Clause, "at the very least, prohibits government from appearing to take a position on questions of religious belief or from 'making adherence to a religion relevant in any way to a person's standing in the political community' " *County of Allegheny* v. *American Civil Liberties Union, Greater Pittsburgh Chapter* (1989), quoting *Lynch* v. *Donnelly* (1984) (O'CONNOR, J., concurring). At least when religious symbols are involved, the question of whether the state is "appearing to take a position" is best judged from the standpoint of a "reasonable observer." It is especially important to take account of the perspective of a reasonable observer who may not share the particular religious belief it expresses. A paramount purpose of the Establishment Clause is to protect such a person from being made to feel like an outsider in matters of faith, and a stranger in the political community. If a reasonable person could perceive a government endorsement of religion from a private display, then the State may not allow its property to be used as a forum for that display. No less stringent rule can adequately protect nonadherents from a well-grounded perception that their sovereign supports a faith to which they do not subscribe.

In determining whether the State's maintenance of the Klan's cross in front of the Statehouse conveyed a forbidden message of endorsement, we should be mindful of the power of a symbol standing alone and unexplained. Even on private property, signs and symbols are generally understood to express the owner's views. The location of the sign is a significant component of the message it conveys. . . .

Like other speakers, a person who places a sign on her own property has the autonomy to choose the content of her own message. Thus, the location of a stationary, unattended sign generally is both a component of its message and an implicit endorsement of that message by the party with the power to decide whether it may be conveyed from that location.

So it is with signs and symbols left to speak for themselves on public property. The very fact that a sign is installed on public property implies official recognition and reinforcement of its message. That implication is especially strong when the sign stands in front of the seat of the government itself. The "reasonable observer" of any symbol placed unattended in front of any capitol in the world will normally assume that the sovereign—which is not only the owner of that parcel of real estate but also the lawgiver for the surrounding territory—has sponsored and facilitated its message. . . .

Because structures on government property—and, in particular, in front of buildings plainly identified with the state—imply state approval of their message, the Government must have considerable leeway, outside of the religious arena, to choose what kinds of displays it will allow and what kinds it will not. Although the First Amendment requires the Government to allow leafletting or demonstrating outside its buildings, the state has greater power to exclude unattended symbols when they convey a type of message with which the state does not wish to be identified. I think it obvious, for example, that Ohio could prohibit certain categories of signs or symbols in Capitol Square—erotic exhibits, commercial advertising, and perhaps campaign posters as well—without violating the Free Speech Clause. . . .

The State's general power to restrict the types of unattended displays does not alone suffice to decide this case, because Ohio did not profess to be exercising any such authority. Instead, the Capitol Square Review Board denied a permit for the cross because it believed the Establishment Clause required as much, and we cannot know whether the Board would have denied the permit on other grounds. Accordingly, we must evaluate the State's rationale on its own terms. But in this case, the endorsement inquiry under the Establishment Clause follows from the State's power to exclude unattended private displays from public property. Just as the Constitution recognizes the State's interest in preventing its property from being used as a conduit for ideas it does not wish to give the appearance of ratifying, the Establishment Clause prohibits government from allowing, and thus endorsing, unattended displays that take a position on a religious issue. If the State allows such stationary displays in front of its seat of government, viewers will reasonably assume that it approves of them. As the picture appended to this opinion demonstrates [omitted], a reasonable observer would likely infer endorsement from the location of the cross erected by the Klan in this case. Even if the disclaimer at the foot of the cross (which stated that the cross was placed there by a private organization) were legible, that inference would remain, because a property owner's decision to allow a third party to place a sign on her property conveys the same message of endorsement as if she had erected it herself.

When the message is religious in character, it is a message the state can neither send nor reinforce without violating the Establishment Clause. Accordingly, I would hold that the Constitution generally forbids the placement of a symbol of a religious character in, on, or before a seat of government. . . .

JUSTICE GINSBURG, dissenting.

We confront here, as JUSTICES O'CONNOR and SOUTER point out, a large Latin cross that stood alone and unattended in close proximity to Ohio's Statehouse. Near the stationary cross were the government's flags and the government's statues. No human speaker was present to disassociate the religious symbol from the State. No other private display was in sight. No plainly visible sign informed the public that the cross belonged to the Klan and that Ohio's government did not endorse the display's message.

If the aim of the Establishment Clause is genuinely to uncouple government from church, a State may not permit, and a court may not order, a display of this character. . . . JUSTICE SOUTER, in the final paragraphs of his opinion, suggests two arrangements that might have distanced the State from "the principal symbol of Christianity around the world"[:] a sufficiently large and clear disclaimer[;] or an area reserved for unattended displays carrying no endorsement from the State, a space plainly and permanently so marked. Neither arrangement is even arguably present in this case. The District Court's order did not mandate a disclaimer. . . . And the disclaimer the Klan appended to the foot of the cross was unsturdy: it did not identify the Klan as sponsor; it failed to state unequivocally that Ohio did not endorse the display's message; and it was not shown to be legible from a distance. The relief ordered by the District Court thus violated the Establishment Clause.

Whether a court order allowing display of a cross, but demanding a sturdier disclaimer, could withstand Establishment Clause analysis is a question more difficult than the one this case poses. I would reserve that question for another day and case. But I would not let the prospect of what might have been permissible control today's decision on the constitutionality of the display the District Court's order in fact authorized.

July

COMMISSION REPORT ON
MILITARY BASE CLOSINGS
July 1, 1995

As part of the continuing cutbacks in U.S. defense spending, President Bill Clinton and Congress agreed in 1995 to close seventy-nine domestic military installations and realign twenty-six others. The cutbacks were projected to save $19.3 billion over twenty years.

The base closings were recommended on July 1 by the eight-member Defense Base Closure and Realignment Commission. Clinton reluctantly accepted the recommendations on July 13, forwarding them to Congress. The House voted 343–75 on September 8 to approve the closings. That vote settled the matter, because the commission recommendations could have been overturned only by a vote of both chambers of Congress.

The 1995 base closings were the fourth round; previous closings had been made in 1988, 1991, and 1993. The 1995 round was the final one mandated in the 1991 defense authorizations law (PL 101–510). However, both Defense Secretary William J. Perry and the commission called for another round of reviews in future years, after all closures had been completed. Those suggestions got a chilly reception on Capitol Hill, where many members were reluctant to face the continued political heat generated by base closings.

As with previous rounds of base closings, the 1995 review set off a political firestorm around the country, with local politicians and members of Congress fighting to protect their bases and urging that Washington look elsewhere for savings.

The furor over the 1995 round was particularly intense because of its potential impact on the 1996 presidential elections. California and Texas, both key states because of their large numbers of electoral votes, faced the biggest cutbacks. Senior Air Force officials lobbied intensely against the closing of large maintenance depots in those states. President Clinton, while ultimately accepting the closings, complained bitterly about the political impact of the base closings process. Under pressure from the California congressional delegation, Clinton reportedly gave serious

*consideration to rejecting at least part of the commission recommenda-
tions.*

*It was to insulate base closings against partisan politics that led Con-
gress to establish the commission review process. In effect, members of
Congress gave themselves the opportunity to blame base closings on an
independent commission. Most observers and members of Congress agreed
that the process worked as well as could be expected, given the economic
and political consequences of the decisions involved.*

The 1995 Closings

*Skirmishing over the 1995 round of base closings began in earnest on
February 28, when Defense Secretary Perry announced plans to close or
realign 146 installations in the United States, including 33 major bases.
Some observers had expected the Pentagon to propose even more closings.
Perry said the military and local communities were having trouble absorb-
ing the impact of previous rounds, and finding the right mix of bases to
close was getting more difficult.*

*Perry's recommendations went to the base closing commission, which
began hearings on March 1. Former Illinois senator Alan Dixon, a Democrat, chaired the eight-member commission, which included several retired
senior military officers.*

*The commission on May 10 added thirty-two bases to a list of those
under review for closing, a step that intensified political scrambling by
local officials and members of Congress. Among the major facilities added
to the potential closing list were McClellan Air Force Base near Sacramento, California; the Portsmouth Naval Shipyard at the Maine-New Hampshire border; and Kelly Air Force Base in San Antonio, Texas.*

*McClellan and Kelly Air Force bases then became the center of attention,
as the commission and the Air Force argued over how much money would
be saved by shrinking or closing them and three other bases. All five bases
were maintenance depots employing thousands of civilians, as well as military personnel. Both the commission and the General Accounting Office,
in an April 13 report, chided the Air Force for using flawed figures to over-
estimate the cost of closing the five depots.*

*During its final round of action the last week of June, the commission
voted to close the five Air Force depots, including the McClellan and Kelly
bases, saying all were underutilized. Closing Kelly would cost about 1,700
military and nearly 12,000 civilian jobs; closing McClellan would mean
2,600 military and nearly 9,000 civilian jobs.*

*Commission chairman Dixon called the vote on the five Air Force depots
"the most significant deviation from the [Defense] secretary's recommendations in the history of base closures." The commission voted to keep open
several other facilities that had been on its tentative hit list. Among the latter were the Portsmouth Naval Shipyard and Tinker Air Force base in
Oklahoma City. In terms of employment, Tinker was the largest on the list,
with 8,200 military and nearly 12,000 civilian jobs. In sparing the*

Portsmouth facility, the commission chose instead to close a naval ship-yard in Long Beach, California.

Pressure on Clinton

The action by the commission shifted the pressure to President Clinton, who faced conflicting political advice from Capitol Hill. On the one hand, lawmakers from California and Texas argued that the president should reject the proposed closings of Kelly and McClellan Air Force bases. Among the most vocal were two key Democrats, California senators Dianne Feinstein and Barbara Boxer.

White House aides hinted in early July that the president might reject the commission recommendations; they cited in particular the political impact of cutting tens of thousands of jobs in California just before a presidential election, fearing that Clinton would be blamed for the loss of jobs.

Most senior congressional leaders of both parties urged the president to accept the commission recommendations—in effect, to refrain from intervening in the base-closing process for political reasons. Perhaps the most influential of those urging this course was Sen. Sam Nunn of Georgia, ranking Democrat on the Armed Services Committee, who was generally considered the most respected voice in Congress on military matters.

Clinton accepted the commission recommendations on July 13, but with the greatest reluctance. He told reporters that the panel's report was "an outrage" motivated by politics, and that the loss of jobs would be most severe in California and Texas.

In an attempt to soften the blow, the administration drew up a plan for the Defense Department to hire private firms to perform much of the maintenance work at the McClellan and Kelly bases. White House spokesman Michael McCurry said that plan could save 8,700 jobs at McClellan and 16,000 at Kelly over a five-year period.

The administration's privatization plan satisfied neither those who wanted to save the Air Force bases nor those who wanted to shut them down. Sen. Feinstein called it "a big letdown." Commission member Josue Robles Jr. said the administration would have a difficult time proving that its plan would save more money than closing the bases and shifting work to other facilities.

Following is the executive summary of the report of the Defense Base Closure and Realignment Commission, issued July 1, 1995:

Closing military facilities is a difficult and painful process. Every installation recommended for closure or realignment has enjoyed a proud history and has offered a priceless service to our nation. At the same time, these installations have become an integral part of their local communities and, in turn, have received strong support from the local citizenry. Rightfully, these citizens are concerned about the effect of base closures on the economic livelihood of their communities.

The undeniable fact remains, however, that U.S. military requirements have been fundamentally altered. The end of the Cold War, combined with the growing urgency to reduce the Federal budget deficit, compels the United States to reduce and realign its military forces. To reduce the number of military installations in the United States, and to ensure the impartiality of the decision-making process, Congress enacted the Defense Base Closure and Realignment Act of 1990 (Public Law 101–510, as amended).

Signed by President George Bush on November 5, 1990, this Act established the independent Defense Base Closure and Realignment Commission (DBCRC). The Commission was established "to provide a fair process that will result in the timely closure and realignment of military installations inside the United States." Authorized to meet only during calendar years 1991, 1993, and 1995, the Commission's authority expires on December 31, 1995.

Because this is the third and final round under Public Law 101–510, the 1995 Commission is proud to have the opportunity to bring this process to a successful and prudent conclusion and to make suggestions regarding the future. The Commission has taken the approach that the base closure process should not be simply a budget-cutting exercise. Base closures must be undertaken to reduce our nation's defense infrastructure in a deliberate way that will improve long-term military readiness and ensure that taxpayer dollars are spent in the most efficient way possible. The Commission's challenge was to develop a list of base closures and realignments that allows the Defense Department to maintain readiness, modernize our military, and preserve the force levels needed to maintain our security. The Commission believes that it has met this challenge.

In compliance with the Defense Base Closure and Realignment Act of 1990, the Secretary of Defense submitted a list of proposed military base closures and realignments to the Commission on February 28, 1995. The Secretary's 1995 recommended actions affected 146 domestic military installations, including 33 major closures, 26 major realignments, and an additional 27 changes prior to base closure round decisions, or "redirects." The statute also required the Secretary of Defense to base all recommendations on a force-structure plan submitted to Congress with the Departments FY 1996 budget request and on selection criteria developed by the Secretary of Defense and approved by Congress. For the 1995 Commission process, the Secretary of Defense announced that the selection criteria would be identical to those used during the 1991 and 1993 base closure rounds.

1995 DoD Selection Criteria

Military Value

1. The current and future mission requirements and the impact on operational readiness of the Department of Defense's [DoD] total force.

2. The availability and condition of land, facilities and associated airspace at both existing and potential receiving locations.
3. The ability to accommodate contingency, mobilization, and future total force requirements at both existing and potential receiving locations.
4. The cost and manpower implications.

Return on Investment

5. The extent and timing of potential costs and savings, including the number of years, beginning with the date of completion of the closure or realignment, for the savings to exceed the costs.

Impacts

6. The economic impact on communities.
7. The ability of both the existing and potential receiving communities' infrastructure to support forces, missions and personnel.
8. The environmental impact.

Upon receipt of the recommendations of the Secretary of Defense, the Commission is required to hold public hearings on the recommendations before making any findings. To change any of the Secretary's recommendations, Public Law 101–510 requires the Commission to find substantial deviation from the Secretary's force-structure plan and the final criteria approved by Congress. Like previous DBCRC rounds, the 1995 Commission's process was a model of open government. Its recommendations resulted from an independent review of the Secretary of Defense's recommendations, without political or partisan influence. As part of its review and analysis process, the Commission solicited information from a wide variety of sources. Most importantly, communities affected by the recommendations played a major role in the Commission's process. Every major site proposed for closure or realignment was visited by at least one commissioner. These visits enabled the commissioners to gain a first-hand look at the installations. Commissioners also heard from members of the public about the effect that closures would have on local communities. The Commission held 13 investigative hearings, conducted 206 fact-finding visits to 167 military installations and activities, held 16 regional hearings nationwide, listened to hundreds of Members of Congress, and received thousands of letters from concerned citizens from across the country. All meetings were open to the public. All data received by the Commission, as well as all transcripts of Commission hearings, were available for public review. Throughout the process, the Commission staff members maintained an active and ongoing dialogue with communities, and met with community representatives at the Commission offices, during base visits, and during regional hearings.

At the Commission's investigative hearings, Commissioners questioned senior military and civilian officials of the Defense Department directly responsible for the Secretary's recommendations. Defense and base closure experts within the Federal government, private sector, and academia provided an independent assessment of the base closure process and the potential impacts of the Secretary of Defense's recommendations. Public Law 101–510, as amended, also requires the General Accounting Office (GAO) to evaluate DoD's selection process and recommendations, and provide the Commission and Congress a report containing their detailed analysis of the process by April 15, 1995. GAO testified before the Commission on April 17, 1995, presenting its findings and recommendations. All of the Commission's hearings and deliberations were held in public. Many were broadcast on national television.

Based on military installation visits, hearings, and its review and analysis, the Commission voted to consider alternatives and additions to the Secretary's list. On March 7, 1995, and again on May 10, 1995, the Commission voted to consider a total of 32 installations as possible alternatives and additions to the 146 bases recommended for closure or realignment by the Secretary of Defense.

Communities that contributed to our country's national security by hosting a military facility for many years should rest assured their concerns were heard, carefully reviewed, and analyzed. The Commission would also like to reassure communities there can be life after a base is closed. Economic recovery is, however, in large part dependent upon a concerted community effort to look towards the future. The same dedicated effort expended by communities over the last several months to save their bases should be redirected towards building and implementing a reuse plan that will revitalize the community and the local economy.

The Department of Defense Office of Economic Adjustment (OEA) was established to help communities affected by base closures, as well as other defense program changes. The OEA's principal objective is to help the communities affected by base closures maintain or restore economic stability. According to an OEA survey, approximately 158,000 new jobs were created between 1961 and 1992 to replace nearly 93,000 jobs lost as a result of base closures. The OEA has also been working with 47 communities located near bases recommended for closure by the 1988 and 1991 Commissions, and has provided $20 million in grants to help communities develop reuse plans.

As part of the 1995 Commission's interest in post-closure activities, the Commission also reviewed and developed recommendations on how to improve the Federal government's performance in the area of conversion and reuse of military installations. The 1988, 1991, and 1993 base closure rounds have resulted in more than 70 major, and almost 200 smaller, base closings. The Federal government has an obligation to assist local communities in the challenge of replacing the base in the local economy. The Commission held two hearings in which local elected officials, private sector groups, and officials from the Federal government presented testimony on post-closure activities of the Federal government. . . .

Costs and Savings of the Commission's Recommendations

After thorough review and analysis, the Commission recommends the closure or realignment of 132 military installations in the United States. This total includes 123 of the 146 closure or realignment recommendations of the Secretary of Defense, and 9 of the 36 military installations identified by the Commission as candidates for consideration during its deliberations.

The Commission estimates that the closure or realignment of these 132 military installations will require one-time, upfront costs of $3.6 billion, and will result in annual savings of $1.6 billion once implemented. Over the next 20 years, the total savings will be approximately $19.3 billion. . . .

While the Commission believes that the one-time costs of implementing its recommendations will exceed the Defense Department's revised estimates by $40 million, the annual savings and 20-year savings from the Commission's recommendations will exceed the Defense Department's revised estimates by $37 million and $323 million, respectively. These 1995 recommendations represent the first time that the Defense Base Closure and Realignment Commission has recommended savings greater than those proposed by the Secretary of Defense.

The following list summarizes the closure and realignment recommendations of the 1995 Defense Base Closure and Realignment Commission.

1995 Defense Base Closure and Realignment Commission Recommendations

Part I: Major Base Closures

Department of the Army

Fort McClellan, AL
Fort Chaffee, AR
Oakland Army Base, CA
Fitzsimons Army Medical Center, CO
Savanna Army Depot Activity, IL
Fort Ritchie, MD
Bayonne Military Ocean Terminal, NJ
Seneca Army Depot, NY
Fort Indiantown Gap, PA
Fort Pickett, VA

Department of the Navy

Naval Air Facility, Adak, AK
Long Beach Naval Shipyard, CA
Ship Repair Facility, GU
Naval Air Warfare Center, Aircraft Division, Indianapolis, IN
Naval Surface Warfare Center, Crane Division Detachment, Louisville, KY
Naval Surface Warfare Center, Dahlgren Division Detachment, White Oak, MD

Naval Air Station, South Weymouth, MA
Naval Air Warfare Center, Aircraft Division, Warminster, PA

Department of the Air Force

McClellan Air Force Base, CA
Ontario International Airport Air Guard Station, CA
Chicago O'Hare International Airport Air Reserve Station, IL
Roslyn Air Guard Station, NY
Bergstrom Air Reserve Base, TX
Reese Air Force Base, TX

Defense Logistics Agency

Defense Distribution Depot, McClellan, CA
Defense Distribution Depot, Memphis, TN
Defense Distribution Depot, San Antonio, TX
Defense Distribution Depot, Ogden, UT

Part II: Major Base Realignments

Department of the Army

Fort Greely, AK
Fort Hunter Liggett, CA
Sierra Army Depot, CA
Fort Meade, MD
Detroit Arsenal, MI
Fort Dix, NJ
Charles E. Kelly Support Center, PA
Letterkenny Army Depot, PA
Fort Buchanan, PR
Red River Army Depot, TX
Fort Lee, VA

Department of the Navy

Naval Air Station, Key West, FL
Naval Activities, GU
Naval Air Station, Corpus Christi, TX
Naval Undersea Warfare Center, Keyport, WA

Department of the Air Force

Onizuka Air Station, CA
Eglin Air Force Base, FL
Malmstrom Air Force Base, MT
Grand Forks Air Force Base, ND
Kelly Air Force Base, TX
Hill Air Force Base, UT (Utah Test and Training Range)

Part III: Smaller Base or Activity Closures, Realignments, Disestablishments or Relocations

Department of the Army

Branch U.S. Disciplinary Barracks, CA
East Fort Baker, CA
Rio Vista Army Reserve Center, CA
Stratford Army Engine Plant, CT
Big Coppett Key, FL
Concepts Analysis Agency, MD
Fort Holabird, MD
Publications Distribution Center, Baltimore, MD
Hingham Cohasset, MA
Sudbury Training Annex, MA
Aviation Troop Command (ATCOM), MO
Fort Missoula, MT
Camp Kilmer, NJ
Camp Pedricktown, NJ
Bellmore Logistics Activity, NY
Fort Totten, NY
Recreation Center #2, Fayetteville, NC
Information Systems Software Center (ISSC), VA
Camp Bonneville, WA

Department of the Navy

Fleet and Industrial Supply Center, Oakland, CA
Naval Command, Control and Ocean Surveillance Center, In-Service Engineering West Coast Division, San Diego, CA
Naval Personnel Research and Development Center, San Diego, CA
Supervisor of Shipbuilding, Conversion and Repair, USN, Long Beach, CA
Naval Undersea Warfare Center-Newport Division, New London Detachment, New London, CT
Naval Research Laboratory, Underwater Sound Reference Detachment, Orlando, FL
Fleet and Industrial Supply Center, GU
Public Works Center, GU
Naval Biodynamics Laboratory, New Orleans, LA
Naval Medical Research Institute, Bethesda, MD
Naval Surface Warfare Center, Carderock Division Detachment, Annapolis, MD
Naval Aviation Engineering Support Unit, Philadelphia, PA
Naval Air Technical Services Facility, Philadelphia, PA
Naval Air Warfare Center, Aircraft Division, Open Water Test Facility, Oreland, PA
Naval Command, Control and Ocean Surveillance Center, RDT&E Division Detachment, Warminster, PA

Fleet and Industrial Supply Center, Charleston, SC
Naval Command, Control and Ocean Surveillance Center, In-Service Engineering, East Coast Detachment, Norfolk, VA
Naval Information Systems Management Center, Arlington, VA
Naval Management Systems Support Office, Chesapeake, VA

Navy/Marine Reserve Activities

Naval Reserve Centers at:
  Huntsville, AL
  Stockton, CA
  Santa Ana, Irvine, CA
  Pomona, CA
  Cadillac, MI
  Staten Island, NY
  Laredo, TX
  Sheboygan, WI
Naval Air Reserve Center at Olathe, KS
Naval Reserve Readiness Commands at:
  New Orleans, LA (Region 10)
  Charleston, SC (Region 7)

Department of the Air Force

Real-Time Digitally Controlled Analyzer Processor Activity, Buffalo, NY

Defense Logistics Agency

Defense Contract Management District South, Marietta, GA
Defense Contract Management Command International, Dayton, OH
Defense Distribution Depot, Columbus, OH
Defense Distribution Depot, Letterkenny, PA
Defense Industrial Supply Center Philadelphia, PA

Defense Investigative Service

Investigations Control and Automation Directorate, Fort Holabird, MD

Part IV: Changes to Previously Approved BRAC Recommendations

Department of the Army

Tri-Service Project Reliance, Army Bio-Medical Research Laboratory, Fort Detrick, MD

Department of the Navy

Marine Corps Air Station, El Toro, CA
Marine Corps Air Station, Tustin, CA
Naval Air Station, Alameda, CA
Naval Recruiting District, San Diego, CA

Naval Training Center, San Diego, CA
Naval Air Station, Cecil Field, FL
Naval Aviation Depot, Pensacola, FL
Navy Nuclear Power Propulsion Training Center, Naval Training Center, Orlando, FL
Naval Training Center, Orlando, FL
Naval Air Station, Agana, GU
Naval Air Station, Barbers Point, HI
Naval Air Facility, Detroit, MI
Naval Shipyard, Norfolk Detachment, Philadelphia, PA
Naval Sea Systems Command, Arlington, VA
Office of Naval Research, Arlington, VA
Space and Naval Warfare Systems Command, Arlington, VA
Naval Recruiting Command, Washington, DC
Naval Security Group Command Detachment Potomac, Washington, DC

Department of the Air Force

Williams Air Force Base, AZ
Lowry Air Force Base, CO
Homestead Air Force Base, FL (301st Rescue Squadron)
Homestead Air Force Base, FL (726th Air Control Squadron)
MacDill Air Force Base, FL
Griffiss Air Force Base, NY (Airfield Support for 10th Infantry Division [Light])
Griffiss Air Force Base, NY (485th Engineering Installation Group)

Defense Logistics Agency

Defense Contract Management District West, El Segundo, CA

Part V: DoD Recommendations Rejected by the Commission

Proposed Closures Rejected by the Commission

Moffett Federal Airfield AGS, CA
Naval Health Research Center, San Diego, CA
North Highlands Air Guard Station, CA
Price Support Center, IL
Selfridge Army Garrison, MI
Naval Air Station Meridian, MS
Naval Technical Training Center Meridian, MS
Naval Air Warfare Center, Aircraft Division, Lakehurst, NJ
Rome Laboratory, Rome, NY
Springfield-Beckley MAP Air Guard Station, OH
Greater Pittsburgh LAP Air Reserve Station, PA
Air Force Electronic Warfare Evaluation Simulator Activity, Fort Worth, TX
Brooks Air Force Base, TX
Defense Distribution Depot, Red River, TX

Proposed Realignments Rejected by the Commission

Robins Air Force Base, CA
Fort Hamilton, NY
Tinker Air Force Base, OK
Hill Air Force Base, UT

Proposed Recommendations Rejected by the Commission at the Request of the Secretary of Defense

Caven Point Reserve Center, NJ
Kirtland Air Force Base, NM
Dugway Proving Ground, UT
Valley Grove Area Maintenance Support Activity (AMSA), WV

JOINT U.S.-RUSSIAN NEWS CONFERENCE FROM SPACE
July 3, 1995

Astronauts aboard the docked American space shuttle Atlantis *and Russian space station* Mir *said on July 3 that their groundbreaking mission was a success that cleared the way for future joint space explorations.*

Atlantis *and* Mir *docked together June 29 and stayed linked for five days. It was the first linking of two space vehicles since the much smaller* Apollo *and* Soyuz *craft were coupled in 1975. More important, the* Atlantis-Mir *mission was the first step toward construction of an international space station, which was scheduled to begin in 1997. Astronaut Norman Thagard celebrated three other important firsts during the mission: he was the first American carried into space on a Russian spaceship; he was the first American to work in the nine-year-old* Mir; *and he set a new American space endurance record of 112 days.*

Thagard and five of his American and Russian colleagues on July 3 participated in a joint news conference from space marking the historic mission. They said their mission demonstrated that cooperation in space could continue despite political squabbles on Earth.

The Cold War Background

The Atlantis *and* Mir *were important symbols of the Cold War—vehicles built as part of that era's competition in all spheres between the United States and the Soviet Union. The shuttle was supposed to have ferried astronauts and equipment to an American space station that was never built. The* Mir, *designed in the 1980s to last no more than five years, instead was kept in service even after the collapse of the Soviet Union, in part to show that Russia would continue to be an international power.*

By 1995 the United States was a benefactor of the Russian space program, which was suffering deep cutbacks due to the severely strained Russian economy. The National Aeronautics and Space Administration was paying the Russian space agency $400 million over four years for use of the Mir *and other services. In Washington, there was a modest debate about* *how reliable a space partner Russia would turn out to be.* (Report on American-Russian space cooperation, p. 222)

The Atlantis-Mir *mission began at the once-secret Baikonur Cosmodrome, located on the frozen steppes of southern Kazakhstan. From that launch facility, the Soviet Union had launched* Sputnik, *the first satellite, into space in 1957; in 1961 Yuri Gagarin began his mission as the first man in space from Baikonur. American U-2 pilot Francis Gary Powers had been on his way to photograph Baikonur when he was shot down and captured in 1960—one of the most infamous events of the Cold War.*

The Atlantis-Mir *Mission Gets Underway*

On March 14, 1995, astronaut Thagard and two Russian cosmonauts aboard a Soyuz spacecraft were lifted into space from Baikonur to start the Atlantis-Mir *mission. Thagard and the two Russians reached the* Mir *two days later, to be met with the traditional Russian welcome of bread and salt.*

Thagard and his Russian colleagues worked for nearly three months to ready the Mir *for its rendezvous with* Atlantis. *That event occurred on June 29, 245 miles above the Earth.* Atlantis *commander Robert "Hoot" Gibson carefully maneuvered his spaceship into a near-perfect docking with* Mir, *just two seconds off the scheduled time. The two vehicles formed an unwieldy looking structure the height of a fifteen-story building and weighing more than 200 tons.*

About two hours after the docking, Gibson floated into the tunnel between the two ships, to be greeted by the Mir *commander, Vladimir N. Dezhurov. The six American and four Russian astronauts then gathered in the cramped* Mir *for a group photo session; it was the biggest assembly ever in space.*

Dezhurov called the docking a "politically important step to strengthening the friendship between the peoples of the United States and Russia." Gibson replied, in Russian: "Together, we will build a future based on cooperation, mutual trust, and friendship. Today, that is our true, important mission."

On July 3, as the Atlantis-Mir *mission was coming to a close, four American astronauts and two Russian cosmonauts participated in an hour-long joint news conference from space, with reporters asking questions from Moscow; Houston, Texas; and Cape Canaveral, Florida.*

Much of the attention was focused on Thagard, a fifty-one-year-old medical doctor and former fighter pilot who joined the space program in 1978 and was on his fifth mission in space. Thagard acknowledged that he sorely missed his family and had been troubled by the "cultural isolation" of not being around English speakers (although he did speak Russian fluently after a year's training near Moscow).

Gibson, Thagard, and other astronauts said the public might not understand how much work was involved aboard a spaceship, from the physical labor of hauling supplies and equipment to the highly technical scientific experiments.

The next day, July 4, the ten astronauts took apart the docking mechanisms and separated the two spaceships. All the Americans, including Thagard, returned to Earth aboard the Atlantis, *while two Russians returned aboard a* Soyuz, *and two Russians stayed behind on the* Mir. *During the five days their ships were docked together, the astronauts conducted twenty-eight experiments, many of them probing the effects on humans of long-duration space flight.*

The Atlantis *and* Mir *docked in space again on November 15 and stayed linked for three days. U.S. and Russian officials said that mission also was a success. At least five other* Atlantis-Mir *dockings were planned before 1997, when the United States, Japan, Canada, Russia, and the European Space Agency were scheduled to begin building the giant international space station. That station was to be used to conduct long-term experiments in space.*

Following are excerpts from the July 3, 1995, joint news conference by four American astronauts and two Russian cosmonauts, in which they discussed the docking of the Atlantis *and* Mir *spaceships. The text was provided by the Federal Document Clearing House Inc. (questions and answers in Russian were not provided):*

GIBSON: Well, . . . it's a pleasure for us to be here and for us to be participating in a ground-breaking mission like this one. And we're all interested to talk to the press today and see what they would like to talk about.

QUESTION: Hi. This is Bill Horowitz, *CBS News,* for Hoot Gibson. Hoot, how do you think this mission will affect or maybe sway detractors of the space station . . . , and should it for that matter? What's your message to the American people after this flight?

GIBSON: I've been real impressed with the fact that the things that we did on this mission are exactly the sorts of things that we need to do with the space station, and I guess in the opinion of the crew here, things have flowed pretty smoothly. Certainly the rendezvous and docking, all of the mechanisms, all of the machinery that had to operate, operated in spectacular function. And I think we've done a pretty good dry run for the sorts of things that we would need to do with an international space station. And so I think I speak for all of us when I say we feel pretty good about the way this mission has gone and what it portends for future space stations.

QUESTION: This is Marcia Dunn of the Associated Press for Dr. Thagard. The sacrifice that astronauts' families make is being talked about. Please discuss that with us, what you've missed back home, and how you plan to make it up to your family when you return?

THAGARD: Well, first of all, I will admit that I owe them a large debt. I, after all, at the end get to fly in space and they don't, but they make the same sacrifice of separation that I do. First of all, we plan to take a vacation the first moment that that's possible. It was not the first time we've done this. I spent a year in Vietnam, so this is just another four months. And I'll promise them it'll be a long time before I'll be this long away from home. . . .

QUESTION: This is Nancy Holland, KHOU-TV, and this is for Bonnie [Dunbar]. What kind of initial information have you gathered on the health of the *Mir* crew, and have there been any surprises so far, anything you didn't expect?

DUNBAR: Well, I think that you can see for yourselves how good they all look. Most of the information that we're collecting in terms of the nautibiotic, physiological samples and so forth are really going to be analyzed once they get all the data down on the ground. And there's a large team of investigators involved in doing that. So it'll take a few months before we actually get the whole picture together, and then I'm sure all of that as we collect more data will be forthcoming.

QUESTION: Jim McKenna, *Aviation Week*, for Dr. Thagard. What is the number one problem or issue that you believe should be addressed before Shannon Lucid arrives at *Mir* next March, as well as with regards to long-duration U.S. space flight?

THAGARD: My impression is [that] psychological aspects probably loom largest. There don't really seem to be big problems physiologically. I think we still have to find out what's happening with mineral loss from bone, for instance. And obviously, radiation is an ongoing problem as long as you're in space. But I think anybody can do three months or four months as I'm doing and six months, in my opinion, and longer is a different matter entirely. I think Shannon won't have any problem, but I think we need to address some things for the folks who plan to be up here six months and longer.

QUESTION: This is Paul Horverston with *USA Today* for Norm Thagard. Sort of following up on the same question. What about the systems on *Mir* or the setup or configuration should absolutely not be done with the international space station, if there is anything?

THAGARD: Well, from what I saw it takes a considerable effort from two folks to keep *Mir* station operating. I think you would want to minimize the amount of maintenance ongoing that was required for a new space station. I don't think I'd run conduits both air and electrical, through hatches which make it difficult, if not impossible, to close those hatches rapidly if you needed to. And lastly, I would certainly pay a lot of attention to storage because if there was a problem that we had, it was finding places to store things. . . .

QUESTION: Todd Halberson of *Florida Today* for Hoot Gibson. Hoot, the mission to date has been remarkably smooth, but like with all enterprises, there's probably room for improvement. What types of lessons have you learned that can be applied to future shuttle-*Mir* missions or the assembly of the space station?

GIBSON: Todd, like you say, it has gone pretty smoothly. There's an aspect of it though that you don't see, and that's how hard we're hustling here on board everyday to accomplish all the things that we need to get done. On a long-duration flight, or a space station flight, you're not going to be able to keep up the kind of pace that we've been keeping up. And a lot of it has been associated with the rather difficult area of transfers of material from the orbiter to the *Mir*, and from the *Mir* back to the orbiter. Both equipment, future test equipment, completed test samples and all those sorts of things.

Now, we expected that this was going to be a pretty big effort, and there was going to be a lot of uncertainty, and there was actually going to be a lot of unknown when we actually got up here and tried to do it, and that [is], in fact kind of what we bumped into. And, we've been working a little bit extra and a little bit harder to accommodate all of those things.

But, that's the one area, and I think for the future docking flights, the transfer plan, the locations, the stowage, all of it needs to be detailed down to a "T" for us to really be able to do it smoothly and efficiently. And, I think that's one of the big lessons that we will have seen out of this flight. Let me finish by saying that was not unexpected. We pretty well knew that that was the kind of situation we were facing when we got up here, and I think we've adapted to it about as well as you could. . . .

QUESTION: This is David Chandler from the *Boston Globe* for Charles Precourt. I understand you're one of the more fluent people in Russian. Can you talk a little bit about what some of the issues have been in working with a multinational crew that speaks different languages, and what you've learned from this mission that you might pass along to people on future multinational missions?

PRECOURT: Well, I appreciate the question. . . .[T]he technical aspects of our language can be achieved easily. Even in spite of language differences, we're able on orbit here to mix our two languages and understand each other really well.

But, in any case, regardless of what we pick for an international language of the space station, we're going to have know each other's languages at least a little bit for many years to come. You say that I'm fluent, [but] I would not call it fluent yet. I've got an awful long way to go before I would consider my Russian skills proficient and fluent. However, if you take a look ten years down the road, and you have a cadre of people, not just crew members, but also in the control centers, who have been working with each other for all that time, and you convey that kind of continuity, eventually, you'll have a situation where you'll have people of all different, from all the different partners who can communicate fluently with each other in a given language. . . .

QUESTION: Earl Lane, *Newsday* for Norm Thagard. When you said psychologically a six-month mission is a different matter entirely, what did you mean? Did you get on each other's nerves or were you starting to get on each other's nerves?

THAGARD: That had nothing to do with the crew relationships. Those remained fine throughout. In fact, I can honestly say there were never any serious disputes among the crew, and probably wouldn't have been even on a six-month mission. For the American on board a Russian space station, you're the only English speaker on board, in general. The cultural isolation is extreme. There were times when I went 72 hours without speaking to an English-speaking person. I didn't get a lot of news up here. All of those things start to weigh heavily after a while. Since I knew from the start I could do anything for three months, it wasn't going to be a problem for me. If I'd been looking at six months, I would have been real worried at about three months that I wasn't going to make it. . . .

QUESTION: This is Beth Dickie with Reuters. I'd like to speak with the three commanders for a second about their impressions of the coordination between the ground control centers and the orbiter in *Mir*, especially with the science crew and [since] Norm seems to have gotten a bit testy at times in the last couple of days over things that you all are being asked to do. And there have been concerns that you have been overbooked. Could each of the commanders, please, talk a little bit about your impressions of that? Do you feel overbooked? Is this a, just a nit that's being picked, or is this a serious problem that will have to be worked out before the next joint mission is flown?

GIBSON: Well, Beth with regard to Norm sounding testy, let me just say that Norm always sounds like that and I don't, I don't believe that Norm has been testy, or meant to sound testy during any of this. I have to give the ground tremendous, tremendous grades on the coordination and the way they've put everything together and the way that things have flowed up here. This is not an easy thing to coordinate the activities of *Mir 18*, *Mir 19*, and *SDS 71*. And I think that both mission control centers, the Suit and Houston, in my view and from what I've seen, have done just a spectacular job of ironing this all out and making this flow smoothly. So, that's what I think about the whole thing. . . .

QUESTION: This is Bill Walsh with Mutual Broadcasting System. I have a question for Norm Thagard. After spending more time in space than any other American, what stands out most in your mind concerning your almost four months in space, and how can you relate the importance of this mission to the American taxpayer?

THAGARD: . . . To the American taxpayer, there are sorts of things that we do up here, and we do them up here usually because this is the only place in which they can be done. There are a number of scientific experiments that we do that are important. They answer important questions. They can only be conducted here in Zero G [gravity]. It's absolutely impossible to conduct them on Earth. And I think that at the least, what we demonstrated here is, this is the way a space station ought to work. You have a space station and you have a good transport vehicle. Our shuttle has solved some of the shortcomings of the *Mir* station, which was lack of ability to transport things back to Earth at the end of the flight. And the space station has provided another goal and task and job for our space shuttle. So, I think it's a good program for the money and I sure hope we expand, continue and expand. . . .

QUESTION: This is James Fork from WFTW in Orlando for Dr. Thagard . . . . What's your concern as you get ready to land and come back into one "G" after being in microgravity so long, and what are going to do once you get back here on Earth?

THAGARD: Well, perhaps the answer to that question explains what was interpreted as being testy with the ground. I did complain this morning that I, because of a task I was assigned, I'd miss my exercise period. I'm concerned about physical condition when I get back on the ground. The Russians believe that you need to exercise with two one-hour periods a day, and that it ought to ramp up in severity toward the end of the flight just before coming home. And I concur. I think that's important, too. So, we ought to do something and we ought to do what we can to protect those exercise periods just before coming home. Other than that, I'm not sure I've been so testy, but that came out of a real concern about being healthy and being able to walk and do well immediately upon return to Earth.

CLINTON SPEECH ON POLITICAL DISCOURSE AND CITIZENSHIP
July 6, 1995

Apparently laying the policy groundwork for his attempt to win a second term, President Bill Clinton on July 6 offered a broad philosophical argument on behalf of moderate and reasoned discussion of political issues and insisted that government can play a positive role in society. Clinton spoke for nearly an hour at his alma mater, Georgetown University, in Washington, D.C. It was the same stage from which Clinton in 1991 delivered a series of speeches outlining his call for a "new covenant" between the American people and their government; those speeches were intended to provide the philosophical basis for his successful 1992 election bid.

In his speech, the president sought to present himself as a moderate genuinely interested in improving the lives of all Americans, in contrast to his critics, some of whom, he said, engaged in extremist rhetoric and excessive partisanship. He generally avoided specific policy issues that were at the forefront of the political battles between Democrats and Republicans at the national, state, and local levels.

Much of the president's speech was extemporaneous, and much was deeply personal. Clinton described growing up in Arkansas in the years after World War II, and the problems of his family, including a stepfather who was an alcoholic and a brother who battled—and eventually recovered from—drug addition.

Clinton related incidents in his own life to national events that have occurred since the 1960s, adding each decade's pluses and minuses and concluding that America changed dramatically during that time. Many changes were positive, he said, such as the civil rights movement and the growing awareness of the environment. He added that, during that time, many Americans found they could no longer reach the middle-class dream of owning their own house and having a secure job, and they became profoundly disillusioned with the government and other societal institutions.

Avoiding Political Extremism

The heart of the president's speech was a call for civility of political debate and the search for "common ground" on the great issues of the day. In arguing that the manner in which issues are debated is as important as the outcome, the president clearly was attempting to respond to widespread public cynicism about American politics and politicians.

Clinton identified two general causes for this cynicism: the increasing stratification of American society into special interest groups, and the use of the mass media to convey intemperate and divisive rhetoric. "Politics has become more and more fractured, just like the rest of our lives," he said.

As examples, Clinton cited the use of "extreme rhetoric" in mass mailings, "semi-hysterical" telephone appeals to voters just before elections, television ads "designed far more to inflame than to inform," and politicians taking language lessons "on how to turn their adversaries into aliens." All those developments are "exciting in some ways," he said, but it is difficult to conclude "that our political system is producing the sort of discussion that will give us the kind of results we need."

The president concluded that the voters have "real reasons" to be angry and frustrated with the political process. "How could our politics not be confusing when people's lives are so confusing and frustrated and seem to be so full of contradictory developments?" he asked.

The solution is a more civil and reflective political debate, where each side is willing to listen to other points of view, Clinton said. "We need to respect our differences and hear them, but it means instead of having the shrill voices of discord, we need a chorus of harmony," he added. "In a chorus of harmony, you know there are lots of differences, but you can hear all the voices."

Clinton said his June 11 debate with House Speaker Newt Gingrich (R-Ga.) in Claremont, New Hampshire, was an example of the kind of "decent, open conversation" he had in mind. He said he had received an "overwhelming" response to that debate, in which the two leaders laid out their sharply conflicting views of the country's political problems.

The president suggested four steps that politicians could take to elevate the level of rhetoric: engage in more conversation and less combat, offer alternatives, look at the long-term and remind the people that problems developed over many years, and do not "berate the worst" in America but spend more time "celebrating the best."

The Role of Government

Clinton devoted a substantial portion of his speech to a discussion of how his view of government differed from the conservative Republicans who won control of Congress in the 1994 elections. In the Contract with America, Clinton said, the Republicans adopted the view that the government is responsible for many of the nation's problems, and therefore it must be cut back as much as possible. The president said he believed in a "more responsive, less bureaucratic" government, but nevertheless a government that has an important role to play in such matters as child support, pensions, and education.

The president cited examples of the differences between him and his political foes on two controversial issues: gun control and AIDS research. In the first case, he quoted the general position of the National Rifle Association (NRA) that guns do not kill people, people do. Clinton said he disagreed with the NRA's opposition to all gun control because the "minor inconvenience" caused gun owners by federal laws had saved lives. In the second case, Clinton quoted a comment by Sen. Jesse Helms (R-N.C.), opposing federal funding for research into a cure for AIDS because, Helms said, AIDS victims brought the disease on themselves. Clinton responded that some people contracted the AIDS virus through no fault of their own. Even if AIDS victims bore some responsibility for their disease, he said, the government should try to find a cure, just as it funds research into lung cancer even though people bring that illness on themselves by smoking.

In both cases, Clinton said, the government had a legitimate right and need to act for the general public good, even if some of the underlying problems were caused by individual behavior. "So I would say to you that there are some things that mere exhortation to good conduct will not solve, that require other responses that are public or that are private but go beyond just saying these are personal or cultural problems," he said.

> *Following are excerpts from a White House text of a speech by President Bill Clinton on July 6, 1995, at Georgetown University in Washington, D.C., in which he called for less partisanship and extremism in political debate and offered a defense of the role of government in public life:*

... Today I want to have more of a conversation than deliver a formal speech about the great debate now raging in our nation, not so much over what we should do, but over how we should resolve the great questions of our time, here in Washington and in communities all across our country. I want to talk about the obligations of citizenship, the obligations imposed on the President and people in power, and the obligations imposed on all Americans.

Two days ago we celebrated the 219th birthday of our democracy. The Declaration of Independence was also clearly a declaration of citizenship: All men are created equal, endowed by their Creator with certain inalienable rights. Among these are life, liberty, and the pursuit of happiness. It was also manifestly a declaration of citizenship in a different way; it was a declaration of interdependence. For the support of this declaration, with a firm reliance on the protection of Divine Providence, we mutually pledge our lives, our fortunes and our sacred honor.

The distinguished American historian, Samuel Eliot Morison, in his *History of the American People*, wrote of these words: "These words are more revolutionary than anything written by Robespierre, Marx, or Lenin, more explosive than the atom; a continual challenge to ourselves as well as an inspiration to the oppressed of all the world." What is the challenge to ourselves at the dawn of the 21st century and how shall we meet it? First of all, we must remember that the Declaration of Independence was written as a commitment for all Americans at all times, not just in time of war or great national crisis. My argument to you is pretty straightforward. I believe we face challenges of truly historic dimensions—challenges here at home perhaps greater than any we faced since the beginning of this century we are about to finish and the dawn of the industrial era. But they are not greater challenges in their own way than the ones we faced at our birth, greater challenges than those of slavery and civil war, greater than those of World War I or the Depression or World War II. And they can be solved, though they are profound. What are they?

Most people my age grew up in an America dominated by middle class dreams and middle class values—the life we wanted to live and the kind of people we wanted to be; dreams that inspired those who were born into the middle class; dreams that restrained and directed the lives of those who were much more successful and more powerful; dreams that animated the strivings of those who were poor because of the condition of their birth or because they came here as immigrants; middle class dreams that there would be reward for work and that the future of our children would be better than the lives we enjoyed. Middle class values, strong families and faith, safe streets, secure futures. These things are very much threatened today, threatened by 20 years of stagnant incomes, of harder work by good Americans for the same or lower pay, of increasing inequity of incomes, and increasing insecurity in jobs and retirement and health care.

They are threatened by 30 years of social problems of profound implications—family break-ups, of a rising tide of violence and drugs, of declining birth rates among successful, married couples, and rising birth rates among young people who are not married. They are threatened by the failure of public institutions to respond; the failure of bureaucracies encrusted in yesterday's prerogatives and not meeting the challenges of today and tomorrow—the schools, the law enforcement agencies, the governments and their economic and other policies. They are threatened by the sheer pace and scope of change as technology and ideas and money and decisions move across the globe at breathtaking rates, and every great opportunity seems to carry within it the seeds of a great problem.

So that we have anomalies everywhere: Abroad, the Cold War ends, but we see the rise and the threat of technology-based destruction—sarin gas exploding in the subway in Japan, the bomb exploding in Oklahoma City. The Soviet Union is no more, and so they worry now in the Baltics about becoming a conduit for drug trafficking, and they worry in Russia about their banks being taken over by organized crime.

And here at home, it all seems so confusing—the highest growth rates in a decade, the stock market at an all-time high, almost 7 million more jobs, more millionaires and new businesses than every before, but most people working harder for less, feeling more insecure. . . .

In 1991, as Father O'Donovan said, I came here to Georgetown to talk about these challenges and laid out my philosophy about how we as a people—not just as a government, but as a people—ought to meet them. I called it the New Covenant. I will repeat briefly what I said then because I don't believe I can do any better today than I did then in terms of what I honestly believe we ought to be doing.

[Working in Partnership]

I think we have to create more opportunity and demand more responsibility. I think we have to give citizens more say and provide them a more responsive, less bureaucratic government. I think we have to do these things because we are literally a community—an American family that is going up or down together, whether we like it or not. If we're going to have middle class dreams and middle class values, we have to do things as private citizens and we have to do things in partnership through our public agencies and through our other associations.

In 1994, when the Republicans won a majority in Congress, they offered a different view which they called their Contract With America. In their view most of our problems were personal and cultural; the government tended to make them worse because it was bureaucratic and wedded to the past and more interested in regulating and choking off the free enterprise system and promoting the welfare state; and, therefore, what we should do is to balance the budget as soon as possible, cut taxes as much as possible, deregulate business completely if possible, and cut our investments in things like welfare as much as possible.

As you know, I thought there were different things that ought to be done because I believed in partnership. I believed in supporting community initiatives that were working and preventing things before they happened, instead of just punishing bad behavior after it occurred, and trying to empower people to make the most of their own lives. So I believed that there were things we could do here in Washington to help, whether it was family leave, or tougher child support enforcement, or reforming the pension system to save the pensions of over 8 million American workers, or investing more in education, making college more affordable.

What I believe grows largely out of my personal history and a lot of it happened to me a long time before I came to Georgetown and read in books things that made me convinced that I was basically right. I grew up in a small town in a poor state. When I was born at the end of World War II, my state's per capita income was barely half the national average. I was the first person in my family to go to college. When I was a boy I lived for a while on a farm without an indoor toilet. It makes a good story—not as good as being born in a log cabin, but it's true. (Laughter.)

I had a stepfather without a high school diploma and a grandfather, whom I loved above all people almost, who had a sixth-grade education. I lived in a seg-regated society, and I lived in a family, as has now been well-documented, with problems of alcohol and later, drug abuse. I learned a lot about what I call the New Covenant, about the importance of responsibility and opportunity.

I lived in a family where everybody worked hard and where kids were expected to study hard. But I also had a lot of opportunity that was given to me by my community. I had good teachers and good schools. And when I needed them, I got scholarships and jobs. I saw what happened to good peo-ple who had no opportunity because they happened to be black, or because they happened to be poor and white and isolated in the hills and hollows of the mountains of my state.

I saw what happened in my own family to people who were good people but didn't behave responsibly. My stepfather was very responsible toward me but not very responsible toward himself. Anybody who's ever lived in a fam-ily with an alcoholic knows that there is nothing you can do for somebody else they are not prepared to do for themselves. And my brother—after all of his struggles with drug addiction, which included even serving some time in jail, I am sometimes more proud of him than I am of what I've done because he has a family and a son and a life—not because of the love and support that we all gave him, but because of what he did for himself.

So my whole political philosophy is basically rooted in what I think works. It works for families and communities, and it worked pretty well for our country for a long time. If you look at recent American history, our country has never been perfect, because none of us are, but we did always seem to be going in the right direction. . . .

Millions of American people go home at night from their work and sit down to dinner and look at their children and wonder what they have done wrong, what did they ever do to fail. And they're riddled with worries about it. Millions more who are poor have simply given up on ever being able to work their way into a stable lifestyle. And that, doubtless, is fueling some of the disturbing increase in casual drug use among very young people and the rise in violence among young people.

That threatens middle class values. In almost every major city in America the crime rate is down—hallelujah. In almost every place in America, the rate of random violence among young people is up, even as the overall crime rate drops. Government is struggling to change, and I'm proud of the changes we have made. But no one really believes that government is fully adjusted to the demands of the 21st century and the information age. It clearly must still be less bureaucratic, more empowering, rely more on incentives, if we still have to reduce spending and we have to find a way to do it while increasing our investment in the things that will determine our ability to live the middle class dreams.

Politics has become more and more fractured, just like the rest of our lives; pluralized. It's exciting in some ways. But as we divide into more and more and more sharply defined organized groups around more and more and more stratified issues, as we communicate more and more with people in extreme rhetoric through mass mailings or sometimes semi-hysterical messages right before election on the telephone, or 30-second ads designed far more to inflame than to inform, as we see politicians actually getting language lessons on how to turn their adversaries into aliens, it is difficult to draw the conclusion that our political system is producing the sort of discussion that will give us the kind of results we need.

But our citizens, even though their confidence in the future has been clouded and their doubts about their leaders and their institutions are profound, want something better. You could see it in the way they turned out for the town meetings in 1992. You could see it in the overwhelming, I mean literally overwhelming, response that I have received from people of all political parties to the simple act of having a decent, open conversation with the Speaker of the House in Claremont, New Hampshire. People know we need to do better. And deep down inside, our people know this is a very great country capable of meeting our challenges.

So what are the conclusions I draw from this? First of all, don't kid yourself. There are real reasons for ordinary voters to be angry, frustrated and downright disoriented. How could our politics not be confusing when people's lives are so confusing and frustrating and seem to be so full of contradictory developments?

Secondly, this is now, as it has ever been, fertile ground for groups that claim a monopoly on middle class values and old-fashioned virtue. And it's easy to blame the government when people don't feel any positive results. It's easy to blame groups of others when people have to have somebody to blame for their own problems when they are working as hard as they can, and they can't keep up.

But there is real reason for hope, my fellow Americans. This is, after all, the most productive country in the world. We do a better job of dealing with racial and ethnic diversity and trying to find some way to bring out the best in all of our people than any other country with this much diversity in the world.

We have an environment that is cleaner and safer and healthier than it used to be. We still have the lead in many important areas that will determine the shape of societies in the 21st century. There is a real willingness among our people to try bold change. And, most important of all, most Americans are still living by middle class values and hanging on to middle class dreams. And everywhere in this country there are examples of people who have taken their future into their own hands, worked with their friends and neighbors, broken through bureaucracy and solved problems. If there is anything I would say to you it is that you can find somewhere in America, somebody who has solved every problem you are worried about.

So there is reason for hope. And I would say, to me, the real heroes in this country are the people that are out there making things work and the people who show up for work every day, even though they're barely at and maybe even below the poverty line, but they still work full-time, obey the law, pay their taxes and raise their kids the best they can. That's what this country is really all about. And so there is really no cause for the kind of hand-wringing and cynicism that dominates too much of the public debate today.

[Solving Problems: Whose Responsibility?]

What do we have to do now? First of all, we've got to have this debate that is looming over Washington. We have to have it. It's a good thing. We are debating things now we thought were settled for decades. We are now back to fundamental issues that were debated like this 50, 60, 70 years ago. There is a group who believe that our problems are primarily personal and cultural. Cultural is a—basically a word that means, in this context, there are a whole lot of persons doing the same bad thing. (Laughter.) And that's what people—and then if everybody would just sort of straighten up and fly right, why, things would be hunky-dory. And why don't they do it?

Now, I—you can see that with just two reasons—I'll give you two examples. And I made you laugh, but let's be serious—these people are honest and genuine in their beliefs. I will give you two examples that are sort of—stand out, but there are hundred more that are more modulated: The NRA's position on gun violence, the Brady Bill and the assault weapons ban.

Their position is guns don't kill people, people do; find the people who do wrong, throw them in jail and throw the key away. Punish wrongdoers. Do not infringe upon my right to keep and bear arms, even to keep and bear arsenals or artillery or assault weapons. Do not do that because I have not done anything wrong and I have no intention of doing anything wrong. Why are you making me wait five days to get a handgun? What do you care if I want an AK-47 or an Uzi to go out and engage in some sort of sporting contest to see who's a better shot? I obey the law. I pay my taxes. I don't give you any grief. Why are you on my back? The Constitution says I can do this. Punish wrongdoers. I am sick and tired of my life being inconvenienced for what other people do.

Second example is the one that dominated the headlines in the last couple of days, what Senator Helms said about AIDS: I'm sick and tired of spending money on research and treatment for a disease that could be ended tomorrow if everybody just straightened up and fly right. I'm tired of it. Why should I spend taxpayer—I've got a budget to balance. We're cutting aid to Africa. We're cutting education. We're cutting Medicare. Why should we spend money on treatment and research for a disease that is a product of people's wrongdoing? Illicit sex and bad drugs, dirty needles—let's just stop it. . . .

Now, I see the Brady Bill in a totally different way because I see these problems as community problems. And I think a public response is all right. And I think saying to people who have the line I said, I think we ought to say to people, look, it is just not out of line for you to be asked to undergo the minor inconvenience of waiting five days to get a handgun, until we can computerize all the records—because, look here, in the last year and a half, there are 40,000 people who had criminal records or mental health histories who didn't get handguns, and they're not out there shooting people because you went through a minor inconvenience. You don't gripe when you go through a metal detector at an airport anymore, because you are very aware of the connection between this minor inconvenience to you and the fact that that plane might blow up, and you don't want the plane to blow up or be hijacked.

Well, look at the level of violence in America. It's the same thing. I don't have a problem with saying, look, these assault weapons are primarily designed to kill people. That's their primary purpose. And I'm sorry if you don't have a new one that you can take out in the woods somewhere, to a shooting contest, but you'll get over it. Shoot with something else. It's worth it. I'm glad you're clapping. I'm glad you agree with me, but remember, the other people are good people who honestly believe what they say. That's the importance of this debate. It's the attitudes. We have to—we're having this debate.

The NRA that I knew as a child, the NRA that I knew as a governor, for years, were the people who did hunter education programs, the people that helped me resolve land boundary disputes when retirees would come to the mountains in the northern part of my state and go into unincorporated areas, and who could and couldn't hunt on whose land. And they actually helped save people's lives and they solved a lot of problems. I mean this is a different—these are deeply held world views about working—but the way I look at it is it's like the airport metal detector.

I'll give you another example. It might not be popular in this group. I agree with the Supreme Court decision on requiring people who want to be on high school athletic teams to take drug tests—not because I think all kids are bad, not because I think they all use drugs, but because casual drug use is going up among young people again. It is a privilege to play on the football team. It is a privilege to be in the band. It is a privilege to have access to all these activities. And I say it's like going through the airport metal detector—you ought to be willing to do that to help get the scourge of drugs out of your school and keep kids off drugs. That's what I believe, because I see it as a common problem.

So we all have to give up a little and go through a little inconvenience to help solve problems and pull the country together and push it forward. But this is a huge debate.

Look at the AIDS debate. You may think it's a little harder. First of all, the truth is not everybody who has AIDS gets it from sex or drug needles. I've got a picture on my desk at the White House of a little boy named Ricky Ray. He and his family were treated horribly by people who were afraid of AIDS when they first got it through blood transfusions, he and his brother. And he died right after my election. I keep his picture on my table to remember that.

Elizabeth Glaser was a good friend of mine. She and the daughter she lost and her wonderful son that survived her, they didn't get AIDS through misconduct. So that's just wrong. I know a fine woman doctor in Texas who got AIDS because she was treating AIDS patients and she got the tiniest pinprick in her finger—a million to one, two million to one chance. But, secondly, and more to the point, the gay people who have AIDS are still our sons, our brothers, our cousins, our citizens. They're Americans, too. They're obeying the law and working hard. They're entitled to be treated like everybody else.

And the drug users—there's nobody in this country that hates that any more than I do because I've lived with it in my family. But I fail to see why we would want to hasten people's demise because they paid a terrible price for their abuse.

You know, smoking causes lung cancer, but we don't propose to stop treating lung cancer or stop doing research to find a cure. Right? Drunk driving causes a lot of highway deaths, but we don't propose to stop trying to make cars safer. Do we? I don't think so.

So I just disagree with this. Why do we have to make this choice? Why can't we say to people, look, you've got to behave if you want your life to work, but we have common problems and we are going to have some common responses. I don't understand why it's got to be an either/or thing. That's not the way we live our lives. Why should we conduct our public debates in this way?

And the best example of all to me that our problems are both personal and cultural and economic, political and social is the whole condition of the middle class economically. I think it requires public and private decision-making. Family values, most families have them. But most families are working harder for less so they have less time and less money to spend with their children. Now, that's just a fact. That's not good for family values. And I don't believe exhortation alone can turn it around. It's going to require some common action. I think that what we did with the family leave law supported family values. I think that we can have a welfare reform law that requires parental responsibility, has tough work requirements, but invests in child care and supports family values. . . .

So I would say to you that there are some things that mere exhortation to good conduct will not solve, that require other responses that are public or that are private but go beyond just saying these are personal or cultural problems.

I also think that if we want to maintain a public response, there must be a relentless effort to change but not to eviscerate the government. We have tried weak government, nonexistent government, in a complex industrial society where powerful interests that are driven only by short-term considerations call all the shots. We tried it decades and decades ago. It didn't work out very well. It didn't even produce a very good economic policy. It had something to do with the onset of the Depression.

On the other hand, we know that an insensitive, overly bureaucratic, yesterday-oriented, special-interest-dominated government can be just as big a nightmare. We've done what we could to change that. The government has 150,000 fewer people working today than it did when I took office. We've gotten rid of thousands of regulations and hundreds of programs. We have a few shining stars like the Small Business Administration, which today has a budget that's 40 percent lower than it did when I took office, that's making twice as many loans, has dramatically increased the loans to women and minorities, has not decreased loans to white males and hasn't made a loan to a single unqualified person. . . .

So that's my side of the argument. That's why I think my New Covenant formulation is better to solve the problems of middle class dreams and middle class values than the Republican contract. But perhaps the most important thing is not whether I'm right or they are, the important thing is how are we going to resolve this and what are citizens going to do. How can we resolve the debate?

I believe—and you've got to decide whether you believe this—I believe that a democracy requires a certain amount of common ground. I do not believe you can solve complex questions like this at the grass-roots level or at the national level or anywhere in between if you have too much extremism of rhetoric and excessive partisanship. Times are changing too fast. We need to keep our eyes open. We need to keep our ears open. We need to be flexible. We need to have new solutions based on old values. I just don't think we can get there unless we can establish some common ground.

[Specific Personal Responsibilities]

And that seems to me to impose certain specific responsibilities on citizens and on political leaders. And if I might, just let me say them. They may be painfully self-evident, but I don't think they're irrelevant. Every citizen in this country's got to say, what do I have to do for myself or my family, or nothing else counts. The truth is that nobody can repeal the laws of the global economy, and people that don't have a certain level of education and skills are not going to be employable in good jobs with long-term prospects. And that's just a fact.

The truth is that if every child in this country had both parents contributing to his or her support and nourishment and emotional stability and education and future, we'd have almost no poor kids, instead of having over 20 percent of our children born in poverty. Those things are true.

The second thing is, more of our citizens have got to say, what should I do in my community. You know, it's not just enough to bemoan the rising crime rate or how kids are behaving and whatever—that's just not enough. It is not enough. Not when you have example after example after example from the LEAP [Learning, Earning, and Parenting] program, the "I Have a Dream" program, to the world-famous Habitat for Humanity program, to all these local initiatives, support corporations, that are now going around the country, revolutionizing slum housing and giving poor, working people decent places to live; to the work of the Catholic social missions in Washington, D.C., and other places.

It is not enough to say that. People have to ask themselves: What should I be doing through my church or my community organizations? People who feel very strongly about one of the most contentious issues in our society, abortion, ought to look at the United Pentecostal Church. They'll adopt any child born, no matter what race, no matter how disabled, no matter what their problems are. There is a positive, constructive outlet for people who are worried about every problem in this country if they will go seek it out. And there is nothing the rest of us can do that will replace that kind of energy.

The fourth thing that I think—the third thing I think citizens have to do that is also important, people have to say, what is my job as a citizen who is a voter? I am in control here. I run the store. I get to throw this crowd out on a regular basis. That's a big responsibility. We're the board of directors of America.

Are we making good decisions? Are we making good decisions? Do we approach these decisions in the right frame of mind? Do we have enough information? Do we know what we're doing? I can tell you, the American people are hungry for information. When I announced my balanced budget and we put it on the Internet, one of our people at the White House told me there were a few hours when we were getting 50,000 requests an hour. The American people want to know things.

So I say to every citizen, do you have the information you need? Do you ever have a discussion with somebody that's different from you? Not just people who agree with you but somebody who's different. You ever listen to one of those radio programs that has the opposite point of view of yours, even if you have to grind your teeth? (Laughter.) And what kind of language do you use when you talk to people who are of different political parties with different views? Is it the language of respect or the language of a suspect? How do you deal with people? This is a huge thing. What do you have to do for yourself and your family? What can you do in your community? What can you do as a citizen?

Thomas Jefferson said he had no fear of the most extreme views in America being expressed with the greatest passion as long as reason had a chance. As long as reason had a chance. Citizens have to give reason a chance.

What do the political leaders have to do? I would argue four things. Number one, we need more conversation and less combat. Number two, when we differ we ought to offer an alternative. Number three, we ought to look relentlessly at the long-term and remind the American people that the problems we have developed over a long period of years. And, number four, we shouldn't just berate the worst in America, we ought to spend more time celebrating the best.

[Responsibilities of Political Leaders]

Those are four things that I think I should do and I think every other leader in this country ought to do. Conversation, not combat is what I tried to do with the Speaker in New Hampshire, and I want to do more of it with others. I'm willing if they are. I think it would be good for America.

Secondly, differ but present an alternative. That's why I presented a balanced budget. A lot of people said, this is dumb politics. The Republicans won the Congress by just saying no: No to deficit reduction, and call it a tax increase. Run away from your own health care plan, say they're trying to make the government take over health care. That may be. But that's because this is a confusing time. It's still not the right thing to do.

Americans don't want "just say no" politics. If they can get the truth, they'll make the right decision 99 times out of 100. And we have to offer an alternative. And so do they. We all should. When we differ, we should say what we're for, not just what we're against.

The third thing is important—looking for the long-term. I was really sad in 1994, I'll be honest with you, on election day I was sad. I kind of felt sorry for myself—I thought, gosh, you know, the real problems in this country are these income problems; and look what we've done with the family leave law; we cut taxes for families with incomes under $28,000 a year by $1,000 a year; we've done—and I reeled it all off. And I said, gosh, I feel terrible. And then I realized, how could they possibly feel anything in two years? These income trends are huge, huge trends. Huge, sweeping over two decades. Fast international forces behind them. Trillions of dollars of money moving across international borders working to find the lowest labor cost and pressing down. Untold improvements in automation—so fast that you just can't create enough high-wage jobs to overcome the ones that are being depressed in some sectors of the economy. These are a huge deal. How could people have felt that?

Nonetheless, our job is not to get reelected, it's to think about the long-term because the problems are long-term problems.

I want to read you what President [Vaclav] Havel [of Czechoslovakia] said in his Harvard commencement speech about this—more eloquent than anything I could say. "The main task of the present generation of politicians is not, I think, to ingratiate themselves with the public through the decisions they take or their smiles on television. Their role is something quite different—to assume their share of responsibility for the long-range prospects of our world, and thus, to set an example for the public in whose sight they work. After all, politics is a matter of serving the community which means that it is morality in practice." I could hardly have said it better.

Fourth, maybe the most important thing is, we should not just condemn the worst, we ought to find the best and celebrate it, and then, relentlessly promote it as a model to be followed. You know, I kept President Bush's Points of Light Foundation when I became President. And we recognize those people every year because I believe in that. I always—I thought that was one of the best things he did. But I tried to institutionalize it in many ways.

That's what AmeriCorps is all about. The national service program gives young people a chance to earn money for college by working in grass-roots community projects all across the country. When I was in New Haven at the LEAP program, I had AmeriCorps volunteers there. I was in Texas the other day walking the streets of an inner city and a girl with a college degree from another state was there working with welfare mothers because she was raised by a welfare mother who taught her to go to school, work hard, and get a college degree, and she did.

We have to find a way to systematically see these things that work sweep across this country with high standards and high expectations and breaking through all this bureaucracy that keeps people from achieving. We can do that. And the President ought to do even more than I have done to celebrate the things that work, and I intend to do it and to do more of it.

Now, I believe, obviously, that my New Covenant approach is better than the Republican contract approach to deal with the problems of middle class dreams and middle class values. But when I ran for this job I said I wanted to restore the American dream and to bring the American people together. I have now come to the conclusion, having watched this drama unfold here and all around our country in the last two-and-a-half years, that I cannot do the first unless we can do the latter. We can't restore the American Dream unless we can find some way to bring the American people closer together. Therefore, how we resolve these differences is as important as what specific position we advocate.

I think we have got to move beyond division and resentment to common ground. We've got to go beyond cynicism to a sense of possibility. America is an idea. We're not one race. We're not one ethnic group. We're not one religious group. We do share a common piece of ground here. But you read the Declaration of Independence and the Constitution: this country is an idea. And it is still going now in our 220th year because we all had a sense of possibility. We never thought there was a mountain we couldn't climb, a river we couldn't ford, or a problem we couldn't solve.

What's that great line in the wonderful new movie, *Apollo 13*, "Failure is not an option." You have to believe in possibility. And if you're cynical, you can't believe in possibility. We need to respect our differences and hear them, but it means instead of having shrill voices of discord, we need a chorus of harmony. In a chorus of harmony you know there are lots of differences, but you can hear all the voices. And that is important.

And we've got to challenge every American in every sector of our society to do their part. We have to challenge in a positive way and hold accountable people who claim to be not responsible for any consequences of their actions that they did not specifically intend—whether it's in government, business, labor, entertainment, the media, religion or community organizations. None of us can say we're not accountable for our actions because we did not intend those consequences, even if we made some contribution to them.

Two days ago, on July the 4th, the people of Oklahoma City raised their flags and their spirits to full mast for the first time since the awful tragedy of April 19th. Governor Keating and Mayor Norick led a celebration in Oklahoma City, which some of you may have seen on television; a celebration of honor and thanks for thousands of Oklahomans and other Americans who showed up and stood united in the face of that awful hatred and loss for what is best in our country.

You know, Oklahoma City took a lot of the meanness out of America. It gave us a chance for more sober reflection. It gave us a chance to come to the same conclusion that Thomas Jefferson did in his first inaugural. I want to read this to you with only this bit of history: Thomas Jefferson was elected the first time by the House of Representatives in a bitterly contested election in the first outbreak of completely excessive partisanship in American history. In that sense it was a time not unlike this time. And this is what he said: "Let us unite with our heart and mind. Let us restore to social intercourse that harmony and affection without which liberty and life itself are but dreary things."

We can redeem the promise of America for our children. We can certainly restore the American family for another full century if we commit to each other, as the Founders did, our lives, our fortunes, and our sacred honor. In our hour of greatest peril and the greatest division when we were fighting over the issue which we still have not fully resolved, Abraham Lincoln said, "We are not enemies but friends. We must not be enemies."

My friends, amidst all our differences, let us find a new, common ground. Thank you very much.

REPORT ON AIDS TESTING FOR PREGNANT WOMEN
July 7, 1995

The federal Centers for Disease Control and Prevention (CDC) recommended July 7 that all pregnant women be offered a chance to be tested to see if they are carrying the virus that causes acquired immune deficiency syndrome, commonly known as AIDS. The recommendation represented a policy shift for the Public Health Service, CDC's parent organization, which had previously recommended voluntary testing only for intravenous drug users, prostitutes, and other women at high risk of carrying the virus. There is no known cure for AIDS.

The recommendation was made after recent studies showed that the risk of transmitting the human immunodeficiency virus (HIV) to babies was substantially reduced if women infected with the virus took the drug AZT during their pregnancy. CDC director David Satcher called this finding "an unprecedented breakthrough in HIV prevention" in a statement released July 6.

HIV-infected women can transmit the virus to their fetuses and newborns during pregnancy, during labor and delivery, and by breastfeeding. The CDC estimated that about 7,000 HIV-infected women give birth each year and that as many as 2,000 babies are born with the infection. The studies found that HIV-infected women who take AZT could reduce the chances of transmission by two-thirds, from about one in four to less than one in ten. The CDC recommended that the AZT therapy start by the fourteenth week of pregnancy, that it be given to the infant for six weeks after birth, and that HIV-infected mothers avoid breastfeeding. The agency also urged that the babies of women who did not receive prenatal medical care be tested so that appropriate treatment can be given to any infected infant.

Studies have shown only minimal, short-term side effects of AZT therapy, but long-term safety is unknown for both women and their babies. The CDC therefore recommended that HIV-infected women be informed about both the benefits and potential risks of using AZT. "Discussions of treat-

ment options should be noncoercive—the final decision to accept or reject [AZT] treatment is the responsibility of the woman," the report said. "Decisions concerning treatment can be complex and adherence to therapy, if accepted, can be difficult; therefore, good rapport and a trusting relationship should be established between the health-care provider and the HIV-infected woman."

The CDC guidelines were intended for use by health-care providers. In addition to the benefits for women found to be HIV-infected, the CDC said that routine HIV counseling and voluntary testing would benefit uninfected women by encouraging them to begin or continue behavior that reduces the risk of acquiring the infection. The agency acknowledged that women who tested positive for HIV infection might be subject to discrimination, domestic violence, and psychological difficulties and urged counseling for women anticipating or encountering such problems.

James Curran, director of HIV/AIDS prevention at the CDC, said voluntary testing "should really be the standard of care for pregnant women in the United States. This should be a routine part of prenatal care." The CDC said it was encouraging private insurers and the federal Medicaid program to cover the costs of the tests.

On July 27, the Senate passed S 64, reauthorizing the Ryan White CARE Act for five years. This federal program provides grants to cities and states for treating and supporting AIDS victims. The bill contained an amendment that would require states receiving the funding to adopt the CDC guidelines. The House passed a similar bill (formerly HR 1872) on September 18, after an amendment that would require states to test newborns for AIDS was withdrawn. The differences between the two versions were not resolved before the year ended.

Earlier in the year, the CDC reported that AIDS had become the leading cause of death among all Americans aged twenty-five to forty-four, ahead of accidents, cancer, and heart disease. Since the epidemic was first recognized in 1981, 440,000 cases of AIDS have been reported to the CDC and more than 250,000 people have died of AIDS or AIDS-related illnesses. About three-fourths of those deaths have been people aged twenty-five to forty-four. The figures were based on data for 1993. AIDS became the leading cause of death among men in this age group in 1992. It was the fourth leading cause of death among women in that age group in 1993 but was expected to rise to second place, ahead of accidents and heart disease, in the next few years, according to the CDC. For the first time more women contracted HIV infection through heterosexual transmission in 1992 than through other routes.

Following are excerpts from the report entitled "U.S. Public Health Service Recommendations for Human Immunodeficiency Virus Counseling and Voluntary Testing for Pregnant Women," issued on July 7, 1995, by the Centers for Disease Control and Prevention:

Introduction

During the past decade, human immunodeficiency virus (HIV) infection has become a leading cause of morbidity and mortality among women, the population accounting for the most rapid increase in cases of acquired immunodeficiency syndrome (AIDS) in recent years. As the incidence of HIV infection has increased among women of childbearing age, increasing numbers of children have become infected through perinatal (i.e., mother to infant) transmission; thus, HIV infection has also become a leading cause of death for young children. To reverse these trends, HIV education and services for prevention and health care must be made available to all women. Women who have HIV infection or who are at risk for infection need access to current information regarding a) early interventions to improve survival rates and quality of life for HIV-infected persons, b) strategies to reduce the risk for perinatal HIV transmission, and c) management of HIV-infection in pregnant women and perinatally exposed or infected children. Results from a randomized, placebo-controlled clinical trial have indicated that the risk for perinatal HIV transmission can be substantially reduced by administration of zidovudine (ZDV [also referred to as AZT]) to HIV-infected pregnant women and their newborns. To optimally benefit from this therapy, HIV infection must be diagnosed in these women before or during early pregnancy.

The U.S. Public Health Service (PHS) encourages all women to adopt behaviors that can prevent HIV infection and to learn their HIV status through counseling and voluntary testing. Ideally, women should know their HIV infection status before becoming pregnant. Thus, sites serving women of childbearing age (e.g., physicians' offices, family planning clinics, sexually transmitted disease clinics, and adolescent clinics) should counsel and offer voluntary HIV testing to women, including adolescents—regardless of whether they are pregnant. Because specific services must be offered to HIV-infected pregnant women to prevent perinatal transmission, PHS is recommending routine HIV counseling and voluntary testing of all pregnant women so that interventions to improve the woman's health and the health of her infant can be offered in a timely and effective manner.

The recommendations in this report were developed by PHS as guidance for health-care providers in their efforts to a) encourage HIV-infected pregnant women to learn their infection status; b) advise infected pregnant women of methods for preventing perinatal, sexual, and other modes of HIV transmission; c) facilitate appropriate follow-up for HIV-infected women, their infants, and their families; and d) help uninfected pregnant women reduce their risk for acquiring HIV infection. Increased availability of HIV counseling, voluntary testing, and follow-up medical and support services is essential to ensure successful implementation of these recommendations. These services can be optimally delivered through a readily available medical system with support services designed to facilitate ongoing care for patients.

Background

HIV Infection and AIDS in Women and Children

HIV infection is a major cause of illness and death among women and children. Nationally, HIV infection was the fourth leading cause of death in 1993 among women 25–44 years of age and the seventh leading cause of death in 1992 among children 1–4 years of age. Blacks and Hispanics have been disproportionately affected by the HIV epidemic. In 1993, HIV infection was the leading cause of death among black women 25–44 years of age and the third leading cause of death among Hispanic women in this age group. In 1991, HIV infection was the second leading cause of death among black children 1–4 years of age in New Jersey, Massachusetts, New York, and Florida and among Hispanic children in this age group in New York.

By 1995, CDC had received reports of >58,000 AIDS cases among adult and adolescent women and >5,500 cases among children who acquired HIV infection perinatally. Approximately one-half of all AIDS cases among women have been attributed to injecting-drug use and one-third to heterosexual contact. Nearly 90% of cumulative AIDS cases reported among children and virtually all new HIV infections among children in the United States can be attributed to perinatal transmission of HIV. An increasing proportion of perinatally acquired AIDS cases has been reported among children whose mothers acquired HIV infection through heterosexual contact with an infected partner whose infection status and risk factors were not known by the mother.

Data from the National Survey of Childbearing Women indicate that in 1992, the estimated national prevalence of HIV infection among childbearing women was 1.7 HIV-infected women per 1,000 childbearing women. Approximately 7,000 HIV-infected women gave birth annually for the years 1989–1992. Given a perinatal transmission rate of 15%–30%, an estimated 1,000–2,000 HIV-infected infants were born annually during these years in the United States. Although urban areas, especially in the northeast, generally have the highest seroprevalence rates, data from this survey have indicated a high prevalence of HIV infection among childbearing women who live in some rural and small urban areas—particularly in the southern states.

Perinatal Transmission of HIV

HIV can be transmitted from an infected woman to her fetus or newborn during pregnancy, during labor and delivery, and during the postpartum period (through breastfeeding), although the percentage of infections transmitted during each of these intervals is not precisely known. Although transmission of HIV to a fetus can occur as early as the 8th week of gestation, data suggest that at least one-half of perinatally transmitted infections from non-breastfeeding women occur shortly before or during the birth process. Breastfeeding may increase the rate of transmission by 10%–20%.

Several prospective studies have reported perinatal transmission rates ranging from 13% to 40%. Transmission rates may differ among studies depending on the prevalence of various factors that can influence the likelihood of transmission. Several maternal factors have been associated with an increased risk for transmission, including low CD4+ T-lymphocyte counts, high viral titer, advanced HIV disease, the presence of p24 antigen in serum, placental membrane inflammation, intrapartum events resulting in increased exposure of the fetus to maternal blood, breastfeeding, low vitamin A levels, premature rupture of membranes, and premature delivery. Factors associated with a decreased rate of HIV transmission have included cesarean section delivery, the presence of maternal neutralizing antibodies, and maternal zidovudine therapy.

HIV Prevention and Treatment Opportunities for Women and Infants

HIV counseling and testing for women of childbearing age offer important prevention opportunities for both uninfected and infected women and their infants. Such counseling is intended to a) assist women in assessing their current or future risk for HIV infection; b) initiate or reinforce HIV risk reduction behavior; and c) allow for referral to other HIV prevention services (e.g., treatment for substance abuse and sexually transmitted diseases) when appropriate. For infected women, knowledge of their HIV infection status provides opportunities to a) obtain early diagnosis and treatment for themselves and their infants, b) make informed reproductive decisions, c) use methods to reduce the risk for perinatal transmission, d) receive information to prevent HIV transmission to others, and e) obtain referral for psychological and social services, if needed.

Interventions designed to reduce morbidity in HIV-infected persons require early diagnosis of HIV infection so that treatment can be initiated before the onset of opportunistic infections and disease progression. However, studies indicate that many HIV-infected persons do not know they are infected until late in the course of illness. A survey of persons diagnosed with AIDS between January 1990 and December 1992 indicated that 57% of the 2,081 men and 62% of the 360 women who participated in the survey gave illness as the primary reason for being tested for HIV infection; 36% of survey participants first tested positive within 2 months of their AIDS diagnosis.

Providing HIV counseling and testing services in gynecologic and prenatal and other obstetric settings presents an opportunity for early diagnosis of HIV infection because many young women frequently access the health-care system for obstetric- or gynecologic-related care. Clinics that provide prenatal and postnatal care, family planning clinics, sexually transmitted disease clinics, adolescent-health clinics, and other health-care facilities already provide a range of preventive services into which HIV education, counseling, and voluntary testing can be integrated. When provided appropriate access to ongoing care, HIV-infected women can be monitored for clinical and immunologic status and can be given preventive treatment and other recommended medical care and services.

Diagnosis of HIV infection before or during pregnancy allows women to make informed decisions regarding prevention of perinatal transmission. Early in the HIV epidemic, strategies to prevent perinatal HIV transmission were limited to either avoiding pregnancy or avoiding breastfeeding (for women in the United States and other countries that have safe alternatives to breast milk). More recent strategies to prevent perinatal HIV transmission have focused on interrupting in utero and intrapartum transmission. Foremost among these strategies has been administration of ZDV to HIV-infected pregnant women and their newborns. Results from a multicenter, placebo-controlled clinical trial (the AIDS Clinical Trials Group [ACTG] protocol number 076) indicated that administration of ZDV to a selected group of HIV-infected women during pregnancy, labor, and delivery and to their newborns reduced the risk for perinatal HIV transmission by approximately two thirds: 25.5% of infants born to mothers in the placebo group were infected, compared with 8.3% of those born to mothers in the ZDV group. The ZDV regimen caused minimal adverse effects among both mothers and infants; the only adverse effect after 18 months of follow-up was mild anemia in the infants that resolved without therapy. As a result of these findings, PHS issued recommendations regarding ZDV therapy to reduce the risk for perinatal HIV transmission. In addition, the Food and Drug Administration (FDA) has approved the use of ZDV for this therapy.

Despite the substantial benefits and short-term safety of the ZDV regimen, however, the results of the trial present several unresolved issues, including a) the long-term safety of the regimen for both mothers and infants, b) ZDV's effectiveness in women who have different clinical characteristics (e.g., CD4+ T-lymphocyte count and previous ZDV use) than those who participated in the trial, and c) the likelihood of the mother's adherence to the lengthy treatment regimen. The PHS recommendations for ZDV therapy emphasize that HIV-infected pregnant women should be informed of both benefits and potential risks when making decisions to receive such therapy. Discussions of treatment options should be noncoercive—the final decision to accept or reject ZDV treatment is the responsibility of the woman. Decisions concerning treatment can be complex and adherence to therapy, if accepted, can be difficult; therefore, good rapport and a trusting relationship should be established between the health-care provider and the HIV-infected woman.

Several other possible strategies to reduce the risk for perinatal HIV transmission are under study or are being planned; however, their efficacies have not yet been determined. These strategies include a) administration of HIV hyperimmune globulin to infected pregnant women and their infants, b) efforts to boost maternal and infant immune responses through vaccination, c) virucidal cleansing of the birth canal before and during labor and delivery, d) modified and shortened antiretroviral regimens, e) cesarean section delivery, and f) vitamin A supplementation.

Knowledge of HIV infection status during pregnancy also allows for early identification of HIV-exposed infants, all of whom should be appropriately tested, monitored, and treated. Prompt identification and close monitoring of such children (particularly infants) is essential for optimal medical management. Approximately 10%–20% of perinatally infected children develop rapidly progressive disease and die by 24 months of age. *Pneumocystis carinii* pneumonia (PCP) is the most common opportunistic infection in children who have AIDS and is often fatal. Because PCP occurs most commonly among perinatally infected children 3–6 months of age, effective prevention requires that children born to HIV-infected mothers be identified promptly, preferably through prenatal testing of their mothers, so that prophylactic therapy can be initiated as soon as possible. CDC and the National Pediatric and Family HIV Resource Center have published revised guidelines for prophylaxis against PCP in children that recommend that all children born to HIV-infected mothers be placed on prophylactic therapy at 4–6 weeks of age. Careful follow-up of these children to promptly diagnose other potentially treatable HIV-related conditions (e.g., severe bacterial infections or tuberculosis) can prevent morbidity and reduce the need for hospitalization. Infants born to HIV-infected women also require changes in their routine immunization regimens as early as 2 months of age.

Despite the potential benefits of HIV counseling and testing to both women and their infants, some persons have expressed concerns about the potential for negative effects resulting from widespread counseling and testing programs in prenatal and other settings. These concerns include the fear that a) such programs could deter pregnant women from using prenatal-care services if testing is not perceived as voluntary, and b) women who have been tested but who choose not to learn their test results may be reluctant to return for further prenatal care. Other potential negative consequences following a diagnosis of HIV infection can include loss of confidentiality, job- or health-care-related discrimination and stigmatization, loss of relationships, domestic violence, and adverse psychological reactions. Although cases of discrimination against HIV-infected persons and loss of confidentiality have been documented, data concerning the frequency of these events for women are limited. Reported rates of abandonment, loss of relationships, severe psychological reactions, and domestic violence have ranged from 4% to 13%. Providing infected women with or referring them to psychological, social, or legal services may help minimize such potential risks and enable women to benefit from the many health advantages of early HIV diagnosis.

Counseling and Testing Strategies

Guidelines published in 1985 regarding HIV counseling and testing of pregnant women recommended a targeted approach directed to women known to be at increased risk for HIV infection (e.g., injecting-drug users and women whose sex partners were HIV—infected or at risk for infection). However, several studies have indicated that counseling and testing strategies that offer testing only to those women who report risk factors fail to identify and offer services to many HIV-infected women (i.e., 50%–70% of infected women in some studies). Women may be unaware of their risk for infection if they have unknowingly had sexual contact with an HIV-infected person. Other women may refuse testing to avoid the stigma often associated with high-risk sexual and injecting-drug-use behaviors.

Because of the advances in prevention and treatment of opportunistic infections for HIV-infected adults and children during the past 10 years, several professional organizations and others have recommended a more widespread approach of offering HIV counseling and testing for pregnant women. This approach can be applied nationally to all pregnant women or to women in limited geographic areas based on the prevalence of HIV infection among childbearing women in those areas. However, a counseling and testing recommendation based on a prevalence threshold (e.g., one HIV-infected woman per 1,000 childbearing women) could delay or discourage implementation of counseling and testing services in areas (e.g., states) where prevalence data are inadequate, outdated, or unavailable, and would miss substantial numbers of HIV-infected pregnant women in areas with lower seroprevalence rates but high numbers of births (e.g., California). A prevalence-based approach also could lead to potentially discriminating testing practices, such as singling out a geographic area or racial/ethnic group. A universal approach of offering HIV counseling and testing to all pregnant women—regardless of the prevalence of HIV infection in their community or their risk for infection—provides a uniform policy that will reach HIV-infected pregnant women in all populations and geographic areas of the United States. Although this universal approach will necessitate increased resources (e.g., funding), effective implementation of HIV counseling and testing services for pregnant women and the ensuing medical interventions will reduce HIV-related morbidity in women and their infants and could ultimately reduce medical costs.

Counseling and testing policies also must address issues associated with provision of consent for testing. Data from universal, routine HIV counseling and voluntary testing programs in several areas indicate that high test-acceptance levels can be achieved without mandating testing. Mandatory testing may increase the potential for negative consequences of HIV testing and result in some women avoiding prenatal care altogether. In addition, mandatory testing may adversely affect the patient-provider relationship by placing the provider in an enforcing rather than facilitating role. Providers must act as facilitators to adequately assist women in making decisions regarding HIV testing and ZDV preventive therapy. Although few studies have addressed the issue of acceptance of HIV testing, higher levels of acceptance have been found in clinics where testing is voluntary but recommended by the health-care provider than in clinics that use a nondirective approach to HIV testing (i.e., patients are told the test is available, but testing is neither encouraged nor discouraged). . . .

Recommendations

The following recommendations have been developed to provide guidance to health-care workers when educating women about HIV infection and the importance of early diagnosis of HIV. . . .

HIV Counseling and Voluntary Testing of Pregnant Women and Their Infants

- Health-care providers should ensure that all pregnant women are counseled and encouraged to be tested for HIV infection to allow women to know their infection status both for their own health and to reduce the risk for perinatal HIV transmission. Pretest HIV counseling of pregnant women should be done in accordance with previous guidelines for HIV counseling. Such counseling should include information regarding the risk for HIV infection associated with sexual activity and injecting-drug use, the risk for transmission to the woman's infant if she is infected, and the availability of therapy to reduce this risk. HIV counseling, including any written materials, should be linguistically, culturally, educationally, and age appropriate for individual patients.

- HIV testing of pregnant women and their infants should be voluntary. Consent for testing should be obtained in accordance with prevailing legal requirements. Women who test positive for HIV or who refuse testing should not be a) denied prenatal or other health-care services, b) reported to child protective service agencies because of refusal to be tested or because of their HIV status, or c) discriminated against in any other way.

- Health-care providers should counsel and offer HIV testing to women as early in pregnancy as possible so that informed and timely therapeutic and reproductive decisions can be made. Specific strategies and resources will be needed to communicate with women who may not obtain prenatal care because of homelessness, incarceration, undocumented citizenship status, drug or alcohol abuse, or other reasons.

- Uninfected pregnant women who continue to practice high-risk behaviors (e.g., injecting-drug use and unprotected sexual contact with an HIV-infected or high-risk partner) should be encouraged to avoid further exposure to HIV and to be retested for HIV in the third trimester of pregnancy.

- The prevalence of HIV infection may be higher in women who have not received prenatal care. These women should be assessed promptly for HIV infection. Such an assessment should include information regarding prior HIV testing, test results, and risk history. For women who are first identified as being HIV infected during labor and delivery, health-care providers should consider offering intrapartum and neonatal ZDV according to published recommendations. For women whose HIV infection status has not been determined, HIV counseling should be provided and HIV testing offered as soon as the mother's medical condition permits. However, involuntary HIV testing should never be substituted for counseling and voluntary testing.

- Some HIV-infected women do not receive prenatal care, choose not to be tested for HIV, or do not retain custody of their children. If a woman has not been tested for HIV, she should be informed of the benefits to

449

her child's health of knowing her child's infection status and should be encouraged to allow the child to be tested. Counselors should ensure that the mother provides consent with the understanding that a positive HIV test for her child is indicative of infection in herself. For infants whose HIV infection status is unknown and who are in foster care, the person legally authorized to provide consent should be encouraged to allow the infant to be tested (with the consent of the biologic mother, when possible) in accordance with the policies of the organization legally responsible for the child and with prevailing legal requirements for HIV testing.

- Pregnant women should be provided access to other HIV prevention and treatment services (e.g., drug-treatment and partner-notification services) as needed. . . .

Recommendations for HIV-Infected Pregnant Women

- HIV-infected pregnant women should receive counseling as previously recommended. Posttest HIV counseling should include an explanation of the clinical implications of a positive HIV antibody test result and the need for, benefit of, and means of access to HIV-related medical and other early intervention services. Such counseling should also include a discussion of the interaction between pregnancy and HIV infection, the risk for perinatal HIV transmission and ways to reduce this risk, and the prognosis for infants who become infected.

- HIV-infected pregnant women should be evaluated according to published recommendations to assess their need for antiretroviral therapy, antimicrobial prophylaxis, and treatment of other conditions. . . . HIV-infected pregnant women should be evaluated to determine their need for psychological and social services.

- HIV-infected pregnant women should be provided information concerning ZDV therapy to reduce the risk for perinatal HIV transmission. . . . HIV-infected pregnant women should not be coerced into making decisions about ZDV therapy. These decisions should be made after consideration of both the benefits and potential risks of the regimen to the woman and her child. Therapy should be offered according to the appropriate regimen in published recommendations. A woman's decision not to accept treatment should not result in punitive action or denial of care.

- HIV-infected pregnant women should receive information about all reproductive options. Reproductive counseling should be nondirective. Health-care providers should be aware of the complex issues that HIV-infected women must consider when making decisions about their reproductive options and should be supportive of any decision.

- To reduce the risk for HIV transmission to their infants, HIV-infected women should be advised against breastfeeding. Support services should be provided when necessary for use of appropriate breast-milk substitutes.

- To optimize medical management, positive and negative HIV test results should be available to a woman's health-care provider and included on both her and her infant's confidential medical records. After obtaining consent, maternal health-care providers should notify the pediatric-care providers of the impending birth of an HIV-exposed child, any anticipated complications, and whether ZDV should be administered after birth. If HIV is first diagnosed in the child, the child's health-care providers should discuss the implication of the child's diagnosis for the woman's health and assist the mother in obtaining care for herself. Providers are encouraged to build supportive health-care relationships that can facilitate the discussion of pertinent health information. Confidential HIV-related information should be disclosed or shared only in accordance with prevailing legal requirements.

- Counseling for HIV-infected pregnant women should include an assessment of the potential for negative effects resulting from HIV infection (e.g., discrimination, domestic violence, and psychological difficulties). For women who anticipate or experience such effects, counseling also should include a) information on how to minimize these potential consequences, b) assistance in identifying supportive persons within their own social network, and c) referral to appropriate psychological, social, and legal services. In addition, HIV-infected women should be informed that discrimination based on HIV status or AIDS regarding matters such as housing, employment, state programs, and public accommodations (including physicians' offices and hospitals) is illegal.

- HIV-infected women should be encouraged to obtain HIV testing for any of their children born after they became infected or, if they do not know when they became infected, for children born after 1977. Older children (i.e., children >12 years of age) should be tested with informed consent of the parent and assent of the child. Women should be informed that the lack of signs and symptoms suggestive of HIV infection in older children may not indicate lack of HIV infection; some perinatally infected children can remain asymptomatic for several years.

Recommendations for Follow-Up of Infected Women and Perinatally Exposed Children

- Following pregnancy, HIV-infected women should be provided ongoing HIV-related medical care, including immune-function monitoring, antiretroviral therapy, and prophylaxis for and treatment of opportunistic infections and other HIV-related conditions. HIV-infected women should receive gynecologic care, including regular Pap smears, reproductive counseling, information on how to prevent sexual transmission of HIV, and treatment of gynecologic conditions according to published recommendations.

- HIV-infected women (or the guardians of their children) should be informed of the importance of follow-up for their children. These children should receive follow-up care to determine their infection status, to initiate prophylactic therapy to prevent PCP, and, if infected, to determine the need for antiretroviral and other prophylactic therapy and to monitor disorders in growth and development, which often occur before 24 months of age. HIV-infected children and other children living in households with HIV-infected persons should be vaccinated according to published recommendations for altered schedule.
- Because the identification of an HIV-infected mother also identifies a family that needs or will need medical and social services as her disease progresses, health-care providers should ensure that referrals to these services focus on the needs of the entire family.

ADDRESS BY NEW NAACP
CHAIRMAN OF THE BOARD
July 9, 1995

Attempting to overcome what some observers said might be the worst crisis in its eighty-six-year history, the National Association for the Advancement of Colored People (NAACP) in 1995 turned to two new leaders. Myrlie Evers-Williams was elected chairman of the sixty-four-member executive board in February. In December the NAACP announced that Rep. Kweisi Mfume (D-Md.) would become president and chief executive officer in February 1996.

Taking Steps Against Scandals and Debt

Evers-Williams, the widow of slain civil rights leader Medgar Evers, ousted the incumbent chairman, William F. Gibson, by a single vote at the February board meeting in New York. Gibson, a dentist from Greenville, South Carolina, and NAACP chairman since 1985, had lost the support of the membership amid allegations that he had mishandled NAACP money and diverted some to his own use.

The allegations against Gibson followed on the heels of the forced resignation of NAACP executive director Benjamin Chavis in 1994 after he admitted to using NAACP money to settle a sexual harassment suit against him. Chavis had taken office only a year and a half earlier, promising to restore the NAACP to its leading position as an influential civil rights organization. In addition, Chavis had drawn fire from some of the NAACP's traditional Jewish and corporate sponsors for his efforts to forge links between the NAACP and the Nation of Islam, headed by the controversial Louis Farrakhan. (Address by NAACP director, Historic Documents of 1993, p. 579)

The Gibson and Chavis scandals compounded anxiety over the association's growing debt, which was estimated at between $3 million and $4 million. The NAACP's annual budget is about $11 million. In addition, the organization was being sued on charges of sexual harassment and salary discrimination against women. Those charges combined with layoffs necessitated by the financial crisis had demoralized the staff.

The board of directors voted for Evers-Williams over Gibson February 18 by a vote of 30–29, after the rank-and-file membership voted no confidence in Gibson's leadership. The board also elected seven new board members and a new treasurer, investment banker Francisco L. Borges, who had served as the state treasurer of Connecticut. The latter action came after the general membership voted not to accept the financial report of the previous treasurer because, they said, it was not specific enough. Gibson remained as a member of the board.

Seeking to show that the NAACP was an active, involved civil rights organization, Evers-Williams announced at a news conference February 20 that NAACP officials would travel to Washington the following week to lobby against the Republican Contract with America and for the nomination of Henry W. Foster Jr. to be surgeon general. "We will be very vocal on issues that deal with welfare reform, that deal with the attitudes and the attempts to roll back many of the gains that we have made over the years . . . particularly affirmative action," she said. (Foster nomination, p. 61)

Evers-Williams expanded upon those themes in a rousing address July 9 to the NAACP's annual convention, held in Minneapolis. "When the nation is in distress," she said, "racism rears up its ugly head . . . once again, and the signs are everywhere. . . ." Evers-Williams noted in particular recent Supreme Court decisions on affirmative action, school desegregation, and legislative redistricting. "This Supreme Court is no longer a friend of civil rights," she said. (Supreme Court on affirmative action, p. 307; Supreme Court on redistricting, p. 369)

To deal with these challenges, Evers-Williams announced that the NAACP would "mount the largest, most effective block-by-block, precinct-by-precinct voter registration and education campaign" that the organization had ever conducted and then do everything possible to get out the vote. On October 1, the association kicked off a campaign to register one million new black voters by the 1996 elections. Evers-Williams also announced an emergency campaign to "save the NAACP" by rebuilding its financial strength, restoring its credibility, and doubling the number of its members and supporters.

The organization took one step toward solving its financial credibility when the board adopted financial controls and an ethics code that bars members from taking any action that might be construed as a conflict of interest. Some of the new rules resulted directly from the findings of an audit conducted by Cooper & Lybrand and released in the summer of 1995. That audit questioned $111,930 in spending by Gibson and found that Chavis had run up $32,459 in personal expenses on an NAACP credit card. The audit also showed that the board of directors had exceeded its travel budget by $264,000 during the previous five years.

Mfume's New Post

With the appointment of Mfume in December, the NAACP clearly hoped that it had found the person to bolster the reinvigoration that Evers-

Williams had begun. "There couldn't be a better person," said C. DeLores Tucker, head of the National Political Congress of Black Women.

Mfume, who was to serve as president and chief executive officer, told the Washington Post why he was giving up his safe seat in the House. "What pushed me into this was my absolute, utter disdain for the ultra-right-wing agenda that is being foisted on our communities without an equal and opposite grass-roots reaction," he said. "It was clear to me that I could do much more outside than I could do inside Congress."

Mfume was a former member of the Baltimore City Council before being elected to Congress in 1986, where he quickly won a reputation as an effective negotiator. He was elected chairman of the Congressional Black Caucus in 1992. Mfume's tenure there was not without controversy. His statement that the black caucus had entered a "covenant" with the NAACP and the Nation of Islam to work toward solving problems in the black community caused a sharp division in the caucus in 1993, with some members shying away from any association with the Nation of Islam and Farrakhan.

Mfume promised to move quickly on several issues important to the NAACP, including putting the organization on a sound financial footing. He also promised to work on the economic problems prevalent in the black community and to emphasize the value of education and individual responsibility. The NAACP "must, without equivocation or timidity, reclaim [its] rightful place as the voice of African-Americans and others who believe in the power and premise that all persons are, in fact, created equal," he told the Post.

> Following is the text of a speech entitled "Celebrating Our Legacy—A Vision for the 21st Century," delivered July 9, 1995, by Myrlie Evers-Williams, chairman of the NAACP board of directors, at the organization's eighty-sixth annual convention in Minneapolis:

It's been a long, interesting and challenging journey from Jackson, Mississippi, where Medgar Evers and I opened the first NAACP state headquarters. I was Medgar's support system and he was the NAACP's "Man in Mississippi." With the full responsibility of organizing branches throughout the state, investigating lynchings, such as the Emmit Till, Rev. George Lee, and others; getting the news of this infant movement from behind the cotton curtain; and sending coded messages by Western Union to the NAACP headquarters in New York where Roy Wilkins and others informed the world as to the happenings in Mississippi, I sat behind that desk at 1072 West Lynch Street and played many roles in keeping that office and my husband on solid footing.

At this moment, I am reminded of the youth who sat in at the lunch counters, fearful yet brave in their actions—challenging the adults, who were more cautious, to move faster because time was short. I recall the elderly members of the NAACP who said, "Those young children are right, and we're gonna march and sit-in side by side with them.

One of the disarming issues was whether we should continue our attack on racism in a non-violent way or resort to more violent means. Before that issue could be settled, Medgar Evers was cut down violently.

I can tell you that way back in 1953 as a secretary/gal-Friday for the NAACP, I never dreamed that in 1995 I would be serving as Chairman of the Board of this beloved organization. In the midst of all of the challenges we face, and the overwhelming hope and support you have all bestowed upon me, it is truly a humbling experience.

To serve our beloved NAACP and you, my friends, in a time when the association is being tested as never before is the greatest challenge of my life— and I have faced many.

When we look back at our legacy, we must not forget the heroes and sheroes of our struggle. Long before there were enough elected black officials in the South to fill a telephone booth, there was a brave and dynamic woman by the name of Ruby Hurley who put her life on the line to organize the NAACP branches in the South. Ruby Hurley, Southeast Regional Division, bravely served this organization and the nation along with W. C. Patton, the Association's Voter Education Director; [they] gave their last ounce of dedication and devotion to our struggle. Today we celebrate the fact that we have over 8,400 black elected officials, more than half in the old South, but let us not forget that this accomplishment did not come into being by elite academicians sitting in comfortable ivory towers or by prognosticators or pontificators, but by the little people who in the rural areas and urban centers stood up for what was just and right.

Our legacy includes a cadre of brilliant legal minds. Charles Houston, Thurgood Marshall, and Robert Carter set forth the strategy for eliminating legal segregation. They were joined by an array of volunteers who successfully challenged the *Plessy v. Ferguson* decision of 1896, which declared that separate but equal facilities were constitutional and the law of the land. Their efforts culminated in the Supreme Court decision of *Brown v. Board of Education* and a score of subsequent decisions which broke the back of legal segregation. Even in the face of recent setbacks, we can celebrate these precedent-setting legal victories and dynamic women, such as Ruby Hurley, who all put their lives on the line to organize the NAACP.

We can look back with pride and celebrate our victories in the legislative arena. It was your NAACP under the leadership of the legendary Clarence Mitchell that succeeded in securing the passage of the Civil Rights Act of 1957, the first Civil Rights legislation enacted since the Civil War. This legislation established the U. S. Commission on Civil Rights. The NAACP Washington Bureau was instrumental in securing the passage of the 1964 Civil Rights Act that called for the elimination of discrimination in employment and public accommodations; the 1965 Voting Rights Act, which made the registration of millions of African-Americans possible; the 1968 Fair Housing Act, which outlawed discrimination in the sale and rental of housing; the Voting Right extensions; and the South African Sanction Bill, which facilitated the fall of apartheid in South Africa.

We owe a debt of gratitude to Clarence Mitchell and Althea Simmons, whose quiet yet effective work on Capitol Hill made a difference in the political landscape of America.

We also owe a debt of gratitude to the hundreds of local and State Conference Officers who lobbied their state legislators [and] city and town councils to make possible the enactment of progressive statutes and ordinances that enhanced economic and social opportunities for African-Americans.

Over the years the NAACP, more than all other Civil Rights groups combined, marched and demonstrated against racial injustice at home and abroad. Today, we are confronted with severe challenges to the progress we have made over these past 86 years, but we have met the enemies of justice before and emerged victorious. We defeated [Governor] Orval Faubus; we defeated Governor George Conley Wallace; we defeated [police officer] Bull Connor and Sheriff Jim Clark; we defeated [associate attorney general nominee] William Bradford Reynolds; we defeated Judge [Robert] Bork; we defeated [Supreme Court nominees G. Harrold] Carswell and [Clemont] Haynesworth; we defeated the mobs who said that we must remain on the outskirts of the American storehouse of opportunity. So tonight, I say to those who are arrayed against affirmative action that we can prevail. I say to those who would cut benefits to the poor and the nation's elderly, we shall prevail. I say to those who would take from the needy to give to the greedy that like the lions who were in the den with Daniel, we have a power on our side that will take away your appetite and your avarice.

I say tonight to those who are celebrating and rejoicing in the current difficulties that the NAACP is experiencing that we met the challenges of the Klan and the White Citizens Council; we met the challenge of the depressions and recessions; we met the challenges of adverse public opinion and predictions of our earlier demise.

Tonight we are imbued with a spirit of renewed optimism. We know that our mission is not yet accomplished and that our task is not complete.

We know that today, the fact is, all of us live in a world of many challenges. Our nation's capital, once a peaceful place of honor, open to the world, is now closed to the public and protected with concrete barricades from "unabombers."

We live in an environment filled with paranoia, doubt and despair—all of which beckon the storm clouds of divisiveness, fear, scapegoating and racism. When the nation is in distress, racism rears up its ugly head, with bravado, once again—and the signs are everywhere, from the thinly-veiled racism implied in the anti-affirmative action attacks of the Republican presidential candidates like Phil Gramm and Pat Buchanan, to the most recent Supreme Court decision, which could wipe out more than half the African-American and Hispanic Members of Congress.

Never has there been a more critical need for the NAACP—a strong and virulent organization with teeth and muscle and intestinal fortitude. And yes, we have our work cut out for us. For example—the U.S. Supreme Court.

For 40 years we looked to the Supreme Court as a sympathetic referee in the struggle for civil rights and social justice. With the recent decisions passed down by this prestigious body, I think we must all agree that today, this Supreme Court is no longer a friend of civil rights.

In the term that just ended, they dismantled federal affirmative action programs that provided minority entrepreneurs and minority businessmen and women the opportunity to create black wealth and compete on an almost level playing field for the first time. Despite the need to make improvements, the intended goal of these programs was being accomplished.

They then delivered a knock-down punch against us when they invalidated the boundaries of a majority African-American congressional district in Georgia. This decision could end the careers of half the elected black and Hispanic officials in the country. There was some good news, however. They did not outlaw affirmative action as "unconstitutional." They may have cut off the head but there's still hope for the body.

This disparaging decision makes racial minorities the only group not allowed to have their group's interests taken into account where reapportionment is concerned.

The Supreme Court also destroyed or severely weakened the gains we had made in federal contracting.

They permitted the dismantling of a University of Maryland scholarship program set up exclusively for African-Americans;

And, perhaps most disturbing of all, they essentially ruled that *Brown v. Board of Education* is dead. That the Supreme Court is no longer in the business of protecting African-American and other minority students from the damage of segregation.

My friends, education is the gateway to opportunity, to self-sufficiency and success in America. But . . . at this critical time when our schools are wracked with violence, infected with an epidemic of teen pregnancy and swamped with the highest drop-out rates in history, the Court is saying to urban kids, parents and educators: you're on your own!

We also live in a time where the Governor of the State of California, a state which is home to the largest diversity of minority groups in the country, has rescinded some affirmative action policies by executive order and is supporting a proposed referendum on the 1996 ballot which would virtually outlaw all government-sponsored affirmative action-based initiatives.

In Newark, New Jersey, and countless other embattled communities across the nation, governors and state legislatures seek to fund suburban schools at the expense of already hard-pressed urban schools.

Across the TV screen of the nightly news we witness the parade of politicians pandering for votes using such racial code words as "welfare reform," "quotas" and "racial preferences."

As critical as good health is to the continued success of our nation's people, we live in a world where the federal program that distributes free vaccine to millions of children has been added to the hit list for dismantling by the

Republican members of Congress. Despite an audit report that cites underestimation of costs to deliver vaccines to doctors and clinics around the country, the program provides free vaccine against such diseases as measles, mumps and polio to children 18 and younger who are eligible for Medicaid, have no health insurance or have private insurance that does not cover vaccine. How can we expose our children and, indeed, all of us to the perils of uncontrolled epidemics? This is incredibly self-destructive leadership.

And over the airwaves, the Rush Limbaughs spew their venom and incite violence and hatred.

We live in a world where a U.S. senator is allowed to call for the abandonment of AIDS research because the victims of AIDS are not worthy of saving due to their engaging in activities he finds unacceptable. Our esteemed Senator Jesse Helms continues to flaunt his ignorance and prejudice without accountability or fear of reprisal.

Who in this room wishes to remain silent?

Do I hear a motion calling for Senator Jesse Helms to be put out to pasture? Can I get an "Amen!"

Yes, my friends, we live in world where it feels as if the Supreme Court, Congress, governors, state legislatures and organized right-wing groups have all decided that their worst enemy is people of color generally, and African-Americans in particular.

SO . . . the question for those of us gathered today in Minneapolis—the hometown of that "happy warrior" Hubert Humphrey and, since the age of four, our very own Roy Wilkins—is this: How do we deal with what is happening to us?

First, let me give you my bottom line answer: No turning back.

—No turning back to the days of Jim Crow!

—No turning back to the days of separate and unequal!

—No turning back to political isolation and segregation!

NOW, let me tell you what we will do.

First priority, we will save our beloved NAACP. Because in times of crisis, like too many in the past, there is no more important, more relevant and more experienced organization than this one.

Beginning today—right here in this hall—all of us must make a commitment to end the backbiting and infighting that has caused us to lose sight of our goal. We didn't keep our eyes on the prize, my brothers and sisters, and we are suffering the consequences for it. But we are an organization and a people of God and we know that *all things are possible for he that believeth.* I believe in the NAACP and I know that you do, too.

We are family and that means we fight and fuss sometimes. It also means we make up because we love one another. It's time for us to get on with the making up and cleaning up our act for the real business at hand. We no longer have the luxury of squandering our precious time and talent fighting each other. The ship has incurred much damage, has taken on water, but there are enough of us bailing that we shall not sink. We can, we will and we must stand together, proud as a people and proud of our legacy of struggle and triumph in our beloved America. It is truly our land, too. I say, hold on to your hats, "Newty-lovers" and the like, because you're in for the fight of your life!

THE NAACP HAS LAUNCHED AN EMERGENCY CAMPAIGN TO SAVE THE NAACP.

The mission of this campaign is to REBUILD our financial strength, RESTORE our credibility and DOUBLE the number of members and supporters.

To date, the members of the board, committees and national staff have worked together to tighten up our overall operations and make the necessary cost-cutting measures to ensure our continued operation over the short term.

As far as old business, the board will review the final and complete audit report from Coopers & Lybrand on Wednesday of this week. The results of that report and our findings and recommendations [for] moving forward will be made public and the matter will be settled. I promised you an organization with integrity and my commitment still stands. Sunshine of disclosure is still the best disinfectant.

To ensure financial integrity from henceforth, we are managing an aggressive plan to reduce our debt and pay off our patient creditors under the direction of a newly appointed Acting Chief Financial Officer who comes to us from Price Waterhouse.

Within the next three months, we will have in place enhanced fundraising capabilities which will allow us to meet our immediate financial needs while also helping put in place an internal fundraising and development structure which will meet the NAACP's future needs.

As you are aware, we have embarked upon a bona fide search for a permanent Executive Director. The Search Committee appointed by the Board is looking to submit its candidate of choice for recommendation for the position at the October Board meeting. Let me assure you, we will, however, take the time needed to identify the best and most qualified person to fill this critical management position.

BUT—even as we work on cleaning up our internal house and putting the past behind us, we have even more important work to do.

The greatest strength of the NAACP lies at the grass roots. Those 2,200 local branches who are hard at work day in and day out. And today, perhaps more than at any time in our history, they are more essential than ever.

As the Gingrich Gang and the Supreme Court return more and more power over our lives to the states, we must be prepared. The decisions which affect our lives and our children's future will not be made just in Washington, D.C., but increasingly by local school boards, county commissions, state legislatures and state executives.

And it is here that your work and the work of your Branches becomes key. And it must be the goal of the National Office to provide the help you need:

- Legal assistance
- Media and communications
- Financial assistance

We are also working to bring you "on line." Yes, the NAACP is going to be a mover and a shaker on the Information Superhighway, too. In fact, we've already started. The Black Information Network has created a World Wide Web page for the NAACP to promote our activities and the news of our leadership on the Internet. It is appalling that less than 10 percent of African-American households have personal computers. Seventy percent of the 24 million USA Internet users today are white males. Surely we must do what we need to, to make a difference here for our community. Internet is currently paid for by all taxpayers. We have a right to be included in the 30 million users worldwide.

We have also been talking with several telecommunications companies who are willing to work with us to network our branches and regional offices with the National Headquarters and our Washington Bureau.

My goal is that, by January 1 of next year, we will have an electronic NAACP Crisis Network in place which links at least 50 percent of our Branches to each other electronically.

This is a powerful technology for sharing information, trading tips on techniques, and, in general, helping us stay politically competitive with those who want to turn back the clock.

Frankly, in recent years we have failed you. It is my pledge to you that this will change. You will get the help you need. The help you deserve.

While we are in the process of rebuilding internally, we will focus on providing the leadership in civil rights mandated by today's crisis. Through the launching of our NATIONAL EMERGENCY CAMPAIGN TO SAVE THE NAACP we will engage in a full-scale crisis mobilization effort to defend our civil rights.

We will:

- Organize Emergency Task forces of experts from the African-American community and other sectors of American life in critical areas such as *media, public relations, finance, corporate support, communications and entertainment.*
- Put these task forces to work on raising the money and building the skills we will need to meet the crisis in civil rights we now face.

Ours is a community rich in talent and resources. The time has come for everyone who has made it in our community to now come forth; to "pay back" those who sacrificed for them yesterday by doing their part to meet today's crisis.

And when it comes to dealing with *crisis* our NAACP has a proud and effective history. So, the central component of our National Emergency Campaign to Save the NAACP is a CRISIS MOBILIZATION, which must get underway at once.

There are two key steps—proven steps—in dealing with the current political crisis faced by African-Americans, other minorities and the women of America:

STEP #1. REGISTER A RECORD NUMBER OF VOTERS

STEP #2. MOBILIZE THE GRASSROOTS TO TURN OUT THE VOTE AND DEMONSTRATE OUR POLITICAL CLOUT

If there's one characteristic all politicians have in common, it's that they can count. Now is the time to put faces and numbers to what is happening to us.

When African-Americans, other minorities and women voted in record numbers in 1992, we made great gains. But when we sat out the 1994 congressional elections, we lost ground—and lost ground badly.

Therefore . . . our top priority, beginning right now, must be [to] mount the largest, most effective block-by-block, precinct-by-precinct voter registration and education campaign ever conducted by the NAACP.

BUT . . . we can't be content with registering record numbers. We must also get out the vote. Consequently, my pledge to you is to work with all the strength and energy in me to build and support the grassroots power of our Branches.

As our organizers and Branches work to register and educate voters, we will work to provide the legal teams and resources needed to counter what I fully expect will be a barrage of challenges and attacks on our franchise and challenges to the make up of legislative districts as a result of the recent Supreme Court decision.

At the same time we must turn to our brothers and sisters in the television and entertainment industries to do everything in their power to popularize and highlight the importance of registering *and* voting.

Of course, there's nothing "new" in all this. We've done it time and time again. And each time we've posted great gains. What is "new" is the clear and unmistakable message that we "get back to basics" in this time of crisis.

Now is the time to go forward, not backward. To remember our martyrs and take strength from their blood and their legacy.

Now is the time to turn our attention outward, to put the internal squabbles of the past behind us.

I urge you to stand—right now—and join hands in unity. This is our first action in our new National Campaign to Save the NAACP. Our first action in aiming our passion toward the future and our children's future.

We won't go back!

REPORT ON THE USE OF GUNS IN CRIME
July 10, 1995

Most incidents of crime do not involve the use of a gun, but those that do usually involve handguns, according to a report released July 10 by the Bureau of Justice Statistics in the Department of Justice. Altogether, 4.4 million violent crimes—defined as rape and sexual assault, robbery, and aggravated assault—were committed in 1993, according to data collected by the National Crime Victimization Survey. Of these, 1.3 million people were victims of a crime committed with a firearm, and 86 percent of those crimes involved handguns. Seventy percent of the 24,526 murders in 1993 were committed with firearms; 57 percent of these involved handguns.

The report, entitled "Guns Used in Crime," was released as some members of Congress were pushing their colleagues to repeal the Brady Law, which required a five-day waiting period for the purchase of a handgun, and a law banning nineteen types of assault weapons. Sarah Brady, the chairman of Handgun Control Inc., a 400,000–member lobbying group, said the Justice Department statistics confirmed the need to keep the two laws in place. "Repealing this legislation now will only lead to more senseless gun deaths in this country," she said. She is the wife of James Brady, a former White House press secretary who was gravely wounded by a handgun in a 1981 assassination attempt on Ronald Reagan.

Use of Handguns, Assault Weapons

According to the Justice Department report, surveys showed that criminals preferred concealable, well-made, large caliber guns. Most handguns used in crimes were revolvers, but a University of Pennsylvania study of murders in Philadelphia showed a significant increase in the use of semiautomatic pistols, from 24 percent in 1985 to 38 percent in 1990. Surveys also showed that juvenile offenders were more likely than adult criminals to own and carry semiautomatic weapons. This last finding was particularly disturbing because the rate of crime among juveniles had been rising dramatically while the rate among adults had been falling and because the juve-

nile crime rate was expected to continue to climb as teenagers accounted for a growing share of the population. (Report on crime statistics, p. 710)

"One thing has shown a dramatic increase in crime statistics: crime by young offenders," said Gene Stephens, a professor at the University of South Carolina College of Criminal Justice. "What might have been an assault with fists and knives in the past now becomes a homicide because kids have automatic and semiautomatic weapons and handguns."

The report acknowledged that little was known about the use of assault weapons in crime and that differing definitions of assault weapons made comparisons difficult. Typically, the report said, assault weapons were defined as semiautomatic firearms—pistols, rifles, or shotguns—that can accommodate a large magazine of ammunition and were designed for rapid fire and combat use.

A study in New York City found that 16 percent of the homicides there in 1993 involved assault weapons, while a study in Virginia found that of the guns used to commit 431 murders between 1989 and 1991, only ten were described as assault weapons.

Effectiveness of the Brady Law

A year after the Brady Law took effect on February 28, 1994, three surveys were released that attempted to assess its effectiveness. The law required a five-day waiting period, while a background check was run on the would-be purchaser. According to the three surveys, as many as 45,000 people, or between 2 percent and 3.5 percent of all who applied to buy handguns, were turned down because they were convicted felons. Felons, along with fugitives from justice, juveniles, illegal aliens, and the mentally ill, were prohibited by law from buying guns. The surveys were conducted by the Treasury Department's Bureau of Alcohol, Tobacco, and Firearms; CBS News; and the International Association of Chiefs of Police, in conjunction with Handgun Control, Inc.

"I believe the Brady Bill has reduced the number of crimes those felons would have committed," a district attorney in Georgia told the New York Times. *The numbers show that "criminals do go to stores to buy guns, and they obviously don't buy handguns to go duck hunting." Others were more skeptical. "The 40,000 people who were stopped were only stopped at that store at that time. . . . So all they had to do was go out on the street corner at midnight and pay more to get a gun," said Bill Bridgewater, the executive director of the National Alliance of Stocking Gun Dealers.*

Although it was too early to assess the effect of the ban on assault weapons, which took effect in November 1994, the Georgia district attorney said the street price of AK-47 rifles had already jumped from $80 to $400 or more in his area, which might price most juveniles out of the market.

Efforts to Repeal Gun Control Laws

Efforts led by the National Rifle Association to repeal the assault weapon ban made little headway in Congress in 1995, despite backing in both par-

ties. Proponents of repealing the ban wanted to add it to a Republican-sponsored crime bill that would also repeal many other provisions of the crime bill passed in 1994. After President Clinton declared in his State of the Union message that he would not let the ban be repealed, House Republican leaders decided to put off a vote on the divisive issue until after the first one hundred days of the new Congress, the time period in which the Republicans had promised to enact their Contract with America. (Clinton's State of the Union address, p. 24; House leaders on the first one hundred days, p. 165)

Although it seemed likely that there were enough votes in the House to repeal the ban, the picture in the Senate was not clear, and Republican leaders apparently decided that they did not want to give President Clinton and the Democrats a political edge on this issue during the presidential election season. The April 19 bombing of a federal office building in Oklahoma city ended any possibility that the ban would be debated on the House floor in 1995. (Oklahoma City bombing, p. 176)

Following are excerpts from "Guns Used in Crime," a report released July 10, 1995, by the Bureau of Justice Statistics:

How often are guns used in violent crimes?

According to the National Crime Victimization Survey (NCVS), almost 43.6 million criminal victimizations occurred in 1993, including 4.4 million violent crimes of rape and sexual assault, robbery, and aggravated assault. Of the victims of these violent crimes, 1.3 million (29%) stated that they faced an offender with a firearm.

In 1993, the FBI's *Crime in the United States* estimated that almost 2 million violent crimes of murder, rape, robbery and aggravated assault were reported to the police by citizens. About 582,000 of these reported murders, robberies, and aggravated assaults were committed with firearms. Murder was the crime that most frequently involved firearms; 70% of the 24,526 murders in 1993 were committed with firearms.

How do we know about the guns used by criminals?

No national collection of data contains detailed information about all of the guns used in crimes. Snapshots of information about the guns used by criminals are available from—

- official police records concerning the guns recovered in crimes and reports gathered from victims
- surveys that interview criminals
- surveys that interview victims of crime.

From these sources, we know how often guns are involved in crime, how guns are used in crime, what general categories of firearms are most often used in crime, and, to a limited extent, the specific types of guns most frequently used by criminals.

Handguns are most often the type of firearm used in crime

- According to the Victim Survey (NCVS), 25% of the victims of rape and sexual assault, robbery, and aggravated assault in 1993 faced an offender armed with a handgun. Of all firearm-related crime reported to the survey, 86% involved handguns.
- The FBI's Supplemental Homicide Reports show that in 1993 57% of all murders were committed with handguns, 3% with rifles, 5% with shotguns, and 5% with firearms where the type was unknown.
- The 1991 Survey of State Prison Inmates found that violent inmates who used a weapon were more likely to use a handgun than any other weapon; 24% of all violent inmates reported that they used a handgun. Of all inmates, 13% reported carrying a handgun when they committed the offense for which they were serving time.

What types of guns do criminals prefer?

Research by Wright and Rossi in the 1980's found that most criminals prefer guns that are easily concealable, large caliber, and well made. Their studies also found that the handguns used by the felons interviewed were similar to the handguns available to the general public, except that the criminals preferred larger caliber guns.

What types of guns are available generally?

The Bureau of Alcohol, Tobacco, and Firearms (ATF) estimates that from 1899 to 1993 about 223 million guns became available in the United States, including over 79 million rifles, 77 million handguns, and 66 million shotguns. The number of guns seized, destroyed, lost, or not working is unknown.

The number of new handguns added to those available has exceeded the number of new shotguns and rifles in recent years. More than half of the guns added in 1993 were handguns. Over 40 million handguns have been produced in the United States since 1973.

Since over 80% of the guns available in the United States are manufactured here, gun production is a reasonable indicator of the guns made available. From 1973 to 1993, U.S. manufacturers produced—

- 6.6 million .357 Magnum revolvers
- 6.5 million .38 Special revolvers
- 5.4 million .22 caliber pistols
- 5.3 million .22 caliber revolvers
- 4.5 million .25 caliber pistols
- 3.1 million 9 millimeter pistols
- 2.4 million .380 caliber pistols

- 2.2 million .44 Magnum revolvers
- 1.7 million .45 caliber pistols
- 1.2 million .32 caliber revolvers.

During the two decades from 1973 to 1993, the types of handguns most frequently produced have changed. Most new handguns are pistols rather than revolvers. Pistol production grew from 28% of the handguns produced in the United States in 1973 to 80% in 1993.

The number of large-caliber pistols produced annually increased substantially after 1986. Until the mid-1980s, most pistols produced in the United States were .22 and .25 caliber models. Production of .380 caliber and 9 millimeter pistols began to increase substantially in 1987, so that by 1993 they became the most frequently produced pistols. From 1991 to 1993, the last 3 years for which data are available, the most frequently produced handguns were—

- .380 caliber pistols (20%)
- 9 millimeter pistols (19%)
- .22 caliber pistols (17%)
- .25 caliber pistols (13%)
- .50 caliber pistols (8%).

Stolen guns are a source of weapons for criminals

All stolen guns are available to criminals by definition. Recent studies of adult and juvenile offenders show that many have either stolen a firearm or kept, sold, or traded a stolen firearm:

- According to the 1991 Survey of State Prison Inmates, among those inmates who possessed a handgun, 9% had acquired it through theft and 28% had acquired it through an illegal market such as a drug dealer or fence. Of all inmates, 10% had stolen at least one gun, and 11% had sold or traded stolen guns.
- Studies of adult and juvenile offenders that the Virginia Department of Criminal Justice Services conducted in 1992 and 1993 found that 15% of the adult offenders and 19% of the juvenile offenders had stolen guns; 16% of the adults and 24% of the juveniles had kept a stolen gun; and 20% of the adults and 30% of the juveniles had sold or traded a stolen gun.
- From a sample of juvenile inmates in four States, Sheley and Wright found that more than 50% had stolen a gun at least once in their lives and 24% had stolen their most recently obtained handgun. They concluded that theft and burglary were the original, not always the proximate, source of many guns acquired by the juveniles.

How many guns are stolen?

The Victim Survey (NCVS) estimates that there were 341,000 incidents of firearm theft from private citizens annually from 1987 to 1992. Because the survey does not ask how many guns were stolen, the number of guns stolen probably exceeds the number of incidents of gun theft.

The FBI's National Crime Information Center (NCIC) stolen gun file contained over 2 million reports as of March 1995. In 1994, over 306,000 entries were added to this file, including a variety of guns, ammunition, cannons, and grenades. Reports of stolen guns are included in the NCIC files when citizens report the theft to law enforcement agencies that submit a report to the FBI. All entries must include make, caliber, and serial number. Initiated in 1967, the NCIC stolen gun file retains all entries indefinitely unless a recovery is reported.

Most stolen guns are handguns

Victims report to the Victim Survey that handguns were stolen in 53% of the thefts of guns. The FBI's stolen gun file's 2 million reports include information on—

- 1.26 million handguns (almost 60%)
- 470,000 rifles (22%)
- 356,000 shotguns (17%).

How many automatic weapons are stolen?

Under the provisions of the National Firearms Act, all automatic weapons such as machine guns must be registered with the ATF. In 1995, over 240,000 automatic weapons were registered with the ATF. As of March 1995, the NCIC stolen gun file contained reports on about 7,700 machine guns and submachine guns.

What types of handguns are most frequently stolen?

Most Frequently Reported Handguns in the NCIC Stolen Gun File

Percent of stolen handguns	Number	Caliber	Type
20.5	259,184	.38	Revolver
11.7	147,681	.22	Revolver
11.6	146,474	.357	Revolver
8.8	111,558	9mm	Semiautomatic
7.0	87,714	.25	Semiautomatic
6.7	84,474	.22	Semiautomatic
5.4	68,112	.380	Semiautomatic
3.7	46,503	.45	Semiautomatic
3.3	41,318	.32	Revolver
3.1	39,254	.44	Revolver
1.5	18,377	.32	Semiautomatic
1.3	16,214	.45	Revolver

Upon request, the ATF traces some guns used in crime to their origin

The National Tracing Center of ATF traces firearms to their original point of sale upon the request of police agencies. The requesting agency may use this information to assist in identifying suspects, providing evidence for subsequent prosecution, establishing stolen status, and proving ownership. The number of requests for firearms traces increased from 37,181 in 1990 to 85,132 in 1994.

Trace requests represent an unknown portion of all the guns used in crimes. ATF is not able to trace guns manufactured before 1968, most surplus military weapons, imported guns without the importer's name, stolen guns, and guns missing a legible serial number.

Police agencies do not request traces on all firearms used in crimes. Not all firearms used in crimes are recovered so that a trace can be done and, in some States and localities, the police agencies may be able to establish ownership locally without going to the ATF.

Most trace requests concern handguns

Over half of the guns that police agencies asked ATF to trace were pistols and another quarter were revolvers. . . . While trace requests for all types of guns increased in recent years, the number of pistols traced increased the most, doubling from 1990 to 1994.

What are the countries of origin of the guns that are traced?

Traced guns come from many countries across the globe. However, 78% of the guns that were traced in 1994 originated in the United States and most of the rest were from—

- Brazil (5%)
- Germany (3%)
- China (3%)
- Austria (3%)
- Italy (2%)
- Spain (2%)

What caliber guns do criminals prefer?

In their 1983 study, Wright, Rossi, and Daly asked a sample of felons about the handgun they had most recently acquired. Of the felons sampled—

- 29% had acquired a .38 caliber handgun
- 20% had acquired a .357 caliber handgun
- 16% had acquired a .22 caliber handgun.

Sheley and Wright found that the juvenile inmates in their 1991 sample in four States preferred large caliber, high-quality handguns. Just prior to their confinement—

- 58% owned a revolver, usually a .38 or .357 caliber gun
- 55% owned a semiautomatic handgun, usually a 9 millimeter or .45 caliber gun
- 51% owned a sawed-off shotgun
- 35% owned a military-style automatic or semiautomatic rifle.

Do juvenile offenders use different types of guns than adult offenders?

A study of adult and juvenile offenders by the Virginia Department of Criminal Justice Services found that juvenile offenders were more likely than adults to have carried a semiautomatic pistol at the crime scene (18% versus 7%). They also were more likely to have carried a revolver (10% versus 7%). The same proportion of adults and juveniles (3%) carried a shotgun or rifle at the crime scene.

Some studies of guns used in homicides provide information about caliber

McGonigal and colleagues at the University of Pennsylvania Medical Center studied firearm homicides that occurred in Philadelphia: 145 in 1985 and 324 in 1990. Most of the firearms used in the homicides studied were handguns: 90% in 1985 and 95% in 1990. In both years, revolvers were the predominant type of handgun used; however, the use of semiautomatic pistols increased from 24% in 1985 to 38% in 1990. The caliber of the handguns used also changed. . . .

The Virginia Department of Criminal Justice Services studied 844 homicides that occurred in 18 jurisdictions from 1989 through 1991. Firearms were identified as the murder weapon in 600 cases. Over 70% of the firearms used were handguns. Of those handguns where the caliber and firing action could be identified, 19% were .38 caliber revolvers, 10% were .22 caliber revolvers, and 9% were 9 millimeter semiautomatic pistols.

The Hawaii Department of the Attorney General, Crime Prevention Division, studied 59 firearms-related homicides in Honolulu from 1988 to 1992. Handguns were used in 48 homicides (over 80%), including 11 handguns of 9 millimeter caliber, 10 of .357 caliber, 10 of .38 caliber, and 5 of .25 caliber.

What caliber guns are used in the killings of law enforcement officers?

From 1982 to 1993, of the 687 officers who were killed by firearms other than their own guns, more were killed by .38 caliber handguns than by any other type of weapon. . . .

How often are assault weapons used in crime?

Little information exists about the use of assault weapons in crime. The information that does exist uses varying definitions of assault weapons that were developed before the Federal assault weapons ban was enacted.

In general, assault weapons are semiautomatic firearms with a large magazine of ammunition that were designed and configured for rapid fire and combat use. An assault weapon can be a pistol, a rifle, or a shotgun. The Federal Violent Crime Control and Law Enforcement Act of 1994 bans the manufacture and sale of 19 specific assault weapons identified by make and manufacturer. It also provides for a ban on those weapons that have a combination of features such as flash suppressors and grenade launchers. The ban does not cover those weapons legally possessed before the law was enacted. The National Institute of Justice will be evaluating the effect of the ban and reporting to Congress in 1997.

In 1993, prior to the passage of the assault weapons ban, the Bureau of Alcohol, Tobacco, and Firearms (ATF) reported that about 1% of the estimated 200 million guns in circulation were assault weapons. Of the gun tracing requests received that year by ATF from law enforcement agencies, 8% involved assault weapons.

Assault weapons and homicide

A New York State Division of Criminal Justice Services study of homicides in 1993 in New York City found that assault weapons were involved in 16% of the homicides studied. The definition of assault weapons used was from proposed but not enacted State legislation that was more expansive than the Federal legislation. By matching ballistics records and homicide files, the study found information on 366 firearms recovered in the homicides of 271 victims. Assault weapons were linked to the deaths of 43 victims (16% of those studied).

A study by the Virginia State Department of Criminal Justice Services reviewed the files of 600 firearm murders that occurred in 18 jurisdictions from 1989 to 1991. The study found that handguns were used in 72% of the murders (431 murders). Ten guns were identified as assault weapons, including five pistols, four rifles, and one shotgun.

Assault weapons and offenders

In the 1991 BJS Survey of State Inmates, about 8% of the inmates reported that they had owned a military-type weapon, such as an Uzi, AK-47, AR-15, or M-16. Less than 1% said that they carried such a weapon when they committed the incident for which they were incarcerated. A Virginia inmate survey conducted between November 1992 and May 1993 found similar results: About 10% of the adult inmates reported that they had ever possessed an assault rifle, but none had carried it at the scene of a crime.

Two studies indicate higher proportions of juvenile offenders reporting possession and use of assault rifles. The Virginia inmate survey also covered 192 juvenile offenders. About 20% reported that they had possessed an assault rifle and 1% said that they had carried it at the scene of a crime. In 1991, Sheley and Wright surveyed 835 serious juvenile offenders incarcerated in six facilities in four States. In the Sheley and Wright study, 35% of the juvenile inmates reported that they had owned a military-style automatic or semiautomatic rifle just prior to confinement.

471

CLINTON ON NORMALIZING
RELATIONS WITH VIETNAM
July 11, 1995

President Bill Clinton on July 11 extended full diplomatic recognition to Vietnam, a step that symbolically ended the Vietnam War more than twenty years after the United States failed to prevent a communist takeover of South Vietnam. Clinton said he hoped his action would "help our own country move forward on an issue that has separated Americans from one another for too long now."

Clinton's move was intended to allow the United States and Vietnam to exchange ambassadors and to open full trade relations. The first visible manifestation of the new policy was a visit to Vietnam in August by Secretary of State Warren Christopher, the highest ranking U.S. official to visit Vietnam in two decades. By year's end Clinton still had not nominated an ambassador, and he was engaged in a dispute with Congress over funding a potential U.S. embassy in Hanoi.

The president won praise for his action from a broad spectrum, starting with the three senators who had been the most prominent supporters of establishing diplomatic ties with Vietnam: John McCain (R-Ariz.), who spent nearly six years as a prisoner of war in North Vietnam; Bob Kerrey (D-Neb.), who lost part of a leg in Vietnam; and John Kerry (D-Mass.), a Vietnam veteran.

Several business groups also supported the move, among them the United States Chamber of Commerce, which had lobbied for diplomatic relations with Vietnam. Those groups hoped formal relations would promote trade relations, including financing by U.S. government lending agencies of American companies wanting to do business in Vietnam.

Senate Majority Leader Bob Dole (R-Kan.), who was a leading candidate for the Republican presidential nomination in 1996, denounced Clinton's action, as did several of his Republican colleagues on Capitol Hill. Opinion was split among veterans groups and organizations representing families of some 1,600 U.S. military personnel still listed as missing in action (MIA) in Vietnam. The American Legion and some family groups opposed diplomatic recognition of Vietnam, while the Veterans of Foreign Wars and other family groups supported it.

The voices of opposition were blunted, to a large degree, by McCain's support for the president's action. A staunch conservative who was by far the most famous of American prisoners of war in Vietnam, McCain provided the political cover that Clinton felt he needed to fend off his conservative foes. The president's uncertainty on the issue stemmed from the continuing controversy over his avoidance of military service during the Vietnam War, which he and millions of others of his generation had bitterly opposed. McCain said Clinton's move "required some courage."

Several of McCain's Republican colleagues were angered by his stance, accusing him of betraying his fellow Vietnam veterans. He shrugged off that criticism, saying that anger over the war was fading and the American people would support the president's move. McCain's prediction was bolstered by a CNN-USA Today poll, conducted by the Gallup organization just before Clinton's announcement, that showed 61 percent of those interviewed supporting recognition of Vietnam, with 27 percent opposed.

Steps Toward Closer Ties

President Clinton's announcement was the culmination of a series of official and unofficial steps taken since the 1980s that lead toward reconciliation between the two enemies. For many years, nearly all the contact between the United States and Vietnam concerned one issue: the fate of U.S. servicemen who were missing in action from the Vietnam War, most of them presumed dead.

Vietnam in the late 1980s stepped up its cooperation with official U.S. efforts to locate the remains of those servicemen and have them returned to the United States. By 1995 Vietnam had turned over to the United States the remains of several dozen personnel and had given U.S. officials information on others. As Vietnam's level of cooperation increased, so did U.S. willingness to deal with the government in Hanoi. Retired general John W. Vessey Jr., who served as chairman of the Joint Chiefs of Staff under President Ronald Reagan, led U.S. negotiations with Vietnam on the MIA issue during the Reagan, Bush, and Clinton administrations.

Partly as a result of Vessey's efforts, President George Bush's administration in April 1991 gave Vietnam a series of steps, called a "road map," leading toward establishment of full diplomatic relations—assuming Vietnam's continued cooperation on the MIA issue. The first major step down that road was the opening, in 1991, of a U.S. office in Hanoi to speed U.S.-Vietnamese cooperation on the issue. The diplomatic and military personnel assigned to that office were the first official U.S. representatives in Vietnam since April 1975, when the United States closed its embassy in Saigon as communist forces were about to take control of the city. The office also was the first official U.S. representation in Hanoi—which had been the capital of North Vietnam—since a consulate was closed in 1955.

The Clinton administration essentially followed steps outlined in Bush's road map, the most important of which was lifting the U.S. trade embargo against Vietnam in February 1994. A year later, in February 1995, the two countries upgraded their missions to the status of "liaison" offices, just short of full diplomatic relations.

In taking each of these steps to upgrade ties with Vietnam, both Bush and Clinton were encouraged by the lack of public protest. Some veterans groups and MIA-support organizations complained, but the most remarkable thing about the public response was the lack of it.

Expanding U.S.-Vietnam Business Ties

In establishing full diplomatic relations with Hanoi, the Clinton administration was recognizing the desire of many American companies to establish operations in Vietnam. Business leaders had argued for years that opening Vietnam to American investment would encourage that country's leaders to abandon communism in favor of free markets—and would give them an extra incentive to resolve the contentious MIA issue. The business leaders also feared they would lose commercial opportunities in Vietnam to firms of other countries that had long since established relations with Hanoi.

Beginning in 1991, the Bush and Clinton administrations took several steps that allowed U.S. firms to begin limited operations in Vietnam, including the signing of contracts in anticipation of the lifting of the trade embargo. According to the General Accounting Office, about thirty American companies already had offices in Vietnam when the embargo was lifted in 1994. The United States Chamber of Commerce reported that the number had increased to three hundred firms by the time Clinton established diplomatic relations.

Energy firms were among the most active in Vietnam, attracted by the possibility of winning the right to explore offshore oil fields in the South China Sea. Firms engaged in banking, insurance, telecommunications, and construction also were increasing their presence in Vietnam. Many of those companies had joined the United States-Vietnam Trade Council, based in Washington, D.C., which was among the groups leading the call for full relations with Vietnam.

Clinton's announcement left several important steps still to be taken before all trade and diplomatic relations would be normalized in fact as well as in name. The most important of these steps were the negotiation of a trade agreement providing mutual "most favored nation" trading status and the establishment of full embassies in each country's capital.

Congressional Action

Congress took several contradictory actions on the Vietnam issue in the months following Clinton's announcement, resulting in at least a partial stalemate in U.S. policy toward Vietnam by the end of 1995. In a voice vote on July 26, the House acted to prohibit funds for an expanded U.S. diplo-

matic presence in Vietnam. Congress in December sent Clinton a fiscal 1997 appropriations bill for the Commerce, Justice, and State departments that banned funds for an embassy in Vietnam unless the president certified that the Vietnamese had been "fully cooperative" on the MIA issue. This was a much weaker position than the House had taken since it gave the president broad discretion to act. Nevertheless, Clinton on December 19 vetoed that bill on several grounds, including the Vietnam provision, which he said interfered with presidential prerogatives.

The Senate proved more receptive to expanded business ties with Vietnam, rejecting, 39–58, a move in September to prohibit formal trade relations unless the president certified that Vietnam was cooperating more fully on the MIA issue.

Following is the text of President Clinton's announcement, on July 11, 1995, of the establishment of full diplomatic relations between the United States and Vietnam:

. . . Today I am announcing the normalization of diplomatic relationships with Vietnam.

From the beginning of this administration, any improvement in relationships between America and Vietnam has depended upon making progress on the issue of Americans who were missing in action or held as prisoners of war. Last year, I lifted the trade embargo on Vietnam in response to their cooperation and to enhance our efforts to secure the remains of lost Americans and to determine the fate of those whose remains have not been found.

It has worked. In seventeen months, Hanoi has taken important steps to help us resolve many cases. Twenty-nine families have received the remains of their loved ones and at last have been able to give them a proper burial. Hanoi has delivered to us hundreds of pages of documents shedding light on what happened to Americans in Vietnam. And Hanoi has stepped up its cooperation with Laos, where many Americans were lost.

We have reduced the number of so-called discrepancy cases, in which we have had reason to believe that Americans were still alive after they were lost to 55. And we will continue to work to resolve more cases.

Hundreds of dedicated men and women are working on all these cases, often under extreme hardship and real danger in the mountains and jungles of Indochina. On behalf of all Americans, I want to thank them. And I want to pay a special tribute to General John Vessey, who has worked so tirelessly on this issue for Presidents Reagan and Bush and for our administration. He has made a great difference to a great many families. And we as a nation are grateful for his dedication and for his service. Thank you, sir.

I also want to thank the presidential delegation, led by Deputy Secretary of Veterans Affairs Hershel Gober, Winston Lord, James Wold, who have helped us to make so much progress on this issue. And I am especially grateful to the leaders of the families and the veterans organizations who have worked with the delegation and maintained their extraordinary commitment to finding the answers we seek.

Never before in the history of warfare has such an extensive effort been made to resolve the fate of soldiers who did not return. Let me emphasize, normalization of our relations with Vietnam is not the end of our effort. From the early days of this administration I have said to the families and veterans groups what I say again here: We will keep working until we get all the answers we can. Our strategy is working. Normalization of relations is the next appropriate step. With this new relationship, we will be able to make more progress. To that end, I will send another delegation to Vietnam this year. And Vietnam has pledged it will continue to help us find answers. We will hold them to that pledge.

By helping to bring Vietnam into the community of nations, normalization also serves our interest in working for a free and peaceful Vietnam in a stable and peaceful Asia. We will begin to normalize our trade relations with Vietnam, whose economy is now liberalizing and integrating into the economy of the Asia-Pacific region. Our policy will be to implement the appropriate United States government programs to develop trade with Vietnam consistent with U.S. law.

As you know, many of these programs require certifications regarding human rights and labor rights before they can proceed. We have already begun discussing human rights issues with Vietnam, especially issues regarding religious freedom. Now we can expand and strengthen that dialogue. The Secretary of State will go to Vietnam in August where he will discuss all of these issues, beginning with our POW and MIA concerns.

I believe normalization and increased contact between Americans and Vietnamese will advance the cause of freedom in Vietnam, just as it did in Eastern Europe and the former Soviet Union. I strongly believe that engaging the Vietnamese on the broad economic front of economic reform and the broad front of democratic reform will help to honor the sacrifice of those who fought for freedom's sake in Vietnam.

I am proud to be joined in this view by distinguished veterans of the Vietnam War. They served their country bravely. They are of different parties. A generation ago they had different judgments about the war which divided us so deeply. But today they are of a single mind. They agree that the time has come for America to move forward on Vietnam. All Americans should be grateful especially that Senators John McCain [R-Ariz.], John Kerry [D-Mass.], Bob Kerrey [D-Neb.], Chuck Robb [D-Va.], and Representative Pete Peterson [D-Fla.], along with other Vietnam veterans in the Congress, including Senator [Tom] Harkin [D-Iowa], Congressman [Jim] Kolbe [R-Ariz.], and Congressman [Wayne] Gilchrest [R-Md.], who just left, and others who are out here in the audience have kept up their passionate interest in Vietnam but were able to move beyond the haunting and painful past toward finding common ground for the future. Today, they and many other veterans support the normalization of relations, giving the opportunity to Vietnam to fully join the community of nations and being true to what they fought for so many years ago.

Whatever we may think about the political decisions of the Vietnam era, the brave Americans who fought and died there had noble motives. They fought for the freedom and the independence of the Vietnamese people. Today the Vietnamese are independent, and we believe this step will help to extend the reach of freedom in Vietnam and, in so doing, to enable these fine veterans of Vietnam to keep working for that freedom.

This step will also help our own country to move forward on an issue that has separated Americans from one another for too long now. Let the future be our destination. We have so much work ahead of us. This moment offers us the opportunity to bind up our own wounds. They have resisted time for too long. We can now move on to common ground. Whatever divided us before let us consign to the past. Let this moment, in the words of the Scripture, be a time to heal and a time to build.

Thank you all. And God bless America.

FRENCH APOLOGY FOR COMPLICITY WITH NAZIS
July 16, 1995

French president Jacques Chirac acknowledged on July 16 that France bore responsibility for helping deport thousands of Jews to German death camps during World War II. Previous French leaders had insisted that Nazi Germany, and the puppet French regime at Vichy, had been to blame for the deportation of French Jews and that the postwar French government need not accept any responsibility.

Chirac's apology, on behalf of the French people, was welcomed by Jewish leaders who had long criticized French reluctance to come to grips with the country's complicity with the Nazis. Joseph Sitruk, chief rabbi of Paris, said he was "fully satisfied" by Chirac's statement.

The Background

In the early hours of July 16, 1942, 450 French police officers, acting under orders of the Vichy collaborationist regime headed by Marshal Henri Philippe Pétain, began rounding up Jewish men, women, and children in Paris. During that day and the next, some 13,000 Jews were arrested and interned at a bicycle racing stadium, the Vélodrome d'Hivier in western Paris. Three days later they were shipped to the German concentration camp at Auschwitz in Poland. In subsequent months, another 63,000 Jews were deported to German concentration camps; reportedly, only 2,500 of those survived.

Some historians have said the Vichy government cooperated in the deportation of the Jews to please the German occupiers and to gain more independence from them. In any event, Jewish leaders have said the French police seemed eager to cooperate; they noted that the Jews interned in the first round were crowded into the stadium and refused food and water. The French police also confiscated all property belonging to the Jews, including money, jewelry, and other valuables. Little, if any, of that property was ever returned and the descendants of those who were deported were never reimbursed. Chirac also pointed out that a number of French police officers had been seen "closing their eyes" to allow some Jews to escape the roundup.

For many years after the war, French officials acknowledged the horror of the deportations but refused to admit any French responsibility, saying the blame rested solely with the Germans. Starting in the 1970s, French officials acknowledged the complicity of the Vichy regime but insisted that was not the legitimate government of France, so the successive French governments need not accept responsibility for Vichy's actions.

Among those taking the latter stance was Chirac's predecessor, François Mitterrand, who attended a ceremony on the fiftieth anniversary of the July 16 roundup but was booed by the crowd. In 1994 Mitterrand had dedicated a monument at the site of the bicycle stadium and declared July 16 a national day of commemoration, but still he refused to admit official French responsibility for deportation of the Jews.

"I will not apologize in the name of France," Mitterrand said in September 1994. "The Republic [of France] had nothing to do with this. I do not believe France is responsible."

Chirac's Statement

Chirac spoke at a ceremony at the Vélodrome site attended by several survivors of the deportations, along with representatives of the Jewish community. His speech was brief and to the point; it offered no excuses for French behavior. While noting the "criminal insanity" of the German occupiers, he did not attempt to shift the blame to them. That insanity, he said, "was assisted by the French people, by the French state."

Chirac spoke of the "black hours" of the Jewish roundup, hours that were followed by the "long and painful journey towards hell." France, he said, "country of the enlightenment and human rights, land of welcome and asylum, France, that day, was committing the irreparable. Breaking her word, she was delivering those she was protecting to the executioners." Of those victims, he added: "We owe them an eternal debt."

The memory of such events must be kept, Chirac said, "so that such atrocities are never ever repeated." Even so, he said, there remains "a spirit of hatred in the air, rekindled here by fundamentalism, sustained there by fear and marginalization." In France today, he said, "certain tiny groups, publications, teachings, political parties reveal themselves to be carriers, some more openly than others, of a racist and anti-semitic ideology."

Despite the past complicity and the present hatreds of a few, France "is in no way an anti-semitic country," Chirac insisted. He noted that some French shielded Jewish families, and he recalled that the roundup of the Jews provided a "jolt" that helped spark the French resistance movement. The France that helped protect Jews, that refused to cooperate with the Germans, "was never that of Vichy," Chirac said. It was the France of the resistance and the Free French forces in northern Africa.

Chirac also drew a parallel between the killing of the Jews during World War II and the war in Bosnia, where, he said, democratic values were

*being flouted "before our very eyes by the proponents of ethnic cleansing."
This was an indirect reference to Bosnian Serbs who vowed to "cleanse"
parts of that country of Muslims, Croats, and other non-Serbs. "Let's learn
the lessons of history," Chirac said. "Let's not accept the role of passive witnesses of, or accomplices to, the unacceptable."*

> *Following is the text, provided by the French Embassy in Wash-
> ington, D.C., of the speech on July 16, 1995, by President
> Jacques Chirac of France in which he acknowledged French
> complicity in the deportation of Jews to German concentration
> camps during World War II:*

There are, in the life of a nation, moments which hurt the memory and idea
people have of their country.

These moments are difficult to talk about, because one doesn't always
know how to find the right words to recall the horror, express the grief of
those for whom they were a living tragedy. Those on whose souls and bodies
the memory of those days of tears and shame have left their indelible mark.

It is difficult to talk about them too because those black hours forever tarnish our history and are an affront to our past and our traditions. Yes, the
criminal insanity of the occupier was assisted by French people, by the
French State.

Fifty-three years ago, on 16 July 1942, 450 French police officers, acting
under the authority of their chiefs, complied with the Nazis' demands.

That day, in the capital and the Paris region, nearly ten thousand Jewish
men, women and children were arrested at their homes, in the early hours of
the morning, and assembled in police stations.

Horrendous scenes were to be seen: families torn apart, mothers separated from their children, old people—including some who had fought in the
great War and shed their blood for France—herded into Paris buses and
police vans.

Seen, too, were police officers closing their eyes, thereby allowing some
to escape.

For all those arrested, there then began the long and painful journey
towards hell. How many were ever to see their homes again? And how many,
at that moment, felt betrayed? How great was their anguish?

France, country of the Enlightenment and Human Rights, land of welcome and asylum, France, that day, was committing the irreparable. Breaking her word, she was delivering those she was protecting to their executioners.

Driven to the Vélodrome d'Hiver, the victims had to wait for several
days, under the terrible conditions we know about, to be sent to one of the
transit camps—Pithiviers or Beaune-la-Rolande—opened by the Vichy
authorities.

Yet, the horror was only beginning.

Other round-ups, other arrests were to follow. In Paris and in the provinces. Seventy-four trains were to leave for Auschwitz. Seventy-six thousand Jews from France were never to return.

We owe them an eternal debt.

Every Jew is duty bound by the Torah to remember. One sentence keeps recurring: "Never forget that you were a stranger and a slave in the land of Pharaoh."

Fifty years later, true to its law, but without a spirit of hatred or vengeance, the Jewish community remembers, and with it the whole of France. So that the six million martyrs of the Shoah live on. So that such atrocities are never ever repeated. So that the blood of the Holocaust becomes, as Samuel Pisar said, the "blood of hope."

When there is a spirit of hatred in the air, rekindled here by fundamentalism, sustained there by fear and marginalization; when on our doorstep, even here, certain tiny groups, publications, teachings, political parties reveal themselves to be carriers, some more openly than others, of a racist and anti-semitic ideology, then that spirit of vigilance which fires you, fires us, must be displayed more strongly than ever.

In this area, nothing is banal, nothing is dissociable. Racist crimes, the defence of revisionist theories, provocation of every kind—cutting remarks, witticisms—draw on the same sources.

By passing on the memory of the Jewish people, the suffering and the camps, witnessing again and again, recognizing the sins of the past, and the sins committed by the State, concealing nothing of the dark hours of our history, we are quite simply upholding an idea of Man, of his freedom and his dignity, we are fighting against the forces of darkness, continually at work.

That constant battle is mine as much as it is yours.

The youngest among you, I am glad, are sensitive to everything to do with the Shoah. They want to know. And with them, now, an increasing number of the French intent on facing up to their past.

France, we all know, is in no way an anti-semitic country.

At this moment of meditation and remembrance, I want to make the choice of hope.

I want to remember that that summer of 1942, which reveals the true face of collaboration, whose racist character, after the anti-Jewish legislation of 1940, is no longer in any doubt, was to give many of our compatriots a jolt, to be for them the starting point for a vast resistance movement.

I want to remember all the hounded Jewish families, shielded from the pitiless searches of the occupier and the militia by the heroic and brotherly action of many French families.

I like to recall that a month earlier, at Bir Hakeim, Koenig's Free French had heroically held out for two weeks against the German and Italian divisions.

Admittedly, errors were made, sins were committed, a collective sin; but there was also France, a certain idea of France, upright, generous, true to her traditions, her genius. That France was never that of Vichy. She was no longer, and for a long time, in Paris. She was in the Libyan sands and wherever the Free French were fighting. She was in London, embodied by General de Gaulle. She was present, one and indivisible, in the heart of those French people, those "Just among the nations", who, at the blackest point in the turmoil, by saving, at the risk of their lives, as Serge Klarsfeld wrote, three quarters of the Jewish community living in France, gave life to her finest attributes: the humanist values, the values of freedom, justice and tolerance, which are the basis of the French identity and commit us for the future.

These values, those which are the foundation of our democracies, are today being flouted in Europe itself, before our very eyes, by the proponents of ethnic cleansing. Let's learn the lessons of history. Let's not accept the role of passive witnesses of, or accomplices to, the unacceptable.

That's the import of the appeal I have issued to our main partners, in London, Washington and Bonn. If we want to, together we can put a stop to an undertaking which is destroying our values and, step by step, risks threatening the whole of Europe.

CLINTON ENDORSEMENT OF AFFIRMATIVE ACTION
July 19, 1995

"Mend it, but don't end it," President Bill Clinton said July 19, in a ring-ing endorsement of federal affirmative action programs. The speech ended several months of uncertainty about the president's position on the volatile issue. Clinton firmly aligned himself with the civil and women's rights groups, which have been two of the main supports of the Democratic party in opposition to the Republican leadership in Congress and the leading GOP presidential contenders.

"Affirmative action has been good for America," Clinton told politicians and civil rights leaders gathered at the National Archives in Washington, D.C. "Affirmative action has not always been perfect, and [it] should not go on forever. It should be changed now to take care of those things that are wrong, and it should be retired when its job is done. . . . But the evidence suggests, indeed, screams that that day has not come."

The Making of a Political Issue

Affirmative action has been controversial since its beginnings in the 1960s when Presidents John F. Kennedy and Lyndon B. Johnson first ordered federal contractors to ensure that their employees were hired and promoted without regard to race or gender. During the next thirty years, the term came to embrace an array of programs designed to help racial minorities and women become full participants in the nation's economic life. At the request of Senate Majority Leader Bob Dole (R-Kan.), the Con-gressional Research Service identified more than one hundred federal pro-grams that could be categorized as affirmative action. These programs were as precise as setting aside a fixed percentage of crime assistance grants for minority or female-owned institutions and as general as urging recipients of federal housing assistance to use minority-owned banks. In addition, state governments and private employers have voluntarily insti-tuted affirmative action programs, while courts have ordered some employers found guilty of discrimination to adopt such plans.

Opponents of affirmative action had long argued that it resulted in reverse discrimination against white males and that too many hiring and promotion decisions were based on race and gender rather than on merit. A growing number of politicians, both Republicans and Democrats, were saying that affirmative action programs were no longer necessary, that the discrimination they were designed to overcome had been greatly diminished.

The 1994 election returns ensured that affirmative action would become a major political issue in the 1996 presidential elections. Three-fifths of white male voters cast their ballots for Republican candidates; it was believed that a primary motivation was their resentment of preference programs for minorities and women. GOP leaders immediately seized on the issue as one that could potentially split apart the coalition of middle-class white males, blacks, and women that had traditionally supported the Democratic party. Dole, Sen. Phil Gramm (D-Texas), and former Tennessee governor Lamar Alexander, all of whom were seeking the Republican presidential nomination, promised to eliminate affirmative action programs if they were elected. Gov. Pete Wilson (R-Calif.), who briefly joined the race for the GOP presidential nomination, lent his support to an initiative to place a referendum issue on the 1996 state ballot that would eliminate all state affirmative action laws. (On July 20, the day after Clinton's speech, the Board of Regents of the University of California, with Wilson's blessing, voted to end race-based admissions practices. The move was a sharp reversal for the university system, which had led the nation in affirmative action practices and as a result had one of the most diverse student populations in the country.)

Recognizing that wooing disaffected white male voters back into the Democratic fold was essential to his reelection, President Clinton in February called for a review of federal affirmative action programs, saying that "we shouldn't be defending things that we can't defend." In a closed-door meeting with Democratic legislators February 22, Clinton warned that the party had to take steps to prevent the GOP from using the issue to break up the Democratic coalition. "We have to help those who deserve help and stand behind the best aspects and principles of opportunity," Clinton was quoted as saying, "But we should also be prepared to recommend modifications where there are problems."

Leaders of civil rights and women's organizations sought to put a good face on Clinton's call for a review, but they were clearly worried that the president might abandon or seriously undermine affirmative action. "A review will corroborate what we've been saying," said Ralph G. Neas, executive director of the Leadership Conference on Civil Rights. "Affirmative action has been an American success story."

Those concerns were heightened on June 12, when the Supreme Court ruled that federal affirmative action programs were subject to the most rigorous level of court review, which required such programs to be "narrowly tailored" to address a "compelling government interest." Although the jus-

tices did not strike down any preference program in Adarand Constructors
v. Peña, *the decision cast doubt on whether several could survive a challenge.* (Supreme Court on affirmative action, p. 307)

The Clinton Speech

*In his speech, Clinton said he was directing all government departments
and agencies to comply with the* Adarand *decision and to apply four standards of fairness to all affirmative action programs: "no quotas in theory
or practice; no illegal discrimination of any kind, including reverse discrimination; no preference for people who are not qualified for any job or
other opportunity; and as soon as a program has succeeded, it must be
retired." Clinton said any program not meeting those four conditions had
to be reformed or eliminated. He noted that the White House review had
assured him of the basic need to continue the preference programs.*

*Clinton also took the opportunity to address the politics of the issue,
declaring that it was "just wrong" to blame affirmative action for the "economic distress" that so many Americans honestly felt. "[I]t is wrong to use
the anxieties of the middle class to divert the American people from the real
causes of their economic distress—the sweeping historic changes taking all
the globe in its path, and the specific policies or lack of them in our own
country which have aggravated those challenges. It is simply wrong to play
politics with the issue of affirmative action. . . ."*

*The speech was greeted with relief by civil and women's rights organizations, who praised the president both for taking a stand on the issue and
for the content of his speech. The Rev. Jesse Jackson, who was contemplating challenging Clinton for the Democratic presidential nomination, said
Clinton had "set a strong moral tone for the country, and I thought it was
presidential in the best sense of the word." Moderate Democrats were more
guarded in their response. Sen. Joseph I. Lieberman of Connecticut, the
chairman of the Democratic Leadership Council, who had called affirmative action programs "patently unfair," praised the president for grappling
with the issue, but said that the* Adarand *decision would put most federal
affirmative action programs out of bounds.*

*Dole said Clinton was dodging the real issue, which Dole said was "the
practice of dividing Americans through any form of preferential treatment. . . ." Dole and Rep. Charles T. Canady (R-Fla.) introduced legislation
July 27 that would undo all federal affirmative action; at hearings in the
House in December, an administration official said the president would
veto the legislation. Efforts to prevent appropriations from being used for
affirmative action also failed in both the House and Senate.*

Complying with the Adarand *Decision*

*Ten days after Clinton's speech, the Justice Department issued a set of
guidelines to help government departments and agencies determine
whether any affirmative action programs within their jurisdiction were
vulnerable to legal challenge under the Supreme Court's ruling in the*

Adarand *case. The Justice Department asked each agency and department to review affirmative action programs under its jurisdiction and inform the Justice Department of any that appeared to be legally vulnerable. The Justice Department would then decide whether to revamp the program, kill it, or find additional justification for it.*

According to the June 29 memo, affirmative action programs designed to address general, historical discrimination or those intended solely to expand racial and ethnic diversity were unlikely to survive judicial scrutiny. Racial- or gender-based preference programs had to target a specific discrimination and entail a narrow remedy designed to overcome that particular discrimination, the memo said. The memo also said that affirmative action programs specifically authorized by Congress were less likely to be vulnerable to challenge than those initiated by the executive branch.

The Federal Communications Commission (FCC) responded to the Supreme Court ruling even before the Justice memo appeared. On June 23, the FCC announced that it was abandoning its preference program for women and minorities in its August auction of wireless telephone licenses and would give all small businesses the same advantages.

On October 23 the Defense Department announced that it was abandoning an affirmative action rule because it was unlikely to meet the judicial scrutiny test required by Adarand. *The "rule of two," which applied to all Defense contracting since 1987, stipulated that if at least two small, disadvantaged companies indicated they wanted to bid on a particular contract, only disadvantaged companies could bid on it. (Virtually all small, disadvantaged companies were minority-owned under affirmative action definitions.) The "rule of two" resulted in minority firms receiving preferential treatment for contracts worth about $1 billion annually. Minority firms would still receive preferential treatment under other Pentagon contracts worth about $5 billion altogether.*

> *Following are excerpts from a speech delivered in Washington, D.C., July 19, 1995, at the National Archives in which President Bill Clinton strongly endorsed affirmative action:*

. . . In recent weeks I have begun a conversation with the American people about our fate and our duty to prepare our nation not only to meet the new century, but to live and lead in a world transformed to a degree seldom seen in all of our history. Much of this change is good, but it is not all good, and all of us are affected by it. Therefore, we must reach beyond our fears and our divisions to a new time of great and common purpose.

Our challenge is twofold: first, to restore the American dream of opportunity and the American value of responsibility; and second, to bring our country together amid all our diversity into a stronger community, so that we can find common ground and move forward as one.

More than ever these two endeavors are inseparable. I am absolutely convinced we cannot restore economic opportunity or solve our social problems unless we find a way to bring the American people together. To bring our people together we must openly and honestly deal with the issues that divide us. Today I want to discuss one of those issues: affirmative action. . . .

Beyond all else, our country is a set of convictions: We hold these truths to be self-evident, that all men are created equal; that they are endowed by their Creator with certain inalienable rights; that among these are life, liberty and the pursuit of happiness.

Our whole history can be seen first as an effort to preserve these rights, and then as an effort to make them real in the lives of all our citizens. We know that from the beginning, there was a great gap between the plain meaning of our creed and the meaner reality of our daily lives. Back then, only white male property owners could vote. Black slaves were not even counted as whole people, and Native Americans were regarded as little more than an obstacle to our great national progress. No wonder Thomas Jefferson, reflecting on slavery, said he trembled to think God is just.

On the 200th anniversary of our great Constitution, Justice Thurgood Marshall, the grandson of a slave, said, "The government our founders devised was defective from the start, requiring several amendments, a civil war, and momentous social transformation to attain the system of constitutional government and its respect for the individual freedoms and human rights we hold as fundamental today."

Emancipation, women's suffrage, civil rights, voting rights, equal rights, the struggle for the rights of the disabled—all these and other struggles are milestones on America's often rocky, but fundamentally righteous journey to close the gap between the ideals enshrined in these treasures here in the National Archives and the reality of our daily lives. . . .

How did this happen? Fundamentally, because we opened our hearts and minds and changed our ways. But not without pressure—the pressure of court decisions, legislation, executive action, and the power of examples in the public and private sector. Along the way we learned that laws alone do not change society; that old habits and thinking patterns are deeply ingrained and die hard; that more is required to really open the doors of opportunity. Our search to find ways to move more quickly to equal opportunity led to the development of what we now call affirmative action.

[The Purpose of Affirmative Action]

The purpose of affirmative action is to give our nation a way to finally address the systemic exclusion of individuals of talent on the basis of their gender or race from opportunities to develop, perform, achieve and contribute. Affirmative action is an effort to develop a systematic approach to open the doors of education, employment and business development opportunities to qualified individuals who happen to be members of groups that have experienced long-standing and persistent discrimination.

487

It is a policy that grew out of many years of trying to navigate between two unacceptable pasts. One was to say simply that we declared discrimination illegal and that's enough. We saw that that way still relegated blacks with college degrees to jobs as railroad porters, and kept women with degrees under a glass ceiling with a lower paycheck.

The other path was simply to try to impose change by leveling draconian penalties on employers who didn't meet certain imposed, ultimately arbitrary, and sometimes unachievable quotas. That, too, was rejected out of a sense of fairness.

So a middle ground was developed that would change an inequitable status quo gradually, but firmly, by building the pool of qualified applicants for college, for contracts, for jobs, and giving more people the chance to learn, work and earn. When affirmative action is done right, it is flexible, it is fair, and it works.

I know some people are honestly concerned about the times affirmative action doesn't work, when it's done in the wrong way. And I know there are times when some employers don't use it in the right way. They may cut corners and treat a flexible goal as a quota. They may give opportunities to people who are unqualified instead of those who deserve it. They may, in so doing, allow a different kind of discrimination. When this happens, it is also wrong. But it isn't affirmative action, and it is not legal.

So when our administration finds cases of that sort, we will enforce the law aggressively. The Justice Department files hundreds of cases every year, attacking discrimination in employment, including suits on behalf of white males. Most of these suits, however, affect women and minorities for a simple reason—because the vast majority of discrimination in America is still discrimination against them. But the law does require fairness for everyone and we are determined to see that that is exactly what the law delivers.

Let me be clear about what affirmative action must not mean and what I won't allow it to be. It does not mean—and I don't favor—the unjustified preference of the unqualified over the qualified of any race or gender. It doesn't mean—and I don't favor—numerical quotas. It doesn't mean—and I don't favor—rejection or selection of any employee or student solely on the basis of race or gender without regard to merit.

Like many business executives and public servants, I owe it to you to say that my views on this subject are, more than anything else, the product of my personal experience. I have had experience with affirmative action, nearly 20 years of it now, and I know it works.

When I was Attorney General of my home state, I hired a record number of women and African American lawyers—every one clearly qualified and exceptionally hardworking. As Governor, I appointed more women to my Cabinet and state boards than any other governor in the state's history, and more African Americans than all the governors in the state's history combined. And no one ever questioned their qualifications or performance. And our state was better and stronger because of their service.

As President, I am proud to have the most diverse administration in history in my Cabinet, my agencies and my staff. And I must say, I have been surprised at the criticism I have received from some quarters in my determination to achieve this.

In the last two and a half years, [in] the most outstanding example of affirmative action in the United States, the Pentagon has opened 260,000 positions for women who serve in our Armed Forces. I have appointed more women and minorities to the federal bench than any other president, more than the last two combined. And yet, far more of our judicial appointments have received the highest rating from the American Bar Association than any other administration since those ratings have been given.

In our administration many government agencies are doing more business with qualified firms run by minorities and women. The Small Business Administration has reduced its budget by 40 percent, doubled its loan outputs, dramatically increased the number of loans to women and minority small business people, without reducing the number of loans to white business owners who happen to be male, and without changing the loan standards for a single, solitary application. Quality and diversity can go hand in hand, and they must.

Let me say that affirmative action has also done more than just open the doors of opportunity to individual Americans. Most economists who study it agree that affirmative action has also been an important part of closing gaps in economic opportunity in our society, thereby strengthening the entire economy.

A group of distinguished business leaders told me just a couple of days ago that their companies are stronger and their profits are larger because of the diversity and the excellence of their work forces achieved through intelligent and fair affirmative action programs. And they said, we have gone far beyond anything the government might require us to do because managing diversity and individual opportunity and being fair to everybody is the key to our future economic success in the global marketplace.

[Continuing Need for Affirmative Action]

Now, there are those who say, my fellow Americans, that even good affirmative action programs are no longer needed; that it should be enough to resort to the courts or the Equal Employment Opportunity Commission in cases of actual, provable, individual discrimination because there is no longer any systematic discrimination in our society. In deciding how to answer that let us consider the facts.

The unemployment rate for African Americans remains about twice that of whites. The Hispanic rate is still much higher. Women have narrowed the earnings gap, but still make only 72 percent as much as men do for comparable jobs. The average income for a Hispanic woman with a college degree is still less than the average income of a white man with a high school diploma.

According to the recently completed Glass Ceiling Report, sponsored by Republican members of Congress, in the nation's largest companies only six-tenths of one percent of senior management positions are held by African

Americans, four-tenths of a percent by Hispanic Americans, three-tenths of a percent by Asian Americans; women hold between three and five percent of these positions. White males make up 43 percent of our work force, but hold 95 percent of these jobs.

Just last week, the Chicago Federal Reserve Bank reported that black home loan applicants are more than twice as likely to be denied credit as whites with the same qualifications; and that Hispanic applicants are more than one and a half times as likely to be denied loans as whites with the same qualifications.

Last year alone the federal government received more than 90,000 complaints of employment discrimination based on race, ethnicity or gender. Less than three percent were for reverse discrimination.

Evidence abounds in other ways of the persistence of the kind of bigotry that can affect the way we think even if we're not conscious of it, in hiring and promotion and business and educational decisions.

Crimes and violence based on hate against Asians, Hispanics, African Americans and other minorities are still with us. And, I'm sorry to say, that the worst and most recent evidence of this involves a recent report of federal law enforcement officials in Tennessee attending an event literally overflowing with racism—a sickening reminder of just how pervasive these kinds of attitudes still are.

By the way, I want to tell you that I am committed to finding the truth about what happened there and to taking appropriate action. And I want to say that if anybody who works in federal law enforcement thinks that that kind of behavior is acceptable, they ought to think about working someplace else.

Now, let's get to the other side of the argument. If affirmative action has worked and if there is evidence that discrimination still exists on a wide scale in ways that are conscious and unconscious, then why should we get rid of it, as many people are urging? Some question the effectiveness or the fairness of particular affirmative action programs. I say to all of you, those are fair questions, and they prompted the review of our affirmative action programs, about which I will talk in a few moments.

Some question the fundamental purpose of the effort. There are people who honestly believe that affirmative action always amounts to group preferences over individual merit; that affirmative action always leads to reverse discrimination; that ultimately, therefore, it demeans those who benefit from it and discriminates against those who are not helped by it.

I just have to tell you that all of you have to decide how you feel about that, and all of our fellow countrymen and women have to decide as well. But I believe if there are no quotas, if we give no opportunities to unqualified people, if we have no reverse discrimination, and if, when the problem ends, the program ends, that criticism is wrong. That's what I believe. But we should have this debate and everyone should ask the question.

[Affirmative Action and Economic Distress]

Now let's deal with what I really think is behind so much of this debate today. There are a lot of people who oppose affirmative action today who supported it for a very long time. I believe they are responding to the sea change in the experiences that most Americans have in the world in which we live.

If you say now you're against affirmative action because the government is using its power or the private sector is using its power to help minorities at the expense of the majority, that gives you a way of explaining away the economic distress that a majority of Americans honestly feel. It gives you a way of turning their resentment against the minorities or against a particular government program, instead of having an honest debate about how we all got into the fix we're in and what we're all going to do together to get out of it.

That explanation, the affirmative action explanation for the fix we're in, is just wrong. It is just wrong. Affirmative action did not cause the great economic problems of the American middle class. And because most minorities or women are either members of that middle class or people who are poor who are struggling to get into it, we must also admit that affirmative action alone won't solve the problems of minorities and women who seek to be a part of the American Dream. To do that, we have to have an economic strategy that reverses the decline in wages and the growth of poverty among working people. Without that, women, minorities and white males will all be in trouble in the future.

But it is wrong to use the anxieties of the middle class to divert the American people from the real causes of their economic distress—the sweeping historic changes taking all the globe in [their] path, and the specific policies or lack of them in our own country which have aggravated those challenges. It is simply wrong to play politics with the issue of affirmative action and divide our country at a time when, if we're really going to change things, we have to be united.

I must say, I think it is ironic that some of those—not all, but some of those who call for an end to affirmative action also advocate policies which will make the real economic problems of the anxious middle class even worse. They talk about opportunity and being for equal opportunity for everyone, and then they reduce investment in equal opportunity on an evenhanded basis. For example, if the real goal is economic opportunity for all Americans, why in the world would we reduce our investment in education, from Head Start to affordable college loans? Why don't we make college loans available to every American instead?

If the real goal is empowering all middle-class Americans and empowering poor people to work their way into the middle class without regard to race or gender, why in the world would the people who advocate that turn around and raise taxes on our poorest working families, or reduce the money available for education and training when they lose their jobs or they're living on poverty wages, or increase the cost of housing for lower-income, working people with children?

Why would we do that? If we're going to empower America, we have to do more than talk about it, we have to do it. And we surely have learned that we cannot empower all Americans by a simple strategy of taking opportunity away from some Americans.

So to those who use this as a political strategy to divide us, we must say, no. We must say, no. But to those who raise legitimate questions about the way affirmative action works, or who raise the larger question about the genuine problems and anxieties of all the American people and their sense of being left behind and treated unfairly, we must say, yes, you are entitled to answers to your questions. We must say yes to that.

Now, that's why I ordered this review of all of our affirmative action programs—a review to look at the facts, not the politics, of affirmative action. This review concluded that affirmative action remains a useful tool for widening economic and educational opportunity. The model used by the military, the Army in particular—and I'm delighted to have the Commanding General of the Army here today because he set such a fine example—has been especially successful because it emphasizes education and training, ensuring that it has a wide pool of qualified candidates for every level of promotion. That approach has given us the most racially diverse and best-qualified military in our history. There are more opportunities for women and minorities there than ever before. And now there are over 50 generals and admirals who are Hispanic, Asian or African-American.

We found that the Education Department targeted on—had programs targeted on under-represented minorities that do a great deal of good with the tiniest of investments. We found that these programs comprised 40 cents of every $1,000 in the Education Department's budget.

Now, college presidents will tell you that the education their schools offer actually benefit from diversity, colleges where young people get the education and make the personal and professional contacts that will shape their lives. If their colleges look like the world they're going to live and work in, and they learn from all different kinds of people things that they can't learn in books, our systems of higher education are stronger.

Still, I believe every child needs the chance to go to college. Every child. That means every child has to have a chance to get affordable and repayable college loans, Pell Grants for poor kids and a chance to do things like join AmeriCorps and work their way through school. Every child is entitled to that. That is not an argument against affirmative action, it's an argument for more opportunity for more Americans until everyone is reached.

As I said a moment ago, the review found that the Small Business Administration last year increased loans to minorities by over two-thirds, loans to women by over 80 percent, did not decrease loans to white men, and not a single loan went to a unqualified person. People who never had a chance before to be part of the American system of free enterprise now have it. No one was hurt in the process. That made America stronger.

This review also found that the executive order on employment practices of large federal contractors also has helped to bring more fairness and inclusion into the work force.

Since President Nixon was here in my job, America has used goals and timetables to preserve opportunity and to prevent discrimination, to urge businesses to set higher expectations for themselves and to realize those expectations. But we did not and we will not use rigid quotas to mandate outcomes.

We also looked at the way we award procurement contracts under the programs known as set-asides. There's no question that these programs have helped to build up firms owned by minorities and women, who historically had been excluded from the old-boy networks in these areas. It has helped a new generation of entrepreneurs to flourish, opening new paths to self-reliance and an economic growth in which all of us ultimately share. Because of the set-asides, businesses ready to compete have had a chance to compete, a chance they would not have otherwise had.

[Need for Some Reforms]

But as with any government program, set-asides can be misapplied, misused, even intentionally abused. There are critics who exploit that fact as an excuse to abolish all these programs, regardless of their effects. I believe they are wrong, but I also believe, based on our factual review, we clearly need some reform. So first, we should crack down on those who take advantage of everyone else through fraud and abuse. We must crack down on fronts and pass-throughs, people who pretend to be eligible for these programs and aren't. That is wrong.

We also, in offering new businesses a leg up, must make sure that the set-asides go to businesses that need them most. We must really look and make sure that our standard for eligibility is fair and defensible. We have to tighten the requirement to move businesses out of programs once they've had a fair opportunity to compete. The graduation requirement must mean something—it must mean graduation. There should be no permanent set-aside for any company.

Second, we must, and we will, comply with the Supreme Court's *Adarand* decision of last month. Now, in particular, that means focusing set-aside programs on particular regions and business sectors where the problems of discrimination or exclusion are provable and are clearly requiring affirmative action. I have directed the Attorney General and the agencies to move forward with compliance with *Adarand* expeditiously.

But I also want to emphasize that the *Adarand* decision did not dismantle affirmative action and did not dismantle set-asides. In fact, while setting stricter standards to mandate reform of affirmative action, it actually reaffirmed the need for affirmative action and reaffirmed the continuing existence of systematic discrimination in the United States.

What the Supreme Court ordered the federal government to do was to meet the same, more rigorous standard for affirmative action programs that state and local governments were ordered to meet several years ago. And the best set-aside programs under that standard have been challenged and have survived.

Third, beyond discrimination we need to do more to help disadvantaged people and distressed communities, no matter what their race or gender. There are places in our country where the free enterprise system simply doesn't reach. It simply isn't working to provide jobs and opportunity. Disproportionately, these areas in urban and rural America are highly populated by racial minorities, but not entirely. To make this initiative work, I believe the government must become a better partner for people in places in urban and rural America [who] are caught in a cycle of poverty. And I believe we have to find ways to get the private sector to assume their rightful role as a driver of economic growth.

It has always amazed me that we have given incentives to our business people to help to develop poor economies in other parts of the world, our neighbors in the Caribbean, our neighbors in other parts of the world—I have supported this when not subject to their own abuses—but we ignore the biggest source of economic growth available to the American economy, the poor economies isolated within the United States of America.

There are those who say, well, even if we made the jobs available, people wouldn't work. They haven't tried. Most of the people in disadvantaged communities work today, and most of them who don't work have a very strong desire to do so. In central Harlem, 14 people apply for every single minimum-wage job opening. Think how many more would apply if there were good jobs with a good future. Our job has to connect disadvantaged people and disadvantaged communities to economic opportunity so that everybody who wants to work can do so.

We've been working at this through our empowerment zones and community develop[ment] banks, through the initiatives of Secretary [Henry] Cisneros of the Housing and Urban Development Department and many other things that we have tried to do to put capital where it is needed. And now I have asked Vice President Gore to develop a proposal to use our contracting to support businesses that locate themselves in these distressed areas or hire a large percentage of their workers from these areas—not to supplement what we're doing in affirmative action, not to substitute for it, but to supplement it, to go beyond it, to do something that will help to deal with the economic crisis of America. We want to make our procurement system more responsive to people in these areas who need help.

My fellow Americans, affirmative action has to be made consistent with our highest ideals of personal responsibility and merit, and our urgent need to find common ground, and to prepare all Americans to compete in the global economy of the next century.

Today, I am directing all our agencies to comply with the Supreme Court's *Adarand* decision, and also to apply the four standards of fairness to all our affirmative action programs that I have already articulated: No quotas in theory or practice; no illegal discrimination of any kind, including reverse discrimination; no preference for people who are not qualified for any job or other opportunity; and as soon as a program has succeeded, it must be retired. Any program that doesn't meet these four principles must be eliminated or reformed to meet them.

But let me be clear: Affirmative action has been good for America.

Affirmative action has not always been perfect, and affirmative action should not go on forever. It should be changed now to take care of those things that are wrong, and it should be retired when its job is done. I am resolved that that day will come. But the evidence suggests, indeed screams, that that day has not come.

The job of ending discrimination in this country is not over. That should not be surprising. We had slavery for centuries before the passage of the 13th, 14th and 15th Amendments. We waited another hundred years for the civil rights legislation. Women have had the vote less than a hundred years. We have always had difficulty with these things, as most societies do. But we are making more progress than many people.

Based on the evidence, the job is not done. So here is what I think we should do. We should reaffirm the principle of affirmative action and fix the practices. We should have a simple slogan: Mend it, but don't end it.

Let me ask all Americans, whether they agree or disagree with what I have said today, to see this issue in the larger context of our times. President Lincoln said we cannot escape our history. We cannot escape our future, either. And that future must be one in which every American has the chance to live up to his or her God-given capacities.

The new technology, the instant communications, the explosion of global commerce have created enormous opportunities and enormous anxieties for Americans. In the last two and a half years, we have seen seven million new jobs, more millionaires and new businesses than ever before, high corporate profits, and a booming stock market. Yet, most Americans are working harder for the same or lower pay. And they feel more insecurity about their jobs, their retirement, their health care, and their children's education. Too many of our children are clearly exposed to poverty and welfare, violence and drugs.

These are the great challenges for our whole country on the home front at the dawn of the 21st century. We've got to find the wisdom and the will to create family-wage jobs for all the people who want to work; to open the door of college to all Americans; to strengthen families and reduce the awful problems to which our children are exposed; to move poor Americans from welfare to work.

This is the work of our administration—to give the people the tools they need to make the most of their own lives, to give families and communities the tools they need to solve their own problems. But let us not forget, affirmative action didn't cause these problems. It won't solve them. And getting rid of affirmative action certainly won't solve them.

If properly done, affirmative action can help us come together, go forward and grow together. It is in our moral, legal and practical interest to see that every person can make the most of his life. In the fight for the future, we need all hands on deck and some of those hands still need a helping hand.

In our national community we're all different, we're all the same. We want liberty and freedom. We want the embrace of family and community. We want to make the most of our own lives and we're determined to give our children a better one. Today there are voices of division who would say forget all that. Don't you dare. Remember we're still closing the gap between our founders' ideals and our reality. But every step along the way has made us richer, stronger and better. And the best is yet to come.

Thank you very much. And God bless you.

GAO ON THE FINANCIAL CRISIS IN THE DISTRICT OF COLUMBIA
July 25, 1995

The nation's capital city sunk into a fiscal crisis in 1995 that threatened not only the financial well-being of the city and its residents, but also home rule, the unique system under which local elected officials and Congress shared responsibility for governing the city. As one member of Congress put it, "Washington, D.C., is coming apart at the seams." Two months after the General Accounting Office (GAO), the investigative arm of Congress, declared the District of Columbia "insolvent," President Bill Clinton signed a law (PL 104–8) setting up a financial control board, appointed by the president, to oversee the District government. Day-to-day operations would remain the responsibility of the city's elected officials, however.

That move offered hope that the city would work itself out of its financial crisis, but late in the year a new crisis emerged when Congress, unable to resolve an unrelated controversy over a voucher system for the city's schools, failed to pass the city's annual appropriation. The District could not spend either local or federal funds without congressional approval.

The Making of a Financial Crisis

Ever since 1800, when it was carved out of Maryland and Virginia to serve as the nation's capital, the District has had an uneasy relationship with Congress, its ultimate overseer. Tensions were particularly high throughout the 1950s and 1960s, when John L. McMillan, a white member of the House from South Carolina who chaired the House District Committee, ran the mostly black city as his personal fiefdom and blocked every proposal for home rule that came his way. A year after McMillan lost his seat in a primary upset, Congress approved a home rule charter that allowed the city to elect its own mayor and city council. It also gave the city responsibility for providing services such as Medicaid and welfare, which most cities share with their state.

At the same time the charter limited the amount of revenue the city could collect by prohibiting the District from imposing an income tax on com-

*muters who worked in the city but lived in the Virginia and Maryland sub-
urbs. By the 1990s, three-fifths of the people who worked in the city did not
live there. The District was also barred from levying property taxes on property owned by the federal government and other nontaxable entities. In lieu
of those taxes, Congress made an annual federal payment to the city.*

*Walter E. Washington became the first elected mayor in 1975. He was
succeeded in 1978 by Marion S. Barry, a black civil rights activist, who in
his first term won praise in the city and in Congress for improving the
management of the city and for running budget surpluses. Barry won
reelection overwhelmingly in 1982, expanded city services, and increased
the number of government workers. The budget surpluses began to dwindle.*

*Two events in the mid- and late 1980s began to multiply the city's bur-
geoning financial woes: the crash of the building boom, which had transformed the city's downtown area both structurally and economically; and the
onset of the crack cocaine epidemic, which fueled drug violence in the city
and accelerated the exodus begun in the 1970s of the black middle class to the
surrounding suburbs. Left behind was a small, well-to-do elite, a shrinking
middle class, and a large and growing underclass; by the mid-1990s, one-
third of the city's population was on some form of public assistance.*

*Beginning in the early 1980s Barry began to be dogged by rumors of
womanizing and drug use. In 1990 Barry was arrested after he was video-
taped in a hotel room smoking crack with a former model. Barry, who was
eventually convicted for possession of crack cocaine, did not seek reelection
that year and was succeeded by Sharon Pratt Kelly, who had won an upset
victory in the Democratic primary with her promise to clean house. It was
a big job. After Kelly's election in November, a blue-ribbon commission
said she was inheriting an overstaffed, inefficient, and cumbersome city
government on the brink of bankruptcy.* (Sentencing of Washington's Mayor,
Historic Documents of 1990, p. 707)

*Kelly was unable to fulfill her promise. Her administration resorted to
various accounting tricks to try to minimize the budget deficit. One of the
most egregious may have been to adjust the property tax year by three
months so that revenues for fifteen months could be used to cover spending
for twelve months. When Barry, who had served a six-month prison sentence and then been elected to the District City Council, was again elected
mayor in 1994, he estimated the city's budget deficit at $400 million.*

*Three months later, on February 1, Barry announced that the shortfall
was $722 million. The next day he asked Congress for help—$267 million
to cover skyrocketing Medicaid costs and a federal takeover of the city's
courts, prisons, and welfare system. In return he promised to eliminate
6,000 jobs and cut the wages of the remaining city workers by 10 percent.*

Creation of a Financial Control Board

*Within two weeks two major investment services lowered their ratings
on the city's credit: Moody's Investor Services, Inc. gave it junk bond status; Standard & Poor's cut its rating on the city's bonds to "triple B minus,"*

the level just above junk bond status. It was also revealed that the Securities and Exchange Commission was investigating whether the city had misrepresented its financial position in December 1994 as it prepared to sell $250 million in short-term bonds.

On February 22, a spokesman for the General Accounting Office told two House subcommittees that the city was "insolvent—it does not have enough cash to pay all of its bills."

This series of events turned even supporters of the District against it. One, Rep. Julian C. Dixon (D-Calif.), had defended the District for years against its harshest critics on Capitol Hill. On February 24 he said he could not "ignore the facts. The District has been deceitful with this committee and with Congress." With some members of Congress talking about putting the city into receivership, the District's delegate to the House of Representatives, Eleanor Holmes Norton, decided to push for creation of a financial control board that could help the city sort out its financial problems without losing home rule altogether.

The legislation (HR 1345) passed quickly through Congress, and on April 17 President Clinton signed the measure into law, setting up a five-member board with broad powers to reorganize city government, slash programs, and reject union contracts in an effort to bring the city's finances under control. The board was also charged with approving the city's borrowing and could veto the mayor's nominees for chief financial officer and an inspector general who would manage an annual audit of the city's finances. Once the city produced four consecutive balanced budgets and earned adequate access to the credit markets, the board would only monitor city actions. It would suspend all its activities once the city had repaid any money it might have borrowed with the review board's help.

The challenges the board faced were formidable, according to the GAO. In testimony before a House subcommittee July 25, a GAO official said the city did not have "needed information to monitor its spending and cash, and is not holding agency managers accountable for spending in their agencies." The financial control board, GAO concluded, would find it difficult even "to establish a financial baseline [from which] to monitor the District's financial condition and improve its financial management."

In other action affecting the District of Columbia, Housing and Urban Development Secretary Henry Cisneros announced on May 4 that a court-appointed receiver would take control of the city's public housing agency for at least three years. On May 22 a federal district court judge took control of the city's child welfare system, a $53 million a year program charged with caring for about 5,000 children. It was the first time a court anywhere had seized control of an entire child welfare system. (Public housing takeovers, p. 294)

Spending Legislation Blocked

The District encountered yet another obstacle to setting its house in order in September, when both the House and Senate added several policy *objectives to the annual spending bill. City officials and their supporters said the policy provisions would kill what remained of the home rule charter. Conferees eventually resolved differences between the two chambers on spending issues and agreed to delay action on most of the policy objectives. Senate conferees balked at a House provision to give some low-income students in the District vouchers to attend the school of their choice, and no further action was taken on the appropriations bill in 1995.*

Without its annual appropriations in place, the District government was forced to shut down in mid-November. City officials said the six-day closure cost the District $7 million in uncollected revenues and lost productivity. Emergency stopgap measures allowed the government to operate using locally generated revenues.

Following are excerpts from the statement by Jeffrey C. Steinhoff, director of planning and reporting in the General Accounting Office's Accounting and Information Management Division, presented July 25, 1995, to the Subcommittee on Surface Transportation of the House Transportation and Infrastructure Committee:

The District of Columbia's Financial Crisis

As we have previously reported, the District of Columbia is insolvent—it does not have enough cash to pay all of its bills. It is spending at a rate in fiscal year 1995 that, based on its own estimates, will exceed its congressional appropriation limit by about $132 million. Millions of dollars in unpaid bills are piling up, threatening basic services provided through private contractors. Some contractors have provided services without contracts. Many District programs are under court order to address basic fundamental weaknesses. And, there is widespread belief that the District has too many employees and does not provide quality service.

The District did not reach this crisis point overnight. Nearly 5 years ago, the Commission on Budget and Financial Priorities of the District of Columbia (commonly known as the Rivlin Commission) noted that the District "confronts an immediate fiscal crisis," and made a multitude of recommendations to the District to deal with that crisis. By and large these recommendations were not followed. In most years since the Rivlin Commission report was issued, until fiscal year 1994, the District's general fund was "balanced"; however, the city's cash position was at the same time declining. This occurred despite receiving additional cash and revenues totaling nearly a billion dollars since 1991.

In June 1994, we issued a report that concluded that the District was faced with both unresolved long-term financial issues and continual short-term financial crises. In that report, we discussed the District's cash and budget situation and explained how cash balances declined even though budgets were balanced. In fiscal year 1994, the District recorded a $335 million deficiency, the largest since Home Rule. . . .

Although between fiscal years 1991 and 1993, the District's general fund showed small surpluses, the District's cash position steadily deteriorated. This decline in cash could have been much worse had the District made all required payments when due. Specifically, in fiscal year 1993, the District deferred nearly $100 million in payments to the pension fund and the Washington Metropolitan Transit Authority. Deferred payments also occurred in fiscal years 1991 and 1992. At the end of fiscal year 1994, deferred payments grew even more. If the District had made all payments when due, it would have run out of cash before the end of fiscal year 1994.

Another demonstration of the District's declining cash situation was that, at the end of each year, the District increasingly relied on the federal payment, which has recently been received in the first month of the fiscal year, to cover bills from the previous fiscal year. For example, in fiscal year 1991, soon after receiving the $331 million general obligation bond for the operating deficit, the previous year's bills were about 39 percent of the federal payment. At the end of fiscal year 1994, the fiscal year 1994 bills were 80 percent of the fiscal year 1995 federal payment. Current trends indicate that the situation will be worse at the end of this fiscal year.

The District Has Not Reduced Expenditures as Directed by the Congress

Last fall, in response to the growing financial crisis, the Congress mandated $140 million in reductions to the District's planned expenditures for fiscal year 1995, thereby capping its appropriated expenditures at $3.254 billion. However, the District has not reduced spending to the congressionally approved level. As we testified on June 21, 1995, at that time, the District was projecting a negative year end cash balance of $236 million and fiscal year 1995 spending of $3.386 billion, which is $132 million over the congressional cap. More than three-fourths of the way through fiscal year 1995, the District had not determined how to allocate the $140 million in mandated cuts to District agencies, and spending controls have largely been ineffective. District agencies were still operating on spending plans based on the original "pre-$140 million cut" budget.

To help with its projected cash shortfall, as permitted by the Financial Responsibility and Management Act of 1995, in June 1995, the District received a $146.7 million advance from Treasury, which is to be repaid by September 30, 1995, or offset against the District's federal payment for fiscal year 1996. Even with this advance, the District is projecting a year end cash shortfall unless there is additional borrowing.

Many of the District's Planned Expenditure Cuts Have Not Been Implemented

For fiscal year 1995, the District proposed a variety of cost cutting initiatives: (1) $224 million in management initiatives in the agencies, (2) $70 million in personnel savings from reductions in pay and furloughs, and (3) $70 million in interest savings resulting from refinancing the debt. Although the District has a system to periodically update the status of the initiatives, agency managers are not accountable for making sure the initiatives are effectively implemented and the savings are realized. We reviewed selected initiatives and noted that much of the savings will not be realized this year, if ever, and a significant number of initiatives have already been dropped.

First, the District has already reduced savings estimates from these initiatives by almost one-third, or $116 million. The $70 million savings from refinancing the debt was abandoned, and the projected personnel savings have been reduced by $6 million to $64 million. And finally, the District's projection of savings from agency management initiatives has been reduced by $39.6 million to $184.4 million. According to District officials, 121 of the initiatives have been completed, saving $89.6 million, and another 100 initiatives are still being implemented, with the estimated savings for these pegged at $94.8 million. However, as we testified on June 21, 1995, some of the completed and remaining initiatives may not result in the level of savings projected. For example:

- About $5.6 million in initiatives related to the transfer of costs from one agency or program to another with no resulting District-wide savings, and another $533,000 in savings were based on eliminating positions that were already vacant.
- The Department of Corrections plans included a $1.3 million savings that would be realized from closing a prison facility, halfway houses, and a drug counseling center. However, the prison facility cannot be closed because of a court order, and the Mayor's Office reversed its decision on closing the halfway houses and drug counseling center.
- Contracting out food services in the Department of Corrections was expected to save $3.8 million in fiscal year 1994. As of May 1995, the action still had not been implemented and projected savings for fiscal year 1995 have been reduced to $315,000.

Poor Financial Information and Controls

The District's financial information and internal controls are poor. As a result, District managers do not have the fundamental information necessary to help control spending and costs and estimate budget and cash needs. As we testified on June 21, 1995, the District does not know the status of expenditures against budgeted amounts, does not know how many bills it owes, is allowing millions of dollars of obligations to occur without required written contracts, and does not know its cash status on a daily basis. Millions of dollars of bills are not entered into the Financial Management System until months and sometimes years after they are paid.

Numerous internal and external audits over a number of years have highlighted problems with various aspects of the District's financial and management controls procedures and practices. The Rivlin Commission

Report recommended a comprehensive financial management improvement program, and both the current acting Chief Financial Officer (CFO) and previous CFO have recommended major improvements in the entire financial management system, including better procedures and improved training.

The District's Financial Management System consists of a 15-year old central system and at least 17 separate program systems. These separate program systems are not integrated with the central system. As a result, District Controller officials must input to the central system thousands of general journal entries that were originally entered into the individual systems. For example, at the Department of Human Services, benefit payments made under programs such as Medicaid, Aid to Families with Dependent Children, General Public Assistance, and Foster Care are computed by these program's own unique systems, which are not integrated with the city's Financial Management System. The benefit payment amounts for these programs and the associated obligations are then manually recorded in the Financial Management System by the D.C. Controllers Office after the payments are made. The result is delays in processing and a lack of timely, accurate information on both expenditures and cash. But while the entire financial management process is antiquated and cumbersome, the lack of effective practices and procedures by District financial officials makes any system even more ineffective.

There are numerous examples of inaccurate financial information:

- The District's fiscal year 1995 second-quarter financial report did not include at least $80 million in Department of Human Services' expenditures that had been incurred.
- District officials have said that the extent of unpaid bills is unknown, but it probably totals tens of millions of dollars. The District's fiscal year 1995 second-quarter financial report said that the District's accounts payable balance of $41.2 million reflects only unpaid invoices accepted into the District's Financial Management System as of March 31, 1995. Tens of millions of dollars in unknown payables also exist but are not in the Financial Management System.
- Some expenditures at the Public Schools were not recorded and paid for months. For example, a 1993 invoice for $200,000 for food from the Defense Logistics Agency was not paid until at least May 1995.
- Information provided by the Department of Human Services' Controller's Office shows that Medicaid payments from October 1994 through May 1995 totaled over $400 million. It was often anywhere from 2 to 12 weeks before these payments were recorded in the Financial Management System. For example, a November 1994 payment of over $6 million went unrecorded for over 12 weeks, and a March 1995 payment of almost $8 million went unrecorded for 11 weeks.
- Aid to Families with Dependent Children payments amounting to $9.7 million and General Public Assistance payments amounting to $775,000

were made on or about January 1, 1995, but were not reflected in the Financial Management System until June 1, 1995—5 months later.

The above examples are not isolated ones. Delays in entering information in the Financial Management System are routine. Our analysis of all general journal entries for May 1995 showed that many payments were recorded months after the checks were written. In fact, over $120 million (44 percent) of the total payments recorded in the Financial Management System using general journal entries were not recorded until over 2 months after the payments occurred.

Other Cities Had to Address Financial Management Weaknesses

In the last 2 decades, other cities have faced financial, management, and structural problems similar to those currently facing the District of Columbia. In March 1995, we testified before the House Government Reform and Oversight Committee's Subcommittee on the District of Columbia on the work we had done on five other cities—Boston, Chicago, Cleveland, New York, and Philadelphia—which had faced financial difficulties. We found that in addition to improving their financial stability, all five cities realized that if they were to avoid more financial difficulties, they also would have to improve the efficiency of city management and operations.

Some of the actions taken included: (1) hiring new financial managers and giving them authority and responsibility to strengthen the cities' accounting, budgeting, and cash management operations and (2) installing or upgrading financial management systems and improving their financial reporting. Among the points most emphasized by officials from these five cities were to establish credible information and know how to use it for making hard decisions to restore financial stability. And, once improved financial systems and practices are established, to use them not only to maintain credible information, but also to improve accountability and performance of government operations.

Conclusions

The District is insolvent and faces many challenges in its efforts to deal with its serious financial problems. The District does not have needed information to monitor its spending and cash, and is not holding agency managers accountable for spending in their agencies. Specifically, agency managers are not accountable to ensure that (1) spending is within prescribed budgets and allotments and (2) management initiatives are effectively implemented with commensurate savings. The problems with District financial management are long-standing, and improvements are essential to providing credible, accurate, and timely information. The new District of Columbia Financial Responsibility and Management Assistance Authority faces a difficult challenge to establish a financial baseline to monitor the District's financial condition and improve its financial management.

As part of the efforts to deal with the District's serious financial problems, improvements in the District's financial information and controls will need to be addressed. As part of our June 21, 1995, testimony, we made a variety of recommendations to the Mayor of the District of Columbia and to the District of Columbia Financial Responsibility and Management Assistance Authority directed at addressing problems with financial information, internal controls, and accountability.

Mr. Chairman, that concludes my statement for the record.

DEDICATION OF KOREAN WAR VETERANS MEMORIAL
July 27, 1995

On the forty-second anniversary of the end of the Korean War, President Bill Clinton and President Kim Young-sam of South Korea dedicated a national memorial in Washington to the 1.5 million Americans who fought in what was often called America's "forgotten war." Clinton paid tribute to Korean War veterans, thousands of whom were at the dedication ceremonies, saying that "when darkness threatened, you kept the torch of liberty alight."

The dedication was timed for the anniversary of the armistice that ended the war and restored the status quo ante: two Koreas—one under a hard-line communist regime in the North, the other under American influence in the South. Ironically, that timing also put the commemoration in the same year that many Americans were focusing renewed attention on two other wars that overshadowed the Korean War: World War II and the Vietnam War. (World War II anniversary events, pp. 55, 216, 302, 478; Vietnam recognition, p. 472)

Some 1.5 million Americans fought in Korea; 54,000 of them died there and another 100,000 were wounded. The Americans fought alongside soldiers from seventeen countries, all under a United Nations mandate. The war devastated much of the Korean peninsula and killed or wounded an estimated 3 million Koreans and Chinese.

A Realistic Memorial

The new memorial is located at the western end of the Mall in Washington, D.C., just east of the Lincoln Memorial and near the popular Vietnam Veterans Memorial. It features nineteen figures (fourteen Army soldiers, three Marines, a Navy medic, and an Air Force forward observer) wearing ponchos and carrying rifles, all appearing tense and weary, as if on an endless patrol. The realistic style of the memorial is in sharp contrast to the Vietnam memorial—a giant wedge of black marble on which are inscribed the names of 55,000 Americans who died in that war.

Korean veterans who attended the July 27 ceremony praised the new memorial as an accurate portrayal of the conditions under which they served, but many said it should have been built years before. "It's way past time," Dick Seeger of Houston, Texas, told the Washington Post.

Korean War Background

The Korean War began on June 25, 1950, with a surprise North Korean attack into the South, across the 38th parallel. The parallel had been the dividing line between the two Koreas, agreed on by the victorious allies of World War II after they drove Japan off the Asian mainland. The United States had responsibility for the South, and the Soviet Union for the North.

The communist regime in the North, headed by Kim Il-Sung, claimed its invasion was justified by an obligation to reunify the Korean peninsula. The offensive rapidly overran the South's defenses and succeeded in pushing the South's forces into an area around the southern port city of Pusan.

The invasion caught the Truman administration off guard, in part because Secretary of State Dean Acheson had declared that Korea was not within the sphere of vital U.S. interests. President Harry Truman quickly reversed that position and declared that North Korea was posing a communist challenge the United States had to resist. The administration then went to the United Nations Security Council to get backing for a resolution condemning the invasion and authorizing a military response. The council's adoption of the resolution was made possible when the Soviet Union, which could have vetoed the measure, instead boycotted the meeting.

By late summer 1950, U.S. forces were able to stabilize the military situation in the Pusan area. In September the United States landed a massive invasion force at Inchon, west of Seoul, and then quickly recaptured the capital. Under allied pressure, the North Korean invading forces collapsed and were driven deep into the North by late November, within a few miles of the border with China.

China responded on November 25, sending more than one million men across the Yalu River, driving the allies back into the South. The military situation eventually stabilized near the old border between North and South, and a demilitarized zone was established with the signing of the armistice on July 27, 1953. The heavily guarded zone was still in effect in 1995.

The outcome represented neither victory nor defeat for the United States and its allies, although it could be viewed as more of the former because the status quo was preserved and North Korea failed to achieve its objective of unifying the two Koreas under its control.

In the United States, the war was generally unpopular, although there were no mass demonstrations comparable to those of the Vietnam War era. The most important political controversy occurred in 1951, when Gen. Douglas MacArthur, commander of UN forces in Korea, publicly supported an invasion of China, a statement at odds with official U.S. policy. Tru-

*man fired MacArthur, helping to make the general a hero among many con-
servatives.*

*Perhaps the most lasting impact of the war was that it hardened U.S.
resolve to oppose communist expansion wherever it occurred. Rather than
scaling back its military after the Korean War—as it did after all previous
wars—Washington maintained a high state of readiness for the next forty
years. A decade after the Korean armistice, the Kennedy and Johnson
administrations responded to increasing communist attacks in South
Vietnam by escalating the U.S. presence there. The Vietnam War had a different outcome, one far less satisfactory from the American point of view.*

*Forty-five years after the start of the war, South Korea was an econom-
ically powerful country, although one beset by political turmoil stemming
from years of nearly authoritarian rule under a democratic guise. North
Korea, still in the grip of Kim Il-Sung's communist dynasty, was still
devoting an extraordinarily high portion of its sources to the military and
was struggling just to feed its people.*

> *Following are the texts of remarks by President Kim Young-sam
> of South Korea and President Bill Clinton at the July 27, 1995,
> ceremony marking the dedication of the Korean War Veterans
> Memorial in Washington, D.C. President Kim's remarks were
> translated from Korean into English:*

KIM'S REMARKS

Your Excellency President Clinton, American congressional leaders, delegates from the Korean War, allies, Korean War veterans, ladies and gentlemen: We are dedicating this Korean War Veterans Memorial in memory of all
the veterans who fought heroically in that war so that all succeeding generations will know how great the sacrifices and devotion of those veterans were,
and how precious freedom and peace are. On behalf of the people of the
Republic of Korea, I pay tribute to all those Korean war veterans who sacrificed their lives, and I pay respect to all those who fought in that war.

I would like to express my profound appreciation to the United States government, Congress, General [Ray] Davis [head of the Korean War Memorial
Board], and others for sponsoring and supporting the building of this profoundly meaningful memorial.

Korean War veterans and distinguished guests, the sacrifices of the Korean War veterans to defend freedom and peace were not in vain. The blood
and sweat shed by the U.S. and the U.N. troops proved to be the prime mover
behind the realization of freedom throughout the postwar world. The free
world's participation in the Korean War, its first resolute and effective action
to stem the expansion of communism, changed the course of history. In this
sense, I would say that the Korean War was the war that heralded the collapse of the Berlin Wall and the demise of communism.

We take pride in the progress of history that has turned the Korean War from a forgotten war into a war most worthy of remembrance. Let all succeeding generations remember the truism engraved in this great memorial—freedom is not free.

Thank you.

CLINTON'S REMARKS

Thank you. Thank you very much, President Kim, for your fine remarks on behalf of all the people of Korea and for your leadership and for your defense of democracy in your country, proving that these sacrifices of the Americans and others were not in vain.

Thank you to all the distinguished guests who are here. I'd like to say also a special word of thanks for those who are responsible for this memorial, for those who designed and built it and conceived it, and those who operate it. It is a magnificent reminder of what is best about the United States. And I thank you all for your contribution.

I also believe that everyone in this crowd, indeed everyone in this country, owes a special debt of gratitude to General Davis and to his predecessor, General [Richard] Stilwell, for their eight-year dream to make this day a reality. General Davis served our country with great distinction in World War II and went on to win the Congressional Medal of Honor in Korea. But he had eight more long years of combat to make this day happen. And all of us who are here owe it to him to say thank you for all of that service.

Today we are surrounded by monuments to some of the greatest figures in our history while we gather at this, our newest national memorial, to remember and honor the Americans who fought for freedom in Korea. In 1950, our nation was weary of war, but 1.5 million Americans left their family and friends and their homes to help to defend freedom for a determined ally halfway around the world or, as the monument says, a place they had never been and a people they had never met.

Together with men and women from 20 other nations, all of whom are represented here today, they joined the first mission of the United Nations to preserve peace, by fighting shoulder to shoulder with the brave people of South Korea to defend their independence, to safeguard other Asian nations from attack, and to protect the freedom that remains our greatest gift.

The Korean War veterans endured terrible hardships—deathly cold, weeks and months crammed in foxholes and bunkers, an enemy of overwhelming numbers, the threat of brutal imprisonment and torture—defending the perimeter at Pusan, braving the tides at Inchon, confronting the world's fastest fighter jets in Mig Alley, enduring hand-to-hand combat on Heartbreak Ridge and Pork Chop Hill, fighting the way back from Chosin Reservoir. They set a standard of courage that may be equaled, but will never be surpassed in the annals of American combat.

If I might recount the deeds of just two men, so as to bring to life today, so many years later, the dimensions of this conflict. One from my home state, 26-year-old Lloyd Burke was trying to lead his company to high ground outside of Seoul. Pinned down by enemy fire, he wiped out three enemy bunkers in a lone assault. Hand grenades were thrown at him, so he caught them and threw them back. Later, he knocked out two enemy mortars and a machine gun position. Despite being wounded, he led his men in a final charge and took the hill. For his extraordinary courage and leadership, Lloyd Burke was awarded the Congressional Medal of Honor.

Corporal Ronald Rosser was forward observer in the hills near Pangil-ri when his platoon came under fire from two directions. With just a carbine and a grenade, he charged the enemy position and knocked out two bunkers and cleared a trench. Twice he ran out of ammunition and twice he crossed through enemy fire to resume his attack. Later, even though he was wounded, Ronald Rosser repeatedly dodged enemy fire to bring other injured soldiers to safety. And for his exceptional bravery, he, too, was awarded the Medal of Honor.

These two great Americans, Lloyd Burke and Ronald Rosser, are with us here today. I ask them to stand and be recognized on behalf of all the veterans of the Korean War.

In this impressive monument we can see the figures and faces that recall their heroism. In steel and granite, in water and earth, the creators of this memorial have brought to life the courage and sacrifice of those who served in all branches of the Armed Forces from every racial and ethnic group and background in America. They represent, once more, the enduring American truth: From many we are one.

Tens of thousands of Americans died in Korea. Our South Korean allies lost hundreds of thousands of soldiers and civilians. Our other U.N. allies suffered grievous casualties. Thousands of Americans who were lost in Korea to this day have never been accounted for. Today I urge the leaders of North Korea to work with us to resolve those cases.

President Kim and I are working together to open the door to better relations between our nations and North Korea. Clarifying these MIA cases is an important step. We have not forgotten our debt to them or to their families and we will never stop working for the day when they can be brought home.

This memorial also commemorates those who made the ultimate sacrifice so that we might live free. And I ask you on this hot, summer day to pause for a moment of silence in honor of those from the United States, our U.N. allies and from our friends in the Republic of Korea who lost their lives in the Korean War. [A moment of silence is observed.] Amen.

On this day 42 years ago, President Dwight Eisenhower called the end of hostilities an armistice on a single battleground, not peace in the world. It's fair to say that when the guns fell silent then, no one knew for sure what our forces in Korea had done for the future of our nation or the future of world freedom. The larger conflict of the Cold War had only begun. It would take four decades more to win.

In a struggle so long and consuming, perhaps it's not surprising that too many lost sight of the importance of Korea. But now we know with the benefit of history that those of you who served and the families who stood behind you laid the foundations for one of the greatest triumphs in the history of human freedom. By sending a clear message that America had not defeated fascism to see communism prevail, you put the free world on the road to victory in the Cold War. That is your enduring contribution. And all free people everywhere should recognize it today.

And look what you achieved in Korea. Today, Korea is thriving and prosperous. From the unbelievable poverty and ruin at the aftermath of the war, this brave, industrious, strong country has risen to become the 11th largest economy in the entire world, with a strong democratic leader in President Kim. In Asia, peace and stability are more firmly rooted than at any time since World War II. And all around the world, freedom and democracy are now on the march.

So to all the veterans here today, and to all throughout our land who are watching, let us all say, when darkness threatened, you kept the torch of liberty alight. You kept the flame burning so that others all across the world could share it. You showed the truth inscribed on the wall, that freedom is not free.

We honor you today because you did answer the call to defend a country you never knew and a people you never met. They are good people. It's a good country. And the world is better because of you.

God bless you and God bless America.

August

FDA ON THE SAFETY OF
SILICONE BREAST IMPLANTS
August 1, 1995

According to David A. Kessler, commissioner of the Food and Drug Administration (FDA), a growing number of studies have shown that silicone gel breast implants do not cause large increases in connective tissue diseases, such as scleroderma, rheumatoid arthritis, and lupus. In testimony August 1 to the House Government Reform and Oversight Subcommittee on Human Resources and Intergovernmental Relations, Kessler could not rule out the possibility that the implants caused some increase in those diseases and that they might be linked to atypical connective tissue disease. The FDA chief also said the rate of rupture of the implants was "much higher" than their manufacturers had initially predicted and that most women with the implants could expect "some degree" of contraction of the scar tissue surrounding the implants. In the worst cases, such contraction can cause pain and hardness of the breast.

Kessler's testimony may have allayed some of the worst fears of the estimated one million women who have had silicone gel breast implants since they first came on the market in 1964. However, it seemed unlikely to affect the tens of thousands of lawsuits women have filed against the manufacturers of the devices. In October three of those companies reached a new agreement to settle many of those cases; the settlement was expected to cost as much as $3 billion. The largest manufacturer of the implants, Dow Corning, declared bankruptcy in May 1995 and was no longer participating in the settlement.

Moratorium, Lawsuits Prompted by Safety Questions

Silicone gel breast implants came on the market before the FDA had authority to review and approve the safety and effectiveness of new medical devices. In 1976 the agency was authorized to investigate the safety of medical devices already on the market, but it was not until 1988 that the FDA held hearings on the implants. By that time women were complaining that the implants were rupturing and leaking silicone gel into their bodies, that the scar tissue was hardening their breasts and causing extreme pain, and that the implants were causing a variety of painful diseases such as rheumatoid arthritis.

In January 1992 the FDA called for a moratorium on the sale of the implants after receiving documentation that the manufacturers had not adequately tested the safety of the devices before putting them on the market and had known for years about potential safety problems. Several doctors and researchers also told the FDA that they suspected an association between the breast implants and some connective tissue disorders. The manufacturers agreed to the moratorium while the FDA and an advisory panel could study the evidence more closely.

In April Kessler 1992 lifted the moratorium, but use was restricted to women participating in clinical studies on the safety of the implants. All women requesting implants for reconstructive purposes were granted access to the clinical trials, but cosmetic implants were strictly limited. Since then, some 12,000 women have enrolled in the clinical trials and received silicone breast implants. Implants filled with saline solution were available for both reconstructive and cosmetic surgery. (FDA on breast implants, Historic Documents of 1992, p. 367)

Although the FDA was careful to say that studies showed no causal link between implants and connective tissue disease, tens of thousands of women had initiated legal suits, complaining of illnesses they said were caused by the implants. In 1993 lawyers for the manufacturers and many of the women agreed to a settlement. Under this agreement, which was the largest single liability settlement in the nation's history, four manufacturers agreed to pay $4.5 billion to settle the claims both of women who were ill and those who sought protection against future illness from the implants. The awards were to range from $200,000 to $2 million, depending on the age of the woman and the severity of her illness. In addition to Dow Corning, the manufacturers were Bristol-Myers Squibb, Baxter Healthcare, and 3M.

Kessler's Testimony

In his testimony Kessler summarized several studies that found no clearcut link between the implants and connective tissue disease, but he would not say that the devices were safe. The studies provided "reasonable assurances" that the implants did not cause "a large increase" in traditional connective tissue diseases, he said, but they "simply cannot rule out either a small but statistically significant increased risk in traditional connective tissue disease or the risk of atypical disease." Many women and their doctors speculated that vague but persistent symptoms such as headaches, pain, and chronic fatigue were signs of connective tissue diseases that were not well understood, perhaps not yet recognized.

More research on how long the implants remain intact within the body, how often they rupture, and the potential health effects of ruptures were needed before the agency could declare the devices safe, Kessler said.

Kessler also reminded the subcommittee that the FDA was authorized to determine only the safety of the specific devices submitted to it for marketing clearance and thus could consider only studies related to the safety of those specific devices. It could not rule on the general safety of all silicone gel implants.

New Legal Settlement

Even as new studies were finding no evidence of large increases in disease caused by implants, the number of women registering for inclusion in the legal settlement was growing. By early 1995, some 100,000 women alleging existing illness had registered, as had 330,000 who were seeking protection against future illness. When Dow Corning declared bankruptcy in May, the federal judge overseeing the settlement told the remaining three companies to come up with a new agreement.

Under that agreement, which the companies announced November 14, individual awards would range from $10,000 to $250,000—significantly lower than those in the first agreement. Still, the manufacturers estimated the agreement could cost as much as $3 billion. Women would be paid according to a plan, approved by the judge, that set specific amounts for certain ailments. Claims against Dow Corning, which accounted for about $2.5 billion of the original settlement agreement, were to be settled by the bankruptcy court. Women choosing not to join the new settlement agreement were free to bring individual lawsuits.

Absent any concrete evidence that the silicone gel breast implants were causally linked to some of the vague symptoms on which many women were basing their legal claims, manufacturers and others raised questions about whether some lawyers and doctors involved in implant cases might be more interested in helping their clients win large settlements than in securing appropriate medical treatment for them. In November a jury in Nevada awarded a woman $14 million in damages not against Dow Corning, the bankrupt maker of her implants, but against its parent company, Dow Chemical. The award was made despite the fact that Dow Chemical said it never worked with the kind of silicone used in the Dow Corning implants. Dow Chemical was expected to appeal the verdict, but it faced 13,000 similar lawsuits. "It used to be that you had to show causation," Lester Brickman of the Cardozo School for Law in New York told Newsweek *magazine. "Today causation is no longer a scientific issue. If you have enough claims to put a company in risk of bankruptcy, you can buy causation."*

> *Following are excerpts from the text of a statement on the safety of silicone breast implants, delivered August 1, 1995, by Dr. David A. Kessler, commissioner of the Food and Drug Administration, to the House Government Reform and Oversight Subcommittee on Human Resources and Intergovernmental Relations:*

... Today I would like to give you an update on the safety of silicone gel breast implants based on the published literature and respond to some of your questions about silicone in general. The good news is that in the three years since 1992, important research on these products has been undertaken, some by FDA [Food and Drug Administration] staff, on some of the critical scientific questions. In these and other areas, more research is still need. FDA has worked with the industry and academic community to encourage needed research and to establish a research agenda.

Let me take you back more than three years, to review with you the kinds of questions facing the Agency in early 1992. At that time, very little was known about the safety of silicone gel implants.

The questions included:

- How frequently do these devices rupture or cause other local complications?
- What do we know about the relationship between silicone gel implants and autoimmune (connective tissue) disease?
- What are the possible mechanisms of silicone gel-mediated immunological reactions?

These questions are very important, and they are not easily answered. But we do have much more information about some of them than we did three years ago. Vigorous research has been conducted over the last three and a half years that has provided a larger body of epidemiological, laboratory and clinical studies than previously existed. We now are beginning to get the kinds of studies that were unavailable in our earlier review of these products.

The safety issues that concern us fall into two categories: local complications which, when they occur, we know are directly attributable to the breast implants. Examples of local complications are implant rupture, capsular contracture, infection, and surgical complications. With the second category of safety issues—systemic disease—the association between breast implants and disease is more difficult to establish. Systemic diseases include autoimmune diseases, particularly connective tissue diseases, such as scleroderma, lupus, and rheumatoid arthritis.

Let me first review what we now know about local complications.

Device Failure and Local Complications

I am going to cite several studies that examine the rupture rate of breast implants. FDA has to be concerned about the durability of any kind of implant—how long it lasts in the body, how often it fails, how frequently it has to be replaced, and what are the consequences of failure.

I want to begin with an important point about rupture rate: today we still do not know what the rupture rate is in women with silicone gel implants, or how that rate changes over time. Several studies, however, suggest that the rate may be such higher than the one percent rate manufacturers originally suggested, and that the rate may increase as the implant ages.

The study that first elevated our concern on the rupture rate issue was conducted by Dr. Judy Destouet and her colleagues and published in 1992 in the *American Journal of Radiology*. They retrospectively analyzed screening mammograms of 350 women with breast implants. In sixteen of the women—five percent—there was evidence of implant rupture. It is very important to keep in mind that women in whom rupture was suspected were specifically excluded from this study—the 5% percent rate, then, was in asymptomatic women who did not suspect a rupture had occurred.

A more recent study was performed by Dr. O. Gordon Robinson, Jr. and others and published in the *Annals of Plastic Surgery* in 1995. Of 495 women who consulted with Dr. Robinson on their silicone breast implants, 300 women decided to have them removed. The study focuses on these 300 women. In some cases the women made the decision because they suspected an implant-related problem, and in other cases the decision was made on the basis of a general concern about silicone gel-filled implants. The investigators found frank ruptures in 154 or 51% of these patients. In a total of 71% of the patients, they found either frank rupture, severe silicone gel bleed, or both. They concluded that the likelihood of rupture increases as the implant ages. As a result, Dr. Robinson recommends to his patients that they have their implants removed prophylactically, preferably within eight years of implantation—prior to rupture.

In another study of 31 women who had 51 implants removed, whether the implant was ruptured was clearly related to the age of the implant. Of those implants aged 1–9 years, 35.7% were ruptured; of those aged 10–17 years, 95.7% had either ruptured or were leaking silicone gel. In a similar study of 57 women who had 102 implants removed, of the implants aged 2–10 years, 25.6% were ruptured; of the implants 11–26 years old, 53.6% were ruptured. These two studies are not representative of the rupture rate in all woman with implants, but rather in women who are going to their doctor because they are having problems with their implants. They indicate, however, that the risk of implant rupture increases as the implants age.

Published studies to date suggest a rupture rate between 5 and 51%—an enormous range—and unfortunately, we do not know with any confidence where within that range the real rupture rate lies.

In addition to rupture rates, I want to mention one other complication that may affect the majority of women with implants: capsular contracture. This occurs when the scar around the implant contracts. In its severest form, it may cause painful, rock hard breasts. The frequency of this complication is unknown. Like rupture, reports in the medical literature vary considerably but suggest that some degree of capsular contracture may occur in the majority of women with implants.

There are other local complications, including infection and surgical complications. While some of these are of greater concern than others, we simply have no solid information at this time about their frequency.

Systemic Diseases

Unlike local complications, which are clearly related to the presence of the implant, there are a constellation of diseases that some suspect silicone gel breast implants also cause. It is more difficult, however, to prove or disprove such a link. It is only within the past year and a half that several epidemiologic studies addressing this issue have been published.

The diseases in question are a type of autoimmune disease called connective tissue disease. Included in this category are very rare diseases, such as scleroderma and lupus, and relatively more common conditions such as rheumatoid arthritis.

The two types of published epidemiologic studies on this subject are— cohort studies and case control studies. Cohort studies compare groups with the exposure of interest—in this case breast implants—with an unexposed group, and assess whether the rate of disease is different in the two groups. In contrast, case control studies take patients who have the disease of interest and then compare the rate of exposure—breast implants—to those who do not have the disease.

Each of these study types has its limitations. Cohort studies are most useful when studying common diseases and are of limited use when the outcome or disease is rare. Case control studies are used when the disease of interest is rare but the exposure may be more common.

The two largest cohort studies published to date are the Mayo Clinic study performed by Dr. Sherine Gabriel and her colleagues and the Nurses Health Study from Dr. Jorge Sanchez-Guerrero and his colleagues at Harvard.

Dr. Gabriel's study was a population-based study of all women in Olmsted County, Minnesota who received a breast implant between 1964 and 1991—a total of 749 women. These women were compared to similar women without breast implants. The study found no association between breast implants and those connective tissue diseases studied.

Dr. Sanchez-Guerrero's study was based on a large survey of nurses that began in 1976. It included 876 women with silicone gel breast implants. It also found no increased risk of common connective tissue diseases in women with silicone gel implants.

Neither of these studies, however, could rule out a small but significant increase in risk for rare connective tissues disease nor could they fully answer the question of whether the implants might lead to atypical symptoms related to the immune system in women.

The only published case-control study we are aware of that examines the association between breast implants and scleroderma is by Dr. Helen Englert and her colleagues in Sydney, Australia. It was published in the *Australian/New Zealand Journal of Medicine* in 1994. This study involved women in Sydney who had scleroderma or a related ailment. These women were compared to similar women without the disease. The authors concluded that they had failed to demonstrate "an association between silicone gel breast implantation and the subsequent development of scleroderma, to a risk level as low as 4.5 with 90% power." This means that this study was large enough to detect whether women with breast implants were 4.5 times more likely to have scleroderma than women in the population. But the study was too small to document any smaller increase in risk. So while ruling out a large increase in scleroderma, this study also was unable to rule out a small, but significant, risk of disease.

There are two important conclusions to draw from these studies. Based on the published studies to date, we now have, for the first time, a reasonable assurance that silicon gel implants do not cause a large increase in traditional connective tissue disease in women who have those implants. This is particularly important for those women who already have implants and have suffered from an absence of scientific information on this subject. The second conclusion, however, is that these published studies simply cannot rule out either a small but statistically significant increased risk in traditional connective tissue disease or the risk of atypical disease. Given the fact that an estimated one million women (an estimate still in question) have received these implants, even one percent translates to 10,000 women. Thus, for some women, we still do not have all the answers.

The Biological Activity of Silicone Gel

It also is important to review the basic science related to the biological activity of silicone gel. Recently published laboratory studies have focused on the potential molecular mechanisms that might be a basis for autoimmune reaction triggered by the silicone gel material in breast implants.

Let me briefly summarize some recent reports.

1. Antibodies to Silicone Gel

Development of an assay for antibodies to silicone gel is a difficult technical challenge, and there is still disagreement over assay reliability. Given this caveat, a significant increase in anti-silicone antibodies has been reported in women with implants compared with groups of women without implants. There was no discussion, however, of health problems in these woman or a possible association between adverse reactions and anti-silicone antibodies. In another study, anti-silicone antibodies were reported in two children who experienced an inflammatory reaction around implanted silicone tubing. It was concluded, however, that antibodies likely were not involved in the inflammatory reaction.

Neither these nor other studies, provide convincing evidence that anti-silicone antibodies, if present, are responsible for adverse effects.

2. Auto-Antibodies to Connective Tissue and Other Proteins

With assays specifically designed to detect auto-antibodies to altered proteins, several reports have provided evidence consistent with the hypothesis that proteins adsorbed to gel can induce auto-antibodies to connective tissue and other proteins in women with breast implants. The question remains, however, whether these or other auto-antibodies can induce clinical manifestations of disease. A recent study on the relationship between auto-anti-bodies and silicone gel implants concluded that "... there is no conclusive evidence that silicone-gel implants are related to the development of connective tissue disease."

Much recent attention has been paid to auto antibodies; less to other potential mechanisms of autoimmunity involving the cellular immune response, cytokines (soluble immune mediators), and effects of chronic inflammation. Although progress has been made, additional well-controlled studies are needed to understand silicone gel's biological activity.

Let me also note that although most reports have focused on silicone gel, other silicones—including low molecular weight contaminants and silicone oil that bleeds through the elastomer shell—also are being studied in experimental animals. One compound of particular interest, D4, was able to enhance the antibody response to a foreign protein in experimental animals, but only at levels exceeding those found in implants. Gel bleed did not have detectable adjuvant activity.

Reaching a Final Conclusion on Safety and Efficacy

A second general topic of interest to the subcommittee involves when FDA will be able to reach a final conclusion on the safety and efficacy of these devices.

Mr. Chairman, the short answer is: when the manufacturers submit data supporting their PMAs [Premarket Approval Applications]. That is quite simply because *sponsors* of medical devices, not the FDA generate data to support product approval. Until such time as a sponsor has submitted a complete application for marketing approval of a breast implant, and there are adequate data to support the safety of the implant, FDA cannot under the law allow the general marketing of silicone gel-filled breast implants. I also should say that any marketing application needs to be product-specific. As part of our evaluation, we would need to examine the implant's specific design characteristics and the way it is to be manufactured.

But that is hardly the entire answer. The FDA has stated publicly the kinds of data we will be looking for in a marketing application for breast implants. We have done this specifically in a written guidance document for breast implants that contain silicone gel. We also are developing guidance for implants that might be filled with alternative materials, based on a major workshop on non-silicone gel implants we held last October. It is fair to say that the data needs are well-known, involving: chemistry, materials science, toxicology, and the clinical data on local complications and systemic diseases, as described above, as well as the product's benefits. We need sufficient data to evaluate the product's safety and prepare informative labeling for surgeons and patients. The manufacturer also must be able to establish adequate quality systems in its manufacturing of the product and pass an onsite FDA inspection. We have been working closely with manufacturers and with the academic community to encourage studies that will provide the information needed on the safety of these products.

Outreach to Women

The uncertainty about the safety of breast implants is alarming, naturally, to women who have or may consider implants. The FDA, as a consumer protection agency, takes their concerns very seriously and has undertaken the following initiatives to both educate consumers with the latest information about implants and ensure their participation in the debate.

- In September 1991, FDA published a notice in the *Federal Register* requiring manufacturers to relay to physicians information on the risks of breast implants. Physicians then would be better able to advise their patients before having implant surgery. I met with consumer groups, health professional groups and manufacturers to discuss this notice.
- Over sixty consumers and consumer representatives testified at the 1991 and 1992 panel meetings on breast implants. Each panel had two members who represented different perspectives from women with implants.
- Following the panel meetings, the Agency established an 800 telephone line dedicated to questions about breast implants. Between February and June 1992, over 40,000 women used this line. Our Office of Consumer Affairs still maintains it and receives approximately 75 calls per week.
- In 1992, the Agency developed *Breast Implants: An Information Update*, which contains current findings about known and possible risks of implants, information about their availability, advice for women with implants, and resources for further information. It has been distributed to over 30,000 women. We have brought copies of our July 1995 update for distribution at this hearing. It includes information on the new published epidemiological studies on the question of connective tissue disease, as described above, as well as the new Patient Information Sheet for Women Considering Saline-Filled Breast Implants, which physicians are to provide to women considering them.
- The Agency reached out to approximately 350 consumer groups for a public (Part 15) hearing on saline breast implants held in July 1994. Twenty-seven consumers and consumer representatives testified.

Throughout this controversy, the Agency has met repeatedly with representatives of patient groups to share information and improve our awareness of the needs and concerns of these women. In addition, we have written articles for newspapers, professional journals, women's magazines and the *FDA Consumer* to provide information to women and their physicians. We have issued press releases, backgrounders and talk papers. We will continue to use these and other vehicles to communicate to the public the most current information about breast implants. . . .

UN TREATY ON CONSERVATION OF WORLD FISHERIES
August 4, 1995

A United Nations conference on August 4 adopted an international treaty to control fishing on the high seas in hopes of conserving several important fish species for the future. The treaty was the result of three years of negotiations by delegates from one hundred nations. It will enter into force when ratified by at least thirty nations, a process the conference expected to take about two years.

Environmentalists and many fishery experts had warned for decades that some of the world's most important commercial fish species were being depleted as a result of increasingly sophisticated commercial fishing techniques. The treaty was an attempt both to curb overfishing and to resolve some international disputes over fishing rights.

Satya Nandan of Fiji, the UN conference chairman, said the treaty would end a "free-for-all situation" in ocean fishing. If the treaty is fully enforced, he said, "there should be no fishing by stealth anymore."

Environmental groups, which had lobbied for an international fishing treaty, offered divergent views on the potential impact of the treaty. Matthew Gianni, a representative of Greenpeace International, called the treaty a "step forward" but said that "it's not going to be enough to reverse the decline of the world's fisheries." On a more optimistic note, Lisa Speer, a scientist with the Natural Resources Defense Council, told the Washington Post that the treaty "spells the end of untrammeled plundering of ocean fisheries" and creates "an enforceable management regime."

Years of Overfishing

The fisheries conference was called to deal with two overriding facts: despite increasingly high-tech means of catching fish, the worldwide catch of ocean fish had been declining by several million tons annually since at least 1989; and, according to the Food and Agriculture Organization, by 1995 about 70 percent of ocean fish stocks were fully depleted, overfished, or just recovering from past overfishing.

524

Especially vulnerable fish species were "straddling" fish that migrate between coastal waters and the high seas. Those included cod, pollack, marlin, tuna, and swordfish. These fish accounted for about 20 percent of the total marine catch, but they were the most sought after.

Industry experts and conference delegates pointed to numerous causes for overfishing. High-powered fishing trawlers and sophisticated technology such as sonar were making it easier to locate and catch fish on the high seas. Many countries heavily subsidized their fishing fleets, thus giving them the financial resources to pursue fish anywhere in the world. Fishermen were growing increasingly aggressive with their tactics, even to the extent of sabotaging their competitors. Modern fishing nets caught millions of tons of unwanted fish, discarding them back into the oceans, a wasteful practice that depleted the overall food chain. Also, the worldwide demand for fish had grown sharply in recent years, especially in Asian countries where fish is a major source of protein and in the West, where fish is becoming more valued as a "healthy" food.

Greenpeace summed up all these causes as "too many boats chasing too few fish." According to the United Nations, six countries accounted for 90 percent of the world's fishing on the high seas: Japan, Poland, Russia, South Korea, Spain, and Taiwan.

The fierce competition had created tense disputes among some nations, almost to the point of conflict. In one highly publicized example, in March 1995 Canada seized one Spanish fishing trawler and cut the nets of another boat. Canada had declared a moratorium on cod fishing off its coast, and it accused the Spanish captains of violating that ban.

Conference Action

In light of those issues, the United Nations in April 1993 convened an international Conference on Straddling Fish Stocks and Highly Migratory Fish Stocks. The goal of the conference was to produce language implementing many of the conservation provisions of the 1982 Law of the Sea treaty. (Law of the Sea Treaty, Historic Documents of 1982, p. 345)

Negotiations began in July 1993 and centered on conflicts between the interests of "coastal states" (such as Argentina and Canada) that were able to control lucrative fishing areas within their 200-mile "exclusive economic zones" and the "distant-water-fishing" countries (such as Spain and Japan) that needed to send their fishing fleets onto the high seas in search of catches. The United States fell into both categories and reportedly served as a mediator between them.

The conference held six formal sessions and dozens of working meetings. After a series of compromises, it produced the treaty that was adopted August 4. The treaty applied only to catches of migratory fish in international waters or inside countries' 200-mile exclusive economic zones. It did not apply to fishing within each country's twelve-mile territorial waters.

The heart of the treaty was a series of requirements for nations and regional organizations to adopt measures promoting the conservation of migratory fish species. Signatory countries and regional organizations would establish quotas for the fishing of straddling species within their jurisdictions. They would have to notify other countries of those quotas, and they would have the right to board boats to ensure the quotas were respected. Countries with distant-water fleets were to take steps to regulate those fleets and to notify other countries of those measures.

Fishing fleets must report catches to their home countries, which in turn must make the statistics available to other countries. The treaty included mandatory dispute-resolution procedures to settle disagreements between signatory countries.

Even as the treaty was being adopted by a "consensus" vote, conference delegates registered concerns over specific provisions, especially those dealing with enforcement. Those provisions were the last ones on which the conference reached compromise decisions.

The most controversial was an authorization for regional organizations and coastal states to use force, if necessary, when boarding fishing vessels to monitor compliance with conservation measures. Delegates from several countries said force should never be used, or should be used only if an inspector's life was in danger. The chief delegate from the European Union objected to what she saw as a lack of legal guidelines for the use of force.

Following are excerpts from a text provided by the United Nations of an August 4, 1995, statement by the Conference on Straddling Fish Stocks and Highly Migratory Fish Stocks on the adoption of an international treaty requiring conservation of several major migratory fish species:

A global treaty to regulate fishing on the high seas was adopted by consensus today at the final session of the United Nations Conference on Straddling Fish Stocks and Highly Migratory Fish Stocks. For the first time, States will be legally bound to conserve and sustainably manage high-seas fisheries and settle fishing disputes peacefully.

The treaty is titled the Agreement for the Implementation of the Provisions of the 1982 United Nations Convention on the Law of the Sea relating to the Conservation and Management of Straddling Fish Stocks and Highly Migratory Fish Stocks.

Calling the Agreement far-sighted, bold and even revolutionary, the Chairman of the Conference, Satya Nandan (Fiji), said it provided for regional, national and global action to address the critical problems facing the world's fisheries. While the Agreement contained innovations that went beyond the Law of the Sea Convention and gave further meaning to some of its basic principles that were not being fully implemented, the Agreement was also realistic and practical and firmly rooted in the Convention.

He said the Agreement was built on three essential pillars: principles for conservation and management based on a precautionary approach and the best scientific information; ensuring that conservation measures were not undermined by those who fished for vulnerable stocks; and the peaceful settlement of disputes. He cited a warning by the Food and Agriculture Organization (FAO) of the disastrous social and economic consequences awaiting the global fishing industry unless the size of fleets were reduced, subsidies eliminated and fleets more effectively regulated. Without the Agreement there would be a further depletion of the world's fish resources, as well as more conflict on the high seas.

The Agreement includes ground-breaking provisions to ensure compatible conservation and management measures between high-seas areas and coastal zones under national jurisdiction. One of its major features is the "precautionary approach" by which States are obligated to act conservatively when there is doubt about the viability of stocks. Other provisions of the Agreement establish detailed minimum international standards for conservation and management of fish stocks. It also includes effective measures for compliance and enforcement on the high seas; it recognizes the special requirements of developing States for assistance in conservation and management.

In the case of conflicts between nations over fishing rights, the treaty calls for compulsory and binding third-party dispute settlement, which is not currently provided by regional organizations. States can choose from the options for dispute settlement established under the Law of the Sea Convention—the International Tribunal for the Law of the Sea, the International Court of Justice or an ad hoc tribunal. The Agreement will enter into force 30 days after its ratification by 30 signatories. It is a process which is expected to take about two years, but in the meantime, countries can apply it provisionally.

While describing the Agreement as a text that balanced the rights and obligations of coastal and distant-water-fishing States, some speakers cautioned that the use of force to ensure the implementation of conservation measures must be only as a last resort. Others said that the derogation of the sovereignty of flag States must be strictly limited.

In other action, the Conference also adopted a Final Act, which includes a resolution requesting the Secretary-General of the United Nations to open the Agreement for signature on 4 December 1995. In addition, the Act contains a resolution recommending that the General Assembly review a report by the Secretary-General on the conservation and management of straddling and highly migratory fish stocks.

The Conference also adopted the report of its Credentials Committee. . . .

Provisions of Agreement

The Agreement legally binds States to the long-term conservation and sustainable use of high-seas fisheries within the framework of the Convention on the Law of the Sea. It also aims to prevent conflicts between coastal States, which have exclusive fishing rights within their 200-mile exclusive economic zones, and countries that maintain fishing fleets on the high seas—the distant-water-fishing States.

It addresses specific problems dealing with conservation of the living resources of the high-seas identified in "Agenda-21"—the programme of action adopted by the 1992 United Nations Conference on Environment and Development (UNCED). Those problems include inadequate fisheries management and overutilization of marine resources, unregulated fishing, over-capitalization and excessive fleet size. The Agreement also deals with vessels which re-flag to escape controls, insufficiently selective fishing gear, unreliable databases on fish stocks and lack of sufficient cooperation between States for ensuring sustainable use of stocks.

It not only sets out principles to underline the better management of the world's fisheries, it also defines methods for enforcing conservation regulations. It recognizes the need for international action to reverse the impact of destructive fishing practices on the marine environment and establishes rules to preserve biodiversity and maintain the marine ecosystems. Conservation measures will be based on the best scientific evidence available, to protect the fish stocks and other species which belong to the same ecosystem. To minimize waste and ecological damage, environmentally safe fishing gear and techniques are required. The interests of artisanal and subsistence fisheries workers are also taken into account.

Countries must collect and share data on their fishing activities, including vessel position, size of catches and the results of research programmes on fisheries management. They will also have to conduct scientific research and develop technologies on sustainable management, as well as enforce conservation measures through monitoring and satellite surveillance.

In emphasizing the precautionary approach, which obliges States to use the best scientific data available, the Agreement says that States cannot use a lack of scientific information as a reason for not taking conservation and management measures.

Compatibility of conservation and management measures for areas under national jurisdiction and those for the high seas is also provided for. While coastal States have the right to exploit and manage fish stocks in their economic zones, they must notify countries fishing in high-seas areas adjacent to those zones about national conservation polices. When adopting conservation measures, States must consider such factors as the biological unity of fish stocks, the economic dependence of different States on those stocks and previously agreed rules for conservation adopted by regional arrangements.

Non-members of regional organizations must still cooperate with the conservation and management measures of subregional or regional organizations. Countries that want to fish in an area managed by a particular organization will have to become members of that organization or agree to abide by its conservation measures. Organizations must be open to all States that have a real interest in the area and must not discriminate against any State or group of States. If there is no fisheries organization to manage a particular stock, concerned States will have to establish one or enter into another management arrangement.

When establishing a subregional or regional organization, States will have to agree on the type of stocks, and the socio-economic, geographical and environmental characteristics of the area as well as their relationship with other fisheries organizations. Members of any new arrangement must keep other countries with a genuine interest in the area informed of their activities.

Regional organizations will decide which countries can fish in their areas, set annual quotas for catches and collect and exchange accurate information on the state of the fish stocks. Organizations will monitor and enforce conservation measures and ensure that disputes are settled peacefully. Due to the waste involved in high-tech fishing methods, organizations are also responsible for assessing the impact of fishing on species caught unintentionally.

In considering the fishing rights of new members of regional organizations, those arrangements will take into account the current level of fishing, as well as the needs of coastal fishing communities, coastal States whose economies are overwhelmingly dependent on the exploitation of marine resources, and the interests of developing States in the area.

In the interests of transparency, subregional and regional fisheries arrangements will allow other intergovernmental and non-governmental organizations to take part in their meetings as observers. States will have to collect and exchange accurate scientific, technical and statistical data on highseas fisheries. Countries conducting scientific research in areas beyond their national jurisdiction will have to share their findings with other interested States.

Countries will have to consider the natural characteristics of enclosed and semi-enclosed seas and take measures to deter activities of vessels of nonparties that undermine the Agreement. Nations fishing in areas of the high seas surrounded entirely by the national waters of a single State must adopt conservation measures which are compatible with those of the coastal State's. Dispute-settlement procedures are to be used when two countries cannot agree on those measures.

Under the duties of flag States, the Agreement provides for such States to exercise control over their vessels fishing in the high seas through a system of licenses and permits, which must be produced for inspection on demand. Also, national records of such licences must be made available to directly interested States, taking into account national laws of disclosure of such information. Fishing vessels and gear must be identified in accordance with internationally recognizable marking systems.

Accurate and verifiable records of vessel position, catch and other data must be kept and inspectors and observers from other States given access to such information. Flag States should develop vessel monitoring mechanisms, including satellite transmitters, which are compatible with subregional, regional or global monitoring systems.

On compliance and enforcement by a flag State, the Agreement calls for flag States to ensure that their registered vessels comply with subregional, regional and global management measures. They must investigate alleged violations, irrespective of where they occur, by physically inspecting the vessel if required and report their findings to the State making the allegation, as well as to the relevant regional organizations. Flag States must act without delay if there is sufficient evidence of a violation and take remedial action, including judicial proceedings and sanctions against the offending vessel.

Under the heading of international cooperation in enforcement, the Agreement provides for flag States enlisting the help of other States or fisheries organizations in investigating alleged violations. They must disseminate the results of the investigation to any interested parties and countries must help each other by identifying offending vessels and providing evidence to prosecuting authorities in other States.

Further, it provides that when a foreign vessel fishes without authorization within the national jurisdiction of another country, the flag State must cooperate with the coastal State in any enforcement action. The flag State can authorize the coastal State to board and inspect the offending vessel on the high seas. In addition, members of a regional organization can take action under international law, including regional procedures set up for this purpose, to stop fishing by vessels violating the accepted conservation measures.

Under subregional and regional cooperation in enforcement, it provides for members to board and inspect vessels of non-members to ensure compliance with regional conservation measures. If there are clear grounds to believe a fishing vessel has committed serious violations of conservation rules set by regional fishing organizations, the inspecting State will notify the flag State. If the flag State does not respond within three working days—during which time the inspectors may stay on the vessel—then the inspecting State can detain the vessel in port for further action. If a flag State believes that enforcement measures have been taken without its consent, it can initiate dispute-settlement procedures.

Serious violations, as defined in the Agreement, include fishing without a license, fishing for prohibited stocks, using illegal fishing gear, and concealing, tampering with or disposing of evidence needed for an investigation.

The Agreement's boarding and inspection procedures provide for an inspecting State to ensure that its inspectors present proper credentials and a copy of the relevant conservation rules when a vessel is being inspected. Inspectors must leave the vessel promptly if no serious violation is found. The use of force should be avoided unless it is necessary to ensure the safety of inspectors or when they are prevented from carrying out their duties. Flag States must allow prompt and safe boarding by inspectors and cooperate in the inspection.

Although most maritime law is enforced by the flag State, the Agreement addresses situations where ships fishing on the high seas are too distant from their flag States to be adequately supervised, or where the flag State is not willing or able to police its vessels. Port States have the right and duty to take measures in favour of global conservation and management measures. They have the right to inspect documents, gear and catch of vessels voluntarily in its ports or offshore terminals. They may prohibit landings and transshipments by vessels which have undermined the effectiveness of those regional measures on the high seas.

To help them fulfil their conservation and management responsibilities, developing States will receive financial and technical assistance from regional organizations and international agencies. The least developed and small island developing States will be helped to participate in high-seas fisheries. The vulnerability of developing nations that depend on living marine resources, as well [as] the needs of subsistence and artisanal fishermen, women fisheries workers and indigenous peoples will be taken into account.

Developing States will not be unfairly burdened by conservation measures. . . .

GOVERNMENT OVERHAUL OF SECURITY CLEARANCES
August 4, 1995

President Bill Clinton on August 4 ordered the most sweeping overhaul in forty years of U.S. government regulations dealing with security clearances for civilian and military officials. One of the changes ended a long-time government practice of prohibiting homosexuals, solely because of their sexual orientation, from having access to classified information. The president's Executive Order 12968 also required officials with security clearances to give the government detailed information about their personal finances.

Although the executive order contained broad provisions on nearly all issues affecting security clearances, most of the public attention was focused on the loosening of restrictions on homosexuals. Gay rights organizations praised the president's action as recognizing that homosexuals do not necessarily pose greater security risks than anyone else. Representatives of some conservative and religious organizations condemned the step, saying that the behavior of homosexuals does make them potential security risks.

In a statement, White House Press Secretary Michael McCurry said the order "strengthens personnel security for all U.S. government agencies and contractors, while insuring fair treatment for the men and women entrusted to protect the nation's secrets."

Ames Case Background

The Clinton administration's review of regulations governing security clearances was sparked by revelations that Aldrich H. Ames, a senior official in the Central Intelligence Agency's directorate of operations, had spied for the Soviet Union since 1985. Ames received more than $2 million for his efforts, payments that enabled him and his wife to live a lavish lifestyle. Despite suspicions about Ames' activities, the CIA took no steps to examine his financial records until 1992. Ames was arrested in February 1994 and two months later he and his wife pleaded guilty to espionage *charges. He was sentenced to life in prison without parole. (Ames case, Historic Documents of 1994, p. 475)*

Administration officials said the Ames case demonstrated the weakness and inconsistency of government regulations on security clearances. For example, they noted that the government had no clear-cut procedures for investigating the finances of high-level officials suspected of engaging in criminal activity. In the wake of the Ames case, the White House ordered all government agencies handling classified information to review their procedures and to recommend changes.

President Clinton's executive order applied both to government officials and to employees of private companies who need to obtain security clearances for their work. As a condition for gaining access to classified information, all these employees were required to provide written consent for federal investigative agencies to have access to their bank records, consumer credit reports, and records relating to foreign travel. Those agencies could examine an employee's financial records under any one of several circumstances, such as when there were reasonable grounds to believe that he or she was disclosing classified information to a foreign country or had acquired "a level of affluence that cannot be explained by other information." McCurry said these last two items had been "indicators of espionage in recent years."

The order also required the filing of annual, detailed financial disclosure statements by all federal employees and private contractors with access to especially sensitive classified information, such as the identities of covert agents, the details of secret codes, and the operations of intelligence-gathering devices such as spy satellites. Unlike financial disclosure statements filed by members of Congress and presidential appointees, these statements would not be made public. The order also authorized the Treasury Department, as part of this effort, to search electronic databases of currency transactions and foreign bank accounts.

Revamped Clearance Regulations

The heart of President Clinton's order was a near-total revamping of procedures for granting security clearances. In the past, each government agency had its own procedures for giving its employees and private contractors access to classified information. That system led to inconsistent and even conflicting standards and often forced government employees to obtain new clearances when they transferred, even temporarily, from one agency to another.

One example was the question of allowing homosexuals to have access to classified information. For decades, all federal agencies restricted security clearances for homosexuals. A General Accounting Office report in March 1995 noted that several agencies had formally or informally dropped such restrictions, while other agencies kept them in place.

The August 4 executive order established government-wide standards for granting, reviewing, and revoking security clearances. The new regu-

lations were to be coordinated by a Security Policy Board, appointed by the president. Clearances granted to employees at one agency were to be honored by other agencies, except where there was "substantial information" indicating that an employee would not satisfy government-wide standards for a clearance.

Clinton's executive order consisted of thirteen single-space, legal-size pages. Only two words dealt with the issue of granting security clearances to homosexuals, but that issue attracted most of the attention when the order was released. Clinton added the words "sexual orientation" to the standard nondiscrimination list, which included race, color, religion, sex, national origin, and disability. Administration officials said homosexuality could still become an issue in a security clearance case if investigating officials found that an employee was so fearful of having his homosexuality disclosed that he could be subjected to blackmail. This had always been one of the reasons cited by government officials for the general discrimination against homosexuals.

The order also loosened restrictions on granting security clearances to individuals who had undergone psychiatric or psychological counseling. It said that "no negative inference" was to be drawn about an employee solely because he or she had undergone such counseling. In fact, the order said, mental health counseling "can be a positive factor" in determining eligibility. Even so, the order said mental health counseling can be considered a factor if it "directly relates" to the standards that would otherwise be applied in determining an employee's eligibility for a security clearance.

Following is the text of Executive Order 12968, signed by President Bill Clinton on August 4, 1995, revising the requirements for granting security clearances to government civilian and military employees for access to classified information:

Executive Order

Access to Classified Information

The national interest requires that certain information be maintained in confidence through a system of classification in order to protect our citizens, our democratic institutions, and our participation within the community of nations. The unauthorized disclosure of information classified in the national interest can cause irreparable damage to the national security and loss of human life.

Security policies designed to protect classified information must ensure consistent, cost effective, and efficient protection of our Nation's classified information, while providing fair and equitable treatment to those Americans upon whom we rely to guard our national security.

This order establishes a uniform Federal personnel security program for employees who will be considered for initial or continued access to classified information.

NOW, THEREFORE, by the authority vested in me as President by the Constitution and the laws of the United States of America, it is hereby ordered as follows:

PART 1: Definitions, Access to Classified Information, Financial Disclosure, and Other Items

Sec. 1.1. Definitions. [Omitted.]

Sec. 1.2. Access to Classified Information. (a) No employee shall be granted access to classified information unless that employee has been determined to be eligible in accordance with this order and to possess a need-to-know.

(b) Agency heads shall be responsible for establishing and maintaining an effective program to ensure that access to classified information by each employee is clearly consistent with the interests of the national security.

(c) Employees shall not be granted access to classified information unless they:

(1) have been determined to be eligible for access under section 3.1 of this order by agency heads or designated officials based upon a favorable adjudication of an appropriate investigation of the employee's background;

(2) have a demonstrated need-to-know; and

(d) All employees shall be subject to investigation by an appropriate government authority prior to being granted access to classified information and at any time during the period of access to ascertain whether they continue to meet the requirements for access.

(e)(1) All employees granted access to classified information shall be required as a condition of such access to provide to the employing agency written consent permitting access by an authorized investigative agency, for such time as access to classified information is maintained and for a period of 3 years thereafter, to:

(A) relevant financial records that are maintained by a financial institution as defined in 31 U.S.C. 5312(a) or by a holding company as defined in section 1101(6) of the Right to Financial Privacy Act of 1978 (12 U.S.C. 3401);

(B) consumer reports pertaining to the employee under the Fair Credit Reporting Act (15 U.S.C. 1681a); and

(C) records maintained by commercial entities within the United States pertaining to any travel by the employee outside the United States.

(2) Information may be requested pursuant to employee consent under this section where:

(A) there are reasonable grounds to believe, based on credible information, that the employee or former employee is, or may be, disclosing classified information in an unauthorized manner to a foreign power or agent of a foreign power;

(B) information the employing agency deems credible indicates the employee or former employee has incurred excessive indebtedness or has acquired a level of affluence that cannot be explained by other information; or

(C) circumstances indicate the employee or former employee had the capability and opportunity to disclose classified information that is known to have been lost or compromised to a foreign power or an agent of a foreign power.

(3) Nothing in this section shall be construed to affect the authority of an investigating agency to obtain information pursuant to the Right to Financial Privacy Act, the Fair Credit Reporting Act or any other applicable law.

Sec. 1.3. Financial Disclosure. (a) Not later than 180 days after the effective date of this order, the head of each agency that originates, handles, transmits, or possesses classified information shall designate each employee, by position or category where possible, who has a regular need for access to classified information that, in the discretion of the agency head, would reveal:

(1) the identity of covert agents as defined in the Intelligence Identities Protection Act of 1982 (50 U.S.C. 421);

(2) technical or specialized national intelligence collection and processing systems that, if disclosed in an unauthorized manner, would substantially negate or impair the effectiveness of the system;

(3) the details of:

(A) the nature, contents, algorithm, preparation, or use of any code, cipher, or cryptographic system or;

(B) the design, construction, functioning, maintenance, or repair of any cryptographic equipment; but not including information concerning the use of cryptographic equipment and services;

(4) particularly sensitive special access programs, the disclosure of which would substantially negate or impair the effectiveness of the information or activity involved; or

(5) especially sensitive nuclear weapons design information (but only for those positions that have been certified as being of a high degree of importance or sensitivity, as described in section 145(f) of the Atomic Energy Act of 1954, as amended).

(b) An employee may not be granted access, or hold a position designated as requiring access, to information described in subsection (a) unless, as a condition of access to such information, the employee:

(1) files with the head of the agency a financial disclosure report, including information with respect to the spouse and dependent children of the employee, as part of all background investigations or reinvestigations;

(2) is subject to annual financial disclosure requirements, if selected by the agency head; and

(3) files relevant information concerning foreign travel, as determined by the Security Policy Board.

(c) Not later than 180 days after the effective date of this order, the Security Policy Board shall develop procedures for the implementation of this section, including a standard financial disclosure form for use by employees under subsection (b) of this section, and agency heads shall identify certain employees, by position or category, who are subject to annual financial disclosure.

Sec. 1.4. Use of Automated Financial Record Data Bases. As part of all investigations and reinvestigations described in section 1.2(d) of this order, agencies may request the Department of the Treasury, under terms and conditions prescribed by the Secretary of the Treasury, to search automated data bases consisting of reports of currency transactions by financial institutions, international transportation of currency or monetary instruments, foreign bank and financial accounts, transactions under $10,000 that are reported as possible money laundering violations, and records of foreign travel.

Sec. 1.5. Employee Education and Assistance. The head of each agency that grants access to classified information shall establish a program for employees with access to classified information to: (a) educate employees about individual responsibilities under this order; and

(b) inform employees about guidance and assistance available concerning issues that may affect their eligibility for access to classified information, including sources of assistance for employees who have questions or concerns about financial matters, mental health, or substance abuse.

Part 2: Access Eligibility Policy and Procedure

Sec. 2.1. Eligibility Determinations. (a) Determinations of eligibility for access to classified information shall be based on criteria established under this order. Such determinations are separate from suitability determinations with respect to the hiring or retention of persons for employment by the government or any other personnel actions.

(b) The number of employees that each agency determines are eligible for access to classified information shall be kept to the minimum required for the conduct of agency functions.

(1) Eligibility for access to classified information shall not be requested or granted solely to permit entry to, or ease of movement within, controlled areas when the employee has no need for access and access to classified information may reasonably be prevented. Where circumstances indicate employees may be inadvertently exposed to classified information in the course of their duties, agencies are authorized to grant or deny, in their discretion, facility access approvals to such employees based on an appropriate level of investigation as determined by each agency.

(2) Except in agencies where eligibility for access is a mandatory condition of employment, eligibility for access to classified information shall only be requested or granted based on a demonstrated, foreseeable need

for access. Requesting or approving eligibility in excess of actual requirements is prohibited.

(3) Eligibility for access to classified information may be granted where
there is a temporary need for access, such as one-time participation in a
classified project, provided the investigative standards established under
this order have been satisfied. In such cases, a fixed date or event for expi-
ration shall be identified and access to classified information shall be limited to information related to the particular project or assignment.

(4) Access to classified information shall be terminated when an
employee no longer has a need for access.

Sec. 2.2. Level of Access Approval. (a) The level at which an access
approval is granted for an employee shall be limited, and relate directly, to
the level of classified information for which there is a need for access. Eligibility for access to a higher level of classified information includes eligibility
for access to information classified at a lower level.

(b) Access to classified information relating to a special access program
shall be granted in accordance with procedures established by the head of
the agency that created the program or, for programs pertaining to intelligence activities (including special activities but not including military operational, strategic, and tactical programs) or intelligence sources and methods,
by the Director of Central Intelligence. To the extent possible and consistent
with the national security interests of the United States, such procedures
shall be consistent with the standards and procedures established by and
under this order.

Sec. 2.3. Temporary Access to Higher Levels. (a) An employee who
has been determined to be eligible for access to classified information based
on favorable adjudication of a completed investigation may be granted temporary access to a higher level where security personnel authorized by the
agency head to make access eligibility determinations find that such access:

(1) is necessary to meet operational or contractual exigencies not
expected to be of a recurring nature;

(2) will not exceed 180 days; and

(3) is limited to specific, identifiable information that is made the subject of a written access record.

(b) Where the access granted under subsection (a) of this section involves
another agency's classified information, that agency must concur before
access to its information is granted.

*Sec. 2.4. Reciprocal Acceptance of Access Eligibility Determina-
tions.* (a) Except when an agency has substantial information indicating that
an employee may not satisfy the standards in section 3.1 of this order, background investigations and eligibility determinations conducted under this
order shall be mutually and reciprocally accepted by all agencies.

(b) Except where there is substantial information indicating that the
employee may not satisfy the standards in section 3.1 of this order, an
employee with existing access to a special access program shall not be
denied eligibility for access to another special access program at the same

sensitivity level as determined personally by the agency head or deputy agency head, or have an existing access eligibility readjudicated, so long as the employee has a need for access to the information involved.

(c) This section shall not preclude agency heads from establishing additional, but not duplicative, investigative or adjudicative procedures for a special access program or for candidates for detail or assignment to their agencies, where such procedures are required in exceptional circumstances to protect the national security.

(d) Where temporary eligibility for access is granted under sections 2.3 or 3.3 of this order or where the determination of eligibility for access is conditional, the fact of such temporary or conditional access shall be conveyed to any other agency that considers affording the employee access to its information.

Sec. 2.5. Specific Access Requirement. (a) Employees who have been determined to be eligible for access to classified information shall be given access to classified information only where there is a need-to-know that information.

(b) It is the responsibility of employees who are authorized holders of classified information to verify that a prospective recipient's eligibility for access has been granted by an authorized agency official and to ensure that a need-to-know exists prior to allowing such access, and to challenge requests for access that do not appear well-founded.

Sec. 2.6. Access by Non-United States Citizens. (a) Where there are compelling reasons in furtherance of an agency mission, immigrant alien and foreign national employees who possess a special expertise may, in the discretion of the agency, be granted limited access to classified information only for specific programs, projects, contracts, licenses, certificates, or grants for which there is a need for access. Such individuals shall not be eligible for access to any greater level of classified information than the United States Government has determined may be releasable to the country of which the subject is currently a citizen, and such limited access may be approved only if the prior 10 years of the subject's life can be appropriately investigated. If there are any doubts concerning granting access, additional lawful investigative procedures shall be fully pursued.

(b) Exceptions to these requirements may be permitted only by the agency head or the senior agency official designated under section 6.1 of this order to further substantial national security interests.

Part 3: Access Eligibility Standards

Sec. 3.1. Standards. (a) No employee shall be deemed to be eligible for access to classified information merely by reason of Federal service or contracting, licensee, certificate holder, or grantee status, or as a matter of right or privilege, or as a result of any particular title, rank, position, or affiliation.

(b) Except as provided in sections 2.6 and 3.3 of this order, eligibility for access to classified information shall be granted only to employees who are United States citizens for whom an appropriate investigation has been completed and whose personal and professional history affirmatively indicates loyalty to the United States, strength of character, trustworthiness, honesty, reliability, discretion, and sound judgment, as well as freedom from conflicting allegiances and potential for coercion, and willingness and ability to abide by regulations governing the use, handling, and protection of classified information. A determination of eligibility for access to such information is a discretionary security decision based on judgments by appropriately trained adjudicative personnel. Eligibility shall be granted only where facts and circumstances indicate access to classified information is clearly consistent with the national security interests of the United States, and any doubt shall be resolved in favor of the national security.

(c) The United States Government does not discriminate on the basis of race, color, religion, sex, national origin, disability, or sexual orientation in granting access to classified information.

(d) In determining eligibility for access under this order, agencies may investigate and consider any matter that relates to the determination of whether access is clearly consistent with the interests of national security. No inference concerning the standards in this section may be raised solely on the basis of the sexual orientation of the employee.

(e) No negative inference concerning the standards in this section may be raised solely on the basis of mental health counseling. Such counseling can be a positive factor in eligibility determinations. However, mental health counseling, where relevant to the adjudication of access to classified information, may justify further inquiry to determine whether the standards of subsection (b) of this section are satisfied, and mental health may be considered where it directly relates to those standards.

(f) Not later than 180 days after the effective date of this order, the Security Policy Board shall develop a common set of adjudicative guidelines for determining eligibility for access to classified information, including access to special access programs.

Sec. 3.2. Basis for Eligibility Approval. (a) Eligibility determinations for access to classified information shall be based on information concerning the applicant or employee that is acquired through the investigation conducted pursuant to this order or otherwise available to security officials and shall be made part of the applicant's or employee's security record. Applicants or employees shall be required to provide relevant information pertaining to their background and character for use in investigating and adjudicating their eligibility for access.

(b) Not later than 180 days after the effective date of this order, the Security Policy Board shall develop a common set of investigative standards for background investigations for access to classified information. These standards may vary for the various levels of access.

(c) Nothing in this order shall prohibit an agency from utilizing any lawful investigative procedure in addition to the investigative requirements set forth in this order and its implementing regulations to resolve issues that may arise during the course of a background investigation or reinvestigation.

540

Sec. 3.3. Special Circumstances. (a) In exceptional circumstances where official functions must be performed prior to the completion of the investigative and adjudication process, temporary eligibility for access to classified information may be granted to an employee while the initial-investigation is underway. When such eligibility is granted, the initial investigation shall be expedited.

(1) Temporary eligibility for access under this section shall include a justification, and the employee must be notified in writing that further access is expressly conditioned on the favorable completion of the investigation and issuance of an access eligibility approval. Access will be immediately terminated, along with any assignment requiring an access eligibility approval, if such approval is not granted.

(2) Temporary eligibility for access may be granted only by security personnel authorized by the agency head to make access eligibility determinations and shall be based on minimum investigative standards developed by the Security Policy Board not later than 180 days after the effective date of this order.

(3) Temporary eligibility for access may be granted only to particular, identified categories of classified information necessary to perform the lawful and authorized functions that are the basis for the granting of temporary access.

(b) Nothing in subsection (a) shall be construed as altering the authority of an agency head to waive requirements for granting access to classified information pursuant to statutory authority.

(c) Where access has been terminated under section 2.1(b)(4) of this order and a new need for access arises, access eligibility up to the same level shall be reapproved without further investigation as to employees who were determined to be eligible based on a favorable adjudication of an investigation completed within the prior 5 years, provided they have remained employed by the same employer during the period in question, the employee certifies in writing that there has been no change in the relevant information provided by the employee for the last background investigation, and there is no information that would tend to indicate the employee may no longer satisfy the standards established by this order for access to classified information.

(d) Access eligibility shall be reapproved for individuals who were determined to be eligible based on a favorable adjudication of an investigation completed within the prior 5 years and who have been retired or otherwise separated from United States Government employment for not more than 2 years; provided there is no indication the individual may no longer satisfy the standards of this order, the individual certifies in writing that there has been no change in the relevant information provided by the individual for the last background investigation, and an appropriate record check reveals no unfavorable information.

Sec. 3.4. Reinvestigation Requirements. (a) Because circumstances and characteristics may change dramatically over time and thereby alter the eligibility of employees for continued access to classified information, reinvestigations shall be conducted with the same priority and care as initial investigations.

(b) Employees who are eligible for access to classified information shall be the subject of periodic reinvestigations and may also be reinvestigated if, at any time, there is reason to believe that they may no longer meet the standards for access established in this order.

(c) Not later than 180 days after the effective date of this order, the Security Policy Board shall develop a common set of reinvestigative standards, including the frequency of reinvestigations.

Part 4: Investigations for Foreign Governments

Sec. 4. Authority. Agencies that conduct background investigations, including the Federal Bureau of Investigation and the Department of State, are authorized to conduct personnel security investigations in the United States when requested by a foreign government as part of its own personnel security program and with the consent of the individual.

Part 5: Review of Access Determinations

Sec. 5.1. Determinations of Need for Access. A determination under section 2.1(b)(4) of this order that an employee does not have, or no longer has, a need for access is a discretionary determination and shall be conclusive.

Sec. 5.2. Review Proceedings for Denials or Revocations of Eligibility for Access. (a) Applicants and employees who are determined to not meet the standards for access to classified information established in section 3.1 of this order shall be:

(1) provided as comprehensive and detailed a written explanation of the basis for that conclusion as the national security interests of the United States and other applicable law permit;

(2) provided within 30 days, upon request and to the extent the documents would be provided if requested under the Freedom of Information Act (5 U.S.C. 552) or the Privacy Act (3 U.S.C. 552a), as applicable, any documents, records, and reports upon which a denial or revocation is based;

(3) informed of their right to be represented by counsel or other representative at their own expense; to request any documents, records, and reports as described in section 5.2(a)(2) upon which a denial or revocation is based; and to request the entire investigative file, as permitted by the national security and other applicable law, which, if requested, shall be promptly provided prior to the time set for a written reply;

(4) provided a reasonable opportunity to reply in writing to, and to request a review of, the determination;

(5) provided written notice of and reasons for the results of the review, the identity of the deciding authority, and written notice of the right to appeal;

(6) provided an opportunity to appeal in writing to a high level panel, appointed by the agency head, which shall be comprised of at least three

members, two of whom shall be selected from outside the security field. Decisions of the panel shall be in writing, and final except as provided in subsection (b) of this section; and

(7) provided an opportunity to appear personally and to present relevant documents, materials, and information at some point in the process before an adjudicative or other authority, other than the investigating entity, as determined by the agency head. A written summary or recording of such appearance shall be made part of the applicant's or employee's security record, unless such appearance occurs in the presence of the appeals panel described in subsection (a) (6) of this section.

(b) Nothing in this section shall prohibit an agency head from personally exercising the appeal authority in subsection (a) (6) of this section based upon recommendations from an appeals panel. In such case, the decision of the agency head shall be final.

(c) Agency heads shall promulgate regulations to implement this section and, at their sole discretion and as resources and national security considerations permit, may provide additional review proceedings beyond those required by subsection (a) of this section. This section does not require additional proceedings, however, and creates no procedural or substantive rights.

(d) When the head of an agency or principal deputy personally certifies that a procedure set forth in this section cannot be made available in a particular case without damaging the national security interests of the United States by revealing classified information, the particular procedure shall not be made available. This certification shall be conclusive.

(e) This section shall not be deemed to limit or affect the responsibility and power of an agency head pursuant to any law or other Executive order to deny or terminate access to classified information in the interests of national security. The power and responsibility to deny or terminate access to classified information pursuant to any law or other Executive order may be exercised only where the agency head determines that the procedures prescribed in subsection (a) of this section cannot be invoked in a manner that is consistent with national security. This determination shall be conclusive.

(f)(1) This section shall not be deemed to limit or affect the responsibility and power of an agency head to make determinations of suitability for employment.

(2) Nothing in this section shall require that an agency provide the procedures prescribed in subsection (a) of this section to an applicant where a conditional offer of employment is withdrawn for reasons of suitability or any other reason other than denial of eligibility for access to classified information;

(3) A suitability determination shall not be used for the purpose of denying an applicant or employee the review proceedings of this section where there has been a denial or revocation of eligibility for access to classified information.

Part 6: Implementation

Sec. 6.1. Agency Implementing Responsibilities. Heads of agencies that grant employees access to classified information shall: (a) designate a senior agency official to direct and administer the agency's personnel security program established by this order. All such programs shall include active oversight and continuing security education and awareness programs to ensure effective implementation of this order;

(b) cooperate, under the guidance of the Security Policy Board, with other agencies to achieve practical, consistent, and effective adjudicative training and guidelines; and

(c) conduct periodic evaluations of the agency's implementation and administration of this order. Including the implementation of section 1.3 (a) of this order. Copies of each report shall be provided to the Security Policy Board.

Sec. 6.2. Employee Responsibilities. (a) Employees who are granted eligibility for access to classified information shall:

(1) protect classified information in their custody from unauthorized disclosure;

(2) report all contacts with persons, including foreign nationals, who seek in any way to obtain unauthorized access to classified information;

(3) report all violations of security regulations to the appropriate security officials; and

(4) comply with all other security requirements set forth in this order and its implementing regulations.

(b) Employees are encouraged and expected to report any information that raises doubts as to whether another employee's continued eligibility for access to classified information is clearly consistent with the national security.

Sec. 6.3. Security Policy Board Responsibilities and Implementation. (a) With respect to actions taken by the Security Policy Board pursuant to sections 1.3(c), 3.1(f), 3.2(b), 3.3(a) (2), and 3.4(c) of this order, the Security Policy Board shall make recommendations to the President through the Assistant to the President for National Security Affairs for implementation.

(b) Any guidelines, standards, or procedures developed by the Security Policy Board pursuant to this order shall be consistent with those guidelines issued by the Federal Bureau of Investigation in March 1994 on Background Investigations Policy/Guidelines Regarding Sexual Orientation.

(c) In carrying out its responsibilities under this order, the Security Policy Board shall consult where appropriate with the Overseas Security Policy Board. In carrying out its responsibilities under section 1.3(c) of this order, the Security Policy Board shall obtain the concurrence of the Director of the Office of Management and Budget.

Sec. 6.4. Sanctions. Employees shall be subject to appropriate sanctions if they knowingly and willfully grant eligibility for, or allow access to, classified information in violation of this order or its implementing regulations. Sanctions may include reprimand, suspension without pay, removal, and other actions in accordance with applicable law and agency regulations. . . .

WILLIAM J. CLINTON
The White House
August 2, 1995

DIRECTIVE ON RELIGION IN PUBLIC SCHOOLS
August 10, 1995

Seeking to diffuse a conservative Republican push for a constitutional amendment permitting prayer and other religious exercises in public schools, the Clinton administration sent an advisory August 10 to the superintendents of the nation's 15,000 public school districts setting out what forms of religious expression were permissible in the schools under current law. The guidelines, which did not carry the force of law, had been requested by President Bill Clinton in a July 12 speech, in which he said that much of the confusion about religion in public schools was caused by widespread misunderstandings and misperceptions about what was and was not allowed.

"It appears that some school officials, teachers, and parents have assumed that religious expression of any type is either inappropriate, or forbidden altogether, in public schools," Clinton told students and parents at James Madison High School in Vienna, Virginia. "As our courts have reaffirmed, however, nothing in the First Amendment converts our public schools into religion-free zones, or requires all religious expression to be left behind at the schoolhouse door."

Clinton and the Republicans were responding to the many stories, circulated in the media and religious rights organizations, of school administrators forbidding students any private religious expression whatsoever in schools, including saying grace in school cafeterias, reading the Bible during recess, and discussing religion with their classmates, all of which were permissible forms of the private religious speech, Clinton said.

A Constitutional Tangle

The First Amendment to the Constitution forbids Congress from making any law "respecting an establishment of religion, or prohibiting the free exercise thereof...." Despite the Establishment Clause, Bible readings, devotional exercises, and prayer were common in public school classrooms across the United States until the Supreme Court handed down two deci-

sions in the early 1960s. In Engle v. Vitale *(1962), the Court held that the New York State Board of Regents had violated the Establishment Clause by recommending that school districts adopt a specific nondenominational prayer to be recited in public schools. The court found that such government sponsorship might have a coercive effect on students, even if they or their families were opposed to such a prayer.*

One year later, in the case of School District of Abington Township v. Schempp *(1963), the Court ruled that government-sponsored Bible readings and recitation of the Lord's Prayer in public schools were violations of the Establishment Clause. The Court found that such exercises infringed on the religious rights of some students and, in some other instances, could tend to advance certain religions over others.*

In subsequent years several cases challenging prayer in the schools and at graduation ceremonies were brought to the Court. The outcomes did not always seem consistent, leading to some confusion about what the law allowed. For example, in the 1992 case of Lee v. Weisman *the Court declared official prayer at high school graduation ceremonies to be unconstitutional. In 1995 it dismissed as moot a lower court's ruling that student-initiated prayers at graduation ceremonies were unconstitutional. That ruling conflicted with a ruling from another appeals court that permitted student-initiated prayer at a public school graduation; the Supreme Court had refused to review that decision.*

Clinton's Directive

Clinton ordered the Department of Education to circulate the memorandum on religion in the schools to help school administrators, students, parents, religious organizations, and public officials who were grappling with this question. The guidelines, which formed the core of Clinton's speech, relied heavily on a paper drafted by a coalition of several mainstream religious organizations, including the American Jewish Congress and the Baptist Joint Committee, and interest groups such as Americans United for Separation of Church and State.

The guidelines said that students in informal settings such as hallways and cafeterias could pray and engage in religious discussion that was not disruptive, but that no student should be compelled to participate in prayer or religious discussion. Under the guidelines, students may also express their religious beliefs in homework, artwork, and other school assignments "free of discrimination based on the religious content of their submissions." Students should also be permitted to display religious messages on their clothing to the same extent that they are permitted to display political or other comparable messages. Students may not be prohibited from wearing particular clothing, such as yarmulkes, as part of their religious practice.

The guidelines also affirmed that, under the Equal Access Act, student religious groups have the same right of access to school facilities as other comparable student groups, even if their meetings include a prayer service, Bible reading, or other devotional exercise.

*In his speech Clinton indicated that he was in general agreement with
the Supreme Court's rulings on school prayer. He recalled that his school
days commonly began with a prayer, but he acknowledged that he gave little thought at the time to whether Catholics and Jews in his class might
have been discomforted by a Protestant prayer. "I do believe that on balance, the direction of the First Amendment has been very good for America and has made us the most religious country in the world by keeping the
government out of creating religion, supporting particular religions . . .
and [from] interfering with other people's religious practices," he said.*

Push for a Prayer Amendment

*While some supporters of a constitutional amendment to permit school
prayer praised the president's speech, most thought the guidelines would
not solve the problem. "I'm just skeptical that the guidelines, which basically amount to a letter being sent out by the Secretary of Education, will
change the environment much," said Rep. Charles T. Canady (R-Fla.).*

*Actually passing a school prayer amendment was likely to be an uphill
road. Most Democrats and many Republicans were opposed to such an
amendment. A proposed amendment was introduced in the House in
November, but no companion legislation was offered in the Senate. If history repeats itself, supporters of a prayer amendment could not be encouraged. A prayer amendment fell short of the two-thirds vote necessary for
passage three times in the past—in 1966 and 1984 in the Senate and in
1971 in the House.*

*Following is the text of the memorandum the Department of
Education sent to all public school districts on August 10, 1995,
setting out guidelines on permissible religious expression in
public schools:*

Nothing in the First Amendment converts our public schools into religion-free
zones, or requires all religious expression to be left behind at the schoolhouse
door. While the government may not use schools to coerce the consciences of
our students, or to convey official endorsement of religion, the public schools
also may not discriminate against private religious expression during the
school day.

Religion is too important in our history and our heritage for us to keep it out
of our schools. . . [I]t shouldn't be demanded, but as long as it is not sponsored
by school officials and doesn't interfere with other children's rights, it mustn't
be denied.

President Clinton
July 12, 1995

Dear Superintendent:

On July 12th, President Clinton directed the Secretary of Education, in
consultation with the Attorney General, to provide every school district in

America with a statement of principles addressing the extent to which religious expression and activity are permitted in our public schools. In response to the President's request, I am sending to you this statement of principles.

In the last two years, I have visited with many educators, parents, students, and religious leaders. I have become increasingly aware of the real need to find a new common ground in the growing and, at times, divisive debate about religion in our public schools. President Clinton and I hope that this information will provide useful guidance to educators, parents, and students in defining the proper place for religious expression and religious freedom in our public schools.

As the President explained, the First Amendment imposes two basic and equally important obligations on public school officials in their dealings with religion. First, schools may not forbid students acting on their own from expressing their personal religious views or beliefs solely because they are of a religious nature. Schools may not discriminate against private religious expression by students, but must instead give students the same right to engage in religious activity and discussion as they have to engage in other comparable activity. Generally, this means that students may pray in a nondisruptive manner during the school day when they are not engaged in school activities and instruction, subject to the same rules of order as apply to other student speech.

At the same time, schools may not endorse religious activity or doctrine, nor may they coerce participation in religious activity. Among other things, of course, school administrators and teachers may not organize or encourage prayer exercises in the classroom. And the right of religious expression in school does not include the right to have a "captive audience" listen, or to compel other students to participate. School officials should not permit student religious speech to turn into religious harassment aimed at a student or a small group of students. Students do not have the right to make repeated invitations to other students to participate in religious activity in the face of a request to stop.

The statement of principles set forth below derives from the First Amendment. Implementation of these principles, of course, will depend on specific factual contexts and will require careful consideration in particular cases.

Although most schools have been implementing these principles already, some problems have arisen where people are unaware of, or do not understand, these obligations. It is my sincere hope that these principles will help to end much of the confusion regarding religious expression in public schools and that they can provide a basis for school officials, teachers, parents, and students to work together to find common ground—helping us to get on with the important work of education. I want to recognize again the efforts of religious and other civic groups who came together earlier this year to issue a statement of current law on religion in the public schools, from which we drew heavily in developing these principles.

I encourage you to share this information widely and in the most appropriate manner with your school community. Accept my sincere thanks for your continuing work on behalf of all of America's children.

Sincerely,
Richard W. Riley
U.S. Secretary of Education

Religious Expression in Public Schools

Student prayer and religious discussion: The Establishment Clause of the First Amendment does not prohibit purely private religious speech by students. Students therefore have the same right to engage in individual or group prayer and religious discussion during the school day as they do to engage in other comparable activity. For example, students may read their Bibles or other scriptures, say grace before meals, and pray before tests to the same extent they may engage in comparable non-disruptive activities. Local school authorities possess substantial discretion to impose rules of order and other pedagogical restrictions on student activities, but they may not structure or administer such rules to discriminate against religious activity or speech.

Generally, students may pray in a non-disruptive manner when not engaged in school activities or instruction, and subject to the rules that normally pertain in the applicable setting. Specifically, students in informal settings, such as cafeterias and hallways, may pray and discuss their religious views with each other, subject to the same rules of order as apply to other student activities and speech. Students may also speak to, and attempt to persuade, their peers about religious topics just as they do with regard to political topics. School officials, however, should intercede to stop student speech that constitutes harassment aimed at a student or a group of students.

Students may also participate in before or after school events with religious content, such as "see you at the flag pole" gatherings, on the same terms as they may participate in other noncurriculum activities on school premises. School officials may neither discourage nor encourage participation in such an event.

The right to engage in voluntary prayer or religious discussion free from discrimination does not include the right to have a captive audience listen, or to compel other students to participate. Teachers and school administrators should ensure that no student is in any way coerced to participate in religious activity.

Graduation prayer and baccalaureates: Under current Supreme Court decisions, school officials may not mandate or organize prayer at graduation, nor organize religious baccalaureate ceremonies. If a school generally opens its facilities to private groups, it must make its facilities available on the same terms to organizers of privately sponsored religious baccalaureate services. A school may not extend preferential treatment to baccalaureate ceremonies and may in some instances be obliged to disclaim official endorsement of such ceremonies.

Official neutrality regarding religious activity: Teachers and school administrators, when acting in those capacities, are representatives of the state and are prohibited by the establishment clause from soliciting or encouraging religious activity, and from participating in such activity with students. Teachers and administrators also are prohibited from discouraging activity because of its religious content, and from soliciting or encouraging antireligious activity.

Teaching about religion: Public schools may not provide religious instruction, but they may teach *about* religion, including the Bible or other scripture: the history of religion, comparative religion, the Bible (or other scripture)-as-literature, and the role of religion in the history of the United States and other countries all are permissible public school subjects. Similarly, it is permissible to consider religious influences on art, music, literature, and social studies. Although public schools may teach about religious holidays, including their religious aspects, and may celebrate the secular aspects of holidays, schools may not observe holidays as religious events or promote such observance by students.

Student assignments: Students may express their beliefs about religion in the form of homework, artwork, and other written and oral assignments free of discrimination based on the religious content of their submissions. Such home and classroom work should be judged by ordinary academic standards of substance and relevance, and against other legitimate pedagogical concerns identified by the school.

Religious literature: Students have a right to distribute religious literature to their schoolmates on the same terms as they are permitted to distribute other literature that is unrelated to school curriculum or activities. Schools may impose the same reasonable time, place, and manner or other constitutional restrictions on distribution of religious literature as they do on nonschool literature generally, but they may not single out religious literature for special regulation.

Religious excusals: Subject to applicable State laws, schools enjoy substantial discretion to excuse individual students from lessons that are objectionable to the student or the student's parents on religious or other conscientious grounds. School officials may neither encourage nor discourage students from availing themselves of an excusal option. Under the Religious Freedom Restoration Act, if it is proved that particular lessons substantially burden a student's free exercise of religion and if the school cannot prove a compelling interest in requiring attendance, the school would be legally required to excuse the student.

Released time: Subject to applicable State laws, schools have the discretion to dismiss students to off-premises religious instruction, provided that schools do not encourage or discourage participation or penalize those who do not attend. Schools may not allow religious instruction by outsiders on school premises during the school day.

Teaching values: Though schools must be neutral with respect to religion, they may play an active role with respect to teaching civic values and virtue, and the moral code that holds us together as a community. The fact that some of these values are held also by religions does not make it unlawful to teach them in school.

Student garb: Students may display religious messages on items of clothing to the same extent that they are permitted to display other comparable messages. Religious messages may not be singled out for suppression, but rather are subject to the same rules as generally apply to comparable messages. When wearing particular attire, such as yarmulkes and head scarves, during the school day is part of students' religious practice, under the Religious Freedom Restoration Act schools generally may not prohibit the wearing of such items.

The Equal Access Act

The Equal Access Act is designed to ensure that, consistent with the First Amendment, student religious activities are accorded the same access to public school facilities as are student secular activities. Based on decisions of the Federal courts, as well as its interpretations of the Act, the Department of Justice has advised that the Act should be interpreted as providing, among other things, that:

General provisions: Student religious groups at public secondary schools have the same right of access to school facilities as is enjoyed by other comparable student groups. Under the Equal Access Act, a school receiving Federal funds that allows one or more student noncurriculum-related clubs to meet on its premises during noninstructional time may not refuse access to student religious groups.

Prayer services and worship exercises covered: A meeting, as defined and protected by the Equal Access Act, may include a prayer service, Bible reading, or other worship exercise.

Equal access to means of publicizing meetings: A school receiving Federal funds must allow student groups meeting under the Act to use the school media—including the public address system, the school newspaper, and the school bulletin board—to announce their meetings on the same terms as other noncurriculum-related student groups are allowed to use the school media. Any policy concerning the use of school media must be applied to all noncurriculum-related student groups in a nondiscriminatory matter. Schools, however, may inform students that certain groups are not school sponsored.

Lunch-time and recess covered: A school creates a limited open forum under the Equal Access Act, triggering equal access rights for religious groups, when it allows students to meet during their lunch periods or other noninstructional time during the school day, as well as when it allows students to meet before and after the school day.

CLINTON ON THE COMPREHENSIVE
TEST BAN TREATY
August 11, 1995

President Bill Clinton announced August 11 that the United States would support an international treaty banning all nuclear weapons tests. Clinton's announcement appeared to break an impasse that had held up agreement on such a treaty, which had been in negotiation for years in Geneva under United Nations sponsorship. Negotiators hoped to conclude the treaty in 1996.

The president's announcement came almost exactly fifty years after the United States dropped the first atomic bomb on Hiroshima. A senior White House aide insisted, however, that the timing was coincidental.

In a related development, the 1995 Nobel Peace Prize was awarded on October 13 to Joseph Rotblat, a British physicist who helped develop nuclear weapons in the 1940s and later campaigned for nuclear disarmament. He shared the prize with the Pugwash Conference on Science and World Affairs, an antinuclear organization he formed with Albert Einstein and Bertrand Russell.

The Norwegian Nobel committee said it awarded the prize to Rotblat to recognize his efforts to "diminish the part played by nuclear arms in international politics and in the longer run to eliminate such arms." Nobel officials also said they hoped, with the prize, to pressure France and China into halting their nuclear testing.

Steps to Limit Testing

The United States and the Soviet Union agreed to a limited ban on nuclear testing in 1963; it was the first arms control agreement of the nuclear age, and it was a major step toward reducing tension between the two superpowers. That treaty barred nuclear tests in the atmosphere.

In 1974 the Nixon administration negotiated a treaty with the Soviet Union prohibiting underground nuclear tests with an explosive power greater than 150,000 tons of TNT. Called the Threshold Test Ban Treaty, it went unratified until 1990, when U.S. and Soviet negotiators tightened some of the provisions and the Senate gave its approval.

In the meantime, the United Nations convened negotiations to broaden those agreements into a comprehensive treaty banning all nuclear weapons tests worldwide. Those negotiations produced agreement on numerous noncontroversial items but bogged down on the basic issue of banning all nuclear tests, no matter what size. None of the five countries that acknowledged having nuclear weapons arsenals—Britain, China, France, the Soviet Union, and the United States—wanted to give up the right to test either existing weapons or new ones before they went into production.

After the collapse of the Soviet Union in 1991, the new Russian government declared a moratorium on nuclear testing, and Congress in 1992 imposed a testing moratorium through June 1993. Once in office, Clinton extended that moratorium three times, with the latest extension effective through September 30, 1996. The U.S. moratorium effectively applied to Britain, which had been conducting its nuclear tests in Nevada. Only China and France continued their testing programs. The French testing was particularly controversial because it involved explosions at a tiny island in the South Pacific—explosions that surrounding nations said caused environmental problems and discouraged tourism, a major part of the region's economy.

Discussion of a test ban treaty picked up in late 1994 and early 1995 during the concluding stages of UN-sponsored negotiations on extending a related treaty: the Treaty on Non-Proliferation of Nuclear Weapons. That treaty, aimed at reducing the spread of nuclear weapons, was due to expire in 1995 unless it was extended.

The United States and the other nuclear weapons states wanted a permanent extension of the nonproliferation treaty, but other countries were reluctant to take such a step unless the nuclear weapons states agreed to a ban on weapons testing. Bowing to that pressure, the nuclear powers agreed to complete negotiations on the weapons testing treaty in 1996. That step cleared the way for final agreement on extending the nonproliferation treaty. (Nonproliferation treaty, p. 239)

Low-Level Testing

The final stumbling block toward agreement on a comprehensive test ban treaty was the issue of "low-level" nuclear tests: those involving explosions equal to only a few hundred tons of TNT. The bomb dropped on Hiroshima was equivalent to about 15,000 tons of TNT; most weapons in the U.S. and Russian nuclear arsenals were hundreds of times more powerful.

Although there was widespread agreement on banning tests of large-scale weapons, military officials in the United States and other countries wanted to have the option to continue smaller tests so they could make sure existing stockpiles remained safe and operable. The U.S. military wanted to be able to test weapons with up to 500 tons of TNT explosive power; the Russian military wanted the right to conduct tests of a few dozen tons.

The Clinton administration tackled the issue in the spring and summer of 1995, with civilian and military officials debating various ways of keeping tabs on the nation's nuclear weapons without testing them.

The solution, at the heart of Clinton's August 11 announcement, was to establish a procedure under which the secretaries of defense and energy would have to certify each year that all critical nuclear weapons systems remained safe and reliable. If these officials could not make such a certification, and if they reported that testing was the only way to determine the status of a weapons system, the president could order a test by invoking a "supreme national interest" clause in the test ban treaty. Robert Bell, special assistant to the president for defense policy, said this provision satisfied military leaders and led them to endorse the president's call for a comprehensive test ban.

Clinton said he did not foresee a need for him or any future president to break the U.S. commitment to the test ban treaty. The reason, he said, was that the United States was developing a "stockpile stewardship program" to monitor the safety and reliability of U.S. weapons with periodic technical check-ups and sophisticated computer simulations.

Bell told reporters it would take about ten years to put this program fully in place, at a cost of "billions of dollars." Clinton, in a written version of his August 11 announcement, said implementing the program would require "sustained bipartisan support" for that decade and longer.

In another move, Clinton acknowledged that current U.S.-intelligence gathering capabilities were not adequate to guarantee detection of very low-yield nuclear tests by other countries. For that reason, he said he was committed to a research and development program to improve the U.S. ability to monitor compliance with the test ban treaty.

Under international pressure to halt its testing entirely, the French government announced on August 10 that it would conclude a series of tests then underway and would embrace a position banning all future tests, no matter how small.

The French and U.S. endorsements of a total test ban left Russia as the only one of the five nuclear weapons states advocating the right to continue low-level tests. China had agreed to a total test ban but wanted to retain the right to conduct "peaceful nuclear explosions," such as those to move massive amounts of earth for a dam project.

Reaction to Clinton's Announcement

Clinton's announcement brought praise from groups that had advocated completion of the test ban treaty. Spurgeon Keeny Jr., president of the Arms Control Association, said the move would "help break the deadlock" in the Geneva treaty negotiations.

Conservative interest groups and their Republican allies in Congress objected strongly to the president's action, saying it would make it more difficult for the United States to ensure the reliability of its nuclear weapons—and thus to deter an enemy nuclear attack. "If there's any doubt about the credibility of our system, it can serve to be an inducement for an enemy to use theirs," said Sen. John Warner (R-Va.), a senior spokesman on military issues.

Even before Clinton's announcement, the Republican-led Senate Armed Services Committee acted to ensure a continued U.S. nuclear weapons testing capability. The committee in June included $50 million in its version of the fiscal 1996 defense authorization bill to prepare for low-yield nuclear tests. That provision remained in the defense bill eventually signed into law, but Congress failed to appropriate the money in a companion Energy Department appropriations bill.

Following is the text of President Bill Clinton's announcement, at the White House on August 11, 1995, of a new United States position supporting a comprehensive ban on all nuclear weapons testing, including "low-yield" tests:

Good afternoon. Today I am announcing my decision to negotiate a true zero yield comprehensive test ban. This is an historic milestone in our efforts to reduce the nuclear threat to build a safer world. The United States will now insist on a test ban that prohibits any nuclear weapons test explosion, or any other nuclear explosion. I am convinced this decision will speed the negotiations so that we can achieve our goal of signing a comprehensive test ban next year.

As a central part of this decision, I am establishing concrete, specific safeguards that define the conditions under which the United States will enter into a comprehensive test ban. These safeguards will strengthen our commitments in the areas of intelligence, monitoring and verification, stockpile stewardship, maintenance of our nuclear laboratories, and test readiness.

They also specify the circumstances under which I would be prepared, in consultation with Congress, to exercise our supreme national interest rights under a comprehensive test ban to conduct necessary testing if the safety or reliability of our nuclear deterrent could no longer be certified.

As a part of this arrangement I am today directing the establishment of a new annual reporting and certification requirement that will ensure that our nuclear weapons remain safe and reliable under a comprehensive test ban.

I appreciate the time, the energy, and the wisdom that the Secretaries of State, Defense, and Energy, the Chairman of the Joint Chiefs of Staff, the Directors of Central Intelligence and the Arms Control and Disarmament Agency have all devoted to the review of this crucial national security issue over the last several months.

American leaders since Presidents Eisenhower and Kennedy have believed a comprehensive test ban would be a major stride toward stopping the proliferation of nuclear weapons. Now, as then, such a treaty would greatly strengthen the security of the United States and nations throughout the world. But now, unlike them, such a treaty is within our reach.

It would build upon the successes we have achieved so far: Securing a permanent extension of the Nuclear Nonproliferation Treaty; freezing North Korea's nuclear program; cutting existing nuclear arsenals by putting the START I Treaty into force; persuading Ukraine, Belarus, and Kazakhstan to give up their nuclear weapons and to reach agreements with Russia that now mean that both our nations no longer target our missiles at each other.

A comprehensive test ban is the right step as we continue pulling back from the nuclear precipice, a precipice which we began to live with 50 years ago this week. It moves us one step closer to the day when no nuclear weapons are detonated anywhere on the face of the earth.

Thank you very much.

BRADLEY ANNOUNCEMENT OF RETIREMENT FROM THE SENATE
August 16, 1995

Most media coverage of Congress in 1995 focused on the new Republican leadership and its drive to dismantle much of the federal government and its social programs. Possibly more important for the long term was another development: the collapse of the political center on Capitol Hill. No single event symbolized that trend more than the August 16 announcement by Sen. Bill Bradley (D-N.J.) that he would retire after three terms. One of the Senate's "glamour" figures because of his basketball stardom, Bradley frequently was mentioned as a possible presidential candidate. Several other important moderate House and Senate members joined Bradley in the exodus, most notably Sen. Sam Nunn (D-Ga.) and Sen. William Cohen (R-Maine).

Moderates Heading for the Exits

The 1995–1996 political season set a record for retirements from Congress. As of late January 1996 thirteen senators and twenty-six House members had announced their retirements; another eleven were expected to leave the House to run for the Senate or governorships.

Many of those departures were predictable, occasioned by age, ill health, or simply a weariness of the hectic life of politics. Several members said it was simply time to move on. Nunn, for example, said he could not bring himself to make another six-year commitment to the Senate. The retirements of Nunn, Bradley, and others were widely viewed as evidence of a deeper trend, that political centrists had lost ground in Congress and were giving up.

Several of the moderates had become deeply frustrated by the increasing partisanship and ideological rigidity in Congress. Bradley was the most direct in voicing his distress, blaming both parties for the fact that "politics is broken" and that Americans had lost faith in the political process.

Sen. John Breaux (D-La.), reacting to Cohen's departure, said it was "symptomatic of the frustration that many moderates are finding in the

Congress. . . . [W]ith the loss of Senator Cohen, it becomes even more difficult to engage a group of moderates in the middle that constitutes a majority."

Cohen and Nunn both had broad influence on a wide range of issues on Capitol Hill. Nunn, who had served as chairman of the Armed Services Committee when Democrats controlled the Senate, arguably was the most influential figure in Washington on military policy.

For decades, as Congress moved fitfully in one direction or another, its course generally was charted by politicians like Nunn and Cohen: pragmatists interested more in getting legislation passed than in scoring ideological or partisan points. Politicians who proudly called themselves liberals or conservatives often came up with the most interesting ideas and were able to put them on the agenda for the future, but political centrists, or moderates, usually were the ones who crafted the compromises needed to get legislation enacted into law.

The list of members of Congress who announced their departures in 1995 and early 1996 included many influential moderates who were not as well known outside their states or Capitol Hill as Bradley, Nunn, or Cohen. Among the Senate retirees were Jim Exon (D-Neb.), Mark O. Hatfield (R-Ore.), J. Bennett Johnston (D-La.), Nancy Landon Kassebaum (R-Kan.), David Pryor (D-Ark.), Paul Simon (D-Ill.), and Alan K. Simpson (R-Wyo.). Among House members were Tom Bevill (D-Ala.), William F. Clinger (R-Pa.), Steve Gunderson (R-Wis.), G. V. "Sonny" Montgomery (D-Miss.), and Pat Williams (D-Mont.).

Also announcing their retirements in 1995 were several members who had made their marks as especially capable or aggressive partisan advocates. Among them were House members Patricia Schroeder (D-Colo.), Gerry E. Studds (D-Mass.), and Robert S. Walker (R-Pa.).

Bradley's Announcement

The media reports on Bradley's retirement announcement generally referred to the senator as "thoughtful." As much as any other, that single word summed up his career in the Senate and the reasons for his departure.

Bradley vaulted into the Senate in 1978 on the strength of his fame as a basketball player. He had been an All-America player for Princeton University, then a Rhodes scholar, then a star forward for the New York Knicks in that team's glory years of the early 1970s. He spent his off-seasons in public service work, such as teaching reading at an Urban League site in Harlem.

As a senator, Bradley seemed to relish delving into weighty policy matters, including many that his colleagues tried to avoid. During the Reagan administration, he became interested in tax policy and was a prime mover behind the massive 1986 tax reform law. Enactment of that law may have marked the height of his legislative influence.

Bradley devoted much of his time to issues that appeared only infrequently on the Senate legislative agenda, such as Third World debt, Western water policy, and race relations. His Senate speeches on those matters often were lengthy and filled with detailed policy prescriptions. Those speeches generated coverage in the New York Times *and won praise from colleagues unwilling to tackle such issues, but they rarely led to any substantive action in Congress. In his retirement announcement, Bradley referred to his fascination with "questions of stature," saying they "always interested me more than issues of marginal gain or questions of blame or strategies for partisan political advantage."*

The heart of Bradley's August 16 announcement was a denunciation of American partisan politics as practiced in the 1990s. Republicans, he said, "are infatuated with the 'magic' of the private sector and reflexively criticize government as the enemy of freedom, and Democrats distrust the market, preach government as the answer to our problems, and prefer the bureaucrat they know to the consumer they can't control. Neither party speaks to people where they live their lives."

Bradley's announcement sparked speculation that he might seek the presidency. In a press conference the following day, he did nothing to squelch that speculation, saying he would not run against President Clinton in the Democratic primaries but was keeping open the option of running as an independent. As the months wore on and it became clear that no groundswell was developing for him, Bradley appeared to drop the notion of an independent presidential bid.

Following is the text of the announcement by Sen. Bill Bradley (D-N.J.) on August 16, 1995, that he would retire from the Senate at the end of his third term:

I have always preferred moving to standing still. As a small forward with the Knicks and then as a U.S. Senator from New Jersey, I've had two of the best jobs in the world. Each kept me on the move, each offered a unique perspective on America, and in each there came a time to go. So today I announce that I am leaving the U.S. Senate at the end of my term and I will not run for re-election.

It's possible to lead from the Senate and to make a difference in people's lives; I've tried to do that. But I've concluded that the U.S. Senate is not the only place to do either of those two things.

I want to thank the people of New Jersey who gave me their votes and their trust. Each of my three senatorial races drew me closer to them and forced me to grow in new and different ways. Election day is democracy's most intimate and important ritual. For all the polling, media and political strategy, I believe there is an essence in any campaign that conveys the bond between the candidate and the electorate on a particular election day, and ultimately, it is the bond that determines the outcome.

For nearly seventeen years my most memorable moments have come from the people I have met. I want to thank those New Jerseyans who told me their stories through their letters and during our encounters along the shore, at commuter terminals, in diners and town meetings, and in countless other settings. It's through the stories of people's lives that I have been moved and that I gained hesitancy about universal solutions. It's from their stories that I saw what a small role government plays in most people's lives and paradoxically it's where I felt the impact of decisions taken in Washington. I have received much more inspiration, insight, and good cheer from them than I could ever say. They reminded me daily of the resilience and power of the human spirit. Their New Jersey stories gave substance and emotion to abstractions about democracy, and each of their stories has now become a part of my story.

I've tried to listen to those I serve while using the judgment that I believe they elected me to exercise. Sometimes they vented their anger and frustration and, just by my listening, they seemed to feel better. I have included young New Jerseyans in my activities as a Senator because democratic participation must burst forth anew in each generation, like flowers in the spring. Unless the seeds are watered there will be no blossoms. I have paid attention to the religious community because I believe the right policy always starts with the right values. I have respected those who disagreed with me, especially when they took the time to write long letters detailing their disagreement.

Flying north from Washington in a small plane as the sun is setting, you reach a point where the sunlight on the Delaware River turns it into a metallic-looking band extending all the way from Trenton to the Water Gap. There lying before you is the New Jersey Peninsula, bordered on the west by the Delaware and on the east by the Atlantic. New Jersey offers unexpected beauty, gives surprising economic opportunity and reveals vital human diversity. I have achieved a greater understanding of the world with all its mixtures of religions and ethnicities by simply representing New Jersey. I have become deeply attached to the Jersey shore, to the mountains of the northwest, the flat farmland of South Jersey and even to certain places on the Garden State Parkway and the Turnpike. These New Jersey places have rooted me and given my life a sense of permanence. It has been an honor to represent our state in the United States Senate.

Over the years, I have been lucky to be assisted by competent staff who took public service seriously and believed they could make a positive difference in the life of our state and our nation. I believe we have.

During my time in the Senate I have tried to balance the private interests and the public interests; the rights of property owners and the needs of society; the big players and the forgotten players. I haven't always pleased everyone but I've tried to be consistent on the big issues such as the economy, race, and America's role in the world. I've also tried to take the long view, often passing up a headline to make sure that when I spoke I knew what I was talking about. Questions of structure, whether on taxes, trade or the environment, always interested me more than issues of marginal gain or questions of blame or strategies for partisan political advantage.

We live in a time when, on a basic level, politics is broken. In growing numbers, people have lost faith in the political process and don't see how it can help their threatened economic circumstances. The political debate has settled into two familiar ruts. The Republicans are infatuated with the "magic" of the private sector and reflexively criticize government as the enemy of freedom, and the Democrats distrust the market, preach government as the answer to our problems, and prefer the bureaucrat they know to the consumer they can't control. Neither party speaks to people where they live their lives. Both have moved away from my own concept of service and my own vision of what America can be. I am saddened on occasion when the media, and politicians themselves, convey that politics is mean, cheap and dirty; that what we hold in common as Americans is somehow less than what we harbor in our hearts and minds for ourselves as individuals. I have never believed that.

As I listen to our current political debate, I feel that among the things missing are the big ambitions that have always guided Americans who settled this continent, ended slavery, won two world wars and saw our liberal democratic ideals triumph around the globe.

I am leaving the U.S. Senate but I am not leaving public life. The quest for a decent life and good wages for all Americans is shaped by many influences that work on many levels. The imperative to engage the world flows through many channels. The fight for justice occurs in many places.

I will expand my dialogue with the American people. I will continue to speak out and call it like I see it on race; on America's role in the world; on the economic plight of the middle class and the poor; and on the need for thorough-going reform that will remove special interests from elections and reduce their influence on government.

In the coming months, I will not lessen my efforts. To the contrary, I will increase them. As I leave the familiar surroundings of the U.S. Senate, I don't know where the future will lead. But, I recall the words of Robert Frost: "The woods are lonely, dark and deep, but I have promises to keep, and miles to go before I sleep; and miles to go before I sleep."

U.S. CENSUS BUREAU ON
FOREIGN-BORN POPULATION
August 29, 1995

The foreign-born population in the United States reached 22.6 million in 1994, or 8.7 percent of the total U.S. population, the Census Bureau reported August 19. Although the percentage of foreign-born had been much higher at the beginning of the century, reaching 14.7 percent in 1910, the 1994 level was the highest since World War II and its announcement intensified an ongoing debate about the appropriate levels of immigration.

Illegal immigrants, estimated at 300,000 or more entrants a year, were the primary target of the debate. "People are fed up," said Sen. Alan J. Simpson (R-Wyo.), chairman of the Senate Judiciary immigration subcommittee. "They see people violating our law come here and be treated hospitably."

Many citizens and politicians were also calling for new restrictions on legal immigration. "We don't need all these people," said a spokesman for the Federation for American Immigration Reform, which called for a temporary moratorium on immigration. In June a federal advisory panel lent substantial credibility to the move for less immigration when it recommended that legal immigration be cut back by one-third.

Immigration was also expected to be an issue in the 1996 presidential elections, in large part because several of the states most affected by immigration were key states in the election process. Voters in California, the state most affected by immigration, had already made illegal immigration a major issue. In 1994 they adopted Proposition 187, which would deny all public benefits to illegal aliens. Implementation of that initiative was on hold pending the outcome of a court challenge. Meanwhile, the House on March 24 passed a bill (HR 4) that would cut off most federal benefits to legal immigrants who were not naturalized citizens, while House and Senate committees were working on legislation that would make major changes in the laws affecting both legal and illegal immigration.

A Profile of the Nation's Foreign-Born

According to the Census Bureau report, the pace of immigration quickened in the early 1990s, with 20 percent of the foreign-born population entering the United States between 1990 and 1994. Mexico was the country of origin for the largest number of immigrants, 6.2 million. California was home to more than one-third of all immigrants—7.7 million. Five other states each had more than a million foreign-born: Florida, Illinois, New Jersey, New York, and Texas.

More than 65 percent of the foreign-born were white, about 20 percent were Asian or Pacific Islander, and fewer than 10 percent were black. Nearly 50 percent of the foreign-born population was of Hispanic origin.

The Census Bureau found high proportions of the immigrant population at both ends of the education scale. Approximately 40 percent of recent immigrants age twenty-five and older had a college degree, compared with 14.7 percent of similarly aged natives. However, 36 percent of immigrants that age had not finished high school, compared with 17.1 percent of natives. Recent immigrants had higher unemployment rates and lower incomes and were more likely to receive public assistance than natives, but the longer the immigrants were in the United States, the closer those rates were to those for natives. Immigrants who arrived before 1970 were less likely than natives to receive public assistance. (Natives were defined as anyone born in the United States, Puerto Rico, or a U.S. territory such as Guam and any person born in a foreign country but who had one parent who was a U.S. citizen. All other people born outside the United States were considered foreign-born. The report included some refugees and immigrants who had entered or remained in the country illegally.)

Cutting Back on the Number of Legal Immigrants

While the number of illegal immigrants had remained about the same, the growth in the overall number of immigrants surprised even some demographers. "It's a very high percentage," said one demographer of the 4.8 million immigrants since 1990. Some of the surge in immigrants as a percentage of the total population was caused by a declining birth rate among native women, but most of it was caused by changes in federal immigration law. In 1965 Congress did away with the national origin quota system and set an annual overall limit on the number of legal immigrants, giving preference to those who already had family members in the United States. Since then Congress had doubled the annual immigration ceiling, from about 320,000 in 1965 to about 700,000 in 1995. When refugees and others allowed in for humanitarian reasons are counted, the number rose to about 830,000.

On June 7 the bipartisan U.S. Commission on Immigration Reform recommended that number be gradually cut back by about one-third to 550,000. It further recommended that visa preferences be granted only to the spouses and young children of legal aliens and not to parents and siblings;

that employment-related immigration be reduced from 140,000 annually to 100,000; and that the number of refugees admitted be cut in half, to 50,000. The commission, which was chaired by former U.S. representative Barbara Jordan (D-Texas), was created by the 1990 immigration act.

The House Judiciary Committee and the Senate Judiciary immigration subcommittee approved bills late in 1995 that roughly followed the commission's recommendations. Both bills also contained provisions to crack down on illegal immigration by increasing the border patrol and enforcing existing sanctions against hiring illegal aliens. Both bills would also prohibit illegal aliens from receiving most federal and state benefits and limit legal immigrants' access to certain benefits.

Political Divisiveness

Reaction to the commission recommendations and the federal legislative proposals illustrated the divisiveness of the immigration issue for both parties. Rep. Lamar Smith (R-Texas), the chief sponsor of the House legislation, said it would protect U.S. workers from undue competition for jobs and save taxpayers the costs of public assistance for illegal immigrants and recent legal arrivals. On the other hand, House Majority Leader Dick Armey, a fellow Texan, argued that legal immigration was an economic boon to the nation and there was no need to curb it. Some Republicans also worried that cutbacks in legal immigration might be perceived as racist and could jeopardize the party's support among some immigrant communities, such as Cuban-Americans in Florida, certain Asian-Americans in California, and Hispanics in Texas.

Business, a traditional ally of the GOP, was lining up against the legislation because of its limits on bringing in skilled workers. "We'd like it stopped dead," said Phyllis Eisen, senior policy director for the National Association of Manufacturers. However, the Republicans were receiving support on that issue from the Clinton administration. "Today, too many companies are reaping huge profits from exploiting foreign workers and laying off skilled American workers," said Labor Secretary Robert B. Reich.

The Clinton administration was at odds with traditional supporters in its own party on other aspects of the immigration reform legislation. President Bill Clinton called the commission's recommended cutback in immigration and changes in visa preferences "pro-family." Other Democrats and ethnic organizations that traditionally support Democrats said the recommendations, especially those changing the visa preferences, would tear families apart. Many in Congress were also concerned about denying benefits to legal immigrants. "If you are a legal immigrant in this country, you are working here, you are paying taxes, and bad times come to you, you ought to be entitled to everything . . . that every American is," said Rep. Jim Walsh (R-N.Y.).

Following is the text of the report issued by the Census Bureau on August 29, 1995, entitled "The Foreign-Born Population: 1994":

Nearly 1 in 11 Americans are foreign-born

In 1994, 8.7 percent of the population of the United States was foreign-born—nearly double the percent foreign-born in 1970 (4.8 percent). While the percent foreign-born is at its highest level since before World War II, much greater proportions of the U.S. population were foreign-born during the early part of this century. From a high of 14.7 percent in 1910, the percent foreign-born declined to a low of 4.8 percent in 1970. Since that time, the percent has steadily increased.

One-third of the foreign-born live in California . . .

The foreign-born population is not distributed evenly throughout the country. California is home to 7.7 million foreign-born persons—more than one-third of all immigrants to the U.S. and nearly one-quarter of all California residents. New York ranks second with 2.9 million and Florida ranks third with 2.1 million foreign-born. Three other States have over 1 million foreign-born residents—Texas, Illinois, and New Jersey.

Year of entry

Twenty percent of the foreign-born population came to the U.S. in the last 5 years. Twice as many came per year during the 1990's than during the 1970's—4.5 million persons arrived in the 5-year period between 1990 and 1994 while 4.8 million came during the decade of the 1970's. Nearly as many came per year during the 1980's (8.3 million total) as in the last 5 years. The remainder of the foreign-born came to the U.S. prior to 1970.

Country of birth . . .

Of the 22,568,000 foreign-born persons living in the United States in March 1994, 6.2 million came from Mexico. Mexico was by far the country of origin with the largest number of immigrants. The next largest group was from the Philippines—1,033,000.

. . . by year of entry

Of the 4.5 million most recent immigrants, over a quarter (1.3 million) came from Mexico and an additional 243,000 came from Russia. Other countries with large numbers of recent immigrants include Vietnam, the Dominican Republic, the Philippines, India, and El Salvador.

During the 1980's, the largest numbers of immigrants came from Mexico (2,671,000) and the Philippines (424,000). China, Korea, the Dominican Republic, and Cuba also contributed large numbers. Prior to 1970, Mexico was still the most frequent country of origin (768,000), but the other top countries of origin were very different from today. They included Germany, Cuba, Italy, Canada, and England.

Citizenship

Foreign-born persons over the age of 18 can become "naturalized citizens" of the United States after they have lived here for a minimum of 5 years and have passed a citizenship exam. Spouses of U.S. citizens (and certain others) can become naturalized after 3 years and children who immigrate generally become citizens when their parents are naturalized. About 31 percent of the foreign-born population in the United States are naturalized citizens.

Foreign-born persons are older than natives . . .

The median age of all foreign-born persons in the United States (37 years) is higher than the median age for natives (33 years). But when the foreign-born population is divided into those who are naturalized citizens and those who are not citizens, a very different picture is formed. Only naturalized citizens are older on average (48 years) than natives.

. . . and younger than natives

Age and year of entry have obvious connections. The most recent immigrants are younger on average than natives. Those who came to the United States between 1990 and 1994 have a median age of only 26 years.

Race and Hispanic origin

More than two-thirds of the foreign-born population are White, about 1 in 5 are Asian or Pacific Islander, and only 7.1 percent are Black. The remainder reported their race as either "American Indian, Eskimo, or Aleut" or "other race." Nearly half (45.5 percent) of all foreign-born persons are of Hispanic origin.

Nearly two-thirds of the Asian and Pacific Islanders in the United States are foreign-born and most of the immigrants (91.7 percent) entered this country since 1970. Although 38.5 percent of the persons of Hispanic origin in this country are foreign-born and most have lived in the U.S. long enough to qualify for naturalization, only 18.3 percent are naturalized citizens.

Fertility

In June 1994, there were 6.2 million foreign-born women 15 to 44 years old, representing 10.4 percent of all women in the United States in the childbearing ages. These women had borne 1.5 children each compared with 1.2 children borne to native-born women. About 68 percent of these women in childbearing ages immigrated to the United States after 1980. Women who became naturalized citizens had borne an average of 1.5 children each, not significantly different from the average reported by non-citizens.

Educational attainment

While it seems a paradox, the foreign-born are both more educated and less educated than natives. Recent immigrants 25 years and over are more likely to have a college degree than either natives or earlier immigrants. While 11.5 percent of recent immigrants have a graduate or professional degree, only about 7.5 percent of natives and immigrants in earlier years have such degrees. Recent immigrants are also more likely to have bachelor's degrees (20.9 percent) than either natives (14.7 percent) or earlier immigrants (13.9 percent).

On the other hand, immigrants are also less likely to have graduated from high school than natives. Only 17.1 percent of natives over the age of 25 are not high school graduates while 36.0 percent of immigrants do not have high school degrees.

Labor force status

The foreign-born population has a higher unemployment rate than do natives (9.1 percent versus 6.8 percent, respectively). However, the unemployment rate of naturalized citizens is no different statistically from that of natives. Foreign-born persons who are not citizens have the highest unemployment rate (10.7 percent).

Income in 1993

Foreign-born persons as a group had a lower median income in 1993 than natives ($12,179 versus $15,876) but this difference seems to be related to length of residence. Foreign-born persons who immigrated during the 1970's have median incomes no different than that of natives. Recent immigrants have the lowest median income ($8,393) of all immigrants by period of entry into the United States.

Receipt of public assistance

Recent immigrants are more likely to receive public assistance income than natives (5.7 percent versus 2.9 percent). The rates drop significantly for immigrants who have been here for 5 or more years. The rates for foreign-born persons who entered during the 1970's and 1980's are not significantly different from those of natives or recent immigrants. Immigrants who arrived before 1970 are less likely to be receiving public assistance (1.4 percent) than natives.

Aid to Families with Dependent Children (AFDC) is the primary source of public assistance income in the CPS [Current Population Survey] data; most natives and immigrants who are receiving some kind of public assistance are receiving AFDC.

Poverty status

While the data on income and receipt of public assistance are limited to persons ages 16 and over, poverty status is based upon family income and persons of all ages are tallied as to whether or not they are in a family above or below the poverty line. The foreign-born are 1.6 times more likely to be in poverty than natives (22.9 versus 14.4 percent). And recent immigrants are over twice as likely to be in poverty (37.1 percent). Only persons who immigrated prior to 1970 are less likely than natives to be in poverty (10.8 percent).

Tenure

Homeownership is one indicator of economic well being. While over two-thirds of natives live in owner-occupied housing units, less than half of the foreign-born live in owner-occupied housing. Homeownership among immigrants increases with length of residence; while persons who immigrated before 1970 have homeownership rates higher than natives, only 17.5 percent of recent immigrants are living in their own homes.

Source of the data

The Current Population Survey began collecting monthly data on nativity in January of 1994. Each respondent was asked where they were born and the country of birth of each of their parents. Persons born outside of the United States were also asked their citizenship status and the year they came to the United States to live. Most of the characteristics of the foreign-born population shown in this brief report are from the March 1994 supplement to the Current Population Survey; the data on fertility are from June 1994.

The foreign-born population in this report include some undocumented immigrants, refugees, and temporary residents such as students and temporary workers as well as the legally admitted immigrants included in data from the Immigration and Naturalization Service.

September

DOLE SPEECH ON SOCIAL ISSUES
September 4, 1995

Senate Majority Leader Bob Dole (R-Kan.), a leading candidate for the 1996 Republican presidential nomination, staked out a range of conservative positions on social issues in a September 4 address to the annual convention of the American Legion, held in Indianapolis. Dole denounced "intellectual elites" who he said were undermining traditional American values, and he endorsed making English the country's official language. The latter step, he said, was necessary to head off "ethnic separatism" in the United States.

Dole's speech covered most of the top social questions on the minds of conservatives, who were expected to dominate the 1996 primaries and caucuses leading to the Republican nomination. Many conservative leaders had been suspicious of Dole because of his past middle-of-the-road stance on some of those social issues and his willingness to embrace legislative compromises. His speech to the American Legion thus was viewed by many as an attempt to burnish his conservative credentials.

Other Republican candidates accused Dole of copying their ideas and attempting to change his ideological stripes. Patrick J. Buchanan, for one, told the Washington Post *that Dole was "violating the copyright laws" with his call to make English the official national language. Buchanan said he had championed that cause for years.*

Dole Under Political Pressure

Dole appeared before the American Legion at a time when his standing as the presumed front-runner for the Republican nomination was beginning to show some slippage. A straw poll in Iowa—the site of the first important Republican caucus—had shown Dole losing ground to Sen. Phil Gramm of Texas. Dole also had been dogged by a controversy over a campaign contribution from a group of gay Republicans, a contribution he returned.

In the late summer of 1995, a year before the Republican convention, Dole also was suffering the fate of nearly all front-runners: an intense examination by the media of his every word and action and consequent speculation that he was not as invulnerable as once thought. A Newsweek *profile in September described Dole as conveying "the air of a man peeved at having to beg for a job he thinks he deserves—and at having to prove an ideological purity he believes no one can reasonably expect him to have."*

Several commentators said Dole faced a long-term political dilemma. To win the Republican nomination, he needed to improve his standing among religious fundamentalists and other hard-line conservatives who had gained control of the party in many states. To defeat President Bill Clinton in the November 1996 elections, Dole had to appeal to a broader public, including moderate Republicans and Democrats who might be repelled by the stands he would have to take in his quest for the nomination.

Addressing Social Issues

In that political context, Dole, wearing the customary American Legion cap, took to the nation's largest veterans organization a message emphasizing contemporary threats to traditional American values. The themes he chose were far from the nuts-and-bolts matters of farm policy, taxation, and budgeting on which he had built his successful Senate career, but they found a receptive audience in fellow veterans, many of them anxious about social trends in the America of the 1990s.

Dole's broad message was that many of the nation's institutions, especially schools and colleges, had come under the control of a liberal "intellectual elite," who he said "seem embarrassed by America" and have no respect for traditional American values. These elites, he said, "have false theories, long dissertations and endless studies to back them up. But they . . . have somehow missed the fact that the United States of America is the greatest force for good the world has ever known, make no mistake about it."

To counter the theories of these "arbiters of political correctness," Dole offered several prescriptions. Among them was the proposal to make English the nation's official language: "Insisting that all our citizens are fluent in English is a welcoming act of inclusion—and insist on it we must." That would mean abandoning "multilingual education as a means of instilling ethnic pride or as a therapy for low esteem or out of elitist guilt over a culture built on the traditions of the West," he said.

Dole accused educators of dwelling on the "dark moments" of the American past and disparaging American traditions and ideals. As an example, he cited a series of national history standards that he said concentrated on McCarthyism and racism while ignoring American heroes and greatness. Such ideas must be scrapped, he said, and schools should be required to teach "Western tradition and American greatness."

Tackling a related issue, Dole denounced "affirmative action," the practice of giving hiring preferences to minorities and women to make up for past discrimination. "We know it has failed and let's stop dividing Americans by race and gender and get back to the simple principle of equal treatment for all Americans," Dole said. Just six weeks before, President Clinton had strongly endorsed continued use of affirmative action programs to offer more opportunities to minorities and women. (Affirmative action, p. 307)

> *Following are excerpts from a speech September 4, 1995, by Sen. Bob Dole (R-Kan.) to the seventy-seventh annual convention of the American Legion, held in Indianapolis:*

... [Y]ou are freedom's heroes and American patriots and I'm proud to be among you. Each of you have answered America's call, whether it was to fight for our freedom or to defend the peace in which we have prospered for so many years. Each of you knows what it's like to wear the uniform of our country, to put your country first and to be willing to bear any sacrifice to keep her free. And I assure you that we will never forget our obligation to those who have worn the uniform in service to this great nation.

I know you all support efforts to balance the federal budget. I know you support efforts to balance the federal budget, to stop the flow of red ink that threatens the futures of our children and our grandchildren. I also know that, as veterans, you are very properly concerned about funding for the activities of the Department of Veteran Affairs. And let me just say this: Yes, we are going to balance the federal budget because it's necessary. And every program is going to be scrutinized, with the exception of Social Security. But the budget will not be balanced on the backs of America's veterans.

We have too much invested. And because you and I know—those who have had the privilege of serving in the armed forces—you know that we are the freest country and the freest people on earth. And you and I know that we must stay that way. We must remain the strongest country on the face of the earth for peace. That's all we want, is peace. Peace.

And that's what I want to talk with you just for a few moments today: keeping America strong in her might and in her heart and in the face of external enemies and in the presence of threats from within. America's still the land of the free and the home of the brave and a great century of hope and opportunity is about to unfold before us.

But to claim that future America needs your help. For some in America believe our might is no longer needed. . . . Can there be any doubt that the world is still a dangerous place? Oh, yes, the Cold War is over. We won one of humanity's greatest struggles against totalitarianism and oppression.

But today peace is threatened and dark forces are multiplying in almost every corner of the world. The evil empire may be gone, that President Reagan talked about, but its missiles still exist in a volatile, unstable and unpredictable region. And despite our protests, Russia's selling nuclear arms to Iran. Iraq is manufacturing gruesome biological and chemical weapons. North Korea will soon have nuclear capability and China is arming Pakistan with nuclear missiles while just across their contested border, India already has them.

And Central Europe is being eaten away by ethnic war and genocide. The United Nations has been impotent and until last week the UN was calling the shots for NATO. And now should be a time for great vigilance, and yet, now Washington seems filled with people who want to dismantle our defenses. And one thing I think is clear, regardless of our political philosophy or party affiliation, I believe [if] we go back and look at what's happened, that our defense budget's been cut too far and too fast.

And I think we're now on a path that would have ended with America's spending about as much as our gross national product on defense as we were when Pearl Harbor was attacked. Now, that's a big, big drop, but the good news is that Congress refused to go along this year.

We rejected the policies that would lead us back to a hollow military. We kept the faith, and we increased spending on defense because I've always felt if I were the President of the United States, and I had a choice of spending maybe a little too much or not spending enough, I'm going to offer spending a little too much because there are no alternatives if we don't spend enough.

And it seems to me that's where the future is and that's what America's all about.

Where the demands of freedom require us to modernize our forces, to maintain our technological edge, and to ensure that America remains the world's one and only superpower. And we will never apologize for that. We will never apologize for that. Our goal is not just to be strong enough to turn back a threat. We must be so strong no one ever again [will even attempt] to threaten us at all, that's what it's all about, that's where we need to be in the future.

[What It Means to Be an American]

But if we're going to return America to greatness . . . [w]e must return as a people to the original concept of what it means to be American. This means tackling subjects the arbiters of political correctness don't even want discussed. For example, English must be recognized as America's official language.

Western tradition and American greatness must be taught in our schools and the federal government must end its war on traditional American values. America's always been more than just a place on a map. It has held a claim on our hearts.

We are a nation dedicated to a proposition that all men and women are created equal, endowed by our creator with certain inalienable rights. Our forefathers rejected race and religion as the forces to form a nation, choosing instead the ideals of freedom and democracy. It was a radical gamble at the time. And ever since we have held it to be an article of faith that those who would be American must first abandon lesser allegiances. And as Franklin Roosevelt said. . . , "Americanism is not and never was a matter of race and ancestry." Succeeding waves of immigrants have been drawn to America by this idea. And lacking the centuries-old primal bonds of other nations, we have used our language, our history, and our code of values to make the American experiment work. We have used them to forge millions of diverse individuals into one people with a common purpose. Language, history and values. These are the strings that bind the hearts of America. These are the forces that have held us together, allowing us to be diverse and yet united, to absorb untold millions of immigrants while coming the closest any country ever has to the classless, upwardly mobile society of our ideals.

But these keys to unity are under attack from our government and from intellectual elites who seem embarrassed by America and what we see as an opportunity, they see as oppression. What we see as a proud past, they see a legacy of shame. What we hold as moral truth, they call intolerance. They have false theories, long dissertations and endless studies to back them up. But they know so much that they have somehow missed the fact that the United States of America is the greatest force for good the world has ever known, make no mistake about it. That's what America is all about.

And yes, we have our faults. But part of what makes me so proud to be an American is the constant effort of our people to do better, to make our country right and good and just. Unfortunately some policies and programs borne out of that desire have gone [awry]. . . .

Affirmative action is one of those programs. Instead of making things better, it has made things worse. No amount of tinkering can rescue it. It was never supposed to be permanent. We know it has failed and let's stop dividing Americans by race and gender and get back to the simple principle of equal treatment for all Americans. All Americans ought to be treated alike, regardless of our background, regardless of our color, regardless of our economic status.

That's why I've introduced legislation which prohibits the federal government from ever using quotas, set asides or other race-based preferences in any form. Whether in employment, contracting or any other federal program, our government must be in the business of bringing our citizens closer together, not tearing us apart, not dividing us into classes. . . .

And that's what America's all about, in my view.

[Teaching Children to Value America]

But nowhere is the focus on what divides us more alarming than what is happening in our schools. The debate about what we teach our children is really a debate about who we are as a people, and whether we are one people anymore at all. Do we embrace ideas that unite us regardless of our sex or color or religion? Or are we just a jostling crowd of competing groups thrown by fate between two oceans?

And one of the most important missions of our schools is to make citizens of our children. . . . Fluency in English should be a central educational goal of every state in our nation. English is the language in which we still speak to each other across the frontiers of culture and race. It is the language of the Constitution. It is the language in which we conduct our great national debates, an essential ingredient of democracy. Insisting that all our citizens are fluent in English is a welcoming act of inclusion—and insist on it we must. Otherwise they're going to fall behind.

And I agree, yes, schools should provide the language class our immigrants and their families need—as long as their purpose is the teaching of English. We have done this since our founding to speed the melding of our melting pot. But we must stop the practice of multilingual education as a means of instilling ethnic pride or as a therapy for low esteem or out of elitist guilt over a culture built on the traditions of the West. With all the divisive forces tearing at our country, we need the glue of language to help hold us together. And if we want to ensure that all of our children have the same opportunities—yours, mine, everyone's in America—the same opportunities in life, alternative-language education should stop and English should be acknowledged once and for all as the official language of the United States of America.

And speaking of elitist guilt: Yes, there have been dark moments in our past. There are still cruel elements in our culture. We should not sanitize them when we teach our children the history of American and Western civilization. But we should not politicize them either, as too many educators and professors in our schools and universities today are attempting to do. There is a shocking campaign afoot among educators at all levels—most evident in the national history standards already distributed to more than 20,000 teachers, administrators and professors—to disparage America and disown the ideas and traditions of the West.

Now let me give you just a couple of examples of what I mean. The history standards—prepared with over $2 million in grants from the U.S. Department of Education and the National Endowment for the Humanities—suggest we teach our students about America by concentrating on some of our most worst moments: the scourge of McCarthyism and the rise of the Ku Klux Klan. George Washington is never even described as our first president in this approach. Alexander Graham Bell and Thomas Edison and Paul Revere disappear from the story of America. And the first time the Constitution is mentioned it is blamed for sidetracking the movement to end slavery.

. . . The purpose of the national history standards seem not to teach our children certain essential facts about our history, but to denigrate America's story while sanitizing and glorifying other cultures. This is wrong and it threatens us as surely as any foreign power ever has. We must use the bully pulpit to make it clear that we will not stand still and allow this campaign to be inflicted upon our children and our grandchildren across America. . . .

. . . We're proud of America, that's why we're here today, that's why you're here today, because we are the greatest [nation] on the face of the earth.

And that's what America is all about. And we won't put up with our tax dollars being used to drag it down or sow doubt about the nobility of America in the minds of our children. They're the future of this country. . . .We must teach them what we were taught and what we know to be true, that this country is one of history's most magnificent ideas.

Our children must come to value freedom as dearly as every refugee fleeing persecution who sailed or swam or scrambled here to find it, as much as every soldier who died to preserve it. America must be in their hearts, as well as in their heads. [It] takes just one generation to snap the chain of freedom. One generation for a nation based on an idea to . . . forget who we are.

And one of the most powerful symbols we use to remind ourselves, of course, is Old Glory, the flag. Our flag is more than a piece of cloth. It is the embodiment of our sacred ideals. I grew up as you all did, holding my hand over my heart and pledging allegiance to it. And perhaps one of our problems is that too few of us do that anymore.

We ought to teach our children at an early age to respect the flag. And we certainly ought to stop its public denigration. . . . And I'm proud to stand with the American Legion in supporting a Constitutional amendment to protect our flag. . . .

And let me just conclude with one other thing. This is a values issue with me and it brings me to the subject of values, something I've spoken a lot about this summer. To put it simply, values do count—not just in our lives but in our society. I don't care how strong our economy will become, in the future or whatever, it'll never be strong enough to transform a neighborhood where 80 percent of the children lack a father and legitimate jobs are dismissed as chump change. There will never be enough prisons or police to enforce order in our society if there is growing disorder in our souls.

And the vast majority of Americans still hold fast to the values that made America great. But now we must do more than just live by them. We must speak out about our values and insist that our culture and our government reflect them. Yes, this means braving the ridicule of the cultural elites and . . . speaking out . . . about our popular entertainment. Our movies and music, advertising and television do have a profound impact on our children—and it's not for the good.

It's much harder to rise out of poverty when the culture derides the values that made that possible. It's much harder for society to control crime when role models preach impulsive violence. And those who would market evil through . . . commerce hate the light of scrutiny. But I will continue my freedom, as you continue your freedom, to call them to account. I will name their names until they feel the shame their actions deserve. Time Warner, the producer of some of the foulest rap music, has already begun to have second thoughts—and others will too. And this is not a matter of right and left, this is a matter of right and wrong.

And we ought to speak out on a matter of right and wrong. I made a speech a while back—it wasn't a partisan speech—and somebody said, "Well, he's just too old-fashioned." What'd I talk about? I talked about love of God and country and family. Commitment to honesty and decency and personal responsibility. And self-reliance tempered by a sense of community.

I thought those were the values that made us the greatest country on the face of the earth. And there's no doubt in my mind that we can get back . . . on the right track if we reassert them again as a people. And if our government returns to them as a matter of national policy. Everywhere in the world we see examples of nations divided against themselves.

[Our Responsibilities as Leader of the Free World]

The tragedy of Bosnia is the most recent, most horrifying example where we waited and waited and waited [and] thousands and thousands of innocent women and children [were] slaughtered. And I'm not suggesting sending ground troops but it seems to me what we're doing now could have been done months and months and months before. And by now we might be having a real peace settlement. But in any event, they are finally doing the right thing. . . .

About four or five years ago when the Berlin wall collapsed, and Communism collapsed, all these people started coming to America from all these different countries, whether it was Poland or Hungary or a former Republic of the Soviet Union. And they were young and they were old and they were men and they were women. And some had been locked up and jailed for years because they stood up and spoke out against the government. And they came to see us as the leaders of the Congress. And almost without exception when they left, they would say something about like this and they would again say it in a very emotional way, with tears streaming down their cheeks in some cases. You know what they said? They said, we want to be like America. We want to be like America. And finally they had the right to vote. They had the right to worship. They had the right to send their children to school. They had a right to travel—something we take for granted. Pick up the telephone—they had that right—without someone tapping the other end.

All these basic rights suddenly were available to these 500 million people. Five hundred million people who have a little taste of freedom because of us, because of people in this audience, because of Presidents Reagan, Bush, and, yes, Carter, who didn't give up and kept the pressure on. And we paid for it with taxes when we increased our defense. But what was the result? Five hundred million people are free.

We have opportunities for a generation of peace. And the point I would make is this: That's why it's so important. You pay a price for leadership. You do it every day in your business, whatever you may do. We pay a price as a country for leadership. President Nixon . . . in a book just before his death, said the American people are tired of the burden of leadership. They would like to give it to somebody else. And you ask yourself, who? Chinese, Japanese, Germans? Nope. It always comes back to us. And we pay a price for it. It's called taxes. You pay a price. But there's no alternative. There's no alternative. And that's why we continue talking about the greatness of America. It's not arrogance. It's not conceit. It's not immodest.

We are the leader of the free world. We have a tremendous responsibility, a tremendous challenge, but also opportunities. We want to avoid war. We want the day to happen someday when there isn't any American Legion or any other veterans group, because there haven't been any wars. That's what America is all about. And that's what the future is all about. And you've made it possible. And I'm honored to be here today to say so. Thank you very much. God bless America.

HILLARY CLINTON'S REMARKS AT THE UN CONFERENCE ON WOMEN
September 5, 1995

Delegates gathering in Beijing for the United Nations' Fourth World Conference on Women adopted a nonbinding "Platform of Action" September 15, asserting that governments should accord women "all human rights and fundamental freedoms," including the right to make their own decisions on matters relating to sexuality and childbearing, to be protected from violence, and to have equal access to economic resources. Although the platform was not binding on governments and some of its key issues were opposed by the Vatican and delegates from some Islamic and Roman Catholic countries, conference leaders seemed to agree that real gains had been made. Women have gone "from claiming handouts, from claiming privileges to demanding rights," Dorothy Thomas of Human Rights Watch told the Washington Post.

Delegates acknowledged that in many instances it was likely to be a long step between demanding rights and actually receiving them. They had only to point to the treatment of women attending the companion forum for nongovernmental organizations (NGOs) as illustration. About 20,000 delegates attended the forum, which ran from August 30 to September 8. The Chinese government refused visas to some groups seeking to attend the NGO forum, and it moved the forum away from downtown Beijing, where the UN conference was held, to Hairou, about an hour away. The meeting facilities were primitive and housing was limited, forcing many women to be bused in from Beijing. Chinese officials placed restrictions on meetings and demonstrations at the NGO forum and searched and otherwise harassed many of the women attending that conference.

In a September 5 speech marking the opening day of the UN conference, first lady Hillary Rodham Clinton was sharply critical of the Chinese government's treatment of the women at the NGO forum. "It is indefensible that many women in nongovernmental organizations who wished to participate in this conference have not been able to attend—or have been prohibited from fully taking part," Clinton said. In words directed toward the

Chinese government but that had broad application, Clinton continued: "Let me be clear. Freedom means the right of people to assemble, organize, and debate openly. It means respecting the views of those who may disagree with the views of their governments. It means not taking citizens away from their loved ones and jailing them, mistreating them, or denying them their freedom or dignity because of the peaceful expression of their ideas and opinions."

'Human Rights Are Women's Rights'

In her speech, which set the tone for the UN conference, Clinton spoke movingly of abuses suffered by women around the world and called on all governments to "accept their responsibility to protect and promote" women's rights. "If there is one message that echoes forth from this conference, it is that human rights are women's rights. And women's rights are human rights," she declared. "It is a violation of human rights," Clinton said, when babies are killed "simply because they are born girls," when women are raped "as a tactic or prize of war," when a leading cause of death among women is domestic violence, when young girls are subjected to the "painful and degrading practice of genital mutilation," and when "women are denied the right to plan their own families, and that includes being forced to have abortions or being sterilized against their wills."

Everyone had a stake in the well-being of women, Clinton said, for "if women are healthy and educated, their families will flourish. If women are free from violence, their families will flourish. If women have a choice to work and earn as full and equal partners in society, their families will flourish. And when families flourish, communities and nations will flourish."

Clinton had been under some pressure not to attend the conference. Human rights activists feared her attendance might be construed as an official U.S. endorsement of China's repressive government. Others were concerned that her visit might damage U.S. relations with China, which were beginning to heal after being strained over several issues, including the Taiwanese president's June visit to the United States and China's recent detention of Chinese American Harry Wu, an outspoken critic of conditions in Chinese prisons.

Clinton herself sought to downplay the effect her speech might have on Sino-U.S. relations. In an interview with reporters afterwards, she said the Clinton administration was "working toward having a very comprehensive and hopefully good relationship with China in many areas. For me, it was important to express how I felt and to do so as clearly as I could."

Platform of Action

In agreeing that women had a right "to have control over and decide freely and responsibly on matters related to their sexuality, including sexual and reproductive health, free of coercion, discrimination and violence," the women's conference took a significant forward step in expand-

ing the definition of human rights. Only a year earlier in September 1994, delegates to the UN Conference on World Population in Cairo had endorsed an action plan encouraging governments to let women assume more control over their lives on the assumption that if women were given a true choice they would opt to have fewer children. At the time the Vatican and several Latin American and Islamic nations objected to the plan, saying that it endorsed abortion. Organizers of the women's conference were concerned that the Cairo language would be reargued in Beijing. "The fear was that we might move backwards from Cairo and that was unfounded," said Patricia Licuanan, chairwoman of the final drafting session. (Conference on world population, Historic Documents of 1994, p. 351)

Another important breakthrough at the Beijing conference was the adoption of language declaring that women should have an equal right with men to inherit; in many countries women were barred legally or culturally from inheriting. Some delegates said this provision did not go far enough because it did not assert that women should inherit equal amounts, only that they should have an equal right to inherit.

As with most such documents, the final Plan of Action contained many compromises. One of the more important involved a tradeoff between delegates from Islamic nations, who had wanted to insert a phrase in the preamble that many thought would subsume women's rights to cultural and religious customs, and delegates from the European Union, who had wanted language in the preamble guaranteeing sexual freedom. The Vatican and many Islamic countries opposed language that could be construed as an endorsement of homosexuality. The final language of the preamble sought to address both issues without direct reference to either:

> *The objective of the platform of action . . . is the empowerment of all women. The full realization of all human rights and fundamental freedoms of all women is essential for the empowerment of women.*
>
> *While the significance of national and regional particularities and various historical, cultural and religious backgrounds must be borne in mind, it is the duty of states regardless of their political, economic and cultural systems to promote and protect all human rights and fundamental freedoms.*
>
> *The implementation of this platform, including through national laws and the formulation of strategies, policies, programs and development priorities, is the sovereign responsibility of each state in conformity with all human rights and fundamental freedoms, and the significance of and full respect for various religious and ethical values, cultural backgrounds and philosophical convictions of individuals and their communities should contribute to the full enjoyment by women of their human rights in order to achieve equality, development and peace.*

The Vatican and several other delegations registered objections to the final document. Vatican spokesman Joaquin Navarro-Valls told reporters that the conference and the plan focused too much on sexual matters and not enough on the main concerns of women, which he said were basic health services and the like. Other delegates said the plan of action would

be meaningless without political action in individual countries to imple-
ment it. Still others acknowledged the correctness of that viewpoint but
said the plan would give new visibility to women's issues and could serve
as a guide for revising national policies.

Following are excerpts from a speech delivered by First Lady
Hillary Rodham Clinton on September 5, 1995, the opening day
of the United Nation's Fourth World Conference on Women, held
in Beijing:

I would like to thank the Secretary General of the United Nations for invit-
ing me to be part of the United Nations Fourth World Conference on Women.
This is truly a celebration—a celebration of the contributions women make
in every aspect of life: in the home, on the job, in their communities, as mothers, wives, sisters, daughters, learners, workers, citizens, and leaders.

It is also a coming together, much the way women come together every
day in every country. We come together in fields and in factories. In village
markets and supermarkets. In living rooms and board rooms.

Whether it is while playing with our children in the park, or washing
clothes in a river, or taking a break at the office water cooler, we come
together and talk about our aspirations and concerns. And time and again,
our talk turns to our children and our families.

However different we may be, there is far more that unites us than divides
us. We share a common future. And we are here to find common ground so that
we may help bring new dignity and respect to women and girls all over the
world—and in so doing, bring new strength and stability to families as well.

By gathering in Beijing, we are focusing world attention on issues that
matter most in the lives of women and their families: access to education,
health care, jobs, and credit, the chance to enjoy basic legal and human rights
and participate fully in the political life of their countries.

There are some who question the reason for this conference. Let them listen to the voices of women in their homes, neighborhoods, and workplaces.

There are some who wonder whether the lives of women and girls matter
to economic and political progress around the globe. . . . Let them look at the
women gathered here and at Hairou . . . the homemakers, nurses, teachers,
lawyers, policymakers, and women who run their own businesses.

It is conferences like this that compel governments and peoples everywhere to listen, look, and face the world's most pressing problems.

Wasn't it after the women's conference in Nairobi ten years ago that the
world focused for the first time on the crisis of domestic violence? . . .

What we are learning around the world is that, if women are healthy and
educated, their families will flourish. If women are free from violence, their
families will flourish. If women have a chance to work and earn as full and
equal partners in society, their families will flourish.

And when families flourish, communities and nations will flourish.

That is why every woman, every man, every child, every family, and every nation on our planet has a stake in the discussion that takes place here. . . .

The great challenge of this conference is to give voice to women everywhere whose experiences go unnoticed, whose words go unheard.

Women comprise more than half the world's population. Women are 70 percent of the world's poor, and two-thirds of those who are not taught to read and write.

Women are the primary caretakers for most of the world's children and elderly. Yet much of the work we do is not valued—not by economists, not by historians, not by popular culture, not by government leaders.

At this very moment, as we sit here, women around the world are giving birth, raising children, cooking meals, washing clothes, cleaning houses, planting crops, working on assembly lines, running companies, and running countries.

Women also are dying from diseases that should have been prevented or treated; they are watching their children succumb to malnutrition caused by poverty and economic deprivation; they are being denied the right to go to school by their own fathers and brothers; they are being forced into prostitution; and they are being barred from the ballot box and the bank lending office.

Those of us who have the opportunity to be here have the responsibility to speak for those who could not.

As an American, I want to speak up for women in my own country—women who are raising children on the minimum wage, women who can't afford health care or child care, women whose lives are threatened by violence, including violence in their own homes.

I want to speak up for mothers who are fighting for good schools, safe neighborhoods, clean air, and clean airwaves; for older women, some of them widows, who have raised their families and now find that their skills and life experiences are not valued in the workplace; for women who are working all night as nurses, hotel clerks, and fast food chefs so that they can be at home during the day with their kids; and for women everywhere who simply don't have time to do everything they are called upon to do each day.

Speaking to you today, I speak for them, just as each of us speaks for women around the world who are denied the chance to go to school, or see a doctor, or own property, or have a say about the direction of their lives, simply because they are women.

The truth is that most women around the world work both inside and outside the home, usually by necessity.

We need to understand that there is no formula for how women should lead their lives. That is why we must respect the choices that each woman makes for herself and her family. Every woman deserves the chance to realize her God-given potential.

We also must recognize that women will never gain full dignity until their human rights are respected and protected.

Our goals for this conference, to strengthen families and societies by empowering women to take greater control over their own destinies, cannot be fully achieved unless all governments—here and around the world—accept their responsibility to protect and promote internationally recognized human rights.

The international community has long acknowledged—and recently affirmed at Vienna—that both women and men are entitled to a range of protections and personal freedoms, from the right to personal security to the right to determine freely the number and spacing of the children they bear.

No one should be forced to remain silent for fear of religious or political persecution, arrest, abuse, or torture.

Tragically, women are most often the ones whose human rights are violated. Even in the late 20th century, the rape of women continues to be used as an instrument of armed conflict. Women and children make up a large majority of the world's refugees. And when women are excluded from the political process, they become even more vulnerable to abuse.

I believe that, on the eve of a new millennium, it is time to break our silence. It is time for us to say here in Beijing, and the world to hear, that it is no longer acceptable to discuss women's rights as separate from human rights.

These abuses have continued because, for too long, the history of women has been a history of silence. Even today, there are those who are trying to silence our words.

The voices of this conference and of the women at Hairou must be heard loud and clear.

It is a violation of human rights when babies are denied food, or drowned, or suffocated, or their spines broken, simply because they are born girls.

It is a violation of human rights when women and girls are sold into the slavery of prostitution.

It is a violation of human rights when women are doused with gasoline, set on fire, and burned to death because their marriage dowries are deemed too small.

It is a violation of human rights when individual women are raped in their own communities and when thousands of women are subjected to rape as a tactic or prize of war.

It is a violation of human rights when a leading cause of death worldwide among women ages 14 to 44 is the violence they are subjected to in their own homes.

It is a violation of human rights when young girls are brutalized by the painful and degrading practice of genital mutilation.

It is a violation of human rights when women are denied the right to plan their own families, and that includes being forced to have abortions or being sterilized against their will.

If there is one message that echoes forth from this conference, it is that human rights are women's rights. And women's rights are human rights.

Let us not forget that among those rights are the right to speak freely. And the right to be heard.

Women must enjoy the right to participate fully in the social and political lives of their countries if we want freedom and democracy to thrive and endure.

It is indefensible that many women in nongovernmental organizations who wished to participate in this conference have not been able to attend— or have been prohibited from fully taking part.

Let me be clear. Freedom means the right of people to assemble, organize, and debate openly. It means respecting the views of those who may disagree with the views of their governments. It means not taking citizens away from their loved ones and jailing them, mistreating them, or denying them their freedom or dignity because of the peaceful expression of their ideas and opinions.

In my country, we recently celebrated the 75th anniversary of women's suffrage. It took 150 years after the signing of our Declaration of Independence for women to win the right to vote. It took 72 years of organized struggle on the part of many courageous women and men.

It was one of America's most divisive philosophical wars. But it was also a bloodless war. Suffrage was achieved without a shot fired. We have also been reminded, in V-J Day observances last weekend, of the good that comes when men and women join together to combat the forces of tyranny and build a better world.

We have seen peace prevail in most places for a half century. We have avoided another world war. But we have not solved older, deeply rooted problems that continue to diminish the potential of half the world's population.

Now it is time to act on behalf of women everywhere.

If we take bold steps to better the lives of women, we will be taking bold steps to better the lives of children and families, too. Families rely on mothers and wives for emotional support and care; families rely on women for labor in the home; and increasingly, families rely on women for income needed to raise healthy children and care for other relatives.

As long as discrimination and inequities remain so commonplace around the world—as long as girls and women are valued less, fed last, overworked, underpaid, not schooled, and subjected to violence in and out of their homes—the potential of the human family to create a peaceful, prosperous world will not be realized.

Let this conference be our—and the world's—call to action. And let us heed the call so that we can create a world in which every woman is treated with respect and dignity, every boy and girl is loved and cared for equally, and every family has the hope of a strong and stable future.

Thank you very much. God's blessing on you, your work, and all who will benefit from it.

RIPKEN ON BREAKING GEHRIG'S CONSECUTIVE GAME RECORD
September 6, 1996

Cal Ripken Jr., an unassuming shortstop for the Baltimore Orioles, on September 6 reached one of the ultimate achievements in American sports, surpassing Lou Gehrig's record of playing in 2,130 consecutive games. Ripken celebrated his achievement by hitting a home run, his third in as many games, helping the Orioles defeat the California Angels 8–0 at home. By the end of the 1995 season Ripken's streak stood at 2,153 games, and he looked forward to playing in 1996 and beyond.

Gehrig was one of baseball's genuine heroes. He played every day for the New York Yankees during their glory years from 1925 through April 1939. The only Yankee more celebrated than Gehrig was Babe Ruth. Gehrig had a .340 lifetime average and hit 493 home runs, in several seasons rivaling Ruth for the American League home run championship.

In setting his record, Gehrig won the description of "Iron Man," and a plaque in his honor at Yankee Stadium said his record "should stand for all time." His streak was stopped by a deadly illness, amyotrophic lateral sclerosis, now known as Lou Gehrig's disease, which claimed his life in 1941. Gehrig began suffering from the disease in 1937, and it progressively affected his playing through the 1938 season. He took himself out of the Yankees lineup after the first eight games of the 1939 season, saying his playing was hurting the team.

Other than Ripken, no player had come close to Gehrig's record. Among modern players, Steve Garvey had the longest streak next to Ripken's— 1,207 games.

Ripken's Record in Baseball History

Gehrig's record was one of two in baseball that long had been considered unsurpassable. The other was Joe DiMaggio's streak of hitting safely in fifty-six consecutive games. Both records were important because they represented endurance, determination, and beating the odds. In theory, either record could have been broken by a player of average ability who plugged *away each day and enjoyed plenty of luck. A player did not need to be a superstar to take the field every day or to get just one hit out of four or five at bats each game over a two-month period. The fact was that Gehrig and DiMaggio were two of baseball's greatest and most beloved superstars, and their records had taken on a mystical quality in a sport that for generations was the closest thing to America's secular religion.*

Cal Ripken Jr. certainly was no ordinary player. He had been an All-Star selection every year of his major league career and twice was voted the most valuable player in the American League. But baseball is a game of statistics, and most of Ripken's statistics fall short of superstar status. As of September 6 his lifetime batting average was a respectable but not spectacular .278; his best offensive year was 1991, when he hit .323, with 34 home runs and 114 runs batted in. Ripken was an excellent shortstop, surpassed defensively in his era only by Ozzie Smith of the St. Louis Cardinals.

For many baseball fans, Ripken's achievement was everyman's: he was a regular guy who showed up for work, did his best, worked well with his teammates, and never tried to call excessive attention to himself. With his modesty and dogged perseverance, Ripken captured the imagination of Americans, whether they were baseball fans or not.

Another factor of the Ripken phenomenon was the fact that many Americans had forsaken baseball, or felt they had been forsaken by baseball. Ripken was a bright light for baseball at one of the sport's lowest points since the Chicago Black Sox gambling scandal of 1919. A players' strike had ended the 1994 season prematurely and delayed the start of the 1995 season. Millions of fans were disgusted by the apparent greed of baseball owners and players. Attendance in 1995 plunged to its lowest point in years, but with his challenge to Gehrig's record, Ripken and the Orioles drew crowds all summer long and he was cheered by fans of rival teams just for playing in their ballparks.

On the Field, Every Day

Ripken began his drive for the record books on May 30, 1982, as a twenty-one-year-old rookie. His manager then was Earl Weaver, who had also been the Orioles manager in 1960, the year Cal Ripken was born; one of Weaver's players that year was Cal Ripken Sr., who spent most of his career as a minor league player and manager. In 1987 Cal Jr. and his brother Billy, a second baseman, both played under their father during his brief tenure as Orioles manager.

Cal Jr. grew up in the Baltimore area and said he never had any desire to play for another team. He won the American League Rookie of the Year award in 1982 and was voted an All-Star by the fans each year thereafter. In 1988 and 1991 he was voted the most valuable player in the American League.

From May 30, 1982, through September 6, 1995, the Baltimore Orioles played 19,386 innings. Ripken was on the field for all but 164 of them—

missing less than 1 percent. As a record of endurance, that achievement matched, and perhaps even surpassed, his record of consecutive games played.

Ripken generally managed to avoid the broken bones, strained muscles, and other injuries that seem inevitable in any sport, especially one in which games are played six days a week for six months. Most of his injuries were minor, and on several occasions his superb physical condition and good luck enabled him to play despite painful strains and bruises that would have sidelined many other players. Colleagues recalled that he never asked to play just to keep his streak alive.

Ripken had the complete support of his team, even a willingness by its majority owner, Peter Angelos, to forfeit an entire season to protect the streak. In the spring of 1995, when the players' strike was underway, other team owners hired replacement players and vowed to start the season using them. Angelos refused to follow suit, saying he would do nothing to jeopardize Ripken's quest for the Gehrig record. If the Orioles had no players, Ripken could not miss any games. The strike was later settled, and Ripken continued his streak.

That kind of loyalty, both Ripken's for his team and the team's loyalty to him, represented for many fans the ideal that had made baseball America's national pastime.

> *Following is the text, provided by the Baltimore Orioles, of a statement by Cal Ripken Jr. on September 6, 1995, after he broke Lou Gehrig's record for the most consecutive games played by a major league baseball player. Ripken's opening reference is to the old B & O railway warehouse next to the Camden Yards ballpark in Baltimore, where the number of his consecutive games was posted on a wall overlooking the park:*

When the game numbers on the warehouse changed during fifth innings over the past several weeks, the fans in this ballpark responded incredibly. I'm not sure that my reactions showed how I really felt. I just didn't know what to do.

Tonight, I want to make sure you know how I feel. As I grew up here, I not only had dreams of being a big league ballplayer, but also of being a Baltimore Oriole. As a boy and a fan, I know how passionate we feel about baseball and the Orioles here. And as a player, I have benefited from this passion.

For all of your support over the years, I want to thank you the fans of Baltimore, from the bottom of my heart. This is the greatest place to play.

This year has been unbelievable. I've been cheered in ball parks all over the country. People not only showed me their kindness, but more importantly, they demonstrated their love of the game of baseball. I give my thanks to baseball fans everywhere.

I also could express my gratitude to a number of individuals who have played a role in my life and my career, but if I try to mention them all, I might unintentionally miss someone and take more time than I should.

There are, however, four people I want to thank specially. Let me start by thanking my Dad. He inspired me with his commitment to the Oriole tradition and made me understand the importance of it. He not only taught me the fundamentals of the game of baseball, but also he taught me to play it the right way, and to play it the Oriole way. From the very beginning my Dad let me know how important it was to be there for your team and to be counted on by your teammates.

My mom—what can I say about my Mom? She is an unbelievable person. She let my Dad lead the way on the field, but she was there in every other way—leading and shaping the lives of our family off the field. She's the glue who held our lives together while we grew up, and she's always been my inspiration.

Dad and Mom laid the foundation for my baseball career and my life, and when I got to the big leagues, there was a man—Eddie Murray—who showed me how to play this game, day in and day out. I thank him for his example and for his friendship. I was lucky to have him as my teammate for the years we were together, and I congratulate him on the great achievement of 3,000 hits this year.

As my major league career moved along, the most important person came into my life—my wife Kelly. She has enriched it with her friendship and with her love. I thank you, Kelly, for the advice, support, and joy you have brought to me, and for always being there. You, Rachel and Ryan are my life.

These people, and many others, have allowed me, day in and day out, to play the great American game of baseball.

Tonight I stand here, overwhelmed, as my name is linked with the great and courageous Lou Gehrig. I'm truly humbled to have our names spoken in the same breath.

Some may think our strongest connection is because we both played many consecutive games. Yet I believe in my heart that our true link is a common motivation—a love of the game of baseball, a passion for our team, and a desire to compete on the very highest level.

I know that if Lou Gehrig is looking down on tonight's activities, he isn't concerned about someone playing one more consecutive game than he did. Instead, he's viewing tonight as just another example of what is good and right about the great American game. Whether your name is Gehrig or Ripken; DiMaggio or Robinson; or that of some youngster who picks up his bat or puts on his glove: you are challenged by the game of baseball to do your very best day in and day out. And that's all that I've ever tried to do.

Thank you.

PACKWOOD RESIGNATION
FROM THE SENATE
September 6 and 7, 1995

Facing the certainty of expulsion for misconduct, Sen. Bob Packwood (R-Ore.) on September 7 gave up his long fight to remain in the Senate and said he would resign. Packwood was one of the few senators ever forced from office by his colleagues.

After an investigation lasting nearly three years, the bipartisan Select Committee on Ethics voted unanimously on September 6 to expel Packwood on charges of sexual harassment and other misconduct. Packwood at first vowed to fight expulsion, but he gave in the next day when fellow senators told him he could not win.

Packwood's colleagues were relieved by his decision to resign rather than face a nasty confrontation on the Senate floor. Majority Leader Bob Dole (R-Kan.), a close friend, said Packwood "made the right decision" because "a protracted debate on the Senate floor may not have changed anything."

After Packwood announced his resignation, Dole argued that Packwood should be allowed to stay in the Senate for three months. Democrats and some Republicans adamantly opposed that plan and forced Packwood to make his resignation effective October 1.

A moderate Republican from Oregon, Packwood long had been one of the most powerful and respected members of the Senate, in large part because of his independent stance on many issues and his ability to bridge differences between the two parties. He had been in the Senate since 1969 and ranked fifth in seniority. At the time of his resignation, Packwood was chairman of the Finance Committee and was one of the Senate's acknowledged experts on the taxation and health care matters over which that committee had jurisdiction.

Sen. William V. Roth (R-Del.) took over the Finance Committee chairmanship. Five months later, in the first congressional election ever conducted entirely by mail, Rep. Ron Wyden, a Democrat, was elected to fill Packwood's unexpired term in the Senate.

A Long and Painful Investigation

Packwood's fall from the heights of American politics began shortly after the November 1992 election in which he won his fifth term in the Senate. The Washington Post *published a lengthy report documenting several cases in which Packwood allegedly forced sexual attentions on female staff members, job-seekers, and others. The incidents included forcible kissing and fondling. Packwood apologized to the women, said he had been guilty of "over-eager kissing," and blamed his behavior on alcohol. He entered a substance-abuse treatment center and stopped drinking.*

Despite Packwood's apology, the Senate ethics committee on December 1, 1992, began a preliminary inquiry into the charges raised by the Washington Post *articles. The investigation dragged on for months, with a key point reached in October 1993, when Packwood mentioned during a deposition that he had kept detailed personal diaries. The committee asked to see the diaries, but Packwood refused, and the issue reached the Senate floor the next month. After two days of debate, the Senate ordered Packwood to turn his diaries over to the committee. He again refused, and the matter went all the way to William H. Rehnquist, chief justice of the Supreme Court, who upheld an appellate court ruling that Packwood yield the diaries. Packwood did so on March 14, 1994.*

While reviewing the diaries, the ethics committee found that Packwood had attempted to alter them to hide incriminating evidence. The committee also discovered that Packwood had solicited jobs for his ex-wife from lobbyists and businessmen with interests before the Finance Committee. Packwood at the time was attempting to reduce his alimony payments.

Republicans took control of the Senate in 1995, but the ethics committee investigation continued. On May 16, 1995, the committee determined that it had "substantial, credible evidence" that Packwood had engaged in sexual misconduct at least eighteen times with seventeen women, that he had altered his diaries to cover up evidence, and that he had improperly asked lobbyists to hire his former wife. The committee announced its findings May 17.

Packwood testified privately before the committee on June 27 and 28 but refused to invoke his right to public hearings. The issue then became whether the committee itself should hold public hearings on the matter. Several of Packwood's Senate colleagues, led by Barbara Boxer (D-Calif.), demanded public hearings. The full Senate on August 2 rejected that demand on a nearly party-line vote of 48–52. The ethics committee then announced it was looking into two additional charges of sexual misconduct by Packwood—an announcement that infuriated Packwood, who said he had been assured the committee's investigation was complete.

On August 25 Packwood reversed course, demanding the public hearings he had so determinedly opposed. His sudden reversal angered many of his colleagues and caused a serious erosion of his support within the Senate.

The ethics committee met on September 6 to decide on a proper punishment for Packwood. The six members quickly found themselves in unanimous agreement that Packwood should be expelled. The committee announced its decision the same day.

Packwood vowed to fight the expulsion resolution, and the next morning he appeared on television news programs announcing his determination to stay in the Senate. One by one, Packwood's colleagues told him he had no chance of winning a fight on the Senate floor. In a dramatic appearance on the Senate floor the afternoon of September 7, Packwood admitted that he had brought dishonor on himself and said, "I do not want to visit further that dishonor on the Senate." As a result, he said, "It is my duty to resign."

Packwood made no specific mention of the charges against him. His speech was a rambling series of recollections of his years in the Senate and the friendships he had made there.

Ethics Committee Charges

The ethics committee listed its formal charges against Packwood in a resolution calling for his expulsion from the Senate. The charges were backed up in an exhaustive report that detailed numerous instances of misconduct by Packwood.

The three main charges against Packwood were the same the committee had found in May: that he tried to obstruct the committee's inquiry by withholding, altering, or destroying evidence; that he "engaged in a pattern of abuse of his position of power and authority" by repeatedly engaging in sexual misconduct; and that he abused his position by soliciting employment for his ex-wife from people who had interest in legislation before his committee.

The sexual misconduct charges were at the heart of the case against Packwood. The committee detailed eighteen instances between 1969 and 1990 in which Packwood made "unwanted and unwelcome sexual advances." Most of the women were members of his staff, Senate employees, or lobbyists. The committee said Packwood's actions "bring discredit and dishonor upon the Senate and constitute conduct unbecoming a United States senator."

The other charges against Packwood also were serious, and the committee said Packwood's attempts to alter evidence might have violated the law as well as Senate rules. Senators said those charges added weight to the overall case against Packwood, helping senators overcome any anxiety about expelling him solely for sexual misconduct.

Packwood was the first senator forced from office by his colleagues since Harrison A. Williams Jr., a New Jersey Democrat, resigned in March 1982 rather than face expulsion. Williams had been convicted in the "Abscam" scandal. (Senate Report on Williams, Historic Documents of 1981, p. 673)

Following are texts of the September 6, 1995, resolution by the Select Committee on Ethics calling for the expulsion of Sen.

Bob Packwood (R-Ore.) from the Senate and of Packwood's speech to the Senate on September 7, 1995, announcing his resignation:

ETHICS COMMITTEE RESOLUTION

Whereas, the Select Committee on Ethics on December 1, 1992, initiated a Preliminary Inquiry into allegations of sexual misconduct by Senator Bob Packwood, and subsequently expanded the scope of its inquiry to include other allegations of misconduct and so notified Senator Packwood; and

Whereas, on December 15, 1993, in light of sworn testimony that Senator Packwood may have altered evidence relevant to the Committee's Inquiry, the Chairman and Vice-Chairman determined as an inherent part of its Inquiry to inquire into the integrity of evidence sought by the Committee and into any information that anyone may have endeavored to obstruct its Inquiry, and so notified Senator Packwood; and

Whereas, on May 11, 1994, upon completion of the Committee staff's review of Senator Packwood's typewritten diaries, the Committee expanded its Inquiry again to include additional areas of potential misconduct by Senator Packwood, including solicitation of financial support for his spouse from persons with an interest in legislation, in exchange, gratitude, or recognition of his official acts; and

Whereas, on May 16, 1995, the Committee unanimously adopted a Resolution for Investigation, finding substantial credible evidence that provides substantial cause for the Committee to conclude that violations within the Committee's jurisdiction as contemplated in Section 2 (a) (1) of S. Res. 338, 88th Congress, as amended, may have occurred; to wit:

(1) Between December 1992, and November 1993, Senator Packwood intentionally altered diary materials that he knew or should have known the Committee had sought or would likely seek as part of its Preliminary Inquiry;

(2) Senator Packwood may have abused his United States Senate Office by improper conduct which has brought discredit upon the United States Senate, by engaging in a pattern of sexual misconduct between 1969 and 1990;

(3) Senator Packwood may have abused his United States Senate Office through improper conduct which has brought discredit upon the United States Senate by inappropriately linking personal financial gain to his official position in that he solicited or otherwise encouraged offers of financial assistance from persons who had a particular interest in legislation or issues that Senator Packwood could influence;

Whereas, the Committee has reviewed all the evidence before it and received the Report of its staff relating to the Investigation concerning Senator Packwood;

It is therefore resolved:

1. That the Committee finds that, on the basis of evidence received during the Inquiry and Investigation, Senator Packwood committed violations of law and rules, within the Committee's jurisdiction as contemplated in Section 2 (a) (1) of S. Res. 338, 88th Congress, as amended, and makes the following determinations:

A. Senator Packwood endeavored to obstruct and impede the Committee's Inquiry by withholding, altering and destroying relevant evidence, including his diary transcripts and audio taped diary material, conduct which is expressly prohibited by 18 U.S.C. sec. 1505 and the Committee's rules. These illegal acts constitute a crime against the Senate, and are reprehensible and contemptuous of the Senate's constitutional self-disciplinary process. Further, Senator Packwood's illegal acts constitute a violation of his duty of trust to the Senate and an abuse of his position as a United States Senator, reflecting discredit upon the United States Senate;

B. Senator Packwood engaged in a pattern of abuse of his position of power and authority as a United States Senator by repeatedly committing sexual misconduct, making at least 18 separate unwanted and unwelcome sexual advances between 1969 and 1990. In most of these instances, the victims were members of Senator Packwood's staff or individuals whose livelihoods were dependent upon or connected to the power and authority held by Senator Packwood. These improper acts bring discredit and dishonor upon the Senate and constitute conduct unbecoming a United States Senator;

C. Senator Packwood abused his position of power and authority as a United States Senator by engaging in a deliberate and systematic plan to enhance his personal financial position by soliciting, encouraging and coordinating employment opportunities for his wife from persons who had a particular interest in legislation or issues that Senator Packwood could influence. These improper acts bring discredit and dishonor upon the Senate and constitute conduct unbecoming a United States Senator.

2. That the Committee makes the following recommendation to the Senate: That Senator Packwood be expelled from the Senate for his illegal actions and improper conduct in attempting to obstruct and impede the Committee's Inquiry; engaging in a pattern of sexual misconduct in at least 17 instances between 1969 and 1990; and engaging in a plan to enhance his financial position by soliciting, encouraging and coordinating employment opportunities for his wife from individuals with interests in legislation or issues which he could influence.

3. The Committee finds that the two additional complaints of sexual misconduct against Senator Packwood, filed after the Resolution for Investigation was adopted, are serious and appear highly credible; however, the Committee concludes that it should proceed on the existing record as outlined in

the Resolution for Investigation, in order to bring this matter to a close without further delay.

PACKWOOD'S RESIGNATION SPEECH

I thank the Chair and the majority leader.

I think many of you are aware of why I am here today. I am aware of the dishonor that has befallen me in the last 3 years, and I do not want to visit further that dishonor on the Senate. I respect this institution and my colleagues too much for that.

For 27 years, I have worked alongside [senators] Bob Dole [R-Kan.], Ted Stevens [R-Alaska], and a few others from that era, and most of all with Mark Hatfield [R-Ore.], who is not just a colleague but a friend of almost 50 years and who I met when I was a teenage Young Republican. He was a bright, young, yet unelected legislator, who turned out to be my teacher, mentor, and friend.

There have been many successes in these 27 years, some failures, some frustrations. Let me remember a few, if I could have your indulgence. Hell's Canyon, that great gash in the Earth that is the boundary between Idaho and Oregon with the Snake River running through it, the deepest gorge in the United States. In the late 1960's, early 1970's, for about 6 years, we had a battle on trying to stop a dam from being built in the gorge and at the same time to create a national recreation area. . . .

I want you to picture this trip. We are on a raft trip in the river. I had been invited by environmentalists, most of whom I did not know. I had not seen the gorge before. They wanted me to see it and become involved in the saving of it. One night around the campfire, I believe it was Brock Evans who, I think, is now with the Audubon Society, then with the Sierra Club—we had a highway map of Oregon and Washington, and he takes out a marking pen, and he says, "I think this is where the boundary is." He draws it. Somebody said, "What about those minerals in Idaho." So he crosses it out and draws that up here. That became the boundaries.

The humor was—realizing this is drawn with a marking pen—that when you take it to the legislative counsel's office, if he says here—do you know how many miles that is? If he would say, "Where are these boundaries?" I would have to smile and say, "You will have to call Brock."

There was truck deregulation, an arcane subject that is probably saving consumers more money than anything in deregulation that we have done. Abortion, early on, was a lonely fight. I remember in 1970, 1971, when I introduced the first national abortion legislation, I could get no cosponsor in the Senate. There was only one nibble in the House from Pete McCloskey [R-Calif.], who did not quite come on as a sponsor. There was a nibble 2 years before *Roe versus Wade*. Those were lonely days.

That is not a fight that is even yet secure.

Israel, and my trips there, the golden domes, the fight that so many of us had made year after year to keep that bastion of our heritage safe and free, and to this date not guaranteed.

Tax reform in 1986. We were up against the verge of failure. The House had passed a middling bill. I was chairman of the Finance Committee. Every day we were voting away $15 or $20 billion in more loopholes.

I finally just adjourned the committee and said, "We are done." I remember Bill Armstrong [R-Colo.] saying, "We are done for the day?" And I said, "No, we are done for the session, we will have no more sessions."

Bill Diefenderfer, my counsel, and I went to the Irish Times for our two famous pitchers of beer. Those were the days I drank. I quit drinking years ago. I know why they call it courage—by the time we finished a second pitcher we drafted out on the napkin an outline and really said, OK, they want tax reform, we will give them tax reform.

Here is an example where this body can move when it wants to move. From the time that committee first saw the bill until they passed it in 12 days, [Sen.] Pat Moynihan [D-N.Y.] was a critical player. The six of us met every morning at 8:30 before the meeting. It passed the Senate within a month. So when people say this body cannot move, this body can move.

Maybe some of the best advice I had came from Bill Roth, successor to [Sen.] John Williams [R-Del.], years ago, when he used the expression—we were having a debate in those days about the filibuster and cloture and how many votes. In those days I was in favor of lowering the number. I am not sure, even though we are in the majority I would favor that now, from two-thirds to 60 votes. John Williams said we make more mistakes in haste than we lose opportunities in delay.

If something should pass, it will pass. It may take 4 or 5 years. That is not a long time in the history of the Republic. Too often in haste we pass things and have to repent.

So for whatever advice I have I hope we would not make things too easy in this body and slip through—I say that as a member of the majority.

Tuition tax credits, a failure. Pat Moynihan and I introduced the first bill in 1977, and have been introducing it ever since. Its day may come. It may be here.

One of the great moments of humor—you have to picture this situation—was in the Carter administration. They were terribly opposed to this tuition tax credit bill. [Health, Education, and Welfare] Secretary [Joseph A.] Califano [Jr.] testified against it twice in the Ways and Means Committee. Came to a Finance Committee hearing and [HEW] Assistant Secretary for Legislative Affairs Dick Warden came to testify. He had previously been with the United Auto Workers and was hired on as a lobbyist, basically for Health and Human Services—HEW as it was called then.

Thirty seconds into his testimony, Senator Moynihan leans forward and said, "Mr. Warden, why are you here? Why are you here?"

Mr. Warden goes, "Why, I am the Assistant Secretary for Legislative Affairs for the Department of Health, Education and Welfare, and I am here representing the Secretary, the administration."

Pat goes, "No, no, Mr. Warden, I did not do the emphasis right. Why are 'you' here? Secretary Califano testified twice in opposition to this bill in the House. In this committee, where there is a more favorable climate, where is the Secretary today?"

Mr. Warden goes, "Why, I think he is in Cleveland speaking."

Pat goes, "Well, where is the Under Secretary? Why is he not here today representing the administration? Mr. Warden, why?"

"I am not sure."

And Pat's voice rising, saying, "Where is the Assistant Secretary for Education? Mr. Warden, I was in the Kennedy administration when that position was created and I can say that man has utterly nothing to do at all. He could be here testifying today. Mr. Warden, I will tell you where they are. They are up on the eighth floor of their building, cowering under their desks, afraid to come and testify on the most important piece of education legislation introduced in this century, and Mr. Warden that is why you are here. Now, please go on."

Poor old Mr. Warden barely went on.

I had more humor in education from Pat than probably anybody here.

Friendships beyond count. The camaraderie is unbelievable. I look at [Sen.] John Chafee [R-R.I.] sitting back here, my squash partner. His secretary, about every 3 months, kicks out our squash matches. Over 15 years, 202 to 199. His secretary not only kicks out the matches, but the games and the scores within the match. John every now and then presents it to me, back we go, back and forth, back and forth, and evenly matched as you can be.

Some here—Senator [Robert C.] Byrd [D-W.Va.] would, Senator [Jim] Exon [D-Neb.] would—some in my age group will remember General [Douglas] MacArthur's final speech at West Point: Duty, honor, country.

It is my duty to resign. It is the honorable thing to do for this country, for this Senate.

So I now announce that I will resign from the Senate, and I leave this institution not with malice but with love, good luck, Godspeed.

UNABOMBER MANIFESTO ON SOCIETY'S ILLS
September 19, 1995

At the request of federal law enforcement officials, the New York Times and the Washington Post on September 19 published a 35,000-word manuscript reportedly written by the "Unabomber," a serial mail bomber. Investigators said the Unabomber was responsible for sixteen bombings, starting in 1978, that had killed three people and injured twenty-three others. He had promised to stop his bombings if either newspaper ran his detailed denunciation of modern technology and industrial society.

The two newspapers jointly financed printing of the Unabomber's manifesto as an eight-page special section, consisting of 232 numbered paragraphs and 36 footnotes. The Post distributed it as part of its regular editions on September 19. Copies of the document also were available on several on-line computer networks, including the Internet.

Publication of the Unabomber's text by two of the country's most prestigious newspapers set off a furious debate among journalists about giving into terrorist blackmail and government pressure. Executives at the newspapers said they were reluctant to publish the text, but officials had convinced them that doing so might help the search for the Unabomber.

As of the end of 1995, the Unabomber had not struck again, and federal investigators were continuing their seventeen-year search for him. The New York Times reported on November 6 that the published manifesto had forced investigators to rethink their theories about the Unabomber's background and motives. The Times reported that some investigators had abandoned the prevailing theory that the Unabomber was a terrorist pursuing an antitechnology political agenda and were instead working on the assumption that he was a serial killer trying to satisfy a psychological need by attacking others.

The Unabomber's Attacks

The Unabomber first struck on May 25, 1978, when a package bomb exploded at the Chicago Circle campus of the University of Illinois, injur-

ing one person. One person was injured by another bomb in May 1979 at the Northwestern University campus in Evanston, Illinois, just north of Chicago. Those early bombings led investigators to believe the Unabomber might have once lived in the Chicago area, possibly as a student. The Federal Bureau of Investigation (FBI) referred to his case as UNABOMB, which led to the general reference to the bomber himself as the Unabomber. In his manifesto, the Unabomber referred to himself as "FC."

Many of the Unabomber's attacks were directed against college campuses. His bombs injured professors at the University of California, Berkeley, in 1982, 1985, and 1993; at the University of California, San Francisco, in 1983; and at Yale University in 1993.

During all those years, the Unabomber acted in silence, issuing no statements and leaving few traces other than his bombs. That changed after the April 19, 1995, bombing of the federal office building in Oklahoma City—an attack that killed 168 people and wounded many more. Two men were charged in connection with that bombing. (Oklahoma City bombing, p. 176)

The next day, the Unabomber mailed four letters, including one to the New York Times, *in which he described the FBI as "surprisingly incompetent." The Unabomber said he was writing a manuscript and that he would stop mailing the bombs if his manuscript was published by the* Times *or another major news organization. At the same time, the Unabomber mailed a bomb that killed Gilbert Murray, a timber industry executive in Sacramento, California. Some investigators theorized that the Unabomber resented the attention paid the Oklahoma City bombing, for which he apparently was not responsible.*

In June, the Unabomber mailed copies of his manifesto to the Times, *the* Washington Post, *and* Penthouse *magazine. It consisted of more than sixty single-spaced pages. He included a letter saying he would send another bomb, to an unspecified location, with the "intent to kill" unless one of the newspapers published his manifesto within three months.*

The FBI analyzed the document and declared it authentic. On September 13, as the Unabomber's deadline approached, Donald E. Graham, publisher of the Post, *and Arthur O. Sulzberger Jr., publisher of the* Times, *met with Attorney General Janet Reno and FBI Director Louis J. Freeh. The two officials urged the newspaper executives to publish the manifesto, in hopes that the Unabomber would keep his word not to bomb again and that publication would produce new leads to his location and identity.*

Graham said his newspaper would not have printed the manifesto for "journalistic reasons" but did so for "public safety reasons." The two newspapers shared the cost of publishing the document, but only the Post *distributed it with its regular editions because the* Times *did not have the mechanical ability to do so.*

The decision to print the Unabomber's manifesto produced intense criticism within journalistic and law enforcement circles. The Post *quoted William Serrin, chairman of the journalism department at New York University, as calling the publication decision "disgraceful, absolutely dis-*

*graceful. You're giving your paper over to a murderer and letting the gov-
ernment dictate what you print in your paper."*

*Others argued that the newspapers were "rewarding" the Unabomber, in
effect giving into his blackmail and encouraging him—and other terrorists
as well—to make similar demands in the future. Still others faulted Reno
and Freeh for pressuring the newspapers to publish the document; doing
so, these critics said, made the newspaper executives feel they would be
responsible if they did not publish the text and the Unabomber struck
again.*

The Unabomber's Arguments

*The Unabomber called his document "Industrial Society and Its Future."
The text referred repeatedly to the author or authors as "we," but federal
investigators said they were convinced it was the work of one man. They
said the Unabomber might have used the plural form to give the impression he was part of a broader group.*

*The opening line established the tone for the remainder, serving as a
succinct summary of a very long and detailed document: "The Industrial
Revolution and its consequences have been a disaster for the human race."
From there, the document reviewed the "suffering" of mankind and nature
as a result of industrial technology, then of more advanced technology such
as computers.*

*Much of the manifesto discussed the political and psychological impact
of technology, focusing in particular on the history of "leftism" in the twentieth century and such trends as feminism. The Unabomber devoted more
than thirty paragraphs to his attack on "leftist" ideologies and movements,
from liberalism to communism, arguing that all were at odds with nature
and personal freedom. His specific complaints ranged from recent antito-
bacco campaigns to the "political correctness" movement that he said was
part of the left's drive for total political power.*

*In his fourth paragraph, the Unabomber advocated a "revolution against
the industrial system," a revolution he said that might or might not make
use of violence. Unlike most other revolutions, he said, this would not be a
political one aimed at governments but would have the object of over-
throwing the "economic and technological basis of the present society."
Factories, laboratories, books, and other sources of technological knowledge
must be destroyed, he said.*

*Although the Unabomber characterized himself as a revolutionary, and
his actions were outside the law, he exhibited a remarkable respect for one
of the most widely violated legal principles: the copyright law. One footnote
included a lengthy quote from a book,* Violence in America: Historical and
Comparative Perspectives, *edited by Hugh Davis Graham and Ted Robert
Gurr. At the end of his document, he acknowledged that copyright laws
might "make it impossible for this long quotation to be printed," and so he
briefly summarized the quotation and said that could be used instead. The
newspapers printed both versions.*

Following are excerpts from the manifesto, "Industrial Society and Its Future," allegedly written by the Unabomber and jointly published on September 19, 1995, by the New York Times *and the* Washington Post:

Introduction

1. The Industrial Revolution and its consequences have been a disaster for the human race. They have greatly increased the life-expectancy of those of us who live in "advanced" countries, but they have destabilized society, have made life unfulfilling, have subjected human beings to indignities, have led to widespread psychological suffering (in the Third World to physical suffering as well) and have inflicted severe damage on the natural world. The continued development of technology will worsen the situation. It will certainly subject human beings to greater indignities and inflict greater damage on the natural world, it will probably lead to greater social disruption and psychological suffering, and it may lead to increased physical suffering even in "advanced" countries.

2. The industrial-technological system may survive or it may break down. If it survives, it MAY eventually achieve a low level of physical and psychological suffering, but only after passing through a long and very painful period of adjustment and only at the cost of permanently reducing human beings and many other living organisms to engineered products and mere cogs in the social machine. Furthermore, if the system survives, the consequences will be inevitable: There is no way of reforming or modifying the system so as to prevent it from depriving people of dignity and autonomy.

3. If the system breaks down the consequences will still be very painful. But the bigger the system grows the more disastrous the results of its breakdown will be, so if it is to break down it had best break down sooner rather than later.

4. We therefore advocate a revolution against the industrial system. This revolution may or may not make use of violence: it may be sudden or it may be a relatively gradual process spanning a few decades. We can't predict any of that. But we do outline in a very general way the measures that those who hate the industrial system should take in order to prepare the way for a revolution against that form of society. This is not to be a POLITICAL revolution. Its object will be to overthrow not governments but the economic and technological basis of the present society.

5. In this article we give attention to only some of the negative developments that have grown out of the industrial-technological system. Other such developments we mention only briefly or ignore altogether. This does not mean that we regard these other developments as unimportant. For practical reasons we have to confine our discussion to areas that have received insufficient public attention or in which we have something new to say. For example, since there are well-developed environmental and wilderness movements, we have written very little about environmental degradation or the destruction of wild nature, even though we consider these to be highly important.

The Psychology of Modern Leftism

6. Almost everyone will agree that we live in a deeply troubled society. One of the most widespread manifestations of the craziness of our world is leftism, so a discussion of the psychology of leftism can serve as an introduction to the discussion of the problems of modern society in general.

7. But what is leftism? During the first half of the 20th century leftism could have been practically identified with socialism. Today the movement is fragmented and it is not clear who can properly be called a leftist. When we speak of leftists in this article we have in mind mainly socialists, collectivists, "politically correct" types, feminists, gay and disability activists, animal rights activists and the like. But not everyone who is associated with one of these movements is a leftist. What we are trying to get at in discussing leftism is not so much a movement or an ideology as a psychological type, or rather a collection of related types. Thus, what we mean by "leftism" will emerge more clearly in the course of our discussion of leftist psychology. . . .

8. Even so, our conception of leftism will remain a good deal less clear than we would wish, but there doesn't seem to be any remedy for this. All we are trying to do is indicate in a rough and approximate way the two psychological tendencies that we believe are the main driving force of modern leftism. We by no means claim to be telling the WHOLE truth about leftist psychology. Also, our discussion is meant to apply to modern leftism only. We leave open the question of the extent to which our discussion could be applied to the leftists of the 19th and early 20th century.

9. The two psychological tendencies that underlie modern leftism we call "feelings of inferiority" and "oversocialization." Feelings of inferiority are characteristic of modern leftism as a whole, while oversocialization is characteristic only of a certain segment of modern leftism; but this segment is highly influential. . . .

Strategy

180. The technophiles are taking us all on an utterly reckless ride into the unknown. Many people understand something of what technological progress is doing to us yet take a passive attitude toward it because they think it is inevitable. But we (FC) don't think it is inevitable. We think it can be stopped, and we will give here some indications of how to go about stopping it.

181. . . . [T]he two main tasks for the present are to promote social stress and instability in industrial society and to develop and propagate an ideology that opposes technology and the industrial system. When the system becomes sufficiently stressed and unstable, a revolution against technology may be possible. The pattern would be similar to that of the French and Russian Revolutions. French society and Russian society, for several decades prior to their respective revolutions, showed increasing signs of stress and weakness. Meanwhile, ideologies were being developed that offered a new world view that was quite different from the old one. In the Russian case, rev-

olutionaries were actively working to undermine the old order. Then, when the old system was put under sufficient additional stress (by financial crisis in France, by military defeat in Russia) it was swept away by revolution. What we propose [is] something along the same lines.

182. It will be objected that the French and Russian Revolutions were failures. But most revolutions have two goals. One is to destroy an old form of society and the other is to set up the new form of society envisioned by the revolutionaries. The French and Russian revolutionaries failed (fortunately!) to create the new kind of society of which they dreamed, but they were quite successful in destroying the existing form of society.

183. But an ideology, in order to gain enthusiastic support, must have a positive ideal [as] well as a negative one; it must be FOR something as well as AGAINST something. The positive ideal that we propose is Nature. That is, WILD nature; those aspects of the functioning of the Earth and its living things that are independent of human management and free of human interference and control. And with wild nature we include human nature, by which we mean those aspects of the functioning of the human individual that are not subject to regulation by organized society but are products of chance, or free will, or God (depending on your religious or philosophical opinions).

184. Nature makes a perfect counter-ideal to technology for several reasons. Nature (that which is outside the power of the system) is the opposite of technology (which seeks to expand indefinitely the power of the system). Most people will agree that nature is beautiful; certainly it has tremendous popular appeal. The radical environmentalists ALREADY hold an ideology that exalts nature and opposes technology. It is not necessary for the sake of nature to set up some chimerical utopia or any new kind of social order. Nature takes care of itself: It was a spontaneous creation that existed long before any human society, and for countless centuries many different kinds of human societies coexisted with nature without doing it an excessive amount of damage. Only with the Industrial Revolution did the effect of human society on nature become really devastating. To relieve the pressure on nature it is not necessary to create a special kind of social system, it is only necessary to get rid of industrial society. Granted, this will not solve all problems. Industrial society has already done tremendous damage to nature and it will take a very long time for the scars to heal. Besides, even pre-industrial societies can do significant damage to nature. Nevertheless, getting rid of industrial society will accomplish a great deal. It will relieve the worst of the pressure on nature so that the scars can begin to heal. It will remove the capacity of organized society to keep increasing its control over nature (including human nature). Whatever kind of society may exist after the demise of the industrial system, it is certain that most people will live close to nature, because in the absence of advanced technology there is [no] other way that people CAN live. To feed themselves they must be peasants or herdsmen or fishermen or hunters, etc., And, generally speaking, local autonomy should tend to increase, because lack of advanced technology and rapid

communications will limit the capacity of governments or other large organizations to control local communities.

185. As for the negative consequences of eliminating industrial society—well, you can't eat your cake and have it too. To gain one thing you have to sacrifice another.

186. Most people hate psychological conflict. For this reason they avoid doing any serious thinking about difficult social issues, and they like to have such issues presented to them in simple, black-and-white terms: THIS is all good and THAT is all bad. The revolutionary ideology should therefore be developed on two levels.

187. On the more sophisticated level the ideology should address itself to people who are intelligent, thoughtful and rational. The object should be to create a core of people who will be opposed to the industrial system on a rational, thought-out basis, with full appreciation of the problems and ambiguities involved, and of the price that has to be paid for getting rid of the system. It is particularly important to attract people of this type, as they are capable people and will be instrumental in influencing others. These people should be addressed on as rational a level as possible. Facts should never intentionally be distorted and intemperate language should be avoided. This does not mean that no appeal can be made to the emotions, but in making such appeal care should be taken to avoid misrepresenting the truth or doing anything else that would destroy the intellectual respectability of the ideology.

188. On a second level, the ideology should be propagated in a simplified form that will enable the unthinking majority to see the conflict of technology vs. nature in unambiguous terms. But even on this second level the ideology should not be expressed in language that is so cheap, intemperate or irrational that it alienates people of the thoughtful and rational type. Cheap, intemperate propaganda sometimes achieves impressive short-term gains, but it will be more advantageous in the long run to keep the loyalty of a small number of intelligently committed people than to arouse the passions of an unthinking, fickle mob who will change their attitude as soon as someone comes along with a better propaganda gimmick. However, propaganda of the rabble-rousing type may be necessary when the system is nearing the point of collapse and there is a final struggle between rival ideologies to determine which will become dominant when the old world-view goes under.

189. Prior to that final struggle, the revolutionaries should not expect to have a majority of people on their side. History is made by active, determined minorities, not by the majority, which seldom has a clear and consistent idea of what it really wants. Until the time comes for the final push toward revolution, the task of revolutionaries will be less to win the shallow support of the majority than to build a small core of deeply committed people. As for the majority, it will be enough to make them aware of the existence of the new ideology and remind them of it frequently; though of course it will be desirable to get majority support to the extent that this can be done without weakening the core of seriously committed people.

190. Any kind of social conflict helps to destabilize the system, but one should be careful about what kind of conflict one encourages. The line of conflict should be drawn between the mass of the people and the power-holding elite of industrial society (politicians, scientists, upper-level business executives, government officials, etc.). It should NOT be drawn between the revolutionaries and the mass of the people. For example, it would be bad strategy for the revolutionaries to condemn Americans for their habits of consumption. Instead, the average American should be portrayed as a victim of the advertising and marketing industry, which has suckered him into buying a lot of junk that he doesn't need and that is very poor compensation for his lost freedom. Either approach is consistent with the facts. It is merely a matter of attitude whether you blame the advertising industry for manipulating the public or blame the public for allowing itself to be manipulated. As a matter of strategy one should generally avoid blaming the public.

191. One should think twice before encouraging any other social conflict than that between the power-holding elite (which wields technology) and the general public (over which technology exerts its power). For one thing, other conflicts tend to distract attention from the important conflicts (between power-elite and ordinary people, between technology and nature); for another thing, other conflicts may actually tend to encourage technologization, because each side in such a conflict wants to use technological power to gain advantages over its adversary. This is clearly seen in rivalries between nations. It also appears in ethnic conflicts within nations. For example, in America many black leaders are anxious to gain power for African Americans by placing back individuals in the technological power-elite. They want there to be many black government officials, scientists, corporation executives and so forth. In this way they are helping to absorb the African American subculture into the technological system. Generally speaking, one should encourage only those social conflicts that can be fitted into the framework of the conflicts of power-elite vs. ordinary people, technology vs. nature.

192. But the way to discourage ethnic conflict is NOT through militant advocacy of minority rights. . . . Instead, the revolutionaries should emphasize that although minorities do suffer more or less disadvantage, this disadvantage is of peripheral significance. Our real enemy is the industrial-technological system, and in the struggle against the system, ethnic distinctions are of no importance.

193. The kind of revolution we have in mind will not necessarily involve an armed uprising against any government. It may or may not involve physical violence, but it will not be a POLITICAL revolution. Its focus will be on technology and economics, not politics.

194. Probably the revolutionaries should even AVOID assuming political power, whether by legal or illegal means, until the industrial system is stressed to the danger point and has proved itself to be a failure in the eyes of most people. Suppose for example that some "green" party should win control of the United States Congress in an election. In order to avoid betraying or watering down their own ideology they would have to take vigorous

measures to turn economic growth into economic shrinkage. To the average man the results would appear disastrous: There would be massive unemployment, shortages of commodities, etc. Even if the grosser ill effects could be avoided through superhumanly skillful management, still people would have to begin giving up the luxuries to which they have become addicted. Dissatisfaction would grow, the "green" party would be voted out of office and the revolutionaries would have suffered a severe setback. For this reason the revolutionaries should not try to acquire political power until the system has gotten itself into such a mess that any hardships will be seen as resulting from the failures of the industrial system itself and not from the policies of the revolutionaries. The revolution against technology will probably have to be a revolution by outsiders, a revolution from below and not from above.

195. The revolution must be international and worldwide. It cannot be carried out on a nation-by-nation basis. Whenever it is suggested that the United States, for example, should cut back on technological progress or economic growth, people get hysterical and start screaming that if we fall behind in technology the Japanese will get ahead of us. Holy robots The world will fly off its orbit if the Japanese ever sell more cars than we do! (Nationalism is a great promoter of technology.) More reasonably, it is argued that if the relatively democratic nations of the world fall behind in technology while nasty, dictatorial nations like China, Vietnam and North Korea continue to progress, eventually the dictators may come to dominate the world. That is why the industrial system should be attacked in all nations simultaneously, to the extent that this may be possible. True, there is no assurance that the industrial system can be destroyed at approximately the same time all over the world, and it is even conceivable that the attempt to overthrow the system could lead instead to the domination of the system by dictators. That is a risk that has to be taken. And it is worth taking, since the difference between a "democratic" industrial system and one controlled by dictators is small compared with the difference between an industrial system and a non-industrial one. It might even be argued that an industrial system controlled by dictators would be preferable, because dictator-controlled systems usually have proved inefficient, hence they are presumably more likely to break down. Look at Cuba.

196. Revolutionaries might consider favoring measures that tend to bind the world economy into a unified whole. Free trade agreements like NAFTA and GATT are probably harmful to the environment in the short run, but in the long run they may perhaps be advantageous because they foster economic interdependence between nations. It will be easier to destroy the industrial system on a worldwide basis if the world economy is so unified that its breakdown in any one major nation will lead to its breakdown in all industrialized nations.

197. Some people take the line that modern man has too much power, too much control over nature; they argue for a more passive attitude on the part of the human race. At best these people are expressing themselves unclear-

ly, because they fail to distinguish between power for LARGE ORGANIZA-TIONS and power for INDIVIDUALS and SMALL GROUPS. It is a mistake to argue for powerlessness and passivity, because people NEED power. Modern man as a collective entity—that is, the industrial system—has immense power over nature, and we (FC) regard this as evil. But modern INDIVIDU-ALS and SMALL GROUPS OF INDIVIDUALS have far less power than primitive man ever did. Generally speaking, the vast power of "modern man" over nature is exercised not by individuals or small groups but by large organizations. To the extent that the average modern INDIVIDUAL can wield the power of technology, he is permitted to do so only within narrow limits and only under the supervision and control of the system. (You need a license for everything and with the license come rules and regulations). The individual has only those technological powers with which the system chooses to provide him. His PERSONAL power over nature is slight.

198. Primitive INDIVIDUALS and SMALL GROUPS actually had considerable power over nature; or maybe it would be better to say power WITHIN nature. When primitive man needed food he knew how to find and prepare edible roots, how to track game and take it with homemade weapons. He knew how to protect himself from heat, cold, rain, dangerous animals, etc. But primitive man did relatively little damage to nature because the COLLECTIVE power of primitive society was negligible compared to the COLLECTIVE power of industrial society.

199. Instead of arguing for powerlessness and passivity, one should argue that the power of the INDUSTRIAL SYSTEM should be broken, and that this will greatly INCREASE the power and freedom of INDIVIDUALS and SMALL GROUPS.

200. Until the industrial system has been thoroughly wrecked, the destruction of that system must be the revolutionaries' ONLY goal. Other goals would distract attention and energy from the main goal. More importantly, if the revolutionaries permit themselves to have any other goal than the destruction of technology, they will be tempted to use technology as a tool for reaching that other goal. If they give in to that temptation, they will fall right back into the technological trap, because modern technology is a unified, tightly organized system, so that, in order to retain SOME technology, one finds oneself obliged to retain MOST technology, hence one ends up sacrificing only token amounts of technology.

201. Suppose for example that the revolutionaries took "social justice" as a goal. Human nature being what it is, social justice would not come about spontaneously; it would have to be enforced. In order to enforce it the revolutionaries would have to retain central organization and control. For that they would need rapid long-distance transportation and communication, and therefore all the technology needed to support the transportation and communication systems. To feed and clothe poor people they would have to use agricultural and manufacturing technology. And so forth. So that the attempt to insure social justice would force them to retain most parts of the technological system. Not that we have anything against social justice, but

it must not be allowed to interfere with the effort to get rid of the technological system.

202. It would be hopeless for revolutionaries to try to attack the system without using SOME modern technology. If nothing else they must use the communications media to spread their message. But they should use modern technology for only ONE purpose: to attack the technological system.

203. Imagine an alcoholic sitting with a barrel of wine in front of him. Suppose he starts saying to himself, "Wine isn't bad for you if used in moderation. Why, they say small amounts of wine are even good for you! It won't do me any harm if I take just one little drink. . . ." Well you know what is going to happen. Never forget that the human race with technology is just like an alcoholic with a barrel of wine.

204. Revolutionaries should have as many children as they can. There is strong scientific evidence that social attitudes are to a significant extent inherited. No one suggests that a social attitude is a direct outcome of a person's genetic constitution, but it appears that personality traits tend, within the context of our society, to make a person more likely to hold this or that social attitude. Objections to these findings have been raised, but objections are feeble and seem to be ideologically motivated. In any event, no one denies that children tend on the average to hold social attitudes similar to those of their parents. From our point of view it doesn't matter all that much whether the attitudes are passed on genetically or through childhood training. In either case [they] ARE passed on.

205. The trouble is that many of the people who are inclined to rebel against the industrial system are also concerned about the population problems, hence they are apt to have few or no children. In this way they may be handing the world over to the sort of people who support or at least accept the industrial system. To insure the strength of the next generation of revolutionaries the present generation must reproduce itself abundantly. In doing so they will be worsening the population problem only slightly. And the most important problem is to get rid of the industrial system, because once the industrial system is gone the world's population necessarily will decrease. . . , whereas, if the industrial system survives, it will continue developing new techniques of food production that may enable the world's population to keep increasing almost indefinitely.

206. With regard to revolutionary strategy, the only points on which we absolutely insist are that the single overriding goal must be the elimination of modern technology, and that no other goal can be allowed to compete with this one. For the rest, revolutionaries should take an empirical approach. If experience indicates that some of the recommendations made in the foregoing paragraphs are not going to give good results, then those recommendations should be discarded. . . .

CLOSING ARGUMENTS IN THE O. J. SIMPSON TRIAL
September 26–29, 1995

The racial divide in the United States was on full display on October 3, when a Los Angeles jury acquitted former football star O. J. (Orenthal James) Simpson of the June 12, 1994, murders of his former wife Nicole Brown Simpson and her friend Ronald L. Goldman. From the time of his arrest until the verdict was handed down more than a year later, the case had millions of Americans closely following the daily televised coverage of the case. A majority of African-Americans seemed to rally to Simpson's side, painting him as a victim of a racist police force and an unjust legal system. A majority of whites, on the other hand, believed that the evidence, including genetic material, proved Simpson's guilt; they saw the acquittal of a man who had allegedly beaten his wife on several occasions as a miscarriage of justice.

Had it not been for Simpson's celebrity status, the murders likely would not have gripped public attention. The fact that Simpson was black and his wife white undoubtedly heightened interest in the trial and its outcome but did not seem to be a shaping factor. As many pundits commented, the trial was not only a process to determine a man's innocence or guilt but also a forum for broader issues—domestic abuse and a corrupt legal system.

Although many whites were appalled by the jubilation with which many blacks greeted the verdict, numerous black spokesmen were quick to divorce those celebrations from the crimes themselves. "The rejoicing is not that somebody got away with murder, but that somebody beat the system," said Lani Guinier, a legal scholar whose nomination to become President Bill Clinton's assistant attorney general for civil rights was withdrawn in June 1993 amid controversy about the content of her academic publications on minority rights.

Simpson "became every black male who's ever been involved in the criminal justice system," Wilbert A. Tatum, editor and publisher of the Amsterdam News, *a prominent black weekly in New York City. "It was the black male in America who was on trial," Tatum said, yet "he was more of a success of white America."*

Indeed, by almost anyone's definition, Simpson appeared to be a success, moving from stardom on the football field to lucrative roles in movies and commercials. His long-running association with the rental car company Hertz brought him instant recognition throughout the country as well as wealth. Yet Simpson, who appeared so earnest and congenial on the television screen, was also an abusive husband, pleading no contest to a charge of spousal battery in 1989, allegedly beating and threatening Nicole Simpson on several other occasions, and allegedly stalking her after they were divorced.

Simpson was arrested on June 17, 1994, five days after a neighbor found the two brutally slashed bodies lying in pools of blood outside Nicole Simpson's townhouse. On June 22, he pleaded "absolutely, 100 percent not guilty."

The Evidence—and Evidence of Contamination

For those who wanted to believe Simpson guilty, the evidence presented at his trial seemed convincing. "He killed her out of jealousy," Christopher Darden argued for the prosecution. "He killed her because he couldn't have her, and if he couldn't have her, he didn't want anyone else to." He also appeared to have the opportunity. The prosecution argued that Simpson was unseen for approximately an hour and a half on the evening of June 12, enough time to drive to his former wife's house, commit the murders, and return to his own house before a limousine driver picked him up to take him to the airport for a scheduled trip to Chicago.

Genetic testing of evidence seemed to support the prosecution's arguments. A glove found on Simpson's estate matched a glove at the crime scene and had blood and hair follicles that genetically matched Nicole Simpson's and Goldman's, as well as fibers identical to those in Goldman's shirt and Simpson's Ford Bronco. Analysis showed that a pair of socks found in Simpson's bedroom had a drop of blood that matched Simpson's and another drop that matched Nicole Simpson's. A blue knit cap at the crime scene contained hairs that seemed to match Simpson's, as well as fibers matching those in his car.

Simpson's defense team countered, both before and during the trial, that Simpson did not have time to commit the crime and that a "cesspool of contamination" had so tainted the evidence that it should be disregarded. Much of the contamination resulted from sloppy handling of blood samples, the defense said, but Simpson's attorneys also argued that one of the bloody gloves had deliberately been moved from the crime scene to Simpson's estate by Los Angeles police detective Mark Fuhrman, in an attempt to frame the former football hero.

Fuhrman, who retired from the police department in August 1995, denied doing any such thing, but he also denied on the witness stand that he had used the word "nigger" at any time in the previous ten years. In late

August defense attorneys showed that Fuhrman was not only a racist but a liar, when they played—out of earshot of the jury—a series of interviews Fuhrman had made with an aspiring screen writer, all taped after 1985, in which he used the racial epithet forty-one times. Fuhrman also boasted on the tapes that he had harassed blacks and interracial couples and that in previous cases he had made up evidence and lied on the witness stand. For blacks listening to the trial, the Fuhrman tapes confirmed what they seemed always to have known: that blacks in general, and Simpson in particular, were the victims of a racist and unjust legal system. Judge Lance A. Ito eventually decided to let the jury hear only two, relatively innocuous, portions of the tapes. Even that was enough to discredit Fuhrman's testimony.

Another significant moment in the trial involved the examination of the bloody gloves. In what was widely considered to be a serious blunder, the prosecution asked Simpson to try on the gloves. He put them on, but only after tugging and pulling at them, leaving the impression that they were too small to have been his gloves. The incident led to the famous line Simpson's chief defense attorney, Johnnie L. Cochran, used again and again in his closing arguments: "If it doesn't fit, you must acquit."

Closing Arguments

Throughout his closing remarks September 27 and 28, Cochran argued that the prosecution had not proved its case beyond a reasonable doubt. The available evidence was tainted, he said, and the prosecution had never produced a murder weapon or the clothes that Simpson had worn when he was allegedly committing the murders. Given the brutality of the murders, much more blood should have been found at Simpson's house or in his car, Cochran said. Furthermore, the evidence showed that Goldman struggled with his assailant. Yet, Cochran said, Simpson showed no sign of injury except for one minor cut, which the prosecution claimed but did not prove was sustained during commission of the crime.

Cochran also appealed to the jury to find the Los Angeles Police Department guilty of covering up for a racist police officer by setting Simpson free. "[T]here are still Mark Fuhrmans in this world, in this country, who hate and yet are embraced by people in power," Cochran said. "But you and I fighting for freedom and ideals and for justice for all, must continue to fight to expose hate and genocidal racism. . . . [I]f you don't speak out, if you don't stand up, if you don't do what's right, this kind of conduct will continue on forever and we will never have an ideal society. . . ."

In his closing remarks September 29, prosecutor Darden reminded the jury that it was Simpson who was on trial, not Fuhrman. "You can't send a message to Fuhrman, you can't send a message to the LAPD, you can't eradicate racism within the LAPD or within the L.A. community or within the nation as whole by delivering a verdict of not guilty," he said.

Marcia Clark, the lead prosecutor, reviewed point by point the evidence that she said proved beyond a reasonable doubt that Simpson had committed the murders. "Usually I feel like I'm the only one left to speak for the vic-

tims," she said. "But in this case, Ron and Nicole are speaking to you. . . . And they both are telling you who did it with their hair, their clothes, their bodies, their blood. They tell you he did it. . . . Will you hear them or will you ignore their plea for justice. . . ." She then replayed tapes of Nicole Simpson calling the emergency 911 line in 1989 and 1993 to seek protection from Simpson and showed pictures of the murdered victims one final time.

Aftermath

The jury of ten women and two men—nine blacks, two whites, and one Hispanic—deliberated for less than four hours before returning their verdict of not guilty and returning to their homes after nearly ninth months of sequestration. In a statement Simpson said he was "relieved that this part of the incredible nightmare" was over, but he still faced further legal action in the form of wrongful death suits from the Brown and Goldman families and a possible battle over custody of his and Nicole's two young children, who lived with their maternal grandparents during the trial.

There was much speculation in the press about Simpson's financial future. His defense in the murder trial was estimated to have cost as much as $10 million; he reportedly earned at least $1 million from a book he wrote before the trial in which he proclaimed his innocence and another $1 million from the tabloid magazine Star *for the exclusive story and photographs of a celebration party at his estate after his acquittal. Whether Simpson could and would continue his lucrative career as an advertising spokesmen was in doubt, as was a proposal for a pay-per-view interview on a cable network, which some said might bring in as much as $100 million.*

There was also a great deal of speculation about various reforms that might result from the Simpson case. Judges expected fewer requests to sequester juries for fear of souring them; tensions caused by sequestration of the Simpson jury came close to causing a mistrial at least once during the case. Judges were expected to exercise more discipline over attorneys in the courtroom. Judge Ito had been severely criticized for not cutting off what many considered to be excessive arguments and thus causing needless delays in the trial. Barely a week after the trial concluded, an ethics rule curbing what attorneys could tell the media outside of the courtroom went into effect in California; several other states were expected to follow suit.

Several defense attorneys said they feared states would rush to enact new laws making it more difficult for defense attorneys to win their case. One proposal was to allow juries to draw an adverse inference from a defendant's failure to testify, something they were forbidden from doing under current law. (Simpson did not testify at his trial.) Another was to allow convictions on less than a unanimous jury. Other proposals would allow only the judge to interview prospective jurors and would end or limit the number of prospective jurors each side could reject without cause.

Still others argued that television cameras should be removed from the courtroom, if only to reduce the circuslike atmosphere that was likely to accompany any trial involving a celebrity or a crime of great national interest, such as the bombing of the federal building in Oklahoma City in April. (Oklahoma City bombing, p. 176)

> *Following are excerpts of closing arguments in the trial of Oren-*
> *thal James Simpson for the first-degree murders of his former*
> *wife Nicole Brown Simpson and her friend Ronald L. Goldman.*
> *Simpson's chief defense attorney Johnnie L. Cochran made his*
> *argument September 27–28, 1995; he was rebutted by prosecu-*
> *tion attorneys Christopher Darden and Marcia Clark on Sep-*
> *tember 29, 1995:*

COCHRAN'S CLOSING ARGUMENTS

[T]heir theory doesn't make sense. And when you are back there deliberating on this case, you're never going to be ever able to reconcile this time line and the fact there's no blood back there. . . . [Under Marcia Clark's] scenario, he still has the knife and the clothes. But what does she tell you yesterday? Well, he still has the knife and he's in these bloody clothes and presumably in bloody shoes, and what does he do? He goes in the house. Now, thank heaven, Judge Ito took us on a jury view. You've seen this house. You've seen this carpet. If he went in that house with bloody shoes, with bloody clothes, with his bloody hands as they say, where's the blood on the doorknob, where's the blood on the light switch, where's the blood on the banister, where's the blood on the carpet? That's like almost white carpet going up those stairs. Where is all that blood trail they've been ranting about in this mountain of evidence? You will see it's little more than a river or a stream. They don't have any mountain or ocean of evidence. It's not so because they say so. That's just rhetoric. We this afternoon are talking about the facts. And so it doesn't make any sense. It just doesn't fit. If it doesn't fit, you must acquit. . . .

And so she talks about O. J. being very, very recognizable. She talks about O. J. Simpson getting dressed up to go commit these murders. . . . It occurred to me how they were going to come here, stand up here and tell you how O. J. Simpson was going to disguise himself. He was going to put on a knit cap and some dark clothes, and he was going to get in his white Bronco, this recognizable person, and go over and kill his wife. That's what they want you to believe. That's how silly their argument is. And I said to myself, maybe I can demonstrate this graphically. Let me show you something. This is a knit cap. Let me put this knit cap on (Indicating). You have seen me for a year. If I put this knit cap on, who am I? I'm still Johnnie Cochran with a knit cap. And if you looked at O. J. Simpson over there—and he has a rather large head—O. J. Simpson in a knit cap from two blocks away is still O. J. Simpson. It's no disguise. It's no disguise. It makes no sense. It doesn't fit. If it doesn't fit, you must acquit. . . .

['The Gloves Didn't Fit']

. . . [L]et's look at some other things that don't fit in this case. As I started to say before, perhaps the single most defining moment in this trial is the day they thought they would conduct this experiment on these gloves. They . . . were going to try to demonstrate to you that these were the killer's gloves and these gloves would fit Mr. Simpson. You don't need any photographs to understand this. I suppose that vision is indelibly imprinted in each and every one of your minds of how Mr. Simpson walked over here and stood before you and you saw four simple words, "The gloves didn't fit." And all their strategy started changing after that. . . . [T]heir case from that day forward was slipping away from them and they knew it and they could never ever recapture it. We may all live to be a hundred years old, and I hope we do, but you will always remember those gloves, when Darden asked him to try them on, didn't fit. They know they didn't fit, and no matter what they do, they can't make them fit. . . . The gloves didn't fit Mr. Simpson because he is not the killer. . . .

[The Police Conspiracy]

. . . Gee, how would all these police officers set up O. J. Simpson? Why would they do that? I will answer that question for you. They believed he was guilty. They wanted to win. They didn't want to lose another big case. That is why. They believed that he was guilty. These actions rose from what their belief was, but they can't make that—the prosecutors can't make that judgment. Nobody but you can make that judgment. So when they take the law into their own hands, they become worse than the people who break the law, because they are the protectors of the law. Who then polices the police? You police the police. You police them by your verdict. You are the ones to send the message. Nobody else is going to do it in this society. . . .

[Fuhrman said that if] he sees an African American with a white woman he would stop them. If he didn't have a reason, he would find one or make up one. This man will lie to set you up. That is what he is saying there. He would do anything to set you up because of the hatred he has his heart. A racist is somebody who has power over you, who can do something to you. People could have views but keep them to themselves, but when they have power over you, that is when racism becomes insidious. That is what we are talking about here. He has power. A police officer in the street, a patrol officer, is the single most powerful figure in the criminal justice system. He can take your life. Unlike the supreme court, you don't have to go through all these appeals. He can do it right there and justify it. And that is why, that is why this has to be routed out in the LAPD and every place. Make up a reason because he made a judgment. That is what happened in this case. They made a judgment. Everything else after that is going to point toward O. J. Simpson. They didn't want to look at anybody else. Mr. Darden asked who did this crime? That is their job as the police. We have been hampered. They turned down our offers for help. But that is the prosecution's job. The judge says we don't have that job. The law says that. We would love to help do that. Who do you think wants to find these murderers more than Mr. Simpson? But that is not our job; it is their job. And when they don't talk to anybody else, when they rush to judgment in their obsession to win, that is why this became a problem. This man had the power to carry out his racist views and that is what is so troubling. Let's move on. Making up a reason. That is troubling. That is frightening. That is chilling. But if that wasn't enough, if that wasn't enough, the thing that really gets you is she goes on to say: "Officer Fuhrman went on to say that he would like nothing more than to see all niggers gathered together and killed. He said something about burning them or bombing them. I was too shaken to remember the exact words he used. However, I do remember that what he said was probably the most horrible thing I had ever heard someone say. What frightened me even more was that he was a police officer sworn to uphold the law." And now we have it. There was another man, not too long ago in the world, who had those same views who wanted to burn people, who had racist views and ultimately had power over people in this country.

People didn't care. People said he was just crazy, he is just a half-baked painter. They didn't do anything about it. This man, this scourge, became one of the worse people in the history of this world, Adolph Hitler, because people didn't care or didn't try to stop him. He had the power over his racism and his anti-religion. Nobody wanted to stop him, and it ended up in World War II, the conduct of this man. And so Fuhrman, Fuhrman wants to take all black people now and burn them or bomb them. That is genocidal racism. Is that ethnic purity? What is that? What is that? We are paying this man's salary to espouse these views? Do you think he only told Kathleen Bell whom he just had met? Do you think he talked to his partners about it? Do you think commanders knew about it? Do you think everybody knew about it and turned their heads? Nobody did anything about it. Things happen for a reason in your life. Maybe this is one of the reasons we are all gathered together this day, one year and two days after we met. Maybe there is a reason for your purpose. Maybe this is why you were selected. There is something in your background, in your character that helps you understand this is wrong. Maybe you are the right people at the right time at the right place to say no more, we are not going to have this. This is wrong. What they've done to our client is wrong. This man, O. J. Simpson, is entitled to an acquittal. You cannot believe these people. You can't trust the message. You can't trust the messengers. It is frightening. It is quite, frankly frightening, and it is not enough for the Prosecutors now to stand up and say, oh, well, let's just back off. The point I was trying to make, they didn't understand that it is not just using the "N" word. Forget that. We knew he was lying about that. Forget that. It is about the lengths to which he would go to get somebody black and also white if they are associated with black. That is pretty frightening. It is not just African Americans, it is white people who would associate or deign to go out with a black man or marry one. You are free in America to love whoever you want, so it infects all of us, doesn't it, this one rotten apple, and yet they cover for him. Yet they cover for him. . . .

... Thank you for your attention during this first part of my argument. I hope that during this phase of it I have demonstrated to you that this really is a case about a rush to judgment, an obsession to win, at all costs, a willingness to distort, twist, theorize in any fashion to try to get you to vote guilty in this case where it is not warranted, that these metaphors about an ocean of evidence or a mountain of evidence is little more than a tiny, tiny stream, if at all, that points equally toward innocence, that any mountain has long ago been reduced to little more than a molehill under an avalanche of lies and complexity and conspiracy. This is what we've shown you. And so as great as America is, we have not yet reached the point where there is equality in rights or equality of opportunity. I started off talking to you a little bit about Frederick Douglass and what he said more than a hundred years ago, for there are still the Mark Fuhrmans in this world, in this country, who hate and are yet embraced by people in power. But you and I, fighting for freedom and ideals and for justice for all, must continue to fight to expose hate and genocidal racism and these tendencies. We then become the guardians of the constitution, as I told you yesterday, for if we as the People don't continue to hold a mirror up to the face of America and say this is what you promised, this is what you delivered, if you don't speak out, if you don't stand up, if you don't do what's right, this kind of conduct will continue on forever and we will never have an ideal society, one that lives out the true meaning of the creed of the constitution or of life, liberty and justice for all. . . . This is a case about an innocent man wrongfully accused. You have seen him now for a year and two days. You observed him during good times and the bad times. Soon it will be your turn. You have the keys to his future. You have the evidence by which you can acquit this man. You have not only the patience, but the integrity and the courage to do the right thing. We believe you will do the right thing, and the right thing is to find this man not guilty on both of these charges. Thank you very, very much. . . .

DARDEN'S REBUTTAL

... The law is a tough thing to enforce in this town. Not everybody, not everybody wants to live up to the law or follow the law. Not everybody thinks that the law applies to them. I have been a Prosecutor for almost fifteen years, and if there is one rule that I have lived by, if there is one rule that means a lot to me, it is this one: No one is above the law; not the police, not the rich, no one. And I hope you agree with that. . . .

O. J. Simpson isn't above the law. . . . [Y]ou can't send a message to Fuhrman, you can't send a message to the LAPD, you can't eradicate racism within the LAPD or within the L.A. community or within the nation as a whole by delivering a verdict of not guilty in a case like this where it is clear and you know it is clear, you feel it, you know it in your heart. . . .

The evidence is there. You just have to find your way through the smoke. You just have to find your way through the smoke. . . . You just need to calm down, take that common sense God gave you, go back in the jury room.

Don't let these people get you all riled up and all fired up because Fuhrman is a racist. Racism blinds you. Those epithets, they blind you. You never heard me use that epithet in this courtroom, did you? I'm not going to put on that kind of show for you know who, for people to watch. That is not where we are coming from. We want you to focus on the evidence. I'm eternally grateful that Mr. Fuhrman was exposed to be what he is, because I think we should know who those people are. I have said it once, I have said it before, we ought to put a big stamp tattooed on their forehead "Racist" so that when we see them we know who they are so that there is no speculation so that we don't have to guess. But what they want you to do and what they have done in this case is they have interjected this racism and now they want you to become impassioned, to be upset, and then they want you to make quantum leaps in logic and in judgment. They want you to say Fuhrman is a racist, he planted the glove. You can't get from point A to point B if you just sit down and use your common sense. If you are logical, if you are reasonable, you can't do that. It is true that Fuhrman is a racist. And it is also true that [Simpson] killed these two people, and we proved that he killed the two people. . . .

CLARK'S REBUTTAL

. . . [T]heir own expert, Mr. MacDonell . . . had some interesting things to say about what kind of blood or how much blood you would ever expect to find, and as a matter of fact, we read the title into the record, "Absence of evidence is not evidence of absence." This makes sense. A crime can happen in many different ways. Use your logic and use your common sense. If you are standing behind somebody cutting their throat, they are bleeding out and they are not bleeding on you, so you will get some on your hands, maybe you will get a little bit of the spatter, but you are not going to be covered in blood and you are certainly not going to be covered in the kind of blood in the Bronco because it is not on your back. When you think about this, think about it logically, but don't let the record mislead you. . . .

[Police Conspiracy Theory Is Mind-Boggling]

What you see, ladies and gentlemen, is a very elaborate effort to make you disbelieve a great wealth of evidence, and what you've heard is basically a conspiracy that extends from Officer Riske to Commander Bushey. Do you realize how many people would have had to have gotten involved in a conspiracy within an hour? Can you imagine how this could happen? Detective Vannatter and Detective Lange never even knew Mark Fuhrman until they met him that night at Bundy, and yet the allegation by the Defense is that they got together that night, meeting the first time, for the very first time, and everybody's covering up and conspiring all of a sudden. Impossible. Not only that, but there are other people involved as well, people we don't even know who they are, according to the Defense, who are willing to get involved in this. You realize how many people have to be involved? I mean it boggles the mind. We don't even know who they're talking about. But that's the contortion you have to go through to believe in this conspiracy theory. That's the contortion you have to go through to step away from the very obvious truth you can see when you look straight on and clear-eyed at this evidence.

If you look at it straight on, you can see the truth. It's very clear and it's very obvious. Mr. Simpson committed these murders, ladies and gentlemen. We don't like it and it's hard, but it's true. . . .

[Equal Justice Under Law]

. . . "Equal justice under the law."

You may recall, that means the law is to be applied equally to all persons in this country regardless of whether one is rich or poor or race or creed or color, famous or otherwise. Not even the President of the United States is above the law. You all agreed with that. We asked you if you had courage to be just to a person. Each of you, each of you said yes, some individually, some responded as a group. And we asked you, you may recall, what equal justice under the law meant to you, and you replied that is the way it should definitely be. And that's right. That is the way it should definitely be. But you see, equal justice under the law is an ideal. It's an abstract principle and it takes you to make this principle a reality. Only you can make this ideal real. I think that with all you've already gone through, you've shown yourselves to be people of remarkable integrity, strength, courage and patience, people who will face the hard questions. And this is one of them.

I think it's been hard for all of us to be here and listen to all of the evidence in this case, evidence that proves Mr. Simpson is guilty because none of us wanted to believe it. We all wanted to believe that our image of him was right. And we all know that we never knew him exactly, but we kind of felt like we did, and it's really kind of hard to have to believe that the man we saw in the movies and commercials could do this. But he did. And the fact that he did doesn't mean that he wasn't a great football player. It doesn't mean he never did a good thing in his life. Nothing takes that away. That's still here. It will always be here. But so will the fact that he committed these murders. And even though it's a hard thing, still it cannot mean, it cannot mean that you let a guilty person go free, that someone who commits murder is not held accountable for it. He had strength and he had weaknesses, and it's his weakness that brought us here today and it's his weakness that's why we're here and Ron and Nicole are not. And Defense would say no motive, no motive. It's one of the oldest motives ever known, ladies and gentlemen; anger, fear of abandonment, jealousy, loss of control of Nicole and of himself. Usually I feel like I'm the only one left to speak for the victims. But in this case, Ron and Nicole are speaking to you. They're speaking to you and they're telling you who murdered them. Nicole started before she even died. Remember back in 1989, she cried to Detective Edwards, "He's going to kill me. He's going to kill me." The children were there. 1990, she made a safe deposit box, put photographs of her beaten face and her haunted look in a safe deposit box along with a will. She was only 30 years old. How many 30 years old you know do that, a will, a safe deposit box? It's like writing in the event of my death. She knew. "He's going to kill me." 1993, the 911 tape, the children were there. He was screaming. She was crying and she was frightened. I think the thing that perhaps was so chilling about her voice is that sound of resignation. There was a resignation to it, inevitability. She knew she was going to die. And Ron, he speaks to you and struggling so valiantly. He forced his murderer to leave the evidence behind that you might not ordinarily have found. And they both are telling you who did it with their hair, their clothes, their bodies, their blood. They tell you he did it. He did it. Mr. Simpson, Orenthal Simpson, he did it. They told you in the only way they can. Will you hear them or will you ignore their plea for justice, or as Nicole said to Detective Edwards, "You never do anything about him." Will you?

I want to play something for you, ladies and gentlemen, that puts it all together. Let me explain what this is. Thank you. This is a compilation of the 1989 tape, 911 call, the 1993 911 call, photographs from the 1989 beating and the photographs from her safe deposit box and the photographs from Rockingham and Bundy. . . .

(At 3:55 P.M., a videotape was played.)

I don't have to say anything else. Ladies and gentlemen, on behalf of the People of the State of California, because we have proven beyond a reasonable doubt, far beyond a reasonable doubt that the Defendant committed these murders, we ask you to find the Defendant guilty of murder in the first degree of Ronald Goldman and Nicole Brown. Thank you very much.

CLINTON, ARAFAT, AND RABIN ON WEST BANK AGREEMENT
September 28, 1995

Israel and the Palestine Liberation Organization (PLO) signed an agreement on September 28 that gave the Palestinians control over much of the West Bank of the Jordan River, which had been occupied by Israel since 1967. The watershed agreement was one that many people thought they would never live to see; others, including extremists on both sides of the great Middle East divide between Arabs and Jews, had fought to ensure the agreement would never happen.

Israeli prime minister Yitzhak Rabin and PLO leader Yasir Arafat signed the Israeli-Palestinian Interim Agreement on the West Bank and the Gaza Strip in a ceremony at the White House, in the presence of President Bill Clinton, King Hussein of Jordan, and Egyptian president Hosni Mubarak. Five weeks later, Rabin was murdered in Jerusalem by an Israeli assassin who accused him of forsaking Israel. Rabin's successor, Shimon Peres, vowed to continue the peace process. (Rabin assassination, p. 689)

The September 28 signing ceremony lacked the drama of an event at the White House two years earlier, when Rabin and Arafat shook hands for the first time. On September 13, 1993, the two leaders issued a "Declaration of Principles" calling for the gradual settling of Israeli-Palestinian issues by the turn of the century. (Peace accord, Historic Documents of 1993, p. 747)

Rabin and Arafat expanded on their 1993 handshake with another agreement signed in May 1994 in Cairo, establishing Palestinian self-rule in the Gaza Strip and the city of Jericho on the West Bank. The September 28, 1995, agreement was the logical extension and was by far the most significant and detailed of those reached to date between the two sides.

With the September 28 agreement, Israel had reached peace with all its major enemies from the past except Syria and Lebanon. Israel and Egypt signed the Camp David peace treaty in 1979, and Israel and Jordan settled on peace in June 1994. U.S.-sponsored negotiations between Israel and Syria took on a new seriousness in the wake of the September 28 agreement, but no breakthroughs were evident by the end of 1995. The main issue in those talks was control of the heavily fortified Golan Heights, which Israel captured from Syria in 1967. (Camp David agreement, Historic Documents of 1978, p. 605; Israeli-Jordanian agreement, Historic Documents of 1994, p. 329)

None of the agreements between Israel and its foes directly addressed the single most intractable issue dividing them: the future of Jerusalem. Israel captured the city in the 1967 war and made it its capital. Arabs claimed the holy city belonged to them. The United States took the position that no country had total claim to Jerusalem and that the city's final status could be settled only through negotiations.

A Tortuous Series of Negotiations

The negotiations between Israel and the PLO probably were the most difficult of any sponsored by the United States in more than twenty-five years of Middle East diplomacy. Israel and the PLO were bitter enemies, separated by seemingly unbridgeable differences over politics, religion, and control of sacred land.

In many ways, Israel held the upper hand. It had control over land the Palestinians wanted (the West Bank), and it was the most militarily powerful state in the region, feared by Arab foes who had lost three major wars to it. After years of infighting and unsuccessful reliance on terrorism, the PLO had no military force of substance and was struggling with more extremist groups for influence among its own people.

Rabin and other peace advocates within Israel had argued for years that the country could not hold onto the West Bank forever and still call itself a democracy. The vast majority of West Bank residents were Palestinians with no rights of citizenship, a statistical fact that was unlikely to change despite a determined settlement campaign by Israel.

After successfully brokering the peace agreement between Israel and Jordan in 1994, the Clinton administration turned its attention to broadening the earlier agreement that gave Palestinians control over the Gaza Strip and Jericho. Negotiators faced dozens of issues dividing Israel and the Palestinians, all centering around control of the West Bank.

As with all previous negotiations, the Israeli-PLO talks were buffeted by occasional walkouts, posturing, and threats by both sides, and by terrorist incidents. Among the latter was a January 23 suicide bombing by Islamic extremists of a bus stop packed with Israeli soldiers in Nordiya, north of Tel Aviv. The bombing killed nineteen people and wounded more than sixty, but it did not stop the peace talks.

At several points, Dennis Ross, the chief U.S. intermediary, and Secretary of State Warren Christopher had to intervene to prevent the collapse of the negotiations. One of those interventions occurred early on September 24, the day the agreement was reached, when Ross negotiated with key Israeli and Palestinian figures for hours by telephone. Arafat reportedly stormed out of the negotiations at one point, declaring that "we are not slaves." Clinton administration officials said credit for the agreement belonged to the Israelis and the PLO and that the U.S. role was primarily one of urging the two parties to keep moving forward.

Arafat and Peres, then Israel's foreign minister, initialed the peace agreement on September 24 at Taba, Egypt, a Red Sea resort that Israel developed during its occupation of the area. The official signing ceremony was held at the White House four days later to give the agreement the full weight of U.S. prestige and backing.

Key Points in the Agreement

The core of the September 28 agreement was Israel's withdrawal from much of the West Bank, along with the election of a Palestinian Council to manage the day-to-day affairs of the Palestinian-controlled areas on such matters as education, taxation, and health care. In essence, the Palestinians gained civil control, but not sovereignty over much of the West Bank. Arafat's dream of a Palestinian state was not yet fulfilled. Israel ceded some of its administrative power but retained ultimate control over security.

The agreement divided the West Bank into three zones, roughly according to their population makeup. Israel was to withdraw its military forces entirely from the heavily populated areas dominated by Palestinians, such as the cities of Bethlehem, Nablus, and Ramallah, by March 30, 1996. In most rural areas, Israel and the Palestinians were to share authority. Israel was to have exclusive control over other areas, including military bases, Jewish settlements, and unpopulated regions.

One of the most difficult issues in the negotiations was the status of Hebron, a Palestinian-dominated city where 450 Jewish settlers had taken up residence, saying they were acting on instructions in the Bible. In a compromise, the city was divided into three security zones, one patrolled by the Israelis, one by the Palestinians, and one patrolled jointly.

Israel agreed to free hundreds of Palestinian prisoners, including women, the young, the sick, the elderly, and those who had served most of their terms, and to negotiate later on other prisoners. Israel also promised to give the Palestinians a greater share of water resources in the West Bank, with further negotiations on water rights to be held later. Palestinians agreed to ensure Jewish access to religious sites in Bethlehem and Nablus, and the two sides were to continue sharing security responsibilities for the Tomb of the Patriarchs in Hebron, sacred to both Jews and Arabs.

The lengthy agreement included hundreds of details about the future of daily life on the West Bank, from what kinds of items the Palestinians could import to the staffing of police stations and the color of propane gas tanks. Both sides had learned from the experience of their 1994 agreement on the Gaza Strip and Jericho that they needed to resolve their differences ahead of time; the 1994 accord had left many issues unsettled, leading to constant disputes.

Even so, the West Bank agreement left unsettled several controversial issues, including long-term water rights and the status of settlements on the West Bank where some 140,000 Jews lived. Those issues were to be taken up in new negotiations starting in the spring of 1996.

Following are excerpts from remarks by President Bill Clinton, PLO chairman Yasir Arafat, and Israeli prime minister Yitzhak Rabin at the White House on September 28, 1995, on the occasion of the signing of the Israeli-Palestinian Interim Agreement on the West Bank and the Gaza Strip. President Clinton spoke before the accord was signed; Arafat and Rabin spoke afterwards:

REMARKS BY CLINTON

I welcome you to the White House for this milestone on the path to reconciliation. Today we make a great stride toward the fulfillment of a vision toward the day when two peoples divided by generations, by conflict, are bound now by peace. Finally, the time is approaching when there will be safety in Israel's house; when the Palestinian people will write their own destiny; when the clash of arms will be banished from God's Holy Land.

Two years ago, on another brilliant September day here at the White House, two men reached across one of history's widest chasms with a simple handshake. That moment is etched forever in our memory.

With the eyes of the world upon you, Mr. Prime Minister, you declared your wish to live side by side with the Palestinian people in dignity, in empathy, as human beings, as free men.

And you, Mr. Chairman, vowed to wage what you called "the most difficult battle of our lives, the battle for peace."

In the days of labor that have followed you have both shown profound courage in bringing us to this moment, and you have kept your word.

The enemies of peace have fought the tide of history with terror and violence. We grieve for their victims, and we renew our vow to redeem the sacrifice of those victims. We will defeat those who will resort to terror. And we revere the determination of these leaders who chose peace; who rejected the old habits of hatred and revenge. Because they broke so bravely with the past, the bridges have multiplied—bridges of communication, of commerce, of understanding. Today, the landscape changes and the chasm narrows. . . .

Mr. Prime Minister and Mr. Chairman, you are showing that it is not by weapons, but by will and by word, that dreams best become reality. Your achievement shines as an inspiration to others all around this world who seek to overcome their own conflicts and to secure for themselves the blessings of peace.

Chapter by chapter, Jews and Arabs are writing a new chapter for their ancient lands. Camp David, the Declaration of Principles, signed here two years ago; the peace of the Arava last year between Jordan and Israel: With each of these, the truth of this book has become clear to the world. As courageous leaders stepped beyond the bounds of convention, they build for their peoples a new world of hope and peace. . . .

All those who doubt the spirit of peace should remember this day and this extraordinary array of leaders who have joined together to bring a new era of hope to the Middle East. The United States is proud to stand with all of them.

Much remains to be done. But we will continue to walk each step of the way with those who work and risk for peace. We will press forward with our efforts until the circle of peace is closed, a circle which must include Syria and Lebanon if peace is to be complete. We will not rest until Muslims and Jews can turn their backs to pray without any fear; until all the region's children can grow up untouched by conflict; until the shadow of violence is lifted from the land of light and gold.

Thank you very much.

STATEMENT BY ARAFAT

. . . We are gathered today under the sponsorship of President Clinton, who has generously offered to host the signing of this agreement. It has been two years since we met at the White House to sign the Declaration of Principles to which we and our Israeli partners have agreed to in Oslo. We meet again today to make new headway in giving hope to this historic process, the process of realizing a credible peace, reconciliation and co-existence between the Palestinian and Israeli peoples, and the peace of the brave, which we achieved on Egyptian land at Taba under President Mubarak's auspices.

A significant portion of Palestinian national rights reverts today to the Palestinian people through their control of the cities, villages, and populated areas. Recovery of this portion is a step in the implementation of the interim agreement, which we are gathered here to witness the signing. It is also a step which paves the way to free and democratic Palestinian elections, capping, thereby, the political components required for the establishment of an independent Palestinian national entity on the Palestinian territories.

These steps which required tremendous efforts, as well as exhausting and relentless work throughout the past months, do not make us oblivious of the fact that added diligence lies ahead to implement this agreement on our land in the West Bank. We still carry on our shoulders many other tasks, such as moving to the permanent status negotiations.

The permanent status negotiations will deal with such issues as settlements, the delineation of the borders, the rights of Palestinian refugees as determined by the international legitimacy, and the fundamental issue concerning the status of Jerusalem, which our people, irrespective of their faith—Muslims, Christians or Jews—consider Jerusalem to be the heart and soul of their entity and the center of their cultural, spiritual and economic life. I would say that the sanctity of Jerusalem for us all dictates that we make it the joint cornerstone and the capital of peace between the Palestinian and the Israeli peoples, inasmuch as it is a beacon for believers all over the world.

We urge you all to recognize the importance of this historic interim step. It demonstrates the irreversibility of the peace process. Its distinct significance lies in the verdict passed by history, the international community and human civilization at the turn of the century, that a just and comprehensive peace be established on this sacred land, whereby the Israeli and Palestinian peoples would coexist on the basis of mutual recognition of the rights, while enjoying a quality and self-determination without occupation or repeated wars, and without terrorism.

At this point, I must tell our Israeli partners from this solemn rostrum and in the presence of our brethren and friends who have come here from the region and from all over the world, particularly those who contributed to the realization of this agreement, that our past experience underscores the need to be more credible and committed to our steps in the future. And the commitment should be precise, honest, and mutual. For our part, we will honor our commitments.

That's why the continuation and expansion of the settlement drive, as the situation in the city of Hebron and elsewhere shows, lead to the persistence of tensions. Likewise, continued qualms about a new and dependent Palestinian birth convey to each and every Palestinian the feeling that his or her life shall remain in jeopardy.

Today, standing before you, I tell you with courage and a sense of responsibility, that our participation in the great peace process means that we are betting everything on the future. Therefore, we must condemn and foreswear violence totally, not only because the use of violence is morally reprehensible, but because it undermines Palestinian aspirations to the realization of peace and the exercise of our political and national options, and the achievement of economic and cultural progress in Palestine and in the region.

From this day on, we do not want to see any waste of, or threat to, any innocent Palestinian life or any innocent Israeli life. Enough killing and enough killing of innocent people.

I urge you, Mr. President, together with all our brethren and friends gathered here, to keep up the drive for a comprehensive and just settlement in our region on all tracks, especially the Syrian and Lebanese tracks, to complete all aspects of the process.

Ladies and gentlemen, we are still striving on two parallel fronts. One is to achieve a just political solution to our problem. The other is to build a homeland on modern and democratic grounds. For us to succeed on both fronts, we are bound to base the emerging Palestinian political system on the principles of liberty, democracy, separation of powers, freedom of expression, and national initiative. We are also bound to continue building Palestinian institutions and the Palestinian national economy. But this enterprise is still in its early stages and our institutions have yet to mature.

The road ahead remains long, indeed. We look forward to your continued support of our people. And we thank all friendly and brotherly donors for their assistance.

Mr. President, as the experience of your great country—the country of freedom, democracy and human rights—taught us that freedom is absolutely indivisible. And here, I would like to emphasize to you and to our people and to our devoted friends that our people's freedom will remain lacking without all our detainees walking free. All the martyrs, the wounded, and the victims shared one dream. They dreamt of a freedom and just peace for their children, for Israeli children, and for the future generations on both sides.

In keeping with that dream, and with that correct vision, we shall continue along this path, the path and reconciliation of the brave, notwithstanding its difficulties.

In conclusion, Mr. President, I thank you deeply for your devotion to this process and the historic reconciliation. I greatly appreciate your personal involvement and the role played by your able aides and by members of your administration who helped us all along to overcome and settle difficulties. . . .

STATEMENT BY RABIN

First, the good news. I'm the last speaker—(laughter)—before, of course, the closing remarks by the President.

. . . Now, after a long series of formal, festive statements, take a look at the stage. The King of Jordan; the President of Egypt; Chairman Arafat; and us, the Prime Minister and the Foreign Minister of Israel, on the one platform with the President of the United States. Please, take a good, hard look. The sight you see before you at this moment was impossible, was unthinkable just three years ago. Only poets dreamt of it. And to our great pain, soldier[s] and civilians went to their death to make this moment possible.

Here we stand before you, men who fate and history have sent on a mission of peace, to end once and for all 100 years of bloodshed. Our dream is also your dream—King Hussein; President Mubarak; Chairman Arafat, all the others, and above, assisting us, President Bill Clinton, a President who is working in the service of peace. We all love the same children, weep the same tears, hate the same enmity and pray for reconciliation. Peace has no borders.

Yes, I know our speeches are already repeating themselves. Perhaps this picture has already become routine. The handshakes no longer set your pulse racing. Your loving hearts no longer pound with emotion as they did then. We have begun to get used to each other. We are like old acquaintances. We can tell all about Arafat's grief. He and his friend can tell you all about ours. We have matured in the two years since we first shook hands here—the handshake that was the sign and symbol of the start of reconciliation.

Today, we are more sober. We are gladdened by the potential for reconciliation, but we are also wary of the dangers that lurk on every side. The enemies of yesterday share a common enemy of today and in the future—the terrorism that sows death in our homes and on the buses that ply the streets. The sounds of celebration here cannot drown out the cries of innocent citizens who traveled those buses to their death. And your eyes shining here cannot erase for a single moment of the sight of the lifeless eyes of the students who were going to their classes and housewives who were on their way to market when hatred struck them down. We are pained by their death, and remember them with love.

I want to say to you, Chairman Arafat, the leader of the Palestinians, together we should not let the land that's flowing with milk and honey become a land flowing with blood and tears. Don't let it happen. If all the partners to the peacemaking do not unite against the evil angels of death by terrorism, all that ... will remain of this ceremony are color snapshots, empty mementos; rivers of hatred will overflow again and swamp the Middle East.

We gentlemen will not permit terrorism to defeat peace. We will not allow it. If we don't have partners in this bitter, difficult war, we will fight it alone. We know how to fight and we know how to win.

My brother Jews speak through the media to you of thousands of years of exile. And the dream of generations have returned us to our historic home in the land of Israel, the land of the prophets. Etched on every vineyard, every field, every olive tree, every flower is the deep imprint of the Jewish history; of the book of the books which we have bequeathed to the entire world; of the values of morality and of justice. Every place in the land of the prophets, every name is an integral part of our heritage of thousands of years of the divine promise to us and to our descendants.

Here is where we were born. Here is where we created a nation. Here we forged a haven for the persecuted and built a model of a democratic country. But we are not alone here on this soil, in this land. And so we are sharing this good earth today with the Palestinian people in order to choose life. Starting today, an agreement on paper will be translated into reality on the ground. We are not retreating; we are not leaving. We are building and we are doing so for the sake of peace.

Our neighbors, the Palestinian people—we who have seen you in your difficulties, we saw you for generations; we who have killed and have been killed are walking beside you now toward a common future, and we want you as good neighbors.

Ladies and gentlemen, this week the Jewish people in each thousands of places of this—has marked a new era, and in their Holy Day prayers, Jews everywhere are saying—(spoken in Hebrew). I'm translating it to the best of my capability. May we be remembered and inscribe before you in the book of life and of blessing and peace and prosperity, of deliverance and comfort and opportunity, we and all your people, the House of Israel, for a good life and peace.

These are my wishes to all the Jewish people. These are my wishes to all the citizens of Israel—a good life and a peace. These are also our wishes to our neighbors, to all the world peoples—a good life and peace.

Ladies and gentlemen, look at us again. Look at the scene on the stage, here in the White House. You are not excited anymore. You have grown up accustomed to it. But in order for peace to be completed, in order for this picture to be completed, and for the Middle East to become a jewel in the world crown, it still lacks two people—the President of Syria and the President of Lebanon. I call upon them to come and join us, to come to the platform of peace.

Ladies and gentlemen, if and when this happens, we will again ask President Clinton to be our gracious host. We will again ask King Hussein, President Mubarak, Chairman Arafat, and all the others to return here to be partners in the glorious picture of all the peoples of the Middle East dwelling in security and peace. Ladies and gentlemen, let me extend my wish to all of us that we may meet here again, and soon. Happy New Year. (Spoken in Hebrew.)

October

CLINTON APOLOGY FOR HUMAN RADIATION EXPERIMENTS
October 3, 1995

Acting on the recommendation of a committee he had appointed, President Bill Clinton on October 3 apologized to the survivors of radiation experiments conducted by U.S. government agencies between 1944 and 1974. The president also accepted the panel's recommendation that the government financially compensate survivors of some of those experiments.

Starting with the development of the atomic bomb and continuing through the height of the Cold War, the Atomic Energy Commission (AEC), the military services, and other agencies sponsored thousands of research studies into the effects of radiation on humans. Many of those experiments involved exposing people to radiation without their knowledge or without any explanation of potential harm. The experiments took place at military bases, prisons, hospitals, and universities.

The recommendations from the President's Advisory Committee on Human Radiation Experiments, and Clinton's apology, received a mixed reaction, especially from survivors of the experiments and their families and representatives. The survivors said they were glad that the government finally was addressing the issue, but some rejected as inadequate the proposed compensation and said the government should have attempted to locate and notify the thousands of people who were subjects of experiments without their knowledge.

Committee Research and Findings

Clinton in January 1994 appointed the committee to study what the government had done and to make recommendations for action. The committee was chaired by Ruth Faden, head of bioethics studies at Johns Hopkins University; most of the other thirteen members were medical historians and ethicists.

Energy Secretary Hazel O'Leary had urged Clinton to appoint the study committee after she learned about some of the experiments conducted by predecessor agencies of her department, primarily the AEC. O'Leary

*ordered an Energy Department study of the matter. A report on its find-
ings, released in February 1995, showed that the AEC and its sister agencies had conducted or sponsored 154 radiation experiments involving
9,000 people.*

*The presidential advisory committee was charged with examining pro-
grams sponsored by all U.S. government agencies, including the Defense
Department and Veterans Administration. The committee and its staff
examined thousands of documents and interviewed researchers, government officials, and survivors of the experiments.*

*Its 906-page report and supporting documents reviewed some 4,000
radiation experiments conducted under government sponsorship during
the 1944–1974 period. Tens of thousands of people were involved in those
experiments. The committee said an exact total will never be known
because some documents gave vague or incomplete information on the
number of people subjected to radiation experiments.*

*In 1974 the Department of Health, Education and Welfare established
rules for protecting human subjects in government research programs.
Those rules prohibited involuntary exposure to radiation and other hazards. In its report the advisory committee said those rules should be
strengthened and some guidelines protecting research subjects should be
put into law.*

*Many of those subjected to radiation were prisoners, mental patients, and
children. Most of those subjects were not fully informed about what the experiments involved, were given misleading information, or were told nothing.*

*The committee found that government officials discussed the potential
harm of radiation experiments as early as 1947 and ordered some procedures to protect both subjects and researchers. For example, the AEC in
1947 ordered that testing on patients would be allowed only if they were
likely to benefit and only if they had given their consent. Those protections
were kept highly secret, however, and some researchers were never told
about them. Although most researchers tried to make their experiments
safe, some of them did not follow recommended safety procedures.*

*Faden said her panel found that much of the radiation research was
conducted in an atmosphere of "arrogance" and showed "a lack of respect
of the American people." Patients trusted their doctors, she said, "but the
doctors who did the research often took advantage of that trust."*

Apology and Compensation

*In accepting the committee's report, Clinton said the underlying theme
was that the American people should be able to rely on their government "to
keep its word, tell the truth, and to do the right thing." The committee's
report was a step forward on all three those counts, he said.*

*Most of the government-sponsored tests were ethical "by any standards,"
Clinton said, but some "were unethical, not only by today's standards, but
by the standards of the time in which they were conducted. They failed both
the test of our national values and the test of humanity."*

Clinton said that "the United States of America offers a sincere apology to those of our citizens who were subjected to these experiments, to their families, and to their communities."

The president cited two cases that had attracted widespread attention. One involved a series of experiments conducted at three universities from 1945 to 1947, in which eighteen people were injected with radioactive plutonium without their knowledge. Clinton also cited a case in which indigent cancer patients were exposed to "excessive doses" of radiation.

One of the most sensitive issues dealt with by the committee involved compensating subjects of the experiments. Compensating all the tens of thousands of subjects would have been enormously expensive and would have required a massive research project to find the survivors.

As an alternative, the committee recommended automatic compensation for a very few survivors and established guidelines for compensating others. In the first category, the committee cited about thirty people who had been subjected to three experiments that exposed them to dangerous levels of radiation without their knowledge. Those people should be awarded compensation, the committee said. Clinton accepted that recommendation, ordering his Cabinet to "devise promptly" a system of relief "that meets the standards of justice and conscience." Details would be worked out with Congress, he said.

Clinton also accepted the committee's recommendation for a set of detailed guidelines for compensating survivors of other experiments that might have exposed them to serious health risks. Most of the experiments, however, did not expose people to dangerous levels of radiation and probably did not cause long-term health problems.

The committee's report, Clinton pledged, "will not be left on a shelf to gather dust."

Following are excerpts from remarks by President Bill Clinton on October 3, 1995, upon accepting the findings of the President's Advisory Committee on Human Radiation Experiments:

... We discovered soon after I entered office that with the specter of an atomic war looming like Armageddon far nearer than it does today, the United States government actually did carry out on our citizens experiments involving radiation. That's when I ordered the creation of this committee. Dr. [Ruth] Faden and the others did a superb job. They enlisted many of our nation's most significant and important medical and scientific ethicists. They had to determine first whether experiments conducted or sponsored by our government between 1944 and 1974 met the ethical and scientific standards of that time and of our time. And then they had to see to it that our research today lives up to nothing less than our highest values and our most deeply-held beliefs.

From the beginning, it was obvious to me that this energetic committee was prepared to do its part. We declassified thousands of pages of documents. We gave committee members the keys to the government's doors, file cabinets and safes. For the last year and a half, the only thing that stood between them and the truth were all the late nights and hard work they had to put in.

This report I received today is a monumental document in more ways than one. But it is a very, very important piece of America's history, and it will shape America's future in ways that will make us a more honorable, more successful and more ethical country.

What this committee learned I would like to review today with a little more detail than Dr. Faden said, because I think it must be engraved on our national memory. Thousands of government-sponsored experiments did take place at hospitals, universities and military bases around our nation. The goal was to understand the effects of radiation exposure on the human body.

While most of the tests were ethical by any standards, some were unethical, not only by today's standards, but by the standards of the time in which they were conducted. They failed both the test of our national values and the test of humanity.

In one . . . experiment . . . scientists injected plutonium into 18 patients without their knowledge. In another, doctors exposed indigent cancer patients to excessive doses of radiation, a treatment from which it is virtually impossible that they could ever benefit.

The report also demonstrates that these and other experiments were carried out on precisely those citizens who count most on the government for its help—the destitute and the gravely ill. But the dispossessed were not alone. Members of the military—precisely those on whom we and our government count most—they were also test subjects.

Informed consent means your doctor tells you the risk of the treatment you are about to undergo. In too many cases, informed consent was withheld. Americans were kept in the dark about the effects of what was being done to them. The deception extended beyond the test subjects themselves to encompass their families and the American people as a whole, for these experiments were kept secret. And they were shrouded not for a compelling reason of national security, but for the simple fear of embarrassment, and that was wrong.

Those who led the government when these decisions were made are no longer here to take responsibility for what they did. They are not here to apologize to the survivors, the family members or the communities [whose] lives were darkened by the shadow of the atom and these choices.

So today, on behalf of another generation of American leaders and another generation of American citizens, the United States of America offers a sincere apology to those of our citizens who were subjected to these experiments, to their families, and to their communities.

When the government does wrong, we have a moral responsibility to admit it. The duty we owe to one another to tell the truth and to protect our fellow citizens from excesses like these is one we can never walk away from. Our government failed in that duty, and it offers an apology to the survivors and their families and to all the American people who must—who must be able to rely upon the United States to keep its word, to tell the truth, and to do the right thing.

We know there are moments when words alone are not enough. That's why I am instructing my Cabinet to use and build on these recommendations, to devise promptly a system of relief, including compensation, that meets the standards of justice and conscience.

When called for, we will work with Congress to serve the best needs of those who were harmed. Make no mistake, as the committee report says, there are circumstances where compensation is appropriate as a matter of ethics and principle. I am committed to seeing to it that the United States of America lives up to its responsibility.

Our greatness is measured not only in how we so frequently do right, but also how we act when we know we've done the wrong thing; how we confront our mistakes, make our apologies, and take action.

That's why this morning, I signed an executive order instructing every arm and agency of our government that conducts, supports or regulates research involving human beings to review immediately their procedures, in light of the recommendations of this report, and the best knowledge and standards available today, and to report back to me by Christmas.

I have also created a Bioethics Advisory Commission to supervise the process, to watch over all such research, and to see to it that never again do we stray from the basic values of protecting our people and being straight with them.

The report I received today will not be left on a shelf to gather dust. Every one of its pages offers a lesson, and every lesson will be learned from these good people who put a year and a half of their lives into the effort to set America straight.

Medical and scientific progress depends upon learning about people's responses to new medicines, to new cutting-edge treatments. Without this kind of research, our children would still be dying from polio and other killers. Without responsible radiation research, we wouldn't be making the progress we are in the war on cancer. We have to continue to research, but there is a right way and a wrong way to do it.

There are local citizens' review boards, there are regulations that establish proper informed consent and ensure that experiments are conducted ethically. But in overseeing this necessary research, we must never relax our vigilance.

The breathtaking advances in science and technology demand that we always keep our ethical watchlight burning. No matter how rapid the pace of change, it can never outrun our core convictions that have stood us so well as a nation for more than 200 years now, through many different scientific revolutions.

I believe we will meet the test of our times—that as science and technology evolve, our ethical conscience will grow, not shrink. Informed consent, community right-to-know, our entire battery of essential human protections—all these grew up in response to the health and humanitarian crises of this 20th century. They are proof that we are equal to our challenges.

Science is not ever simply objective. It emerges from the crucible of historical circumstances and personal experience. Times of crisis and fear can call forth bad science, even science we know in retrospect to be unethical. Let us remember the difficult years chronicled in this report, and think about how good people could have done things that we know were wrong.

Let these pages serve as an internal reminder to hold humility and moral accountability in higher esteem than we do the latest development in technology. Let us remember, too, that cynicism about government has roots in historical circumstances. Because of stonewallings and evasions in the past, times when a family member or a neighbor suffered an injustice and had nowhere to turn and couldn't even get the facts, some Americans lost faith in the promise of our democracy. Government was very powerful, but very far away and not trusted to be ethical.

So today, by making ourselves accountable for the sins of the past, I hope more than anything else, we are laying the foundation stone for a new era. Good people, like these members of Congress who have labored on this issue for a long time, and have devoted their careers to trying to do the right thing, and having people justifiably feel confidence in the work of their representatives. They will continue to work to see that we implement these recommendations.

And under our watch, we will no longer hide the truth from our citizens. We will act as if all that we do will see the light of day. Nothing that happens in Washington will ever be more important in anyone's life affected by these experiments, perhaps, than these reports we issue today. But all of us as Americans will be better off because of the larger lesson we learned in this exercise and because of our continuing effort to demonstrate to our people that we can be faithful to their values.

Thank you very much.

UN SPEECH ON HUMAN RIGHTS BY POPE JOHN PAUL II
October 5, 1995

As part of the celebration of the fiftieth anniversary of the founding of the United Nations, Pope John Paul II on October 5 offered a philosophical roadmap for promoting human rights and freedom into the twenty-first century. The pope told the UN General Assembly that, even with the end of the Cold War, the world faced grave threats to peace. One of the foremost challenges, he said, was the widespread aversion to accepting cultural, religious, and other differences among people. "Unhappily, the world has yet to learn how to live with diversity, as recent events in the Balkans and Central Africa have painfully reminded us," he said. (UN fiftieth anniversary ceremony, p. 350)

The pope's address to the United Nations was his second in sixteen years, and only the third by a pontiff in UN history. Pope Paul VI offered the United Nations an emotional antiwar message in 1965, a time of regional conflicts stemming from the Cold War. (Address to the UN, Historic Documents of 1979, p. 748)

John Paul spent five days in the United States, delivering several major speeches, including homilies before capacity crowds at the Giants football stadium in New Jersey and the Camden Yards baseball park in Baltimore. In several of those speeches he sharply criticized moral standards in the United States, citing especially abortion, the death penalty, and the rise of anti-immigration sentiment.

While celebrating mass at Giants stadium, a few hours after his speech at the United Nations, John Paul noted that he was just a few miles from the Statue of Liberty, "which stands as an enduring witness to the American tradition of welcoming the stranger. . . ." He asked, "is present-day America becoming less sensitive, less caring toward the poor, the weak, the stranger, the needy? It must not. Today, as before, the United States is called to be a hospitable society, a welcoming culture. If America were to turn in on itself, would this not be the beginning of the end of what constitutes the very essence of 'the American experience'?"

The Rights of Nations

In his speech to the United Nations, the pope focused on broad trends in recent world history and offered moral guidance, while generally avoiding specific issues of the day. He referred only in passing to the bloody ethnic conflicts in Bosnia and Rwanda that were capturing headlines at the time of his speech.

To bolster his call for respect for diversity, the pope delivered parts of his speech in each of the six official languages of the United Nations: Arabic, Chinese, English, French, Russian, and Spanish. As was his custom, he read only part of his lengthy speech to the UN delegates; the rest was entered into the official record of the General Assembly.

At the heart of the pope's speech was a plea for acceptance of differences among people, whether they were gathered as nation-states or as distinct ethnic or cultural groups within nations or regions. The pope insisted that the "rights of nations"—most importantly the right to exist—applied to minority groups within nations, as well as to nation-states. "The fundamental right to existence does not necessarily call for sovereignty as a state," he said, noting that minorities can have distinct identities within a state or can survive within confederations. Along with its right to exist, he said, each nation has a right to its own language and culture.

John Paul warned that these rights are threatened around the world by a lack of respect for diversity. "The fact of 'difference,' and the reality of 'the other,' can sometimes be felt as a burden, or even as a threat," he said. "Amplified by historic grievances and exacerbated by the manipulation of the unscrupulous, the fear of 'difference' can lead to a denial of the very humanity of 'the other,' with the result that people fall into a cycle of violence in which no one is spared, not even the children." The conflict in Bosnia was an example of this trend, he said.

Related to the refusal to accept diversity, he said, is "an unhealthy form of nationalism, which teaches contempt for other nations and cultures. . . ." That kind of nationalism, he added, is different from true patriotism, "which is a proper love of one's country" and which "never seeks to advance the well-being of one's own nation at the expense of others."

The Use of Freedom

The collapse of communism accelerated the "quest for freedom" worldwide, John Paul said, but that event did not settle the issue of how freedom is used once it is attained. "Living the freedom sought by individuals and peoples is a great challenge to man's spiritual growth and to the moral vitality of nations," he said. "The basic question which we must all face today is the responsible use of freedom, in both its personal and social dimensions."

Unless it is governed by what the pope called "the truth about the human person," freedom "deteriorates into license in the lives of individuals and, in political life, it becomes the caprice of the most powerful and the arrogance of power."

Freedom also is threatened by "utilitarianism," which he described as "the doctrine which defines morality not in terms of what is good but of what is advantageous." On an international level, utilitarianism inspires an "aggressive nationalism" that subjugates small and weak nations in the "national interest" of the strong. Economic utilitarianism, he said, leads powerful countries to manipulate and exploit weaker ones.

Although the Vatican and the United Nations often had been at odds over such issues as abortion and women's rights, the Pope challenged the United Nations to expand its role in world affairs. The world body, he said, should "rise above the cold status of an administrative institution and become a moral center, where all the nations of the world feel at home and develop a shared awareness of being, as it were, a family of nations."

Following are excerpts from the address by Pope John Paul II to the United Nations General Assembly on October 5, 1995, in which he laid out a moral basis for the conduct of international affairs:

I'm grateful for your presence and for your kind attention. Ladies and gentlemen, on the threshold of a new millennium we are witnessing an extraordinary global acceleration of that quest for freedom which is one of the great dynamics of human history.

This phenomenon is not limited to any one part of the world, nor is it the expression of any single culture. Men and women throughout the world, even when threatened by violence, have taken the risk of freedom, asking to be given a place in social, political, and economic life, which is commensurate with their dignity as free human beings.

This universal longing for freedom is truly one of the distinguishing marks of our time. It is important for us to grasp what might be called the inner structure of this worldwide movement. It is precisely its global character which offers us its first and fundamental key—and confirms that there are indeed universal human rights rooted in the nature of the person, rights which reflect the objective and inviolable demands of a universal moral law.

These are not abstract points. Rather, these rights tell us something important about the actual life of every individual and every social group.

They also remind us that we do not live in an [irrational] and meaningless world. On the contrary, there is a moral logic which is built into human life and which makes possible dialogue between individuals and peoples.

If we want a century of violent coercion to be succeeded by a century of persuasion, we must find a way to discuss the human future [intelligibly]. The universal moral law written on the human heart is precisely that kind of grammar which is needed if the world is to engage in this discussion of its future.

The moral dynamics of this universal quest for freedom clearly appeared in central and eastern Europe during the non-violent revolutions of 1989.

Unfolding [in specific] times and places, those historical events nonetheless told a lesson which goes far beyond a specific geographical location. For the non-violent revolutions of 1989 demonstrated that the quest for freedom cannot be suppressed. It arises from a recognition of the inestimable dignity and value of the human person. And it cannot fail to be accompanied by a commitment on behalf of the human person.

Modern totalitarianism has been first and foremost an assault on the dignity of the person—an assault which has gone even to the point of denying the inalienable value of the individual's life. The revolutions of 1989 were made possible by the commitment of brave men and women, inspired by a different and ultimately more profound and powerful vision: The vision of man as a creature of intelligence and free-will, amassed in a mystery which transcends his own being and endowed with the ability to reflect and the ability to choose, and thus capable of wisdom and virtue. A decisive factor in the success of those non-violent revolutions was the experience of social solidarity: in the face of regimes backed by the power of propaganda and terror, solidarity was the moral core of the power of the powerless—a beacon of hope and an enduring reminder that it is possible for man's historical journey to follow a path which is true to the finest aspirations of the human spirit. . . .

The universal declaration of human rights, adopted in 1948, spoke eloquently of the rights of persons. But no similar international agreement has yet adequately addressed the rights of nations. This situation must be [carefully pondered] for it raises urgent questions about justice and freedom in the world today.

A study of these rights is certainly not easy, [particularly if] we consider the difficulty of defining the very concept of nations, which cannot be identified a priori or necessarily . . . with the state. [A start] must nonetheless be made if we wish to avoid the errors of the past and ensure a just world order. A [presupposition] of a nation's rights is certainly its right to exist. Therefore, no one—neither a state nor another nation, nor an international organization—is ever justified in . . . asserting that an individual nation is not worthy of existence.

This fundamental right to existence naturally implies that every nation also enjoys the rights to its own languages and culture through which a people expresses and promotes that which I would call its fundamental. History shows that in extreme circumstances such as those which occurred in the land where I was born, it is precisely its culture that enables a nation to survive the loss of political and economic independence.

Every nation, therefore, has also the right to shape its life according to its own traditions, excluding of course, every abuse of basic human rights and in particular, oppression of minorities.

Every nation has to build its future by providing an appropriate education for the younger generation.

During my pastoral pilgrimages to the communities of the catholic church over the past 17 years, I have been able to enter into dialogue with the rich diversity of nations and cultures in every part of the world. Unhappily, the world has yet to learn how to live with diversity, as recent events in the Balkans and Central Africa have painfully reminded us.

The fact of 'difference,' and the reality of 'the other,' can sometimes be felt as a burden or even as a threat.

Amplified by historic grievances, and exacerbated by the manipulations of the unscrupulous, the fear of 'difference' can lead to a denial of the very humanity—the very humanity—of 'the other,' with the result that people fall into a cycle of violence in which no one is spared, not even the children.

We are all very familiar today with such situations. At this moment, my heart and my prayers turn in a special way to the sufferings of the sorely-tried peoples of Bosnia-Herzegovina.

From bitter experience, then, we know that the fear of 'difference,' especially when it expresses itself in a narrow and exclusive nationalism which denies any rights to 'the other,' can lead to a true nightmare of violence and terror. And yet, if we make the effort to look at matters subjectively, we can see that transcending all the differences which distinguish individuals and peoples, there is a fundamental commonality.

For different cultures are but different ways of facing the question of the meaning of personal existence. And it is precisely here that we find one source of the respect which is due to every culture and every nation. Every culture is an effort to ponder the mystery of the world and, in particular, of the human person. It is a way of giving expression to the transcendent dimension of human life. The heart of every culture is its approach to the greatest of all mysteries—the mystery of God.

Our respect for the culture of others is, therefore, rooted in our respect for each community's attempt to answer the question of human life.

And here we can see how important it is to safeguard the fundamental right to freedom of religion and freedom of conscience as the corner stones of the structure of human rights and the foundation of every truly free society.

No one is permitted to suppress those rights by using coercive power, to impose an answer to the mystery of man. We must clarify the essential difference between the [unhealthy] form of nationalism, which teaches contempt for other nations or cultures, and patriotism, which is a proper love of one's country.

True patriotism never seeks to advance the well-being of one's own nation at the expense of others. For in the end this would harm one's own nation as well, doing wrong damages both to aggressor and victim.

Nationalism, particularly in its most radical forms, is thus the antithesis of true patriotism. And today, we must ensure that extreme nationalism does not continue to give rise to new forms of the aberrations of totalitarianism.

Ladies and gentlemen, freedom is the measure of man's dignity and greatness. Living the freedoms sought by individuals and people is a great challenge to man's spiritual growth and to the moral vitality of nations.

The basic question which we must all face today is the responsible use of freedom in both its personal and social dimensions. Our reflection must turn then to the question of the moral structure of freedom which is the inner architecture of the culture of freedom.

Freedom is not simply the absence of tyranny or oppression. Nor is freedom a license to do whatever we like. Freedom has an inner logic which distinguishes it and ennobles it. Freedom is ordered to the truth, and is fulfilled in man's quest for truth and in man's living in the truth. Detached from the truth about the human person, freedom deteriorates into license in the lives of individuals and in political life it becomes the caprice of the most powerful and the arrogance of power.

Far from being a limitation upon freedom or a threat to it, reference to the truth about the human person, a truth universally knowable through the moral law, written on the hearts of all, is in fact the guarantor of freedom's future.

In the light of what has been said, we understand how utilitarianism, the doctrine which defines morality not in terms of what is good, but of what is advantageous, threatens the freedom of individuals and nations and obstructs the building of a true culture of freedom. Utilitarianism often has devastating political consequences because it inspires an aggressive nationalism on the basis of which the subjugation, for example, of a smaller or weaker nation is claimed to be a good thing, solely because it corresponds to the national interest.

No less grave are the results of economic utilitarianism, which drives more powerful countries to manipulate and exploit weaker ones. Nationalistic and economic utilitarianism are sometimes combined, a phenomenon which has too often characterized relations between the North and the South.

For the emerging countries the achievement of political independence has too frequently been accompanied by a situation of de facto economic dependence on other countries. Such situations offend the conscience of humanity, and pose a formidable challenge to the human family.

Yes, distinguished ladies and gentlemen, the international economic scene needs an ethic of solidarity if participation, economic growth, and a just distribution of goods are to characterize the future of humanity.

The international cooperation, called for by the charter of the United Nations, for solving international problems of an economic, social, cultural or humanitarian character cannot be conceived exclusively in terms of help and assistance, or even by considering the eventual returns on the resources provided. When millions of people are suffering from a poverty which means hunger, malnutrition, sickness, illiteracy and degradation, we must not only remind ourselves that no one has a right to exploit another for his own advantage, but also and above all, we must recommit ourselves to that solidarity which enables others to live out the actual circumstances of their economic and political lives, the creativity which is a distinguishing mark of the human person, and the true source of the wealth of nations in today's world.

As we face these enormous challenges, how can we fail to acknowledge the role of the United Nations Organization. The United Nations Organization needs to rise more and more above the cold status of an administrative institution and to become a moral center where all nations of the world feel at home and develop a shared awareness of being, as it were, a family of nations. . . .

It is one of the great paradoxes of our time that man, who began the period we call modernity with a self-confident assertion of his coming of age and autonomy, approaches the end of the 20th century fearful of himself, fearful of what he might be capable of, fearful for the future. Indeed, the second half of the 20th century has seen the unprecedented phenomenon of a humanity uncertain about the very likelihood of a future, given the threat of nuclear war. That danger, mercifully, appears to have receded, and everything that might make it return needs to be rejected firmly and universally. All the same, fear for the future and of the future remains.

In order to ensure that the new millennium, now approaching, will witness a new flourishing of the human spirit, mediated through an authentic culture of freedom, men and women must learn to conquer fear. We must learn not to be afraid. We must rediscover a spirit of hope and a spirit of trust. Hope is not empty optimism springing from a naive confidence that the future will necessarily be better than the past.

Hope and trust are the premise of responsible activity and are nurtured in that inner sanctuary of conscience where man is alone with God, and thus perceives that he is not alone amid the enigmas of existence, for he is surrounded by the love of the Creator.

Hope and trust—these may seem matters beyond the purview of the United Nations, but they are not. The politics of nations, with which your organization is principally concerned, can never ignore the transcendent spiritual dimension of the human experience, and could never ignore it without harming the cause of man and the cause of human freedom. Whatever diminishes man harms the course of freedom. . . .

CLINTON PLEA TO END RACISM IN AMERICA
October 16, 1995

While hundreds of thousands of African-American men gathered on the Mall in Washington in a day of atonement and reconciliation, President Bill Clinton, speaking a thousand miles away in Austin, Texas, implored Americans to "clean our house of racism." The speech came at a time when national sensitivity to racial divisiveness was at a peak. Just two weeks earlier a Los Angeles jury had acquitted football celebrity O. J. Simpson of the murders of his former wife and her friend in a trial that often focused on race and racism. The Million Man March going on in Washington as Clinton spoke had been organized by Nation of Islam leader Louis Farrakhan, whose racist and separatist views made him anathema to many Americans.

Clinton made it clear that racism by whites or blacks was intolerable. Referring to former Los Angles police detective Mark Fuhrman, a white whose racial slurs figured prominently in the Simpson trial, the president said that "the taped voice of one policeman should fill you with outrage." While praising the men participating in the Million Man March for "standing up for personal responsibility," Clinton, in an indirect reference to Farrakhan, said that "one million men do not make right one man's message of malice and division." (Simpson trial, p. 611; Million Man March, p. 655)

Clinton's speech seemed timed to take advantage of the public acknowledgment of the racial rift by trying to help blacks and whites better understand each other's fears and begin a real dialogue with each other. Aides said the president debated for several days about what he should say. In the end, he opted for a more philosophical tone than most presidential speeches adopt. In part that was because government's role in bridging the gap between the races is limited. "At its base, this issue of race is not about government or political leaders, it is about what is in the heart and the minds and the life of the American people," Clinton told the largely white audience at the University of Texas in Austin.

Understanding Each Other's Fears

Racial divisions were caused by racism, the president said, but they were also caused by "the different ways we experience the threats of modern life" and by the "fact that we still haven't learned to talk frankly, to listen carefully, and to work together across racial lines." He called on "every citizen—in every workplace and learning place and meeting place all across America—to take personal responsibility for reaching out to people of different races; for taking time to sit down and talk through this issue; to have the courage to speak honestly and frankly; and then to have the discipline to listen quietly with an open mind and an open heart. . . ."

The president called on whites to understand "the roots of black pain." Acknowledging the suspicion that many African-Americans hold for the legal system, which became strikingly evident during the Simpson trial, Clinton said they had reason to distrust a system "that in too many cases has been and continues to be less than just." He also cited the continuing economic disparity between blacks and whites, and said that whites who think that blacks "are getting more than their fair share" under affirmative action programs were mistaken. The truth, the president said, was that blacks still earned about 60 percent of what whites earned.

By the same token, Clinton continued, "blacks must understand and acknowledge the roots of white fear in America." The fear of violence was "legitimate," the president said. "It isn't racist for whites to say they don't understand why people put up with gangs on the corner or in the projects, or with drugs being sold in the schools or in the open. It's not racist for whites to assert that the culture of welfare dependency, out-of-wedlock pregnancy, and absent fatherhood cannot be broken by social programs unless there is first more personal responsibility."

Clinton said the Million Man March was a great opportunity for the white community to see "that most black people share their old-fashioned American values"—working hard, caring for their families, paying their taxes, and obeying the law, "often under circumstances which are far more difficult than those their white counterparts face."

Reaction

Senate Majority Leader Bob Dole (R-Kan.), the leading contender for the Republican presidential nomination, said he was "shocked and dismayed" that Clinton "did not find the moral courage to denounce Louis Farrakhan by name. . . . Farrakhan is a racist and anti-Semite, unhinged by hate. He has no place in American public life, and all who would lead must say so." Dole added that he resented "the implication by the President of the United States that ours is a racist nation."

Farrakhan referred to Clinton's speech in his own two-hour address at the Million Man March. "I must hasten to tell you, Mr. President, that I'm not a malicious person, and I'm not filled with malice," Farrakhan said.

"But, I must tell you that I come in the tradition of the doctor who has to point out, with truth, what's wrong."

Following are excerpts from a speech delivered by President Bill Clinton on October 16, 1995, at the University of Texas at Austin, in which he called on all Americans to put aside their racial prejudices:

In recent weeks, every one of us has been made aware of a simple truth—white Americans and black Americans often see the same world in drastically different ways—ways that go beyond and beneath the Simpson trial and its aftermath, which brought these perceptions so starkly into the open.

The rift we see before us that is tearing at the heart of America exists in spite of the remarkable progress black Americans have made in the last generation, since Martin Luther King swept America up in his dream, and President Johnson spoke so powerfully for the dignity of man and the destiny of democracy in demanding that Congress guarantee full voting rights to blacks. The rift between blacks and whites exists still in a very special way in America, in spite of the fact that we have become much more racially and ethnically diverse, and that Hispanic Americans—themselves no strangers to discrimination—are now almost 10 percent of our national population.

The reasons for this divide are many. Some are rooted in the awful history and stubborn persistence of racism. Some are rooted in the different ways we experience the threats of modern life to personal security, family values, and strong communities. Some are rooted in the fact that we still haven't learned to talk frankly, to listen carefully, and to work together across racial lines.

Almost 30 years ago, Dr. Martin Luther King took his last march with sanitation workers in Memphis. They marched for dignity, equality, and economic justice. Many carried placards that read simply, "I am a man." The throngs of men marching in Washington today, almost all of them, are doing so for the same stated reason. But there is a profound difference between this march today and those of 30 years ago. Thirty years ago, the marchers were demanding the dignity and opportunity they were due because in the face of terrible discrimination, they had worked hard, raised their children, paid their taxes, obeyed the laws, and fought our wars.

Well, today's march is also about pride and dignity and respect. But after a generation of deepening social problems that disproportionately impact black Americans, it is also about black men taking renewed responsibility for themselves, their families, and their communities. It's about saying no to crime and drugs and violence. It's about standing up for atonement and reconciliation. It's about insisting that others do the same, and offering to help them. It's about the frank admission that unless black men shoulder their load, no one else can help them or their brothers, their sisters, and their children escape the hard, bleak lives that too many of them still face.

Of course, some of those in the march do have a history that is far from its message of atonement and reconciliation. One million men are right to be standing up for personal responsibility. But one million men do not make right one man's message of malice and division. No good house was ever built on a bad foundation. Nothing good ever came of hate. So let us pray today that all who march and all who speak will stand for atonement, for reconciliation, for responsibility. . . .

Today we face a choice—one way leads to further separation and bitterness and more lost futures. The other way, the path of courage and wisdom, leads to unity, to reconciliation, to a rich opportunity for all Americans to make the most of the lives God gave them. This moment in which the racial divide is so clearly out in the open need not be a setback for us. It presents us with a great opportunity, and we dare not let it pass us by. . . .

The two worlds we see now each contain both truth and distortion. Both black and white Americans must face this, for honesty is the only gateway to the many acts of reconciliation that will unite our worlds at last into one America.

White America must understand and acknowledge the roots of black pain. It began with unequal treatment first in law and later in fact. African Americans indeed have lived too long with a justice system that in too many cases has been and continues to be less than just. The record of abuses extends from lynchings and trumped up charges to false arrests and police brutality. The tragedies of Emmett Till and Rodney King are bloody markers on the very same road.

Still today too many of our police officers play by the rules of the bad old days. It is beyond wrong when law-abiding black parents have to tell their law-abiding children to fear the police whose salaries are paid by their own taxes.

And blacks are right to think something is terribly wrong when African American men are many times more likely to be victims of homicide than any other group in this country; when there are more African American men in our corrections system than in our colleges; when almost one in three African American men in their twenties are either in jail, on parole or otherwise under the supervision of the criminal justice system—nearly one in three. And that is a disproportionate percentage in comparison to the percentage of blacks who use drugs in our society. Now, I would like every white person here and in America to take a moment to think how he or she would feel if one in three white men were in similar circumstances.

And there is still unacceptable economic disparity between blacks and whites. It is so fashionable to talk today about African Americans as if they have been some sort of protected class. Many whites think blacks are getting more than their fair share in terms of jobs and promotions. That is not true. That is not true.

The truth is that African Americans still make on average about 60 percent of what white people do; that more than half of African American children live in poverty. And at the very time our young Americans need access to college more than ever before, black college enrollment is dropping in America.

On the other hand, blacks must understand and acknowledge the roots of white fear in America. There is a legitimate fear of the violence that is too prevalent in our urban areas; and often by experience or at least what people see on the news at night, violence for those white people too often has a black face.

It isn't racist for a parent to pull his or her child close when walking through a high-crime neighborhood, or to wish to stay away from neighborhoods where innocent children can be shot in school or standing at bus stops by thugs driving by with assault weapons or toting handguns like old west desperadoes.

It isn't racist for parents to recoil in disgust when they read about a national survey of gang members saying that two-thirds of them feel justified in shooting someone simply for showing them disrespect. It isn't racist for whites to say they don't understand why people put up with gangs on the corner or in the projects, or with drugs being sold in the schools or in the open. It's not racist for whites to assert that the culture of welfare dependency, out-of-wedlock pregnancy and absent fatherhood cannot be broken by social programs unless there is first more personal responsibility.

The great potential for this march today, beyond the black community, is that whites will come to see a larger truth—that blacks share their fears and embrace their convictions; openly assert that without changes in the black community and within individuals, real change for our society will not come.

This march could remind white people that most black people share their old-fashioned American values—for most black Americans still do work hard, care for their families, pay their taxes, and obey the law, often under circumstances which are far more difficult than those their white counterparts face.

Imagine how you would feel if you were a young parent in your twenties with a young child living in a housing project, working somewhere for $5 an hour with no health insurance, passing every day people on the street selling drugs, making 100 times what you make. Those people are the real heroes of America today, and we should recognize that.

And white people too often forget that they are not immune to the problems black Americans face—crime, drugs, domestic abuse, and teen pregnancy. They are too prevalent among whites as well, and some of those problems are growing faster in our white population than in our minority population.

So we all have a stake in solving these common problems together. It is therefore wrong for white Americans to do what they have done too often—simply to move further away from the problems and support policies that will only make them worse.

Finally, both sides seem to fear deep down inside that they'll never quite be able to see each other as more than enemy faces, all of whom carry at least a sliver of bigotry in their hearts. Differences of opinion rooted in different experiences are healthy, indeed essential, for democracies. But differences so great and so rooted in race threaten to divide the house Mr. Lincoln gave his life to save. As Dr. King said, "We must learn to live together as brothers, or we will perish as fools."

Recognizing one another's real grievances is only the first step. We must all take responsibility for ourselves, our conduct and our attitudes. America, we must clean our house of racism.

To our white citizens, I say, I know most of you ever[y] day do your very best by your own lights—to live a life free of discrimination. Nevertheless, too many destructive ideas are gaining currency in our midst. The taped voice of one policeman should fill you with outrage. And so I say, we must clean the house of white America of racism. Americans who are in the white majority should be proud to stand up and be heard denouncing the sort of racist rhetoric we heard on that tape—so loudly and clearly denouncing it, that our black fellow citizens can hear us. White racism may be black people's burden, but it's white people's problem. We must clean our house.

To our black citizens, I honor the presence of hundreds of thousands of men in Washington today, committed to atonement and to personal responsibility, and the commitment of millions of other men and women who are African Americans to this cause. I call upon you to build on this effort, to share equally in the promise of America. But to do that, your house, too, must be cleaned of racism. There are too many today—white and black, on the left and the right, on the street corners and radio waves, who seek to sow division for their own purposes. To them I say, no more. We must be one.

Long before we were so diverse, our nation's motto was E Pluribus Unum—out of many, we are one. We must be one—as neighbors, as fellow citizens; not separate camps, but family—white, black, Latino, all of us, no matter how different, who share basic American values and are willing to live by them.

When a child is gunned down on a street in the Bronx, no matter what our race, he is our American child. When a woman dies from a beating, no matter what our race or hers, she is our American sister. And every time drugs course through the veins of another child, it clouds the future of all our American children.

Whether we like it or not, we are one nation, one family, indivisible. And for us, divorce or separation are not options.

Here, in 1995, on the edge of the 21st century, we dare not tolerate the existence of two Americas. Under my watch, I will do everything I can to see that as soon as possible there is only one—one America under the rule of law; one social contract committed not to winner take all, but to giving all Americans a chance to win together—one America.

Well, how do we get there? First, today I ask every governor, every mayor, every business leader, every church leader, every civic leader, every union steward, every student leader—most important, every citizen—in every workplace and learning place and meeting place all across America—to take personal responsibility for reaching out to people of different races; for taking time to sit down and talk through this issue; to have the courage to speak honestly and frankly; and then to have the discipline to listen quietly with an open mind and an open heart, as others do the same.

This may seem like a simple request, but for tens of millions of Americans, this has never been a reality. They have never spoken, and they have never listened—not really, not really. I am convinced, based on a rich lifetime of friendships and common endeavors with people of different races, that the American people will find out they have a lot more in common than they think they do.

The second thing we have to do is to defend and enhance real opportunity. I'm not talking about opportunity for black Americans or opportunity for white Americans; I'm talking about opportunity for all Americans. Sooner or later, all our speaking, all our listening, all our caring has to lead to constructive action together for our words and our intentions to have meaning. We can do this first by truly rewarding work and family in government policies, in employment policies, in community practices.

We also have to realize that there are some areas of our country—whether in urban areas or poor rural areas like south Texas or eastern Arkansas— where these problems are going to be more prevalent just because there is no opportunity. There is only so much temptation some people can stand when they turn up against a brick wall day after day after day. And if we can spread the benefits of education and free enterprise to those who have been denied them too long and who are isolated in enclaves in this country, then we have a moral obligation to do it. It will be good for our country.

Third and perhaps most important of all, we have to give every child in this country, and every adult who still needs it, the opportunity to get a good education. . . .

But let us remember, the people marching in Washington today are right about one fundamental thing—at its base, this issue of race is not about government or political leaders; it is about what is in the heart and the minds and life of the American people. There will be no progress in the absence of real responsibility on the part of all Americans. Nowhere is that responsibility more important than in our efforts to promote public safety and preserve the rule of law.

Law and order is the first responsibility of government. Our citizens must respect the law and those who enforce it. Police have a life and death responsibility never, never to abuse the power granted them by the people. We know, by the way, what works in fighting crime also happens to improve relationships between the races. What works in fighting crime is community policing. We have seen it working all across America. The crime rate is down. The murder rate is down where people relate to each other across the lines of police and community in an open, honest, respectful, supportive way. We can lower crime and raise the state of race relations in America if we will remember this simple truth.

But if this is going to work, police departments have to be fair and engaged with, not estranged from, their communities. I am committed to making this kind of community policing a reality all across our country. But you must be committed to making it a reality in your communities. We have to root out the remnants of racism in our police departments. We've got to get it out of our entire criminal justice system. But just as the police have a sacred duty to protect the community fairly, all of our citizens have a sacred responsibility to respect the police; to teach our young people to respect them; and then to support them and work with them so that they can succeed in making us safer.

Let's not forget, most police officers of whatever race are honest people who love the law and put their lives on the line so that the citizens they're protecting can lead decent, secure lives, and so that their children can grow up to do the same.

Finally, I want to say, on the day of this march, a moment about a crucial area of responsibility—the responsibility of fatherhood. The single biggest social problem in our society may be the growing absence of fathers from their children's homes, because it contributes to so many other social problems. One child in four grows up in a fatherless home. Without a father to help guide, without a father to care, without a father to teach boys to be men and to teach girls to expect respect from men, it's harder. There are a lot of mothers out there doing a magnificent job alone—(applause)—a magnificent job alone, but it is harder. It is harder. This, of course, is not a black problem or a Latino problem or a white problem; it is an American problem. But it aggravates the conditions of the racial divide. . . .

For those who are neglecting their children, I say it is not too late; your children still need you. To those who only send money in the form of child support, I say keep sending the checks; your kids count on them, and we'll catch you and enforce the law if you stop. But the message of this march today—one message is that your money is no replacement for your guiding, your caring, you[r] loving the children you brought into this world.

We can only build strong families when men and women respect each other; when they have partnerships; when men are as involved in the homeplace as women have become involved in the workplace. It means, among other things, that we must keep working until we end domestic violence against women and children. I hope those men in Washington today pledge among other things to never, never raise their hand in violence against a woman.

So today, my fellow Americans, I honor the black men marching in Washington to demonstrate their commitment to themselves, their families, and their communities. I honor the millions of men and women in America, the vast majority of every color, who without fanfare or recognition do what it takes to be good fathers and good mothers, good workers and good citizens. They all deserve the thanks of America.

But when we leave here today, what are you going to do? What are you going to do? Let all of us who want to stand up against racism do our part to roll back the divide. Begin by seeking out people in the workplace, the classroom, the community, the neighborhood across town, the places of worship to actually sit down and have those honest conversations I talked about—conversations where we speak openly and listen and understand how others view this world of ours. . . .

. . . While leaders and legislation may be important, this is work that has to be done by every single one of you. And this is the ultimate test of our democracy, for today the house divided exists largely in the minds and hearts of the American people. And it must be united there in the minds and hearts of our people.

Yes, there are some who would poison our progress by selling short the great character of our people and our enormous capacity to change and grow. But they will not win the day; we will win the day. . . .

FARRAKHAN'S REMARKS AT THE MILLION MAN MARCH
October 16, 1995

Heeding the call of Nation of Islam leader Louis Farrakhan, at least 400,000 African-American men came to the Mall in Washington, D.C., on October 16 and pledged to take more responsibility for themselves, their families, and their communities. Although the number fell short of Farrakhan's prediction of a "Million Man March," it was nonetheless the largest civil rights demonstration in the nation's history. In comparison, the March on Washington in 1963, when the Rev. Martin Luther King gave his famous "I Have a Dream" speech, drew 250,000.

Farrakhan had put both white and black leaders in a ticklish situation with his call for the Million Man March. Many were reluctant to endorse the rally for fear of legitimizing Farrakhan, a black separatist whose racist comments about whites in general and Jews in particular had made him anathema to many. At the same time, leaders did not want to appear to be spurning the marchers, who were gathering in a spirit of fellowship for a day of atonement and reconciliation. In the end most leaders compromised by praising the message while deploring the chief messenger.

"One million men are right to be standing up for personal responsibility," President Bill Clinton told an audience at the University of Texas in Austin, where he made a major speech on racism shortly before Farrakhan spoke in Washington. "But one million men do not make right one man's message of malice and division." (Clinton speech on racism, p. 646)

Many of the men attending the march also separated the message from the messenger. According to a Washington Post *poll of those attending, more than half came to show support for the black family and for black men who take responsibility for their families, while 25 percent came to demonstrate black unity; only 5 percent came to show support for Farrakhan. Farrakhan "offers a strong message of hope," said one marcher, "but when it's mixed with prejudice, the message gets watered."*

A Mixed Message

Farrakhan's message was indeed mixed. During his fiery, but often rambling, keynote address, which lasted more than two hours, he declared that the "real evil in America" was white supremacy, which gave whites the idea that they should rule because they were white. At the same time he took a tentative step toward reconciliation with the Jewish community, saying that "maybe it's time to sit down and talk." He urged the marchers to go home and help register the 8 million eligible but unregistered blacks so that political candidates, whether white or black, would be forced to "speak to our agenda."

(At a news conference on October 18, Farrakhan announced that he would join forces with a recently organized group of African-American women in Operation Big Vote. "We in the Nation of Islam have never before become thoroughly involved politically," Farrakhan said. "We intend to make practically all of our membership registrars.")

Farrakhan's speech, delivered from the steps of the Capitol, was liberally sprinkled with biblical imagery, numerology, Masonic symbolism, and Afrocentrism. Sections of it had the rhythm of rap; others the tone of a gospel preacher. Often he spoke directly to the national television audience, estimated at 2.2 million viewers. Throughout he characterized himself as God's messenger. "Whenever a nation is involved in sin to the point that God intends to judge and destroy that nation, he always sends someone to make that nation or people know their sins, to reflect on it, to acknowledge, to confess, to repent, and to atone that they might find forgiveness with God," Farrakhan said at one point.

Farrakhan spoke at the end of a long day of celebration and speeches from ministers, businessmen, civil rights activists, and politicians, such as Rep. Kweisi Mfume (D-Md.) and Marion Barry, mayor of Washington, D.C. The Rev. Jesse Jackson was the only widely known national politician to take part in the march, which was shunned by such major black organizations as the Urban League and the National Association for the Advancement of Colored People (which, in December, would name Mfume its next president). (New NAACP leadership, p. 453)

Women, whom Farrakhan deliberately excluded from his call to march, generally stayed away, but three well-known African-American women spoke: the poet Maya Angelou; Rosa Parks, the Atlanta woman whose refusal to give up her seat on a public bus was credited as the spark that led to enactment of the Civil Rights Act of 1964; and Betty Shabazz, the widow of Malcolm X.

Many of the speakers preached the need for African-American men to atone for abandoning their wives and children and to assume responsibility for their lives. Others voiced their anger at decades of white oppression. "Where is economic justice," asked Mfume, "when we are condemned to the bottom of the pay scale and government abandons its commitment to affirmative action?" Gus Savage, a former representative from Chicago, said black men should be angrier than they were at white racism and "incipient fascism."

Farrakhan and the Nation of Islam

Farrakhan is the leader of a small group of men (estimates range between 10,000 and 20,000) that believes a black man created whites and that white rule will end sometime in the twentieth century, when blacks return to a position of leadership. The Nation of Islam, which is not acknowledged by orthodox Islam, was founded in the 1930s by Elijah Muhammad, who preached a gospel of black separatism and self-sufficiency. Farrakhan, born Louis Eugene Walcott in 1933, was a calypso singer when he joined the Nation of Islam as Louis X in 1955. He was tutored by Malcolm X, who in 1964 broke with the Nation. At the time, Farrakhan denounced his former tutor. He later acknowledged that his remarks may have helped to create the climate that led to Malcolm X's assassination in 1965.

Elijah Muhammad died in 1975. In 1978 Farrakhan split from the movement, which was moving toward mainstream Islam, and vowed to revive Muhammad's separatist teachings. Since then Farrakhan had come to national attention largely for his extremist remarks. His one foray into national politics before the Million Man March came in 1984, when he supported the Rev. Jesse Jackson's presidential campaign, but he was quickly shunned after making a speech in which he appeared to praise Hitler and referred to Judaism as a "gutter religion."

Reaction

Senate Majority Leader Bob Dole's comments on the march and its leader were fairly typical of those heard from many Republicans. "There are probably a lot of well-intentioned people coming to Washington," said Dole, a contender for the Republican presidential nomination. "And I like the talk about self-reliance, about picking yourself up, cleaning up our cities and getting kids off drugs. But I don't think Farrakhan should be the leader of the march. He spreads suspicion, separatism and hate wherever he goes. No cloak can cover the ugliness of Farrakhan's purpose." Dole also criticized President Clinton for not condemning Farrakhan by name.

Retired general Colin Powell, who at the time was still exploring the possibility of entering the presidential race, said he decided not to appear on stage with Farrakhan because, he said, "I deplore the message of Minister Farrakhan, and I don't want to be associated with it." Like Dole, Powell praised the marchers, saying several hundred thousand black men who "care about themselves, care about their future, care about the future of this country" could not be ignored.

David Garrow, who wrote a Pulitzer Prize-winning biography of Martin Luther King, said Farrakhan had hurt himself by speaking for so long. "He is showing to a national audience that he doesn't have full control of himself," Garrow told a New York Times *reporter.*

Historian Roger Wilkins suggested that Farrakhan was becoming a powerful voice in the African-American community largely by default. "Responsible black people have been trying to get the attention of the Democratic party and the Republican party for a long time to tell them that black people were unemployed at double digit levels for two decades, that black teen-agers are in trouble, black families are falling apart largely because they do not have adequate incomes. White people have not listened. Their response was [House Speaker Newt] Gingrich's programs to punish the poor. By ignoring moderate black leaders they sowed the seeds for the emergence of Farrakhan as a more important figure in American life," Wilkins told the New York Times.

Following are excerpts from a speech by Nation of Islam leader Louis Farrakhan, delivered October 16, 1995, at the Million Man March in Washington, D.C.:

. . . I would like to thank all of those known and unknown persons who worked to make this day of atonement and reconciliation a reality. . . .

Now, where are we gathered? We're standing at the steps of the United States Capitol.

I'm looking at the Washington Monument and beyond it to the Lincoln Memorial. And, beyond that . . . the Jefferson Memorial. Abraham Lincoln was the 16th president of these United States and he was the man who allegedly freed us. . . .

Abraham Lincoln, when he saw this great divide, he pondered a solution of separation. Abraham Lincoln said he was never in favor of our being jurors or having equal status with the Whites of this nation. Abraham Lincoln said that if there were to be a superior or inferior, he would rather the superior position be assigned to the White race. There, in the middle of this mall is the Washington Monument, 555 feet high. But if we put a one in front of that 555, we get 1555, the year that our first fathers landed on the shores of Jamestown, Virginia, as slaves.

In the background is the Jefferson and Lincoln Memorial, each one of these monuments is 19 feet high.

Abraham Lincoln, the sixteenth president. Thomas Jefferson, the third president, and 16 and three make 19 again. What is so deep about this number 19? Why are we standing on the Capitol steps today? That number 19—when you have a nine you have a womb that is pregnant. And when you have a one standing by the nine, it means that there's something secret that has to be unfolded.

Right here on this mall . . . slaves used to be brought in chains to be sold up and down the eastern seaboard. Right along this mall, going over to the White House, our fathers were sold into slavery. But, George Washington, the first president of the United States, said he feared that before too many years passed over his head, this slave would prove to become a most troublesome species of property.

Thomas Jefferson said he trembled for this country when he reflected that God was just and that his justice could not sleep forever. Well, the day that these presidents feared has now come to pass, for on this mall, here we stand in the capital of America. And the layout of this great city, laid out by a Black man, Benjamin Banneker. This is all placed and based in a secret Masonic ritual. And at the core of the secret of that ritual is the Black man. . . .

. . . George Washington, who was a grand master of the Masonic order, laid the foundation, the corner stone, of this capitol building where we stand. George was a slave owner. . . . Now [President Clinton] spoke today and he wanted to heal the great divide. But I respectfully suggest to the President, you did not dig deep enough at the malady that divides Black and White in order to effect a solution to the problem. . . .

Look at our division, not here, out there. We are a people who have been fractured, divided, and destroyed, and because of our division must move toward a perfect union. But let's look at a speech delivered by a White slave holder on the banks of the James River in 1712. . . .

Sixty-eight years before our former slave owners permitted us to join the Christian faith. Listen to what he said. He said, "In my bag I have a fool proof method of controlling black slaves. I guarantee every one of you, if installed correctly, it will control the slaves for at least 300 years. My method is simple. Any member of your family or your overseer can use it. I have outlined a number of differences among the slaves and I take these differences and I make them bigger. I use fear, distrust, and envy for control purposes."

I want you to listen. What are those three things? Fear, envy, distrust. For what purpose? Control. To control who? The slave. Who is the slave? Us. . . .

"Gentlemen, these are your keys to control. Use them. Never miss an opportunity. And if used intensely for one year, the slaves themselves will remain forever distrustful. Thank you, gentlemen." End of quote. So spoke Willie Lynch 283 years ago.

And so, as a consequence, we as a people now have been fractured, divided and destroyed, filled with fear, distrust and envy. Therefore, because of fear, envy and distrust of one another, many of us as leaders, teachers, educators, pastors, and persons are still under the control mechanism of our former slave masters and their children.

And now, in spite of all that division, we responded to a call and look at what is present here today. We have here those brothers with means and those who have no means. Those who are light and those who are dark. Those who are educated, those who are uneducated. Those who are business people, those who don't know anything about business. Those who are young, those who are old. Those who are scientific, those who know nothing of science. Those who are religious and those who are irreligious. Those who are Christian, those who are Muslim, those who are Baptist, those who are Methodist, those who are Episcopalian, those of traditional African religion. We've got them all here today.

And why did we come? We came because we want to move toward a more perfect union. And if you notice, the press triggered every one of those divisions. You shouldn't come, you're a Christian. That's a Muslim thing. You shouldn't come, you're too intelligent to follow hate! You shouldn't come, look at what they did, they excluded women, you see? They played all the cards, they pulled all the strings.

Oh, but you better look again, Willie. There's a new Black man in America today. A new Black woman in America today. Now brothers, there's a social benefit of our gathering here today. That is, that from this day forward, we can never again see ourselves through the narrow eyes of the limitation of the boundaries of our own fraternal, civic, political, religious, street organization or professional organization. We are forced by the magnitude of what we see here today, that whenever you return to your cities and you see a Black man, a Black woman, don't ask him what is your social, political or religious affiliation, or what is your status? Know that he is your brother.

You must live beyond the narrow restrictions of the divisions that have been imposed upon us. Well, some of us are here because it's history-making. Some of us are here because it's a march through which we can express anger and rage with America for what she has and is doing to us. So, we're here for many reasons but the basic reason why this was called was for atonement and reconciliation. So, it is necessary for me in as short a time as possible to give as full an explanation of atonement as possible.

. . . [A]tonement is the fifth stage in an eight stage process. So, let's go back to the first stage of the process that brings us into perfect union with God. And the first stage is the most difficult of all because when we are wrong, and we are not aware of it, someone has to point out the wrong. I want to, I want to say this again, but I want to say it slowly. And I really want each one of these points to sink in. How many of us in this audience, at some time or another have been wrong? Would we just raise our hands?

OK. Now, when we are wrong, Lord knows we want to be right. The most difficult thing is when somebody points it out, do we accept it, do we reject it, do we hate the person who pointed out our wrong? How do we treat the person who points out our wrong? Now, I want you to follow me. When you go to a doctor, you're not feeling well, the doctor says, what's wrong? Well, I don't know, doc. Well, where is the pain? Tell me something about the symptoms. You want the doctor to make a correct diagnosis. You don't smack the doctor when he points out what's wrong.

You don't hate the doctor when he points out what's wrong. You say, thank you, doctor. What's my prescription for healing? We all right? Now, look, whoever is entrusted with the task of pointing out wrong, depending on the nature of the circumstances, is not always loved.

In fact, more than likely, that person is going to be hated and misunderstood. Such persons are generally hated because no one wants to be shown as being wrong. Particularly when you're dealing with governments, with principalities, with powers, with rulers, with administrations. When you're dealing with forces which have become entrenched in their evil, intractable and unyielding, their power produces an arrogance. And their arrogance produces a blindness. And out of that evil state of mind, they will do all manner of evil to the person who points out their wrong. Even though you're doing good for them by pointing out where America went wrong.

Now, Martin Luther King, Jr. was probably the most patriotic American. More patriotic than George Washington. More patriotic than Thomas Jefferson. More patriotic than many of the presidents because he had the courage to point out what was wrong in the society. And because he pointed out what was wrong, he was ill spoken of, vilified, maligned, hated and, eventually, murdered.

Brother Malcolm had that same road to travel. He pointed out what was wrong in the society, and he had to suffer for pointing out what was wrong, and he ultimately died on the altar for pointing out what was wrong. Inside the Nation, outside the Nation, to the greater nation and to the smaller nation. . . .

[The Meaning of Atonement]

But, atonement means satisfaction or reparation for a wrong or injury. It means to make amends. It means penance, expiation, compensation and recompense made or done for an injury or wrong.

So, atonement means we must be willing to do something in expiation of our sins, so we can't just have a good time today, and say we made history in Washington. We've got to resolve today that we're going back home to do something about what's going on in our lives and in our families and in our communities.

Now, we all right? Can you hang with me a few more? Now, brothers and sisters, if we make atonement it leads to the sixth stage. And the sixth stage is forgiveness. Now, so many of us want forgiveness, but we don't want to go through the process that leads to it. And so, when we say we forgive, we forgive from our lips, but we have never pardoned in the heart.

So, the injury still remains. My dear family. My dear brothers. We need forgiveness. God is always ready to forgive us for our sins. Forgiveness means to grant pardon for, or remission of, an offense or sin. It is to absolve, to clear, to exonerate and to liberate. Boy, that's something!

See, you're not liberated until you can forgive. You're not liberated from the evil effect of [your] own sin until [you] can ask God for forgiveness and then forgive others, and this is why in the Lord's Prayer you say, forgive us our trespasses as we forgive those who trespass against us.

So, it means to cease to feel offense and resentment against another for the harm done by an offender. It means to wipe the slate clean. And then, that leads to the seventh stage. . . .

. . . The seventh tone, the leading tone that leads to the perfect union with God is reconciliation and restoration because after forgiveness, now, we are going to be restored to what? To our original position. To restore, to reconcile means to become friendly, peaceable again, to put hostile persons into a state of agreement or harmony, to make compatible or to compose or settle what it was that made for division.

It means to resolve differences. It can mean to establish or re-establish a close relationship between previously hostile persons. So, restoration means the act of returning something to an original or unimpaired condition. Now, when you're back to an unimpaired position, you have reached the eighth stage, which is perfect union. And when we go through all these steps, there is no difference between us that we can't heal. . . .

We are a wounded people but we're being healed, but President Clinton, America is also wounded. And there's hostility now in the great divide between the people. Socially the fabric of America is being torn apart, and it's black against black, black against white, white against white, white against black, yellow against brown, brown against yellow. We are being torn apart. And we can't gloss it over with nice speeches, my dear Mr. President.

Sir, with all due respect, that was a great speech you made today. And you praised the marchers and they're worthy of praise. You honored the marchers and they are worthy of honor. But of course, you spoke ill indirectly of me, as a purveyor of malice and hatred.

I must hasten to tell you, Mr. President, that I'm not a malicious person, and I'm not filled with malice. But, I must tell you that I come in the tradition of the doctor who has to point out, with truth, what's wrong. And the pain is that power has made America arrogant. Power and wealth have made America spiritually blind and the power and the arrogance of America makes you refuse to hear a child of your slaves pointing out the wrong in your society. . . .

. . . [W]henever a nation is involved in sin to the point that God intends to judge and destroy that nation, He always sends someone to make that nation or people know their sins, to reflect on it, to acknowledge, to confess, to repent and to atone that they might find forgiveness with God. America, oh America. This great city of Washington is like Jerusalem. And the Bible says, "Jerusalem, oh Jerusalem, you that stoneth and killeth the prophets of God."

Right from this beautiful Capitol and from the beautiful White House have come commands to kill the prophets. David's trouble came from this house. Martin Luther King's trouble came from this house. Malcolm's trouble came from this house. W. E. B. Dubois' trouble came from this house. And from this house, you stoned and killed the prophets of God that would have liberated Black people, liberated America. But I stand here today knowing, knowing that you are angry. My people have validated me. I don't need you to validate me.

I don't need to be in any mainstream.

I want to wash in the river of Jordan and the river that you see and the sea that is before us and behind us and around us.

It's validation. That's the mainstream. You're out of touch with reality. A few of you in a few smoke-filled rooms, calling that the mainstream while the masses of the people, white and black, red, yellow, and brown, poor and vulnerable are suffering in this nation.

Well, America, great America. Like Jerusalem that stoned and killed the prophets of God. A work has been done in you today unlike any work that's ever been done in this great city. I wonder what you'll say tomorrow?

I wonder what you'll write in your newspapers and magazines tomorrow. Will you give God the glory? Will you give God the glory? Will you respect the beauty of this day? All of these black men that the world sees as savage, maniacal, and bestial. Look at them. A sea of peace. A sea of tranquillity. A sea of men ready to come back to God. Settle their differences and go back home to turn our communities into decent and safe places to live.

America. America, the beautiful. There's no country like this on the earth. And certainly if I lived in another country, I might never have had the opportunity to speak as I speak today. I probably would have been shot outright. . . .

But because this is America you allow me to speak even though you don't like what I may say. Because this is America, that provision in the constitution for freedom of speech and freedom of assembly and freedom of religion, that is your saving grace.

Because what you're under right now is grace. And grace is the expression of divine love and protection which God bestows freely on people.

God is angry, America. He's angry, but His mercy is still present. Brothers and sisters, look at the afflictions that have come upon us in the Black community. Do you know why we're being afflicted? God wants us to humble ourselves to the message that will make us atone and come back to Him and make ourselves whole again. But why is God afflicting America? Why is God afflicting the world? Why did Jesus say there would be wars and rumors of wars, and earthquakes in diverse places and pestilence and famine, and why did He say that these were just the beginning of sorrows?. . .

[The Evil of White Supremacy]

Now brothers, sisters, I want to close this lecture with a special message to our President and to the Congress. There is a great divide, but the real evil in America is not white flesh, or black flesh. The real evil in America is the idea that undergirds the set-up of the western world. And that idea is called white supremacy.

Now wait, wait, wait. Before you get angry. Those of you listening by television. You don't even know why you behave the way you behave.

I'm not telling you I'm a psychiatrist, but I do want to operate on your head. White supremacy is the enemy of both White people and Black people because the idea of white supremacy means you should rule because you're white. That makes you sick. And you've produced a sick society and a sick world. The founding fathers meant well, but they said, "toward a more perfect union." So, the Bible says, we know in part, we prophesy in part, but when that which is perfect is come, that which is in part shall be done away with.

So Mr. Clinton, we're going to do away with the mind-set of the founding fathers. You don't have to repudiate them like you've asked my brothers to do me. You don't have to say they were malicious, hate-filled people. But you must evolve out of their mind-set. You see their minds was limited to those six European nations out of which this country was founded. But you've got Asians here. How are you going to handle that? You've got children of Africa here. How are you going to handle that?

You've got Arabs here. You've got Hispanics here. I know you call them illegal aliens, but hell, you took Texas from them by flooding Texas with people that got your mind. And now they're coming back across the border to what is northern Mexico, Texas, Arizona, New Mexico, and California. They don't see themselves as illegal aliens. I think they might see you as an illegal alien. You have to be careful how you talk to people. You have to be careful how you deal with people. The Native American is suffering today. He's suffering almost complete extinction. Now, he learned about bingo. You taught him. He learned about black jack. You taught him. He learned about playing roulette. You taught him. Now, he's making a lot of money. You're upset with him because he's adopted your ways. What makes you like this? See, you're like this because you're not well. You're not well. And in the light of today's global village, you can never harmonize with the Asians. You can't harmonize with the islands of the Pacific.

You can't harmonize with the dark people of the world who outnumber you eleven to one, if you're going to stand in the mind of white supremacy. White supremacy has to die in order for humanity to live.

Now, oh, I know. I know. I know it's painful, but we have to operate now, just, just take a little of this morphine and you won't feel the pain as much. You just need to bite down on something, as I stop [these] last few minutes, just bite down on your finger. Listen, listen, listen, listen, white supremacy caused you all, not you all, some White folk to try to rewrite history and write us out. White supremacy caused Napoleon to blow the nose off of the Sphinx because it reminded you too much of the Black man's majesty.

White supremacy caused you to take Jesus, a man with hair like lamb's wool and feet like burnished brass and make him White. So that you could worship him because you could never see yourself honoring somebody Black because of the state of your mind. You see, you, you really need help. You'll be all right. You'll be all right. You will be all right. Now, now, now, you painted the Last Supper, everybody there White.

My mother asked the man that came to bring her the Bible. He said, look there, the pictures in the Bible. You see, Jesus and all his disciples are at the Last Supper—my mother in her West Indian accent said, you mean ain't nobody Black was at the Last Supper?

And the man said, yes, but they was in the kitchen. So now you've whitened up everything.

Any great invention we made you put white on it, because you didn't want to admit that a Black person had that intelligence, that genius. You try to color everything to make it satisfactory to the sickness of our mind.

So you whitened up religion, Farrakhan didn't do that. You locked the Bible from us, Farrakhan didn't do that. Your sick mind wouldn't even let you bury us in the same ground that both of us came out of. We had to be buried somewhere else. That's sick. Some of us died just to drink water out of a fountain marked White. That's sick. Isn't it sick?

You poisoned religion. And in all the churches, until recently, the master was painted white. So, you had us bowing down to your image. Which ill-affected our minds. You gave us your version of history. And you whitened that up. Yes, you did. Yes, you did. . . .

I'm almost finished. White supremacy has poisoned the bloodstream of religion, education, politics, jurisprudence, economics, social ethics and morality.

And there is no way that we can integrate into white supremacy and hold our dignity as human beings because if we integrate into that, we become subservient to that. And to become subservient to that is to make the slave master comfortable with his slave. So, we got to come out. . . . Come out of a system and a world that is built on the wrong idea. An idea that never can create a perfect union with God.

The false idea of white supremacy prevents anyone from becoming one with God. White people have to come out of that idea, which has poisoned them into a false attitude of superiority based on the color of their skins. The doctrine of white supremacy disallows Whites to grow to their full potential. It forces White people to see themselves as the law or above the law. And that's why [former Los Angeles police detective Mark] Fuhrman could say that he is like a god. See, he thinks like that, but that idea is pervasive in police departments across the country. And it's getting worse and not better because white supremacy is not being challenged.

And I say to all of us who are leaders, all of us who are preachers, we must not shrink from the responsibility of pointing out wrong, so that we can be comfortable and keep White people comfortable in their alienation from God. And so, White folks are having heart attacks today because their world is coming down. And if you look at the Asians, the Asians have the fastest growing economies in the world. The Asians are not saying, bashing White people. You don't find the Asians saying the White man is this, the White man is that, the White man is the other.

He don't talk like that. You know what he does? He just relocates the top banks from Wall Street to Tokyo. He don't say, I'm better than the White man. He just starts building his world and building his economy and challenging white supremacy. . . .

[Turning Black Communities into Productive Places]

Black man, you don't have to bash White people, all we gotta do is go back home and turn our communities into productive places. All we gotta do is go back home and make our communities a decent and safe place to live. And if we start dotting the Black community with businesses, opening up factories, challenging ourselves to be better than we are, White folk, instead of driving by, using the "N" word, they'll say, look, look at them. Oh, my God. They're marvelous. They're wonderful. We can't, we can't say they're inferior anymore.

But, every time we drive-by shoot, every time we carjack, every time we use foul, filthy language, every time we produce culturally degenerate films and tapes, putting a string in our women's backside and parading them before the world, every time we do things like this we are feeding the degenerate mind of white supremacy, and I want us to stop feeding that mind and let that mind die a natural death.

And so, to all the artists that are present, you wonderful gifted artists, remember that your gift comes from God. And David the Psalmist said, praise him on the timbrel, praise him on the lute, praise him on the harp, praise him in the sultry, praise in the song, praise him in the dance, let everything be a praise of God.

So, when you sing, you don't have to get naked to sing. Demonstrate your gift, not your breast. Demonstrate your gift, not what is between your legs. Clean up, Black man, and the world will respect and honor you. But, you have fallen down like the prodigal son and you're husking corn and feeding swine.

Filthy jokes. We can't bring our children to the television.

We can't bring our families to the movies because the American people have an appetite like a swine. And you are feeding the swine with the filth of degenerate culture. We got to stop it.

We're not putting you down, brothers, we want to pick you up so with your rap, you can pick up the world. With your song, you can pick up the world. With your dance, with your music, you can pick up the world. . . .

So, my beloved brothers and sisters, here's what we would like you to do. Every one of you, my dear brothers, when you go home, here's what I want you to do. We must belong to some organization that is working for and in the interest of the uplift and the liberation of our people.

Go back, join the NAACP if you want to, join the Urban League, join the All African People's Revolutionary Party, join us, join the Nation of Islam, join PUSH, join the Congress of Racial Equality, join SCLC—the Southern Christian Leadership Conference, but we must become a totally organized people, and the only way we can do that is to become a part of some organization that is working for the uplift of our people.

We must keep the local organizing committees that made this event possible, we must keep them together. And then all of us, as leaders, must stay together and make the National African American Leadership Summit inclusive of all of us.

I know that the NAACP did not officially endorse this march. Neither did the Urban League. But, so what? So what? Many of the members are here anyway. I know that Dr. Lyons, of the National Baptist Association USA, did not endorse the march, nor did the Reverend Dr. B. W. Smith, nor did Bishop Chandler Owens, but so what?

These are our brothers and we're not going to stop reaching out for them simply because we feel there was a misunderstanding. We still want to talk to our brothers because we cannot let artificial barriers divide us. . . .

[Call for Voter Registration Drive]

Brothers, when you go home, we've got to register eight million eligible but unregistered brothers, sisters. So you go home and find eight more like yourself. You register and get them to register. Should I register as Democrat? Should I register as a Republican? Should I register as independent?

If you're an independent, that's fine. If you're a Democrat, that's fine. If you're a Republican, that's OK. Because in local elections you have to do that which is in the best interest of your local community. But what we want is not necessarily a third party, but a third force.

Which means that we're going to collect Democrats, Republicans and independents around an agenda that is in the best interest of our people. And then all of us can stand on that agenda and in 1996, whoever the standard-bearer is for the Democratic, the Republican, or the Independent party should one come into existence, they've got to speak to our agenda.

We're no longer going to vote for somebody just because they're Black. We tried that. We wish we could. But we got to vote for you, if you are compatible with our agenda.

Now many of the people that's in this House right here are put there by the margin of the Black vote. So in the next election, we want to see who's in here do we want to stay and who in here do we want to go.

And we want to show them that never again will they ever disrespect the Black community. We must make them afraid to do evil to us and think they can get away with it.

We must be prepared to help them if they are with us or to punish them if they're against us. And when they are against us, I'm not talking about color. I'm talking about an agenda that's in the best interest of the Black, the poor and the vulnerable in this society.

Now atonement goes beyond us. I don't like this squabble with the members of the Jewish community. I don't like it. The honorable Elijah Muhammad said in one of his writings that he believed that we would work out some kind of an accord. Maybe so. Reverend Jackson has talked to the twelve presidents of Jewish organizations and perhaps in the light of what we see today, maybe it's time to sit down and talk. Not with any preconditions. You got pain. Well, we've got pain, too. You hurt. We hurt, too.

The question is: if the dialogue is proper then we might be able to end the pain. And ending the pain may be good for both and ultimately good for the nation. We're not opposed to sitting down. And I guess if you can sit down with [Yasir] Arafat where there are rivers of blood between you—why can't you sit down with us and there's no blood between us. It don't make sense not to dialogue. It doesn't make sense. . . .

[Proposed Economic Development Fund]

Now brothers, the last thing we want to say, we want to develop an economic development fund. Suppose the nearly two million here, and ten million more back home that support us gave ten dollars a month to a national economic development fund.

Inside of one month, we would have over $100 million. And in one year, we would have $1 billion, $200 million. What will we do with that? I would love for the leadership up here to form a board and call in [Myrlie] Evers Williams [chairman of the NAACP board of directors] and ask her, what is the budget of the NAACP for this year? It's $13 million. It's $15 million, write a check. Now, next year you have to become accountable to the board, and the members of the NAACP will be on the board too, which means that no Black organization will be accountable to anybody outside of us.

Be accountable to us and we will free the NAACP, the Urban League and all Black organizations to work in the best interest of our people. How many of you would like to see all our Black organizations free? Now, look brothers, an economic development fund for $10 a month is not a big price to ask to begin to build an economic infrastructure to nurture businesses within the Black community. Soon the leadership is going to meet and work out the details of an Exodus, Exodus Economic Fund.

And we're going to get back to you. This is not a one day thing. A task force will be formed right out of this leadership to make sure that the things that we say today will be implemented so that next year on the day of atonement, which will take place each and every year from now on until God says, well done. Now, you saw the money that was taken up today, didn't you? How many of you gave some money today? I see some hands that wanted to give, but didn't get that box to them.

Well, let me tell you something brothers, we want an outside accounting firm to come in and scrutinize every dollar that was raised from your pockets to make the Million Man March a success. And if there is any overage, it will not be spent. We will come back to this board of leadership and we will account for every nickel, every dime, every dollar. . . .

[Pledge of Self-Improvement]

Is that agreeable, black man? Now, brothers, I want you to take this pledge. When I say I, I want you to say I, and I'll say your name. I know that there's so many names, but I want you to shout your name out so that the ancestors can hear it.

Take this pledge with me. Say with me please, I, say your name, pledge that from this day forward I will strive to love my brother as I love myself. I, say your name, from this day forward will strive to improve myself spiritually, morally, mentally, socially, politically, and economically for the benefit of myself, my family, and my people. I, say your name, pledge that I will strive to build business, build houses, build hospitals, build factories, and then to enter international trade for the good of myself, my family, and my people. I, say your name, pledge that from this day forward I will never raise my hand with a knife or a gun to beat, cut, or shoot any member of my family or any human being, except in self-defense.

I, say your name, pledge from this day forward I will never abuse my wife by striking her, disrespecting her, for she is the mother of my children and the producer of my future. I, say your name, pledge that from this day forward I will never engage in the abuse of children, little boys, or little girls for sexual gratification. But I will let them grow in peace to be strong men and women for the future of our people. I, say your name, will never again use the B word to describe any female, but particularly my own Black sister.

I, say your name, pledge from this day forward that I will not poison my body with drugs or that which is destructive to my health and my well being.

I, say your name, pledge from this day forward, I will support Black newspapers, Black radio, Black television. I will support Black artists, who clean up their acts to show respect for themselves and respect for their people, and respect for the ears of the human family.

I, say your name, will do all of this so help me God. Well, I think we all should hold hands now. . . .

FDA CHIEF ON PROPOSED
CIGARETTE REGULATIONS
October 20, 1995

Accepting a Food and Drug Administration (FDA) finding that nicotine was an addictive and dangerous drug, President Bill Clinton on August 10 announced a set of proposed regulations to heighten restrictions on the marketing and sale of tobacco products. Among other things, the proposal would ban all cigarette vending machines, bar cigarette brand name advertising on nontobacco items such as T-shirts, and restrict cigarette ads on billboards.

Cigarette manufacturers immediately filed suit, challenging the FDA's assertion that it could regulate cigarettes under a federal law that authorizes the agency to regulate medicines, medical devices, and pharmaceutical products. The FDA had based its assertion on internal documents from several of the tobacco companies, in which researchers and company officials acknowledged that nicotine was an addictive drug and indicated that nicotine levels were deliberately manipulated.

Declaring that the FDA's real intent was eventually to ban all cigarette smoking, Steve Parrish, senior vice president of corporate affairs for Philip Morris Companies, Inc., the country's largest cigarette maker, declared that FDA commissioner David Kessler "is trying to sneak through the back door." The proposed regulations, Parrish said, "can only be described as a Trojan horse, set forward under the guise of preventing youth smoking."

Calling the lawsuit "the last gasp of the tobacco industry," Dr. Sidney C. Smith Jr., president of the American Heart Association, added: "When 3,000 children start smoking every day, I think we've got a problem with the front door, not the back door. And when over 400,000 Americans die yearly from tobacco-related illnesses, it's hardly a Trojan horse, particularly when we know that 90 percent of smokers start before the age of 18."

The proposed regulations were among several assaults on the tobacco industry in 1995. The cigarette makers also faced new legal threats and had to respond to the latest scientific studies that underlined the damage caused by tobacco products.

The Proposed FDA Regulations

The FDA's assertion that it had legal authority to regulate cigarettes was not a surprise. At congressional hearings in March 1994, Kessler had said that "accumulating evidence" suggested that cigarette makers controlled the nicotine levels in their products "in a manner that creates and sustains an addiction in the vast majority of smokers." Much of the evidence, which Kessler detailed in an October 20, 1995, speech at St. Jude's Children's Hospital in Memphis, came from internal tobacco company memos and patent applications. One document, for example, written by an R. J. Reynolds research and development executive in 1972, said, "In a sense, the tobacco industry may be thought of as being a specialized, highly ritualized, and stylized segment of the pharmaceutical industry. Tobacco products uniquely contain and deliver nicotine, a potent drug with a variety of physiological effects." (Testimony on the Addictive Nature of Tobacco, Historic Documents of 1994, p. 205)

Noting that 3,000 young people begin to smoke every day and that one-third of them would eventually die of tobacco-related illness, Clinton said August 10 that the proposed regulations were aimed at children because they were "especially susceptible" to tobacco and its marketing. "When Joe Camel tells young children that smoking is cool, when billboards tell teens that smoking will lead to true romance, when Virginia Slims tells adolescents that cigarettes may make then thin and glamorous, then our children" need protection, the president said.

To keep minors from easily obtaining cigarettes, the proposed regulation would ban cigarette vending machines, self-service displays, mail orders, and free samples. Buyers of cigarettes or smokeless tobacco would have to prove they were at least eighteen years old. Cigarette companies would not be allowed to use their brand names or logos on such products as T-shirts, hats, and gym bags; they would also be barred from using their brand names in sponsoring sports and entertainment events. Outdoor advertising within 1,000 feet of a school or playground was banned outright; all other outdoor advertising would be restricted to black-and-white text. Color and pictorial ads would not be permitted in any publication with a significant readership (15 percent or two million) under eighteen years of age. The tobacco industry would also be required to fund and mount a $150 million education campaign aimed at reducing teenage smoking. (Earlier in the summer Philip Morris had announced that it was launching a national campaign against underage smoking and was ending its practice of giving away 25 million cigarettes a year.)

Clinton stressed that the FDA was not seeking to ban adult smoking or advertising aimed at adults. He said he would have preferred some route other than regulatory action but had concluded that the cigarette makers were unlikely to act voluntarily. He noted that these regulations would be unnecessary if Congress would enact the restrictions into law, but it appeared more likely that if Congress took any action on the issue it

*would be to amend or veto the proposed regulations. Many House and Sen-
ate Republicans in leadership positions represented tobacco-growing
states or congressional districts, and the tobacco lobby was an influential
force as well as a major campaign contributor. House Commerce Committee Chairman Thomas J. Bliley Jr. (R-Va.), a longtime defender of the
tobacco industry, indicated that he would stay out of the matter: "Whether
the FDA has the legal authority to regulate tobacco is a question for the
courts, not Congress."*

Legal Actions

*Several other legal actions were brought against members of the tobacco
industry in 1995. Among them were the following:*

- *The state of Florida filed suit February 21 against the tobacco industry seeking to recover $1.4 billion in Medicaid it had spent in the pre-
  vious five years for treating thousands of smokers. Florida was at
  least the fourth state to file such a suit. "While big tobacco goes to the
  bank and deposits enormous profits from the lives they're ruining,
  Florida's taxpayers consistently have to make withdrawals from their
  wallets to pay for the carnage," said Gov. Lawton Chiles. R. J.
  Reynolds and Philip Morris Inc. filed suits that same day challenging
  the constitutionality of a Florida law enacted in 1994 that allowed
  Florida to seek reimbursement from tobacco companies for smoking-
  related health costs. Under the law, the state used statistical models
  and federal health data to determine the number of Medicaid patients
  treated for various diseases related to smoking and then seek compensation from each tobacco company, based on its share of the Florida cigarette market.*

- *On June 6, Philip Morris, manufacturer of Marlboro and other
  brands, signed a consent agreement with the Justice Department
  agreeing to position advertising billboards and other advertising out
  of the range of television cameras at several sports arenas and stadiums around the country. The Justice Department said the company
  had been effectively skirting the 1971 restrictions on television advertising of cigarettes by placing billboards advertising its products is
  strategic locations, such as the scorers' tables in professional basketball arenas or behind home plate in major league baseball stadiums.*

- *On July 24, the Justice Department convened a grand jury in New
  York to investigate whether cigarette manufacturers misrepresented
  the contents and ill effects of cigarettes to federal regulators. A second
  panel was expected to be convened to see whether they lied to Congress. The grand jury investigations grew out of testimony before a
  congressional committee in April 1994, when executives from seven
  tobacco companies said under oath that they did not think that nicotine was addictive, that it caused disease, or that their companies
  manipulated nicotine levels. Shortly after that, the first of several doc-*

uments was released showing that the companies had known for years, through their own research, that nicotine was addictive and harmful. Several lawmakers then asked Attorney General Janet Reno to investigate whether the executives had perjured themselves.

Mounting Medical Evidence

Several studies detailing the harmful effects of smoking were released during the year. The results of a study on secondhand smoking was released by Stanton A. Glantz, professor of medicine at University of California at San Francisco and an avowed opponent of smoking. After reviewing more than eighty other studies, he concluded that nonsmokers were much more sensitive than smokers to heart damage from secondhand smoke because their bodies had not built up tolerances to the poisons in tobacco. Although passive smokers might breathe only about 1 percent of the smoke that smokers do, their risk of heart disease was proportionately much higher than that of smokers. Glantz said smoking doubled or tripled a person's risk of heart disease, while a passive smoker's risk of heart disease went up by about 30 percent. According to one analysis, approximately 47,000 people died each year from heart disease caused by second-hand smoke, while 150,000 passive smokers suffered nonfatal heart attacks.

Another survey of more than one hundred studies concluded that between 19,000 and 141,000 miscarriages annually in the United States could be linked to smoking. Mothers who smoked gave birth to an estimated 26,000 low-weight babies who required intensive care.

Following is the text of a speech made October 20, 1995, at St. Jude's Children's Hospital in Memphis by David Kessler, commissioner of the Food and Drug Administration, in which he discussed the evidence that led the FDA to assert the authority to regulate cigarettes and propose restrictions on marketing and selling cigarettes to children:

As pediatricians, we learn to listen to the voices of our patients. Recently, I have been listening to the voices of children. Children who are addicted to nicotine. Children who smoke. These voices echo with the sadness that is made all the more haunting because they appear not in a publication about the perils of smoking, but in two studies commissioned by the Canadian affiliates of a major American tobacco company.

These studies, one entitled Project Sixteen, question why young people start to smoke and why they want to quit. Listen, listen to what the tobacco industry heard from these children. "I liked this. Now, I hate it. But I still got the habit. We all said we'd do it for a few years and then quit. And we really meant it. Now, it's what, five years later and I'm not so sure. I never thought it would become a habit. After you get smoking for a while, you realize what it is then it's too late." Too late indeed.

Smokers almost always become addicted during their teenage years. The story rarely varies. Experimentation followed by addiction and only later the realization that the addiction is real. There exists a window, an opening into the world of addiction. While that window is open during the adolescent years nearly 90 percent of the people who become addicted to nicotine begin to use tobacco. Once that window is closed at the end of the adolescent years, few begin to smoke.

One of the tobacco industry documents speaking of high school students observed that "the desire to quit seems to come even prior to the end of high school and take hold as soon as the recent starter admits to himself that he is hooked on smoking." However, the desire to quit and actually carrying it out are two quite different things, as the would-be quitter soon learns.

This epidemic of youth addiction has enormous public health consequences. A casual decision at a young age to use tobacco products leads all too often to addiction, serious disease, and premature death, as an adult.

Every day, every day another 3,000 children begin to smoke and become regular smokers. As adults, 1,000 of them, 1,000 of the 3,000 who begin, every day 1,000 of them will die before their time, because of their smoking. This translates into more than 400,000 deaths each year due to smoking. It is statistics like these that compel[led] the Food and Drug Administration [FDA] to launch an 18-month investigation early last year into the role of nicotine in tobacco.

On August 10, 1995, President Clinton announced the FDA's proposed rule based on that investigation to reduce the use of tobacco by young people. The President's announcement was both historic and precedent setting. And many people have asked me why the FDA took so long to act. After all, by the early 1990s there was almost universal agreement in the scientific and medical communities that nicotine was an addictive drug.

But this knowledge was not sufficient by itself. In order to oversee tobacco products, the FDA believed it must demonstrate that tobacco companies intend to produce nicotine's pharmacological effect. As our investigation proceeded, piece after piece of evidence fell into place.

We learned how the industry controls and manipulates nicotine to achieve adequate delivery. And we learned that the industry engaged in 30 years of sophisticated research on nicotine pharmacology. The sheer magnitude of these efforts helps to explain why one industry official concluded, "We are in a nicotine rather than a tobacco industry." Our first clue that the tobacco industry understood that people smoked to obtain the pharmacological effect of nicotine and that the industry was highly focused on controlling nicotine levels came from a search of the industry's patents.

These patents revealed that beginning in the early 1960s the tobacco industry conducted extensive research on controlling the precise amount of nicotine delivered by a cigarette. Perhaps the most interesting of these patents was one on the addition of certain chemicals to tobacco. For example, organic acid, levulinic acid, for one, used to mask the harsh flavor of nicotine. The stated purpose was to increase the amount of nicotine in a cigarette through the use of high nicotine tobacco without creating an [excessively] harsh cigarette.

These patents seemed to contradict the industry's claim that nicotine was used in cigarettes solely for taste. Here was research being conducted on how to increase nicotine levels despite the taste. Almost from the beginning, we've had evidence that the tobacco industry was manipulating nicotine.

An analysis of data published by the Federal Trade Commission showed that the nicotine content for all marketed cigarettes on a sales rated basis began to rise in 1982, while tar levels continued to drop. This was in direct conflict with industry statements, that if tar levels are reduced, so too are nicotine levels. We found that the industry is able to control and manipulate nicotine levels even before the manufacturing process begins.

As one tobacco lobbyist out it, "it all begins in the field." Each tobacco plant has leaves located at various stalk positions and the higher up on the stalk that you go, the more nicotine you will find. By blending different stalk positions from different tobacco varieties over several crop years, the companies have literally dozens and dozens of nicotine combinations from which to choose. We soon learned that at least one company had gone beyond reliance on existing nicotine levels.

We had received a tip to check the patent files in foreign countries. We discovered a Brazilian patent written in Portuguese, held by Brown and Willamson for a new tobacco variety with twice the nicotine content of normal tobacco. The new tobacco was called "Y-1". We knew that Brown and Willamson had a corporate affiliate in Sousa Cruz, Brazil. We needed to find out whether the patent had ever been put into practice. The patent named [three] individuals as inventors.

We tracked one of them to a small genetic engineering firm in New Jersey and began to put together the pieces of a rather remarkable story. The scientist told us that Brown and Willamson had developed a high nicotine tobacco plant. [They] hired her company to produce a version of the plant that did not produce seeds. This would prevent the plant from being stolen by competitors. She told us that as part of her job, she has shipped several pounds of Y-1 seeds to Brazil, and had actually been to Sousa Cruz and seen the Y-1 growing in the field.

Although it was a long shot, we sent one of our investigators to check U.S. Customs records for evidence that Y-1 had been brought into the United States. A few days later, he telephoned in. He found two invoices showing that in September 1992, Brown and Willamson had shipped over 500,000 pounds of "your order, project Y-1" into the United States. It was like finding a needle in a haystack. When confronted with this evidence, Brown and Willamson executives acknowledged that they had on-hand as much as four million pounds of this high nicotine tobacco.

And that it, it already had been used commercially. More important, they admitted that Y-1 was intended as a "blending tool to lower the tar yield in certain products while maintaining the nicotine level."

We next learned that the industry also uses chemicals to increase the amount of nicotine absorbed by the smoker. In a plain white envelop, we anonymously received one company's handbook on leaf blending and product development.

The handbook describes how industry uses ammonia to "liberate free nicotine from the blend," which is associated with increases in impact and satisfaction reported by smokers.

Furthermore, we found that in the early 1980s, Philip Morris forced one of its scientists to withdraw a manuscript he had submitted to the journal *Psychopharmacology*, which described research at Philip Morris. The research was significant in that it was the first study to determine that rats will self-administer nicotine, one of the hallmark properties of an addictive substance.

The scientist . . . testified last year about the lab that he had run at Philip Morris between 1980 and 1984. He testified that while at Philip Morris, he conducted tests on nicotine analogs, chemicals that could be substituted for nicotine if the tobacco industry was ever forced to remove nicotine from its products.

The central focus of this research was the search for a substitute that could duplicate nicotine's psychoactive and reinforcing effects. [The scientist's] testimony gave us important evidence that Philip Morris both knew of nicotine's pharmacological properties and understood that those properties were essential to the success of tobacco products.

At this point, all we had were pieces of a puzzle. It was only when 30 years worth of internal industry documents were uncovered that the pieces of the puzzle began to fit together. The documents reveal sophisticated research enterprises by the tobacco industry to understand the pharmacology of nicotine, including the minimum dose needed to satisfy smokers.

The documents contain hundreds of internal statements by tobacco company officials revealing their understanding that most people use tobacco for nicotine. The documents reveal 30 years of research into the manipulation of nicotine and that the research had been applied in marketed products.

On May 9, 1994, the *New York Times* published an article that described a series of internal documents from Brown and Williamson and its parent company, the British American Tobacco Company, dating back to the 1960s and given to the *New York Times* by an anonymous source.

These documents were later made public along with many additional company documents. They included hundreds of statements by company officials at all levels of the corporate structure recognizing that many, even most, people use cigarettes to obtain the pharmacological effect of nicotine.

For example, a 1962 document includes this description of nicotine's effect on smokers by a senior executive: "It is my conviction that nicotine is a very remarkable significant drug that both helps the body to resist external stress and also can as a result show a pronounced tranquilizing effect."

"Nicotine is not only a very fine drug, but the techniques of administration of smoking, by smoking has considerable, psychological advantage and a built in control against excessive absorption." The Brown and Willamson documents thus show for the first time that a major tobacco company privately viewed the pharmacological effects of nicotine as critical to the success of the tobacco, of their tobacco products.

Just two weeks before we published our proposed regulations, another large body of internal tobacco documents was unanimously delivered to Congress. This time the company was Philip Morris. The documents revealed that, like Brown and Willamson, Philip Morris conducted a long-term, highly sophisticated research program on nicotine pharmacology and nicotine manipulation. And like the Brown and Willamson documents, the Philip Morris documents showed company officials making repeated statements acknowledging nicotine's central role in sustaining tobacco use.

A draft of remarks by the then vice president for research and development to the Philip Morris board of directors states, "We are of the conviction that the ultimate explanation for the perpetuated cigarette habit resides in the pharmacological effect of smoke upon the body of the smoker. Thus the evidence before the agency, at that time showed that Philip Morris, like Brown and Willamson, has long understood that the pharmacological effects of nicotine are critical to the success of the tobacco industry."

Just as you listened earlier to the voices of the children, listen now to the voices of industry. "We are then in the business of selling nicotine, an addictive drug." Think of the cigarette pack as a storage container for a day's supply of nicotine. Think of the cigarette as a dispenser for a dose unit of nicotine. Think of a puff of smoke as the vehicle for nicotine. Smoke is beyond question, the most optimized vehicle of nicotine.

And "in a sense, the tobacco industry [may be] thought of as being a specialized, highly ritualized and stylized segment of the pharmaceutical industry. Tobacco products uniquely contain and deliver nicotine, a potent drug with a variety of physiological effects." Key industry officials knew it and said it long before we did.

We are providing an opportunity for comment on our findings and an analysis and continue to seek additional relevant evidence.

A second phase of our investigation examined the way the industry markets its products to young people, for youth remains its primary source of new customers.

A Canadian affiliate of an American tobacco company states the case with callous indifference. "If the last ten years have taught us anything, it is that the industry is dominated by the companies who respond most effectively to the needs of the younger smokers."

In the United States, an even more revealing document has just come to light. Quoting from an internal RJR Reynolds document, a national newspaper reported, "Evidence is now available to indicate that the 14 to 18-year old group is an increasing segment of the smoking population. RJRT must soon establish a successful new brand in this market if our position in the industry is to be maintained over the long-term."

The company said this was not its policy. However, RJR later introduced their Joe Camel character, which rapidly boosted the sale of Camels among young people, and our investigation revealed the central role that Joe Camel promotional items played in what RJR called its YAS program—its young adult smokers program.

As part of this program, the RJR sales force in at least two states was instructed to place promotional items such as hats and tee shirts bearing the likeness of Joe Camel in stores close to high schools. With this evidence before us, the next step was to propose what could be done to reduce the use of tobacco by young people.

The President has proposed a program that has two goals. The first is to minimize the easy access that children have to tobacco. The second is to minimize the appeal that tobacco products exert on children as a direct result of this $6 billion annually spent by [the] industry [on] marketing and promotion.

The essence of the access proposal is to restrict the sale of cigarettes and smokeless tobacco to face-to-face transactions. To do this, we have proposed to ban the sale of tobacco in vending machines, by mail order sale, self-service displays, and free samples. The advertising proposals are designed to reduce the appeal of smoking that advertising portrays as fun, rebellious and glamorous—scenes with a particular appeal to adolescents.

These ads send a message that is fundamentally contrary to the advice that we as pediatricians and parents give to young people. The President's proposal would ban outdoor advertising within a thousand feet of playgrounds and schools. All other outdoor advertising, in-store advertising and print ads and publications with a significant youth readership would be restricted to a black and white text only format. That . . . would reduce the imagery so appealing to young people while preserving the information considered useful by adults.

The President's proposal would also eliminate brand name promotion on non-tobacco items such as hats and tee shirts. These items are so popular with young people that currently one half of kids who smoke and one quarter of those who don't own a tobacco promotional item. Further, the proposal would limit the sponsorship of sporting events by tobacco companies to use of the corporate name, not the brand name. These events are viewed in person and on television by millions of youngsters each year, who have come to associate smoking with exciting and athletic activities.

Finally, the President's proposal would require the tobacco companies to spend $150 million each year on a media-based educational campaign that would counsel young people on the hazards of smoking. This is what the President has proposed and I encourage all of you to participate in the process by contributing your comments to the agency on the issues that I have discussed today.

Remember the voices that you heard today. Remember the voices of the tobacco industry. "We are in the business of selling nicotine, an addictive drug. Of course it's addictive, that's why you smoke. Realistically, if our company is to survive and prosper over the long term, we must get our share of the youth market."

And, remember the voices of the children. In high school you never think that you're gambling with death. It's just a challenge to see if you can get away with it. You never think you're doing any damage to yourself. You'll know how to control it. What we hear in those voices is the unwillingness of the young to consider their own mortality. Each young person is sure that he or she is the one who will not become addicted.

But, as one industry voice stated with chilling accuracy more than a decade ago, "Addicted, they do indeed become." Thank you.

ELECTION REMARKS BY
NEW AFL-CIO PRESIDENT
October 26, 1995

Suffering from declining membership, the American Federation of Labor-Congress of Industrial Organizations, commonly known as the AFL-CIO, underwent a major change of leadership in 1995. Dissidents forced the retirement in August of Lane Kirkland, who had served sixteen years as president. In the first election contest in the AFL-CIO's forty-year history, the membership chose John J. Sweeney, the head of the Service Employees International Union and an old-fashioned organizer, to head the 13-million-member federation of national and international labor unions in the United States. In his acceptance speech October 26, Sweeney promised to "organize every working woman and man who needs a better deal and a new voice" and to "use old-fashioned mass demonstrations as well as sophisticated corporate campaigns to make worker rights the civil rights issue of the 1990s."

Sweeney and the AFL-CIO had their work cut out for them. Overall, union membership had fallen from more then 30 percent of all workers in its heyday in the 1950s to about 15 percent in 1995. The number of strikes had declined from an average of about 350 a year in the 1950s to fewer than 50 a year since 1987. During a period when many American companies were shifting jobs overseas and others were downsizing, unions were perceived as powerless, unable to stem the layoffs or raise stagnant wages and benefits.

Sweeney and the new AFL-CIO leadership planned to spend $20 million a year on training and organizing new members—eight times the $2.5 million spent annually under Kirkland. They also promised to be more confrontational. Several observers questioned whether these steps would be enough to overcome the forces that were weakening organized labor. For more than a decade unions had been confronted with competition from abroad; Republican initiatives hostile to the union movement; technological change that was eliminating jobs, many of them once high-paying manufacturing jobs; and management's increasingly sophisticated meth-

ods of holding union organizers at bay. "This is their last chance; I hope they realize that," Monsignor George Higgins, who has long worked with the labor movement, told the Washington Post. "They'll never get another chance."

Kirkland's Departure

Kirkland, successor to the legendary George Meany, was poised to run for a ninth term, but at a February meeting of the thirty-five-member executive council of the AFL-CIO, several union leaders made it clear they were unhappy with his presidency, in particular his failure to organize more aggressively. Led by Sweeney and George W. McEntee, president of the American Federation of State, County and Municipal Employees (AFSCME), eleven union leaders representing about half of the AFL-CIO membership urged Kirkland to abandon his plans to seek reelection. After a five-hour, closed-door meeting in which the union leaders detailed their complaints and Kirkland defended his leadership, Kirkland said he would make a decision "in the fullness of time."

In May he announced that he would run again, but by June several more union leaders had lined up against him and it was clear that he would not have enough votes to win reelection. On June 12 Kirkland announced that he was retiring as of August 1; that Thomas R. Donohue, who had served as secretary-treasurer of the AFL-CIO throughout Kirkland's term, would complete his term; and that Donohue would seek election as president in the fall. The next day McEntee announced that Sweeney would run against Donohue.

Sweeney's Election

The outcome of the election was foreordained even before Kirkland's retirement announcement. Twenty-one union leaders, representing 7.3 million AFL-CIO workers, voted for Sweeney; leaders representing 5.6 million members supported Donohue. Donohue, who had recruited Sweeney for his first union job in a Service Employees local, had left the Sheraton Hotel convention hall in New York City before the voting and was not present to turn the gavel over to Sweeney. That honor was left to Albert Shanker, president of the American Federation of Teachers and a Donohue supporter, who offered Sweeney no public congratulations.

Richard Trumka, president of the United Mine Workers, was elected secretary-treasurer; he defeated Barbara Easterling, a coal miner's daughter who had been the first women to hold executive office in the labor federation. To keep a woman in the ruling hierarchy, the convention created a third office, that of executive vice president, and immediately elected Linda Chavez-Thompson to fill it. An organizer and vice president of AFSCME, Chavez-Thompson was one of the few Hispanics in a union leadership position. The convention also increased the size of its policymaking council and ensured that one-quarter of the slots would be filled by women and minorities.

Sweeney worked his way up through the ranks at Local 32B of the Service Employees Union in New York, becoming president before moving to Washington D.C., where he headed the international union for fifteen years. His was one of the few unions that actually grew during the 1980s and early 1990s, nearly doubling to 1.1 million members.

Sweeney was known for being soft-spoken but a militant on behalf of workers at the bottom end of the wage scale. Criticized by Donohue at the end of the election campaign for blocking bridges in Washington to call attention to his union's efforts to organize janitors, Sweeney responded: "I believe in building bridges, whenever the shelling lets up long enough for us to put up steel and pour concrete. We need to be a full partner with our employers. But I believe in blocking bridges whenever these employers and those communities turn a deaf ear to the working families that we represent."

That militancy was an inspiration to some, but a worry to others. Stephen P. Yokich, the new president of the United Auto Workers, said after the election: "This is the first time in 20 years there's excitement. I heard someone say we have to defend the middle class. Well, that's right. But we've got to defend from the middle class on down."

In an editorial, the New York Times *wrote that Sweeney's election represented the AFL-CIO's "recognition that it must change or continue to shrivel." The* Times *cautioned that Sweeney should not "waste his fresh start on convulsive" and dated organizing tactics when what was needed was a "more sophisticated understanding of the global economy and the changing workplace to which it must adapt. . . . Demonizing corporations, while emotionally satisfying, will not deliver the new skills and productivity increases needed to give American workers more jobs at higher wages."*

"The fundamental message of trade unionism still resonates with most American workers," said Ronald Seeber, a professor at Cornell University School of Industrial and Labor Relations. "They would like someone arguing on their economic behalf in the workplace; that's almost a universal truth. But when you attach the word 'union' to it, that turns a lot of people off. Unions will have to go back to core fundamentals to figure out how to reach these people."

Following is the acceptance speech delivered October 26, 1995, by John J. Sweeney upon his election as president of the AFL-CIO:

Brothers and sisters, in just six months we've changed the labor movement. Now we're going to change America.

At this historic moment, I'm filled with gratitude, humility and hope. To those who supported us and fought for us and made history at this convention, I thank you; and I will honor you by implementing the changes that you have mandated.

To Tom Donahue and Barbara Easterling, we honor you by pledging our respect and our commitment to the work that you've devoted your lives to.

Tom Donahue and I share a fierce dedication to that work. We began a friendship more than 35 years ago in a union hall not very far from here. I hope that we can repair that friendship and continue it for many years, because Tom Donahue is the most principled, caring and committed trade unionist that I know.

Barbara Easterling broke the glass ceiling in this federation, and history will mark hers as a singular achievement. We will find more such roles for Barbara in this movement which cannot afford to squander her experience.

I want to express my sincere congratulations to this distinguished Executive Council which has united together on behalf of all of the members of this great federation.

To my teammates who represent the new American work force, Richard Trumka and Linda Chavez-Thompson, you are two of the best things that ever happened to the trade union movement.

And we owe you a great deal for our success.

I've spent a lifetime in this labor movement, and all along life's journey I've tried not to forget where I came from. This movement gives all of us something rare and wonderful.

We have the chance to even the odds for people who give the world an honest day's work but don't have power over their own lives.

I thank God every day that I have the chance to do work that I love. I'm a lucky man, but this movement and this moment isn't about me or Rich or Linda or the members of this united Executive Council. This movement is about all of you and the working people that we have met along the way.

People like Machinist Bill Damaron who joined us for our kickoff and shouted in a voice cracking with desperation, "Workers like me have been on the losing end too long."

Or janitor Maria Hererra, who described through an interpreter the futility of trying to raise a family on $5 an hour.

For the sake of Bill and Maria and hundreds of thousands of American workers like them, we begin today to build a new AFL-CIO that will be a movement of, by and for working Americans.

To the more than 13 million workers we represent and to millions more who are not represented, our commitment is firm and clear. When you struggle for justice, you will not struggle alone. Our problem is your stagnant wages. America needs a raise. The solution is a bigger, stronger labor movement.

The problem is American companies that export jobs instead of products. The solution is a union movement that fights for American workers as well as American values. The problem is that we all want to do our jobs better, but our employers too often care only about the bottom line. The solution is a union movement that fights for quality in the products we make and the services we provide. We're going to make sure that everyone knows that "union made" is another way of saying "world class."

The problem is the decline of democracy in America. We all know that the power of big money is shouting down the voices of workers and their families. The solution is all of us working together in a labor movement where we all can raise our voices from our workplaces to Washington.

Finally, the problem is that America is coming apart. We're fracturing along the lines of race, ethnicity, and income. The solution is American workers coming together as never before, because this movement is for everyone, women and men, black and white, Asian-Pacific American and Latino, white collar and blue collar and new collar.

Our unions are all that stand between America and shrinking paychecks, disappearing jobs, vanishing health care, increasing inequality, and more racism, rancor, and resentment.

Rich, Linda and I ran on a powerful and detailed plan for reviving American labor, and with your help we're going to put it into action.

But I'm here to tell you that the most important thing we can do starting right now, today, is to organize every working woman and man who needs a better deal and a new voice. As long as we speak for scarcely one-sixth of the work force, we will never be able to win what we deserve at the bargaining table or in the legislative process. That is why we're going to pour resources into organizing at a pace and a scale that is unprecedented and to offer . . . our hands and open our ranks to workers from the Rust Belt to the Sun Belt. We're going to spread the union message from coast to coast and border to border; from clothing workers to manufacturing workers and from health care to high tech to hard hat. If anyone denies American workers their constitutional right to freedom of association, we will use old-fashioned mass demonstrations as well as sophisticated corporate campaigns to make worker rights the civil rights issue of the 1990s.

We're going to spend whatever it takes, work as hard as it takes, and stick with it as long as it takes to help American workers win the right to speak for themselves in strong unions. That is what we mean by a New Voice for American workers. And we mean more than just changing the leadership of our labor Federation at the top. We mean building a strong new movement from the ground up.

And as we win higher wages, better benefits and more dignity and opportunity for more workers, other workers will benefit, our current members and our future members alike.

For too long we've been caught in a downward spiral of defeat and retreat where some lose their jobs, others give back benefits and everyone becomes less secure. We've learned the hard way that an injury to one is an injury to all. We're going to start proving that a victory for one is a victory for all.

To our employers we say, if you are wise, labor's victories can be your victories. With decent paychecks we can buy your products and your services. We prefer cooperation to confrontation, but we are prepared for both.

To our nation's leaders we say, American labor is a proud part of the American community. To every officeholder in America we say, when you do the right thing, we will be the best friends that you've ever had. But when you do the wrong thing, we will be the first in line with our criticism and last in line with our money and our people. (Standing ovation)

Next year we're determined to go from a union summer to an American autumn. It is then that we will reelect a President and elect a Democratic Congress committed to the people who work hard and play by the rules. To the new leadership of this movement, Linda, Rich and I say we have a mandate and a mission, and they are to fight and to win in organizing campaigns, contract struggles, political and legislative fights, and the battle to shape public opinion. Together we can meet the awesome challenges that we face.

My sisters and brothers, if you will invest your passion, your energy and your commitment, Rich, Linda and I can live up to our commitment, together with the elected members of our Executive Council, to revitalize the labor movement at every level and to our pledge to continue to change its face to represent the faces of all American workers.

Together we can write a proud new chapter, not just in labor history, but in American history. Together we can create a strong, new voice for American workers. And with your help, we will be heard.

Thank you very much. (Standing ovation)

November

WORLD LEADERS ON DEATH OF PRIME MINISTER RABIN
November 4 and 6, 1995

President Bill Clinton and Middle East leaders on November 6 eulogized slain Israeli prime minister Yitzhak Rabin as a brave soldier for peace, and they vowed to carry on his battle for accommodation between Israel and its Arab neighbors. Jordan's King Hussein, for nearly forty years the leader of a country officially at war with Israel, shed tears as Rabin was laid to rest at Mount Herzl cemetery in Jerusalem and said he was determined to "continue the legacy for which my friend fell."

Rabin was gunned down on November 4 by a former Israeli soldier, Yigal Amir, who said the prime minister had betrayed Israel by making peace concessions to Arabs. Just five weeks earlier, Rabin had signed a peace agreement with Yasir Arafat, chairman of the Palestine Liberation Organization (PLO), under which Israel was to turn over substantial portions of the West Bank of the Jordan River to Palestinian authority. (West Bank peace agreement, p. 622)

The assassination sparked an intense period of soul-searching in Israel, which was sharply divided on all questions concerning peace with the Arabs. Extremists on the right had openly denounced Rabin and his government, with some religious leaders appearing to condone any actions that would halt the peace process. Amir said at a court hearing on November 6 that killing Rabin "was my obligation according to religious law."

Despite the political upheaval in Israel caused by the assassination, the government continued the peace policies Rabin had championed. His interim successor as prime minister was Shimon Peres, who as foreign minister had helped negotiate peace agreements in 1994 and 1995 with Jordan and the Palestinians. Peres had served as prime minister in the 1980s, but he lacked Rabin's political standing as a former solider. He told Hussein and other Arab leaders gathered at Rabin's funeral that "the course of peace is irreversible."

The Peres government began implementing the peace agreement with the Palestinians. The Palestinians would go to the polls for the first time Jan-

uary 10, 1996, to elect an assembly that would be responsible for many civil functions on the West Bank.

Rabin: A Warrior and Peacemaker

Yitzhak Rabin was a man of history for Israel, the one man who had the political stature and iron determination to lead his country into a broad peace with its Arab neighbors. At age seventy-three, he was old enough to have been in public service to his country ever since its founding in 1948. Born in Jerusalem in 1922, Rabin became the first native-born, or sabra *in Hebrew, to serve as prime minister.*

Rabin served as army chief of staff during the Six Day War of 1967, when Israel fought off a united Arab attack and captured significant sections of territory, including Jerusalem and all of the West Bank. After serving as Israel's ambassador to the United States during the Nixon administration, Rabin ran for the Knesset as a Labor party member in 1973, becoming prime minister a year later following domestic upheaval over the government's bungling of the Yom Kippur war. Rabin served as prime minister for three difficult years, during which he negotiated "disengagement" agreements that separated the Israeli and Arab armies in the wake of the Yom Kippur war. Those negotiations led Rabin to the conclusion that a true peace between Israel and its Arab neighbors was unattainable.

Rabin fell victim in 1977 to a corruption scandal, fueled in part by the revelation that his wife, Leah, illegally kept a bank account in the United States. The right-wing Likud party, headed by Menachem Begin, took over the government.

Seven years later, in 1984, Rabin returned to government as defense minister in a coalition government with Likud. Rabin's biggest challenge in that post came from within: the Palestinian uprising, known as the intifada, *which began in 1987 and led to massive protests in the occupied territories. Rabin was in charge of putting down the unrest, and he took a hard-line approach, characterized by his controversial order to Israeli soldiers to break the arms and legs of Palestinian protesters and to demolish Palestinian homes in retaliation for attacks on Israelis. He called his policy "force, might, and blows."*

That tough policy failed to stem the intifada, *which dragged on for years, at great cost to both Israel and the Palestinians. In the process, Rabin gradually changed his view of how Israel should deal with the Palestinians. By the early 1990s he had adopted much of the "land for peace" philosophy of those in the left wing of his Labor party. Leading his party into the elections in July 1992, Rabin advocated a peace platform and won just enough votes to be able to form a government.*

In 1993 Rabin entered into secret talks with the PLO, sponsored by the Norwegian government. Those negotiations led to a peace declaration that Rabin and Arafat signed at the White House in November 1993. The signing ceremony was the occasion for a dramatic handshake by the two old enemies, with President Clinton looking on. Rabin, Peres, and Arafat shared the 1994 Nobel Peace Prize for their steps toward peace. (Peace treaty, Historic Documents of 1994, p. 330)

Rabin negotiated a peace agreement with Jordan in 1994, and in November 1995 signed the formal agreement with Arafat that lead to an Israeli military withdrawal from much of the West Bank. More than any of the previous agreements, the West Bank accord provoked cries of outrage from Israeli rightists, who said God meant the territory to be under Jewish control.

Rabin refused to back down, insisting that peace would strengthen Israel morally and militarily. Rabin was shot following a giant peace rally in Tel Aviv. He told the thousands of people gathered at the rally that "the people of Israel want peace and support peace. I always believed that most of the people want peace and are ready to take a risk for it."

Eulogies for Rabin

On November 6, Rabin was buried in Jerusalem following a memorial service attended by kings, presidents, prime ministers, and leaders from eighty nations. It was the largest gathering of world political leaders in Israel's history. Joining President Clinton were two of his predecessors, who had sponsored earlier moves for peace between Israel and its neighbors: Jimmy Carter and George Bush.

Among the speakers at the outdoor service were Egyptian president Hosni Mubarak and Jordan's King Hussein, leaders of the two Arab nations that had signed formal peace agreements with Israel. Arafat did not attend, citing security concerns; he watched the service on television at PLO offices in the Gaza Strip.

In their remarks, Clinton and the other leaders praised Rabin's willingness to risk his life for peace, and they said they would not abandon his cause. For millions of people around the world who watched the service on television, the most moving moment was a short speech by Rabin's seventeen-year-old granddaughter, Noa Ben-Artzi Philosof. Barely able to hold back her tears, she talked of Rabin as a grandfather and a hero. "Grandfather, you were the pillar of fire in front of the camp, and now we are left in the camp alone, in the dark, and we are so cold and so sad," she said.

Following is a statement by President Bill Clinton on November 4, 1995, after he learned of the assassination of Israeli prime minister Yitzhak Rabin, and excerpts from speeches by acting Israeli prime minister Shimon Peres, King Hussein of Jordan, and Egyptian president Hosni Mubarak during memorial services for Rabin at Mount Herzl cemetery in Jerusalem on November 6, 1995:

CLINTON STATEMENT

The world has lost one of its greatest men, a warrior for his nation's freedom and now a martyr for his nation's peace.

To Leah Rabin and her children, Hillary and I send our love and our prayers. To the people of Israel, I want you to know that the hearts and prayers of all Americans are with you. Just as America has stood by you in moments of crisis and triumph, so now we all stand by you in this moment of grieving and loss.

For half a century, Yitzhak Rabin risked his life to defend his country. Today, he gave his life to bring it a lasting peace. His last act, his last words were in defense of that peace he did so much to create.

Peace must be and peace will be Prime Minister Rabin's lasting legacy. Tonight, the land for which he gave his life is in mourning, but I want the world to remember what Prime Minister Rabin said here at the White House barely one month ago.

And I quote: "We should not let the land flowing with milk and honey become a land flowing with blood and tears. Don't let it happen."

Now it falls to us, all those in Israel, throughout the Middle East, and around the world who yearn for and love peace to make sure it doesn't happen.

Yitzhak Rabin was my partner and my friend. I admired him, and I loved him very much. Because words cannot express my true feelings, let me just say *"shalom chaver."* Good-bye, friend.

PERES REMARKS

Yitzhak, the youngest of Israel's generals, and Yitzhak, the greatest of peacemakers: the suddenness of your passing illuminated the abundance of your accomplishments.

You resembled no one; nor did you seek to emulate anyone. You were not one of the "joyous and merry."

You were one who made great demands—first of yourself, and therefore also of others.

You refused to accept failures, and you were not intimidated by pinnacles.

You knew every detail, and you grasped the overall picture. You shaped the details one by one to form great steps, great decisions.

All your life, you worked hard, day and night. But the last three years were unparalleled in their intensity. You promised to change priorities. Indeed, a new order has arrived, a priority of openness.

New crossroads have been opened, new roads paved; unemployment has declined; immigrants have been absorbed; exports have increased and investments expanded; the economy is flourishing; education has doubled; and science has advanced.

And above all, perhaps at the root of it all, the mighty winds of peace have begun to blow.

Two agreements with our neighbors the Palestinians will enable them to hold democratic elections, and will free us from the necessity of ruling another people—as you promised.

A warm peace with Jordan invited the great desert between us to become a green promise for both peoples.

The Middle East has reawakened, and a coalition of peace is taking shape: a regional coalition supported by a world coalition, to which the leaders of America and Europe, of Asia and Africa, of Australia and of our region standing alongside your fresh grave bear witness.

They came, as we did, to salute you, and to declare that the course that you began will continue.

This time, Leah is here without you. But the whole nation is with her, and with the family.

I see our people in profound shock, with tears in their eyes. But also a people who know that the bullets that [slew] you could not slay the idea which you embraced. You did not leave us a last will, but you left us a path on which we will march with conviction and faith. The nation today is shedding tears. But these are also tears of unity and of spiritual uplifting.

I see our Arab neighbors, and to them I say: the course of peace is irreversible. Neither for us, nor for you. Neither we nor you can stop, delay or hesitate when it comes to peace—a peace that must be full and comprehensive, for young and old, for all the peoples.

From here, from Jerusalem, where you were born, the birthplace of the three great religions, let us say in the words of the lamentation for Rachel, who passed away on the very day you were slain:

"Refrain thy voice from weeping, and thine eyes from tears; for thy work shall be rewarded, and there is hope for thy future, saith the Lord." (Jeremiah 31:16–17)

Goodbye, my older brother, hero of peace. We shall continue to bear this great peace, near and far, as you sought during your lifetime, as you charge us with your death.

HUSSEIN REMARKS

My sister, Mrs. Leah Rabin, my friends, I had never thought that the moment would come like this when I would grieve the loss of a brother, a colleague and a friend—a man, a soldier who met us on the opposite side of a divide whom we respected as he respected us. A man I came to know because I realized, as he did, that we have to cross over the divide, establish a dialogue, get to know each other and strive to leave for those who follow us a legacy that is worthy of them. And so we did. And so we became brethren and friends.

I've never been used to standing, except with you next to me, speaking of peace, speaking about dreams and hopes for generations to come that must live in peace, enjoy human dignity, come together, work together, to build a better future which is their right. Never in all my thoughts would it have occurred to me that my first visit to Jerusalem and response to your invitation, the invitation of the Speaker of the Knesset, the invitation of the president of Israel, would be on such an occasion.

You lived as a soldier, you died as a soldier for peace and I believe it is time for all of us to come out, openly, and to speak our piece, but here today, but for all the times to come. We belong to the camp of peace. We believe in peace. We believe that our one God wishes us to live in peace and wishes peace upon us, for these are His teachings to all the followers of the three great monotheistic religions, the children of Abraham.

Let's not keep silent. Let our voices rise high to speak of our commitment to peace for all times to come, and let us tell those who live in darkness who are the enemies of life, and through faith and religion and the teachings of our one God, this is where we stand. This is our camp. May God bless you with the realization that you must join it and we pray that He will, but otherwise we are not ashamed, nor are we afraid, nor are we anything but determined to fulfill the legacy for which my friend fell, as did my grandfather in this very city when I was with him and but a young boy. He was a man of courage, a man of vision, and he was endowed with one of the greatest virtues that any man can have. He was endowed with humility. He felt with those around him and in a position of responsibility, he placed himself, as I do and have done, often, in the place of the other partner to achieve a worthy goal. And we achieved peace, an honorable peace and a lasting peace. He had courage, he had vision, and he had a commitment to peace, and standing here, I commit before you, before my people in Jordan, before the world, myself to continue with our utmost, to ensure that we leave a similar legacy. And when my time comes, I hope it will be like my grandfather's and like Yitzhak Rabin's.

The faces in my country amongst the majority of my people and our armed forces and people who once were your enemies are somber today and their hearts are heavy. Let's hope and pray that God will give us all guidance, each in his respective position to do what he can for the better future that Yitzhak Rabin sought with determination and courage. As long as I live, I'll be proud to have known him, to have worked with him, as a brother and as a friend, and as a man, and the relationship of friendship that we had is something unique and I am proud of that.

On behalf of the people of Jordan, my large Jordanian family, my Hashemite family, all those who belong to the camp of peace, to all those who belong to the camp of peace, our deepest sympathies, our deepest condolences as we share together this moment of remembrance and commitment, to continue our struggle for the future of generations to come, as did Yitzhak Rabin, and to fulfill his legacy. Thank you.

MUBARAK REMARKS

... [I]t is with deep regret that we assemble here today to pay our last respects to Prime Minister Yitzhak Rabin, a courageous leader and a recognized statesman. His earnest efforts to achieve peace in the Middle East are a testament to his vision, which we share, to end the suffering of all the peoples of our region.

He defied the prejudices of the past to tackle the most complicated of problems, namely the Palestinian problem, in a forthright manner. The success he achieved in this regard has firmly laid the foundations of peaceful coexistence between Palestinians and the Israelis in a climate of trust and a mutual respect. These achievements have undoubtedly established him as a true hero of peace.

The untimely loss of Prime Minister Yitzhak Rabin at this important juncture in the history with the Middle East has dealt a severe blow to our noble cause. We must, therefore, redouble our efforts and reaffirm our obligation to continue the sacred mission to achieve a just and lasting peace. We must deprive those treacherous hands hostile towards our goal from reaping the rewards of their vile actions. Only through our unwavering commitment to this objective can we truly honor the memory of this fallen hero of peace.

And I could say that the message memorial for Yitzhak Rabin is to continue what he started, which is the peace process and, of course, as we mentioned several times, peace is so precious for the whole people all over the world. On this sad occasion, ladies and gentlemen, I extend the condolences of the people and the government [of] Egypt, and my personal condolences, to the government and the people of Israel and the family of Mr. Yitzhak Rabin. Thank you.

U.S. RESPONSE TO HANGING OF DISSIDENTS IN NIGERIA
November 10, 1995

The military dictatorship in Nigeria on November 10 executed play-wright Ken Saro-Wiwa and eight other dissidents, prompting a chorus of protests from the Clinton administration and many world leaders. Saro-Wiwa and his colleagues were the latest victims of a harsh crackdown by the government headed by General Sani Abacha. The Abacha regime, which seized power in 1993, had systematically arrested and imprisoned many of the country's political leaders. The execution of Saro-Wiwa, the country's most vocal human rights activist, was generally viewed as an effort to intimidate potential government foes.

The United States joined several major countries in withdrawing their ambassadors from Nigeria to protest the executions. The British took the unprecedented step of suspending Nigeria's membership in the British Commonweath. A United Nations committee representing the members of the UN General Assembly voted on December 14 to condemn the executions.

Despite the condemnations, world leaders hesitated to take stronger actions. Some human rights advocates suggested boycotting Nigerian oil, which was the basis of the country's economy. Nigeria exported nearly one-half of its oil to the United States; this oil represented about 10 percent of U.S. oil imports. Diplomats said international embargoes were difficult to organize and enforce and a unilateral embargo, even by as important a country as the United States, might have little long-term impact on a dictatorship such as the one in Nigeria.

Nigeria's Slide into Dictatorship

Since its independence from Britain in 1960, Nigeria had gone through cycles of civil war, democracy, and dictatorship. Although the most popu-lous nation in Africa, and once the wealthiest because of its oil resources, Nigeria had become politically and economically unstable.

A civil war, starting in 1970, set the stage for the country's subsequent slide. After suffering several massacres, the Ibo people of eastern Nigeria declared independence as the state of Biafra. The resulting three-year civil war, and a devastating famine, made Biafra a worldwide symbol of man's inhumanity to man. The central government eventually won the war and forced the surrender of the Biafran independence movement.

A boom in oil production speeded economic recovery in the 1970s, but by the next decade Nigeria fell into a cycle of military coups that halted economic development. Several of the military dictators saw their stewardship of Nigeria's oil resources as opportunity for personal aggrandizement. Since seizing power, General Abacha had reportedly become a billionaire and his senior military commanders had amassed sizable fortunes as well. Their plundering left little money for broader growth of the economy.

The Crackdown on Dissidents

It was the economic issue that made the political crusade of Saro-Wiwa threatening to the Abacha regime. A playwright who long had been critical of military governments headed by leaders from northern Nigeria, Saro-Wiwa founded the Movement for the Survival of the Ogani People. The group's goal was to promote the rights of his ethnic group, which was based in the southern part of the country where most of the oil was produced. Saro-Wiwa protested environmental damage caused by oil companies and demanded a more equitable distribution of oil revenues.

The government arrested Saro-Wiwa in 1994, accusing him of inciting the brutal murders of four tribal leaders in his own region, the Rivers State at the extreme south of Nigeria. The murders apparently were carried out by supporters of Saro-Wiwa, but he insisted that he had nothing to do with the slayings. Most observers concluded that the government used the murders as an excuse to put Saro-Wiwa behind bars. After a trial at which Saro-Wiwa was given little chance to defend himself, the government sentenced him and eight associates to death.

In the month before Saro-Wiwa was to be executed, the government faced a decision about how to handle another group of imprisoned dissidents. That group included a former military president, Olusegun Obasanjo. Several had been sentenced to death, and the rest sentenced to life in prison, on charges of plotting against the government. Hardliners in Abacha's regime reportedly wanted to carry out those tough sentences, fearing that not doing so would be seen as a sign of weakness. Under international pressure and the threat of sanctions, Abacha backed down and reduced the sentences to long prison terms; Obasanjo was given a fifteen-year sentence.

International pressure on behalf of Saro-Wiwa and his colleagues was less intense, however, in part because they were not as well known outside Nigeria as was Obasanjo. The United States and other countries appealed to Abacha to spare Saro-Wiwa but did not threaten sanctions if he was executed. South African president Nelson Mandela, who might have been able to influence the Nigerian government because of his enormous international prestige, chose a course of quiet diplomacy that did not include public pressure.

The execution, by hanging, of Saro-Wiwa and his eight colleagues brought a swift, if limited, reaction from world leaders. The White House issued a statement condemning the executions and imposing several modest sanctions, such as broadening a ban on visits to the United States by Nigerian military officials. The fifteen member-nations of the European Union voted to withdraw their ambassadors from Lagos to protest the executions. The World Bank also withdrew its backing for a $100 million loan for a liquefied natural gas project.

Nigeria became the first nation suspended from the fifty-two-member British Commonwealth. Meeting in Queenstown, New Zealand, the day after Saro-Wiwa's execution, Commonwealth leaders voted to suspend Nigeria until it had taken steps to adhere to a set of principles for democracy and rule of law that had been adopted by the Commonwealth in 1991. An angry Mandela led the move for Nigeria's suspension, saying international pressure was needed if there was to be any chance for the return of democracy in Nigeria.

The United States asked the UN Security Council, which had the power to impose international sanctions, for a strong condemnation of Nigeria. The council declined to act because of opposition by China, which had veto power, and the reluctance of several African nations to take tough actions against a sister country.

The only action by the United Nations was the adoption, on December 14, of a resolution by the Social, Humanitarian and Cultural Committee condemning the "arbitrary" execution of Saro-Wiwa and his colleagues. The committee represented all countries belonging to the United Nations. The vote was 98 to 12, with 42 abstentions.

Following is the text of a statement issued by the White House on November 10, 1995, condemning the execution by the Nigerian government of Ken Saro-Wiwa and eight other dissidents:

The United States strongly condemns the execution today of environmental and human rights activist Ken Saro-Wiwa and eight others accused of murder in May 1994. These executions demonstrate to the world the Abacha regime's flaunting of even the most basic international norms and universal standards of human rights.

Mr. Saro-Wiwa was a champion of the rights of his fellow Ogani people and a world leader in the struggle to preserve our environment. He was a distinguished author, an Amnesty International Prisoner of Conscience and the recipient of many international awards. The United States extends its sincere condolences to the families of those executed. Their deaths will be mourned around the world.

The United States deplores the gravely flawed process by which Mr. Saro-Wiwa and his associates were convicted and executed. They were condemned outside the traditional judicial system and without regard for due process. This latest action follows the 1 October announcement by the government of Nigeria of a transition to democracy that lacks credibility. In addition, we have strongly condemned the imposition of harsh sentences last month on the alleged coup plotters. In that case, a secret trial also denied the defendants due process.

In response to these actions, President Clinton has decided:

To recall Ambassador Carrington from Lagos for consultations; To protest the executions to the Nigerian Ambassador to the United States, Zubair Mahmud Kazaure;

To ban the sale and repair of military goods and services to Nigeria;

To extend our ban on visas, which currently prohibits the entry into the United States of senior military officers and senior government officials and their families, to include also all military officers and civilians who actively formulate, implement or benefit from the policies that impede Nigeria's transition to democracy;

To ask his Ambassador to the United Nations, Madeleine Albright, to begin consultations immediately on appropriate United Nations measures to condemn these actions; and

Henceforth, to require Nigerian government officials visiting the United Nations or the international financial institutions to remain within 25 miles of those organizations;

We will continue to oppose International Monetary Fund loans and credits and debt relief for Nigeria.

The United States reiterates its call on the Nigerian leadership to speed the transition to democracy starting by releasing all political detainees immediately and unconditionally. We again urge the Nigerian government to take bold, credible steps to restore Nigeria promptly to civilian democratic rule, and will keep additional measures under review.

NEW ETHICS LEGISLATION PASSED BY HOUSE AND SENATE
November 16, 1995

Attempting to restore public trust in Congress, both the House and Senate in 1995 imposed tough new limits on gifts that members could accept and passed legislation forcing lobbyists to disclose their clients and other interests. These steps long had been advocated by reformers but had been kept on the congressional back burner. The sudden action in 1995 came despite the new Republican leadership in both chambers; although they proclaimed their interest in congressional reform, the Republican leaders were forced to act by more junior members of their own party and by Democrats.

Although the Senate acted first on both issues, resistance was deepest there because senior members of both parties were not anxious to embrace reforms they had stalled for many years. The Senate adopted a much weaker limit on gifts than the House version, and Senate Republicans had killed ethics legislation during their pre-election political maneuverings in 1994.

Limits on Gifts to Members

For decades, political reform groups such as Common Cause had decried the fact that members of Congress could accept meals, expensive trips, entertainment, and other gifts from lobbyists who were hoping to influence legislation. Both chambers in the 1970s required members to report many of those gifts in their annual financial disclosure statements—but that step did little to stop lobbyists from wining and dining legislators.

When Congress took up the issue in 1995, both chambers had some restrictions on gifts. The Senate, for example, prohibited its members from accepting more than $250 annually from any one person. Individual gifts valued at less than $100 did not count toward that limit, and meals were exempt from any limit. As a result, a lobbyist theoretically could give a senator $99 per day every day of the year, for a total of $36,135, and buy him or her three meals a day.

The Senate worked from two competing proposals to put new limits on gifts. The stronger, by Carl M. Levin (D-Mich.) and William S. Cohen (R-Maine), would have prohibited senators from receiving free meals, entertainment, or gifts of any value from lobbyists. Anyone other than a lobbyist could buy senators meals valued at less than $20. A milder proposal by Mitch McConnell (R-Ky.) would have allowed any gifts from any source up to $100 in value per gift.

Weeks of backroom negotiations on the issue produced a compromise brokered by John McCain (R-Ariz.). That compromise set a $20 limit on any single gift, meal, or other item a senator could receive from anyone other than relatives and close friends. It set a $50 annual limit on gifts a senator could accept from any one source.

During its debate on that proposal, on July 28, the Senate came close to undoing the reforms. By a 54–46 vote, it adopted an amendment by Majority Whip Trent Lott (R-Miss.) that would have allowed an unlimited number of gifts valued at under $50, but with an annual cap of $100 on gifts worth more than $50. Among those supporting Lott's amendment was Majority Leader Bob Dole (R-Kan.).

The Senate's vote shocked reform-minded senators, who put together a new compromise setting an annual $100 limit on gifts worth $10 or more and limiting any single gift to $50 in value. In effect reversing its vote on the Lott amendment, the Senate accepted that compromise by voice vote and then adopted the overall rule (S Res 158) limiting gifts by a 98–0 vote. The rule took effect on January 1, 1996, and it applied to senators and their aides. None of the limits applied to campaign contributions.

The House was slower to act on gift limits, largely because of opposition from Republican leaders. After the Senate vote, House Majority Leader Richard Armey (R-Texas) insisted the House was too busy to deal with the issue in 1995. That stance was not credible to many junior House members of both parties, who began pushing for House action on the gifts issue. Pressure mounted through the summer and fall, reaching a peak on October 25 when Democrats and junior Republicans threatened to attach the Senate's gift ban to a pending legislative branch appropriations bill. Faced with a majority of members demanding action, the House leadership gave in and promised a vote on the issue by November 16.

On that day, the House considered a resolution incorporating the same gift restrictions the Senate had adopted more than three months earlier. By that time, House Speaker Newt Gingrich (R-Ga.) had joined those calling for an absolute ban on all gifts to House members. Gingrich argued that the Senate's restrictions were too complex; for example, a member could inadvertently forget about a $10 gift and later be accused of trying to hide it. The Speaker's support proved crucial. In its deliberations, the House at first defeated, 154–276, an amendment by Dan Burton (R-Ind.) that would have dropped any tougher gift limits and instead strengthened disclosure requirements.

By a 422–6 vote, the House then adopted H Res 250, barring members from accepting any gifts except from family members and close personal friends. Under the resolution, members could attend meetings, dinners, and other privately sponsored events if doing so was part of their official duties.

Lobbyist Registrations

In both chambers, the gift restrictions were coupled with a move to force lobbyists to register and to disclose such information as their clients and legislative interests. Congressional reformers for decades had targeted lobbyists—many of them former government officials or members of Congress—because of their enormous behind-the-scenes influence.

Congress in 1946 required the registration of lobbyists seeking to influence legislation on Capitol Hill, but that law had more loopholes than substance; for example, it applied only to people who devoted a majority of their time to lobbying members of Congress directly, a threshold that enabled most lobbyists to claim they were not covered. The General Accounting Office reported that fewer than 4,000 of the 13,500 people listed in a directory of Washington representatives had registered as lobbyists. Those who did register often provided little information on their activities, largely because Congress never seriously enforced even the limited provisions of the 1946 law.

Attempts to toughen the lobbyist registration law rarely got past the hearing stage in Congress. Sentiment for action built in the early 1990s, and both chambers approved tougher legislation during the 104th Congress. That effort failed in late 1994 when Senate Republicans filibustered a House-Senate compromise on the issue.

Senate Republican leaders clearly had no appetite to tackle the issue again in 1995, but their hand was forced when Sen. Levin and others threatened to bring lobbyist registration amendments to the floor during consideration of a popular telecommunications deregulation bill. Under pressure, Majority Leader Dole brought the lobbyist bill to the floor on July 25, and it was passed by a 98–0 vote.

As with the issue of gifts to members of Congress, House leaders at first said their chamber was too busy in 1995 to deal with the Senate-passed legislation. Once again, Democrats and junior Republicans forced the House leaders to act. They received a boost from President Clinton, who announced on August 4 that he was unilaterally putting the Senate provisions into place with regard to lobbying of the executive branch. Clinton accused Gingrich of stalling action on the matter.

Gingrich and his fellow House leaders eventually succumbed to the political pressure, allowing the Senate bill (S 1060) to be brought to the floor on November 27. The House rejected several attempts to weaken the measure or to add amendments that would have delayed its eventual adoption. Among the latter was a controversial proposal by Rep. Ernest J. Istook Jr. (R-Okla.) to curtail lobbying by nonprofit organizations and political advocacy groups that received federal grants. The House passed the bill by a 421–0 vote, sending it to Clinton for his signature.

The new law required semiannual registrations with the House and the Senate by anyone who devoted at least 20 percent of his or her time to lobbying members of Congress, their staffs, or executive branch officials, and who received at least $5,000 from any single client in any six-month period. The law also applied to companies whose in-house lobbyists spent at least $20,000 in any six-month period. In their registrations, lobbyists were required to disclose the names of individuals they contacted, the issues on which they lobbied, how much they spent on lobbying, and whether they were acting on behalf of any foreign government or entity.

Following are excerpts from the Congressional Record *text of H Res 250, adopted by the House of Representatives on November 16, 1995, which prohibited members of the House from accepting gifts, except from family members and close personal friends:*

Resolved,

SECTION 1. AMENDMENT TO HOUSE RULES.

Rule LII of the Rules of the House of Representatives is amended to read as follows:

"Rule LII

"GIFT RULE

"1. (a) (1) No Member, officer, or employee of the House of Representatives shall knowingly accept a gift except as provided in this rule. . . .

"(b)(1) For the purpose of this rule, the term 'gift' means any gratuity, favor, discount, entertainment, hospitality, loan, forbearance, or other item having monetary value. The term includes gifts of services, training, transportation, lodging, and meals, whether provided in kind, by purchase of a ticket, payment in advance, or reimbursement after the expense has been incurred.

"(2)(A) A gift to a family member of a Member, officer, or employee, or a gift to any other individual based on that individual's relationship with the Member, officer, or employee, shall be considered a gift to the Member, officer, or employee if it is given with the knowledge and acquiescence of the Member, officer, or employee and the Member, officer, or employee has reason to believe the gift was given because of the official position of the Member, officer, or employee.

"(B) If food or refreshment is provided at the same time and place to both a Member, officer, or employee and the spouse or dependent thereof, only the food or refreshment provided to the Member, officer, or employee shall be treated as a gift for purposes of this rule.

"(c) The restrictions in paragraph (a) shall not apply to the following:

"(1) Anything for which the Member, officer, or employee pays the market value, or does not use and promptly returns to the donor.

"(2) A contribution, as defined in section 301(8) of the Federal Election Campaign Act of 1971 (2 U.S.C. 431 et seq.) that is lawfully made under that Act, a lawful contribution for election to a State or local government office, or attendance at a fundraising event sponsored by a political organization described in section 527(e) of the Internal Revenue Code of 1986.

"(3) A gift from a relative as described in section 109(16) of title I of the Ethics in Government Act of 1978 (Public Law 95–521).

"(4)(A) Anything provided by an individual on the basis of a personal friendship unless the Member, officer, or employee has reason to believe that, under the circumstances, the gift was provided because of the official position of the Member, officer, or employee and not because of the personal friendship.

"(B) In determining whether a gift is provided on the basis of personal friendship, the Member, officer, or employee shall consider the circumstances under which the gift was offered, such as:

"(i) The history of the relationship between the individual giving the gift and the recipient of the gift, including any previous exchange of gifts between such individuals.

"(ii) Whether to the actual knowledge of the Member, officer, or employee the individual who gave the gift personally paid for the gift or sought a tax deduction or business reimbursement for the gift.

"(iii) Whether to the actual knowledge of the Member, officer, or employee the individual who gave the gift also at the same time gave the same or similar gifts to other Members, officers, or employees.

"(5) Except as provided in clause 3(c), a contribution or other payment to a legal expense fund established for the benefit of a Member, officer, or employee that is otherwise lawfully made in accordance with the restrictions and disclosure requirements of the Committee on Standards of Official Conduct.

"(6) Any gift from another Member, officer, or employee of the Senate or the House of Representatives.

"(7) Food, refreshments, lodging, transportation, and other benefits—

"(A) resulting from the outside business or employment activities (or other outside activities that are not connected to the duties of the Member, officer, or employee as an officeholder) of the Member, officer, or employee, or the spouse of the Member, officer, or employee, if such benefits have not been offered or enhanced because of the official position of the Member, officer, or employee and are customarily provided to others in similar circumstances;

"(B) customarily provided by a prospective employer in connection with bona fide employment discussions; or

"(C) provided by a political organization described in section 527(e) of the Internal Revenue Code of 1986 in connection with a fundraising or campaign event sponsored by such an organization.

"(8) Pension and other benefits resulting from continued participation in an employee welfare and benefits plan maintained by a former employer.

"(9) Informational materials that are sent to the office of the Member, officer, or employee in the form of books, articles, periodicals, other written materials, audiotapes, videotapes, or other forms of communication.

"(10) Awards or prizes which are given to competitors in contests or events open to the public, including random drawings.

"(11) Honorary degrees (and associated travel, food, refreshments, and entertainment) and other bona fide, nonmonetary awards presented in recognition of public service (and associated food, refreshments, and entertainment provided in the presentation of such degrees and awards).

"(12) Donations of products from the State that the Member represents that are intended primarily for promotional purposes, such as display or free distribution, and are of minimal value to any individual recipient.

"(13) Training (including food and refreshments furnished to all attendees as an integral part of the training) provided to a Member, officer, or employee, if such training is in the interest of the House of Representatives.

"(14) Bequests, inheritances, and other transfers at death.

"(15) Any item, the receipt of which is authorized by the Foreign Gifts and Decorations Act, the Mutual Educational and Cultural Exchange Act, or any other statute.

"(16) Anything which is paid for by the Federal Government, by a State or local government, or secured by the Government under a Government contract.

"(17) A gift of personal hospitality (as defined in section 109(14) of the Ethics in Government Act) of an individual other than a registered lobbyist or agent of a foreign principal.

"(18) Free attendance at a widely attended event permitted pursuant to paragraph (d).

"(19) Opportunities and benefits which are—

"(A) available to the public or to a class consisting of all Federal employees, whether or not restricted on the basis of geographic consideration;

"(B) offered to members of a group or class in which membership is unrelated to congressional employment;

"(C) offered to members of an organization, such as an employees' association or congressional credit union, in which membership is related to congressional employment and similar opportunities are available to large segments of the public through organizations of similar size;

"(D) offered to any group or class that is not defined in a manner that specifically discriminates among Government employees on the basis of branch of Government or type of responsibility, or on a basis that favors those of higher rank or rate of pay;

"(E) in the form of loans from banks and other financial institutions on terms generally available to the public; or

"(F) in the form of reduced membership or other fees for participation in organization activities offered to all Government employees by professional organizations if the only restrictions on membership relate to professional qualifications.

"(20) A plaque, trophy, or other item that is substantially commemorative in nature and which is intended for presentation.

"(21) Anything for which, in an unusual case, a waiver is granted by the Committee on Standards of Official Conduct.

"(22) Food or refreshments of a nominal value offered other than as a part of a meal.

"(23) An item of nominal value such as a greeting card, baseball cap, or a T-shirt.

"(d)(1) A Member, officer, or employee may accept an offer of free attendance at a widely attended convention, conference, symposium, forum, panel discussion, dinner, viewing, reception, or similar event, provided by the sponsor of the event, if—

"(A) the Member, officer, or employee participates in the event as a speaker or a panel participant, by presenting information related to Congress or matters before Congress, or by performing a ceremonial function appropriate to the Member's, officer's, or employee's official position; or

"(B) attendance at the event is appropriate to the performance of the official duties or representative function of the Member, officer, or employee.

"(2) A Member, officer, or employee who attends an event described in subparagraph (1) may accept a sponsor's unsolicited offer of free attendance at the event for an accompanying individual if others in attendance will generally be similarly accompanied or if such attendance is appropriate to assist in the representation of the House of Representatives.

"(3) A Member, officer, or employee, or the spouse or dependent thereof, may accept a sponsor's unsolicited offer of free attendance at a charity event, except that reimbursement for transportation and lodging may not be accepted in connection with the event.

"(4) For purposes of this paragraph, the term 'free attendance' may include waiver of all or part of a conference or other fee, the provision of local transportation, or the provision of food, refreshments, entertainment, and instructional materials furnished to all attendees as an integral part of the event. The term does not include entertainment collateral to the event, nor does it include food or refreshments taken other than in a group setting with all or substantially all other attendees.

"(e) No Member, officer, or employee may accept a gift the value of which exceeds $250 on the basis of the personal friendship exception in paragraph (c)(4) unless the Committee on Standards of Official Conduct issues a written determination that such exception applies. No determination under this paragraph is required for gifts given on the basis of the family relationship exception.

"(f) When it is not practicable to return a tangible item because it is perishable, the item may, at the discretion of the recipient, be given to an appropriate charity or destroyed.

"2. (a)(1) A reimbursement (including payment in kind) to a Member, officer, or employee from a private source other than a registered lobbyist or agent of a foreign principal for necessary transportation, lodging and related expenses for travel to a meeting, speaking engagement, factfinding trip or similar event in connection with the duties of the Member, officer, or employee as an officeholder shall be deemed to be a reimbursement to the House of Representatives and not a gift prohibited by this rule, if the Member, officer, or employee—

"(A) in the case of an employee, receives advance authorization, from the Member or officer under whose direct supervision the employee works, to accept reimbursement, and

"(B) discloses the expenses reimbursed or to be reimbursed and the authorization to the Clerk of the House of Representatives within 30 days after the travel is completed.

"(2) For purposes of paragraph (a)(1), events, the activities of which are substantially recreational in nature, shall not be considered to be in connection with the duties of a Member, officer, or employee as an officeholder.

"(b) Each advance authorization to accept reimbursement shall be signed by the Member or officer under whose direct supervision the employee works and shall include—

"(1) the name of the employee;

"(2) the name of the person who will make the reimbursement;

"(3) the time, place, and purpose of the travel; and

"(4) a determination that the travel is in connection with the duties of the employee as an officeholder and would not create the appearance that the employee is using public office for private gain.

"(c) Each disclosure made under paragraph (a)(1) of expenses reimbursed or to be reimbursed shall be signed by the Member or officer (in the case of travel by that Member or officer) or by the Member or officer under whose direct supervision the employee works (in the case of travel by an employee) and shall include—

"(1) a good faith estimate of total transportation expenses reimbursed or to be reimbursed;

"(2) a good faith estimate of total lodging expenses reimbursed or to be reimbursed;

"(3) a good faith estimate of total meal expenses reimbursed or to be reimbursed;

"(4) a good faith estimate of the total of other expenses reimbursed or to be reimbursed;

"(5) a determination that all such expenses are necessary transportation, lodging, and related expenses as defined in paragraph (d); and

"(6) in the case of a reimbursement to a Member or officer, a determination that the travel was in connection with the duties of the Member or officer as an officeholder and would not create the appearance that the Member or officer is using public office for private gain.

"(d) For the purposes of this clause, the term 'necessary transportation, lodging, and related expenses'—

"(1) includes reasonable expenses that are necessary for travel for a period not exceeding 4 days within the United States or 7 days exclusive of travel time outside of the United States unless approved in advance by the Committee on Standards of Official Conduct;

"(2) is limited to reasonable expenditures for transportation, lodging, conference fees and materials, and food and refreshments, including reimbursement for necessary transportation, whether or not such transportation occurs within the periods described in subparagraph (1);

"(3) does not include expenditures for recreational activities, nor does it include entertainment other than that provided to all attendees as an integral part of the event, except for activities or entertainment otherwise permissible under this rule; and

"(4) may include travel expenses incurred on behalf of either the spouse or a child of the Member, officer, or employee subject to a determination signed by the Member or officer (or in the case of an employee, the Member or officer under whose supervision the employee works) that the attendance of the spouse or child is appropriate to assist in the representation of the House of Representatives.

"(e) The Clerk of the House of Representatives shall make available to the public all advance authorizations and disclosures of reimbursement filed pursuant to paragraph (a) as soon as possible after they are received.

"3. A gift prohibited by clause 1(a) includes the following:

"(a) Anything provided by a registered lobbyist or an agent of a foreign principal to an entity that is maintained or controlled by a Member, officer, or employee.

"(b) A charitable contribution (as defined in section 170(c) of the Internal Revenue Code of 1986) made by a registered lobbyist or an agent of a foreign principal on the basis of a designation, recommendation, or other specification of a Member, officer, or employee (not including a mass mailing or other solicitation directed to a broad category of persons or entities), other than a charitable contribution permitted by clause 4.

"(c) A contribution or other payment by a registered lobbyist or an agent of a foreign principal to a legal expense fund established for the benefit of a Member, officer, or employee.

"(d) A financial contribution or expenditure made by a registered lobbyist or an agent of a foreign principal relating to a conference, retreat, or similar event, sponsored by or affiliated with an official congressional organization, for or on behalf of Members, officers, or employees.

"4. (a) A charitable contribution (as defined in section 170(c) of the Internal Revenue Code of 1986) made by a registered lobbyist or an agent of a foreign principal in lieu of an honorarium to a Member, officer, or employee shall not be considered a gift under this rule if it is reported as provided in paragraph (b).

"(b) A Member, officer, or employee who designates or recommends a contribution to a charitable organization in lieu of honoraria described in paragraph (a) shall report within 30 days after such designation or recommendation to the Clerk of the House of Representatives—

"(1) the name and address of the registered lobbyist who is making the contribution in lieu of honoraria;

"(2) the date and amount of the contribution;

"(3) the name and address of the charitable organization designated or recommended by the Member.

The Clerk of the House of Representatives shall make public information received pursuant to this paragraph as soon as possible after it is received.

"5. For purposes of this rule—

"(a) the term 'registered lobbyist' means a lobbyist registered under the Federal Regulation of Lobbying Act or any successor statute; and

"(b) the term 'agent of a foreign principal' means an agent of a foreign principal registered under the Foreign Agents Registration Act.

"6. All the provisions of this rule shall be interpreted and enforced solely by the Committee on Standards of Official Conduct. The Committee on Standards of Official Conduct is authorized to issue guidance on any matter contained in this rule."

[Section 2 omitted]

SEC. 3. EFFECTIVE DATE.

This resolution and the amendment made by this resolution shall take effect on and be effective for calendar years beginning on January 1, 1996.

FBI REPORT ON CRIME
November 19, 1995

Both the rate and incidence of crime, including violent crime, declined in 1994, according to statistics released by the Federal Bureau of Investigation on November 19, but crime was still substantially higher in 1994 than it had been ten years before. Some criminology experts believed that the rate was poised to go higher during the next ten years.

Fourteen million offenses were committed in 1994, 1 percent fewer than in 1993 but 13 percent more than were reported in 1985. The crime rate was 5,374 per 100,000 population, 2 percent below the 1993 rate but 3 percent above that of 1985. The violent crime rate (murder, forcible rape, robbery, and aggravated assault) reached its lowest level since 1989. The murder rate was 9 per 100,000 population. On December 17 the FBI reported that the murder rate for the first six months of 1995 had dropped 12 percent over the same period in 1994, the largest decline in at least thirty-five years.

The data came from the FBI's annual report, "Crime in the United States," which is a compilation of the crimes reported to police departments throughout the country. Justice Department studies show that more than half of all crimes, even violent crimes, go unreported to authorities, although murder is thought to be reported more often than other types of crimes.

In both 1994 and the first half of 1995, the murder rate dropped significantly in the nation's largest cities; in the first half of 1995 the number of murders in cities with populations of 1 million or more fell 17 percent. According to Alfred Blumstein, a professor at Carnegie-Mellon University in Pittsburgh, murders in the nine largest cities account for one-quarter of the total. The decline in the big cities "probably reflects the maturing of the drug markets," Blumstein said. In the 1980s, the homicide rate rose as drug traffickers fought over turf; in the 1990s, Blumstein said, "they have found ways to settle disputes without so much lethal violence."

Others, including Attorney General Janet Reno, gave a large share of the credit to law enforcement officials, including the FBI and the Drug

Enforcement Administration. The experts also agreed that a major cause of the decline was demographic—the baby boom generation had reached middle age, past the most violence-prone years.

Rise in Juvenile Criminals

That respite was expected to be short-lived, however. Many experts believe that changing demographics could lead to an upsurge in the murder rate. "The overall crime rate hides the grim truth because it mixes together two crime trends going in opposite directions," James Alan Fox, dean of the College of Criminal Justice at Northeastern University, said May 22, when the FBI released some earlier statistics on serious crime. Fox noted that murders by those aged twenty-five and older had fallen steadily for fifteen years, from 8.4 per 100,000 in 1981 to 5.2 per 100,000 in 1993, while the number of murders committed by eighteen- to twenty-four-year-old males rose 65 percent. The number of homicides committed by males aged fourteen to seventeen shot up 165 percent. If those trends continued, Fox predicted a "crime storm," noting that by the year 2005 the number of teenagers in the country will have increased 23 percent.

The problem seemed to be confined to young males using guns. The murder rate for teenagers with guns had quadrupled since 1984, while the murder rate among female teenagers and among teenagers using other kinds of weapons remained the same. (Report on guns used in crime, p. 463)

A report on juvenile offenders released September 8 by the National Center for Juvenile Justice in Pittsburgh corroborated Fox's predictions. "What you see here is a road map to the next generation of crime," said Attorney General Reno when the report was released. "Unless we act now to stop young people from choosing a life of violence and crime, the beginning of the twenty-first century could bring levels of violent crime to our community that far exceed what we have experienced."

Incarceration Rates

One factor contributing to the drop in the crime rate may be the increase in the number of people incarcerated. According to a Justice Department report released August 27, more than 5.1 million Americans were either in prison or on parole or probation in 1994. That number represented nearly 2.7 percent of the adult population and was a 3.9 percent increase over 1993, according to the Bureau of Justice Statistics. Nearly 3 million adults were on probation. Another 690,000 were on parole; they could be returned to prison if they violated the terms of their parole or committed other offenses.

On August 9 the Bureau of Justice Statistics reported that 1.5 million people were in prison or jail in 1994—a record number. In 1980 one of every 453 residents was incarcerated; in 1993 the rate was one of every 189. Nearly a million, 958,704, were in state prisons; 95,034 were in federal prison, and the rest were in local jails. Although jails usually hold peo-

*ple awaiting trial or serving sentences of a year or less, convicted crimi-
nals with longer sentences were being housed in some jails to reduce over-
crowding in state prisons. The prison population was up 8.6 percent overall, the second biggest one-year increase ever; in 16 states it was up at least
10 percent. In Texas the increase was 28.5 percent. Texas also had the
largest number of adults on probation and parole.*

*The incarceration rate of blacks was seven times that of whites. Violent
offenders were the fastest growing prison population between 1980 and
1993, numbering 405,240 in the latter year; drug offenders were the second fastest growing population, at 234,554. Women accounted for only 6.1
percent of all prisoners, but the incarceration rate of females was increasing faster, at 10.6 percent in 1994, than that of males, which stood at 8.5
percent.*

> *Following is a press release issued by the Federal Bureau of
> Investigation on November 19, 1995, which accompanied
> release of the FBI's annual report, "Crime in the United States,"
> and summarized the data for 1994:*

Final 1994 crime statistics released today by FBI Director Louis J. Freeh
showed that 14 million Crime Index offenses were reported to law enforcement across the Nation. The 1994 total represents a rate of 5,374 offenses for
every 100,000 United States inhabitants. The number of crimes was down 1
percent from 1993, while the crime rate declined 2 percent. The number of
violent crimes dropped 3 percent, while the rate of violent crimes dropped 4
percent. In the nine U.S. cities with more than one million population, the
decrease in the number of violent crimes was 8 percent. In the 66 largest
cities, with populations over 250,000, Crime Index totals dropped 4 percent.

"The modest decreases in crime are, in large part, a tribute to the men and
women in law enforcement who daily risk their lives for the public's safety,"
said FBI Director Freeh. "The ominous increase in juvenile crime coupled
with population trends portend future crime and violence at nearly unprecedented levels. Indeed, all Americans, especially those of us in law enforcement, must remain vigilant, or else the scourge of illegal drugs and violence
directly attributable to drugs will dramatically worsen," Freeh said.

The statistics are based on a Crime Index of selected violent and property
offenses reported to the FBI's Uniform Crime Reporting Program by over
16,000 law enforcement agencies, covering 96 percent of the Nation's population. Estimates are included for nonreporting areas. The 1994 data appear in
the FBI's annual publication, "Crime in the United States," released today. . . .

Crime Volume

- In 1994, the Crime Index total of 14 million offenses was 1 percent lower
  than in 1993 and 3 percent below the 1990 total. A comparison with 1985

figures, however, showed a 13 percent increase over the last 10-year period.

- By region, the Southern States recorded 35 percent of all Crime Index offenses reported to law enforcement. The lowest volume was reported in the Northeastern States, accounting for 20 percent of the total. Among the regions, only the Midwest recorded an increase from 1993 to 1994, 1 percent.
- Property valued at $15.6 billion was stolen in connection with all Crime Index offenses.

Crime Rate

- The 1994 Crime Index rate, 5,374 per 100,000 population, was 2 percent lower than in 1993. For 5- and 10-year trend increments, the 1994 rate was 8 percent lower than the 1990 rate, but 3 percent above that of 1985.
- Geographically, the total Crime Index rates ranged from 6,152 in the West to 4,344 in the Northeast. The rates declined in all regions except the Midwest where virtually no change was reported from 1993 to 1994.
- The Crime Index rate was 5,894 per 100,000 inhabitants in the Nation's Metropolitan Statistical Areas (MSAs) and 5,318 per 100,000 for cities outside MSAs. The lowest rate was registered by the collective rural counties at 2,034 per 100,000 inhabitants.

Violent Crime

- Violent crimes (murder, forcible rape, robbery, and aggravated assault) reported to the country's law enforcement agencies during 1994 dropped below 1.9 million offenses for the first annual period since 1990. The rate of 716 violent crimes for every 100,000 inhabitants was the lowest since 1989.
- From 1993 to 1994, violent crimes collectively decreased by 3 percent. The 1994 total was, however, 2 percent higher than the 1990 figure and 40 percent above the 1985 level.
- Data collected on weapons used in connection with murder, robbery, and aggravated assault showed that firearms were used in 31 percent of the offenses and personal weapons (hands, fists, feet, etc.) in another 31 percent. The proportion of violent crimes committed with firearms has remained relatively constant in recent years.
- Aggravated assaults accounted for 60 percent and robberies comprised 33 percent of all violent crimes reported to law enforcement in 1994.

Crime Clearances

- Law enforcement agencies nationwide recorded a 21 percent Crime Index clearance rate in 1994. The clearance rate for violent crimes was 45 percent, and for property crimes, 18 percent.

- Among the Crime Index offenses, the clearance rate was highest for murder, at 64 percent, and lowest for burglary, at 13 percent.
- Offenses involving only offenders under 18 years of age accounted for 22 percent of the overall Crime Index clearances, 14 percent of the violent crime clearances, and 25 percent of the property crime clearances.

Arrests

- During the year, law enforcement agencies made an estimated 14.6 million arrests for all criminal infractions other than traffic violations. The highest arrest counts were for larceny-theft, 1.5 million; drug abuse violations and driving under the influence, each 1.4 million; and simple assaults, 1.2 million.
- Relating the number of arrests to the total U.S. population, the rate was 5,715 arrests per 100,000 population.
- The total number of arrests for all offenses except traffic violations increased 6 percent from 1993 to 1994. Adult arrests increased 5 percent, and those of juveniles were up 11 percent.
- Of all persons arrested in 1994, 45 percent were under the age of 25, 80 percent were male, and 67 percent were white.
- Larceny-theft was the offense resulting in the most arrests of persons under the age of 18, while adults were most often arrested for driving under the influence.
- A special study focusing on the decline in persons arrested for prostitution and commercialized vice from 1970 through 1993 is included in this year's publication.

Murder

- The murder count for 1994 totaled 23,305, the lowest since 1989. The murder rate was 9 per 100,000 inhabitants.
- Based on supplemental data received, 79 percent of the murder victims in 1994 were males, and 88 percent were persons 18 years of age or older. By race, 51 percent were black, and 47 percent were white.
- Data based on a total of 25,052 murder offenders showed 91 percent of the assailants were males, and 84 percent were 18 years of age or older. Fifty-six percent of the offenders were black, and 42 percent were white.
- Forty-seven percent of murder victims were related to (12 percent) or acquainted with (35 percent) their assailants. Among all female murder victims in 1994, 28 percent were slain by husbands or boyfriends.
- By circumstance, 28 percent of the murders resulted from arguments and 18 percent from felonious activities such as robbery, arson, etc.
- Firearms were the weapons used in approximately 7 of every 10 murders reported during 1994.
- A special study entitled "Child Homicide Victims, 1980–1994," included in the publication, addresses the increasing numbers of children (12 and under) as victims of murder.

Forcible Rape

- The total of 102,096 forcible rapes reported to law enforcement during 1994 was the lowest total since 1989. The 1994 count was 4 percent lower than in 1993.
- In the Uniform Crime Reporting Program, the victims of forcible rape are always female, and in 1994, an estimated 77 of every 100,000 females in the country were reported rape victims.

Robbery

- In 1994, law enforcement recorded nearly 619,000 robberies, for a crime rate of 238 robberies per 100,000 population nationwide.
- Monetary loss attributed to property stolen in connection with this offense was estimated at $496 million. Bank robberies resulted in the highest average losses, $3,551 per offense; convenience store robberies the lowest, $387.
- Robberies on streets or highways accounted for more than half (55 percent) of the offenses in this category. All robbery types declined in 1994 as compared to 1993 totals.
- In 1994, 42 percent of all robberies were committed with firearms and 39 percent through the use of strong-arm tactics.

Aggravated Assault

- After increasing steadily since 1983, aggravated assaults dropped 1 percent in 1994 to an estimated total of 1,119,950. Aggravated assaults comprised 60 percent of the violent crimes in 1994.
- There were 430 victims of aggravated assault for every 100,000 people nationwide in 1994.
- In 1994, 32 percent of the aggravated assaults were committed with blunt objects or other dangerous weapons. Personal weapons such as hands, fists, and feet were used in 26 percent, firearms in 24 percent, and knives or cutting instruments in the remainder.

Burglary

- Over 2.7 million burglaries were reported to law enforcement agencies in 1994, with 2 of every 3 being residential in nature.
- Sixty-seven percent of all burglaries involved forcible entry. Over half (52 percent) of burglaries occurred during the daylight hours.
- The value of property stolen during burglaries was estimated at $3.6 billion in 1994.

Larceny-theft

- Larceny-theft, with an estimated total of nearly 7.9 million offenses, comprised 56 percent of the Crime Index total.

715

- The total dollar loss to victims nationwide was estimated at $4 billion during 1994. The average value of property stolen was $505 per incident.
- Thefts of motor vehicle parts, accessories, and contents made up the largest portion of reported larcenies, 37 percent.

Motor Vehicle Theft

- In 1994, over 1.5 million thefts of motor vehicles, or an average of 1 theft for every 130 registered motor vehicles, were reported.
- The estimated monetary loss due to these crimes was nearly $7.6 billion, for an average of $4,940 per vehicle.
- Seventy-nine percent of all motor vehicles reported stolen in 1994 were automobiles.

Arson

- A total of 102,139 arson offenses was reported in 1994.
- As in previous years, structures were the most frequent targets of arsonists in 1994, comprising 52 percent of the reported incidents. Residential property was involved in 60 percent of the structural arsons during the year.
- The average dollar loss was $9,761 per reported arson in 1994.
- Of the arsons cleared during the year, 48 percent involved only young people under the age of 18, a higher percentage of juvenile involvement than for any other Index offense.

Law Enforcement Employees

- A total of 13,124 city, county, and state police agencies submitting Uniform Crime Reporting data reported employing 561,543 officers and 220,567 civilians in 1994.
- The average rate of 2.3 full-time officers for every 1,000 inhabitants across the country in 1994 remained unchanged from the 1993 figure.
- Geographically, the highest rate of officers to population was recorded in the Southern States, where there were 2.6 officers per 1,000 inhabitants.

CLINTON ON U.S. ROLE IN BOSNIA PEACEKEEPING MISSION
November 27, 1995

An ethnic civil war in Bosnia—the bloodiest fighting in Europe since World War II—came to an halt in December 1995, thanks to a U.S.-brokered peace agreement. A massive NATO peacekeeping force, including some 20,000 U.S. troops, began pouring into Bosnia-Herzegovina just before Christmas. The NATO mission was intended to enforce a fragile agreement ending a war that had killed more than 200,000 people, had left more than two million homeless, and had torn apart the tiny republic of the former Yugoslavia.

President Bill Clinton, who exerted strong U.S. pressure to end the war after nearly three years of fruitless international diplomacy, praised the Bosnians for finally moving toward peace and pledged American support. "The people of Bosnia, our NATO allies, and people all around the world are now looking to America for leadership," Clinton said in a November 27 televised address from the White House. "So let us lead. That is our responsibility as Americans."

Clinton won grudging congressional approval for U.S. participation in the NATO peacekeeping mission. The congressional reluctance mirrored public sentiment, as shown by numerous opinion polls, that the United States had no business sending armed troops to try to quash an ethnic dispute that had roots extending back hundreds of years.

The Bosnian Civil War

The Bosnian war began on February 29, 1992, when the Muslim-led government of Bosnia-Herzegovina declared independence from the central Yugoslavian government, which was dominated by Serbs. Bosnia's declaration followed similar independence moves by the regions of Slovenia and Croatia in the summer of 1991. Those moves left the remnants of Yugoslavia, especially the army, in the hands of Serbs, headed by Slobodan Milosevic, president of Serbia.

Serbs inside Bosnia declared their own independent state, headquartered in Palé, and in April began a siege of Sarajevo, the Bosnian capi-

tal. Bosnian Croats also began fighting—sometimes along with the Muslim-led government forces, at other times against them. The fighting splintered what, under the rule of Yugoslavia's communist government, had been a remarkably peaceful sharing of power and territory among three ethnic groups with ancient grievances against one another: the Muslims, who since the days of Turkish rule in the 1300s had been the dominant force in Bosnia; the Croatian Catholics; and the Eastern Orthodox Serbs.

The Bosnian Serbs, who had the backing of the former Yugoslavian army, quickly dominated the fighting and captured much of the territory held by the Muslims. The Serbs began a relentless campaign to rid the captured territory of Muslims and Croats. Often referred to as "ethnic cleansing," this campaign included emptying villages, summary executions, and the establishment of concentration camps where Muslim and Croat prisoners were held in primitive conditions. The United Nations established a tribunal to investigate Bosnian war crimes; in April 1995 it identified Bosnian Serb leader Radovan Karadzic and his military commander, Ratko Mladic, as leading war criminals. (Serb aggression, Historic Documents of 1994, p. 550; Human rights report, Historic Documents of 1993, p. 561; Ethnic cleansing, Historic Documents of 1992, p. 771)

The brutality of the war horrified the rest of the world, especially Europeans who had believed that the lessons of World War II had made unthinkable a renewal of such events on their continent. For three years, outside powers proved incapable of taking effective action to stop the fighting.

The United Nations in 1992 sent in a peacekeeping force whose primary missions were to provide food and other supplies to the besieged city of Sarajevo and to prevent the Serbs from capturing several Muslim and Croatian enclaves. The UN called these latter areas "safe havens" and it warned the Serbs not to attack them. Starting in May 1994, the UN was able to call on NATO warplanes for air strikes against Serbian positions, often in retaliation for Serb attacks on the safe havens. The UN offered little real protection and the NATO air strikes had little effect, however, and the Serbs captured the safe havens of Srebrenica and Zepa in eastern Bosnia and laid siege to three others: Gorazde, Tuzla, and Sarajevo. (UN relief mission, Historic Documents of 1992, p. 765)

Even with NATO airpower behind it, the UN peacekeeping force was ineffective because there was no international agreement on how to stop the war. Leading European nations, who had the greatest direct interest, were unwilling to commit the massive military power that was required to separate the three Bosnian armies. The Bush administration, and then the Clinton administration, were reluctant to force the United States into a leadership position. Russia, which had ancient ethnic and political alliances with the Serbs, refused to allow the UN Security Council to take a tougher position on the war. (European summit, Historic Documents of 1994, p. 584)

Movements Toward Peace

By late 1994 and early 1995, the war was nearly ripe for a settlement. All three sides in Bosnia were exhausted and weakened from the fighting, and the Serbs—widely seen by the outside world as the aggressors—had achieved most of their objectives in capturing Bosnian territory. At Christmastime in 1994, former president Jimmy Carter negotiated a cease-fire that lasted for four months. Although it did not bring a permanent end to the fighting, the Carter initiative showed that outsiders could have influence in Bosnia and that there was an interest among the parties there in ending the war.

After the cease-fire lapsed in May 1995, the fighting resumed with all its savage fury, as Croatian forces captured significant chunks of land from Serbs, and Serbs overran the Muslim enclaves of Srebrenica and Zepa. The renewed fighting gave all sides new incentives to look for peace and spurred U.S. diplomatic efforts. The Clinton administration arranged a temporary cease-fire and indirect talks, starting on November 1 in Dayton, Ohio, among the presidents of Bosnia, Croatia, and Serbia.

The Dayton talks lasted for three weeks and nearly collapsed at several points, but ultimately they produced an agreement dividing Bosnia into two ethnic regions, establishing a new multiethnic system of government, and providing for a massive NATO peacekeeping mission to enforce the agreement. The three presidents—Alija Izetbegovic of Bosnia, Franjo Tudjman of Croatia, and Serbia's Milosevic—initialed the accord in Dayton on November 21 and formally signed it in Paris on December 14.

The peace agreement formally retained the international boundaries of Bosnia-Herzegovina and its official status as a unified state, but it also recognized the facts of what had happened during the war, especially the Serbian domination of half the country. The agreement established two distinct ethnic areas of Bosnia: a Bosnian-Croatian federation controlling about 51 percent of the country's territory, and a Serbian republic controlling the rest. An elected group presidency and parliament, with representatives from each of the three ethnic factions, would be in charge of foreign relations, a national currency, a national court system, and other nationwide issues. The elections were to be held six to nine months after the December 14 signing.

The agreement's numerous provisions did not resolve all political issues about the future of Bosnia. For example, it left open the question of how the Bosnian Muslims and Croats—who were sometimes enemies and sometimes allies in the war—would cooperate to govern their jointly held territory. The agreement also raised the prospect that the Serbs might simply secede from Bosnia and align themselves with neighboring Serbia.

The agreement provided for a NATO peacekeeping force to take the place of the discredited UN contingent. The 60,000 NATO troops—about one-third of them from the United States—would separate the warring parties and attempt to ensure that they did not resume the war. The NATO mis-

sion was to last just one year, after which Bosnia presumably would be pacified.

Clinton Seeks Support

In his November 27 speech, President Clinton appealed for public support of the NATO peacekeeping mission. Many Republicans and some Democrats on Capitol Hill were highly critical of the extent of U.S. participation in the NATO mission, and Clinton hoped to avoid congressional votes that would tie his hands or undermine U.S. leadership of the Bosnia peace effort.

To reassure the critics, Clinton promised that the U.S. military mission "will be limited, focused, and under the command of an American general." To explain the reason for U.S. participation, Clinton said the rest of the world was looking for American leadership, just as it had on many other international issues since World War II.

"There are times and places where our leadership can mean the difference between peace and war, and where we can defend our fundamental values as a people and serve our most basic, strategic interests," Clinton said. "My fellow Americans, in this new era there are still times when America and America alone can and should make the difference for peace. The terrible war in Bosnia is such a case."

Polls showed that Clinton's speech had little impact on public opinion and that a substantial portion of Americans did not understand or were opposed to a U.S. role in the peacekeeping mission. On Capitol Hill, even those members who opposed the mission or were highly skeptical of it realized that they had no choice but to go along with Clinton's commitment. "Our friends and enemies don't discriminate between Republican and Democratic presidents when the word of an American president is given," Sen. John McCain (R-Ariz.) said. "When the president's word is no longer credible abroad, all Americans are less safe."

On December 13, as the first NATO peacekeeping units were arriving in Bosnia, Congress gave its assent to U.S. participation in the mission. Both the House and Senate adopted resolutions that neither endorsed nor opposed the peacekeeping mission but expressed support for American troops. The resolutions amounted to acquiescence to a risky mission already under way, and they sought to thrust entirely on President Clinton any political consequences should the mission fail.

Following are excerpts from a televised address to the nation by President Bill Clinton on November 27, 1995, in which he explained U.S. participation in a NATO peacekeeping mission in Bosnia and appealed for public and congressional support:

Good evening. Last week, the warring factions in Bosnia reached a peace agreement, as a result of our efforts in Dayton, Ohio, and the support of our

European and Russian partners. Tonight, I want to speak with you about implementing the Bosnian peace agreement, and why our values and interests as Americans require that we participate.

Let me say at the outset, America's role will not be about fighting a war. It will be about helping the people of Bosnia to secure their own peace agreement. Our mission will be limited, focused and under the command of an American general.

In fulfilling this mission, we will have the chance to help stop the killing of innocent civilians, especially children; and at the same time, to bring stability to Central Europe, a region of the world that is vital to our national interests. It is the right thing to do.

From our birth, America has always been more than just a place. America has embodied an idea that has become the ideal for billions of people throughout the world. Our founders said it best: America is about life, liberty, and the pursuit of happiness.

In this century especially, America has done more than simply stand for these ideals. We have acted on them and sacrificed for them. Our people fought two world wars so that freedom could triumph over tyranny. After World War I, we pulled back from the world, leaving a vacuum that was filled by the forces of hatred. After World War II, we continued to lead the world. We made the commitments that kept the peace, that helped to spread democracy, that created unparalleled prosperity, and that brought victory in the Cold War.

Today, because of our dedication, America's ideals—liberty, democracy and peace—are more and more the aspirations of people everywhere in the world. It is the power of our ideas, even more than our size, our wealth and our military might, that makes America a uniquely trusted nation.

With the Cold War over, some people now question the need for our continued active leadership in the world. They believe that, much like after World War I, America can now step back from the responsibilities of leadership. They argue that to be secure we need only to keep our own borders safe and that the time has come now to leave to others the hard work of leadership beyond our borders. I strongly disagree.

As the Cold War gives way to the global village, our leadership is needed more than ever because problems that start beyond our borders can quickly become problems within them. We're all vulnerable to the organized forces of intolerance and destruction; terrorism; ethnic, religious and regional rivalries; the spread of organized crime and weapons of mass destruction and drug trafficking. Just as surely as fascism and communism, these forces also threaten freedom and democracy, peace and prosperity. And they, too, demand American leadership.

But nowhere has the argument for our leadership been more clearly justified than in the struggle to stop or prevent war and civil violence. From Iraq to Haiti, from South Africa to Korea, from the Middle East to Northern Ireland, we have stood up for peace and freedom because it's in our interest to do so and because it is the right thing to do.

Now, that doesn't mean we can solve every problem. My duty as President is to match the demands for American leadership to our strategic interest and to our ability to make a difference. America cannot and must not be the world's policeman. We cannot stop all war for all time; but we can stop some wars. We cannot save all women and all children; but we can save many of them. We can't do everything; but we must do what we can.

There are times and places where our leadership can mean the difference between peace and war, and where we can defend our fundamental values as a people and serve our most basic, strategic interests. My fellow Americans, in this new era there are still times when America and America alone can and should make the difference for peace.

The terrible war in Bosnia is such a case. Nowhere today is the need for American leadership more stark or more immediate than in Bosnia. For nearly four years a terrible war has torn Bosnia apart. Horrors we prayed had been banished from Europe forever have been seared into our minds again. Skeletal prisoners caged behind barbed-wire fences; women and girls raped as a tool of war; defenseless men and boys shot down into mass graves, evoking visions of World War II concentration camps; and endless lines of refugees marching toward a future of despair.

When I took office, some were urging immediate intervention in the conflict. I decided that American ground troops should not fight a war in Bosnia because the United States could not force peace on Bosnia's warring ethnic groups, the Serbs, Croats, and Muslims. Instead, America has worked with our European allies in searching for peace, stopping the war from spreading, and easing the suffering of the Bosnian people.

We imposed tough economic sanctions on Serbia. We used our air power to conduct the longest humanitarian airlift in history, and to enforce a no-fly zone that took the war out of the skies. We helped to make peace between two of the three warring parties, the Muslims and the Croats. But as the months of war turned into years, it became clear that Europe alone could not end the conflict.

This summer, Bosnian Serb shelling once again turned Bosnia's playgrounds and marketplaces into killing fields. In response, the United States led NATO's heavy and continuous air strikes, many of them flown by skilled and brave American pilots. Those air strikes, together with the renewed determination of our European partners and the Bosnian and Croat gains on the battlefield convinced the Serbs, finally, to start thinking about making peace.

At the same time, the United States initiated an intensive diplomatic effort that forged a Bosnia-wide cease-fire and got the parties to agree to the basic principles of peace. Three dedicated American diplomats—Bob Frazier, Joe Kruzel and Nelson Drew—lost their lives in that effort. Tonight we remember their sacrifice and that of their families. And we will never forget their exceptional service to our nation.

Finally, just three weeks ago, the Muslims, Croats and Serbs came to Dayton, Ohio, in America's heartland, to negotiate a settlement. There, exhausted by war, they made a commitment to peace. They agreed to put down their guns; to preserve Bosnia as a single state; to investigate and prosecute war criminals; to protect the human rights of all citizens; to try to build a peaceful, democratic future. And they asked for America's help as they implement this peace agreement.

America has a responsibility to answer that request, to help to turn this moment of hope into an enduring reality. To do that, troops from our country and around the world would go into Bosnia to give them the confidence and support they need to implement their peace plan. I refuse to send American troops to fight a war in Bosnia, but I believe we must help to secure the Bosnian peace.

I want you to know tonight what is at stake, exactly what our troops will be asked to accomplish, and why we must carry out our responsibility to help implement the peace agreement. Implementing the agreement in Bosnia can end the terrible suffering of the people—the warfare, the mass executions, the ethnic cleansing, the campaigns of rape and terror. Let us never forget a quarter of a million men, women and children have been shelled, shot and tortured to death. Two million people, half of the population, were forced from their homes and into a miserable life as refugees. And these faceless numbers hide millions of real personal tragedies. For each of the war's victims was a mother or daughter, a father or son, a brother or sister.

Now the war is over. American leadership created the chance to build a peace and stop the suffering. Securing peace in Bosnia will also help to build a free and stable Europe. Bosnia lies at the very heart of Europe, next-door to many of its fragile new democracies and some of our closest allies. Generations of Americans have understood that Europe's freedom and Europe's stability is vital to our own national security. That's why we fought two wars in Europe. That's why we launched the Marshall Plan to restore Europe. That's why we created NATO and waged the Cold War. And that's why we must help the nations of Europe to end their worst nightmare since World War II, now.

The only force capable of getting this job done is NATO, the powerful, military alliance of democracies that has guaranteed our security for half a century now. And as NATO's leader and the primary broker of the peace agreement, the United States must be an essential part of the mission. If we're not there, NATO will not be there. The peace will collapse. The war will reignite. The slaughter of innocents will begin again. A conflict that already has claimed so many victims could spread like poison throughout the region, eat away at Europe's stability and erode our partnership with our European allies.

And America's commitment to leadership will be questioned if we refuse to participate in implementing a peace agreement we brokered right here in the United States, especially since the Presidents of Bosnia, Croatia and Serbia all asked us to participate and all pledged their best efforts to the security of our troops.

When America's partnerships are weak and our leadership is in doubt, it undermines our ability to secure our interests and to convince others to work with us. If we do maintain our partnerships and our leadership, we need not act alone. As we saw in the Gulf War and in Haiti, many other nations who share our goals will also share our burdens. But when America does not lead, the consequences can be very grave, not only for others, but eventually for us as well.

As I speak to you, NATO is completing its planning for IFOR—an international force for peace in Bosnia of about 60,000 troops. Already, more than 25 other nations, including our major NATO allies, have pledged to take part. They will contribute about two-thirds of the total implementation force, some 40,000 troops. The United States would contribute the rest, about 20,000 soldiers.

Later this week, the final NATO plan will be submitted to me for review and approval. Let me make clear what I expect it to include, and what it must include, for me to give final approval to the participation of our Armed Forces.

First, the mission will be precisely defined with clear, realistic goals that can be achieved in a definite period of time. Our troops will make sure that each side withdraws its forces behind the front lines and keeps them there. They will maintain the cease-fire to prevent the war from accidentally starting again. These efforts, in turn, will help to create a secure environment, so that the people of Bosnia can return to their homes, vote in free elections and begin to rebuild their lives. Our Joint Chiefs of Staff have concluded that this mission should and will take about one year.

Second, the risks to our troops will be minimized. American troops will take their orders from the American general who commands NATO. They will be heavily armed and thoroughly trained. By making an overwhelming show of force, they will lessen the need to use force. But unlike the UN forces, they will have the authority to respond immediately, and the training and the equipment to respond with overwhelming force to any threat to their own safety or any violations of the military provisions of the peace agreement.

If the NATO plan meets with my approval, I will immediately send it to Congress and request its support. I will also authorize the participation of a small number of American troops in a NATO advance mission that will lay the groundwork for IFOR, starting sometime next week. They will establish headquarters and set up the sophisticated communication systems that must be in place before NATO can send in its troops, tanks and trucks to Bosnia.

The implementation force itself would begin deploying in Bosnia in the days following the formal signature of the peace agreement in mid-December. The international community will help to implement arms control provisions of the agreement so that future hostilities are less likely and armaments are limited, while the world community, the United States and others, will also make sure that the Bosnian Federation has the means to defend itself once IFOR withdraws. IFOR will not be a part of this effort.

Civilian agencies from around the world will begin a separate program of humanitarian relief and reconstruction, principally paid for by our European allies and other interested countries. This effort is also absolutely essential to making the peace endure.

It will bring the people of Bosnia the food, shelter, clothing and medicine so many have been denied for so long. It will help them to rebuild—to rebuild their roads and schools, their power plants and hospitals, their factories and shops. It will reunite children with their parents and families with their homes. It will allow the Bosnians freely to choose their own leaders. It will give all the people of Bosnia a much greater stake in peace than war, so that peace takes on a life and a logic of its own.

In Bosnia we can and will succeed because our mission is clear and limited, and our troops are strong and very well-prepared. But, my fellow Americans, no deployment of American troops is risk-free, and this one may well involve casualties. There may be accidents in the field, or incidents with people who have not given up their hatred. I will take every measure possible to minimize these risks, but we must be prepared for that possibility.

As President my most difficult duty is to put the men and women who volunteer to serve our nation in harm's way when our interests and values demand it. I assume full responsibility for any harm that may come to them. But anyone contemplating any action that would endanger our troops should know this: America protects its own. Anyone—anyone—who takes on our troops will suffer the consequences. We will fight fire with fire—and then some.

After so much bloodshed and loss, after so many outrageous acts of inhuman brutality, it will take an extraordinary effort of will for the people of Bosnia to pull themselves from their past and start building a future of peace. But with our leadership and the commitment of our allies, the people of Bosnia can have the chance to decide their future in peace. They have a chance to remind the world that just a few short years ago the mosques and churches of Sarajevo were a shining symbol of multiethnic tolerance; that Bosnia once found unity in its diversity. Indeed, the cemetery in the center of the city was just a few short years ago a magnificent stadium which hosted the Olympics, our universal symbol of peace and harmony. Bosnia can be that kind of place again. We must not turn our backs on Bosnia now.

And so I ask all Americans, and I ask every member of Congress, Democrat and Republican alike, to make the choice for peace. In the choice between peace and war, America must choose peace.

My fellow Americans, I ask you to think just for a moment about this century that is drawing to a close and the new one that will soon begin. Because previous generations of Americans stood up for freedom and because we continue to do so, the American people are more secure and more prosperous. And all around the world, more people than ever before live in freedom. More people than ever before are treated with dignity. More people than ever before can hope to build a better life. That is what America's leadership is all about.

We know that these are the blessings of freedom. And America has always been freedom's greatest champion. If we continue to do everything we can to share these blessings with people around the world, if we continue to be leaders for peace, then the next century can be the greatest time our nation has ever known.

A few weeks ago, I was privileged to spend some time with His Holiness, Pope John Paul II, when he came to America. At the very end of our meeting, the Pope looked at me and said, "I have lived through most of this century. I remember that it began with a war in Sarajevo. Mr. President, you must not let it end with a war in Sarajevo."

In Bosnia, this terrible war has challenged our interests and troubled our souls. Thankfully, we can do something about it. I say again, our mission will be clear, limited and achievable. The people of Bosnia, our NATO allies, and people all around the world are now looking to America for leadership. So let us lead. That is our responsibility as Americans.

Good night and God bless America.

CLINTON ON PEACE EFFORTS
IN NORTHERN IRELAND
November 30, 1995

Seeking to bring U.S. influence to bear in the search for peace in North-ern Ireland, President Bill Clinton on November 30 became the first sitting president to visit that embattled region. Clinton declared that "America will stand with you as you take risks for peace."

Clinton's visit came during a period of hope that twenty-five years of sectarian violence might be nearing an end. The Catholic-based Irish Republican Army (IRA) and its militant Protestant counterparts for more than a year had observed a cease-fire in their mutual campaigns of bombings, shootings, and other violent attacks. It appeared that direct negotiations among all the parties to Northern Ireland's conflict might be in the offing.

A Generation of Violence

Britain retained control of the six counties of Northern Ireland, collec-tively known as Ulster, after it granted independence to the Republic of Ire-land in 1920. The republican south was primarily Roman Catholic; the northern counties were primarily Protestant. Many Catholics in the north felt they were treated as second-class citizens and were discriminated against in employment, housing, and other services.

Many Catholics wanted Ulster incorporated within the Republic of Ire-land and called themselves "Republicans." Most Protestants, and some Catholics, favored continued union with Great Britain, and so were called "Unionists" or "Loyalists." Extremists, representing minorities on both sides, armed themselves and in the late 1960s engaged in a civil war that tore the region apart. The IRA attacked British government targets within Ulster and in Britain; paramilitary Protestant organizations responded with violence against Catholic neighborhoods.

Until the war in Bosnia overshadowed it, the conflict in Northern Ire-land was Europe's bloodiest sectarian dispute of the modern age. More than 3,000 people had died since the outbreak of fighting in 1969. The violence peaked in 1971 and 1972, but continued through the years, severely dam-aging the region's economy and turning much of the main city, Belfast, into a bombed-out, boarded-up wasteland. (Bosnia conflict, p. 717)

During the 1970s and 1980s, several efforts were made to end the civil war or at least get negotiations under way, but none had much success. In 1994 the Clinton administration decided to step up U.S. diplomacy on the issue, despite objections by the British government against outside inter-ference in its internal affairs. The administration granted a visa for a visit to the United States by Gerry Adams, head of Sinn Fein, the political arm of the IRA. That high-profile U.S. visit led to a series of political maneuvers, including secret, indirect talks among British officials and Sinn Fein, that produced an IRA cease-fire starting August 31, 1994.

The cease-fire led to a general relaxation of tension, including a compa-rable cease-fire on the part of the Protestant militias. In December 1994 the British government and Sinn Fein held their first direct talks in more than twenty years. On May 24, 1995, Sir Patrick Mayhew, the British secretary of state for Northern Ireland, met Adams in Washington during a U.S.-sponsored conference on international investment in Northern Ireland. The most direct contact between the two sides since 1972, the meeting sym-bolized a new willingness by old enemies to talk about peace.

Britain in the meantime had cast aside its reluctance to engage in direct talks about the Northern Ireland question with the Republic of Ire-land. On February 22, 1995, the two sides brought forth a long-term plan for peace in Northern Ireland, called the "Framework Document." The most ambitious of a series of peace plans in recent decades, it called for a new legislative assembly for Northern Ireland, with provisions aimed at pre-venting the Protestant majority from dominating the Catholic minority. The Irish government pledged to revise its constitution, which claimed sov-ereignty over the whole of the island. The plan also gave the Dublin gov-ernment a role in areas of mutual interest between the north and south, such as agriculture, tourism, and environmental policy. This proposal was referred to as the "Irish dimension," and it drew the sharpest criticism from hard-line Protestant leaders in the north who feared it was the first step toward unification with the south.

The direct talks between Sinn Fein and the British government were less productive, however, ultimately foundering on November 3. The central issue was Britain's demand that the IRA begin turning over some of its weapons before the start of all-party negotiations on a political solution to the conflict. The IRA refused and demanded, in turn, that the British gov-ernment disarm its military forces in Northern Ireland.

Clinton's Visit

The collapse of the British-Sinn Fein talks threatened to halt the peace process and to spoil the planned visit to Northern Ireland by President Clinton in November. Although nearly one-third of all U.S. presidents had Irish ancestry, and several had visited the Republic of Ireland, none had set foot in Ulster while in office. Clinton's planned visit had great symbolic importance and served as a stimulus to renewed negotiations.

On November 28, hours before Clinton was due to leave Washington, the British and Irish governments agreed to a new plan calling for "preparatory talks" involving the governments and all factions from Northern Ireland, including Sinn Fein. Those talks were to lead to full-scale negotiations among all parties in February 1996.

That agreement enabled Clinton to visit Northern Ireland on November 30 in a moment of hope for the peace process. Clinton gave two major speeches in Belfast, one at the Mackie International textile machinery plant in West Belfast and another at a ceremony for the lighting of a Christmas tree Clinton had brought with him from Nashville, Tenn., Belfast's twin city.

The president also visited Londonderry, where IRA violence against British rule began in 1969. There, Clinton inaugurated a chair in peace studies at the University of Ulster. The professorship was named after Thomas P. O'Neill Jr., who as Speaker of the U.S. House of Representatives sought for years to stem the flow of American aid to the IRA military wing.

In his remarks, Clinton praised those who were taking the "risk" of peace, contrasting them with extremists on both sides who seemed to favor continued violence and intransigence. He told his audience at the Mackie plant: "There will always be those who define the worth of their lives not by who they are, but by who they aren't, not by what they're for, but by what they are against. They will never escape the dead-end street of violence. But you, the vast majority, Protestant and Catholic alike, must not allow the ship of peace to sink on the rocks of old habits and hard grudges."

Clinton was praised by many on both sides of the divide between Catholics and Protestants. One of the most respected moderate Catholic leaders, John Hume, called the president's visit "the most historic day ever" for Northern Ireland.

Following is the text of a speech by President Bill Clinton, on November 30, 1995, at the Mackie International textile machinery plant in Belfast, Northern Ireland:

. . . At this holiday season all around the world, the promise of peace is in the air. The barriers of the cold war are giving way to a global village where communication and cooperation are the order of the day. From South Africa to the Middle East, and now to troubled Bosnia, conflicts long thought impossible to solve are moving along the road to resolution. Once-bitter foes are clasping hands and changing history, and long-suffering people are moving closer to normal lives.

Here in Northern Ireland, you are making a miracle, a miracle symbolized by those two children who held hands and told us what this whole thing is all about. In the land of the harp and the fiddle, the fife and the lambeg drum, two proud traditions are coming together in the harmonies of peace. The cease-fire and negotiations have sparked a powerful transformation.

Mackie's plant is a symbol of Northern Ireland's rebirth. It has long been a symbol of world-class engineering. The textile machines you make permit people to weave disparate threads into remarkable fabrics. That is now what you must do here with the people of Northern Ireland.

Here we lie along the peace line, the wall of steel and stone separating Protestant from Catholic. But today, under the leadership of Pat Dougan, you are bridging the divide, overcoming a legacy of discrimination where fair employment and integration are the watchwords of the future. On this shop floor, men and women of both traditions are working together to achieve common goals.

Peace, once a distant dream, is now making a difference in everyday life in this land. Soldiers have left the streets of Belfast; many have gone home. People can go to the pub or the store without the burden of the search or the threat of a bomb. As barriers disappear along the border, families and communities divided for decades are becoming whole once more.

This year in Armagh on St. Patrick's Day, Protestant and Catholic children led the parade together for the first time since The Troubles began. A bystander's words marked the wonder of the occasion when he said, "Even the normal is beginning to seem normal."

The economic rewards of peace are evident as well. Unemployment has fallen here to its lowest level in 14 years, while retail sales and investment are surging. For from the gleaming city center to the new shop fronts of Belfast, to the Enterprise Center in East Belfast, business is thriving, and opportunities are expanding. With every extra day that the guns are still, business confidence grows stronger, and the promise of prosperity grows as well.

As the shroud of terror melts away, Northern Ireland's beauty has been revealed again to all the world, the castles and coasts, the Giant's Causeway, the lush green hills, the high white cliffs, a magical backdrop to your greatest asset which I saw all along the way from the airport here today, the warmth and good feeling of your people. Visitors are now coming in record numbers. Indeed, today the air route between Belfast and London is the second busiest in all of Europe. . . .

Last year's ceasefire of the Irish Republican Army, joined by the combined Loyalist Military Command, marked a turning point in the history of Northern Ireland. Now is the time to sustain that momentum and lock in the gains of peace. Neither community wants to go back to the violence of the past. The children told of that today. Both parties must do their part to move this process forward now.

Let me begin by saying that the search for common ground demands the courage of an open mind. This twin-track initiative gives the parties a chance to begin preliminary talks in ways in which all views will be represented and all voices will be heard. It also establishes an international body to address the issue of arms decommissioning. I hope the parties will seize this opportunity. Engaging in honest dialog is not an act of surrender, it is an act of strength and common sense.

Moving from cease-fire to peace requires dialog. For 25 years now, the history of Northern Ireland has been written in the blood of its children and their parents. The cease-fire turned the page on that history. It must not be allowed to turn back.

There must also be progress away from the negotiating table. Violence has lessened, but it has not disappeared. The leaders of the four main churches recently condemned the so-called punishment beatings and called for an end to such attacks. I add my voice to theirs.

As the church leaders said, this is a time when the utmost efforts on all sides are needed to build a peaceful and confident community in the future. But true peace requires more than a treaty, even more than the absence of violence. Those who have suffered most in the fighting must share fairly in the fruits of renewal. The frustration that gave rise to violence must give way to faith in the future.

The United States will help to secure the tangible benefits of peace. Ours is the first American administration ever to support in the Congress the international Fund for Ireland, which has become an engine for economic development and for reconciliation. We will continue to encourage trade and investment and to help end the cycle of unemployment.

We are proud to support Northern Ireland. You have given America a very great deal. Irish-Protestant and Irish-Catholic together have added to America's strength. From our battle for independence down to the present day, the Irish have not only fought in our wars, they have built our Nation, and we owe you a very great debt. . . .

It is so much easier to believe that our differences matter more than what we have in common. It is easier, but it is wrong. We all cherish family and faith, work and community. We all strive to live lives that are free and honest and responsible. We all want our children to grow up in a world where their talents are matched by their opportunities. And I believe those values are just as strong in County Londonderry as they are in Londonderry, New Hampshire; in Belfast, Northern Ireland as in Belfast, Maine.

I am proud to be of Ulster Scots stock. I am proud to be, also, of Irish stock. I share these roots with millions and millions of Americans, now over 40 million Americans. And we rejoice at things being various, as Louis MacNeice once wrote. It is one of the things that makes America special.

Because our greatness flows from the wealth of our diversity as well as the strength of the ideals we share in common, we feel bound to support others around the world who seek to bridge their own divides. This is an important part of our country's mission on the eve of the 21st century, because we know that the chain of peace that protects us grows stronger with every new link that is forged. . . .

Those who work for peace have got to support one another. We know that when leaders stand up for peace, they place their forces on the line and sometimes their very lives on the line, as we learned so recently in the tragic murder of the brave Prime Minister of Israel. For, just as peace has its pioneers, peace will always have its rivals. Even when children stand up and say what these children said today, there will always be people who, deep down inside, will never be able to give up the past.

Over the last 3 years, I have had the privilege of meeting with and closely listening to both Nationalists and Unionists from Northern Ireland, and I believe that the greatest struggle you face now is not between opposing ideas or opposing interests. The greatest struggle you face is between those who deep down inside are inclined to be peacemakers and those who deep down inside cannot yet embrace the cause of peace, between those who are in the ship of peace and those who are trying to sink it. Old habits die hard. There will always be those who define the worth of their lives not by who they are but by who they aren't, not by what they're for but by what they are against. They will never escape the dead-end street of violence. But you, the vast majority, Protestant and Catholic alike, must not allow the ship of peace to sink on the rocks of old habits and hard grudges.

You must stand firm against terror. You must say to those who still would use violence for political objectives, "You are the past. Your day is over. Violence has no place at the table of democracy and no role in the future of this land." By the same token, you must also be willing to say to those who renounce violence and who do take their own risks for peace that they are entitled to be full participants in the democratic process. Those who do show the courage to break with the past are entitled to their stake in the future.

As leaders for peace become invested in the process, as leaders make compromises and risk the backlash, people begin more and more—I have seen this all over the world—they begin more and more to develop a common interest in each other's success, in standing together rather than standing apart. They realize that the sooner they get to true peace, with all the rewards it brings, the sooner it will be easy to discredit and destroy the forces of destruction.

We will stand with those who take risks for peace in Northern Ireland and around the world. I pledge that we will do all we can, through the International Fund for Ireland and in many other ways, to ease your load. If you walk down this path continually, you will not walk alone. We are entering an era of possibility unparalleled in all of human history. If you enter that era determined to build a new age of peace, the United States of America will proudly stand with you.

But at the end of the day, as with all free people, your future is for you to decide. Your destiny is for you to determine. Only you can decide between division and unity, between hard lives and high hopes. Only you can create a lasting peace. It takes courage to let go of familiar divisions. It takes faith to walk down a new road. But when we see the bright gaze of these children, we know the risk is worth the reward.

I have been so touched by the thousands of letters I have received from schoolchildren here, telling me what peace means to them. One young girl from Ballymena wrote, and I quote, "It is not easy to forgive and forget, especially for those who have lost a family member or a close friend. However, if people could look to the future with hope instead of the past with fear, we can only be moving in the right direction." I couldn't have said it nearly as well.

I believe you can summon the strength to keep moving forward. After all, you have come so far already. You have braved so many dangers. You have endured so many sacrifices. Surely, there can be no turning back. But peace must be waged with a warrior's resolve, bravely, proudly, and relentlessly, secure in the knowledge of the single greatest difference between war and peace: In peace, everybody can win.

I was overcome today, when I landed in my plane and I drove with Hillary up the highway to come here, by the phenomenal beauty of the place and the spirit and the good will of the people. Northern Ireland has a chance not only to begin anew but to be a real inspiration to the rest of the world, a model of progress through tolerance.

Let us join our efforts together as never before to make that dream a reality. Let us join our prayers in this season of peace for a future of peace in this good land.

Thank you very much.

December

CLINTON, REPUBLICANS ON BUDGET IMPASSE
December 6, 1995

President Bill Clinton and the new Republican leadership of Congress sparred all during 1995 on the central issue of how to reshape the federal government. They did so primarily on terms set by the Republicans, who demanded a balanced budget in seven years and drastic cutbacks in welfare and other social programs. After initially vacillating in response to the Republicans and then embracing the concept of a balanced budget, Clinton later stood his ground to protect his party's priorities.

The net result of the year's feuding was a general consensus on the goal of achieving a balanced budget in seven years, but with little agreement on the specifics of how to reach that objective. Republicans forced two expensive partial shutdowns of the federal government in November and December in hopes of pressuring Clinton to accept their terms. That tactic failed, backfiring politically on the Republicans, who were forced at the start of 1996 to allow the government to remain open while they engaged in negotiations with the Clinton administration on a more conventional basis.

One of many low points in relations between the administration and Congress came on December 6, when Clinton vetoed a sweeping balanced-budget plan crafted by the Republicans. He called it an "extreme approach" that "would hurt average Americans and help special interests." Republican leaders responded that Clinton had missed a chance to jump on their balanced-budget bandwagon.

All year long, both sides wavered between cutting a deal, to demonstrate to the increasingly disillusioned voters that Washington politicians could accomplish something, and battling it out so they would have an issue for the 1996 elections. Nearly all the posturing and rhetoric reflected the politics of the moment: whether each side saw greater political advantage in compromising or refusing to budge. Polls showed that most voters were unimpressed by what they saw, but in the latter part of 1995 Clinton had the public relations edge.

Early Skirmishing

Upon taking over Congress in January, the Republicans were determined to undo much of the legislation that previous Congresses and presidents of both parties had enacted into law since the New Deal. House Republicans sought to pass more than a dozen items in their Contract with America, which promised a drastic scaling-back of the federal government's role in American society. (Contract with America, Historic Documents of 1994, p. 374)

One of the chief methods for cutting back the government was to be a balanced budget, achieved in seven years. Republicans argued that the government was spending billions on wasteful, unnecessary, or unworkable programs and that the only way to get rid of them was by demanding a balanced budget, thereby leaving only enough money for truly necessary spending.

Clinton had said he agreed with the goal of a balanced budget, but he rejected any approach mandating that goal within a set time period. In February he sent Congress a status quo budget for fiscal year 1996 that essentially left it to the Republicans to take the first step.

Led by Speaker Newt Gingrich (R-Ga.), the House Republicans quickly seized the initiative. The House approved a constitutional amendment requiring a balanced budget; that measure fell short in the Senate by one vote. While acting on the rest of their legislative agenda, House and Senate Republicans negotiated with each other on a giant package of changes that would lead to a balanced budget in seven years, by fiscal year 2002. Even though the Republicans shared an overall political philosophy, those negotiations were difficult, involving sharply conflicting priorities between the conservatives in the House and some of the Senate's more moderate leaders.

As the Republicans worked on their plan, Clinton began to play a more active role than he had in the weeks after the Republicans took over Congress. On June 7 he vetoed a short-term plan by the Republicans to cut $16.4 billion from previously appropriated spending. It was his first veto, and it demonstrated a new determination by the president to stand up to the Republican-led Congress.

On June 13 Clinton took a giant step toward the Republicans, offering a plan to balance the budget in ten years, by fiscal 2005. Republican leaders said Clinton's plan was inadequate, in part because it was based on overly optimistic economic assumptions. The president's proposal angered many Democrats, who accused him of giving into Republican demands for draconian budget cuts.

Clinton's move gave Republicans an incentive to complete their own proposal, which they did on June 22. It was a massive rewrite of federal legislation, involving sharp cuts in federal programs to reach a balanced budget by 2002. Its most controversial provision mandated cuts of more than $450 billion in Medicare and Medicaid—but with no details on how those cuts would be made. It was approved June 29 in back-to-back votes in the

*House and Senate, mostly along party lines. Passed as a concurrent reso-
lution, it was a congressional statement of principle that did not go to the
White House for presidential action.*

More Vetoes and Government Shut-Downs

*The budget struggle got under way in earnest in November. Congress sent
to the White House two pieces of legislation intended to keep the government
functioning: a continuing resolution to fund government departments
whose appropriations bills for fiscal 1996 had not yet been enacted into law,
and a short-term borrowing extension for the Treasury Department. Both
measures included budget-cutting and other legislative provisions Clinton
said he would not accept, and he vetoed them on November 13.*

*That step led to a shutdown of much of the federal government the next
day; some 800,000 "nonessential" government workers were told to stay
home. The shutdown lasted seven days—twice as long as any of the nine
previous closings in U.S. government history.*

*Gingrich said November 16 that he had precipitated the crisis, in part
out of pique that Clinton had snubbed him and Senate Majority Leader
Robert Dole (R-Kan.) during a flight on Air Force One, when Clinton and
the leaders were returning from the funeral of Israeli prime minister
Yitzhak Rabin. Gingrich admitted that his complaint against Clinton was
"petty," and Democrats had a field day accusing the Speaker of "childish"
behavior. Gingrich's misstep was reflected in opinion polls, which showed
that most of the public blamed Republicans, not Clinton, for the government shutdown.*

*The Gingrich controversy also took some of the public impact away from
the Republicans' next step: passage by Congress on November 17 of a massive "reconciliation" bill implementing the Republican balanced-budget
strategy. The bill would have cut $894 billion from projected federal spend-
ing by 2002 by radically overhauling welfare, Medicare, Medicaid, other
social welfare programs, and farm subsidies. It also would have allowed
$245 billion worth of tax cuts. The bill also contained numerous nonbud-
get provisions, such as opening the Arctic National Wildlife Refuge in Alaska to oil exploration—long a major goal of the oil industry.*

*Two days later, on November 19, Clinton and the Republicans agreed on
a general "framework" for negotiating a balanced budget in seven years. It
marked the first time Clinton agreed to that time frame. The agreement
also allowed the government to reopen through December 15.*

*It was then Clinton's turn to take action. On December 6, he vetoed the
Republican budget-balancing bill, saying it would have made "extreme cuts
and other unacceptable changes in Medicare and Medicaid" and would
have raised taxes "on millions of working Americans." The next day, Clinton offered his own plan to balance the budget in seven years. The White
House said the new plan made $141 billion more in cuts than the presi-
dent's June 13 plan; even so, Republicans insisted that it fell short of a balanced budget.*

A week later, on December 15, Republicans walked out of budget talks with the White House, accusing the president of reneging on his promise to say how he would close a $365 billion gap between the two sides. Much of the government was forced to shut down again the next day because short-term funding had expired and Congress and the president still had not settled on six appropriations bills for fiscal 1996.

By this point, both sides had become so entrenched in their positions and had justified themselves with such inflammatory rhetoric that making a deal had become increasingly difficult. In addition, Gingrich found himself hostage to his own creation: the House Republican freshmen, whom he had helped get elected but who now refused to make any concessions to Clinton. On December 20, the House Republicans blocked a leadership plan to allow the government to reopen temporarily while budget talks continued. Congress left Washington two days later for its Christmas recess, with the budget issue unresolved and much of the government still closed.

Clobbered in the public opinion polls for forcing the government shutdowns, Republicans abandoned that strategy on January 5, 1996, allowing the federal workers to return to their jobs, with full back pay. Budget negotiations between the two sides continued well into the year, despite repeated setbacks. With the 1996 presidential and congressional elections looming, both sides seemed to have concluded that a long-term resolution of the balanced budget impasse would not be possible until after the voters had one more chance to choose sides on election day.

Following is the text of President Bill Clinton's December 6 message explaining his veto of the "reconciliation" bill mandating budget cuts and a balanced budget by fiscal 2002, followed by remarks the same day by Senate Majority Leader Robert Dole (R-Kan.) and House Speaker Newt Gingrich (R-Ga.) at a press conference:

CLINTON VETO

TO THE HOUSE OF REPRESENTATIVES:

I am returning herewith without my approval H.R. 2491, the budget reconciliation bill adopted by the Republican majority, which seeks to make extreme cuts and other unacceptable changes in Medicare and Medicaid, and to raise taxes on millions of working Americans.

As I have repeatedly stressed, I want to find common ground with the Congress on a balanced budget plan that will best serve the American people. But, I have profound differences with the extreme approach that the Republican majority has adopted. It would hurt average Americans and help special interests.

My balanced budget plan reflects the values that Americans share—work and family, opportunity and responsibility. It would protect Medicare and retain Medicaid's guarantee of coverage; invest in education and training and other priorities; protect public health and the environment; and provide for a targeted tax cut to help middle-income Americans raise their children, save for the future, and pay for postsecondary education. To reach balance, my plan would eliminate wasteful spending, streamline programs, and end unneeded subsidies; take the first, serious steps toward health care reform; and reform welfare to reward work.

By contrast, H.R. 2491 would cut deeply into Medicare, Medicaid, student loans, and nutrition programs; hurt the environment; raise taxes on millions of working men and women and their families by slashing the Earned Income Tax Credit (EITC); and provide a huge tax cut whose benefits would flow disproportionately to those who are already the most well-off.

Moreover, this bill creates new fiscal pressures. Revenue losses from the tax cuts grow rapidly after 2002, with costs exploding for provisions that primarily benefit upper-income taxpayers. Taken together, the revenue losses for the 3 years after 2002 for the individual retirement account (IRA), capital gains, and estate tax provisions exceed the losses for the preceding 6 years.

Title VIII would cut Medicare by $270 billion over 7 years—by far the largest cut in Medicare's 30-year history. While we need to slow the rate of growth in Medicare spending, I believe Medicare must keep pace with anticipated increases in the costs of medical services and the growing number of elderly Americans. This bill would fall woefully short and would hurt beneficiaries, over half of whom are women. In addition, the bill introduces untested, and highly questionable, Medicare "choices" that could increase risks and costs for the most vulnerable beneficiaries.

Title VII would cut Federal Medicaid payments to States by $163 billion over 7 years and convert the program into a block grant, eliminating guaranteed coverage to millions of Americans and putting States at risk during economic downturns. States would face untenable choices: cutting benefits, dropping coverage for millions of beneficiaries, or reducing provider payments to a level that would undermine quality service to children, people with disabilities, the elderly, pregnant women, and others who depend on Medicaid. I am also concerned that the bill has inadequate quality and income protections for nursing home residents, the developmentally disabled, and their families; and that it would eliminate a program that guarantees immunizations to many children.

Title IV would virtually eliminate the Direct Student Loan Program, reversing its significant progress and ending the participation of over 1,300 schools and hundreds of thousands of students. These actions would hurt middle- and low-income families, make student loan programs less efficient, perpetuate unnecessary red tape, and deny students and schools the free-market choice of guaranteed or direct loans.

Title V would open the Arctic National Wildlife Refuge (ANWR) to oil and gas drilling, threatening a unique, pristine ecosystem, in hopes of generating $1.3 billion in Federal revenues—a revenue estimate based on wishful thinking and outdated analysis. I want to protect this biologically rich wilderness permanently. I am also concerned that the Congress has chosen to use the reconciliation bill as a catch-all for various objectionable natural resource and environmental policies. One would retain the notorious patenting provision whereby the government transfers billions of dollars of publicly owned minerals at little or no charge to private interests; another would transfer Federal land for a low-level radioactive waste site in California without public safeguards.

While making such devastating cuts in Medicare, Medicaid, and other vital programs, this bill would provide huge tax cuts for those who are already the most well-off. Over 47 percent of the tax benefits would go to families with incomes over $100,000—the top 12 percent. The bill would provide unwarranted benefits to corporations and new tax breaks for special interests. At the same time, it would raise taxes, on average, for the poorest one-fifth of all families.

The bill would make capital gains cuts retroactive to January 1, 1995, providing a windfall of $13 billion in about the first 9 months of 1995 alone to taxpayers who already have sold their assets. While my Administration supports limited reform of the alternative minimum tax (AMT), this bill's cuts in the corporate AMT would not adequately ensure that profitable corporations pay at least some Federal tax. The bill also would encourage businesses to avoid taxes by stockpiling foreign earnings in tax havens. And the bill does not include my proposal to close a loophole that allows wealthy Americans to avoid taxes on the gains they accrue by giving up their U.S. citizenship. Instead, it substitutes a provision that would prove ineffective.

While cutting taxes for the well-off, this bill would cut the EITC for almost 13 million working families. It would repeal part of the scheduled 1996 increase for taxpayers with two or more children, and end the credit for workers who do not live with qualifying children. Even after accounting for other tax cuts in this bill, about eight million families would face a net tax increase.

The bill would threaten the retirement benefits of workers and increase the exposure of the Pension Benefit Guaranty Corporation by making it easy for companies to withdraw tax-favored pension assets for nonpension purposes. It also would raise Federal employee retirement contributions, unduly burdening Federal workers. Moreover, the bill would eliminate the low-income housing tax credit and the community development corporation tax credit, which address critical housing needs and help rebuild communities. Finally, the bill would repeal the tax credit that encourages economic activity in Puerto Rico. We must not ignore the real needs of our citizens in Puerto Rico, and any legislation must contain effective mechanisms to promote job creation in the islands.

Title XII includes many welfare provisions. I strongly support real welfare reform that strengthens families and encourages work and responsibility. But the provisions in this bill, when added to the EITC cuts, would cut low-income programs too deeply. For welfare reform to succeed, savings should result from moving people from welfare to work, not from cutting people off and shifting costs to the States. The cost of excessive program cuts in human terms—to working families, single mothers with small children, abused and neglected children, low-income legal immigrants, and disabled children—would be grave. In addition, this bill threatens the national nutritional safety net by making unwarranted changes in child nutrition programs and the national food stamp program.

The agriculture provisions would eliminate the safety net that farm programs provide for U.S. agriculture. Title I would provide windfall payments to producers when prices are high, but not protect family farm income when prices are low. In addition, it would slash spending for agricultural export assistance and reduce the environmental benefits of the Conservation Reserve Program.

For all of these reasons, and for others detailed in the attachment, this bill is unacceptable.

Nevertheless, while I have major differences with the Congress, I want to work with Members to find a common path to balance the budget in a way that will honor our commitment to senior citizens, help working families, provide a better life for our children, and improve the standard of living of all Americans.

WILLIAM J. CLINTON
The White House,
December 6, 1995.

DOLE REMARKS

Someone said it was ironic that the President would use the pen that created Medicare to veto a bill that would have saved it. But, I guess the President understands what he was doing.

He missed a very historic opportunity today to give America [its] first balanced budget in a generation. Now, the veto didn't come as a surprise, but I think some of the rhetoric came as a surprise. He could have written into law a prosperous future for America, a future for our children, the next generation taking us into the next century. But despite his veto today, I look forward to seeing what he'll offer tomorrow; whether it's going to be a warmed over same-budget we had that didn't get a single vote in the United States Senate—or whether he is really going to take a step in the right direction toward a balanced budget over the next seven years.

We're obviously ready, willing. We've been ready and willing the past ten days when virtually nothing has happened. And both [Rep.] John Kasich [R-Ohio] and [Sen.] Pete Domenici [R-N.M.] and the Speaker and myself are prepared. We want to get this done. We believe America deserves it. We believe our children deserve it. It means lower interest rates, whether you buy a car, or farm machinery, a house, take out a student loan.

We're talking about things that matter to the American people, that make a difference in their lives, that affect their values. So, while we're disappointed in the President's action today, we look forward to hopefully a different response tomorrow.

GINGRICH REMARKS

Let me say, first of all, that we knew the President would veto the balanced budget act. We're still very proud of the fact that—as a team—House and Senate Republicans passed the first balanced budget in a generation. And we did it working together, solving a tremendous number of problems. We did it honestly, using the Congressional Budget Office which was tough.

And both Senator Domenici and Congressman Kasich will tell you, it was difficult at times because we'd love to [have] found a fudge factor; we'd love to have found a way to just get a little more money. And it wasn't there.

And yet, I have to say that I have mixed emotions today. On the one hand the President said yesterday he's going to send up a seven-year balanced budget. It won't yet be scored by the Congressional Budget Office. But they've agreed the Congressional Budget Office would do the scoring.

Now, just to make clear why that's important. The so-called "balanced budget" of the President over here, when scored by the Congressional Budget Office, suddenly became a $200 billion a year deficit. So, we can't rely on some phony White House score. And we want to just make clear that our first principle is that whatever the President sends up, we're going to insist on honest scoring to get honest numbers, which were the ground rules that we wrote the balanced budget act by.

Second, we want to establish today we're not going to spend a lot of time answering the President. He had a nice gimmick down at the White House and he had another photo opportunity. Instead of leading, instead of governing, he played games with the American people. But the fact is, the President needs to recognize that Lyndon Johnson's "Great Society" has failed.

The people know that a Washington-based, Washington-spending, Washington bureaucracy, Washington red-tape "Great Society" isn't the answer. And that's why, I think, these five principles, which are really the core of what we're going to be working on in the next ten days, are so vital.

And this is how we're going to measure, in addition to having honest numbers, we're going to measure the President's budget proposal by these facts first:

Does it reduce Washington's spending and cut taxes for families and promote economic growth? Very basic. Is the President going to ask for higher taxes of the American people to spend more money on Washington bureaucracies, or is he prepared to join us in restraining the Washington bureaucracies so families get a $500 per child tax credit, so parents can spend money on their own children, and so the economy grows because people have a reason to invest and create jobs?

Second, is he going to go work with us to ensure Medicare solvency? I don't think he mentioned once today in his photo opportunity that our bill

744

actually saves Medicare from going broke. Our bill, by every test of the actuaries, moves Medicare in to solvency. It preserves and protects Medicare, and we're going to ensure that Medicare is protected.

Third, we are committed to reforming welfare. We want to see what he sends up. He's already indicated he may veto our welfare reform bill. We believe in reestablishing the work ethic and in making sure that welfare is truly reformed.

Fourth, and I think this is going to be, I think, maybe one of the most difficult issues of the negotiations. We believe that money should return to the states, to the local governments and to citizens. We believe that, wherever possible, we should begin to move power out of the Washington high-rise bureaucracies, out of the local offices you see all around this capital, and we should move that power back to the state governments, the local governments and to private citizens. And we want to see whether the President sticks to the same old Washington-based, Washington mentality that we know now doesn't work.

Finally, we are committed to getting the job done now, not next year, not after the election, not someday down the road. We believe the American people want a balanced budget. We believe they deserve a balanced budget, and we believe the American people support the idea of getting it done now. . . .

HOUSE ETHICS COMMITTEE ON SPEAKER GINGRICH
December 6, 1995

Speakers of the U.S. House of Representatives rarely are household names, but the man who took over the Speakership in 1995 quickly became known everywhere by his unusual nickname: Newt. Republican Newt Gingrich of Georgia, the first of his party to be Speaker in more than forty years, led a Republican revolution that swept Democrats from power on Capitol Hill and set out to reverse a half century's worth of federal legislation.

In the process, Gingrich's sharp-elbowed, high-decibel approach won him notoriety and the ire of many. At the end of 1995, Gingrich was facing an inquiry into alleged ethical violations that threatened to undermine his credibility. At least one charge also had the potential to force Gingrich from power. The last time a Speaker had faced such scrutiny was in 1989, when Gingrich had been the driving force in pursuing charges against Speaker Jim Wright (D-Texas), who was ultimately driven from office. Gingrich's involvement then had made him a major actor in the Republican party.

The House Committee on Standards of Official Conduct, known as the ethics committee, on December 6 unanimously found Gingrich guilty of three violations of House rules, but recommended no punishment. The committee also voted to hire an outside counsel to investigate whether Gingrich violated federal tax laws by using tax-deductible donations to subsidize a college course he taught in Georgia, while in Congress. The committee dismissed two other complaints against Gingrich but strongly questioned the propriety of his actions in one of those cases.

The findings, included in a December 6 letter to Gingrich and detailed in a report made public on December 12, represented the first time the ethics committee had formally accused a Speaker of violating House rules. Speaker Wright resigned before the committee completed its inquiry in 1989. The committee in 1978 also said Speaker Thomas P. "Tip" O'Neill Jr. had engaged in "questionable" activity by attending two private parties related to a South Korean influence peddling scandal, but O'Neill was not accused of violating any rules. (Wright case, Historic Documents of 1989, p. 329)

Gingrich's First Year in Power

After his election in 1989 as House minority whip (the number two Republican leadership post), Gingrich worked with the Christian Coalition and other conservative groups on a strategy to capture the House from the Democrats. Many in both parties believed Gingrich's campaign was futile, but his determination and intellectual leadership inspired scores of conservatives to challenge entrenched Democrats. Gingrich convinced Republican colleagues in 1994 to sign the Contract with America—a collection of conservative legislative priorities such as a constitutional amendment requiring a balanced budget—and to use it as a battering ram against Democrats. Heavily financed by contributions from conservatives and other special interest groups, and benefiting from strong public dissatisfaction with President Bill Clinton, the Republicans swept to power in the 1994 elections, winning control of the House and Senate. (Contract with America, Historic Documents of 1994, p. 374)

In their Contract with America, the House Republicans promised that the House would pass all of their legislative priorities in the first one hundred days of the 104th Congress. With few exceptions, they managed to do so. Gingrich also took personal control of the House, stripping committee chairmen of much of their influence and amassing more power than any Speaker in decades. (First one hundred days, p. 165*)*

While he retained the loyalty of junior Republicans whom he had helped elect to office, Gingrich increasingly found himself a target of unflattering publicity. Gingrich's high-profile, harshly partisan attacks on Democrats gave him more public exposure than any Speaker in recent memory, and many people did not like what they saw. An ABC/Washington Post poll in November put Gingrich's disapproval rating at 65 percent—extraordinarily high for any politician, especially one who had been in the public eye nationally for little more than a year.

At the end of 1995, Gingrich was leading his Republican colleagues in a high-risk campaign to force President Clinton to accept Republican priorities for reaching a balanced federal budget in seven years. Their tactic was to force a shutdown of the federal government until Clinton conceded. Clinton was more resistant than the Republicans foresaw, however, and in January 1996 they were forced to abandon that approach in favor of longer-term negotiations. (Budget battle, p. 737*)*

Many of Gingrich's House colleagues urged him to lower his profile during the 1996 election season so that Democrats would have less success in using his unpopularity to attack other Republican candidates. In December he said he would do so, but most observers doubted that Gingrich would be able to stay out of the limelight for very long.

Ethics Charges Against Gingrich

Even before he assumed the Speakership, Gingrich was dogged by complaints that he had improperly used his political influence for personal gain and had made improper use of a political action committee he headed, GOPAC. The first formal complaint was filed with the ethics committee in February 1994 by several House Democrats. Other complaints were lodged in September 1994 and January 1995 by former representative Ben Jones, whom Gingrich defeated in the 1994 elections, and in February and March 1995 by Reps. George Miller (D-Calif.) and David Bonior (D-Mich.), the minority whip.

The bipartisan ethics committee wrestled with those charges in 1994, when the House was under Democratic control, and all through 1995, when Republicans were in charge. The committee held forty-seven meetings on the Gingrich charges but could not overcome a partisan deadlock. At several points in 1995, Democrats complained that Republicans were trying to block action to protect the Speaker.

The logjam started to break loose in November, when the Federal Election Commission (FEC) filed a lawsuit alleging that Gingrich's GOPAC had been involved in congressional elections at a time when it legally was allowed only to help state and local candidates. In filing its suit, the FEC released thousands of pages of documents that showed, among other things, that all five Republican members of the ethics committee had some relationship with GOPAC or had benefited from GOPAC activities.

Embarrassed by the disclosure, the Republican ethics committee members on December 6 gave in to demands by Democrats for action against Gingrich, including hiring an outside counsel to investigate at least one of the charges against him. The committee acted unanimously and sent its findings to Gingrich in a letter signed by Chairman Nancy L. Johnson (R-Conn.), a Gingrich ally, and ranking Democrat Jim McDermott of Washington.

The committee said Gingrich violated House rules on three counts:

- *He used the House floor on four occasions in 1993 and 1994 to promote a course he taught at Kennesaw State College and Reinhardt College, both in Georgia. In a floor speech on April 12, 1994, for example, Gingrich gave out a toll-free number to order tapes of his course. The committee said Gingrich had made an "improper solicitation."*
- *He used House floor speeches on several occasions to promote a nationally televised program, the American Opportunity Workshop, that was sponsored by GOPAC. The committee said this also was an improper use of the House floor.*
- *He allowed Joseph Gaylord, a Republican political consultant and close ally, to help interview candidates for congressional staff positions, even though Gaylord was not on the House payroll. The committee said this action violated a House rule prohibiting the use of private funds to pay for congressional operations.*

The ethics committee recommended no punishment for Gingrich, and it dismissed two other complaints. Even so, the committee sharply criticized Gingrich's actions in one of the complaints it eventually dismissed: his lucrative and controversial book contract with media giant Rupert Murdoch. Gingrich had accepted a $4.5 million advance from Murdoch's HarperCollins publishers for a book about his political philosophy. Gingrich was widely criticized for the book deal, and he later decided to turn down the advance in favor of accepting royalties. In its letter, the ethics committee told Gingrich that it strongly questioned "the appropriateness of what some could describe as an attempt by you to capitalize on your office."

Special Counsel Hired

Of potentially greater long-term significance than any of those issues was another matter on which the committee decided to turn to an outside counsel. Democrats had charged that Gingrich violated federal tax laws in raising money for the courses he taught at the two Georgia colleges, and they demanded that the committee hire a special counsel to look into the matter.

Republican members of the ethics committee adamantly refused the call for an outside counsel until after the embarrassing disclosures about GOPAC in the FEC documents. During the committee's December 6 meeting, Republicans agreed to hire a counsel, although they tried to limit the scope of what the counsel could investigate. At the insistence of Democrats, the committee cited the one charge against Gingrich as the counsel's mandate but did not specifically limit his scope—in effect giving the counsel broad discretion to investigate Gingrich's activities. The committee on December 22 named James M. Cole, a former Justice Department prosecutor, as its outside counsel. He was expected to begin work in January 1996.

As a result of its deliberations on the Gingrich case, the committee decided to try to change House rules to limit book royalties that members could receive. Over the opposition of Republican leaders, the committee proposed to include book royalties in the $20,040 annual limit on outside income that members could earn in addition to their congressional salaries. The House rejected that proposal on December 22, adopting a milder alternative prohibiting advance payments on book contracts and requiring members to receive ethics committee approval for any book contracts signed after January 1, 1996.

Following is the text of a letter sent December 6, 1995, by the House Committee on Standards of Official Conduct to Speaker Newt Gingrich (R-Ga.), in which the committee cited three violations of House rules by Gingrich but dismissed other complaints against him:

Dear Mr. Speaker:

The Committee has met for many months on the various complaints which have been filed against you. Pursuant to Committee rule 15(g), the Committee hereby provides notice of a Committee resolution pertaining to these complaints adopted by unanimous vote of the Committee.

In reference to those complaints filed by Mr. Ben Jones on Sept. 12, 1994, and Jan. 26, 1995, relating to your teaching a course under the auspices of the Kennesaw State College Foundation and the Progress and Freedom Foundation at Kennesaw State College and Reinhardt College, the Committee has voted a Preliminary Inquiry to review whether your activities in relation to the course entitled "Renewing American Civilization" were in violation of section 501(c)(3) of title 26, United States Code, or whether any section 501(c)(3) entity, with respect to the course, violated its status with your knowledge and approval. The Committee will hire special counsel to assist the Investigative Subcommittee. With respect to the allegations involving improper use of official resources in connection with the course, the Committee notified you of its dismissal on October 31, 1994. With respect to the allegations of connection between official action and contribution to the course, these portions of the complaint are dismissed.

In reference to the complaint filed by Mr. Jones on January 26, 1995, concerning the publication of your book "To Renew America," while the amount involved greatly exceeds the financial bounds of any book contract contemplated at the time the current rules were drafted, the Committee concludes that your book contract was in technical compliance with the "usual and customary" standard as set out in House Rule 47. However, the Committee strongly questions the appropriateness of what some could describe as an attempt by you to capitalize on your office. As recent events demonstrate, existing rules permit a Member to reap significant and immediate financial benefit which appears to be based primarily on his or her position. At a minimum, this creates the impression of exploiting one's office for personal gain. Such a perception is especially troubling when it pertains to the office of the Speaker of the House, a constitutional office requiring the highest standards of ethical behavior. The Committee has drafted an amendment to House rules to treat income from book royalties as part of outside earned income subject to the annual limit of House Rule 47. The Committee will propose this resolution to take effect January 1, 1996, and will ask that it be scheduled for Floor consideration prior to the end of this session.

The Committee finds that the auction process was customary and has dismissed all portions of the complaint in relation to the book and the Murdoch meeting. [Rupert Murdoch's News Corp. owns Gingrich's publisher, Harper-Collins. Murdoch was lobbying Congress on telecommunications law changes. HarperCollins at first offered Gingrich a $4.5 million book advance. Gingrich also had a meeting with Murdoch.]

The Committee has dismissed that portion of the complaint referencing improper solicitation by you to the Business Roundtable and the Managed Futures Association.

The Committee has dismissed the allegation of improper intervention with the Executive branch for a donor to the Progress and Freedom Foundation (Direct Access Diagnostics).

In reference to the complaint filed by Rep. George Miller [D-Calif.], on February 13, 1995, the Committee has found that your use of Mr. Joseph Gaylord was in violation of House Rule 45, which prohibits the use of unofficial resources for official purposes. Specifically the Committee found that Mr. Gaylord's activities during the transition of interviewing prospective staff violate our rules and that his regular, routine presence in congressional offices, while in and of itself not a violation of House rules, creates the appearance of the improper commingling of political and official resources. Such activities, if they are continuing, should cease immediately. The Committee will take no further action.

In reference to the complaint filed by Representatives [Patricia] Schroeder [D-Colo.], [Cynthia A.] McKinney [D-Ga.], and [Harry A.] Johnston [D-Fla.], on February 23, 1994, the Committee has dismissed the complaint alleging that the broadcasting of the course was either improperly solicited by you or a gift to you.

In reference to the complaint filed by Representative [David E.] Bonior [D-Mich.], on March 8, 1995, the Committee has found a misuse of the House Floor in Count I. The House Floor should not be used for commercial purposes, and since a caller to this number was offered only the option of buying a set of tapes, the Committee finds the use of a 1–800 number to be an improper solicitation. The Committee will take no further action on this matter and has dismissed Counts II through V.

In reference to the complaint filed by Representative Bonior on May 8, 1995, the Committee has found a similar violation in your references on the House Floor in 1990 regarding a nationwide town meeting sponsored by GOPAC. You were using the House Floor to publicize a political meeting sponsored by a political organization. The Committee will take no further action.

With regard to the use of the House Floor, the Committee will ask that House rules be clarified to guide Members with greater precision on the appropriate use of Special Orders.

The Committee will make this letter public and will issue a report to the House discussing in more detail the findings stated above.

Sincerely,
Nancy L. Johnson [R-Conn.], Chairman
Jim McDermott [D-Wash.], Ranking Democratic Member

CUMULATIVE INDEX, 1991–1995

A

entrapment of **1992** 313
as mayor of Washington **1995** 498
Barzun, Jacques **1991** 344-345
Baseball
cancellation of the season **1994** 360-362
Ripken on breaking Gehrig's consecutive
game record **1995** 588-590
Schott suspension for racist remarks **1993**
167-170
Vincent resignation as commissioner **1992**
855-858
Basketball, Magic Johnson's retirement **1991**
747-749, **1992** 335, 340
Basle Accords (1988) **1992** 115
Battle, Parris C. **1992** 88
Baxter Healthcare **1995** 516
Bazemore v. Friday **1992** 582
BCCI. *See* Bank of Credit and Commerce
International
Beasley, Michele **1995** 277
Beauharnais v. Illinois **1992** 546
Beck, George **1993** 304
Beck, Harry F. **1992** 345-347
Beck v. Alabama **1993** 150
Beckel, Bob **1992** 909
Becker, Judith **1992** 509
Becker, Lance **1993** 671-675
Beer v. United States **1993** 472
Belarus, Commonwealth Pact **1991** 787-791
Belize **1992** 267-275
Bell, Griffin B. **1994** 9
Bell v. Hood **1992** 192, 196, 198
Bell v. Wolfish **1992** 178
Benitez, Jose Federico **1994** 564
Bennett, Charles **1992** 382
Bennett, Charles E. **1991** 5
Bennett, Robert **1993** 168
Bentsen, Lloyd **1992** 1021
at Tokyo economic summit **1993** 541
Bergalis, Kimberly **1992** 709
Berkowitz, David **1991** 813-825
Berliner, Lucy **1992** 386
Berman, Howard L. (D-Calif.) **1992** 1047
Bernardin, Cardinal Joseph **1992** 507-518
Bernstein, Jared **1993** 271
Berry, Steven K. **1992** 1046
Bertrand v. Sava **1992** 460
Bessmertnykh, Alexander **1991** 288
Betancur, Belisario **1993** 237
Bethlehem Steel **1992** 409
Biafra, independence movement **1995** 697
Biden, Joseph R. (D-Del.)
on Foster, surgeon general nomination
1995 62
on Freeh, FBI director nomination **1993**
611
on Glaspie-Hussein prewar meeting **1991**
1161
Thomas confirmation hearings **1991**
557-561, 575-576, 582-583, 592-595,
615-616

"Big Bang" theory **1992** 379-383
Billington, James H. **1993** 339-345
Bioethics
euthanasia, Catholic teaching on **1995** 146,
155-158
genetically engineered foods **1992** 469-473
physician-assisted suicide **1994** 501-512
Pope's encyclical on moral theology **1993**
843-850
Biological weapons
Clinton's UN address **1993** 811-812
economic summit (London) **1991** 451-456
Gulf War syndrome **1994** 264-275
Iraq warfare research **1991** 193
Biotechnology
Earth Summit (Rio) **1992** 499-506
genetically engineered foods **1992** 469-473
Scope document **1992** 471
Birth control. *See* Abortion; Contraception
Black, Creed C. **1991** 129
Blackburn v. Alabama **1991** 179
Blackley, Ronald **1994** 403
Blackmun, Harry A.
abortion **1993** 339
abortion clinics
advice issue **1991** 258-259, 266-272
blockades **1993** 93, 101-102
protests **1994** 312-320
asset forfeiture
drug trafficking **1993** 432-438
pornography seized **1993** 432, 440-446
coastal property rights **1992** 616
coerced confessions **1991** 175-176
compensation law **1991** 815, 823
damages for tobacco-related ills **1992** 564-
573
on deaf parochial student **1993** 400, 403-
406
death penalty, renunciation of **1994** 161-
171
death row, appeals **1993** 142, 149-152
entrapment in child pornography case **1992**
313-322
Haitian refugees returned **1993** 414, 421
hate crimes **1992** 544-551, **1993** 385-389
impeachment authority **1993** 82-91
job discrimination
fetal protection **1991** 144, 146-150
involving African-Americans **1993** 424,
424-430
jury selection **1994** 223, 237-231
legislative intent **1993** 250-253
libel from misquotation **1991** 329
monetary damages for sexual harassment
1992 188-197
murder case sentencing **1991** 391-395
on prison inmates, beaten by guards **1992**
176-182
prisoner appeals **1991** 205, 215-218
public lands and developers **1994** 299, 306-
309

Brady v. Maryland **1991** 208-209
Bram v. United States **1991** 179
Branch Davidians
   Waco cult compound attack **1993** 293-301
   Waco investigations **1993** 819-840
Brandeis, Louis **1993** 395
Branstad, Terry E. **1993** 484-486
Bray v. Alexandria Women's Health Clinic
   1993 93-112
Brazil
   Earth Summit (Rio) **1992** 499-506
   report on smoking **1992** 267-275
   student test scores **1992** 90, 92, 94, 95
Breast cancer. *See* Cancer
Breaux, John B. (D-La.)
   on Hurricane Andrew **1992** 534
   response to Clinton State of the Union
     address **1995** 26
Brennan, William J., Jr., retirement of **1991**
   175
Brewster v. Gage **1992** 462
Breyer, Stephen G.
   affirmative action **1995** 309, 323-326
   congressional term limits **1995** 260
   drug testing of students **1995** 339-346
   endangered species on private lands **1995**
     359-368
   gun-free school zone **1995** 184, 190-191,
     196-200
   race-based redistricting **1995** 371, 380-384
   religious publications **1995** 386, 393-395
   religious symbols **1995** 387, 396-404
   Supreme Court appointment **1993** 393, 396
Brezhnev, Leonid **1993** 772
Brickman, Lester **1995** 517
Bridgeport (Conn.), mayor on city bankruptcy
   1991 303-307
Bridgewater, Bill **1995** 464
Brinker, Nancy A. **1993** 907
Briseno, Theodore J. **1992** 409, **1993** 633-
   637, 639, 641-642, 647, 650
Bristol-Myers Squibb **1995** 516
Brittain, Leon **1993** 542
Broccoli
   calcium in **1992** 399, 403
   as cancer preventative **1992** 277-281
Broder, David S. **1995** 24
Brookings Institution, on succession in Saudi
   Arabia **1992** 227
Brooks, Jack
   crime bill **1994** 576
   on Twenty-seventh Amendment **1992** 440
Brown, Edmund G. "Jerry," Jr. **1992** 669, 686
Brown, Jesse
   on Gulf War syndrome **1994** 266
   radiation testing on citizens **1993** 988
Brown, Lee P. **1995** 341
Brown, Ronald H.
   Democratic convention (1992) **1992** 669
   on labor-management relations report **1995**
     15, 17

Brown v. Board of Education **1991** 23, 27,
   29, **1992** 577, 578, 579, 581, 585, 599, **1995**
   456, 458
   effect on Thomas's career **1992** 35, 41, 42
Brown, Willie L. **1991** 444-445
Browner, Carol M. **1993** 64-65
Browning-Ferris Industries of Vermont,
   Inc. v. Kelco Disposal, Inc. **1993** 433-434,
   437, 440
Brush, Peter **1993** 987-995
Bryant, Anne **1993** 355
Bryant, Barbara E. **1991** 443
Bryant, John (D-Texas) **1993** 489
Brzezinski, Zbigniew **1992** 260, **1993** 114
Buchanan, Patrick J.
   attacks Clinton on draft issue **1992** 158
   on English as official language **1995** 573
   in 1992 presidential primaries **1992** 56
Buckley, William **1991** 753
Budget deficit
   Bush administration **1991** 67-68, 69
   CEA report on **1991** 87
   Democratic party platform on **1992** 691
   and Omnibus Budget Reconciliation Act
     1993 182
   reduction of
     Clinton plan for **1995** 72-73
     and investment **1995** 80-81
   State of the Union address, Democratic
     response to **1991** 48
Budget (U.S.)
   Bush's message **1991** 67-71
   See also Balanced budget amendment
Buerganthal, Thomas **1993** 237
Bulgaria, Warsaw Pact dissolution **1991** 399-
   401
Bureau of Justice Statistics (BJS)
   on rape **1993** 386, 389-390
   on violent crime **1993** 377
Bureau of Labor Statistics (BLS), data on
   young families **1992** 356
Bureau of Land Management (BLM), logging
   in Oregon **1992** 490
Burger, Warren E. **1993** 339-340
Burnet v. Colorado Oil & Gas Co. **1991** 389
Burnham, Frederic B. **1992** 381
Burt, Martha **1994** 253
Burton, Dan (R-Ind.) **1995** 701
Burton, Harold H. **1993** 340
Burundi, Ntaryamira assassination **1994** 541
Bush, George
   campaigns and elections
     acceptance speeches **1992** 781-794
     postelection statement **1992** 1019, 1023-
       1024
     presidential debates **1992** 907-977
     on Republican party platform **1992** 799
    challenge from Perot **1992** 717
    collapse in Japan **1992** 12, 17-18
    defense policy
     Iraq war resolution **1991** 3, 6

C

Senate POW/MIA report **1993** 120-122, 124-125

UN report on refugees **1991** 672-673

UN role in **1995** 355

Campbell, Carroll A. **1992** 46-47, 48-49

Campbell, Kim **1993** 541-557

Campbell, William **1994** 214-217

Campolo, Tony **1994** 49

Canada

economic summit (Munich) **1992** 637-648

ozone depletion **1992** 79-80

report on smoking **1992** 267-275

student test scores **1992** 90

Canaday, Charles T. (R-Fla.)

affirmative action programs **1995** 485

school prayer amendment **1995** 548

Cancer

breast cancer report **1993** 905-922

prevention strategies with diet **1992** 277-281

secondhand smoke, EPA report on **1993** 63-69

skin **1992** 82

smoking and damage suits **1992** 563-573

Cannon v. University of Chicago **1992** 189, 190, 191-192, 194-195, 198

Cantwell v. Connecticut **1992** 546

Capital gains taxes **1991** 75, **1992** 56-57, 63

Capital punishment. *See* Death penalty

Capitol Square Review v. Pinette **1995** 385, 387, 396-404

Card, Andrew H., Jr. **1992** 534, 844

Carey v. Piphus **1992** 193

Carey v. Population Services International **1992** 594

Caribbean area, report on smoking **1992** 267-275

Carlson, Arne **1993** 486

Carnahan, Mel **1993** 486

Carnegie Foundation, international math and science test **1992** 85-96

Carroll, Ted **1994** 410

Carroll v. President and Commissioners of Princess Anne **1994** 316, 317

Carswell, G. Harrold **1994** 164

Carter, Jimmy

Bosnia cease-fire negotiations **1995** 719

Middle East peace negotiations **1993** 748, 749

Panama Canal and **1992** 650

Reagan presidential library dedication **1991** 735, 744-746

Casey, Robert P. **1992** 590

Casey, William J.

fatal illness of **1994** 20, 60 652

Iran-contra affair **1991** 652, **1994** 17

"October Surprise" report **1993** 4-5, 7, 10-11

Castor, Betty **1992** 144

Cataracts, UV radiation and **1992** 77, 81-82

Catholic Bishops' Conference (Ireland) **1992** 250

Catholic Church

diplomatic accord with Israel **1993** 1033-1040

economic questions, Pope's encyclical on **1993** 229-241

on homosexual rights laws **1992** 723-730

moral theology, Pope's encyclical on **1993** 843-850

Pope's Denver visit **1993** 659-669

sexual abuse of children by priests **1993** 407-411

Catholic clergy

ban on female priests **1994** 276-280

sexual abuse by priests **1992** 507-518, **1993** 407-411

Cavazos, Lauro F. **1991** 219

Cedras, Raoul **1993** 454

Census Bureau (U.S.)

on foreign-born population **1995** 563-569

health insurance report **1994** 463-471

portrait of the nation's social, economic status **1992** 475-478

undercount **1991** 443-449

young families data **1992** 356

Center on Budget and Policy Priorities **1991** 827-842

Center for Science in the Public Interest (CSPI), Chinese food and nutrition report **1993** 689-694

Center for Study of the States **1991** 827-842

Centers for Disease Control and Prevention

adolescent AIDS **1992** 339-343

AIDS cases and deaths **1993** 447

AIDS testing of pregnant women **1995** 441-452

cigarette smoking **1993** 64, 65

sedentary lifestyle **1993** 625-628

tuberculosis control program **1993** 853, 859-865

Central and Eastern European countries (CEECs), Munich economic summit on **1992** 644-645

Central Intelligence Agency (CIA)

Ames espionage case **1994** 475-497

Center for the Study of Intelligence **1992** 3

Gates nomination hearings **1991** 651-669

government secrets **1994** 525-526

Iran-contra affair, role of officials **1992** 1073-1079, **1994** 17

Noriega of Panama and **1992** 651

North Korea **1994** 602-603

Office of Public Affairs **1992** 3

reform of **1992** 3-10

Chabad-Lubavitch v. Burlington **1995** 397

Chabad-Lubavitch v. Miller **1995** 397

Chad, human rights in **1993** 559-560

Channell, Carl R.

Iran-contra affair, role in **1994** 15

Iran-contra conviction **1991** 619, **1994** 12

H